THINK
HUMAN SEXUALITY

KELLY WELCH

Kansas State University

Allyn & Bacon

Boston   Columbus   Indianapolis   New York   San Francisco   Upper Saddle River
Amsterdam   Cape Town   Dubai   London   Madrid   Milan   Munich   Paris   Montreal   Toronto
Delhi   Mexico City   Sao Paulo   Sydney   Hong Kong   Seoul   Singapore   Taipei   Tokyo

Executive Editor: Susan Hartman
Editorial Assistant: Laura Berry
Executive Marketing Manager: Jeanette Koskinas
Marketing Assistant: Shauna Fishweicher
Senior Production Project Manager: Patrick Cash-Peterson
Manufacturing Buyer: Debbie Rossi
Cover Administrator: John Christiana
Editorial Production and Composition Service: Words & Numbers
Interior Design: John Christiana
Photo Researcher: Words & Numbers
Cover Designer: John Christiana

To my husband, Dave.
I'm so glad we're in this together.

Credits appear on page 402, which constitutes an extension of the copyright page.

Library of Congress Cataloging-in-Publication Data

Welch, Kelly.
Think human sexuality / Kelly J. Welch.
    p. cm.
Includes bibliographical references and index.
ISBN-13: 978-0-205-77771-6 (student : alk. paper)
ISBN-10: 0-205-77771-6 (student : alk. paper)
ISBN-13: 978-0-205-77772-3 (exam copy : alk. paper)
ISBN-10: 0-205-77772-4 (exam copy : alk. paper)
1. Sex. 2. Sex customs–United States. I. Title.
HQ21.W564 2011
613.9071--dc22

2010018575

10 9 8 7 6 5 4 3 CKV 13 12

Allyn & Bacon
is an imprint of

www.pearsonhighered.com

Student ISBN-13:   978-0-205-77771-6
Student ISBN-10:   0-205-77771-6
Exam Copy ISBN-13: 978-0-205-77772-3
Exam Copy ISBN-10: 0-205-77772-4

BRIEF CONTENTS

CONTENTS

06 SEXUAL DEVELOPMENT FROM INFANCY THROUGH EARLY ADULTHOOD 102

07 SEXUAL ORIENTATION DEVELOPMENT: GAY, STRAIGHT, OR BISEXUAL? 126

08 THE PATH TO COMMITMENT: ATTRACTION, DATING, AND THE EXPERIENCES OF LOVE 150

09 COMMUNICATION: ENRICHING INTIMATE RELATIONSHIPS 170

I didn't do this on my own. There are many people who deserve to be recognized for their roles in creating this dynamic, cutting-edge book.

The Reviewers

Although I have never met the reviewers, I owe you much gratitude and many, many thanks for the insight and direction you provided. It's not easy to read criticisms of my work, but your comments and suggestions gave me clear direction and focus. Thank you, Andrea Zabel, Midland College; Keith Davis, University of South Carolina; Jerry Green, Tarrant County College; Amanda Woods, Georgia State University; Jason Daniel, San Diego Mesa College; Catherine Sherwood-Laughlin, Indiana University; Shani Peterson, Spelman College; Florence Denmark, Pace University; Kathleen Dolan, North Georgia College and State University; Juline Koken, Hunter College; Kathy Erickson, Pima Community College; Debra Golden, Grossmont College; Christina McKittrick, Drew University; Susan Cardenas, Texas Woman's University; Grace Pokorny, Long Beach City College; Richelle Frabotta, Miami University; Lester Wright, Western Michigan University; Cheryl Robinson, The University of Tennessee at Chattanooga; Jason McCoy, Cape Fear Community College; O'Neal Weeks, Eastern Kentucky University; and Heather Martarella, Agrosy University.

The A-Team

I can't imagine a greater group of people to work with! I don't know how to thank Susan Hartman, executive editor for Psychology (Pearson) for her vision and for her unwavering confidence in me. Susan, your encouragement and belief in me are what kept me from throwing in the towel when things seemed impossible. I can't even begin to put into words my gratitude for you. Anyone who ever has the opportunity to work with you is so fortunate! I am also so very thankful to LeeAnn Doherty, associate editor (Pearson), who organized and synthesized all of the reviews, as well as Amber Mackey (Pearson), senior editor, Psychology, and Paige Clunie, editorial assistant (Pearson), for getting us to the finish line! Thank you, Claudine Bellanton and Patrick Cash-Peterson, production editors (Pearson), and Ally Brocious (Words & Numbers), who shepherded this book through the production process and found ways to make the improbable possible, and many thanks to John Christiana, title design (Pearson). I am so grateful for the folks at Pearson—you will always be my second family.

First and foremost, I give a heartfelt thank you (!!) to Dr. Sharon Ballard and Dr. Kevin Gross, College of Human Ecology, East Carolina University, who coauthored this book's coverage about sexually transmitted infections, contraception, and aging, and who contributed to the sexual orientation and sexual variations chapters. Sharon and Kevin, I turned to you not only because of your expertise in Family Life Education, but also because you are master educators and mentors. Each of us is passionate and committed to our students, and we have one united purpose: To promote the sexual health and well-being of the students we serve. I am very grateful for your collaborative efforts on this book. Thank you!

Bob Keller, senior content director (Words & Numbers), brought this project to life and kept it on schedule. Bob, you brought this book to reality, and for that I am so very thankful! You were the voice of reason and a calming presence, and always seemed to intuitively know the best next step. It was a true pleasure to work with you! My husband and I look forward to continuing the friendship we have with you.

And finally, to Staci Wolfson, assistant editor and content lead (Words & Numbers): How do I ever thank you? *You are incredible!* You "got" the vision of this book early on—your photo selections, your graphic designs, your ability to massage the text to get the most possible out of our very limited word count, and your diligent work in preparing the manuscript for production . . . *You* are the force behind this book. I thank you and I thank you and I thank you!

To Those Closer to Home

First, I thank my students: *You* are the reason I do this every day! You breathe life and energy into me, you make me look forward to coming to class every week, you laugh at my stupid jokes, you put up with my crazy schedule . . . and you always, always brighten my day when you say, "Hey Dr. Dub, wassup?!" I hope you know how much I truly love you.

I also owe a word of gratitude to Dr. Larry Moeller, physician (Lafene Student Health Center, KSU) and STI/HIV content expert. Larry, thank you for reviewing the information presented in Chapter 14. Because of your expertise, students have the most relevant, current facts. With this knowledge, they are better able to make informed choices, and protect and more fully enjoy their sexuality. Your compassion for students is evident, and I am so very fortunate to know you!

I am very appreciative and grateful for my colleagues, especially Dr. Farrell Webb, whose frequent "Keep going, gurl!" really did keep me going. Farrell, so much of this book is the result of your always-welcomed feedback—thank you! Thank you, Dr. Ginny Moxley (dean of the College of Human Ecology), Dr. Morey MacDonald (chair, School of Family Studies & Human Services), and Dr. Emily Lehning (assistant vice president for Student Life). Each of you has guided me in ways to make this book possible. Thank you!

And to my family: You alone know the sacrifices you made so that this book could be written:

- My husband, Dave. Who knew that "paradise" is wherever you are?
- My guys and gals, Eric and Gretchen, Shawn, Danny and Kateland, and Kyle. I held your hands when you were little. . . . you held mine as you walked me through this past year.
- My siblings and their spouses, Terri and Pete, Tim and Michele, Dan and Roxanne. As the saying goes, "I'm smiling because you're my siblings. I'm laughing because you can't do anything about it!" Never has a sister been as blessed as I am.

I sincerely hope that you enjoy reading and teaching from this book. I've worked so diligently to incorporate everything on your wish lists, and I have given my best to ensure that issues facing us today are included. At the end of the day, I hope that students are presented a realistic picture of today's sex and sexuality, and that they hold in their hands a book that is relevant to their lives.

Kelly

ABOUT THE AUTHOR

DR. KELLY WELCH is an assistant professor in the School of Family Studies and Human Services at Kansas State University. She is a Certified Family Life Educator (CFLE), and her teaching and research background includes human development, sexuality, and marriage and family. Her knowledge in life span development and intimate relationships provides a fresh voice and unique approach—because of her expertise in areas, such as love, intimacy, interpersonal relationships, and communication, she ably presents a holistic approach to the study of sexuality, an approach that recognizes that sex and sexuality encompass so much more than body parts and the acts of sex alone.

Prior to her work at Kansas State University, Dr. Welch served her community as a Women's and Maternal Health Specialist, and devoted her time to serving at-risk impoverished women in their childbearing years. Her work in community clinics is evident as she sensitively describes diversity issues, men's and women's anatomy and physiology, changes associated with male and female puberty, pregnancy and childbirth, contraception options, and sexually transmitted infections and HIV/AIDS. Her long-term goal is to open similar clinics in Ethiopia, where fetal and maternal outcomes are dismal.

Dr. Welch is the recipient of numerous teaching awards, including the Presidential Award for Outstanding Undergraduate Teaching, and she has been recognized by the Pew Foundation for her cutting-edge "hands-on, minds-on" pedagogy and course design. Her many awards and nominations recognize her distinct, innovative, and energetic teaching style—a style students say puts them on the edge of their seats.

As you thumb through this book, you will find a voice that is simultaneously informative and rigorous, humorous and entertaining, and always compassionate and heartfelt. Dr. Welch brings your students the most current, relevant information and presents a candid, sensitive, inclusive, nonjudgmental balance of research and "real life." It is her hope that you find this to be a natural partner to your course, and that your students discover a resource to help them make informed decisions about their sexuality.

Dr. Welch's previous works include, *Development: Journey of a Lifetime*, *Development: Journey through Childhood and Adolescence*, and *Family Life Now*.

THINK
HUMAN SEXUALITY

SEXUAL LIFE NOW

WHAT IS SEXOLOGY?
WHAT ARE THE CHARACTERISTICS OF ANCIENT SEXOLOGY?
WHAT ARE THE THREE DOMAINS OF SEXUALITY AND WHAT IS THEIR SIGNIFICANCE?
HOW DOES CULTURE INFLUENCE EXPERIENCES OF SEXUALITY AND SEX?

The year

1977 marked the freshman year of my university experience. The clothing that is today considered "retro" (low-rise, flared bottom, frayed jeans) was then *the style*. Sex was no longer considered taboo. People more readily talked about it, it was readily available, and the prior perceived consequences of premarital sex were no longer viewed as an obstacle. Abortion had been legal for about four years and was relatively easy and inexpensive to obtain; cohabitation before marriage was becoming a common and popular thing to do; the more serious sexually transmitted infections (STIs) could be treated with a dose of penicillin; and the AIDS pandemic was still a decade away.

But with all the sexual freedom my generation was enjoying and with the more freethinking, socially driven attitudes toward the expression of sexuality, *Playboy* magazine was still displayed in brown paper wrappers on magazine stands. Even though individuals were expressing their sexuality more openly, aspects of sex and sexuality were still hidden from society. In fact, at colleges and universities— usually located among more open-minded communities—sex was still a controversial subject. The first human sexuality course I took at the university is a case in point. Although the course was available, it was offered under a cloud of secrecy. It was not listed in the course offerings schedule printed and distributed to every student each semester. The human sexuality course was a "secret society" of sorts— students knew about it by word of mouth, and parents did not! The course was wrapped in "brown paper," hidden away from society.

Still today on college campuses across the country, sexuality courses are taught in filled-to-capacity rooms. What is it about sex and sexuality that generates such interest, such heated political debate, and such media attention? We will explore these questions and much, much more throughout this book.

Source: Author's files

STUDYING SEXUALITY AND SEX

Characterizing sexuality and sex is a tall order. I was recently asked, "How is it possible to write an entire textbook about sex? Doesn't everyone do it? Do people really need to be *taught* about sex?" The answers to these questions are complex, because the study of sexuality is a web of interwoven aspects that are influenced by factors such as intimacy, love, gender roles, sexual orientation, communication styles, variations in sexual expression, sexual behaviors, sexual health, aging, and a wide range of realistic and not-so-realistic expectations. In addition to this potentially endless list of influences, we all experience our sexual lives from a different perspective: Each of us is an expert in our own interpretations and experiences of "sex" and intimate relationships. Often, we approach our first serious intimate relationship thinking we know enough about sex to get started, that we'll learn together what we don't know, or that we'll somehow figure it all out.

EXPLORING SEXUALITY AND SEX: A PATH TO SELF-DISCOVERY

But realistically speaking, none of us is equipped to tackle the "everything" that comes with sex and intimate relationships. Couples argue with each other, and more often than not, they're tired when they come home from work and the demands they face quickly erase the idea of having sex after the kids are in bed. Sometimes, a woman experiences infertility or the loss of a pregnancy. In the course of relationships, we may experience family or partner violence; we may find our partner has had a secret affair, leaving us feeling devastated. We change. Relationships change. We grow. And the "everything" we expected in our relationships is different.

There's little denying that our sexual lives are integral aspects of who we are. Most of us don't need a course in sexuality to experience satisfying, enjoyable sexual lives. After all, is it really possible to *prepare* for sexual life? Can we *learn* how to have an orgasm (or a better orgasm)? Is it possible to understand how and why people communicate sexually the way they do? If our sexual relationship is in crisis, does our understanding of sexual life make a difference?

Realistically speaking, I can't really "teach" you how to develop rewarding sexual relationships with your partner or change the dynamics of your sexual life.

What I can do, however, is point you toward a path that will help you make your own discoveries, which, in turn, will help you gain insight into the intricacies of sexual life. In the end, it is my sincere hope that you use this book to gain a solid understanding of your sexuality, the sexuality of others, and sex.

WHAT IS SEXOLOGY?

The concept of education for people to better understand their relationship dynamics or to maximize their relationship's effectiveness is certainly not new to the 20th and 21st centuries. *Any* time social conditions change—especially within complex societies, such as the United States—the teachings from previous generations may be ineffective, inappropriate, or insufficient (Arcus, Schvaneveldt, & Moss, 1993). Given the fact that none of us comes into intimate, committed, or sexual relationships with a how-to instruction manual, we either go it alone or seek out some type of "help." And in the United States, sexual living is, without a doubt, changing.

Consider how television representations of sex have changed over the past 50 years or so. In the 1950s and 1960s, popular television shows such as *I Love Lucy*, *Leave It to Beaver*, and *The Dick Van Dyke Show*, TV censors mandated that couples had twin beds in their studio-set bedrooms—and that at least one actor had at least one foot on the floor at all times if one or both of the actors were in bed. Only Fred and Wilma of *The Flintstones* and Herman and Lily Munster of *The Munsters* were allowed to share a bed (and that's because they were not "real" characters!). It wasn't until the early 1970s that parents were shown in the same bed on *The Brady Bunch*. In the 1960s TV sitcom *I Dream of Jeannie*, censors required that actress Barbara Eden's belly button be covered with flesh-covered putty. Fast-forward to the 1990s and later, where shows like *Sex and the City* and

<<< **Representations of sex on television have come a long way since** Ricky and Lucy Ricardo occupied separate twin beds in their own bedroom.

OWN IT! I Hope to Discover . . .

There is so much to discover about sexuality and sex over the course of our study. Although sexual relationships can be quite complex, it is possible to gain a better understanding of how we become sexual beings and how we experience our sexuality and the sexuality of others.

Take a moment to respond to the following questions:

1. Quickly jot down five things you hope to learn about sex and sexual life over this course.

2. Why did you choose these particular five areas? What makes these issues or processes more important to you than others?

The Girls Next Door not only describe sexual acts, but also show characters acting many of them out.

To better understand societal changes, the complex and diverse experiences of sexuality in today's global society, and the shifts in trends in sexuality (such as increased rates of oral sex among adolescents and college students), we must look at sexuality from an academic viewpoint, or through the science of *sexology*.

SEXOLOGY: A SCIENTIFIC QUEST

Sexology involves the systematic, organized study of human sexual behavior in all aspects. A **sexologist** is a person who has expert academic knowledge in sexual science and who devotes himself or herself to the objective, empirical study of sexuality (Institute for Advanced Study of Human Sexuality, 2007). Many people incorrectly assume that the primary focus of sexology is the study of the mechanics of sexual intercourse, sexual function, and/or sexual variants, such as *paraphilias* (sexual practices that are outside social norms). We discuss these variants in Chapter 15. But according to the Institute for Advanced Study of Human Sexuality (IASHS), modern sexology includes much more than studying only sex parts and sex acts, as demonstrated in Table 1.1. For example, today's sexology includes the study of human sexual development, relationship development, relationship processes, the sexuality of certain groups, and sexual pathologies (IASHS, 2007). We will explore all of these issues throughout our course of study.

Sexology is also a multidisciplinary science, and professionals from a number of fields of study contribute to modern sexology. These disciplines include the medical field and biology, as well as psychology, sociology, and education—or what I refer to as "the other side of the microscope." The science of sexology necessitates that professionals from these multiple disciplines use their research, knowledge, and

expertise to further the sexual health of all people, in the United States and cultures around the world. Through their efforts, sexologists continue to better understand the sexological and non-sexological aspects people's lives.

Even though an interest in sexuality and sexual expression was present throughout many ancient cultures, Western culture was slow to begin its quest of understanding sexuality.

>>> "What makes you curl your **toes during sex?**"

TABLE 1.1
Contributors to Sexology

Source: American Academy of Clinical Sexologists (2007)

A number of disciplines contribute to our understanding of sexology today. These include:

- *Medicine:* This study includes embryology and genetics (the study of the formation, early growth, and development of living organisms) and gynecology (the science of women's reproductive organs).

- *Evolutionary Biology:* Why do we do what we do? This discipline helps us understand the causes of sexual behavior across cultures.

- *Psychiatry:* This science seeks to understand certain disorders in sexual behavior, from sexual dysfunctions to sexual variants, such as paraphilias.

- *Epidemiology:* This science helps us better understand sexually transmitted infections.

- *Psychology:* This discipline helps us understand all aspects of human development, including sexual development.

- *Neuroscience:* This new contribution to the field of sexology examines the basic sexual reflexes. This science gives insight into the sexual responses in certain disabled people, such as those with spinal cord injuries.

- *Sociology:* This study examines the roles and functions of sexuality across cultures.

- *Criminology:* Criminologists study many sexual offenses, such as rape and child sexual abuse.

- *Biology* and *Ethology:* Together, biology and ethology (which means *beginnings*) look at the sexual behavior of different animals; the scientists then compare these behaviors with human sexual behaviors.

- *Education:* Educators, such as certified sexuality educators affiliated with the American Association of Sexuality Educators, Counselors, and Therapists (AASECT), and other instructors and professors help promote sexual health through education.

ANCIENT SEXOLOGY

Attempts to systematically investigate or document the attributes of sex have been around for thousands of years. The oldest sex manual known to the world was written in the Greco-Roman era, somewhere between the third and first centuries BCE. Written by Philaenis of Samos, *The Art of Love* was the first-of-a-kind manual that was circulated widely in the ancient world. This work was one of the few to be written by a woman, and at the time it was *the* authoritative guide for all matters pertaining to sex. The pragmatic work included discussions and depictions of sexual positions, the description of *aphrodisiacs* (substances that are said to arouse sexual desire), *abortifacients* (substances and methods to terminate an unwanted pregnancy), and even described the use of cosmetics to entice a lover (The Egypt Exploration Society, 2007).

The **Kama Sutra** (also known as *Kamasutram*) is notoriously thought to be an ancient sex manual, although only 10 of the 36 chapters are devoted to sex. Written in the first to sixth centuries, the *Kama Sutra* is an ancient Indian text that addresses the Hindu aims and priorities of life; the content of the chapters center on sexual union, the acquisition of a wife, proper conduct of wives, the wives of other people, how to choose lovers, and how to make oneself attractive to potential partners (Avari, 2007).

The word *kama* means wish, desire, and intention; it also means pleasure and sexual love (Sudhir & Doniger, 2003). The types of pleasure that arise from human contact (such as sexual contact) are called *kama*. The word *sutra* signifies a thread, or threaded discussions about concise rules. The *Kama Sutra* is thus a work about the rules of pleasure, desire, and intentions (Sudhir & Doniger, 2003).

The *Kama Sutra* is often confused with tantric sex. Broadly stated, *tantric sex* involves the sexual practices that originated with Buddhist folklore whereby men

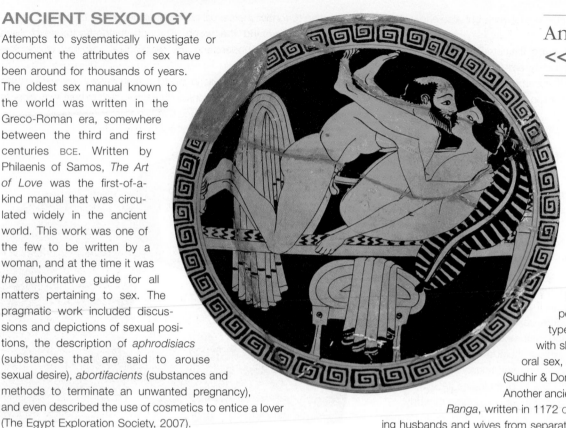

Ancient Greek
<<< Erotic Art

use their abdominal muscles to delay orgasm (Anad, 2003). More accurately, though, the 10 chapters in the *Kama Sutra* describe 64 types of sexual acts that include highly descriptive information on stimulating sexual desire, types of embraces, different types of caressing and kissing, marking or scratching with fingernails, biting and marking with teeth, sexual positions, slapping by hand and the types of moaning that correspond with slapping, sexual potency in women, oral sex, and preludes to the game of love (Sudhir & Doniger, 2003).

Another ancient Indian love manual, the *Ananga Ranga*, written in 1172 CE, is aimed specifically at preventing husbands and wives from separating. Its content includes the seats of passion for women, the temperaments of women, and the "internal" and "external" enjoyments of women.

Written somewhere between 1410 and 1434, *The Perfumed Garden of Sensual Delight* is an Arabic sex manual and an erotic work of literature. Replete with advice on sexual techniques, warnings about sexual health, remedies for sexual problems, and even a brief discussion about sex between animals, translators believe what makes this ancient prose unique is the clinical, serious nature in which the most provocative and "obscene" matters are detailed (Burton, 1886; Coville, 1999).

There are variations in how this erotic work has been translated and interpreted. Sir Richard Francis Burton (1821–1890), an English linguist and author, completed the most well-known interpretation. *The Perfumed Garden* provides explicit details to "praiseworthy" (sexually desirable) men and women:

Praiseworthy Men: "[The penis], to please women, must have at most a length of the breadth of twelve fingers, or three hand-breadths, and at least six fingers, or a hand and a half breadth. A man whose member is of less dimensions cannot please women" (Burton, 1886, p. 2).

Image from >>>
the Kama Sutra

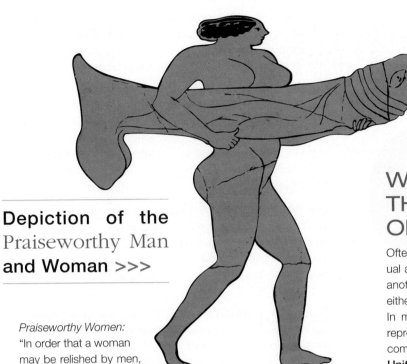

Depiction of the Praiseworthy Man and Woman >>>

Praiseworthy Women:
"In order that a woman may be relished by men, she must have a perfect waist, and must be plump and lusty. Her bust and belly [must be] large; her breasts must be full and firm, her belly in good proportion; the lower part of the belly is to be large, the vulva projecting and fleshy . . . the conduit [vagina] must be narrow and not moist, soft to the touch, and emitting a strong heat and no bad smell; she must have thighs and buttocks hard, the hips large and full; plump arms, and well-developed shoulders. If one looks at a woman with those qualities in front, one is fascinated; if from behind, one dies with pleasure" (p. 15).

There's no doubt about it—interest in sexuality and sexual expression has been present throughout ancient cultures, and ancient erotic art gives us a glimpse into other eras-old cultural understandings of sexuality. But despite the existence of these primitive sex manuals in other cultures, Western culture was slow to begin its quest of understanding sexuality. The science of sexology in the Western world is only about 100 years old. In Chapter 2, we will explore sexology through the 19th and 20th centuries, and its impact on our understanding and experiences of sexuality today.

WHAT IS SEXUALITY? THE INTERRELATED DOMAINS OF SEXUALITY

Often when people define human sexuality, they define it in terms of sexual anatomy and physiology, different sexual behaviors, or attraction to another person. Others understand their sexuality as the quality of being either a male or a female, or of being either heterosexual or homosexual. In most species, sexual behavior essentially serves the purposes of reproduction (Bancroft, 2002). In humans, however, sexuality is far more complex. The **Sexuality Information and Education Council of the United States (SIECUS)** defines human sexuality as a dimension of our personality that encompasses our sexual beliefs, attitudes, values, behaviors, and knowledge (SIECUS, 2009). Sexuality is a part of who we are as a person, a part of our personality, and part of what makes each of us unique. A lifelong learning process, sexuality integrates the physical, emotional, social, and cultural experiences of our lives (Alberta Society for the Promotion of Sexual Health, 2007). SIECUS affirms that sexuality is a fundamental part of being human, and it is worthy of dignity and respect (2009). It is this foundational belief from which we engage in our exploration of sexuality.

Sexuality involves three interrelated domains that all play an equal role in how we experience and express our sexuality: the *biological*, *psychosocial/psychosexual*, and *sociocultural* dimensions

sex talk

What Is Your Definition of Sexuality?

At the beginning of each semester in my sexuality course, I ask students to define "sex." Here are some of their responses:

"Sex is just that—sex. Intercourse. Penis into vagina. A few hot, sweaty moments of passion. Euphoria afterward. And then you repeat the process, either within a few minutes, a few days, a few weeks, or a few months."

"I think sex is an innate, inborn drive, in every species. Humans are just lucky—we get to do it because we *want* to, not because we *have* to!"

"When you think about it, sex is everything that love is; it's companionship, trust, respect, intimacy, jealousy, humor, communication, friendship, commitment. How can you separate any of these components from sex?"

"I think there is a difference between sex and sexual intercourse. I think sex is sinful, but I think sexual intercourse is OK for the purposes of procreation."

"Sex can be anything. The key to great sex, though, is that that each partner has the same definition!"

"Sex is ... AWESOME!"

>>> TALK ABOUT IT

1. At this point in your academic career, how would you define "sex"?
2. In your experiences, does your culture shape your sexuality and your sexual experiences? If so, how?

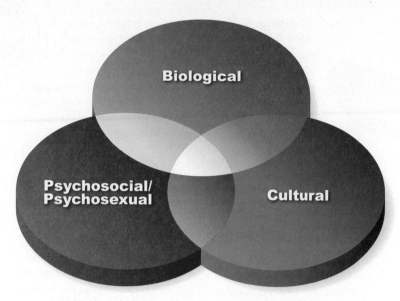

Figure 1.1 Interrelated Domains of Sexuality

(see Figure 1.1). All three of these domains are in constant interaction and are continuously growing and changing; each domain is multifaceted. Our sexuality is thus an ongoing, fluid process that undergoes change as we age. In the sections that follow, we'll take a brief look at each of these dimensions that make up our sexuality.

THE BIOLOGICAL DOMAIN

The **biological domain** (see Figure 1.2) of sexuality explores areas such as male and female anatomy and physiology, gender, and genetics, including the contributions of hereditary factors that contribute to sexuality experiences. We give considerable attention to these facets of the biological domain and more throughout this text. The following is a preview of sorts into what we will study throughout this course.

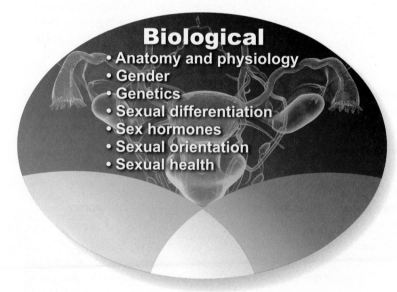

Figure 1.2 The Biological Domain of Sexuality

John Bancroft, MD, former director of The Kinsey Institute, has been involved in various aspects of sex research for the past 30 years. He provides a comprehensive review of the key concepts relative to understanding the role of biology in shaping human sexuality.

- **Sexual differentiation** refers to the prenatal physiological and anatomical differentiation into male and female. Throughout the prenatal period of human development, certain hormones are produced in the developing baby, which direct the development of the reproductive organs, as well as the central nervous system. In Chapter 3, we will thoroughly explore these hormonal influences.

- **Sex hormones** not only direct sexual differentiation in the womb, but they also continue to influence sexual maturation through puberty. Sex hormones also play key roles in sexual response and the experiences of sexual pleasure, pregnancy, childbirth, breast-feeding, and sexuality through the aging process (see Chapters 4, 5, 12, and 16).

- **Sexual orientation** refers to whether a person is a heterosexual, homosexual, or bisexual. In Chapter 7, we explore in depth the biological contributions to sexual orientation. This discussion includes a comprehensive look at the role of genetics, prenatal hormonal influences and brain differentiation, and hormonal levels after birth.

- **Sexual health** is not merely the absence of a disease, some type of sexual dysfunction, or illness related to the reproductive organs (see Chapters 13 and 14), but physical and emotional well-being in relation to sexuality (Bancroft, 2002).

But biological influences alone are not sufficient to describe and explain how we experience sexuality today. We must also consider the interacting influences from the *psychosocial/psychosexual* domain of sexuality.

THE PSYCHOSOCIAL/ PSYCHOSEXUAL DOMAIN

How our bodies sexually develop and how we experience sexual pleasure or sexual arousal and response are, without question, important to understanding sexuality. But in order to more fully understand sexuality and sex, we must go beyond biological influences. How we think and feel, how we experience these thoughts and feelings *intrapersonally* (within ourselves), as well as *interpersonally* (within our relationships with others), are integral parts of our sexuality equation and sexual health. The **psychosocial domain** (see Figure 1.3) of human sexuality refers to the social and emotional/psychological aspects of sexuality. This domain takes into consideration our *psychological* development and experiences in the context of our *social* development and experiences. The **psychosexual domain** is a blending of sorts of the sexual aspects of our personality with other psychological factors.

As we explore the psychosocial/psychosexual domain of sexuality throughout our time together, among other issues we will examine the following:

- **Feelings and emotions:** This multifaceted dimension includes intimacy development and maintenance across the life span (refer to Chapter 6); experiences of love and loving (see Chapter 8); body image; self-concept and self-worth; gender identity; feelings associated with sexual trauma (abuse, rape, harassment, and coercion) (Chapter 17); and feelings and emotions associated with sexual orientation (such as coming out).

- **Interpersonal relationships:** This area of the psychosocial/psychosexual domain includes such topics as the development of gender roles; interrelationships with family and how they shape our sexuality; the significance of friends to our psychosocial and psychosexual development; dating, hooking up, nonmarital cohabitation, marriage, and divorce; heterosexual, homosexual, and bisexual relationships; and sexuality and aging.

- **Sexual health:** Within the psychosocial/psychosexual domain of sexuality, sexual health refers to the development of healthy attitudes about sexuality and sexual behavior. This domain also includes sexual decision making and interpersonal communication skills (Chapter 9).

As you are beginning to see, who you are as a sexual being is the result of individual biophysical factors that are intricately intertwined with psychological and social factors. But, to understand sexuality fully, we need an understanding of one more critical influence: *culture*.

THE CULTURAL DOMAIN

How individuals understand and practice their sexuality and sexual behaviors is influenced by the culture in which they live. It is important to understand that a person's sex and sexuality are determined in large part by his or her *social identity*. Social identity can be looked at in two different ways.

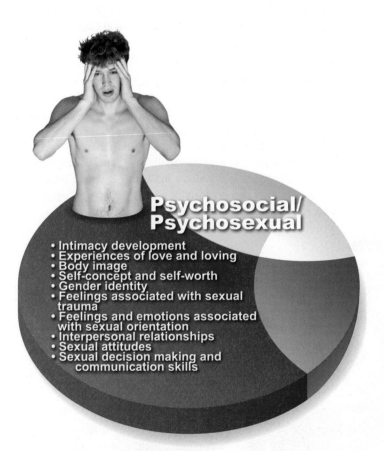

Psychosocial/ Psychosexual

- Intimacy development
- Experiences of love and loving
- Body image
- Self-concept and self-worth
- Gender identity
- Feelings associated with sexual trauma
- Feelings and emotions associated with sexual orientation
- Interpersonal relationships
- Sexual attitudes
- Sexual decision making and communication skills

Figure 1.3 The Psychosocial/ Psychosexual Domain of Sexuality

∧
∧ The thoughts and emotions that
∧ accompany sexuality, **both within ourselves and toward others, make up the psychosocial/psychosexual domain.**

Social psychologists Henri Tajfel and John Turner (1979), for example, introduced the **social identity theory** to help us understand how people identify and define themselves through the social groups to which they belong, such as a racial or ethnic group, their friends, and their families. On the other hand, sociologists seek to determine whether the culture defines its social identity as a *collectivist* culture or an *individualistic* culture, because culturally approved beliefs influence our expectations, experiences, attitudes, and behaviors (Neto, 2007).

In **collectivist cultures**, individuals define their identity in terms of the relationships they hold with others. For instance, if asked the question, "Who are you?" a collectivist is likely to respond by giving the family's name or the region from which he or she originates (Triandis & Suh, 2002). The goals of the *collective*—the whole society—are given priority over individual needs, and group membership is important (Myers, 2008). In these cultures, members strive to be equal, contributing, beneficial members of the society (Triandis & Suh, 2002), and a feeling of obligation and duty to the society drives their personal behavior (Johnson et al., 2005). Because of the desire to maintain harmony within the group, collectivist cultures stress harmony, cooperation, and the promotion of feelings of closeness (Kupperbusch, et al., 1999).

For example, Asians accentuate the importance of the collective whole, and they therefore emphasize family bonds in their experiences of love, including extended family members. People's self-concepts, personal goals, mate selection, sexual attitudes, sexual behaviors, and the larger society are inseparable in collectivist societies (Johnson et al., 2005).

In **individualistic cultures**, people define their identity or sense of self in terms of personal attributes (such as wealth, social status, education level, and marital status) and promote individual over group goals (Myers, 2008). Unlike in collectivist cultures, *individualists* view themselves as truly independent entities from the society in which they live, and their personal needs and rights—rather than the needs of the society—guide their behaviors (Johnson et al., 2005). Individualistic cultures promote the idea of autonomy and individuation from the family,

^
^
^ **The media bombards us with multiple images of sex daily,** influencing our gender roles and identities.

Cultural

- Social identity
- Cultural roots and heritage
- Race
- Ethnicity
- Sexual attitudes, knowledge, and norms
- Religion
- Media
- Sexuality education

Figure 1.4   The Cultural Domain

which, in turn, affects relationship satisfaction, the ease with which intimacy is established, and "love" as a basis for marriage (Dion & Dion, 1993). Partners are free, by society's standards, to choose relationship partners that best suit their needs; it is thought that this freedom of choice enhances relationship satisfaction and the experiences of love, intimacy, and sex.

There are other cultural factors (see Figure 1.4) that significantly influence and shape sexuality and sex, particularly in Western cultures. As we continue our study together across this term, we will discuss each of these factors at length:

- **Media:** We are exposed to a number of sources across our life spans, from parents and other family members to the classroom, from music to Hollywood icons, from peers to books or magazines, from the Internet to the fashion industry, from TV to movies. In Chapter 3, we'll take a serious look at how media influence our gender roles and gender identities. In Chapter 18, we'll examine the sex industry, which includes print and Internet pornography, erotic literature, most adult films, and sex workers.

- **Religion: Spirituality** reflects the depth to which a person experiences the sacred or a deity (Guralnik, 1982). **Religiosity** refers to an individual's preference for religious expression. Religious principles and spirituality can have a marked effect on the conduct of individuals in all areas of their lives. As you will see in Chapter 2, these religious principles significantly shape and influence many people's sexual attitudes, values, beliefs, and behaviors.

- **Sexuality education:** Sexuality education is one of several methods that are used to influence the sexual health and sexual quality of life for people. The goal of programmatic sexuality education is to help children, youth, adolescents, and adults develop a sense of responsibility for their sexuality, their sexual knowledge, and their sexual health; it is believed that this education promotes a high level of wellness in individuals. In Chapter 2, we will explore the cultural meanings and contexts of sexuality education, as well as how this factor shapes our sexuality in the United States.

>>> Social identity determines how people define them-selves, impacting their sexuality and sexual behaviors.

In collectivist cultures, **sexual decisions are inextricably tied to the impact they will have on family bonds.**

Healthy Selves / Healthy Sex

Healthy Body, Great Sex!

Research shows us that healthy sexuality and sex contribute not only to healthy relationships, but to our overall happiness, too. For example, one study from England indicated that the happiness people get from increasing their sexual activity from one time per month to once a week is equivalent to the happiness they would feel if they received a $50,000 raise at work (Davis, 2006)! Without question, there is a strong relationship between overall health, overall lifestyle, and great sex. Here's how health affects your sex life:

- Losing small amounts of weight can stimulate the production of sex hormones. Keep your weight as close to ideal as possible.

- Eat a healthy, nutritious diet. High cholesterol and high blood pressure may affect sexual response levels, particularly as we age.

- Alcohol and drugs affect your sexual response levels. Stick to the adage, "everything in moderation" for optimal sexual health.

- Exercise regularly. Not only does exercise strengthen your heart and other muscles, the release of the feel-good hormones (endorphins) stabilizes your mood.

- Get seven to eight hours of sleep each night. It's hard to be in the mood for sex when you're tired all the time!

- Keep a positive attitude. Accept your body as it is.

- Protect your sexuality. Don't put yourself in dangerous situations at parties or have unprotected sex.

- Believe in yourself as a sexual person.

Some of these changes are small, and some of these changes may require a change in your overall lifestyle. But all of these can go a long way toward improving both your sex drive and sexual desire!

It is without question that sexual behavior cannot be isolated from the cultural contexts in which we live (Bowleg, Lucas, & Tschann, 2004). Throughout this textbook, you will see how a culture's social identity shapes and directs the sexual attitudes, norms, and behaviors of its members.

SEXUAL LIFE EDUCATION

Today, there are substantial differences in how people experience and enjoy their sexuality. And certainly, broader social changes also influence the experience of our sexuality. As the United States moved into the second half of the 20th century, a number of social and cultural changes occurred that continue to have impact on 21st-century sexuality, including:

- Lowered birth rates
- Delays in marriage
- An increase in the woman's ability to control her fertility through contraceptive drugs or devices
- Changes in attitudes toward abortion
- Changes in attitudes regarding marriage and divorce
- Increased rates and social acceptance of nonmarital cohabitation and same-sex relationships
- The role of feminism in attempting to overcome the tradition of patriarchy in the home and in society

All of these factors work together to change the ways in which Americans experience and practice their sexuality, and, throughout our study in this book, we will examine all of these changes in depth.

Although we are not far historically from that first year of my college experience, in another sense, we are worlds away from that time. Long gone is the "secret society" of human sexuality courses. After this brief introduction to the topic, I hope you are ready to deal with issues of sexual life in an open and honest way and to unpack the complexities of sexual attitudes, expressions, and experiences.

Sexuality, of course, is so much more than just perfect body parts and perfectly timed orgasms. It also doesn't exist in a vacuum, nor is it isolated to just one aspect of our relational lives. As we change through the life course, so too do our experiences of our sexuality. Clearly, our sexuality is an inseparable part of our being that affects every other area of our lives, including our biological, psychosocial/psychosexual, and cultural lives.

Each of you comes to this course with your own sexual history. But regardless of your sexual beliefs, attitudes, or experiences, our study of sexuality and sex will equip you and strengthen your knowledge base as

Broad societal changes have impacted how people view and experience sexuality, particularly in the United States.

you prepare for a career in the helping professions or for your intimate relationships. There is much to discover about sex—about *real* sex in today's complex, global society. We have a lot to learn, so let's roll up our sleeves and get busy!

Should Abstinence-Until-Marriage Be the Only Sex Education?

Is it great to wait? A hotly debated topic among religious leaders and organizations, educations, and political groups, few topics bring such polarity as the issue of abstinence education. At issue is whether such educational programs keep preteens and teens from having sex until marriage, or whether a lack of education and information serves only to put teens at greater risk for unwanted pregnancies and STIs and HIV/AIDS. Should abstinence-until-marriage be the only sex education youth and teens receive?

YES!

- Three million teens—one-fourth of all sexually active teens in America—have a sexually transmitted disease (Guttmacher Institute, 2007).

- Teenage moms are more likely to live under the constraints of poverty, because 41 percent will drop out of school (Maher, 2004). Their poverty and limited education have a profound effect on *their* children, who are more likely to have lower grades, be abused, and drop out of school themselves.

- According to the Family Research Council, kids having kids costs American taxpayers over $7 billion per year in lost tax revenue and support services, such as welfare.

- Evidence shows abstinence-only programs (AOP) work. An AOP adopted by the Georgia State Board of Education for use in all eighth-grade classes in Columbus, Georgia, over a period of four years found a marked drop in pregnancies over a two-year period, an increase in pregnancies in non-AOP districts, and a positive effect of virginity pledges (the commitment to remaining a virgin until marriage).

NO!

- Supporters of sex education maintain that AOPs: provide fear-based education that tries to scare adolescents into sexual abstinence; are unrealistic (adolescents will have sex and should protect their health); omit critical information, including the use of condoms and other forms of birth control; and risk alienating bisexuals, gays, lesbians, single moms, and sexually active teens.

- Advocates of sex education note that AOPs exclusively address vaginal intercourse (which is the commonly agreed-upon requirement for losing virginity), but make no mention of other sexual activity that can also lead to disease, such as oral and anal sex.

- In contrast, Comprehensive Sexuality Education (CSE) addresses these areas, all the while maintaining several core principles: every person is valuable and has worth; sexual activity should never be exploitative or coercive; sexual decisions have consequences; and every person has a right and an obligation to make responsible sexual decisions.

- After completing a comprehensive sex education program, a majority of teens (70 percent) are more likely to use protective measures. This means fewer pregnancies, fewer instances of STIs, and healthy teens.

>>> WHAT DO YOU THINK?

1. Do abstinence-only programs put adolescents at risk for unwanted consequences of sex, such as pregnancy and STIs?
2. In your opinion, what is the most effective sex education: abstinence only, birth control/prevention only, or a combination of both programs? Why did you reach this decision?

Sources: Alford, S. (2001). Transitions, rights, respect, responsibility. Retrieved August 19, 2009, from www.advocatesforyouth.org; Maher, B. (2004). Abstinence until marriage: the best message for teens. The Family Research Council. Retrieved August 19, 2009, from www.frc.org; National Guidelines Task Force (1994). *Guidelines for comprehensive sexuality education.* New York: SIECUS.

01

Summary

WHAT IS SEXOLOGY? 4

• Sexology is a scientific quest to know and to understand how and why people experience their sexuality and sex the ways they do. It is a multidisciplinary science that includes the study of human sexual development, relationship development, relationship processes, the sexuality of certain groups, and sexual pathologies.

WHAT ARE THE CHARACTERISTICS OF ANCIENT SEXOLOGY? 6

• For thousands of years, people have written and illustrated manuals and literary works that document the attributes of sex and included advice on sexual techniques, information about sexual health and problems.

WHAT ARE THE THREE DOMAINS OF SEXUALITY AND WHAT IS THEIR SIGNIFICANCE? 7

• Sexuality involves three interrelated domains that all play an equal role in how we experience and express our sexuality: the biological, psychosocial/psychosexual, and sociocultural dimensions. All three of these domains are in constant interaction and are continuously growing and changing.

HOW DOES CULTURE INFLUENCE THE EXPERIENCES OF SEXUALITY AND SEX? 9

• The understanding and practices of sexuality and sexual behaviors are influenced by culture. In order to understand sexuality, it is important to consider the impact of social factors such as media, religion, race, ethnicity, heritage, and concepts of social identity.

Key Terms

sexology the systematic, organized study of human sexual behavior in all aspects 5

sexologist a person who has expert academic knowledge in sexual science and who devotes himself or herself to the objective, empirical study of sexuality 5

Kama Sutra an ancient Indian text that addresses the rules of pleasure, desire, and intentions 6

Sexuality Information and Education Council of the United States (SIECUS) council that defines human sexuality as a dimension of our personality that encompasses our sexual beliefs, attitudes, values, behaviors, and knowledge 7

biological domain of sexuality sexual exploration of areas such as male and female anatomy and physiology, gender, and genetics, including the contributions of hereditary factors that contribute to sexuality experiences 8

psychosocial domain of sexuality the social and emotional/psychological aspects of sexuality 8

psychosexual domain of sexuality a blending of the sexual aspects of our personality with other psychological factors 8

social identity theory theory constructed by Tajfel and Turner to help us understand how people identify and define themselves through the social groups to which they belong, such as

a racial or ethnic group, their friends, and their families 9

collectivist culture culture in which individuals define their identity in terms of the relationships they hold with others 9

individualistic culture culture in which people define their identity or sense of self in terms of personal attributes (such as wealth, social status, education level, and marital status) and promote individual over group goals 9

spirituality reflection of the depth to which a person experiences the sacred or a deity 10

religiosity an individual's preference for religious expression 10

Sample Test Questions

MULTIPLE CHOICE

1. Which is NOT true regarding sexology?

   a. It includes the study of human development and relationship processes.

   b. It is multidisciplinary.

   c. It has ancient origins.

   d. Its primary focus is on the mechanics of intercourse.

2. How has sexuality changed in the United States over the last 50 years?

   a. Sexuality is censored more than ever in the media.

   b. Sexuality has become more prominent in the media.

   c. Sexuality is no longer censored by network television.

   d. Sexuality has become a topic that society no longer cares about.

3. What is the oldest known sex manual?

   a. *Perfumed Garden*

   b. *Kama Sutra*

   c. *Art of Love*

   d. *Sexual Behavior in the Human Male*

4. Sexual differentiation is a topic of interest under which domain of sexuality?

   a. Biological

   b. Psychosocial/Psychosexual

   c. Cultural

   d. Interpersonal

5. Which BEST describes human sexuality?

   a. It is limited to the purpose of reproduction.

   b. It is the quality of being either male or female.

   c. It involves an identity independent of cultural influences.

   d. It includes sexual beliefs, values, behaviors, and knowledge.

6. Which is NOT studied in the psychosocial domain of sexuality?

   a. Intrapersonal feelings

   b. Self-concept and self-worth

   c. Hormones that direct sexual differentiation

   d. The influence of family relationships on sexuality

7. Which is TRUE about the relationship of culture to human sexuality?

   a. Culture shapes the sexual attitudes, norms, and behaviors of its members.

   b. Sexual behavior can be fully understood without reference to cultural influences.

   c. Culture determines the biological and physiological character of human sexuality.

   d. All cultures have essentially the same attitude toward human sexuality.

8. What is a way to maintain healthy sexual response levels?

   a. Having unprotected sex

   b. Exercising regularly

   c. Eating foods high in fat

   d. Drinking alcohol to excess

SHORT RESPONSE

1. Using what you learned in this chapter, respond to a friend who thinks that there is little need for a course in human sexuality.

2. Identify two different approaches to sex education in the United States.

3. Provide an example of one aspect of sexuality in which the psychosocial/psychosexual domain would be useful.

4. Describe the difference between collectivistic and individualistic cultures.

5. In your opinion, what has the largest influence on sexual behaviors? Why?

KNOWING WHAT WE KNOW
Understanding Sexual Life through Research and Theory

<<< The Eromatique sex toy vending machine in Tilburg, Netherlands, is an example of the Dutch's relatively open attitudes toward sexuality.

WHAT CONTRIBUTIONS DID EARLY SEXOLOGISTS MAKE TO OUR UNDERSTANDING OF SEXUALITY TODAY?

WHAT IS EMPIRICAL RESEARCH IN THE SOCIAL SCIENCES?

HOW DOES BRONFENBRENNER'S ECOLOGICAL MODEL EXPLAIN OUR DIFFERENCES IN SEXUALITY?

HOW DO THE VARIOUS THEORETICAL PERSPECTIVES OFFER INSIGHT INTO THE STUDY OF SEXUALITY?

I am

a 19-year-old male who attends a university in the Midwest. Because of my unusual upbringing, I'm having a really tough time coming to terms with "who" I am sexually.

My father was an executive for a corporation that took us to the Netherlands when I was four or five years old. Within the past year, I moved back to the States to go to college, so most of my life was spent in the Netherlands.

In the Netherlands, sexuality and sex aren't taboo, something you can't openly talk about or enjoy—the Dutch have a very practical attitude toward sex. The Netherlands is a very socially liberal country. Nothing is "shocking" or off-limits. The age of consent for sex is 12, not 18 like it is in the United States, and "official" sex education in the Netherlands begins in preschool.

As far as my personal experiences, from as young as I can remember, I grew up watching my mom and her friends tan in the nude in our backyard [and later had fantasies about them]. Every Sunday afternoon, my parents listened to a three-hour radio talk show where people called in and asked anything about sex, and today I can still remember things I heard and learned.

Now that I'm back in [the United States], I'm starting to understand that my sexuality and my sexual behaviors were dictated by Dutch culture. In that culture, it was no big deal to have sexual fantasies about your mom and her friends or to fool around with your guy friends—two things that are waaaay off-limits in U.S. culture. I guess what I'm trying to say, is that for 19 years of my life, I thought I was a normal, healthy guy who had a normal, healthy sexual appetite. Now, the sexual values of this country make me feel like I'm some [pervert] who needs some serious therapy. Am I gay? Bisexual? Incestuous? How do I change to fit into this culture? How can I change to fit into this culture? Believe me, I've learned the hard way that sex in one part of the world isn't necessarily sex in another part of the world. Sex is not sex is not sex . . .

Source: Author's files

CHAPTER 02

Science is humankind's exploration of how the world works. Often, the exploration to discover and understand begins with a simple inquiry, such as the questions posed by the college student in the opening vignette. How is our sexuality shaped by the culture in which we are raised? And, if we move to a different culture that embraces differing views of sex and sexuality, how does *that* culture influence our sexual expression?

When examining social and individual behaviors by using methods beyond our logical common sense or reason alone, we engage in the practice of **empirical research**. Today, sexology researchers adhere to rigorous standards, and they do not face as many challenges as the pioneers of sexuality research in the 19th and 20th centuries. In this chapter, we'll first take a look at the early history of sexology in Europe and the United States, and then look at different theories that help us better understand how the culture in which we live shapes and directs our sexual beliefs, attitudes, behaviors, and norms.

EARLY SEXUALITY RESEARCH: PAVING THE WAY TO UNDERSTANDING SEXUALITY AND SEX

Sex research has an irregular history (see Figure 2.1) because many people have ambivalent or conflicting feelings about sex, and because of Western societies' long-standing taboo on eroticism and sexuality

Figure 2.1 A Historical View of Sex through the Ages

| 1000 BCE | | 1 CE | | 500 CE |

The Greeks
1000 BCE to 200 BCE

- Ancient Greek culture was a culture of wild indulgences, and today it is widely known for its historical temples of sex and homosexuality.

- In their studies of Corinthian sacred prostitutes, or **pornai**, historians have discovered that these slaves were dedicated to temples as forms of religious offerings, servants to Aphrodite, the patron sexual goddess (Perrottet, 2007). *Pornai* engaged in uninhibited, pagan sexual free-for-alls with sailors who came to the Greek port, Corinth.

- Homosexuality was prevalent in ancient Greece, particularly among warriors and in the militaries. The prevalence of homosexuality is also observed in the Greek arts.

- The majority of homosexual relationships took place within the socially approved institution of **pederasty**, sexual relationships between an adult man and a male youth. The **erastes**, a male in his 20s or 30s, educated, protected, loved, and provided a role model for his lover, a beardless boy, the **eromenos**. In turn, the *eromenos* offered his *erastes* beauty, youth, admiration, and love (Dover, 1989).

- Greek males regarded their wives as suitable only for raising children, not as someone with whom to have sex. For pleasurable sex, Greek males went to *pornai* or *eromenos*.

The Roman Empire
27 BCE to 385 CE

- During the rise and fall of the Roman Empire, love went from guilt-free sexual indulgence to a somber, joyless, guilt-ridden experience intertwined with the act of sex.

- Exit (out and sinful) love as the Greeks related it to sensuality and sexuality.

- Enter Christianity where the call to love one another in a self-sacrificing way dominated.

Early Christianity
50 CE to 1000 CE

- The apostle Paul (who died in 66 CE) emphasized in his writings in the New Testament that sex outside of marriage and homosexual sex were sins against God; people who engaged in these acts could not inherit the Kingdom of God.

- Later in church history, the bishop Augustine (354–430 CE) proclaimed that lust is what caused "the fall" of Adam and Eve, and he declared that their lust (and hence, the sex that resulted because of the lust) as "original sin."

- Bishop Augustine's writings formalized church doctrine that sex outside of marriage, and sex for any purposes other than procreation was sin—the "sex as sinful" movement war born (Bullough, 2001). This sex-as-sinful theology prevailed for 1,000 years, and persisted throughout the Middle Ages.

(Bullough, 2004; Haeberle, 1983; Money, 1976). For example, mid-20th century sexologist Vern Bullough was under suspicion of the United States FBI, who monitored his activities in the field of sex research. He was regarded as a "dangerous subversive" (Bullough, 2004). Despite these hurdles, scholarly attempts to understand sexuality, eroticism, and sex emerged in the 19th century.

19TH-CENTURY SEXUALITY RESEARCH

Aristotle (384 BCE–322 BCE) wrote about a number of different subjects, including poetry, theater, politics, ethics, and biology. He was one of the first to offer sexual theories regarding sexual responses, reproduction, contraception, abortions, the legislation of sex, and sexual ethics. Though he didn't write it, *Aristotle's Masterpiece*, one of the most wide-

ly read sex manuals in the 18th and 19th centuries, bears his name (Bullough, 2004; Fissell, 2003). This work described sex, pregnancy, and childbirth. Many young boys and adolescent males received their first understanding of sex from the manual, and historians believe that young brides sometimes received the manual from their mothers (Fissell, 2003). *Aristotle's Masterpiece* advised male lovers to pay particular attention to the woman's clitoris "because blowing the coals of the amorous fires" leads to greater sexual pleasure for both partners (Bullough, 1973, p. 242). The manual was so explicit in detail and provocative that its publication was banned in Britain until the 1960s (Fissell, 2003).

Although attitudes toward sex and sexuality were largely negative throughout the 18th and 19th centuries in the West, there were still a number of European and American pioneers in sex research. These sex-

---

1000 CE   **1500 CE**   **2000 CE**

The Middle Ages
476 CE to 1400 CE

- People were concerned with faith, the church, piety, and salvation (Gilmour-Bryson, 2007). It was an era wherein the only acceptable sex was between a man and a woman — with her assuming the submissive, on-the-bottom position — and only for the purposes of procreation. It is from this era the Western world came to demand chastity, not only from unmarried women, but from priests, monks, and nuns, too (Gilmour-Bryson, 2007).

- Theologian Thomas Aquinas (1224–1274) maintained that any human sexual contact other than penis/vagina intercourse was sinful, a "crime against nature," and violated God's will for men and women (Gilmour-Bryson, 2007).

- In the 1400s, Pope Gregory IX gave standards on what constituted sexual sin: masturbation, mutual masturbation, interfemoral intercourse (the placement of the penis between the thighs of the passive partner), oral sex, and anal intercourse (Blacksmith, 2001). During this era, sex was taught as an "evil" introduced by the Devil.

- Church law in the Middle Ages dictated when it was permissible to have sex with one's wife—and when it was forbidden to do so.

- When caught in acts of homosexuality, the Church punished the "guilty" with penances (a religious devotion) of fasting on bread and water for seven years, a fine, or even a forfeit of life. The Medieval Church was against any form of contraception. (Blacksmith, 2001).

Coming to America
1500 CE to 1600 CE

- As the British emigrated to New England during the 16th and 17th centuries to pursue religious reformation and freedom, contrary to popular belief, the Puritans and Pilgrims showed themselves to be romantically sentimental — and thoroughly enjoyed sex within the confines of marriage. During this historical era, the ideals of love and romance were combined with the expectancy of (enjoyable) sex within marriage (Hunt, 1959).

- Such freedoms, however, were short-lived as 18th century Puritans gave way to the oppressive, stuffy, formality of the Victorians — in love, romance, and sexual practices.

Modern Day
1800 CE to 1900 CE

- The Victorian era derived its name from the British Queen Victoria (1819–1901). The virginal, shy, virtuous, spiritual woman was the epitome of the attitude toward sexuality and the role of women during this timeframe in history.

- In a society where saying "leg" in public was a mark of impropriety, any premarital activity beyond a stolen kiss was strictly forbidden (Tingsten, 1966).

- To be sure, virginity was nearly sacrosanct. This is not to say, however, that there was not a glaring double standard of virginity. Indeed, men were more easily excused for their frivolous sexuality, their drinking, their smoking, and their sexual joking (Tingsten, 1966).

- In Victorian England and America, sex was publicly dichotomized between the proper woman's distaste for sex and the normal man's active sexual appetite. Since it was a proper woman's natural state to be chaste, it was only reasonable to expect that the inevitable honeymoon intrusion upon such purity would be horrid. As one mother was famously credited with saying before her daughter's marriage experience, "Close your eyes and think of England!" (Marsh, 2006).

- The Victorian era was short-lived and quickly gave way to the emergence of sexual research in the 19th and 20th centuries.

ology forefathers were the first to publicly discuss and write about sexual theories, sexual dysfunctions or abnormalities, and sexual response (Bullough, 1994). These 19th century sex researchers greatly expanded the understanding of human sexuality (Matte, 2005). Just as importantly, many of the terms and concepts developed by these sexology reformers are still used today (see Table 2.1) to help us understand human sexuality (Matte, 2005). The following sex researchers significantly influenced sexology. They are not discussed in order of their importance or in chronological order.

Iwan Bloch (1872–1922): The Father of Sexology

The "father of sexology," Iwan Bloch, was devoted to understanding sex in a scientific and scholarly way (Haeberle, 1983). Bloch coined the term *sexualwissenschaft*, or **sexology**, which refers to the theoretical and scientific study of sex. This concept of sexology differed from the older concept of **erotology**, such as erotic writings like *Aristotle's Masterpiece*. Bloch also believed that previous attempts to understand sexuality strictly from a medical perspective were restrictive. He believed that scientific explanations were needed as to why sexual "perversions" existed throughout all cultures and through time (Matte, 2005). This new centralized viewpoint was the *sexologist*—and the empirical science and quest to understand sexuality across multiple disciplines was launched.

Karl Heinrich Ulrichs (1825–1875): A Political Activist

Karl Heinrich Ulrichs contributed to the field of sexology through his publications about his theories on *Uranism*, or "third gender" men whom he believed possessed female souls and were thus attracted to other men (Kennedy, 1981). Ulrichs became a public activist for issues associated with sexual minorities (such as same-sex attraction and gender ambiguity). His theories, however, were based in large part on his own sexuality and sexual experiences (Matte, 2005). Because of the public nature of his writings, others (such as Richard von Krafft-Ebing) contacted him and adapted his initial theories.

Richard von Krafft-Ebing (1840–1902): A Promoter that Sex Is Deviant

Richard von Krafft-Ebing advanced the idea that the purpose of sexual desire was for procreation and that any sexual desire or behavior for any purpose other than producing children was perversion. Although much of Krafft-Ebing's work focused on the negative aspects of sexuality and "seems to many students of today to be an encyclopedia of horror stories" (Bullough, 2004, p. 377), perhaps the greatest contribution Krafft-Ebing made to the field of early sexology was his extensive case histories, which numbered more than 300 (Matte, 2005). Over time, Krafft-Ebing corrected himself and came to believe that homosexuality was not a pathological, deviant form of

TABLE 2.1
Sexuality Studies in the United States

Several sexuality studies have given us great insight into our current understanding of human sexuality.

The Janus Report	Perhaps one of the most comprehensive sexuality studies in the U.S. since Kinsey's studies in the 1950s, the Janus Report was based on the data of nearly 3,000 surveys. Samuel and Cynthia Janus asserted that Americans were more willing to talk about and engage in wider varieties of sexual behaviors, and that older Americans had a greater interest in sex than previously thought. The study has been criticized because of the sampling technique used (it was not a random sample).
The National Health and Social Life Survey	The AIDS epidemic in the 1980s spurred the U.S. Department of Health and Human Services to call for proposals to study the sexual norms of Americans. Researchers from the University of Chicago created a survey that was administered to nearly 3,500 people, making the NHSLS the largest study of Americans' sexuality in history. The researchers used sophisticated sampling techniques to ensure a representative sample and had a striking 79 percent response rate.
The Youth Risk Behavior Survey	The YRBS is a report provided by the Centers for Disease Control and Prevention (CDC). Every two years, the YRBS surveys students in grades nine through 12 to determine six categories of health risk behaviors among high school students. Sexual behaviors and trends in teen pregnancy and STIs comprise one of the six categories of health that are studied.
Pfizer Global Study of Sexual Attitudes and Behaviors	More than 27,000 men and women, aged 40 to 80 years, from 29 different countries participated in the Pfizer study. This study assesses the role and importance of sex and intimacy in people's lives, the sexual attitudes and beliefs of middle-aged and older adults, and treatment-seeking behaviors for sexual dysfunction among men and women. The data provide an international baseline about sexual attitudes and beliefs; this data can be used in the future to compare changes in attitudes.

behavior, but rather a process that developed during the prenatal period (Oosterhuis, 2000).

Clelia Duel Mosher (1863–1940): An Advocate for Women's Sexual Health

Clelia Duel Mosher challenged stereotypes about the physical weaknesses and maladies of Victorian women (Jacob, 1981). Her personal goal was to debunk the prevailing idea that female menstruation was an insurmountable barrier that kept women at home and out of the workforce. She studied healthy women to better understand what normal menstruation was, what factors made menstruation painful or abnormal, and whether or not certain factors could be modified to make menstruation less painful (Jacob, 1981). Her preliminary findings were groundbreaking at the time: "There was no physiological reason why most normal, healthy women should be incapacitated by menstruation" (Jacob, 1981).

Through her research findings, Mosher believed she physically emancipated women; no longer were women sent to bed during their menstrual periods, but instead, they were encouraged to understand and to know how their bodies functioned (Jacob, 1981). Her second publication in 1923, "Woman's Physical Freedom," focused on middle-aged women who were experiencing menopause.

But Mosher's most provocative, first-of-its-kind research was not published until 1974, some 34 years after her death. As far back as 1892, Mosher began to collect data from 19th century, Victorian-era women about their sexual practices, values, and beliefs; some of the women were born before the Civil War. Mosher's data revealed some interesting findings; despite that fact that women of the Victorian era were expected to live under a repressive, restrictive sexual code, Mosher's pioneering sexual research shows us that many of the women did not reluctantly engage in sex as part of their wifely responsibilities. To the contrary—they desired the experiences of intercourse and orgasm (Jacob, 1981).

Havelock Ellis (1859–1939): An Agitator for Sexual Reform

Havelock Ellis is viewed by some in the field of sexology as an agitator for sexual reform (Matte, 2005). Ellis was one of the first to recognize the existence of female sexuality and that women had a right to sexual pleasure (Jackson, 1983). Ellis himself claimed to be asserting the "erotic rights of women on their behalf" (Jackson, 1983, p. 3). Furthermore, Ellis was adamant in his belief that homosexuality was a natural occurrence in the sexual world and that it should be accepted by society (Matte, 2005). His ideas broadened the range of what was considered to be "legitimate" sexual behavior; these theories, in turn, promoted a greater tolerance of sexual differences (Jackson, 1983; Matte, 2005).

Albert Moll (1862–1939): A Social Conservative

Albert Moll was second only to Iwan Bloch and Magnus Hirschfeld as a great promoter of sexology. Moll was not a sexual activist or reformer; he was politically conservative and believed that Freud and Hirschfeld put forth false claims about sexuality, and every chance he got, he debunked their work as the work of frauds (Archive for Sexology, 2007).

Moll introduced the idea that our sexual nature is made up of two entirely distinct parts, *genital impulse* and *sexual attraction*. Simply stated, Moll was as interested in the biological, physical aspects of sexuality as he was in the emotional aspects of sexuality, but he regarded these two aspects as equally important in understanding sexuality, and did not separate attraction from other sexual behaviors.

^
^ 20th century sexuality research
^ **helped to user in the 1960s sexual revolution.**

Magnus Hirschfeld (1868–1935): A Gay Rights Champion

Magnus Hirschfeld proved to be one of the most significant, influential people in the 19th and early 20th centuries sexology movement. Hirschfeld used extensive case histories, interviews, and consultations to develop his theories about sexual orientation and sexual variations (Matte, 2005). In 1897, Hirschfeld founded the *Scientific Humanitarian Committee*, the world's first gay rights organization, to petition changes in German law that criminalized homosexual relations between men. Contrary to prevailing views that someone was either male or female, and either heterosexual or homosexual, Hirschfeld challenged these notions and advanced the idea that gender ran along a continuum. He developed the term "sexual intermediary" to describe people who were not heterosexual, such as homosexuals, bisexuals, and people who were otherwise gender variant; was a self-proclaimed "intermediary" (Matte, 2005). In 1910, Hirschfeld coined the term *transvestite* to describe a person who habitually or frequently adopts the dress and/or behavior of the opposite sex.

Although their research methodologies may not have withstood the rigorous research standards and ethics present in the scientific community today, it is important to understand the influences of the forefathers of the study of sexuality and to appreciate their international collaboration. Each of these individuals not only contributed to our present understanding of many of the variances observed in sexuality, but they also paved the way for the organized, systematic study of sexuality in the 20th century (see Table 2.1).

20TH-CENTURY SEXUALITY RESEARCH

Although they fought opposition and often faced negative social reception for their ideas and their work, these 19th-century sexuality researchers initiated the international social reform that was necessary for those who followed in their footsteps to carry the sexology torch into the 20th century (Matte, 2005). Even though sexology today still appears to many to be a science without sound theoretical foundation, much less a legitimate academic endeavor, sexologists of the 20th century worked to develop an understanding of sexuality, sexual freedom, and sexual rights.

The work of the sexologists we discuss in the sections that follow helped to usher in the **sexual revolution**, the changing trends in social thought that relaxed sexual taboos about sexuality from the 1960s into the 1970s. Sexuality historian David Allyn (2002) suggests that the sexual revolution was a time of "coming out" for the United States, a time that involved major changes in how people thought about and talked about sexuality and sex. To be sure, during this time America did come out: about premarital sex, masturbation, sexual fantasies, pornography, and homosexuality (Allyn, 2002).

Sigmund Freud (1856–1939): An Influential Thinker

Sigmund Freud sought to anchor all aspects of sexuality, including sexual development, sexual orientation, and sexual behaviors, in the dynamics of the human mind. We'll discuss Freud's theory and stages of psychosexual development at length in Chapter 7; the point to keep in consideration here is that Freud moved beyond the medical paradigm of sexuality that was so prominent in the 19th century and explored sexuality as an integral part of his broader theory of human personality development.

Freud developed his five-stage theory of sexuality based on his assumption that all children have a sexual love for their mothers and sexual jealousy of their fathers. Central to Freud's theory of the mind (personality development) is the concept of *libido*. According to Freud, the human mind has a fixed amount of psychic energy—or **libido**. Although most people today use the term to refer solely to sexual urges, Freud originally suggested that libido fuels our thought processes, perception, imagination, memory, and our sexual urges (Stevenson, 1996). The amount of libido is fixed; however, the mind can transfer the psychic energy from one function to another (Stevenson, 1996). Freud argued that libido can become fixated on specific objects throughout the course of development, such as pleasure in breastfeeding as an infant (the oral stage) and pleasure in having a bowel movement as a toddler (the anal stage).

Freud differed with some of the prevailing views of the time. He believed that his predecessors in sexuality research defined human sexuality too narrowly. He contradicted the popular opinions on sexuality by noting that sexual life doesn't begin at puberty, but soon after birth; that being "sexual" includes activities that have nothing to do with the genitals; and that sexual life serves both reproduction and pleasure.

At the beginning of the 20th century, Freud ushered in a new paradigm about human sexuality. His perspectives helped broaden Victorians' prim attitudes about sexuality and sex, and today many practitioners continue to adhere to the tenets of his theories.

∧∧ Sigmund Freud

Alfred Kinsey (1894–1956): A Sexual Liberalizer

Alfred Kinsey was perhaps one of the most influential Americans of the 20th century. His landmark research that sought to understand male and female sexual behavior helped bring about the "sexual revolution" that took place in the 1960s and 1970s (Brown & Fee, 2003). Kinsey believed that to truly understand human sexuality, it was necessary for a scholarly approach that included not just case histories, but also research from other disciplines, such as the social sciences, law, education, the arts, music, and literature (Bullough, 2004).

The key to Kinsey's research was the interviews he used to gather his data (Bullough, 2004). He inquired about:

- Menstruation history
- Anatomical changes associated with puberty (timing and development)
- Masturbation/masturbatory techniques
- Erotic fantasies

Interspersed throughout each interview were questions that gave the interviewers hints about the participant's sexual preference (Bullough, 2004). From this research, Kinsey developed his sexual orientation scale. We'll discuss this continuum of sexual orientation at length in Chapter 7.

To some extent, Kinsey created the sexuality we know today. Beyond this, however, Alfred Kinsey was an instrumental force in bringing homosexuality out of the closet, and he encouraged gays and lesbians to do just that—to come out. Just as importantly, Kinsey's research dispelled long-held myths about female sexual behaviors and response; this research was the launching pad for the feminist movement in the mid-20th century, which eventually led to greater equality for the sexes (Bullough, 2004).

William Masters (1915–2001) and Virginia Johnson (1925–): Promoters of Change

William Masters and Virginia Johnson pioneered research into the physiological responses of human sexuality, as well as the diagnosis and treatment of sexual disorders and dysfunctions. Within our sex-saturated society today, it is difficult to imagine or envision how startling and alarming Masters and Johnson's research was in the 1960s and 1970s when their landmark, classic books, *Human Sexual Response* (1966) and *Human Sexual Inadequacy* (1970) were published (Kolodny, 2001).

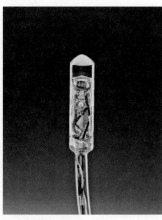

∧
∧ **The penile strain gauge** and the
∧ **photoplethysmograph** provide data
about sexual arousal in men and
women.

Unlike their predecessors, Masters and Johnson did not rely on case histories and interviews to gather their information about sexual behaviors; instead, they provided definitive laboratory evidence regarding such things as the origin of vaginal lubrication. The Masters and Johnson research team used EKG (**electrocardiogram**) machines to measure their subjects' heart rates and blood pressures. They also used polygraph-like machines to gather never-before-seen human sexual response data, such as the **penile strain gauge** that measured erections of the penis, and the **photoplethysmograph**, which measured vaginal

lubrication in women. With these tools, Masters and Johnson measured 700 men and women during sexual intercourse and masturbation. Based on the data they collected in their study, Masters and Johnson outlined their revolutionary *Four Phases of Human Sexual Response*, which we study in Chapter 11.

Beyond their laboratory findings, however, Masters and Johnson further promoted our understanding of sexuality by developing a revolutionary clinical approach to the treatment of sexual problems and dysfunctions. They incorporated a holistic approach to understanding and treating sexual problems.

Undeniably, Masters and Johnson made incredible strides to further our understanding of sexuality and to promote the objective science of sexology. Few who preceded them and few scientists in the future will achieve what Masters and Johnson did. Although their work evoked harsh criticisms from some, the team was "the ultimate scientific pioneer[s] who had a combination of remarkable vision, scientific fervor, and willingness to work against the odds to reach [their] goals" (Kolodny, 2001, p. 276).

As our study has shown us so far, the sexologists from the 19th and early 20th centuries strived to investigate sex and sexuality with a scientific approach. By using case histories, for example, sexologists were able to categorize different sexual behaviors and attitudes. Masters and Johnson then took this scientific quest to a different level when they were able to systematically measure the sexual responses of men and women.

Today, all sexologists are held to rigorous research standards, which are shown in Table 2.2. These standards not only ensure the research findings, but they also ensure the safety and well-being of research participants. Researchers today also follow a step-by-step process to ensure that the results they obtain in their studies are valid and reliable. The **scientific method** details the sequential, interrelated investigative steps the research will follow; this is illustrated for you in Figures 2.2 and 2.3 on page 24.

TABLE 2.2
Research Ethics

Ethics refers to the rules and standards that govern researchers' conduct as they examine human behaviors, feelings, and attitudes (National Academy of Sciences, 1995). Academic institutions and other research institutions have established research review committees, or **Institutional Review Boards for the Protection of Human Subjects (IRB)**. IRBs are often referred to as *human subjects committees.* Before pursuing a research plan, scientists must first gain the approval of their institution's IRB. IRBs are concerned with the following (National Academy of Sciences, 1995):

- *Safety:* There is a saying in research communities: *Above all, do no harm.* Researchers and social scientists must be careful to minimize any risks to the research participants.

- *Informed consent:* The research investigator must obtain consent, or permission, from the research participant before they involve them in a study of inquiry. Study participants must be fully informed of the true nature of the research, as well as of the risks and benefits associated with the research. Ethical informed consent includes: 1) full disclosure of the risks and benefits of the research; 2) understanding the research and being provided the opportunity to ask questions; 3) voluntary participation; 4) competence to agree to participate; and 5) written consent.

- *Privacy and confidentiality:* The research plan must detail how the privacy and confidentiality of the research participants will be protected. This ensures that unauthorized observers will not have access to the information gained from research participants. Researchers must ensure that no identifying information of the study participants is provided to unauthorized observers.

- *Injury:* Ethical research plans consider how potential injuries (physical or emotional) will be handled, such as who will pay for medical treatment if an injury occurs and who will provide that care.

Figure 2.2 The Research Process from Start to Finish

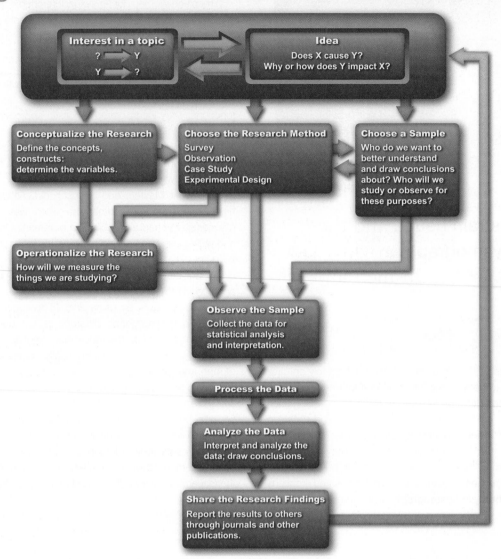

Source: From The Practice of Social Research (with CD-ROM and Info Trac) 10th edition by BABBIE. © 2004. Reprinted with permission of Wadsworth, a division of Thomson Learning: www.thomsonrights.com. Fax 800 730.2215.

Figure 2.3 The Experimental Design Research Method

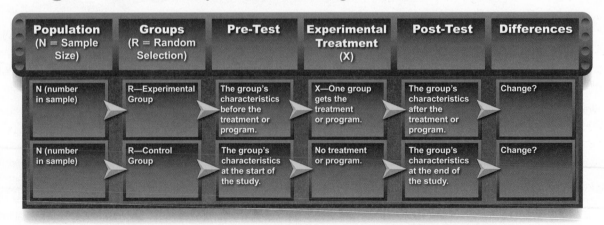

Source: From The Practice of Social Research (with CD-ROM and Info Trac) 10th edition by BABBIE. © 2004. Reprinted with permission of Wadsworth, a division of Thomson Learning: www.thomsonrights.com. Fax 800 730.2215.

UNDERSTANDING THE MULTIPLE INFLUENCES ON OUR SEXUALITY: THE ECOLOGICAL MODEL

The opening vignette of this chapter illustrates that we do not develop in isolation. What we have not yet discussed, though, is the idea that there are *multiple* cultural influences with which we are in constant interaction. A **social ecology** perspective recognizes that our individual backgrounds (such as our sexual history, experiences with our **family of origin**—the family in which we are raised), as well as outside social and cultural factors and policies, significantly affect the quality and the nature of personal and sexual relationships (Alberts, 2002). In his **ecological model**, Urie Bronfenbrenner (1979) sought to understand how these multiple, interacting **contexts**, or areas of individual and family development, play a role in the relationship between people and their environments. Bronfenbrenner recognized that the influence on relationships is **bi-directional**; not only does the environment influence the individual, but the individual influences the environment. For example, a new baby in a family has an impact on the parents just as much as the parents have an impact on the baby.

Figure 2.4 presents the ecological model. Notice that the individual is located in the center of four concentric, nested circles that expand outward. Each of those circles represents a different layer of societal interactions and influences external to the individual. The circles nearest the individual have more immediate impacts on the individual, whereas those farther out are more distant and may have less influence on the individual's development. To help guide this process, we will discuss each context, or **ecosystem**, within the ecological model.

THE INDIVIDUAL

Bronfenbrenner recognized that a person's development is not simply a matter of biology, cognition, or social interaction. Development is instead an intricate intertwining of *all three* components. Individual influences include, but are not limited to, race, ethnicity, genetics, health, nutrition, and physiological abilities or disabilities. By using this context, it allows us to see that someone who is born with a chromosomal disorder, such as Down syndrome, will have genetically determined influences on his or her sexual development and future sexual interactions that a person born without such disabilities will not have.

It is also important to note that in the United States, we tend to practice our sexuality at the individual, or *micro level*. In other words, our sexual attitudes, values, norms, beliefs, and behaviors are driven more by our *individual* needs and desires; they are not based on the overarching norms of society as is common in other cultures; these overarching norms are referred to as the *macro level*.

MICROSYSTEM

The **microsystem** is the developmental context nearest the individual and represents those interactions to which people are directly exposed. The elements that comprise this ecosystem are the individuals, groups, and agencies that have the earliest and most immediate influences on the individual. These include the family of origin; day care/schools; the neighborhood; workplaces; the community; and the church, synagogue, mosque, or temple. Each of us also has an impact on our environment. As we comply or rebel, agree or disagree, or express our views, we exert influence on the elements with which we interact. In short, we affect and are affected by the contexts of living.

MESOSYSTEM

The **mesosystem** retains all the elements that are present in the microsystem, but now focuses on the interaction *between* the various elements, rather than on the individual. For instance, how does the school impact sexuality?

Consider a public school district in the Northeast that establishes a sex education program that offers condom distribution to sixth graders, or

Healthy Selves / Healthy Sex

Are Ethics in Sexuality Research Important?

Given that sexuality research involves human subjects and given the sensitivity of sex research, high standards of research ethics that protect the physical, emotional, cognitive, and spiritual aspects of human subjects are essential.

According to Resnik (1998), ethical research behavior includes:

- **Honesty.** All scientific communication requires truthfulness and honesty. There should never be deception, falsification, or fabrication of data, results, research methods, or status of publications that report the findings of the study.

- **Objectivity.** True empirical research strives to avoid bias of any kind in the research plan, gathering data, data analysis/interpretation, and any other aspects of research.

- **Integrity.** Conduct all research with sincerity and consistency.

- **Carefulness.** Avoid careless errors and accept constructive criticism from peers. Keep accurate—honest—records of all activities associated with research.

- **Attribution.** Respect others' work. Give credit where credit is due!

- **Human Subjects.** Do no harm. Minimize risks associated with research, and be cautious with vulnerable populations, such as children.

- **Social Responsibility.** Strive to do research that promotes the social good and that strives to alleviate social ills.

Source: Based on Resnik, D. (1998). *The ethics of science: An introduction.* New York: Routledge.

Figure 2.4
Bronfenbrenner's Ecological Model

Macrosystem
Cultural Context

Exosystem
Socioeconomic Context

Mesosystem

Microsystem

Media

Education Institutions

Person Biological Context

Family
School
Religious Affiliation
Neighborhood

Religious Institutions

Political Institutions

Government Institutions

Overarching Beliefs and Values

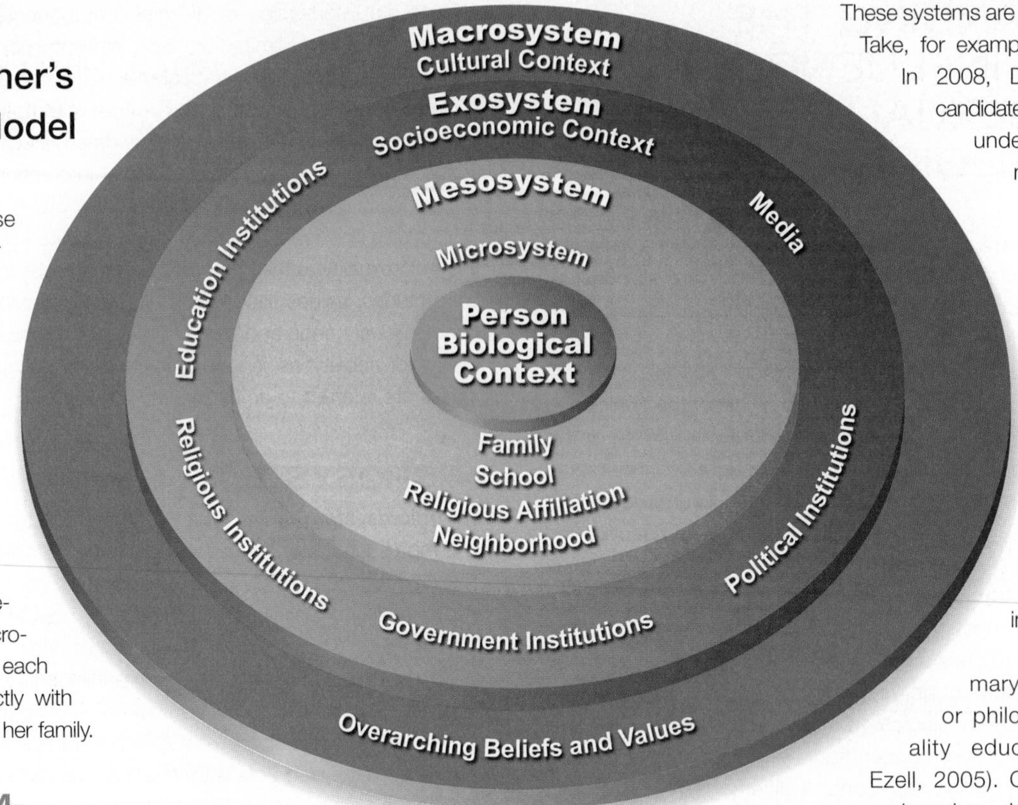

Source: Urie Bronfenbrenner (1979)

a school health nurse who makes referrals for teens to health clinics for birth control. Is it likely that a conservative community in the South would endorse these practices in a similar way that a community in Vermont might? These scenarios are examples of how elements within the microsystem interact with each other rather than directly with an individual and his or her family.

EXOSYSTEM

The **exosystem** consists of the fabrics of society in which policies are made and influenced that ultimately have an impact on the microsystem and the individual (Alberts, 2002). As Figure 2.4 illustrates, the exosystem serves as an umbrella for all of the "systems" in a society: educational, religious, economic, media, political, transportation, and government.

Think about, for example, the State Board of Education, which establishes policies and selects curricula that are used in each of the local school districts. At the same time, the hierarchies of various religious denominations determine the central tenets of their faith, which include and determine what sexual behaviors are deemed to be appropriate or inappropriate according to those tenets. In turn, those religious beliefs in large part determine what is taught in the public schools. As a result of this influence, a public school education may be vastly different in one state compared to another, depending on the components of the exosystem.

These systems are not without controversy. Take, for example, sexuality education. In 2008, Democratic presidential candidate Barack Obama came under fire when he announced that he was in favor of supporting sexuality education in schools as early as kindergarten. The reason for the debate? Many people believe that sexuality education entices kids to have sex (Anspaugh & Ezell, 2005) and that these courses involve little more than teaching the act of intercourse.

There are two primary schools of thought, or philosophies, about sexuality education (Anspaugh & Ezell, 2005). One position supports comprehensive, kindergarten-through-12th grade sexuality and health education; the other group advocates abstinence from sex until marriage. Table 2.3 shows the differences between the two philosophies. The *Sexual Life Now* feature box provides further insight into this decades-old debate.

Currently, 35 states mandate that public schools provide either sex education or education about HIV/AIDS and other sexually transmitted infections (Guttmacher Institute, 2006). Of these schools that have a policy to teach sexuality education, 86 percent require that abstinence-until-marriage be promoted. This is not to say, however, that comprehensive sexuality education cannot be taught or is not taught in these public schools. In American public schools, about 35 percent require abstinence to be taught as the *only option* for people who are unmarried; further, these schools do not allow the discussion of contraception, or if there is discussion, it focuses on the ineffectiveness of contraception (Guttmacher Institute, 2006). Most educators prefer a middle ground on

OWN IT! Sex is not sex is not sex . . .

Bronfenbrenner's ecological model shows us that our sexuality is the result of many interacting cultural influences. Every thought and every behavior is linked to and influenced by the culture in which we are raised.

Take a moment to jot down those factors from each ecosystem that shaped your sexuality today.

- *Microsystem:* How did your family of origin influence your sexuality? Your school? Your church, temple, or mosque? Have your friends influenced your sexuality?

- *Mesosystem:* Were there any influences in your microsystem that interacted with your family of origin? For instance, did your youth

group or school have sexuality education seminars that included your parents?

- *Exosystem:* List the ways your sexuality was influenced by the religious, political, and media systems in your culture.

- *Macrosystem:* What are the overarching cultural beliefs and values of the country in which you were raised? How did these affect your sexuality?

- *Chronosystem:* Do you think your sexuality would be different if you were raised at a different point in history? If so, in what ways?

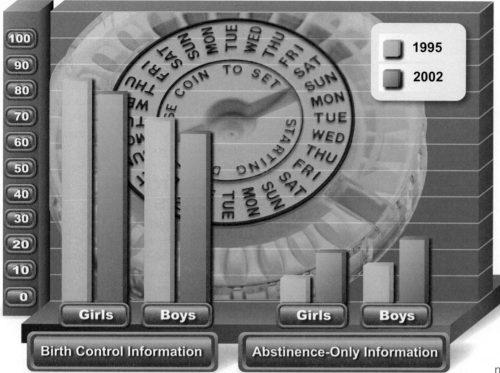

Figure 2.5 Shifts in Sexuality Education Information

Birth Control Information | Abstinence-Only Information

1995
2002

Girls | Boys | Girls | Boys

Source: Guttmacher Institute, 2006

information about abstinence has increased (Guttmacher Institute, 2006). This is an interesting finding, because there is a large gap between what teachers *want* to teach or what they believe should be covered and what they *actually* teach. Today, more than nine in 10 teachers think that students should be provided contraception education, but one in four is prohibited from doing so because of state and/or local policies (Guttmacher Institute, 2006).

MACROSYSTEM

The **macrosystem** represents the next layer in Bronfenbrenner's model and recognizes that a society has a set of overarching cultural values and beliefs that affect individual development by establishing either implicit or explicit rules about what is acceptable behavior. In a population as diverse as the United States, there are hundreds of different religious, racial, and ethnic groups, and each group may have specific cultural norms that do not conform to a broader, national set of values. Additionally, not all groups that fall within a general ethnic category will be the same. For instance, not all Latinos share the same belief system. Christians have different values than Jews, Muslims, or Buddhists. Republicans have different values than Democrats. Cultural values may vary across place (United States versus the Middle East) and across time (generations within one family).

what should be covered in sexuality education curricula (Anspaugh & Ezell, 2005). They encourage abstinence—but they also have a realistic understanding that today's youth are sexually active, and therefore need accurate, up-to-date information that helps them protect themselves from unwanted pregnancies, sexually transmitted infections, and HIV. Since 1995, however, there has been an increase in the number of teachers who teach that abstinence is the only way to prevent pregnancy and STIs. As Figure 2.5 shows us, the proportion of teens that receives information about birth control has declined, while the proportion receiving

TABLE 2.3
Comparison of Content of Abstinence-Only and Comprehensive Sexuality Education

Source: Collins, C., Alagiri, P., & Summers, T. (2002). *Abstinence only vs. comprehensive sex education: What are the arguments? What is the evidence?* San Francisco, CA: AIDS Research Institute.

Comprehensive Sex Ed	Abstinence-Only Sex Ed
Comprehensive sex ed programs explore the context for and meanings involved in sex.	Abstinence-only sex ed programs include discussions of values, character-building, and refusal skills.
Promote delay of first sexual experiences	Promote abstinence from sex as a way to avoid STIs, HIV and unplanned pregnancies
Acknowledge that many teens will become sexually active	Do not acknowledge that teens will become sexually active
Teach about contraception and condom use	Do not teach about contraception or condom use
Include discussions about contraception, abortion, STIs, HIV, and sexual orientation	Avoid abortion discussions

The broader point to keep in mind here is that macro-level influences such as religious and cultural roots influence every aspect of our sexuality, from sexual orientation, to contraception and abortion, to sex in and outside marriage.

CHRONOSYSTEM

The **chronosystem**, the next, outermost layer, reflects the changes that happen over time. It accounts for the collective historical precursors of current social attitudes (Dutton, 1998), such as social and economic discrimination, women's rights to reproductive choice, and the debate over the definition of marriage.

Bronfenbrenner's framework, as conveyed in this model, allows us to grasp both the nature of the main interacting influences on our lives and to examine the role that each plays on us and our relationships or our families. It is with this knowledge of the ecological model that we explore sexual life in various contexts through the remainder of this book.

UNDERSTANDING SEX AND SEXUALITY THROUGH THEORY

A solid, foundational knowledge base in *social science theory* is essential for students and professionals interested in the field of sexual life. A **theory** is an organized set or group of interrelated ideas that provide a lens through which to view behavior and interactions. Theories profoundly affect what we know about sexual life and intimate relationships because they provide structure for how we think, what we observe, how we interpret what we observe, and how we subsequently create programs and

introduce policies (Smith, 1995). Theories allow us to move beyond our everyday, common beliefs and move toward an objective, scientific understanding of sexuality.

There are two general kinds of theories, each of which aids in our overall understanding of sexual life (White & Klein, 2007). One kind *describes* certain phenomena (such as the frequency of sexual intimacy), and the other kind of theory *explains* (at least in part) behaviors (for example, the frequency of sexual intimacy impacts relationship satisfaction). In the section that follows, we'll take a brief look at today's theories that help us begin to understand sexuality and sex.

AN INTRODUCTION TO SEXUALITY THEORIES

We develop theories to explain things such as how our concepts of gender and sexual orientation develop, why we are attracted to one person and not another, and how and why we fall in love. Theories also reflect our attempts to explain the workings of sexuality. White and Klein (2008) discuss today's prevailing theories that help us understand sexuality within interpersonal relationships. As you're studying these theories, it's important to keep in mind that no one theory is adequate to explain our understanding of human sexual behavior.

- **Ecological Theory:** This theory is concerned with the many social and cultural contexts that impact and influence our sexual lives. As you now understand, these contexts range from immediate influences on the individual (schools, churches or temples, and neighborhoods) to broader contexts such as government, educational, and political systems.

- **Family Development Theory:** This theory is concerned with understanding the changes in family structures (such as the birth of children) and the roles of family members across each stage of family development. According to this theory, healthy relationships are able to adapt to changes across time.

- **Family Systems Theory:** The family systems theory views the family as an interconnected group of individual members. What happens to one family member, such as an illness or a loss of a job, affects every family member.

- **Symbolic Interaction Theory:** Symbolic interaction theory concerns itself with how people form and share meanings in their communication efforts. This theory's primary focus is the use of *symbols* to convey meaning through verbal and nonverbal communication.

- **Social Exchange Theory:** This theory maintains that people weigh costs and rewards before they act on a decision—we engage in behavior in which our rewards are maximized and our costs are minimized. According to this theory, we form relationships with other people if we anticipate that the relationship will be rewarding.

- **Structural-Functionalism Theory:** Structural functionalism emphasizes the traditional, heterosexual nuclear family and highlights two primary functions of the family in society: socialization of children to society's culture and norms and the stabilization of adult personalities.

<<< Gay parents and straight parents—**who better serves the "function" of parenting?** Can both?

This view revolves around the idea that the family is organized and governed by unchanging, fixed role configurations—and these gender-specific family functions benefit the family and the greater good of the society. This theory raises interesting questions. When two women or two men rear children and do not abide by clearly outlined, specialized gender roles, what happens to the family structure? By traditional structural-functionalism assumption, the lesbian/gay family form deviates from the ideal family form and, as such, should turn out children who are nonconforming to societal values and norms. But is this an accurate conclusion? We'll explore this at length in Chapter 7.

- **Conflict Theory: Conflict theory** supports the basic theme that human beings are prone to conflict—that conflict is expected, natural, and inevitable. Why is there conflict? According to the conflict perspective, *inequality* is a defining trait built in to any society. Dominant and subordinate groups are always in *competition* for society's limited resources and for whatever society deems important. It is the competition for resources—with the "haves" competing to keep what they possess and the "have-nots" trying to gain what they do not have—that produces conflict. Although conflict theory is not frequently used in sexuality studies to shed light on

sexual life now

Is Abstinence-Only Education Effective?

Since 1997, three federal programs have provided well over half a billion dollars in abstinence-only education funding to public schools (Government Accountability Office, 2006). Still, the question remains: Is abstinence-only education effective?

YES!

Rebecca Ray, director of Healthy Futures, an abstinence-only education program in Boston, maintains that abstinence-only-until-marriage education programs are essential to the health of today's teens. Such programs not only educate teens about the physical and emotional risks of adolescent sexual activity, but they also help students acquire the skills that are necessary to make abstinence an informed and attainable choice (American Federation of Teachers, 2004).

Research into abstinence-only education programs bolsters the case for the effectiveness of such programs in reducing sexual activity, smoking, and substance use. In particular, one study found that teens who participated in abstinence-only education were significantly less likely than their friends to engage in high-risk behaviors (Lerner, 2004). Furthermore, junior high and high school girls, when compared to their peers who did not participate in such programs, were:

- 6.5 times more likely to remain sexually abstinent through high school

- Almost two times more likely to abstain from drinking

- Eight times more likely to abstain from drugs

- More than two times more likely to abstain from smoking

Other abstinence-only education programs have been effective in reducing teen birth rates and teen pregnancies. For example, one study found that increased abstinence among 15- to 19-year-old teens accounted for a 67 percent decline in teen pregnancy rates; increased abstinence also accounted for more than 51 percent of the decline in teen birth rates (Mohn, Tingle, & Finger, 2003).

NO!

Advocates for Youth (2008) is an organization that creates programs and advocates for policies that help youth and teens make informed and responsible decisions about their health. They assert that abstinence-only education programs are dangerous, ineffective, and inaccurate. And there is research that provides strong support for their claims. Analysis of abstinence-only curricula found that over 80 percent contained false, misleading, or distorted information about the effectiveness of contraceptives, the risks of abortion, and other medical facts.

For instance, the following quote is an example of an inaccurate medical statement contained in one abstinence-only program: "The outward direction of sperm cells is supported by emphasis on an outward direction in the male's personality. The ovum, by contrast, is receptive and inward-directed [similar to the female personality]" (Wilson et al., 2005).

Further, research regarding abstinence-only education programs have found that (Brückner & Bearman, 2005; Bearman & Brückner, 2001) 88 percent of abstainers ("virginity pledgers") initiated sex prior to marriage and that pledge-takers were less likely to seek STI testing and use contraception when they did have sex.

>>> WHAT DO YOU THINK?

1. What are your experiences with sexuality education? Did you have comprehensive sexuality education that taught a broad spectrum of health and sexuality, such as information about contraception, STIs, abortion, and the like? Or did you have abstinence-only education?
2. Should sexuality education in public schools be continued or halted?

Learning About Sex and Sexuality

There are so many topics to explore in a class about sex and sexuality. Although you may have great interest in some topics, understandably other topics may make you uneasy or uncomfortable.

I took this class because _____

_____ .

My goals for this class include _____

_____ .

I am most interested in the topics of _____

_____ .

I am most apprehensive to learn about _____

_____ .

The Bible or Koran shape and direct many people's sexual attitudes, beliefs, and behaviors. I think religious influences are

_____ .

I am comfortable/uncomfortable examining other cultures' experiences of sex and sexuality. This is because

_____ .

At this point in my development, the most positive influential people on my sexuality are

_____ .

I have had negative influences on my sexuality. These include _____

_____ .

If there was one influence on my sexuality I could change up to this point in my life, it would be

_____ .

If there was one thing I could change about sexuality in my culture, it would be _____

_____ .

---

interpersonal relationships and sexual life, its application is of great value when examining the inequalities in human relationships and factors such as gender, ethnicity, race, and socioeconomic class. Conflict theory survives today in its contemporary form: feminist theory.

- **Women's Studies/Feminist Theory: Feminist theory** is one that embraces the conflict approach to understanding inequalities in the male/female relationships. There is no single feminist theory. A theory is deemed feminist theory if it centers on the experiences specific to women, views experiences from a woman's vantage point and advocates on behalf of women (Lengermann & Brantley, 1988). Types of feminist theory include (Schwartz & Scott, 2003):

- *Marxist feminist theory*—This perspective maintains that the inequality and oppression that women experience is a result of the women's subordinate class position.

- *Radical feminist theory*—According to this viewpoint, the universal oppression that women experience is a result of patriarchy (male-dominated society). Violence against women is one consequence of patriarchy.

- *Liberal feminist theory*—This theoretical perspective focuses on how **sexism**—the belief that men are superior and women are inferior—and promotes equal opportunity, such as in the workplace and in education.

- *Lesbian feminist theory*—This viewpoint focuses primarily on the predominance of heterosexuality in patriarchal (male-dominated) societies and insists that attention be given to the oppression of lesbians.

- *Women-of-color feminist theory*—According to this perspective, women do not share common experiences; instead, they are thought to be molded by their unique experiences of race, class, and societal and cultural influences.

Many researchers use these theories to acknowledge that there is great diversity not just between men and women, but *among* women. There are a number of ways in which the feminist perspective can be applied to study family and intimate relationships.

- **Men's Studies** Like women's studies, men's studies investigate the multiple social and cultural forces and issues that affect men, and what it means to "be" a male in today's society. It is an umbrella term for a field that encompasses a number of issues specific to men's lives and encourages scholarship in an effort to generate theory specific to the study of masculinity, as well as to shun all forms of oppression—sexism, racism, homophobia, and classism (Willis, 2005).

SEXUAL LIFE EDUCATION

As we work our way through our study, we will focus on the foundations of these theories and add to them. The study of sexuality is fascinating.

^
^ A woman uses her body to oppose a bill lowering
^ the limit for **abortions by four weeks to 20 weeks
at a pro-choice rally.**

Throughout the 19th and 20th centuries, sexologists used the tools of scientific inquiry they had at the time to examine human sexuality by relying on things other than their logic and intuition. There is no question that the efforts of these early sexologists, researchers, and philosophers greatly influenced what we know about sexuality today. Contemporary sexologists, psychologists, sociologists, health educators, and family scientists use the step-by-step scientific method to seek out answers that pertain to sexuality. This solid research methodology provides researchers and consumers with reliable scholarship and allows us to look beyond our own personal sexual experiences or the experiences common in the culture in which we are raised, to examine and understand the influences of the multiple cultural facets on our sexual lives.

By using the many theoretical frameworks and models, we have different lenses through which we can view and better understand sexuality, sex, and sexual relationships. So far, we have given attention to Bronfenbrenner's ecological model, because it provides a framework that helps us understand the different social contexts that surround and influence an individual and his or her family. As the college student in the opening vignette reveals, we do not experience sexuality and our sexual lives separately from our surroundings, and the sexual attitudes of one culture are not necessarily the same sexual attitudes of another culture. "Sex is not sex is not sex . . ." By using the many theoretical frameworks and models, we can better understand sexuality, sex, and sexual relationships. Throughout our study together, we will look at the theories that seek to explain sexuality and sexual life.

By employing the practice of social science research, we can explore, explain, and develop—with confidence, not fear—a deeper understanding of sex. In essence, we can "know" sex and sexual life.

▶▶▶ TAKING SIDES

Do Shared Religious Beliefs Affect a Couple's Sexuality?

Bronfenbrenner observed that religion and religious organizations play key roles in shaping our sexuality. Given this, should couples who have nothing in common spiritually marry, or will their relationship be fraught with difficulties?

Her Side: Religion is not important to me. It's not that we share different faiths, like some of our friends do, it's that I don't have any religious beliefs. I respect his individual practice of his religion, and I respect his choices to worship and his devotion to his religion. Believe it or not, his devotion to his faith is something that attracted me to him in the first place. In all honesty, it's just not for me. I don't understand why he feels I need to participate with him. I love him. I support him. I encourage him. I think our intimacy levels are deep and strong, because we communicate often. And I have to believe that our sex life is strong because of this communication. I just can't believe that our religious differences can influence our sexuality that much—not if we don't let these differences divide us.

His Side: I don't think she understands that religion is not just something I participate in—it's a *way of life* for me. It informs and shapes nearly every decision I make in my life, including my sexuality. I firmly believe that religion is something that can unify us and strengthen our intimacy. Like, I really believe that praying together as a couple is one of the most intimate things they can do together. For example, let's say a couple is having sexual difficulties in their marriage. I really believe that sitting down and praying about the problem together is the first step they should take in tackling the problem. How can I ignore the fact that she doesn't believe in *a Higher Power?*

Your Side: Taking into consideration what you have learned about Bronfenbrenner's model in this chapter, along with your personal life experiences:

1. Do you believe that couples who have opposing religious beliefs should marry? Why or why not?

2. In your opinion, do you think that religion can affect a couple's sex life? In what ways?

02

Summary

WHAT CONTRIBUTIONS DID EARLY SEXOLOGISTS MAKE TO OUR UNDERSTANDING OF SEXUALITY TODAY? 18

• Early sexologists laid the cornerstone of modern sexology, bringing to light topics such as same-sex attraction, gender ambiguity, stereotypes about women, and sexual reform.

WHAT IS EMPIRICAL RESEARCH IN THE SOCIAL SCIENCES? 18

• Empirical research is objective; true empirical research strives to avoid bias of any kind in the research plan, gathering data, data analysis/ interpretation, and any other aspects of research.

HOW DOES BRONFENBRENNER'S ECOLOGICAL MODEL EXPLAIN OUR DIFFERENCES IN SEXUALITY? 25

• Bronfenbrenner's model explains how multiple, interacting contexts of individual and family development play a role in the bi-directional relationship between people and their environments.

HOW DO THE VARIOUS THEORETICAL PERSPECTIVES OFFER INSIGHT INTO THE STUDY OF SEXUALITY? 30

• Theoretical frameworks and models allow us a variety of different lenses through which we can view and better understand sexuality, sex, and sexual relationships.

Key Terms

empirical research examination of social and individual behaviors by using methods beyond logical common sense or reason alone *18*

sexology the theoretical and scientific study of sex *20*

erotology older concept than sexology that dealt primarily with erotic writings *20*

sexual revolution the changing trends in social thought that relaxed sexual taboos about sexuality from the 1960s into the 1970s *22*

libido a fixed amount of psychic energy, as defined by Sigmund Freud *22*

electrocardiogram, or **EKG** machines used to measure the subjects' heart rates and blood pressures *23*

penile strain gauge measurement of erections of the penis *23*

photoplethysmograph machine used to measure vaginal lubrication in women *23*

scientific method the sequential, interrelated investigative steps that research follows *23*

ethics the rules and standards that govern researchers' conduct as they examine human behaviors, feelings, and attitudes *23*

social ecology perspective that recognizes that our individual backgrounds (such as our sexual history, experiences with our family of origin—the family in which we are raised)

as well as outside social and cultural factors and policies significantly affect the quality and the nature of personal and sexual relationships *25*

family of origin the family in which we are raised *25*

ecological model model in which Urie Bronfenbrenner sought to understand how multiple, interacting contexts play a role in the relationship between people and their environments *25*

contexts areas of individual and family development *25*

bi-directional descriptive of two-sided influence on relationships *25*

ecosystem a context in the ecological model *25*

microsystem the developmental context nearest the individual and represents those interactions to which people are directly exposed *25*

mesosystem the developmental context that retains all the elements that are present in the microsystem, but also focuses on the interaction between the various elements, rather than on the individual *25*

exosystem the developmental context that consists of the fabrics of society in which policies are made and influenced that ultimately

have an impact on the microsystem and the individual *26*

macrosystem the developmental perspective that recognizes that a society has a set of overarching cultural values and beliefs that affect individual development by establishing either implicit or explicit rules about what is acceptable behavior *27*

chronosystem the developmental perspective that this outermost layer reflects the changes that happen over time. It accounts for the collective historical precursors of current social attitudes, such as social and economic discrimination, women's rights to reproductive choice, and the debate over the definition of marriage *28*

theory an organized set or group of interrelated ideas that provide a lens through which to view behavior and interactions *28*

conflict theory theory that supports the basic theme that human beings are prone to conflict—that conflict is expected, natural, and inevitable *29*

feminist theory theories that embrace the conflict approach to understanding inequalities in the male/female relationships *30*

sexism belief that men are superior and women are inferior *30*

Sample Test Questions

MULTIPLE CHOICE

1. What step typically comes *after* selecting a population and sampling?
   a. Using operational/empirical definitions
   b. Creating the research question
   c. Choosing the research method
   d. Collecting, processing, and analyzing the data

2. What is an *adequate* response rate for analyzing data?
   a. 30 percent
   b. 50 percent
   c. 70 percent
   d. 90 percent

3. The concern that a researcher is able to provide a definition that reflects the true meaning of the construct being considered is one of:
   a. reliability
   b. validity
   c. probability
   d. conceptualization

4. If you wanted to study the unusual college experience of a recent graduate from your campus because you do not believe anyone has a similar story, which method would be a logical starting point?
   a. Survey
   b. Experiment
   c. Case study
   d. Observation

5. Which is NOT true of probability samples?
   a. They involve random selection
   b. They are representative of the population being studied
   c. Each person has an equal chance of being selected
   d. They are known as "convenience samples"

6. Human subjects committees are also known as:
   a. Institutional Review Boards
   b. Inquiry Research Boards
   c. Institutional Revision Boards
   d. Integrity Review Boards

7. A consideration of one's family of origin is part of which level of Bronfenbrenner's ecological model?
   a. Mesosystem
   b. Microsystem
   c. Macrosystem
   d. Chronosystem

8. Which theoretical perspective embraces the conflict approach to understanding relationships?
   a. Feminist theory
   b. Structural functionalism
   c. Family systems theory
   d. Symbolic interaction theory

SHORT RESPONSE

1. What is meant by the idea that social research involves the "other side of the microscope"?

2. Identify three characteristics of a well-constructed survey.

3. Assume you are hired to study "sexual behavior" of students at your university. Create what you feel would be a sufficient operational definition of the concept to get you started with your research.

4. Discuss an example of how the macrosystem layer of Bronfenbrenner's model might play a role in attitudes toward gay marriage.

5. Using the structural functionalist approach, argue either for or against abstinence-only sexual education.

Answers: 1. d; 2. b; 3. b; 4. c; 5. d; 6. a; 7. b; 8. a

Remember to check www.thethinkspot.com **for additional information, downloadable flashcards, and other helpful resources.**

THINK READINGS

THE NEW YORK TIMES

The Opposites Of Sex: The 'Normal' And the Not

By DINITIA SMITH
Published: May 13, 2000

When it comes to sex, who decides what constitutes normal? Who decides what's too little and who says what's too much? For years, sociologists, psychologists and other experts have charted the continual shifts in sexual attitudes and practices. Now, two feminist historians are trying to upend conventional assumptions about sex, one of them studying celibacy, the other nymphomania.

Consider, for example, ideas about whether men or women have the stronger sex drive. Carol Groneman, a history professor at John Jay College of Criminal Justice at the City University of New York, and Elizabeth Abbott, dean of women at Trinity College at the University of Toronto, agree that the notion that men are by nature more highly sexed than women is a fairly recent one. In the classical world, women were seen as the highly sexed ones. Ms. Abbott, whose book, "A History of Celibacy" (Scribner) is being published this month, cites the myth of Teiresias. Having been male and female, Teiresias was asked by Zeus and Hera to settle their argument as to who had most pleasure in sex. Women did,

he replied; they experienced nine-tenths of the pleasure of intercourse, and men only one-tenth.

The early Christians inherited the Roman idea that women were carnal creatures, Ms. Abbott writes. Although celibacy was at the center of Christianity (as with many religions), celibacy outside the church was suspect. In the 14th century, the ecclesiastical authorities crushed the Beguinage movement, in which women chose celibacy to minister to the needy but lived outside the cloister. Church fathers, she says, believed that "women are weak and are temptresses, and if they are not locked up behind walls and monitored, they're constitutionally incapable of maintaining vows of celibacy."

Ms. Groneman, whose book "Nymphomania: A History" (W. W. Norton) is due out in August, says that in the United States the idea that men have a stronger sex drive than women came into being only in the 19th century. The shift was connected to the egalitarian promise of the French and American Revolutions, she said. The notion that human beings are born with inalienable rights had to be reconciled with the fact that

women could not vote and did not have equal property rights. So the ideal of the "passionless" woman, who was "the angel of the house," was born as a rationalization for preserving the traditional hierarchy. "From this exalted position, her unique role in the new republic would be to tame men's passions and maintain the purity of the home," Ms. Groneman writes.

As for definitions of sexual normalcy, Ms. Groneman says that doctors—traditionally men— became the arbiters. "They weighed in with their understanding that women's too delicate nervous system, monthly 'illness' and smaller brain, as well as their reproductive organs, all made it unhealthy for them to vote, work outside the home, write books, go to college or participate in the public arena."

As medicine became professionalized, too much sexual desire in women became a "disease." The cures were drastic. Ms. Groneman cites an 1841 article in The Boston Medical and Surgical Journal about a "Miss T." who exhibited uncontrolled "libidinous feelings." When doctors examined Miss T. vaginally, they determined that she bore the signs of

---

"Celibacy" means to abstain from sexual activity, usually for religious or spiritual reasons.

The concept of nymphomania—extreme, uncontrollable hypersexuality in women—was first introduced by French physician Bienville in 1771. Although some researchers and clinicians may still support the idea that some women experience sex at levels high enough to be considered clinically significant (i.e., "sex addicts"), sexologists today support the idea that there is nothing "abnormal" about women who enjoy frequent sex and/or sex with multiple partners.

These were closed, nun-like communities where women dedicated their lives to God. Authorities in the early church believed that women were too weak to overcome their sexual desires, and that if they didn't live in convents they were physically incapable of staying away from sex. But what about the men?

During the Victorian era (1837–1901), the virginal, shy, virtuous woman was considered ideal. General feelings toward sexuality were prim and stuffy. In fact, saying "leg" in public was a mark of impropriety, and any premarital activity beyond a stolen kiss was strictly forbidden. Not only were unmarried women expected to be pure, they were also expected to maintain a certain level of innocence when it came to sexual matters, even after they were married.

"nymphomania," including an enlarged uterus and genitalia. So they bled her, applied caustics to her genitals and prescribed cold-water douches.

Indeed, doctors used the term "nymphomaniac" to describe a wide range of behavior, including women who confessed to having sexual dreams and to asylum inmates who tore off their clothes and masturbated. From the 1870's, doctors regularly performed ovariotomies and even, in a few instances, clitorodectomies to cure it. Until the 1990's, Ms. Groneman writes, nymphomania was admitted into court during rape trials as evidence, the theory being that the female victim "wanted" sex.

A persistent theme in histories of sexuality is the link between sex and power. As Ms. Groneman and Ms. Abbott show, women discovered they could achieve power by withholding their sexuality, or by strategically using it.

Ms. Abbott argues that to gain power, women and men have often had to sacrifice their sexuality. For example, the vestal virgins of Rome took 30-year vows of celibacy in return for their elevated status and legal independence.

Later, she writes, Christian women "recast the misogynist bachelor world of the Church Fathers into a splendid, challenging one where virgins were honorable and could also be powerful, and where God's love empowered the humblest women."

At the beginning of the sixth century, upper-class women who gave up sex and marriage could be abbesses in convents, and thus could study and administer property. Celibacy signified "they're not going to be a challenge," Ms. Abbott said in an interview, and above all, would not bear sons on

whose behalf they might conspire to gain property.

In ancient China, males were forcibly castrated, sometimes as punishment for seducing unmarried women, and then trained to work in the imperial palace. But records show that by the 17th century, Chinese men were voluntarily submitting to castration in a desperate desire to escape poverty and gain civil service positions.

Another reason for male celibacy has been the equation of semen with the life force. That concept drove the male purity movement of 1830's America, which coincided with increasing social mobility and the decline of parental control over sons. Celibacy became a form of social control, and was thought to curb excesses like masturbation that could lead to a depletion of energy and potency. Sylvester Graham, a founder of the movement, invented the Graham cracker, and Dr. John Harvey Kellogg, another advocate of celibacy, created his breakfast cereal as aids in curbing lust. There is also a long tradition of athletes foregoing sex before sports events to conserve power and energy.

Ms. Abbott says she found herself "intensely moved" by accounts of people who have chosen celibacy to devote their energies to art, literature and science. Divorced twice and with a grown son, she decided to give up sex herself. "I realized that at this stage in my life, I value even more the independence and serenity chaste solitude brings me," she writes in her book.

If celibacy has been used as a tactic to gain more independence, sexual freedom has also been a central tenet of the women's movement. It was at the turn of the century, when women

were campaigning for equal rights and birth control devices were more widely distributed that the concept of sexual compatibility in marriage first became popular. Freud proclaimed the centrality of sex, and the experts declared that women should enjoy it. Theodore Van de Velde's popular 1926 advice book, "Ideal Marriage," decreed that married women should experience "a fully equal and reciprocal share in love making."

Nonetheless, Ms. Groneman points out, women's sexuality occupied a very narrow band.

On the one hand, the term "frigidity" became popular, indicating a concern that women achieve sexual pleasure with their husbands. On the other, a woman was expected to be the "passive" recipient of the orgasm "given" her by her husband. Women who exhibited a greater sexual drive than their husbands, or not enough desire, were seen as abnormal or deviant.

Today, in the post-sexual revolution, Ms. Groneman says, nymphomania has been replaced by "sex addict" or "love addict"— the last phrase more commonly used in popular literature in connection with women.

The implication, in some quarters at least, is that sexual desire in women is still seen as a sickness, with the "love addict" as a "codependent," giving sex to get love, or because of a childhood trauma of sexual abuse.

But "love addict" is as simplistic and misleading as "nymphomaniac," says Ms. Groneman. They are new names for an old idea, but the same old stereotypes are at work. As she says, the questions "How much is too much? How much is enough? And who decides?" have still not been satisfactorily answered.

Prior to the 20th century, blood-letting was a common medical practice, where considerable amounts of blood were drawn in an attempt to cure disease. "Caustics" were agents that burned the flesh.

The next time you grab a graham cracker for a quick snack or have a bowl of Kellogg's Corn Flakes for breakfast, remember why these products were created!

When it comes to sex and sexuality, is there such a thing as "normal" or "abnormal"? And who does decide?

Do you think that women gain power by withholding sex? By having sex? What about men?

GENDER NOW

WHAT ARE THE ROLES OF BIOLOGY (NATURE) AND ENVIRONMENT (NURTURE) IN THE PRODUCTION OF GENDER?

HOW DOES SEXUAL DIFFERENTIATION OCCUR PRENATALLY, AND WHAT CHROMOSOMAL AND HORMONAL DISORDERS MAY RESULT?

HOW ARE MASCULINITIES AND FEMININITIES CREATED BY CULTURES?

WHAT IS THE SIGNIFICANCE OF GENDER IDENTITY TO MALE AND FEMALE?

There's not

really a typical [transgender] story. A lot of people will say that they have always felt they were trapped in the wrong body, that their body was wrong, or that their gender identity was at odds with what their genitals said they should be. [I was born a male in 1955 and] . . . in my early 20s it became clear to me that I wanted to express my gender differently from how I was expressing it [as a male]. I remember wishing I could express more femininity, but at that time there wasn't much [information] about being transgender.

I thought of myself as being in the middle [somewhere between "male" and "female"] for quite a while, and that's where I identified. I think maybe that was just safer for me. Then I began to make little changes over time . . . from cropped pants, to earrings, to wearing a skirt in public. Being a woman is complicated and multidimensional, but I finally thought, "I can feel comfortable there." I wasn't sure I wanted to do the physical changes, but eventually I did . . . I think I finally just threw in the towel on trying to be intergender, in-between . . . it just didn't feel OK. But now, being transgender is a hard place to be. People just don't get it. Gender is a social construction, and people respond to us differently . . . despite the fact that we're doing a gender and we present to others that *this* is our gender, *this* is our identity . . . but what do they give us? It leaves you in this weird space because no one can make sense of you. Unless my body looks "this way," people won't get me. But I've told myself that I would do this for myself . . . I'm experiencing gender my own way, on my own terms—internally and externally. I'm different and that's OK.

Can we as a culture learn to respond to other gender cues? I don't know, but we should give it a try. I don't want to keep waiting for society to change . . . whether a person is transgender or not, we're just trying to find comfort being who we are.

Source: Author's files

CHAPTER 03

Abraham Lincoln once posed the following question to a group of intellectuals. "If you call the tail of a donkey a leg, how many legs does the donkey then have?" The group replied, "Sir, of course it would have five legs." Lincoln replied, "No, gentlemen. Simply calling it a leg does not make it a leg." Could the same hold true in a discussion about gender? Does labeling someone "male" or "female" make him or her so?

Simple questions often bring complex answers, so it is not surprising that the study of *gender* is interdisciplinary and multidisciplinary in scope (Muehlenhard et al., 2003). To more fully understand the intricacies involved in human interpersonal and sexual relationships, this chapter examines the **nature** (biological) influences of gender and the **nurture** (environmental) influences of gender. We'll also explore the **psychosocial** influences of gender (how a person feels about what nature and nurture impose).

IT MATTERS: THE BIOLOGICAL FOUNDATIONS OF GENDER

As each of my children inched their way into the world, anticipation filled my heart as I waited to discover the sex of each baby. Minutes away from the delivery of our fourth child—a *fourth son?*—my obstetrician quipped, "Boy, girl, what does it matter?" As we'll see below, gender *does* matter in a variety of ways.

SEX IS NOT GENDER

There has been much debate over the years about which comes first: Do boys act "boyish" (active, aggressive) and girls "girlish" (cuddly, chatty) because of inborn personality traits? Or does the presence or absence of a penis at birth bring about certain parental and societal expectations and, thus, reinforcement of socially created, expected, and maybe even anticipated gender behaviors?

Sex and *gender* are two distinct terms, although in our culture the traits are used interchangeably. **Sex** refers to biological traits that distinguish males from females, such as the internal and external reproductive anatomy, chromosomes, hormones, and other physiological characteristics. At birth, a person's sex is assigned when these *biologically* determined characteristics are observed. Without complicated surgical procedures and artificial hormone supplements, sex cannot be changed. **Gender** is thought of as the sum of our developmental and life course experiences and encompasses a number of characteristics. In essence, gender is the position from which we play our roles in the community and society. As you'll discover in this chapter, gender is not an either/or concept, but rather it runs along a continuum and can be experienced however a person wishes to express it, as the opening vignette shows us.

We'll give considerable attention to the cultural influences of gender later in this chapter, but for now, we begin with the study of gender and prenatal development. We launch our study of gender and gendered behavior here, because biology is the basis of all social and cultural influences that ultimately have impact on gender roles and gender identity—and subsequently our experiences of sexuality.

BIOLOGICAL SEX: THE FOUNDATION OF GENDER

A unique person is created when the genes of two individuals are mixed through the process of **sexual reproduction**, the sexual union that produces offspring. A person's biological sex is determined at the instant the gametes fuse together in the process of **fertilization**. **Gametes** are the specialized reproductive cells through which parents pass their genetic material to their offspring (Cummings & Kavlock, 2004). The microscopic **sperm** (the male reproductive cell) and the microscopic egg or **ovum** (the female reproductive cell) each contains one half of the developing person's genetic blueprint.

The developing embryo receives either two X sex chromosomes or one X and one Y sex chromosome. Females are a **homogametic sex**, because they can only pass X sex chromosomes to offspring; males are a **heterogametic sex** because they can pass on either an X or a Y chromosome (Johnson, 2007). The XX sex chromosome combination results in a female genetic blueprint for the developing embryo, and the XY combination results in a male one. The coupling of the XX or XY chromosomes determines a fetus sex characteristics (Ovaries or testes? Clitoris or penis?), both internally and externally. From the moment of fertilization, the development of gender—and perhaps even the subjective experiences of gender—is put into motion.

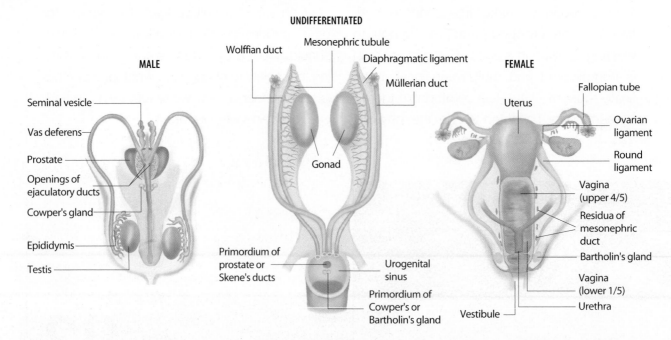

Figure 3.1 Internal Sex Organs: Male and Female, Undifferentiated

Figure 3.2 Sex Differentiation of Males and Females

MALE AND FEMALE

When a Y sex chromosome is present, tissue begins to develop into testes in the male (see Figure 3.1). The testes then begin to produce **androgens** (testosterone), the masculinizing **sex hormones**, as presented in Table 3.1. These increasing levels of testosterone then direct the development of the *internal male reproductive organs*, which include the seminal vesicles, vas deferens, and testes. At some point during the third month of pregnancy, the *external male genitalia*, the penis and scrotum, form under the direction of the androgens, primarily **testosterone**.

It was once believed that, without hormonal influences, the overall pattern for prenatal sexual development was female (among many others: Cummings & Kavlock, 2004; Pinel, 1997). In 1989, however, the scientific community mapped the **SRY** gene, the **S**ex-Determining **R**egion of the **Y** chromosome. This arm of the Y chromosome plays the critical role in the development of male internal and external sex structures. In essence, the SRY is the "maleness" gene (Barsoum & Yao, 2006), or the "baton of masculinity" in the gender relay (Johnson, 2007, p. 12).

Today, we know that when a Y sex chromosome is not present and thus testosterone is not produced, the tissue continues to develop into the *internal female reproductive organs*, which includes the ovaries, uterus, fallopian tubes, and vagina (see Figure 3.1). So, it is not the presence of **estrogen**, the feminizing sex hormone, that produces the biological sex female; it is the *absence of the testosterone* that ultimately results in the creation of a female.

As you can see in Figure 3.2, females and males are more biologically similar than many people think, because the internal

Males and females are more biologically similar than most people think. Notice the similarity of the undifferentiated tissue.

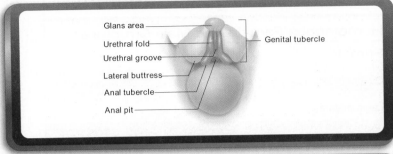

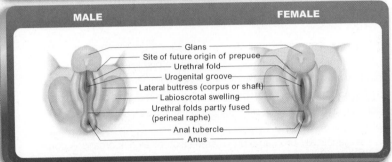

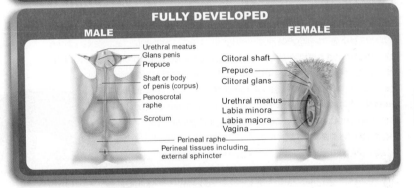

TABLE 3.1
Male and Female Sex Hormones

Around the eighth week of pregnancy, the gonads begin to produce sex hormones, which orchestrate the development and differentiation of both the internal and external sex organs.

Class of Hormone	Associated Sex	Characteristics
Estrogens	Female	• a group of hormones (estriol, estrone, and estradiol) produced mainly within the ovaries • direct female sexual development within the womb and are responsible for the control of the menstrual cycle • largely responsible for a woman's sexual response and pleasure, certain elements in pregnancy, and the development of breast tissue
Progesterone	Female	• a hormone manufactured in the ovaries, released, and carried throughout the bloodstream • works in tandem with estrogens to play a key role in a woman's menstrual cycle and sexual response • high levels cause symptoms that some women experience with their menstrual cycles, such as feeling bloated, mood swings, and breast tenderness
Androgens	Male	• a wide range of androgens are found in males, but in humans the most potent are testosterone and DHT (dihydrotestosterone) • trigger male puberty and are responsible for the more aggressive nature of men and their sex drives

TABLE 3.2
List of Homologous Structures

Homologous Female and Male Structures	
Female	**Male**
Ovaries	Testes
Labia majora	Scrotal sac
Labia minora	Penis shaft (urethral tube)
Clitoris	Glans (Penis)

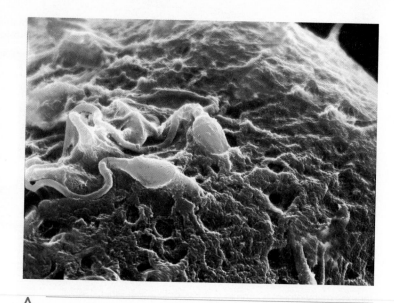

and external sex organs begin with the same primitive tissues in developing embryos. Therefore, many of the sex parts of males and females are **homologous**, or corresponding. The *clitoris* of the female corresponds with the *glans* (head) of the penis in the male, and so on, as illustrated in Table 3.2.

The genetically programmed differentiation of all sex organs is completed around the 12th week of pregnancy. Although we certainly cannot control everything in our environments, there are many things parents can do to create a safe womb for the developing baby. **Teratogens** are substances (such as alcohol or cigarettes) or environmental factors (such as lead paint) that can cause prenatal damage, leading to **congenital birth defects**, or those present at birth. The third week through about the eighth or ninth weeks of pregnancy is the **sensitive period** of development, when organs and structures undergo rapid development; teratogens pose the most risk to the structures that develop the most rapidly (Moore & Persaud, 2007). The embryo's external genitalia are highly sensitive to the effects of teratogens from about the seventh through the 12th weeks of pregnancy.

But there's more to becoming a male or a female than the development of the sex organs. Crucial to our experiences of male or female is the sex differentiation that occurs in the prenatal brain—specifically, the influences of sex hormones on the developing embryo's brain. There is a great deal that can be discussed about the differences between the male and female brains (see Chapters 4 and 5), but here we'll focus on those factors that masculinize and feminize the human brain.

SEX DIFFERENTIATION IN THE PRENATAL BRAIN

The central nervous system and primitive brain development begin during the third week of prenatal development. Brain development becomes quite rapid from the ninth

> ^
> ^ When sperm fertilizes an egg, **a
> ^ person's biological sex is decided.**

week of pregnancy until birth, generating as many as 250,000 brain cells per minute! The prenatal brain is significantly influenced in structure and function by the exposure to sex hormones during pregnancy (Sato et al., 2004; Swaab, Gooren, & Hofman, 1995; Wilson & Davies, 2007).

Within every brain there are androgen and estrogen receptors (Sato et al., 2004). As Takashi Sato and others (2004) explain, a *receptor* is a protein within a brain cell that binds to a specific molecule; in the case of sex differentiation in the brain, the receptor binds itself to a sex hormone. Researchers have found that the testosterone (androgens) produced by the gonads during the prenatal period not only orchestrates the formation of the internal and external genitalia, but also masculinizes and defeminizes the male brain (Sato et al., 2004; Wallen, 2005; Wilson & Davies, 2007).

Sex differentiation of the brain is dependent on the presence or absence of *estradiol*, an estrogen. Through an immensely complex, intricate series of biochemical processes in the developing prenatal brain, in a male (XY) fetus, the androgen receptors in the brain convert some of the androgen into estrogen. This process masculinizes the male brain; it becomes larger than a female brain and establishes a different metabolic pattern (Wilson & Davies, 2007).

You might be wondering, "Since a developing female's gonads produce estradiol, why isn't the female brain masculinized

> ^
> ^ A fertilized ovum becomes a zygote, **the
> ^ cells divide, and an embryo develops.**

An intersexual, whose biological sex is unclear, **does not fit a male or female label.** >>>

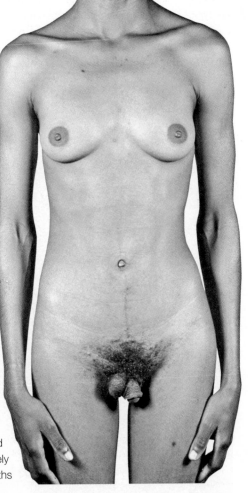

from the effects of the estradiol, just like a male's brain is?" To prevent a female (XX) fetus brain from being masculinized by the estradiol, *alpha-fetoprotein (AFP)* binds the circulating estradiol and disables it so it cannot reach the developing female's brain; the developing brain is unaffected by the estradiol (Bakker et al., 2007).

Sex differentiation of the brain is important to our understanding of gender for several reasons (Wilson & Davies, 2007):

1. The masculinized/feminized differentiation sets the stage for secretion of certain hormones in the brain that regulate puberty in adolescence, as well as the lifelong cyclical production of testosterone in males and estrogen in females (see Chapters 4 and 5).

2. Brain sex differentiation is responsible for sex-specific gendered behaviors, such as the male-typical behaviors of aggression and a high sex drive.

3. Prenatal brain sex differentiation may be responsible for determining a person's sexual orientation (we explore this at length in Chapter 7).

In short, the conversion of androgen to estrogen in the prenatal brain is the underlying cause of brain sex differentiation. Such progressive research leaves the door open for more research into understanding the complex differences between the male and female brains.

SOMEWHERE BETWEEN "MALE" AND "FEMALE"

When a baby is born, the doctor or midwife is charged with the responsibility of assigning the biological sex of *either* male or female to that child. At the moment of birth, we are branded *one* genetic sex *or* the other; we are then raised in the gender brand of our assigned sex. For most babies born in the United States, this either/or sex assignment accurately describes their biologic sex (Evans, 2004); that is to say, the genitals match up with the sex-linked brand of "male" or "female." But what happens when the genetic sex of a child is unclear? Is that child a boy, a girl—or somewhere in between? And, just as importantly, does it matter?

An **intersex** person, or **intersexual**, is someone who is anatomically somewhere along the continuum between male and female. These variations can occur due to a person acquiring both male and female anatomical structures and/or sex chromosomes, or to an off-balance exposure to sex hormones during pregnancy, causing *ambiguous* (not easily distinguishable as male or female) genitalia. The average number of intersex births in the United States is approximately one in 2,000 live births (Lewis, 2000).

An intersex individual could be a **hermaphrodite**, which means that the individual may be born with both ovarian and testicular tissue, or have a combination of an ovary and a testicle as one structure, referred to as an *ovatestes* (Kim et al., 2002). They may also be born with both male and female genitalia. A true hermaphrodite is an extremely rare occurrence, with only about 350 to 450 known cases in the world. A **female pseudohermaphrodite** has an XX sex chromosomal structure and has normal female internal reproductive organs; however, the external genitalia are masculinized, giving them a more male than female appearance. This genetic anomaly occurs in about one in every 14,000 births (Evans, 2004). **Male pseudohermaphrodites** have an XY sex chromosomal structure and testes (although typically located within the pelvis), giving them the appearance of being a female. Other intersex

OWN IT! "Should Parents be Able to Select the Sex of Their Child?"

Thanks to advances in technology, companies such as MicroSort are becoming increasingly popular among hoping-to-become-pregnant couples. Used for the purposes of genetic disease prevention (such as in hemophilia or forms of muscular dystrophy) and family balancing (referred to as "gender variety" in offspring), sperm-sorting technology allows couples today the option of selecting the sex of their children. Although there are currently no laws in the United States that ban sex selection, potential concerns arise, such as sex ratio imbalances in the future, which already exist in China and India.

Take a moment to jot down your opinions on the following questions:

1. How might selection create a climate in which sex discrimination can flourish?

2. How does sex selection create a push for "designer" babies?

3. Would you choose sex selection? Would your parents?

conditions are presented in Figure 3.3. As you can see, these conditions are typically the result of sex chromosome or sex hormone variations.

Although certainly, intersex conditions are not medical emergencies that threaten a child's overall health, often these infants are seen as "social emergencies" in need of "fixing" in some way.

SEX REASSIGNMENT: THE "JOHN/JOAN" CASE

There is perhaps no other case that has brought as much attention to intersex conditions as the infamous *John/Joan* case. In 1965 in Winnipeg, infant identical twin boys (Bruce and Brian Reimer) underwent

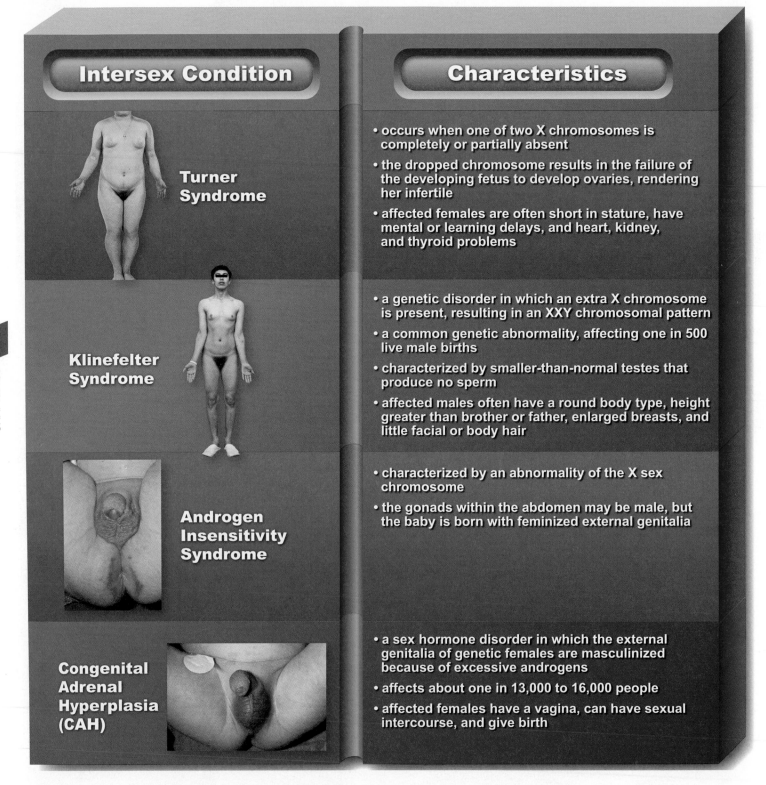

Intersex Condition	Characteristics
Turner Syndrome	• occurs when one of two X chromosomes is completely or partially absent • the dropped chromosome results in the failure of the developing fetus to develop ovaries, rendering her infertile • affected females are often short in stature, have mental or learning delays, and heart, kidney, and thyroid problems
Klinefelter Syndrome	• a genetic disorder in which an extra X chromosome is present, resulting in an XXY chromosomal pattern • a common genetic abnormality, affecting one in 500 live male births • characterized by smaller-than-normal testes that produce no sperm • affected males often have a round body type, height greater than brother or father, enlarged breasts, and little facial or body hair
Androgen Insensitivity Syndrome	• characterized by an abnormality of the X sex chromosome • the gonads within the abdomen may be male, but the baby is born with feminized external genitalia
Congenital Adrenal Hyperplasia (CAH)	• a sex hormone disorder in which the external genitalia of genetic females are masculinized because of excessive androgens • affects about one in 13,000 to 16,000 people • affected females have a vagina, can have sexual intercourse, and give birth

Figure 3.3 **Types of Intersex Conditions**

routine circumcision (see Chapter 5 for a description of this procedure). Through a horrific medical mistake, Bruce's penis was so badly burned that it could not be repaired; it was virtually nonexistent.

Famed American doctor John Money was convinced that "gender" was a learned behavior and was a result of environmental, not biological, influences. Dr. Money believed that then 2-year-old Bruce was a perfect candidate for sex reassignment. **Sex reassignment** is a routine procedure whereby "abnormal" genitalia were surgically corrected; supplemental sex hormones later sustained the surgically assigned "gender." In Bruce's case, the testicles were removed, and the Reimers began to raise Bruce as a girl, Brenda. They dressed him in frilly clothing, grew out his hair, and surrounded him with "girl" toys, such as dolls. Over the next 13 years, Dr. Money touted Bruce's sex reassignment to be a success (Money, 1975). By age 15, Bruce retransitioned to a male and later underwent four surgeries in an attempt to regain his male genitalia. He lived as a male, David, until his death by suicide at age 38. David's case study is now referred to as *John/Joan*.

CURRENT MEDICAL MANAGEMENT

Why do the majority of cultures settle into an *either/or* categorization of male/female? In such contexts, what do we, a two-sex-categories-only culture, do when a condition makes it difficult to determine a child's "sex?"

Since the formation in 1993 of the Intersex Society of North America and the testimony of adults who underwent sex reassignment surgery, the medical field now understands that it takes more than external genitalia to constitute gender. Despite this knowledge base about the development of gender, however, the standard of care is slow to change (Arana, 2005; Diamond, 2004). Current medical protocol regarding

ambiguous genitalia or intersex children is that gender assignment is based on DNA (genetic male or female), not the appearance of genitals (Arana, 2005). Furthermore, advocates for intersex children maintain that the outward appearance of a child's sexual anatomy should not rest on *others'* needs (what others need genitalia to look like), but instead should be left for an individual to decide when he or she is old enough to do so (Arana, 2005).

As the parent of an intersex child observes, "If we [as a culture] truly acknowledge the complexity of [sex], we would understand that biologically there are more than just the two choices society offers. While most of us acknowledge racial, ethnic, religious, and other types of diversity, [our culture] is blind to sex diversity because we continue to live in this either-or world."

IT MATTERS: THE CULTURE OF GENDER

The concept of gender is significantly more complex than biological attributes alone. Although "sex" refers to the biological attributes of male and female, "gender" refers to the *socially* or *culturally* determined traits, characteristics, and expectations of male and female, or how we learn to be male and female; it is a social conceptualization, culturally specific, experienced differently in different cultures.

GENDER ROLES: THE MAKING OF MALE OR FEMALE, MASCULINE OR FEMININE

Gender is multidimensional and it is *created* by people's culture. It includes a number of characteristics, shown in Figure 3.4. Each individual

Male	Female
Aggressive	Passive/kind
Competitive	Polite and ladylike
Independent	Relationship-oriented
Dominating	Submissive
Hides Emotions	Talkative
Confident	Empathetic
Protective	Nurturing
Risk-taker	Risk-avoider
One-track mind	Multitasker
Rational	Led by emotions
Secret-keeper	Gossiper
Disorganized	Responsible
Leader	Follower

Figure 3.4 Characteristics of Gender

Is It Possible to Raise Gender-Neutral Children?

Although most people adhere to the socially and culturally determined gender roles ascribed to them, today more and more individuals are filling nontraditional gender roles. This flexibility and fluidity between the genders has some researchers today questioning whether it is possible to raise gender-neutral children, in whom there are no clear-cut lines between "male" and "female."

YES!

Psychologist and researcher Sandra Lipsitz Bem contends that it is possible to raise gender-neutral children, and she uses her own children as examples in her scholarly writings. Bem and her husband sought to retard the stereotypical gender messages in their children's environments.

Intent on exposing their children to nontraditional gender roles, Bem and her husband did all they could to eliminate the common correlations between a person's biological sex and day-to-day tasks. For example, the Bems took turns doing certain household tasks, caring for the children, and driving the car. They went out of their way to show their children men and women engaging in nontraditional occupations, such as driving by a construction site every day so their children would see the female construction worker. So gender-neutral were they in their parenting that their son referred to individuals as "heorshe," implying there were not two genders, but one.

Throughout childhood and adolescence, the Bems

- encouraged their children to be skeptical of conventional cultural messages about gender by emphasizing diversity;

- helped them understand that all gender messages are created by culture and society.

NO!

Sociologists Denise Segura and Jennifer Pierce (1993) maintain that gender identity and gender roles are very closely tied to family and cultural expectations; because of this, they contend that gender-specific role fulfillment is critically vital to certain cultures. To support their claim, they examined the Chicana/Chicano culture of Mexico in which the features of *familism* (emphasis on family unity and multigenerational ties), *compardrazgo* (interaction between godparents and fictive kin), and *nonexclusive mothering* (mothering by other trusted individuals) play an influential role on the development of gendered personalities.

Unlike European American mothers, Chicana mothers rear their children to act communally, or to think and act in ways that benefit the family and the community. The collective needs of the culture drive the development of gender identity; the Chicana or the Chicano's gendered personality development is closely intertwined with one's cultural or ethnic identity—it would be difficult to disentangle the two. Sons and daughters in this Mexican culture are raised to believe they are extensions not of their *parents*, but of their *culture*. Consider how females are reared in this culture:

- With multiple mother figures (*nonexclusive mothering*), daughters' gender identification centers on Mexican cultural practices and beliefs, such as appropriate mothering roles, knowledge of cultural traditions, behaviors, and values, and honoring other kin ties. These roles are referred to as "doing Chicana." The Chicana believes that these roles complement the role of men, which is to be the provider for the family.

Consider how males are reared in the Mexican culture:

- Because of the presence of several female role models in the sons' lives, the transmission of culture and gender expectations is accomplished by a process known as "becoming masculine." Chicana women repeat the centuries-old Mexican saying, "*feo, fuerte y formal.*" Roughly translated, the young boy is to be rugged and strong, to be a man who is steadfast and responsible, and a good provider for his family. The young Chicano boy learns how to be a male by *not* being a female.

In the Mexican culture, these unique family constellations ultimately contribute to the acquisition of gender identity, a gender identity that is nearly inseparable from group, ethnic, and cultural identity.

>>> **WHAT DO YOU THINK?**

1. Is it possible to raise gender-neutral children in societies where gender messages abound?
2. Is it necessary to raise gender-neutral children?
3. What are the advantages of a gender-neutral society? What are the disadvantages?

Sources: Bem, S. L. (1998); Segura, D. A., & Pierce, J. L. (1993).

society orchestrates, directs, and dictates the expected gender roles, gender presentations, and gender stereotypes of male and female. From these, gender identity is shaped. In essence, we *learn* what it means to be male and female, masculine and feminine, from cultural cues. Societal roles are therefore *gendered*, meaning that differences are assigned to each biological sex.

From birth, we are repeatedly exposed to culturally driven beliefs, ideas, perceptions, and opinions about the differences between genders. Because this continuous flow of cultural information informs us of what is "appropriate" behavior and what is "inappropriate" behavior, we eventually internalize (make part of ourselves) these prototypes for behavior and adopt them (see Figure 3.5). We are *taught* from our culture how to be "male" or "female" (Bem, 1981; Bussey & Bandura, 1999). We then use these models to organize and categorize all social information, including relationships. **Gender socialization** refers to the specific messages and practices we receive from our culture concerning the nature of being a male or a female, of being feminine or masculine.

Societal expectations establish criteria to which its members are to adhere to ensure the longevity and the continuation of that society. **Gender roles** are the cultural norms for male and female attitudes and

> Bandura's research highlighted the role of cognition in acquisition of gender. He maintained there are three reciprocal interacting components in acquiring any behavior (Bandura, 1977).

Person – your genetics, race, ethnicity, age, biological sex

Behavior – the choices and decisions you make, your responses and reactions to the incoming information in your daily life

Environment – your parents, school, peers, neighborhood, the media, the religous hierarchy, and the political structure of the culture in which you live

Figure 3.5 Bandura's Learning and Social Theory

behaviors; these roles delineate what is considered to be appropriate for people of a particular sex. They are the explicitly expressed and implicitly implied behaviors, feelings, attributes, and traits that society expects of a male or a female. Typically, gender roles are referred to as either masculine or feminine. When we refer to *masculinity* or *femininity*, we are talking about the configurations of how we practice our biological sex.

MASCULINITY: "DOING" MALE

Although the term *male* can be used to describe the genetic sex of any species, **masculinity** is a socially/culturally constructed set of beliefs, values, and opinions that shape manly character, or manliness; it prescribes and defines how men should act and feel. Every culture also has an ideal, dominant standard of masculinity for which men are to aim. This is referred to as **hegemonic** (pronounced heh-je-mon'-ick) **masculinity** (Connell, 1987). Although hegemonic masculinity isn't necessarily the most prevalent form of manliness found in a culture, it is the most socially endorsed and desired; this standard changes over time (see Figure 3.6). Today in the United States, images of hegemonic masculinity abound in popular culture media representations, such as *American Gladiators* and

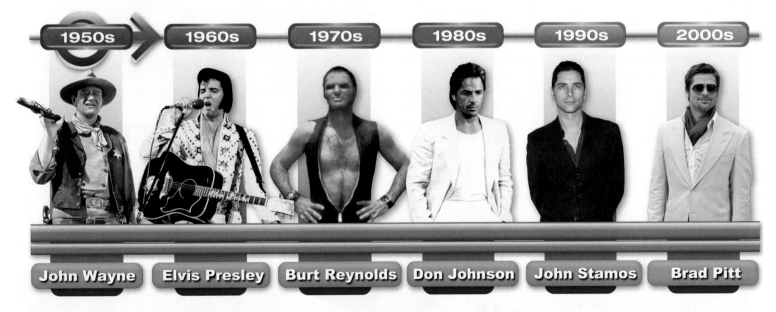

| 1950s | 1960s | 1970s | 1980s | 1990s | 2000s |

John Wayne · **Elvis Presley** · **Burt Reynolds** · **Don Johnson** · **John Stamos** · **Brad Pitt**

Figure 3.6 Historical Timeline of Hegemonic Masculinity

Λ
Λ
Λ Parents influence gender **by exposing children to certain activities.**

Λ
Λ
Λ **A casual glance at any magazine or TV show** clearly illustrates contemporary society's design **on what constitutes** "maleness" and "femaleness."

WWE Wrestling. Throughout their lives, boys learn and acquire these masculine characteristics and traits through language, the toys they play with, certain behaviors that are rewarded or discouraged, and occupations they are encouraged to pursue (Jandt & Hundley, 2007).

Of course, one problem with this characterization of masculinity is that it most often describes white, middle-class conceptions of what being a "man" is supposed to look like. Most of the existing empirical science tends to overlook men of color and their construction of masculinity (Wester et al., 2006).

European American (white) masculinity stresses *individual* success and economic achievement, often excluding collaborative or group efforts (Wester et al., 2006). But within traditional black cultures, cooperation and the promotion of the collective good are promoted, as is *group* success. Because of these conflicting masculine gender expectations, many men of color in the United States have had to adopt *both* the Euro American ideal of "success through competition" while at the same time expressing their black cultural beliefs that highlight support, community, and the importance of interpersonal

>>> Born male, Bruce Reimer underwent sex reassignment surgery and was raised as a girl. **He later transitioned back to being a male, but ultimately killed himself at 38 (see page 43).**

relationships (Wester et al., 2006). This blending of two cultural masculinities among African Americans and Afro-Caribbeans has resulted in a new, exaggerated version of masculinity for them. This is referred to as **cool pose**; black masculinity "presents a powerful face to the world," while at the same time entails the expected cooperative behaviors of black culture (Canales, 2000; Wester et al., 2006).

Societies that emphasize hegemonic masculinity (such as the United States, Australia, Japan, and Latin American cultures) are characterized by high degrees of male dominance, independence, aggression, achievement, and endurance (Williams & Best, 1990). These types of cultures are referred to as *masculine cultures*.

There is perhaps no better example of masculine cultures than Latin America. Embedded within these cultures is machismo, deeply held traditions that influence gender behaviors and attitudes. **Machismo** refers to the idea that men are superior over women, and that men are socially and physically dominating. Machismo is not necessarily an act per se, but it is more of an attitude that can range from a sense of sexual power to masculinity to male superiority. This machismo cultural attitude translates to many areas of interpersonal relationships, including choosing whom to date and to marry, and the role of power to decide birth control and/or contraceptive behaviors during sex (Afable-Munsuz & Brindis, 2006; Villarruel & Rodriquez, 2003).

FEMININITY: "DOING" FEMALE

Femininity refers to qualities, behaviors, and attitudes that are deemed by a particular culture to be ideal for girls and women. Femininity is most often associated with nurturing, life-giving attributes, such as kindness, gentleness, and patience.

But do contemporary women affirm the traditional ideals of femininity? The *Femininity Ideology Scale (FIS)* survey contains statements such as "Women should have soft voices"; "A woman's natural role should be the caregiver of the

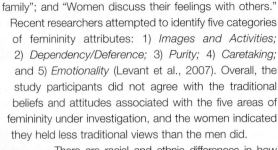

∧
∧
∧ Rapper 50 Cent **demonstrates the exaggerated masculinity of cool pose.**

family"; and "Women discuss their feelings with others." Recent researchers attempted to identify five categories of femininity attributes: 1) *Images and Activities;* 2) *Dependency/Deference;* 3) *Purity;* 4) *Caretaking;* and 5) *Emotionality* (Levant et al., 2007). Overall, the study participants did not agree with the traditional beliefs and attitudes associated with the five areas of femininity under investigation, and the women indicated they held less traditional views than the men did.

There are racial and ethnic differences in how cultures define and socialize "femininity." In Hispanic cultures, for example, the female equivalent of machismo is *marianismo*, the essence of Latina femininity. Based on the Catholic church's belief that Mary gave birth to Jesus and is thus the mother of God, **marianismo** teaches that women are semi-divine, and are morally superior to and spiritually stronger than men (Noland, 2006). The Latino male thus wants a "Maria" (Mary) for a wife—a wife that is observant of religious laws and who is emotional, kind, instinctive, passive, compliant, and unassertive.

In white, westernized cultures, gender roles are largely delineated by divisions of labor based on a person's biological sex— there are separate spheres of labor for men (protection and provision) and women (nurturing and caregiving). However, for more than 200 years, black women functioned in similar capacities to their male counterparts (Buckley & Carter, 2005). That is to say, as a necessary means of survival, black women traditionally had to adopt both masculine and feminine gender roles, such as hard work, self-reliance, resistance, and perseverance (masculine) and care and nurturance (feminine) (Collins, 2004). Today, black men and women still tend to adopt more flexible and less restrictive gender roles. For example, one study found that black adolescent girls today take on both masculine and feminine gender roles by assuming roles and traits of worker, independence, and assertiveness, as well as that of mother and caregiver (Buckley & Carter, 2005). The researchers observed that adolescent girls today continue to adopt these more traditional black gender roles, because the roles—and the characteristics associated with them—are consistent with their cultural histories and teachings (Buckley & Carter, 2005).

<<< **Boys prefer to engage in rough and aggressive types of play,** while girls prefer to engage in fantasy, imaginary, and relational play.

Examining the role of gender in a study of marital, family, and intimate relationships is important, because gender carries with it socially sanctioned, approved, and endorsed prescribed *life roles* (housewife or provider?), *occupations* (flight attendant or pilot?), *relationships* (heterosexual marriage or same-sex union?), and *abilities* (verbal or mathematical?) (Bussey & Bandura, 1999; Howard & Hollander, 1997). Changes in ideal female body shapes are charted in Figure 3.7. It is these commonly held beliefs that lead to **gender stereotypes**, or long-held assumptions or labels about male and female capabilities and limitations. When we pigeonhole gender characteristics and gender roles, it is very difficult to move toward change.

This discussion leads us to another concept about masculinity and femininity that we haven't yet looked at, *gender polarization*.

GENDER POLARIZATION: COMPLEMENTARY OPPOSITES— OR INEQUALITY?

Views of masculinity and femininity present men and women as complementary, polar opposites. Rather than emphasize the *similarities* between men and women, cultural viewpoints almost always emphasize the *differences* between men and women. This "opposite" model

sex talk

Socialized Gender Roles and Sexual Behaviors

With the never ending barrage of social gender messages, it is not surprising that gender roles orchestrate and direct every aspect of daily life—including your sexual life. All aspects of sexuality and sex develop over time. Take time to examine your individual attitudes toward socialized gender roles and how these influence your sexual behavior by completing the relevant statements in the following inventory.

Gender Role Sexual Behavior Inventory

I would describe our sexual gender roles as _____. This makes me feel _____

In general, I believe men are more sexually aggressive than women. This makes me feel _____.

In general, I believe women are more sexually aggressive than men. This makes me feel _____.

When you are passive during sex, it makes me feel _____

When you are aggressive during sex, it makes me feel _____

To me, casual sex outside our relationship makes me feel _____
I haven't had as many sex partners as you have. Knowing this makes me _____

I've had more sex partners than you have. Knowing this makes me _____

When you exhibit traditional masculine traits (such as aggression and assertiveness) during our sex times, I feel _____

When you exhibit traditional feminine traits (such as caring and affection) during our sex times, I feel _____

I have a difficult time speaking up for what I want during sex. How does this make you feel? _____

I have a hard time connecting emotionally during sex. How does this make you feel? _____

If I were to ask for something daring and dirty during sex, it makes me feel _____. How would this make you feel? _____
Sexual fantasies are _____
When you want to talk and cuddle before, during, and after sex, it makes me wish _____

When you don't want to talk and cuddle before, during, and after sex, it makes me wish _____

If I were to sum up gender roles in our sexual behaviors, I would characterize them as _____

Figure 3.7 Body Shapes and the Media

Today, advertisers and television go to great lengths to portray the "ideal" woman, in an attempt to sell their products. A look through history shows us how the ideal female body shape has changed over time.

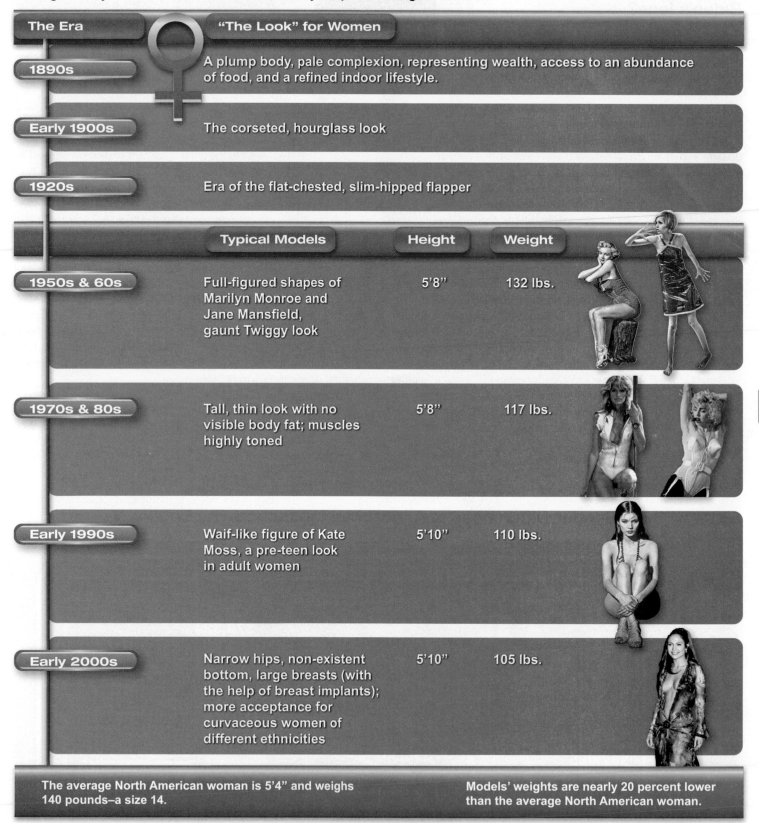

The Era	"The Look" for Women
1890s	A plump body, pale complexion, representing wealth, access to an abundance of food, and a refined indoor lifestyle.
Early 1900s	The corseted, hourglass look
1920s	Era of the flat-chested, slim-hipped flapper

	Typical Models	Height	Weight
1950s & 60s	Full-figured shapes of Marilyn Monroe and Jane Mansfield, gaunt Twiggy look	5'8"	132 lbs.
1970s & 80s	Tall, thin look with no visible body fat; muscles highly toned	5'8"	117 lbs.
Early 1990s	Waif-like figure of Kate Moss, a pre-teen look in adult women	5'10"	110 lbs.
Early 2000s	Narrow hips, non-existent bottom, large breasts (with the help of breast implants); more acceptance for curvaceous women of different ethnicities	5'10"	105 lbs.

The average North American woman is 5'4" and weighs 140 pounds—a size 14.

Models' weights are nearly 20 percent lower than the average North American woman.

Source: Based on Peel Public Health. Available: www.region.peel.on.ca/health/commhlth/bodyimg/media.htm [2007, August 6].

>>> Would photographers have photographed **through Joe Biden's legs?**

is referred to as **gender polarization**, or **bipolar gender** (Bem, 1993).

Many problems crop up when cultures polarize gender. For instance, when we emphasize masculine/feminine differences and categorize them as total opposites, if a person deviates from the "typical" cultural characteristics, that person is then seen as belonging to the *other* category (Bem, 1993). If a man, for example, freely expresses his emotions, he is not only seen as less masculine, but also more feminine. Similarly, if a woman shows aggression, she is seen as less feminine and more masculine.

Gender polarization is also problematic because there are individuals who are somewhere "in between" on this continuum, as the story in the opening vignette showed us. This view also poses difficulties because traditional views of masculinity and femininity as opposites can cause a number of different types of **inequality** or gaps, such as inequality in societal status wages, education, employment opportunities and advancement, and social and intimate relationships.

Society's division of gender into either/or categories leads to **gender inequality**, which can be obvious or hidden disparities or discrimination in opportunities or advancements among individuals; these differences are based solely on a person's gender. Inequality between the sexes is often referred to as sexism. **Sexism** is defined in a number of different ways:

- A prejudice or discrimination based on biological sex

- A belief system that assumes a hierarchy of human worth based on the social construction of the differences between the sexes

- An ideology of male supremacy, superiority, authority, and beliefs/behaviors that support and sustain this ideology

Sexism, then, supports the belief that people of one sex (typically, males) are inherently superior to people of the other sex. These attitudes and beliefs lead to the unfair treatment or discrimination of the "weaker" sex (typically, females), and the cultural dominance of one sex over the other leads to disadvantages and/or unequal opportunities. In short, people are treated differently because of their biological sex. For example, during the 2008 U.S. presidential election, vice presidential candidate Sarah Palin was photographed through her legs. Would this same type of photo have been taken of her rival, Joe Biden? If so, would the photos have elicited the same response? Furthermore, the media extensively discussed her wardrobe and its cost. The media failed, however, to mention the cost of the male candidates' tailor-made suits. This type of treatment is referred to as **sexist**, because Palin was treated differently due to her sex.

These types of inequalities and differences in how a person is treated are manifest in a number of dimensions in a person's daily life, but today in the United States, it is still particularly apparent in the work

Figure 3.8 Gender Differences in Annual Median Income, by Education

Source: Sax, L. J. (2008). *The gender gap in college: Maximizing the developmental potential of women and men.* San Francisco: Jossey-Bass.

Figure 3.9 Self-Confidence of First-Year College Students, by Gender 2006

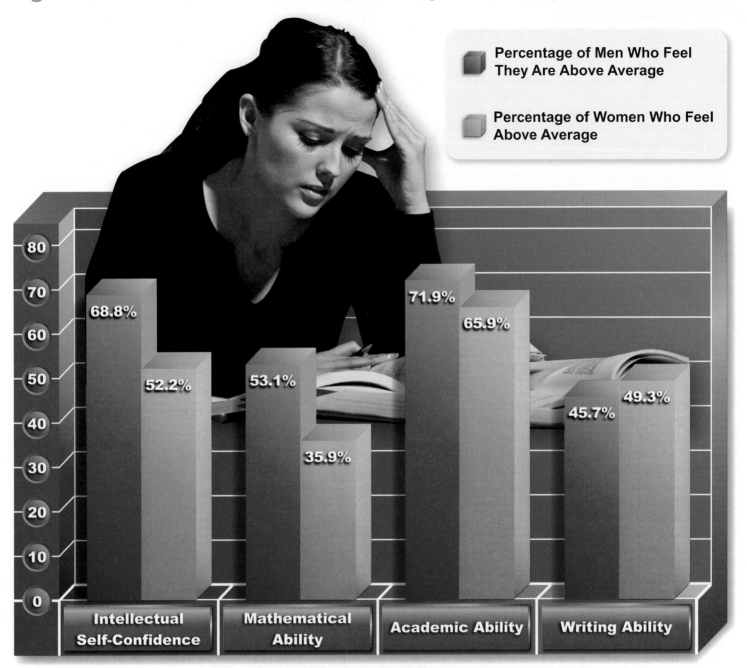

Percentage of Men Who Feel They Are Above Average

Percentage of Women Who Feel Above Average

	Men	Women
Intellectual Self-Confidence	68.8%	52.2%
Mathematical Ability	53.1%	35.9%
Academic Ability	71.9%	65.9%
Writing Ability	45.7%	49.3%

Source: Sax, L. J. (2008). *The gender gap in college: Maximizing the developmental potential of women and men.* San Francisco: Jossey-Bass.

and education arenas. Our country also still struggles with equality in the workforce, particularly in wages. This inequality in wages is referred to as the **wage gap**. On average, today a woman earns about 77 cents for every dollar a man makes (U.S. Department of Labor Statistics, 2008). Even the highest levels of education don't necessarily mean a higher income for women, as the data in Figure 3.8 show us. Whether a woman has a high school diploma, a college bachelor's degree, a master's degree or doctorate, or a professional degree, she still earns less than a man. There are also racial differences in women's wages.

Using data gathered from millions of college students nationwide in the freshman survey, Linda Sax found that men and women have different confidence levels in their academic abilities; these findings are presented in Figure 3.9 (Sax, 2008). In every area other than writing ability, freshmen women have less confidence than men do. These are very interesting findings, because women's self-ratings aren't consistent with data that showed that they actually do better academically than men do. So, it's not that men *perform* better than women do in these areas—they don't. Instead, it's that men have *much more confidence* in their academic abilities than women do. Sax (2008)

Gender, Emotion, and Sexual Life

Understanding stereotyped gender roles is important to a person's emotional and physical health, because sometimes these culture-specific roles are personally limiting or socially divisive. Often, if a person does not conform to his or her society's gender expectations, the person feels that his or her behavior is wrong or unacceptable; as the transgender female in the opening vignette tells us, these feelings become internalized and affect well-being and overall health.

The broader point here is that any time one trait is deemed more valuable than another trait, inequality exists. Socialized behaviors and expectations limit *both* men and women by confining them to rigid, stereotyped gendered roles and rules for living.

Too often in sexual life, socialized behavior causes misunderstandings, hurt feelings, disappointment, frustration, and anger. For healthy selves and healthy sex, minimize gender role stereotypes in family living:

- *Discuss* bothersome issues. For example, if a woman feels that sex is always so rushed that she never feels satisfied, or if a man is tired of the same routine sexual positions, she or he should express those concerns and work toward a solution that is beneficial to the couple.

- *Challenge* stereotypical gender roles—disregard socialized roles and do what is in the best interest of the couple and the family.

- *Do not allow* demeaning sexist language or actions to become acceptable in couple or family behaviors.

- *Respect* the different values and opinions of *every* family member.

Source: Welch, K. J. (2007).

refers to this new phenomenon as the **confidence gap**. Of particular concern to Sax is that women have difficulty believing that they are "as competent as their performance would suggest." Unfortunately for women, the confidence gap appears to grow and widen throughout college.

These findings are so new that no other social or family scientists have had an opportunity to further research the confidence gap. How does it form? What reinforces it? Why is it so prevailing? Do lower confidence levels influence the college majors/career choices of women? Much more research needs to be conducted in this area so that we have a more complete understanding of those issues that may create and perpetuate the glass ceiling and the wage gap.

This discussion leads us to an unanswered question. What happens if our cognitive conceptions of our gender do not line up with what our family or society says our gender *should* be, as talked about in the opening vignette of this chapter? And what happens in the instances where a person displays both male and female traits?

IT MATTERS: GENDER IDENTITY

Gender identity refers to our intuitive sense of our maleness or our femaleness (White, 2003), our internal feelings of what it is to be a man or a woman. Gender identity speaks to how a person settles in to society's assigned gender roles. In other words, it is a *subjective*, continuous, persistent sense of who we are as a male or a female.

<<< The *"glass ceiling"* that Hillary Clinton spoke of in 2008 **is an invisible barrier that determines the level to which women or other minorities can rise in an organization.**

Gender identity doesn't define *gender*—it defines how a person *experiences* it in *his or her* particular culture.

Gender identity does not refer to sexual orientation. **Sexual orientation** refers to the focus of a person's erotic desires or fantasies, or a person's affectionate or romantic feelings toward a particular gender. This is the term most often used by family practitioners, therapists, and the medical community, because the word *orientation* implies that one's gender preference is biologically predetermined. Those who believe that sexuality is fluid and is more a matter of choice than biology use the alternate term **sexual preference**. The erotic and amorous desires for heterosexuals focus on the opposite of one's gender. For homosexuals, the focus is toward those of the same gender. The focus for bisexuals is potentially toward either gender. Asexuals have no sexual attraction to either gender.

ANDROGYNY

When referring to the concept of **androgyny**, we mean that something either has neutral gender value assigned to it, or that a person possesses traits, behaviors, or characteristics that are typically associated with the opposite gender. It occurs as a result of the two primary concepts associated with gender, the biological influences of gender and the social influences of gender.

There are three types of androgyny. The first is *physiological androgyny*, which deals with physical or biological traits, such as in the cases of intersex individuals. The second is *behavioral androgyny*, which involves the blending of masculine and feminine traits; an androgynous person might display traits and behaviors that are typically associated with male and female—not one or the other. The third type of androgyny is *psychological androgyny*, which involves the individual's gender identity.

Some cultures make room for androgyny. This means that there are no rigid gender roles guiding men and women's behaviors. The Hijras of India, Pakistan, and Bangladesh are often described, for example, as "neither male nor female." Serena Nanda (1990) discusses the fascinating lives of the Hijras. Raised as boys, the ritualistic

HIJRAS ARE WOMEN

<<< Hindus fear and revere the neither male nor female Hijras, allowing for androgyny in societies in India, Pakistan, and Bangladesh.

removal of the genitals takes place between the ages of 10 and 15. The Hijras have a separate social category—they are not male, and they are not female. The social role of Hijras is to dress and act as women and perform at weddings and religious ceremonies after the birth of a boy. Hijras are feared and revered in Hindu society, as they are thought to ward off both impotence and infertility. Nanda points out, however, that a significant number of the Hijras were chosen because of pre-existing "sexual and gender conditions," such as ambiguous sexual anatomy, intersexuality, and homosexuality.

Usually, a person's gender identity matches his or her assigned biological sex, but this is not always the case.

- *FTM* (female to male) are people who were born female but see themselves as partly to fully masculine; also referred to as *transman* (Landén et al., 1996)

- *MTF* (male to female) are people who were born male but see themselves as partly to fully feminine; also referred to as *transwoman* (Landén et al., 1996)

- *Intersexuals*, as discussed earlier in this chapter, are born with some combination of male and female physiology (similar to a hermaphrodite), who may accept as natural their mixed gender.

TRANSGENDER

Transgender, an umbrella term, refers to people who feel that their biologically assigned gender is a false or incomplete description of themselves. There are several types of transgender individuals: FTM, MFT, and intersexuals.

People often confuse a transgender person with a transsexual. A **transsexual** is a person whose sexual identity is opposite to the one assigned at birth. This phenomenon is stereotypically described as a woman feeling that she is "trapped inside a man's body," or vice versa.

Most transsexuals report that this intense longing to be a different sex begins early in life and intensifies over time (Rudacille, 2005). Although the medical science community today still does not understand the precise reasons behind such feelings, it does recognize that some people experience a *gender identity disorder*, in particular, **gender dysmorphia**, a mental health classification that describes this longing to live as and be accepted as the opposite sex.

Transsexual men and women work toward transition from the gender of their birth to a permanent identity of the opposite gender through a complex process called *gender reassignment*. The gender transitioning process is complex and lengthy, and it requires the involvement of medical and mental health professionals. In most cases, gender reassignment involves psychological counseling, hormonal supplements, and **sex reassignment surgery (SRS)**, where a surgical alteration to the body is performed. This is also called *genital surgery*. Most people considering SRS are required to make a gradual transition to their preferred gender over a period of several months.

Unlike transsexuals who seek a permanent gender change, transvestites do not. Broadly speaking, a **transvestite** dresses and acts in the manner of a person of the gender opposite from his or her own. Popular culture refers to transvestites as *cross-dressers*. The sexual orientation of transvestites varies.

As we have discussed throughout this chapter, gender is not a case of either/or. But another important question remains to be answered. By what processes do we "become" male or female, andrygynous, or transgender? We address these questions in Chapter 6.

SEXUAL LIFE EDUCATION

As the opening vignette shows us, the issue of gender does matter to a transgender female who feels she doesn't conform to society's gender expectations.

The simple truth is gender matters! It matters in our examination of sexuality and sex because the socially sanctioned, approved, and endorsed gendered behaviors affect the roles we play within our intimate relationships, including our sexual relationships. It matters because of the countless social and environmental gender cues that surround us from the moment we are born, infusing us with a sense of what it means to be "male" or "female." It matters because sometimes "boy" or "girl" isn't always a clear-cut determination. It matters because sometimes the outward signs of the biological sex are not congruent with how someone feels internally about his or her gender. It matters, because as you'll discover as you work your way through this course, everything you learned in this chapter affects and influences how you love, how you experience intimacy, how you choose intimate or lifelong partners, how you respond sexually, and how you experience your unique sexuality. It matters.

Having undergone sex reassignment surgery, **Tom Beatie became the world's first pregnant man.**

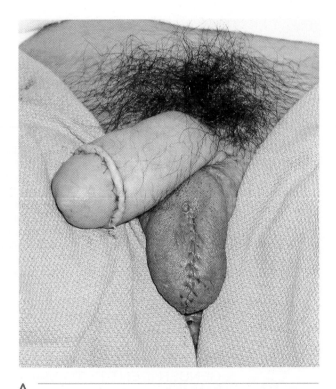

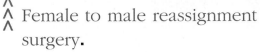
^^^ Female to male reassignment surgery.

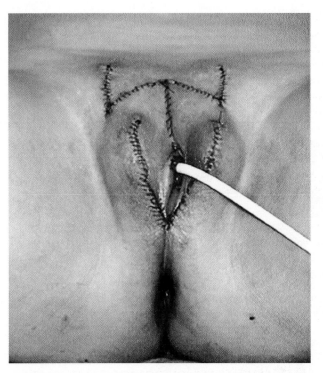
^^^ **Male to female reassignment surgery.**

▶▶▶ **TAKING SIDES**

Should Boys Play with Dolls? Should Girls Be Allowed to Play in Male-Dominated Sports, such as Football?

Meredith is a 14-year-old freshman in high school. A gifted, talented athlete, Meredith excels in every sport she plays. She began playing football in elementary school and played on flag football teams for a number of years. Now that she is in high school, she wants to continue playing football. This has started a heated battle between her parents.

Mom's Side: We have always taught Meredith that she can do *anything* she puts her mind to, whether it is in sports, in academics, or in her career some day. I think it's fine for Meredith to continue to play football. She is extremely talented in sports, and football is no exception to that. She excels in the sport and even has aspirations of playing Division I college football someday. No, we don't see female running backs in collegiate football. Who's to say Meredith won't be the one to change that someday? I fully embrace her decision to play high school football.

Dad's Side: I was OK when Meredith wanted to play football in elementary and junior high school, but I cannot endorse her decision to play high school football or college football. In the lower grades, Meredith's physical stature was similar to boys—one gender was not necessarily more muscular or taller than the other. But in high school those same boys are now becoming men. It is not about "gender" to me—it is about her getting hurt. Some of those young men will weigh over 300 pounds, and Meredith barely weighs 130 pounds. Can a developing woman's body take that kind of impact?

Your Side: If you were Meredith's parents, would you allow her to play high school football? In your decision-making process, consider the following questions:

1. Can/should young women physically compete against young men?

2. Is football socially constructed? In other words, has society defined the roles of the actors in football—that women are to be on the sidelines as cheerleaders or dancers and men are to be on the field as coaches, players, and referees?

3. Do existing beliefs about gender differences affect your decision? If so, how?

Summary

WHAT ARE THE ROLES OF BIOLOGY (NATURE) AND ENVIRONMENT (NURTURE) IN THE PRODUCTION OF GENDER? 38

- Sex and gender are not interchangeable. The term *sex* refers to a person's biological traits, while *gender* encompasses one's life experiences that result in a certain set of characteristics. In other words, sex is associated with nature, while gender is associated with nurture.
- One's biology will determine the hormones with which the brain interacts. Sex differentiation in the brain is often responsible for gender-typical behaviors and possibly for sexual orientation.

HOW ARE MASCULINITIES AND FEMININITIES CREATED BY CULTURES? 43

- Because gender is a social concept, culture largely determines what is deemed "feminine" or "masculine." A repetitive exposure to what is culturally appropriate for a male or female causes people to internalize such behavior.
- Different cultures often polarize gender, making masculine and feminine traits opposites. This causes problems when a person deviates from the perceived norm or when a person finds himself or herself somewhere along the gender continuum, rather than at one end or the other.

HOW DOES SEXUAL DIFFERENTIATION OCCUR PRENATALLY, AND WHAT CHROMOSOMAL AND HORMONAL DISORDERS MAY RESULT? 41

- Sexual differentiation occurs prenatally when a developing embryo receives either two X sex chromosomes or an X sex chromosome with a Y sex chromosome. These blueprints determine a fetus' internal and external sex characteristics.
- Intersex conditions occur when a person is neither anatomically fully male nor fully female, but instead somewhere along the continuum.

WHAT IS THE SIGNIFICANCE OF GENDER IDENTITY TO MALE AND FEMALE? 52

- Gender identity refers to how a person experiences his or her gender within that particular culture.
- Although nature does not necessarily determine a person's gender, it plays a large role in developing it. The type of sexual anatomy a person is born with will have a great impact on how society relates to him or her.

Key Terms

nature biological   *38*

nurture environmental   *38*

psychosocial how a person feels about what nature and nurture impose   *38*

sex biological trait   *38*

gender the sum of our developmental and life course experiences   *38*

sexual reproduction the sexual union that produces offspring   *38*

fertilization process that fuses gametes   *38*

gametes cells through which parents pass their genetic material to their offspring   *38*

sperm the male reproductive cell   *38*

ovum the female reproductive cell   *38*

homogametic sex females, can only pass X sex chromosomes to offspring   *38*

heterogametic sex males, can pass on either an X or a Y chromosome   *38*

gonads the male or female sex glands   *38*

germ cells male or female reproductive cells   *38*

androgens masculinizing sex hormones   *39*

sex hormones orchestrate the development and differentiation of sex organs   *39*

testosterone androgen   *39*

SRY sex-determining region of the Y chromosome   *39*

estrogen feminizing sex hormone   *39*

homologous corresponding   *40*

teratogens factors that can cause prenatal damage   *40*

congenital birth defects defects present at birth   *40*

sensitive period period of development in which organs and structures undergo rapid development   *40*

intersex or **intersexual** someone who is anatomically along the continuum between male and female   *41*

hermaphrodite an individual born with both ovarian and testicular tissue   *41*

female pseudohermaphrodite a person born with an XX sex chromosomal structure and has normal female internal reproductive organs but masculinized external genitalia   *41*

male pseudohermaphrodite a person born with an XY sex chromosomal structure and testes, giving the appearance of being a female   *41*

sex reassignment a routine procedure whereby "abnormal" genitalia were surgically corrected and supplemental sex hormones later sustained the surgically assigned "gender"   *43*

gender socialization the specific messages and practices we receive from our culture concerning the nature of being feminine or masculine   *45*

gender roles the cultural norms for male and female attitudes and behaviors   *45*

masculinity a socially/culturally constructed set of beliefs, values, and opinions that shape manliness   *45*

hegemonic masculinity an ideal, dominant standard of masculinity   *45*

cool pose a new, exaggerated version of masculinity for black men   *47*

machismo the attitude that men are superior over women, and that men are socially and physically dominating *47*

femininity qualities, behaviors, and attitudes that are deemed by a particular culture to be ideally appropriate for girls and women *47*

marianismo the essence of Latina femininity that teaches that women are semi-divine and are morally superior to and spiritually stronger than men *47*

gender stereotypes long-held assumptions or labels about male and female capabilities and limitations *48*

gender polarization, or **bipolar gender** opposite model in which men and women are separated by their differences *50*

inequality gaps caused by differences in how men and women are treated and viewed *50*

gender inequality disparities or discrimination in opportunities or advancements among individuals based gender *50*

sexism the belief that people of one sex are inherently superior to people of the other sex *50*

sexist treating people differently based solely on sex *50*

wage gap a woman earns about 77 cents for every dollar a man makes in the United States *51*

confidence gap women have less confidence than men do *52*

gender identity a person's intuitive sense of maleness or femaleness *52*

sexual orientation the focus of a person's erotic desires or fantasies, or a person's affectionate or romantic feelings toward a particular gender *53*

sexual preference alternate term for sexual orientation *53*

androgyny a concept with no gender value assigned *53*

transgender people who feel that their biologically assigned gender is false or incomplete description *53*

transsexual a person whose sexual identity is opposite to the one assigned at birth *53*

gender dysmorphia a mental health classification that describes longing to live as and be accepted as the opposite sex *54*

sex reassignment surgery (SRS) surgery in which alteration to the genitals is performed to change the patient's sex *54*

transvestite a person who dresses and acts in the manner of a person of the gender opposite from his or her own *54*

Sample Test Questions

MULTIPLE CHOICE

1. Which of the following is NOT true regarding the hormone progesterone?
   a. It is actually a group of hormones rather than a single hormone.
   b. It is manufactured in the ovaries.
   c. It affects female sexual response.
   d. It plays a key role in the menstrual cycle.

2. In a male, what is the homologous structure to the female clitoris?
   a. Glans
   b. Scrotum
   c. Testes
   d. Penis shaft

3. The sex chromosome disorder that results in an XXY chromosome pattern and renders men infertile is known as:
   a. Turner Syndrome
   b. Congenital Adrenal Hyperplasia
   c. Androgen Insensitivity Syndrome
   d. Klinefelter Syndrome

4. According to Bandura, which component affects how children learn gender behavior?
   a. Parents
   b. Media
   c. Peers
   d. All of the above

5. Masculine ideals in Latin America are referred to as:
   a. Hegemonic masculinity
   b. Marianismo
   c. Machismo
   d. Cool pose

6. Hijras of India:
   a. Are biologically intersexed.
   b. Are socially ostracized.
   c. Are raised as boys and perform the social role of women.
   d. Are exclusively homosexual.

7. Gender dysmorphia is defined as:
   a. Male-to-female sex reassignment surgery
   b. Cross-dressing
   c. A desire to live as the opposite sex
   d. Androgyny

8. The differentiation of internal and external sex organs is complete by which week of pregnancy?
   a. 2
   b. 12
   c. 20
   d. 32

SHORT RESPONSE

1. Identify three teratogens and describe their potential effects on a developing fetus.

2. Based on what you learned in this chapter, how would you respond to a comment that a female friend obviously acts in stereotypically feminine ways because she was raised by two lesbian parents?

3. What was your favorite movie as a child? How does it challenge or reinforce the arguments regarding gender representations in films discussed in the section on media and socialization?

4. Explain the differences between sex and gender.

5. Describe Sax's confidence gap phenomenon.

Answers: 1. a; 2. a; 3. d; 4. d; 5. c; 6. c; 7. c; 8. b

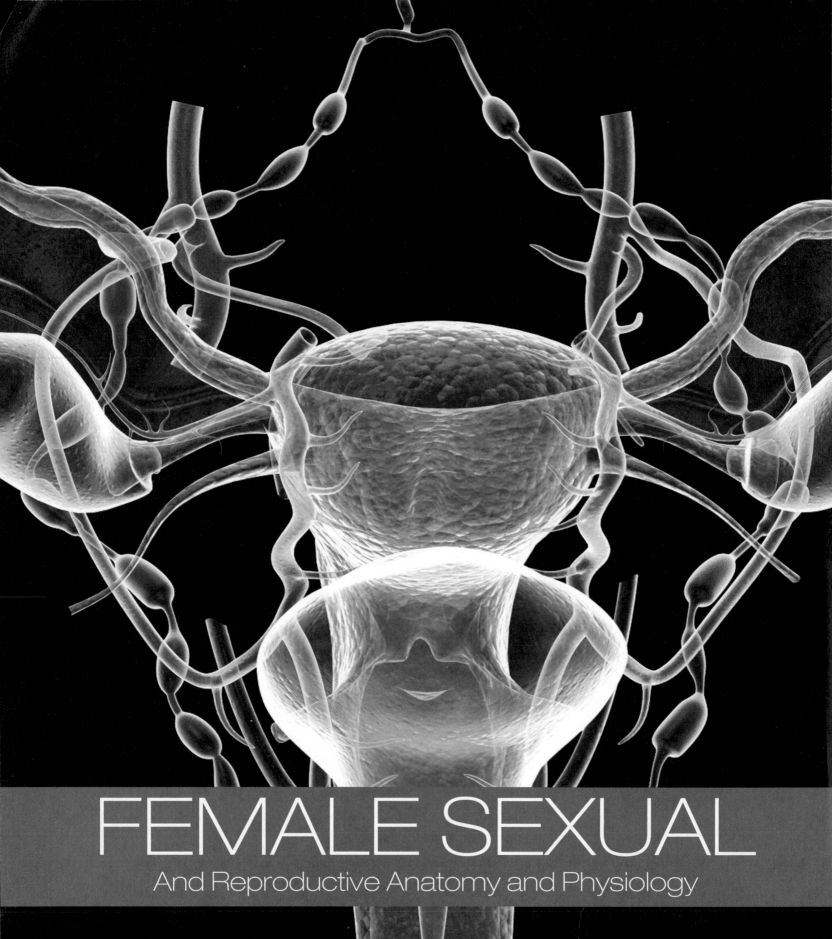

FEMALE SEXUAL

And Reproductive Anatomy and Physiology

HOW DO THE VARIOUS INTERNAL AND EXTERNAL SEXUAL AND REPRODUCTIVE STRUCTURES FUNCTION?

HOW DOES THE MENSTRUAL CYCLE WORK AND WHAT ARE THE COMPLICATIONS ASSOCIATED WITH IT?

WHAT ARE THE BASICS OF BREAST CARE?

WHAT MEASURES OF SELF-CARE AND PROFESSIONAL HEALTH CARE CAN WOMEN USE TO ENSURE SEXUAL AND REPRODUCTIVE HEALTH?

This past

year, my mom died of ovarian cancer. She was only 47. Her mom died of ovarian cancer, too. Given our family history, my sister and I promised Mom that we would get tested to see if we carry the gene that puts us at an increased risk. My sister didn't test positive for the gene. I did. So here I am, 22 years old, knowing that I will get breast or ovarian cancer, or even both, at some point. No one survives if she gets ovarian cancer.

I have two options. I can go to the doctor every six months and have biopsy after biopsy, CAT scans, and sonograms to make sure I'm not developing cancer in my ovaries or in my breasts. Or, I can have my ovaries and breasts removed NOW—and never really worry again about cancer or

dying young. I don't like the idea of having my breasts removed . . . If I have my ovaries removed, I won't have estrogen anymore . . ., which would certainly affect my sex life. But worse, I wouldn't be able to have children. And the thought of not having ovaries or breasts . . . I mean, would I even be a woman anymore? Or would I just be a hollowed-out nothing?

I don't even know how to start to make this decision. All I know is this—if I have the surgeries done to remove my ovaries and my breasts, I'll feel cheated out of my sex life and children. But if I don't, I'll almost certainly get cancer, and I could die. Why is this happening to me?

Source: Author's files

CHAPTER **04**

It's important to gain an understanding about the anatomy and functioning of the male and female sexual and reproductive systems because this knowledge offers guidance and direction for your sexual functioning. Just as importantly, understanding how and why your bodies work the way they do enhances your sexual lives, and also helps protect your sexual health and well-being (Georgia Reproduction Specialists, 2005). Most of the content in this chapter, and the next, can be applied in ways that improve your intimate and sexual relationships.

In this chapter, we further our understanding of the biophysical factors as we examine the female sexual and reproductive *anatomy and physiology*, two branches of science that help us understand the human body and how it works. **Anatomy** refers to the science of the *structure* of human body parts. **Physiology** refers to the biological study of the *functions* of the different body parts and how they carry out these functions. After our study of the external and internal sexual and reproductive structures and functions, we'll examine female sexual maturation and menstruation. We will then turn our attention to the breasts and breast care, and we'll conclude our discussion with a comprehensive review of sexual and reproductive health care.

Throughout these next two chapters, you will see photographs of actual female and male anatomical structures. It is understandable that for some, these photos may cause feelings of uneasiness or embarrassment. If you do experience these feelings, it is helpful to remember that gaining a realistic knowledge and understanding of the human body is an essential component in your sexual health and well-being. You will begin to learn about one of the most fascinating scientific subjects there is—your own body.

"Let's Talk About Sex, Baby"

Although sex and images of the female body are everywhere today, and although you can hardly turn on your iPod without hearing a song or two about sex, research tells us that most people are uncomfortable when it comes to studying the female body or talking about menstruation. When talking about sex, it's vitally important to be aware of the things that make you excited, as well as the things that make you apprehensive.

When I was growing up, if I had a question about my body, I would ask _____
_____ .

When I asked my parents a question about my body, they would _____
_____ .

When I was growing up, I was curious about what my mom and dad, my siblings, or other adults looked like naked. These thoughts made me feel _____
_____ .

When it comes to studying female sexual and reproductive anatomy and physiology, I feel _____
_____ .

When I look at the photos of women's sexual and reproductive anatomy, I feel _____
_____ .

My religious and/or cultural upbringing makes studying the female body _____ . This is because _____
_____ .

Studying the female sexual and reproductive anatomy sexually arouses/repulses me. This makes me feel _____
_____ .

Regarding the female sexual and reproductive anatomy, I have always wanted to know/ask _____
_____ .

I think menstrual periods are _____ .

I learned about menstrual periods from _____ .

When I have my menstrual period, I do/do not try to hide it from everyone. This is because _____ .

The one question I have about the menstrual cycle is _____
_____ .

The one question I have about the female body is _____
_____ .

The most important thing I hope to learn in this chapter is _____
_____ .

THE VULVA: EXTERNAL SEXUAL AND REPRODUCTIVE ANATOMY

The **vulva**—"covering" in Latin—encompasses all of the external female genital structures, which includes the pubic hair, folds of skin, vaginal opening, urinary opening, clitoris, perineum, and anus. To aid our discussion, Figure 4.1 illustrates these structures. Some medical resources also refer to the vulva as the *pudendum*, which means "shameful" (Marieb & Hoehn, 2007). There is great diversity in the size, shape, and color of women's sexual and reproductive anatomical structures.

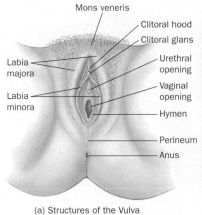

(a) Structures of the Vulva

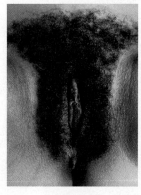

(b) Variations in the Appearance of the Vulva

Figure 4.1 **The Vulva** The appearances of female external genitalia **vary from woman to woman.**

THE MONS VENERIS

The **mons veneris**, or "the mound of Venus" (the Roman goddess of love and beauty) is also referred to as the **mons pubis** ("mountain on the pubis"). The mons is the soft, fatty, rounded area that covers and protects the pubic bone and is more distinct in women because the fatty tissue is sensitive to estrogen; the size of the mons correlates with the amount of body fat a person has. The mons is covered by pubic hair, which has the distinctive sexual function of trapping the scent of a woman's vaginal secretions, enhancing sexual arousal.

THE LABIA MAJORA

The mons veneris divides into the **labia majora**, or outer, larger lips; the labia majora are two thick, fatty folds of skin that extend from the mons to the anus. They begin near the base of the center of the mons and extend down toward the inner thighs. They are covered with strong, crisp, coarse pubic hair, and they contain oil-secreting glands. The labia majora enclose the labia minora. The labia majora are the female counterpart of the male scrotum.

Healthy Selves / Healthy Sex

Don't Like Your Genitals? Female Genital Cosmetic Surgery (FGCS)

There is great variation in the appearance of female genitalia. But today, some women are opting for cosmetic surgery of their external genitalia to "normalize" their appearance, boosting the acceptance of their body and their confidence in the bedroom. *Female sexual enhancement* surgeries, such as breast augmentations, are surgical procedures that enhance a woman's sexuality by improving her self-image. There are different surgical procedures for different "problem" areas.

Labiaplasty Labiaplasty is also referred to as *labia beautification*, because some contemporary women are seeking the surgical sculpting of their labia to achieve a more aesthetically pleasing look for themselves. In this surgical procedure, the cosmetic surgeon removes and/or reshapes the labia minora and/or majora to reduce their outward appearance.

Vaginoplasty Vaginoplasty is often referred to as *vaginal rejuvenation*. In this surgery, the vaginal area and the surrounding muscles are tightened. Vaginoplasty procedures are increasing in number because the renewal of the vaginal tissues/muscular structures often enhances the sexual experiences of women.

Hoodectomy In the hoodectomy procedure, a surgeon removes the clitoral hood. This procedure is also thus referred to as **clitoral unhooding**. Women may opt to have their clitoral hood removed so the clitoris is exposed at all times. This procedure is said to heighten the clitoral sensations, as well as a woman's sexual arousal.

Hymenoplasty In the hymenoplasty surgery, surgeons are able to stitch the hymen tissue back together, thus repairing and restoring it; tiny blood vessels will grow into the restored hymen tissue. When the woman has vulva intercourse, the tissue will "tear" again and the small blood vessels will break—she will "bleed," and her partner will think that she is a virgin. This surgery is also referred to as *virginity restoration*.

Vaginal cosmetic surgical procedures are becoming increasingly popular as the cosmetic and reconstructive procedures become more mainstream. However, if a woman is contemplating any of these surgical procedures, she should seek out only board-certified cosmetic surgeons, urologists, or plastic surgeons to perform the procedures.

Source: Based on American Society of Plastic Surgeons (ASPS). (2008). Retrieved February 5, 2008, from www.plasticsurgery.org.

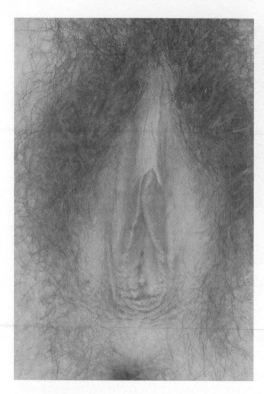
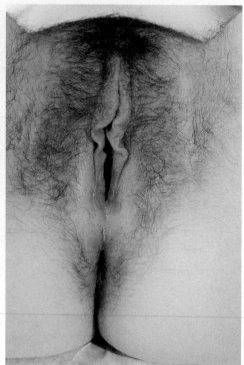

^
^ **Different women have** labia of different thicknesses
^ and lengths.

covers the head of the clitoris, the **glans** (head), and the **shaft** (length). The glans contains 6,000 to 8,000 sensory nerve endings, which are estimated to be nearly twice the number of nerve fibers found in the penis (O'Connell, 2005). These nerve endings make the clitoris highly sensitive to touch and serve the sole function of contributing to females' sexual arousal and orgasm. When masturbating, most women achieve arousal and orgasm by clitoral stimulation, not by inserting something into the vagina. Direct stimulation is generally too intense for women.

When the hood is removed, the clitoris looks like a small penis. Within the shaft of the clitoris are two sponge-like spaces that are called the **corpora cavernosa**, which contain a rich supply of blood vessels. When a female becomes sexually aroused, blood rushes into the sponge-like tissue in the cavernous bodies and the tissue becomes engorged, resulting in a clitoral erection. On average, the size of the clitoris is smaller than a pencil eraser, although there is great variation among women (O'Connell, 2005).

The **urethra** is a muscular tube that empties urine from the bladder and then carries the urine out of the body (Marieb & Hoehn, 2007). The opening of the urethra is called the *external urethral orifice*. It lies above the vaginal opening and just below the clitoris.

THE LABIA MINORA

The **labia minora** are the smaller, "minor," inner lips that are situated within the labia majora. They are thin, smooth, hairless folds of skin that contain sweat and oil glands. They also have a great number of blood vessels and nerve endings, which play a key role in women's sexual arousal (see Chapter 11). The labia minora join at the clitoral hood, or **prepuce**, and extend downward on either side past the clitoris, the urinary opening, and the opening to the vagina. There is considerable variation in the appearance of labia minora. The *Healthy Selves/Healthy Sex* feature box discusses two common plastic or cosmetic surgeries today among women: *labial reduction* and *labial augmentation*. Although some women in Western cultures seek to "normalize" the appearance of their labia through surgical procedures, in other cultures elongated labia minora are considered to be a sign of beauty and voluptuousness. For example, the *Hottentot* women of a tribal group near Namibia, South Africa, were thought by Dutch seamen in the 1600s to have additional appendages that hung from the vulva; it may have been, however, that the men had a lack of awareness of the differences in female genitalia (Long, 2007).

THE CLITORIS

The **clitoris**—translated as "little hill" in Greek—is an anatomical structure in females that functions solely to induce sexual pleasure. In slang, it is sometimes referred to as *clit* or *pink*. As you learned in Chapter 3, the clitoris is *homologous* to the penis because the two share similar structures (Francoeur, 2000). It is located just below the mons where the labia minora, or the inner lips, join together.

The clitoris is a complex structure that is composed mostly of erectile tissue, and it is comprised of the clitoral hood (prepuce), which

FEMALE GENITAL MUTILATION

Female genital mutilation (FGM) is a term used to refer to any practice that removes or alters the female genitalia to suppress sexual desire in females. Between 8 and 10 million women and girls in the Middle East and Africa are at risk for some type of genital cutting; about 10,000 girls in the United States are at risk for this practice (Sarkis, 2003). Although FGM is practiced mostly in Islamic countries (affecting about 75 million females all together), it is a cross-cultural and cross-religious ritual. There are many sociological reasons why families want FGM for their daughters, particularly because of the identification with their cultural heritage and the social integration of their daughters (World Health Organization, 2000). Some uncircumcised women may not marry; others are accused of being possessed by the devil (Aldeeb Abu-Sahlieh, 1994).

Starting from the top left and going clockwise, Figure 4.2 illustrates the three types of FGM practiced throughout the world.

Type I: Sunna Circumcision

The least invasive type of FGM is the *sunna circumcision*. A religious ritual and tradition as taught by the Islamic prophet, Muhammad, in sunna, the prepuce—the clitoral hood—is removed, with or without removing part or all of the clitoris (World Health Organization, 2000). Girls may be circumcised as early as one week after birth, but certainly before the onset of menstruation (Aldeeb Abu-Sahlieh, 1994). Midwives or barbers often perform the procedure, which is done with crude instruments and without anesthesia (World Health Organization, 2000).

Type II: Clitoridectomy

In the second type of FGM, Type II, a *clitoridectomy* is performed, removing the prepuce and all or part of the clitoris and scraping away the labia minora. Any remaining skin is then sewn together. Invented by Sudanese midwives in 1946, today this procedure is commonly performed on female Sudanese infants, children, and adolescents. It is performed by midwives in crude conditions with no anesthesia.

Type III: Infibulation or Pharaonic Circumcision

The most invasive type of FGM is Type III. *Infibulation* or *pharaonic circumcision* (referring to the pharaohs who were believed to practice this ritual) involves the removal of the entire clitoris and labia minora and majora. The remaining skin is held together with thorns or thread with a small opening to allow urine passage and menstrual flow. On a woman's wedding night, the infibulated woman is cut open

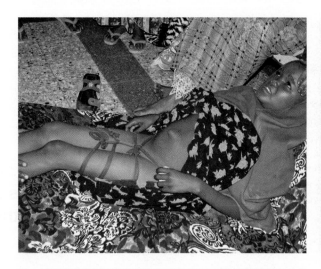

ˆˆˆˆ **Fay Mohammed of Somalia, who was circumcised several days ago,** lies with her legs bound so the wound will heal.

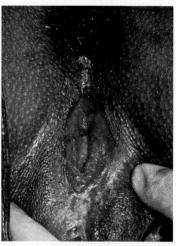

ˆˆˆˆ A woman's circumcised vagina **is reopened to allow her to reproduce.**

to allow sexual intercourse to take place then closed again to secure fidelity (Sarkis, 2003). It is reopened during childbirth.

But does clitoral circumcision always negatively affect women's sexual desire and response? Interestingly, one study of 300 women in Sudan found that the women reported sexual desire, sexual pleasure, and orgasm, despite their extreme genital mutilation (Lightfoot-Klein & Hanny, 1989). Another study found that women reported infibulation as a source of empowerment and strength because it freed their bodies from their "masculine properties" (Abusharaf, 2001). Although it may seem barbaric to some, looking at the *cultural contexts* reveals how the practice is an acceptable and expected tradition in other parts of the world. Today, in countries such as Ghana and Kenya,

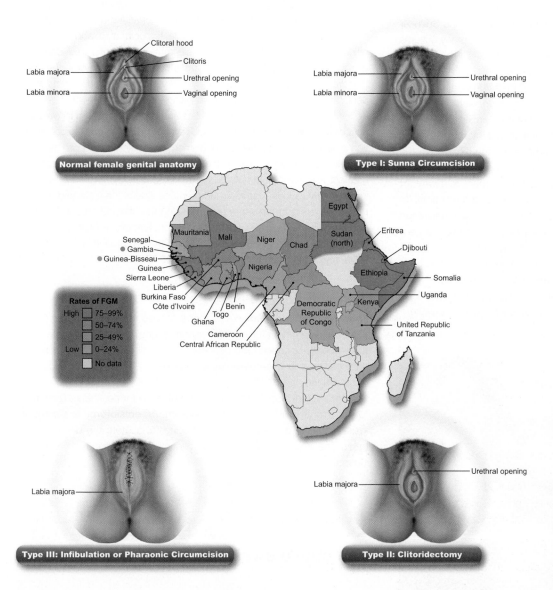

Figure 4.2 Female Genital Mutilation
There are three types of FGM practiced throughout the world. **Compare them with the anatomy of a normal woman's genitals.**

the celebrations and rituals take place, but without genital cutting (Sarkis, 2003).

Effects of Female Genital Mutilation

Aside from the initial pain and trauma of the female genital cuttings, there can be other short- and long-term effects including intense pain, shock, uncontrolled bleeding (and possible death), infections (including HIV), complications with urination, painful intercourse, and lasting effects on psychological and psychosexual development (Sarkis, 2003; World Health Organization, 2000). This practice has triggered a passionate debate in the international community.

THE INTROITUS AND THE HYMEN

The **introitus** forms the mouth of the vagina, and lies between the opening of the urethra and the anus. There is a thin layer of tissue—a mucous membrane—that partially covers the external vaginal opening. This tissue membrane is called the **hymen** (see Figure 4.3). Popular slang words for the hymen are *cherry*, *popping the cherry*, and *maidenhead*. An intact hymen is a sign of virginity, a sign that penetration by a male has not taken place. An intact hymen has many social implications in some parts of the world because it is seen as a "sexual purity code" for some (Ortner, 1978). For example, it was announced to the world that Diana Spencer was indeed a virgin before she married Prince Charles. In many cultures today, it is still customary to examine a woman to see if her hymen remains intact before her wedding day, and in some cultures, parents demand to see blood-stained sheets as "proof" the bride was a virgin on her wedding night. Today, some girls have a *hymenoplasty*, a surgical reconstruction of the hymen, to hide the loss of their virginity.

Although in about 43 percent of women sexual intercourse is the most common way the hymen is torn, in the remaining 57 percent the hymen is so elastic that is stretches enough during sex so as not to tear (Emans, 2000). Students frequently ask me if there is a way for women to stretch the hymen before they have sex for the first time. To do this, a woman (and/or her partner) can insert one or two moistened fingers into the introitus and gradually move them around until a gentle stretching is felt (the key is to go slowly). Some women may feel a little sore or tight, and some women may bleed. When she does have sex for the first time, it's important for she and her partner to engage in plenty of foreplay to ensure that she is sufficiently lubricated. First intercourse doesn't have to be painful—it can be fun and enjoyable!

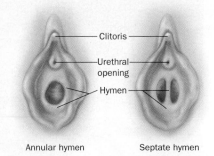

Clitoris

Urethral opening

Hymen

Annular hymen   Septate hymen   Cribriform hymen   Parous (intact) hymen

Figure 4.3 Variations in Hymens The hymen is a thin tissue membrane **that partially covers the opening of the vagina.**

THE BARTHOLIN GLANDS

Bartholin glands are pea-sized glands situated within the vestibule and found in the labia minora at either side of the vaginal opening in the 4 and 8 o'clock positions. These glands secrete a drop or two of fluid when a woman becomes sexually aroused. It was once thought that the Bartholin glands lubricated the vagina during sexual arousal; however, the belief now is that this fluid moistens the vestibule area, making contact more comfortable in this erogenous zone (Marieb & Hoehn, 2007).

The Bartholin glands can become infected or irritated, and these conditions can result in swelling and a considerable amount of pain. A Bartholin gland *cyst* is a fluid-filled lump that forms in the gland itself or in the duct that drains the gland. A cyst typically grows very slowly and does not cause pain; often it will go away on its own without medical treatment.

If the fluid continues to accumulate and does not drain on its own, an *abscess*, or infection, will result. If such an infection occurs, medical attention is needed. About 2 percent of women will develop a Bartholin gland or duct abscess at some point in their life; women ages 20 to 29 are at the greatest risk (Omole, Simmons, & Hacker, 2003). Symptoms of a non-infected cyst include a painless lump on one side of the vulva and/or redness or swelling in the same area. Soaking the affected area with warm compresses may help alleviate the discomfort. Symptoms of an abscessed gland/duct include pain, fever and chills (flu-like symptoms), swelling in the vulva, and draining from the cysts (Toth, 2000).

THE PERINEUM

In women, the **perineum** is a diamond-shaped region of skin that is situated between the anus and the vagina. In English slang, it is called the *taint*, *gooch*, or *cooch*. The perineum has an abundant supply of nerve endings, so it is quite pleasurable to have this area stroked, touched, or massaged.

In childbirth today, it is a common practice for healthcare providers to perform an episiotomy in the perineum. An **episiotomy** is a surgical incision that enlarges the vaginal opening to facilitate the delivery of a baby. The implications for this procedure are discussed at length in Chapter 12.

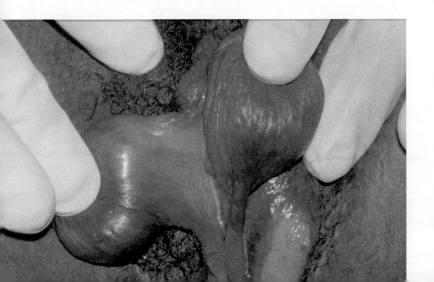

<<< A Bartholin gland infection or cyst **can cause swelling and pain.**

THE PELVIC FLOOR MUSCLES

The **pelvic floor muscles** provide support for the pelvic organs, such as the uterus and the bladder, and promote the voluntary closure of the openings to the urethra and the anus (Rosenbaum, 2007). The triangle of pelvic floor muscles extend from the top of the clitoral shaft to the base of the anal opening. The pelvic floor is a complex network of blood vessels, nerve endings, and multidirectional musculature. The medical term for these muscles is *pubococcygeals*, often shortened to "**PC**."

It is of absolute necessity that women do what they can to maintain the integrity of their pelvic floor muscles. For instance, strong pelvic floor muscles help prevent *urinary incontinence* (leaking of urine when a woman laughs, sneezes, or coughs). Urine can also leak during sexual intercourse, and this often decreases a woman's overall sexual satisfaction (Handa et al., 2004). Pregnancy, childbirth, being overweight, and aging can cause the pelvic floor muscles to weaken in women. Weak pelvic floor muscles can also cause pelvic pain, pain during sexual intercourse, and inhibit orgasmic response (Rosenbaum, 2007).

KEGEL EXERCISES

In 1952, gynecologist Arnold Kegel (1894–1981) developed a series of exercises, now referred to as *Kegel exercises*, to help women regain urinary control after giving birth. These exercises can be done anywhere at any time. Here is how to do the exercises (The Mayo Clinic, 2008a):

- *Locate* the PC muscle. Insert a finger inside the vagina and try to squeeze it with the surrounding muscles. You will feel the pelvic floor lift and your vagina tighten.

- *Squeeze* the muscles for 10 seconds. Relax the muscles. Repeat 10 times.

- *Squeeze* the muscles as rapidly as possible, counting quickly to 25, contracting the muscles with each count.

Do these exercises three times a day (even while having sexual intercourse!). Women will notice differences within eight to 12 weeks.

INTERNAL FEMALE SEXUAL AND REPRODUCTIVE ANATOMY

The female reproductive physiology is far more complex than that of a male, because her body must also nourish and nurture a developing baby (Marieb & Hoehn, 2007). In the sections that follow, we'll discuss the internal female sexual and reproductive anatomy and physiology: the vagina, cervix, uterus, and ovaries.

THE VAGINA

The **vagina** is the muscular canal that begins at the end of the *cervix*, and extends about three to five inches to outside the female body. The vagina

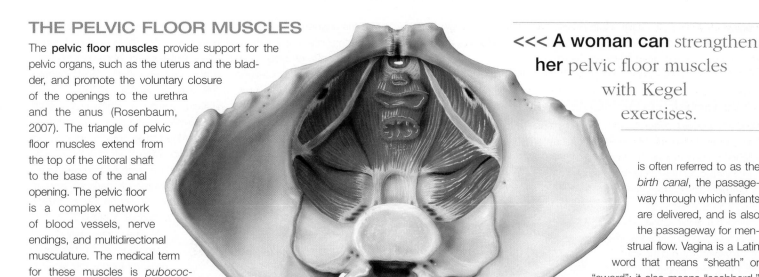

<<< A woman can strengthen **her** pelvic floor muscles with Kegel exercises.

is often referred to as the *birth canal*, the passageway through which infants are delivered, and is also the passageway for menstrual flow. Vagina is a Latin word that means "sheath" or "sword"; it also means "scabbard," something into which a sword would go. Contrary to what many people think, the vagina is not a continually open space or a hole, but is made of layers of expandable tissue (Marieb & Hoehn, 2007). It's best to think of the vagina as a *potential* space. When a woman is not sexually aroused, the walls of the vagina touch. The differing tissue structures in the vagina allow it to expand and contract to accommodate anything that is in it, such as a tampon, a finger, any size of penis, or a baby during childbirth. There are very few nerve endings in the length of the vagina, so the vagina itself is not very sensitive to touch (this lack of nerve endings makes childbirth easier as the baby makes its way through the vagina).

VAGINAL SECRETIONS

Just as saliva moistens the mouth, mucosa cells produce secretions, **vaginal discharge**, that cleanse and regulate the vaginal environment. The amount and consistency of the secretions are affected by factors such as age, menstrual cycle, emotional stress, nutrition, pregnancy, cancer treatments, and use of medications, such as birth control. Healthy discharge may appear clear or cloudy, and it may dry a yellowish color on clothing; it has a fleshy smell, similar to that of menstruation. Its consistency varies, from smooth and silky to simply moist. Unhealthy discharge may appear thick and greenish; it also has a foul odor, or "fishy" smell. The chemical balance of the vagina is quite acidic, which is necessary to keep the vagina free of infection and bacteria.

VAGINAL LUBRICATION DURING SEXUAL AROUSAL

Within a matter of a few seconds of becoming sexually aroused, droplets of clear, slippery, silky fluid, called *vaginal lubrication*, are released from the vaginal mucosa. Women and their partners often refer to this process as becoming *juicy* or *wet*. Women can become sexually aroused by tactile (touch), psychological, or visual stimuli. The tissues of the vagina are endowed with blood vessels; during sexual arousal, blood rushes to these tissues and the blood vessels *engorge*, or fill, with blood. This engorgement is referred to as **vasocongestion**. During vasocongestion, the engorged blood vessels press against vaginal tissues and apply pressure to them, and this pressure forces the clear, slippery fluid to seep from the congested tissue to the vaginal walls.

Vaginal lubrication serves vital functions in women's sexual and reproductive processes. It makes vaginal and vulval play more comfortable for a woman and thereby increases her sexual enjoyment. Lubrication also aids reproduction by aiding the travel of sperm to the *fallopian tubes*.

It adjusts the normally highly acidic chemical balance of the vagina—an environment that is hostile to sperm—to more balanced levels at which sperm can survive (Marieb & Hoehn, 2007).

THE GRAFENBERG SPOT

Although popular culture widely accepts and purports the existence of the G-spot, today scientists can't agree on the existence and function of the Grafenberg spot, or **G-spot**. Some speculate that the G-spot is a small area that lies behind the pubic bone, about an inch or two up inside the wall of the vagina, toward the front of the body (see Figure 4.4), just behind the bladder. The general area is thought to be that of the **urethral sponge**, the spongy cushion of tissue that surrounds the urethra. Some evidence shows that if the urethral sponge is sufficiently stimulated, women can experience **female ejaculation** and intense orgasms.

Female Ejaculation

Buried within the urethral sponge near each side of the urethral opening are **Skene glands**, or *paraurethral glands* (which means *along-*

side the urethra). The Skene glands drain into the urethra as well as near the urethral opening. It is through these glands that the expulsion of noticeable amounts of clear secretions—ejaculation—is observed in some women when they experience orgasm (Addiego et al., 1981; Cabello, 1997; Heath, 1984; Zaviacic, 1999; Zaviacic & Ablin, 2000; Zaviacic, Jakubovska, & Belosovic, 2000). Female ejaculation is commonly referred to as *squirting* or *gushing*. Two different studies have found that between 54 and 60 percent of women experience ejaculation (Bullough et al., 1984; Kratochvil, 1994).

The Skene glands are homologous to the male *prostate gland*, the gland in which fluid is produced to nurture and aid the mobilization of sperm (Zaviacic & Ablin, 2000). Chemical analyses of the female ejaculate reveal that the secretions contained properties that are found in male ejaculate, such as sugars (see Zaviacic's studies, 1994, 1997, 2000).

The existing empirical evidence concerning the female prostate gland, the paraurethral glands, and female ejaculation is perhaps what confounds the issue as to whether the G-spot truly exists in women. Although science supports the existence of Skene

Figure 4.4 The G-Spot Scientists have not agreed on the **existence and function of the G-spot.**

Uterus
Bladder
Vagina
Skene's glands and erectile tissue
Clitoris
Urethra
G-spot

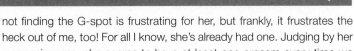

▶▶▶ **TAKING SIDES**

Research vs. Pop Culture: Is There Really a G-Spot? Is It Worth Searching for?

Yana and Doug are a committed couple in their mid-20s who enjoy exploring their sexuality. Yana experiences orgasms regularly through masturbation, intercourse, and oral sex, but she has yet to experience the intense G-spot-triggered orgasm she has heard and read about. She has encouraged Doug to help her in her quest and he has complied. It seems that no matter how hard Doug tries, he can't seem to hit that spot with his penis or fingers and trigger an orgasm worthy of a *Cosmo* cover.

Her Side: I'm frustrated! I know they say you shouldn't believe everything you read on the Internet. But many of my friends, too, claim they have had intense orgasms when their partners' penises stimulate the G-spot area. We've tried lots of different positions so that Doug's penis would be touching the correct area during intercourse. I know Doug is trying really hard to hit the right spot with his penis or when fingering me. Sometimes I enjoy the intensity of his effort and I purposely moan more loudly than usual, but I don't "see fireworks." What am I doing wrong?

His Side: I think I've tried every angle and every position imaginable with Yana to try to trigger a G-spot orgasm. I know that

not finding the G-spot is frustrating for her, but frankly, it frustrates the heck out of me, too! For all I know, she's already had one. Judging by her responsiveness, she seems to have at least one orgasm every time we have sex. I have a lot of sexual experience and have never had trouble pleasing a woman. If she's enjoying herself, why doesn't she just sit back and "enjoy the ride" so we can both quit trying so hard?

Your Side: Should Yana and Doug continue their quest to find Yana's G-spot and trigger that elusive mind-numbing orgasm? In your decision-making process, consider the following questions:

1. What kinds of information have you seen, read, or heard about the G-spot? Where did you encounter the information?

2. Were you surprised to read in this chapter that current research does not support the existence of a G-spot that triggers ejaculation and intense orgasms? How do you explain the difference between the research and popular culture?

3. Could the G-spot controversy affect a couple's sexual relationship either negatively or positively? If so, how?

You can't pick up a woman's magazine (or even a men's magazine for that matter) without finding tips on how to locate and stimulate a woman's G-spot. Reporting that the G-spot is *the* Holy Grail of sexual experiences, and reporting that finding the G-spot will give a woman *the most* powerful and explosive orgasms, pop culture continues to assert that every woman has a G-spot, and it's just a matter of practice, practice, practice to find it. But as our study has shown us, claims about the existence of the G-spot go well beyond the available scientific evidence. Based on your personal experiences, respond to the following questions:

1. Do you believe that women do have a G-spot, and that science has just not found the evidence of its existence yet?

2. Do you think that pop culture has perpetuated a myth about the existence of the G-spot based on faulty/scant research?

3. Do you agree with Hines' comments when he states that ". . . many women have been seriously misinformed about their bodies and their sexuality"? Have you ever felt sexually inadequate or that something is "wrong" with you because you or your partner couldn't "find" your G-spot?

glands, a female prostate gland, and female ejaculation, there is no evidence that a G-spot exists.

MYTH OR REALITY?

There is still no widespread proof of the G-spot, but scientific evidence is beginning to emerge. To produce the types of intense orgasms said to originate from the G-spot, there must also be nerve endings in the vaginal area where the G-spot is located (Hines, 2001). However, studies suggest that there is no vaginal location with increased nerve density (Hilliges et al., 1995; Pauls et al., 2006).

Why does the "realness" of the G-spot matter? As one researcher notes, "The G-spot is not just a point of minor anatomic interest. The G-spot seems to be widely accepted as being real . . . if the G-spot does not exist, then many women have been seriously misinformed about their bodies and their sexuality. Women who fail to 'find' their G-spot, because they fail to respond to stimulation as the G-spot myth suggests they should, may end up feeling [sexually] inadequate and abnormal" (Hines, 2001, p. 361). In short, the widespread pop culture claims about the existence of the G-spot go well beyond the available scientific evidence.

THE UTERUS

The **uterus**, or womb, is a hollow, pear-shaped organ that lies at the top of the vagina in the pelvis. The purpose and function of this muscular organ is to receive a fertilized ovum and nourish and protect the baby as it develops. With walls that are about one inch thick, the non-pregnant uterus is about the size of a woman's closed fist, or about three inches long; it is about three inches wide at the *fundus*, or the top. The body of the uterus, or about the upper two-thirds, is called the

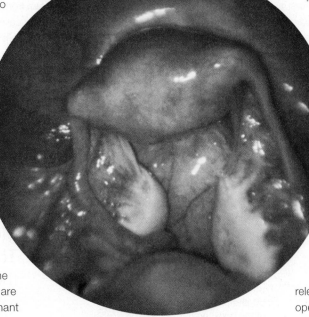

∧
∧ **An endoscope view of the**
∧
female reproductive organs.

corpus. The corpus extends toward the vagina and narrows to the **cervix**, or neck. In a non-pregnant woman, the cervix is about the size of a quarter, is pinkish in color, and feels like the tip of your nose. The *os* of the cervix is the mouth or opening to the uterine body.

The uterine wall is made up of three layers:

- *Perimetrium:* The outermost layer, which is a thin membrane.

- *Myometrium:* The inner layer, made up of many bulky, interlacing muscle fibers; some muscle fibers go up-and-down, while others are circular. During pregnancy, these muscles contract to expand the uterus, to accommodate the growing baby; during childbirth, the muscles contract to expel the baby.

- *Endometrium:* The innermost layer, which undergoes monthly changes in response to changes in hormones; this layer thickens in preparation to receive and nourish a fertilized ovum.

Ligaments support the uterus in the abdominal cavity.

THE FALLOPIAN TUBES

At the fundus, the uterus opens into the **fallopian tubes**, or **oviducts**, to the left and the right sides. Each tube is about four inches long, and the outside edges extend to the *ovary* on each side of the pelvis. The *ampullas* curve toward the ovaries and end in finger-like projections that are called *fimbriae*, or "fringe," that drape over the ovary. Interestingly, the fallopian tubes do not come into contact with the ovaries. When an egg is released from the ovary, it is projected into an open cavity. The fimbriae stiffen and literally sweep the egg into the tube. *Cilia*, tiny, hair-like structures, help the ovum travel through the fallopian tube to its destination, the endometrium in the uterus. A fertilized egg will then embed in the rich, nourishing endometrium uterine lining and continue to develop; an unfertilized egg will disintegrate there, to be expelled later during menstruation.

THE OVARIES

Positioned at the end of each fallopian tube, the ovary produces and stores the *ova*, or eggs. The **ovaries** are the female endocrine glands that produce female sex hormones: the estrogens, progesterone, and testosterone. At birth, a girl's ovaries contain from 40,000 to over 400,000 immature ova (*oocytes*). Between the first release of mature eggs at *puberty* and menopause, ovaries will mature and release approximately 400 ova. The maturation and release of ova is a complex process that takes place during a woman's menstrual cycle.

FEMALE SEXUAL MATURATION AND DEVELOPMENT

Puberty is a transitional period of life between childhood and adulthood during which muscles and bones grow to adult size. This growth is stimulated by hormone signals (in women, estradiol) from the brain that in turn signal the ovaries to produce sex hormones.

In females, the first sign of puberty is the development of breast buds, or the initial growth of breast tissue. Breast budding generally begins between the ages of eight and 13 years (Marieb & Hoehn, 2007). Following the development of breast buds, girls develop underarm and pubic hair and fat deposits in their hips and bellies. Sexual organs also mature to adult size, becoming functional and capable of creating and sustaining human life.

MENARCHE

The first *menses*, or monthly menstrual cycle of a female, is called **menarche**. The age of onset of menarche varies from population to population and is dependent on a number of factors, such as nutrition. For example, in underdeveloped Haiti, the average age of menarche is 15.37 years (Thomas et al., 2001). In the past 150 years or so, the average age of menarche in the West has declined, probably because of improvements in nutrition and living conditions (Blumstein Posner, 2006). In the

contemporary United States, the "normal range" for onset of menarche is between the ages of 10 and 14; this age range has remained stable over the past 50 years (American Academy of Pediatrics, 2006; Lerner, Lerner, & Finkelstein, 2001). Today, the median age at menarche in the United States and across the world is between 12 and 13 years among well-nourished populations (Chumlea et al., 2003). There are racial and ethnic differences seen in the age of menarche, although these differences are not statistically significant (Blumstein Posner, 2006):

- Whites: 12.43 years
- African Americans: 12.06 years
- Hispanics: 12.25 years

On average, 98 percent of girls in the United States are menstruating by age 15 (National Center for Health Statistics, 2006).

Early menstrual life is irregular, because it is characterized by the absence of **ovulation**, the monthly process in which an ovum matures and is released. This is because ovulation is dependent upon the maturation and regulation of hormonal controls in the brain and the ovaries—this maturation may take nearly two or more years after menarche (Marieb & Hoehn, 2007; Blumstein Posner, 2006).

Menarche initiates the menstrual cycle. Absent health problems or pregnancy, a girl will have a monthly menstrual cycle until she approaches **menopause**—the time in life when her menstruation ceases—between the ages of 45 and 55 (we discuss menopause at length in Chapter 16).

MENSTRUAL PHYSIOLOGY

At some time during puberty, the hypothalamus begins to release *gonadotropin-releasing hormone (GnRH)*, which in turn stimulates the pituitary gland to release two different hormones: *follicle-stimulating hormone (FSH)* and *luteinizing hormone (LH)*. FSH stimulates the production and secretion of estrogen in the ovary, and stimulates an ovum to mature in follicles (tiny sacs) within the ovary. LH triggers ovulation, which is the release of a mature ovum from the ovary, and transforms the ruptured follicle into a yellowish body called the **corpus luteum**. The corpus luteum is an endocrine gland that produces progesterone and estrogen and causes the two layers of the endometrium to thicken, preparing it to nourish an implanted fertilized ovum.

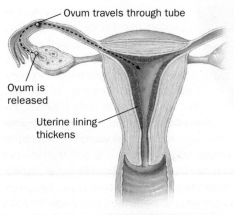

Ovum travels through tube

Ovum is released

Uterine lining thickens

(a) Follicular Phase
(First Half of Menstrual Cycle)

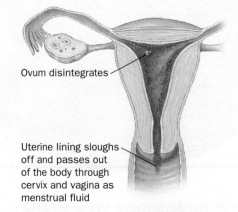

Ovum disintegrates

Uterine lining sloughs off and passes out of the body through cervix and vagina as menstrual fluid

(b) Luteal Phase
(Second Half of Menstrual Cycle)

Figure 4.5 **The Menstrual Cycle** Throughout each month, the endometrium responds to fluctuating hormones, **and the resulting changes make up a woman's menstrual cycle.**

>>> **Female athletes and women with eating disorders sometimes experience difficulties with their menstrual cycles, such as** amenorrhea, or the absence of their periods.

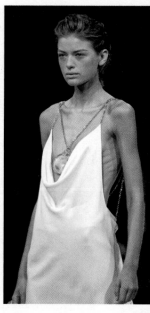

THE MENSTRUAL CYCLE

The **menstrual cycle** (see Figure 4.5) is a series of cyclic changes that the endometrium goes through each month in response to the fluctuating levels of sex hormones in the bloodstream (Marieb & Hoehn, 2007). The length of an entire cycle is said to be 28 days, but there is great variation. The *menstrual cycle* is regulated by hormones during three distinct phases: menstrual, proliferative, and secretory.

The Menstrual Phase: Days 1–5

Triggered by reduced levels of progesterone and estrogen, the uterus sheds the endometrium in the process of **menstruation**. The resulting blood flow (that also contains tissue and mucous) from the vagina generally lasts from three to five days (Healy, 2004). During this phase, FSH levels begin to increase.

The Proliferative Phase: Days 6–14

In the *proliferative phase*, or *follicular phase*, the production of FSH increases, which stimulates five to seven follicles to mature. Near the end of the proliferative phase, at about Day 14 in the cycle, LH triggers ovulation. Ovulation is a process where the ovary bursts and expels the egg, which makes its way through the fallopian tube to the uterus. Each month, only one egg is released from one or the other ovary. It takes 14 days for menstruation to begin after ovulation occurs.

The Secretory Phase: Days 15–28

In the *secretory (postovulatory) phase*, if an ovum is not fertilized or if a fertilized ovum fails to imbed in the endometrium, LH levels decrease and the corpus luteum begins to disintegrate and progesterone production decreases. Because there is no longer hormonal support for the endometrium, it is signaled to slough off through the process of menstruation. Menstrual bleeding initiates Day 1 of a new menstrual cycle.

DIFFICULTIES AND CHANGES IN THE MENSTRUAL CYCLE

With the complicated physiology involved in the menstrual cycle, it is not surprising that some women experience pain or problems. We'll discuss four difficulties women commonly experience during their menstrual cycles: *premenstrual syndrome*, *dysmenorrhea*, *amenorrhea*, and *toxic shock syndrome*.

PREMENSTRUAL SYNDROME

Premenstrual syndrome (PMS) refers to a wide range of difficulties that women experience throughout their menstrual cycles. About 80 percent of women of childbearing age experience PMS at some point (Dickerson, Mazyek, & Hunter, 2003; Mayo Clinic, 2008b). There are nearly 200 different symptoms (U.S. Department of Health and Human Services, 2007). Although researchers still do not know exactly what causes PMS, fluctuations in hormones, chemical changes in the brain, low levels of vitamins and minerals, tobacco and caffeine intake, and infections play a role (Bertone-Johnson, 2008; Doyle, Ewald Swain, & Ewald, 2007). In many cases, women can manage their PMS symptoms with lifestyle changes, such as changes in diet and exercise. For debilitating symptoms, physicians or nurse practitioners may prescribe medications to help alleviate PMS symptoms.

DYSMENORRHEA

Dysmenorrhea, which means "difficult monthly flow" in Greek, is a term that is commonly used to refer to painful menstruation cramps. It occurs most commonly in women between the ages of 20 and 24 (Hudson, 2006).

Primary dysmenorrhea occurs during menstruation, and it usually appears within six to 12 months after an adolescent has her first menstrual period. The pain is typically the most severe on the first day or two of a woman's menstrual period. Women experience pain/cramping in their lower abdomen, and often the pain radiates (travels) to the back, inner thighs, and vaginal area. In addition to the cramping, more than 50 percent of women also experience dizziness, nausea, vomiting, diarrhea, headache, fatigue, irritability, and nervousness (Hudson, 2006).

Secondary dysmenorrhea is more chronic in nature; that is, the pelvic pain is not necessarily associated with a few days during the menstrual cycle. Constant, spasmodic lower abdominal pain that extends to the back and inner thighs often characterizes secondary dysmenorrhea (Latthe, Mignini, & Gray, 2006). The causes of secondary dysmenorrhea vary, but include: pelvic inflammatory disease (or PID; see Chapter 14); internal scar tissue; sexual abuse (see Chapter 17); pregnancy loss; drug and alcohol use (Latthe et al., 2006); and **endometriosis**, a condition in which tissue similar to the endometrium implants outside the uterus in the abdominal cavity (see Figure 4.6).

AMENORRHEA

Amenorrhea is a term used to describe the absence of menstruation. There are two types of amenorrhea. *Primary amenorrhea* refers to girls who do not experience menarche by age 16. It can be caused by genetic conditions such as Turner syndrome, AIS, and partial/incomplete sexual development (see Chapter 3) and also by hormonal imbalances, impoverished living conditions, and poor nutrition (Clinician Reviews, 2007). *Secondary amenorrhea* occurs when menstruation ceases for three to six consecutive cycles. This is common during the first two years following menarche, pregnancy, breastfeeding, and perimenopause and menopause. Amenorrhea also occurs in female athletes and women with eating disorders (Thompson, 2007).

TOXIC SHOCK SYNDROME

Toxic shock syndrome (TSS) is an extremely rare but serious infection that is the result of the production of toxins that occur during the bacterial growth of *Staphylococcus* (staph). Some symptoms include fever, widespread rash, vomiting, and diarrhea (United States Centers for Disease Control and Prevention, 2005).

The first series of TSS cases reported in the United States were associated with tampon use (Chesney, 1989; Mellish & Cherry, 1992). Women today are encouraged to use low-absorbency tampons and wear menstrual pads for 24 hours during a menstrual cycle (Farley, 1999).

Figure 4.6 Endometriosis: Causes, Symptoms, and Treatment Options Fragments of the endometrium, highlighted in blue, **can attach to organs outside of the uterus, causing the painful condition.**

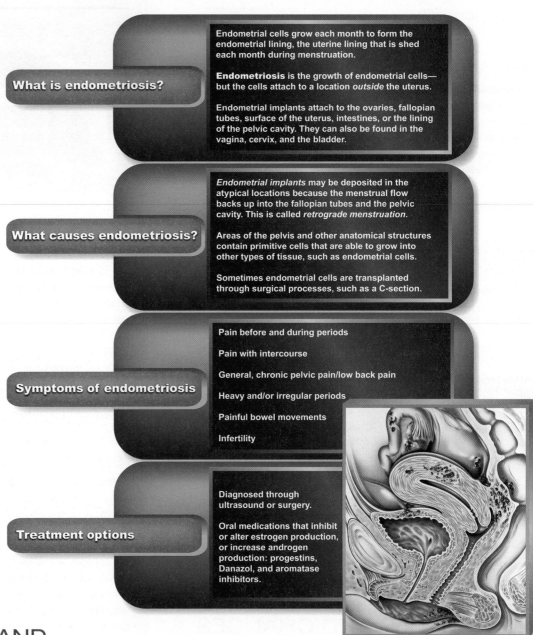

What is endometriosis?

Endometrial cells grow each month to form the endometrial lining, the uterine lining that is shed each month during menstruation.

Endometriosis is the growth of endometrial cells—but the cells attach to a location *outside* the uterus.

Endometrial implants attach to the ovaries, fallopian tubes, surface of the uterus, intestines, or the lining of the pelvic cavity. They can also be found in the vagina, cervix, and the bladder.

What causes endometriosis?

Endometrial implants may be deposited in the atypical locations because the menstrual flow backs up into the fallopian tubes and the pelvic cavity. This is called *retrograde menstruation*.

Areas of the pelvis and other anatomical structures contain primitive cells that are able to grow into other types of tissue, such as endometrial cells.

Sometimes endometrial cells are transplanted through surgical processes, such as a C-section.

Symptoms of endometriosis

Pain before and during periods

Pain with intercourse

General, chronic pelvic pain/low back pain

Heavy and/or irregular periods

Painful bowel movements

Infertility

Treatment options

Diagnosed through ultrasound or surgery.

Oral medications that inhibit or alter estrogen production, or increase androgen production: progestins, Danazol, and aromatase inhibitors.

MENSTRUATION AND THE 21ST CENTURY

Although it is a normal, expected biological event in the life of a female, menstruation is an event that is anchored in often contradictory cultural value systems (Hensel, Fortenberry, & Orr, 2007). It is not surprising, then, that each semester when I teach my sexuality course a student asks me: "Is it OK to have sex during my/her period?"

SEXUAL BEHAVIOR AND MENSTRUATION

Generally speaking, there is relative infrequency of sexual intercourse during a woman's menstrual period (Fortenberry et al., 2005; Hensel et al., 2004; Hensel, Fortenberry, & Orr, 2007). But why? Some research suggests it's because women and men incorporate the social and cultural taboos of menstruation into their sexual behaviors (Hensel, Fortenberry, & Orr, 2007). What all of this research tells us is that if culture deems a menstrual period to be "embarrassing," "dirty," and "painful," then it is also considered to be "embarrassing," "dirty," and "painful" to have sex while a woman is on her period. These negative attitudes are formed early in the sexual lives of adolescents and are anchored in their meanings of sexuality (Hensel, Fortenberry, & Orr, 2007).

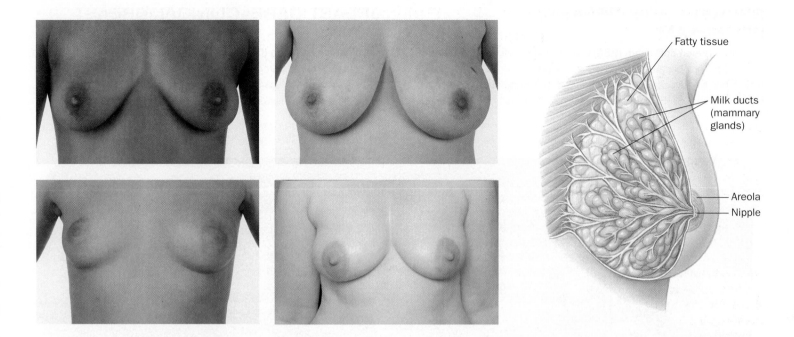

Figure 4.7 **The Female Breasts** Like other female sex organs, **breasts vary in size and shape.**

Labels on diagram:
- Fatty tissue
- Milk ducts (mammary glands)
- Areola
- Nipple

There are a number of other factors that influence whether a person engages in sexual behavior during menstruation. Positive attitudes about menstruation and lower levels of menstrual "disgust" are associated with higher frequencies of sex play and sexual intercourse during menstruation, as is positive partner attitude (Rempel & Baumgartner, 2003; Forbes et al., 2003). The simple answer to "Is it OK to have sex during my/her period," is yes. As long as each partner is comfortable, there is no physical or medical reason why a woman cannot have sex during her period.

All of these findings are interesting, because they speak to the contemporary negativity associated with menstruation. These negative attitudes are leading toward an increasing trend among adolescents and young adult women who prefer to forgo menstruation altogether. The interest in *menstrual suppression* is on the increase in Western cultures today.

MANIPULATING MENSTRUATION: IS HAVING A PERIOD OBSOLETE?

Indeed, women have many reasons for wanting to have less frequent periods (or no periods, for that matter)—and today they can do something about it. **Menstrual suppression** is a process in which oral contraceptives are used every day of the month to totally eliminate a woman's menstrual period. In September 2003, the U.S. Food and Drug Administration (FDA) approved a new oral contraceptive medication, *Seasonale*. With this contraceptive, women only have four periods in a 12-month timeframe (Johnston-Robledo, Barnack, & Wares, 2006). It is crucial to point out, however, that no long-term studies have been performed to determine whether menstrual suppression over a significant period of time (such as two or three years) is safe (Hitchcock & Johnston-Robledo, 2007).

A number of studies have found that women don't necessarily mind the monthly bleeding as much as they do the symptoms that often accompany menstruation, such as bloating, headaches, and cramping. If an oral contraceptive could control her menstrual symptoms, a woman doesn't mind the amount of bleeding she experiences (Miller & Notter, 2001; Miller & Hughes, 2003; Kwiecien et al., 2003).

THE BREASTS

The sex organs are referred to as *primary sex characteristics*. During puberty, increasing levels of sex hormones exert their influence and *secondary sex characteristics*, like breasts (see Figure 4.7), develop.

BREAST ANATOMY AND PHYSIOLOGY

Female breasts are composed of fat tissue and **mammary glands**. Mammary glands are essentially modified sweat glands that lie just below the surface of the skin. Each mammary gland consists of about 15 to 25 *lobes* that are padded and separated from each other by fat. Inside each lobe are *alveoli glands* that produce milk after a woman has a baby; the milk is then stored within the **ducts**. When a baby breastfeeds, milk passes through the ducts, then the **nipple**. The ring of pigmented skin around the nipple is called the **areola**.

In lovemaking, partners often concentrate their sex play on the nipple/areola structure. This is understandable, because the breasts constitute an *erogenous zone*, or an area of the body that has heightened sensitivity. Erogenous zones normally elicit some type of sexual response, because they are endowed with ample nerve endings that are close to the surface of the skin. Some women, however, find breast and/or nipple stimulation to be too intense. In Chapter 10 we'll explore in more detail breasts as erogenous zones.

BREAST CARE: BREAST SELF-EXAM

A monthly **breast self-exam (BSE)** is an important aspect of a woman's self-health care because it teaches a woman about her body—and it makes her an advocate of her own health. The steps of a BSE are outlined in Figure 4.8, "Five Steps of a Breast Self-Exam."

BREAST CARE: CLINICAL BREAST EXAMS

A **clinical breast exam (CBE)** is performed by a physician or other health care professional as part of a woman's periodic health examination.

As the health care professional exams a woman's breasts, she palpates the tissue within the breasts and the nearby lymph

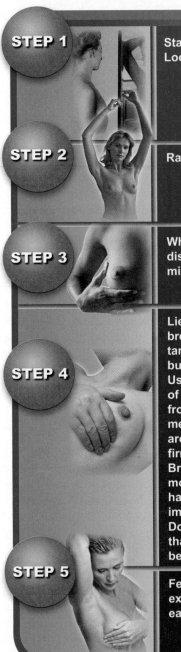

STEP 1 Stand in front of a mirror with your shoulders straightened and your hands on your hips. Look at your breasts.
- Are your breasts their usual size, shape, and color?
- Are they evenly shaped without visible swelling?
- Is there any dimpling, puckering, or bulging in the skin?
- Has a nipple changed position or begun to push inward?
- Is there any redness, soreness, rash, or swelling?

STEP 2 Raise your arms above your head and look for the same changes.

STEP 3 While standing, gently squeeze each nipple between your finger and thumb to check for nipple discharge. If a woman is pregnant or breastfeeding, she will have a sticky, yellow discharge or milk. Is there any blood in the discharge?

STEP 4 Lie down. Use your right hand to feel your left breast, then your left hand to feel your right breast. Make the number "3" with your fingers. Keep your fingers flat and together. Envision a target with a bull's-eye in the center, and larger and larger circles that go outward from the bull's-eye.

Using a firm, pressing touch, with the three fingers of your hand begin at the nipple (the center of the "target"), and go out from circle to circle of the entire target. Examine your entire breast from top to bottom, side to side. Cover the area from your collarbone to the top of your abdomen, and from your armpit to your cleavage. You can either do this in a circular motion (going around the "target"), or you can go up and down. You'll want to make sure that your touch is firm enough to feel the deeper tissue, down to the ribcage.

Breasts have different "neighborhoods." The area near the armpit tends to be the area where most lumps and bumps are found. The lower half of a woman's breasts can often feel like they have grains of sand in them. The area under the nipple can feel like it has tiny pebbles in it. The important thing is to know what your breasts feel like.

Don't panic if you find a lump. Watch it over the course of your menstrual cycle; it will more than likely go away. Only changes that last beyond one full menstrual cycle or get worse or become painful over time need to be examined further by your doctor.

STEP 5 Feel your breasts while you are standing, sitting, or in the shower. Many women prefer to examine their breasts while they're in the shower because the wet, slippery skin makes it easier to perform the exam.

Figure 4.8 Five Steps of a Breast Self-Exam Beginning in their 20s, women should become aware of how their breasts normally look and feel. **The best time for a woman to examine her breasts is when the breasts are not tender or swollen, such as during her menstrual cycle.** Women who are pregnant, breastfeeding, or who have breast implants can do self-breast exams. **A change does not mean there is cancer in the breast,** but a woman should report any changes to her doctor or health care practitioner.

Figure 4.9
Recommendations by Major Health Organizations for the Performance of CBEs

Physicians or other health care professionals perform a clinical breast exam **as a part of a woman's periodic health examination.**

Recommendations

Organization	Age (years)		
	20–39	40–49	50 and older
American College of Obstetrics and Gynecolgy	None	Annually	Annually
American College of Family Physicians	None	None	None
American College of Radiology	None	Annually	Annually
American Medical Association	None	Every one to two years	Annually
American Cancer Society	As part of periodic health examination. Preferably at least every three years	As part of periodic health examination	As part of periodic health examination
Susan G. Komen Breast Cancer Foundation	At least every three years	Annually	Annually
Canadian Task Force on Preventive Health Care	None	None	Every one to two years
Scottish Intercollegiate Guidelines Network	Annually among high-risk women	Annually among high-risk women	Annual screenings

There are two different types of mammograms (Radiological Society of North America, 2008). A *screening mammogram* is a periodic X-ray that is used to detect changes in women who may have no signs or symptoms of breast cancer. If a lump or other breast irregularities are found in a CBE, a *diagnostic mammogram* is used to further examine the area(s) in question. Some women forgo mammograms because they believe the process will be painful, but the benefits of an accurate diagnosis far outweigh any discomfort.

node systems to search for lumps, noting the shape, consistency, and movement of any kind. She also visually inspects the breasts, looking at the *contour of the skin* (is it dimpling or puckering?), *the color* (is there an area that is more discolored than another area?), *the texture* (is there an area that is thicker than another area?), and whether there is any *drainage from a nipple*. Figure 4.9 presents recommendations by major health organizations for obtaining a clinical breast exam.

BREAST CARE: MAMMOGRAM

A **mammogram** is a highly sensitive type of X-ray imaging that is used to examine breast tissue and the areas that surround it.

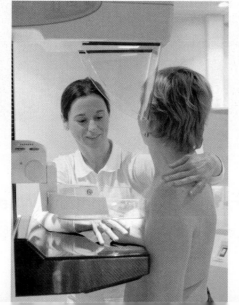

>>> **A woman undergoes a mammogram,** an X-ray to detect any changes indicative of breast cancer.

BREAST LUMPS

Breast lumps are actually very common in women who are still in their childbearing years. *Fibroadenomas* are movable, solid, rounded lumps that may grow but are not cancerous. About eight out of 10 breast lumps are fibroadenomas (Susan G. Komen for the Cure, 2007). *Cysts* are fluid-filled masses in the breast tissue. They are also very common and rarely associated with cancer. *Calcifications* are like tiny grains of salt that sometimes form in the soft tissue of the breasts. They usually cannot be felt because they are so small, but they do appear on mammogram. If the suspicious area is a solid lump, or tumor, a *biopsy* might be necessary.

BREAST CANCER

Current rates suggest that one in eight women born today will be diagnosed with *breast cancer* at some point in her life (National Cancer Institute, 2008). A woman's risk of being diagnosed with breast cancer increases with her age (National Cancer Institute, 2008). Although it is uncommon for a woman in her 20s to be diagnosed with breast cancer, women in this age group tend to have a much higher death rate because these types of breast cancer are usually quite aggressive. This is why women such as the college student in the opening vignette of this chapter face such difficult decisions.

BREAST AUGMENTATION

There is almost a universal association of women's breasts with sexuality and eroticism—and in Westernized cultures, the bigger the breasts are, the greater the attraction.

Breast augmentation is a procedure in which saline- or silicon-filled implants are used to help women surgically achieve their desired breast size and shape. Some women have **breast reconstruction** following the removal of a breast because of breast cancer. In 2008, breast augmentation was the most popular surgical cosmetic procedure performed in the United States, with nearly 307,000 women opting for the surgery (American Society of Plastic Surgeons, 2008).

BREAST REDUCTION

Despite our cultural fascination with size, women who have very large breasts often suffer from back, neck, and shoulder pain as well as social stigmatization. **Breast reduction** can involve the use of *liposuction*, a process in which excess fat is sucked out of the body, surgical removal of tissue, or a combination of both procedures. In 2006, breast reduction surgery was the fifth most common surgical cosmetic procedure performed in the United States, with nearly 146,000 women having the procedure (American Board of Plastic Surgeons, 2006).

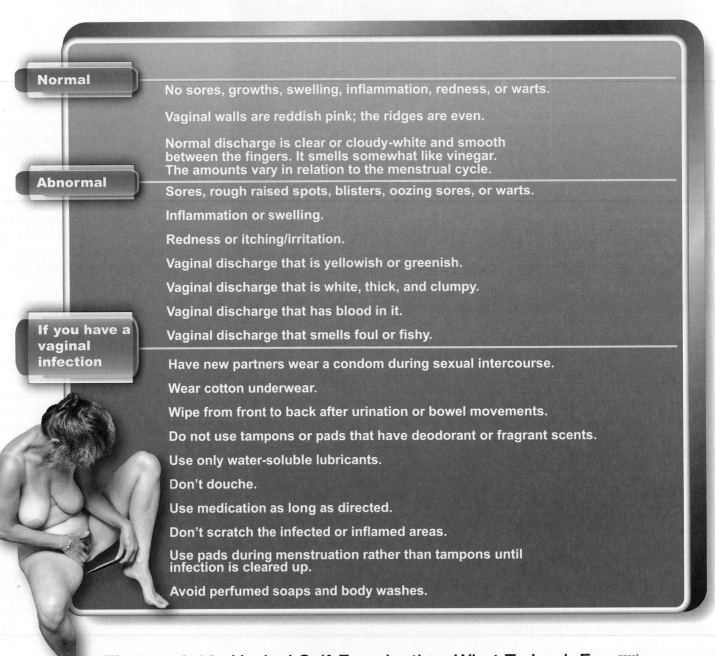

Normal

No sores, growths, swelling, inflammation, redness, or warts.

Vaginal walls are reddish pink; the ridges are even.

Normal discharge is clear or cloudy-white and smooth between the fingers. It smells somewhat like vinegar. The amounts vary in relation to the menstrual cycle.

Abnormal

Sores, rough raised spots, blisters, oozing sores, or warts.

Inflammation or swelling.

Redness or itching/irritation.

Vaginal discharge that is yellowish or greenish.

Vaginal discharge that is white, thick, and clumpy.

Vaginal discharge that has blood in it.

Vaginal discharge that smells foul or fishy.

If you have a vaginal infection

Have new partners wear a condom during sexual intercourse.

Wear cotton underwear.

Wipe from front to back after urination or bowel movements.

Do not use tampons or pads that have deodorant or fragrant scents.

Use only water-soluble lubricants.

Don't douche.

Use medication as long as directed.

Don't scratch the infected or inflamed areas.

Use pads during menstruation rather than tampons until infection is cleared up.

Avoid perfumed soaps and body washes.

Figure 4.10 **Vaginal Self-Examination: What To Look For** When performing a genital self-exam, **using a mirror and flashlight can be helpful.**

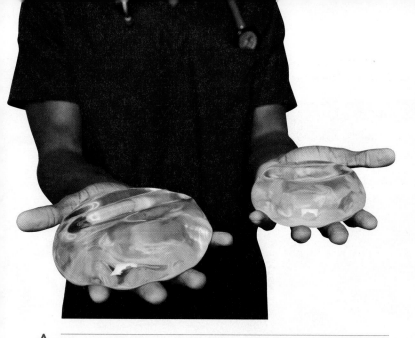

^ ^ ^ ^ **Saline-filled breast implants.**

SEXUAL AND REPRODUCTIVE HEALTH

Sexual and reproductive health, or **gynecological health**, allows you to take action to do all you can to protect yourself from cancer, infections, and sexually transmitted infections. By providing you baseline information of how you look and feel when you're healthy, routine self-health care helps you better distinguish when to seek professional medical attention. Here, we briefly discuss those areas of health that are of concern to women in their childbearing years.

GENITAL SELF-EXAM

A **genital self-exam (GSE)** (see Figure 4.10) is a simple examination of the vulva. It helps a woman learn about her body, detect vaginal sores,

early signs of cancer, abnormal discharges, or other problems, such as *genital warts* (see Chapter 14). A GSE requires that a woman is nude and that she touches and explores her genitals; this notion makes a lot of women uncomfortable, because they have been taught from a young age that they should not touch their "private" parts. But be assured that this is necessary to ensure overall health and well-being.

Doing a genital self-exam is easy. All a woman needs to get started is a mirror; some health care providers also suggest that she uses a small flashlight:

- **Position:** Hold the mirror in one hand and position it so that the entire vulva can be seen.

- **Check the mons:** Look and use the fingers to sense any bumps, warts, blisters, pimples, new moles, or changes in skin color.

- **Check the clitoris:** First examine the clitoral hood, then pull up the hood and examine the clitoris by sight and touch for redness or irritation.

- **Examine the labia:** Look for any bumps, sores, blisters, or inflamed areas. Do the same for the perineum and anus.

- **Examine the vagina:** Using the fingers to spread apart the lips, adjust the light and mirror until the inside of the vagina can be seen. The vaginal walls will appear to be reddish-pink, the discharge clear to cloudy white.

- **Make a note:** Jot down any concerns and contact a health care practitioner.

Genital diseases are typically easily, safely, and successfully treated if they are discovered early. Genital self-exams are a practical way for a woman to guard her health and protect her sexual life.

THE ANNUAL EXAM: PELVIC EXAM AND PAP SMEAR

The American College of Obstetrics and Gynecologists (ACOG) recommends annual exams for every woman as soon as she is sexually active (2007). During the yearly clinical exam, the doctor or health care practitioner will give the woman a pelvic exam, Pap smear, and clinical breast exam.

During a **pelvic exam** (see Figure 4.11), the doctor places two gloved fingers into the vagina while her other hand presses down on the lower abdomen to assess the size, shape, and location of the uterus, fal-

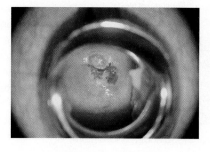
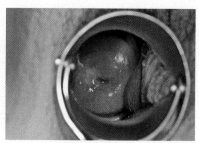

(a) Internal View of the Pap Test Procedure   (b) Abnormal Cervix   (c) Normal Cervix

Cervical swab or brush · Speculum · Cervix · Bladder · Uterus · Rectum

Figure 4.11 Clinical Pelvic Exam Along with a Pap smear and breast exam, **a woman should have a yearly clinical pelvic exam.**

>>> There is a wide array of feminine hygiene products **easily available to women.**

lopian tubes, and ovaries. After removing her fingers from the vagina, the doctor will gently insert a *speculum*, which widens the vagina so the doctor can examine the upper portion of the vagina and cervix for any inflammation or infection.

While the speculum is still inserted into the vagina, the clinician will do a **Pap smear**, which is a way that doctors can examine cells from the cervix. The purpose of the Pap smear is to detect cancer in the cervix or any abnormal cell growth that might lead to cancer. A sample of cells is taken from the cervix with a wooden scraper; the "smear" is then placed on a glass microscope slide and sent to the lab for examination. Women should have a Pap smear at least every three years (National Cancer Institute, 2008).

INFECTIONS

Nearly 70 percent of all women get a vaginal infection at some point in their lives (American Social Health Association, 2008). These infections, or **vaginitis**, occur when the vaginal environment is changed by medications, douches, sexual intercourse, sexually transmitted infections, stress, or a change in sexual partners. Three vaginal infections are the most common: *bacterial vaginosis*, *yeast infections*, and *trichomoniasis*.

- **Bacterial vaginosis (BV):** BV is the most common cause of vaginitis, caused by an overgrowth of the naturally occurring bacteria in the vagina. The most common symptom of BV is vaginal discharge that has a fishy smell, accompanied by intense itching, rash, and/or burning with urination.
- **Yeast infections:** Although normally a small amount of yeast, or *Candida* fungus, exists in the vagina, sometimes there is an overabundance. Symptoms include an increased amount of discharge that may look similar to cottage cheese, redness, itching, and burning.
- **Trichomoniasis:** Trichomoniasis is caused by a single-cell protozoan parasite. This parasite causes a sexually transmitted infection, which causes a vaginal infection. We'll discuss trichomoniasis in Chapter 14.

Vulvitis involves the external genitalia (the labia, clitoris, and the entrance to the vagina). Like vaginitis, vulvitis can be caused by a number of different infections.

URINARY TRACT INFECTION

The urinary system is made up of the kidneys, bladder, and urethra. A **urinary tract infection (UTI)** is an infection of any part of the urinary system. Most women develop an infection in the urethra or the bladder (Mayo Clinic, 2006). UTIs typically develop when bacteria enter the urethra and begin to multiply.

Women can reduce their risk of urinary tract infections by (Mayo Clinic, 2006):

- Drinking plenty of liquids, including water and cranberry juice.
- Urinating as soon as the urge arises.
- Wiping from front to back.
- Emptying their bladder as soon as possible after intercourse.
- Avoiding the use of feminine products, such as sprays and powders.

FEMININE HYGIENE

Feminine hygiene refers to a woman's care and cleaning of her genitals and her genital area. *Feminine hygiene products* are products that women use during their menstrual periods to absorb the blood flow, such as tampons, sanitary pads, and liners. For decades, women have been misled by advertisers into believing they need other special products to "hide" their normal vaginal odor. These products are unnecessary.

The goal of feminine hygiene is to keep bodies functioning the way they should (University of Iowa, 2006). Because the vagina naturally maintains a certain acidity level, using chemicals found in douches and perfumed sprays can break down the natural bacterial level of the vagina; this increases a woman's risk of developing vaginal infections. When a woman tries to remove these natural vaginal secretions through the use of douches, she is removing the best line of defense against infections. Nature has provided a woman all that she needs to protect her sexual and reproductive organs: skin. The skin surrounding a woman's vulva does what it is designed to do, which is to protect the area from germs.

SEXUAL LIFE EDUCATION

I am often asked by my students why we need to go into such detail when we study female and male anatomy and physiology in a class about sex.

Cut Off My Breasts, Pluck Out My Ovaries: Save My Life?

Women who are at an increased risk of developing breast and/or ovarian cancer often need to make decisions about the medical management of their cancer risk at relatively young ages. There are essentially two routes a woman can choose: 1) She can opt for increased medical surveillance, which includes increased clinical exams, mammography, ultrasound, and blood tests (although intensive screening for ovarian cancer is typically not effective); 2) She can opt for the surgical removal of her breasts and/or ovaries to significantly reduce her cancer risks. The surgical removal of both breasts is referred to as a *bilateral mastectomy*; the surgical removal of both ovaries is referred to as an *oophorectomy*.

Should women who are at high risk to develop breast and/or ovarian cancer have these anatomical and reproductive structures preventively removed?

The reduction in cancer risk is substantial among women who opt for bilateral mastectomy or oophorectomy. A number of studies indicate that:

- Ovarian cancer is the fifth leading cause of cancer death in women and the leading cause of death from gynecologic cancer. Preventive oophorectomy reduces ovarian cancer risk to between 1.2 and 1.4 percent (Antoniou et al., 2003; Eisen et al., 2005; Ozcan et al., 1998).

- In women who have the BRCA 1 and/or BRCA 2 mutations, those who choose a preventive bilateral mastectomy achieve a greater than 90 percent reduction in their breast cancer risk (Antoniou, 2003; Eisen, 2005; Rebbeck and others, 2004; Narod & Offit, 2005).

- The prophylactic removal of the breasts and/or ovaries provides women psychological reassurance, as well as a sense of control over their health.

Some researchers and medical ethics experts contend that prophylactic mastectomy and oophorectomy are not strictly medical questions, but that the surgeries raise ethical concerns as well. There are several areas of particular concern:

- A risky condition—being at high risk to the development of breast or ovarian cancer—is *not* a disease. Prevention does not necessarily improve a woman's well-being (Eisinger, 2007).

- There are psychological costs of mastectomy and oophorectomy. These include lessened body image, feelings of being sexually unattractive and unwanted, and confusion with gender identity (Hallowell et al., 2004; Welch, 1999).

- The removal of estrogen due to prophylactic "castration" causes increased rates of heart disease and loss of bone mass in women. This lack of estrogen also causes a decrease in the production of brain cells, increasing a woman's risk to Parkinson's disease (Rocca et al., 2008).

One thing is certain: The decision to have breasts or ovaries preventively removed must be carefully balanced against the effects of removing healthy organs.

>>> WHAT DO YOU THINK?

1. Are you, or anyone you know, at risk to the development of breast and/or ovarian cancer? Has a family member been diagnosed with either of these cancers?

2. If you are a female, would you consider the preventive removal of your breasts and/or ovaries to reduce your risk of developing these cancers? If you are a male, would you support your sexual partner's desire to undergo the removal of her breasts and/or ovaries? Why or why not?

3. How might these surgeries negatively affect a sexual relationship? How might these surgeries enhance a sexual relationship?

Undeniably, this was a challenging chapter because we covered a lot of biological and medical functions and terminology. But to better understand "who" you are as a sexual person and to better understand "how" and "why" you sexually function the way you and your partner do, you *have to* have knowledge of the complexity and intricacies of the female sexual and reproductive anatomy.

The college student in the opening vignette of this chapter asked a lot of challenging questions. Clearly, the decision to have preventive breast and ovarian removal is beyond difficult. There's no right or wrong answer. But knowing the anatomy and physiology of these sexual and reproductive organs equips her with the knowledge to make an informed decision. And to perhaps save her life.

04

Summary

HOW DO THE VARIOUS INTERNAL AND EXTERNAL SEXUAL AND REPRODUCTIVE STRUCTURES FUNCTION?   61

- The vulva, which encompasses the external sexual and reproductive structures, functions to protect other structures, house glands, facilitate urination, and provide sexual pleasure and support for other internal organs.
- The internal sexual and reproductive structures primarily facilitate reproduction, playing parts in menstruation, birth, intercourse, sexual pleasure and the production, storage, and movement of a woman's eggs.

HOW DOES THE MENSTRUAL CYCLE WORK AND WHAT ARE THE COMPLICATIONS ASSOCIATED WITH IT?   69

- Following puberty, hormones regulate the menstrual cycle into three phases, the menstrual, proliferate, and secretory phases.

WHAT ARE THE BASICS OF BREAST CARE?   71

- An important way that a woman can be proactive in taking care of her breasts is to perform regular self-exams.
- Regular clinical breast exams and mammograms can help women detect any irregularities in an attempt to catch a malignancy early on.

WHAT MEASURES OF SELF-CARE AND PROFESSIONAL HEALTH CARE CAN WOMEN USE TO ENSURE SEXUAL AND REPRODUCTIVE HEALTH?   75

- Just like a woman can perform a breast self-exam, she can also perform a genital self-exam.
- Along with clinical breast exams, yearly clinical exams should include pelvic exams and Pap smears. During pelvic exams, physicians can make sure a woman's internal sexual organs are healthy, and a Pap smear is used to check for abnormal cell growth that could lead to cancer.

Key Terms

anatomy the science of the structure of human body parts   60

physiology the biological study of the functions of the different body parts   60

vulva the external female genital structures   61

mons veneris or **mons pubis** the soft, fatty, rounded area that covers and protects the pubic bone   61

labia majora outer lips, or two thick, fatty folds of skin that extend from the mons to the anus   61

labiaplasty the surgical sculpting of the labia   61

vaginoplasty vaginal rejuvenation surgery   61

hoodectomy or **clitoral unhooding** removal of the clitoral hood   61

hymenoplasty surgery in which hymen tissue is stitched back together   61

labia minora inner lips, or thin, smooth, hairless folds of skin that contain sweat and oil glands   62

prepuce the clitoral hood   62

clitoris functions solely to induce sexual pleasure   62

glans head of the clitoris   62

shaft length of the clitoris   62

corpora cavernosa two sponge-like spaces within the shaft of the clitoris   62

urethra a muscular tube that empties urine from the bladder   62

female genital mutilation (FGM) any practice that removes or alters the female genitalia to suppress sexual desire   62

introitus the mouth of the vagina   64

hymen mucous membrane that partially covers the external vaginal opening   64

Bartholin glands pea-sized glands situated within the vestibule and found in the labia minora at either side of the vaginal opening   64

cyst fluid-filled lump that forms in the gland itself or in the duct that drains the gland   64

perineum region of skin between the anus and the vagina   64

episiotomy a surgical incision that enlarges the vaginal opening to facilitate the delivery of a baby   64

pelvic floor muscles or **PC muscles** muscles that provide support for the pelvic organs   65

vagina the muscular canal that begins at the end of the cervix and extends about three to five inches to outside the female body   65

vaginal discharge secretions that clean and regulate the vaginal environment   65

vasocongestion engorgement of blood vessels during sexual arousal   65

G-spot a small area that may be behind the pubic bone   66

urethral sponge the spongy cushion of tissue that surrounds the urethra   66

female ejaculation a release of fluids when a woman is sexually aroused   66

Skene glands paraurethral glands near each side of the urethral openings that expel ejaculation   66

uterus womb; hollow, pear-shaped organ that lies at the top of the vagina in the pelvis   67

cervix neck   67

fallopian tubes or **oviducts** one of two tubes leading from the uterus to an ovary   67

ovaries the female endocrine glands that produce female sex hormones   68

menarche the first monthly menstrual cycle   68

puberty a transitional period of life between childhood and adulthood   68

ovulation the monthly process in which an ovum matures and is released   68

menopause the time in life when a woman's menstruation ceases—between the ages of 45 and 55   68

corpus luteum an endocrine gland that produces progesterone and estrogen   68

menstrual cycle a series of cyclic changes that the endometrium goes through each month in response to the fluctuating levels of sex hormones in the bloodstream 69

menstruation process by which the uterus sheds the endometrium 69

premenstrual syndrome (PMS) a wide range of difficulties that women experience throughout their menstrual cycles 69

dysmenorrhea menstruation cramps 69

endometriosis a condition in which tissue similar to the endometrium implants outside the uterus in the abdominal cavity 69

amenorrhea the absence of menstruation 70

toxic shock syndrome (TSS) infection that is the result of the production of toxins 70

menstrual suppression a process in which oral contraceptives are used to eliminate a menstrual period 71

mammary glands modified sweat glands that along with fat tissue, make up female breasts 71

ducts the place in the breast where milk is stored 71

nipple body part that supplies milk to a baby 71

areola ring of pigmented skin around the nipple 71

breast self-exam (BSE) an important aspect of a woman's self-health care 72

clinical breast exam (CBE) exam performed by a physician or other health care professional 72

mammogram type of X-ray imaging that is used to examine breast tissue 73

breast augmentation a procedure in which saline- or silicone-filled implants are used to help women surgically achieve their desired breast size and shape 74

breast reconstruction a procedure following the removal of a breast 74

breast reduction a procedure to decrease the size of a woman's breasts 74

gynecological health sexual and reproductive health 75

genital self-exam (GSE) examination of the vulva 75

pelvic exam exam performed by doctor 75

Pap smear method for doctors to examine cells from the cervix 76

vaginitis vaginal infection 76

bacterial vaginosis (BV) an overgrowth of naturally occurring bacteria in the vagina 76

yeast infection vaginitis caused by an over-abundance of yeast or Candida fungus 76

vulvitis infection of the external genitalia 76

urinary tract infection (UTI) infection of the urinary system 76

feminine hygiene the care and cleaning of a woman's genitals and her genital area 76

Sample Test Questions

MULTIPLE CHOICE

1. The soft, fatty area that covers and protects the pubic bone is known as the:
   a. Labia Majora
   b. Labia Minora
   c. Mons Veneris
   d. Vulva

2. Which of the following describes sunna FGM?
   a. It is the least invasive form of FGM.
   b. It is also referred to as Type III.
   c. The prepuce and clitoris are removed, and the labia minora are scraped away.
   d. The remaining skin is sewn together and reopened on a woman's wedding night.

3. This part of a woman's body is often cut during childbirth in order to facilitate the passage of the baby through the birth canal.
   a. Vestible
   b. Introitus
   c. Hymen
   d. Perineum

4. Exercises that strengthen the pelvic floor muscles were named after which individual?
   a. Kegel
   b. Grafenberg
   c. Skene
   d. Bartholin

5. Women typical reach menopause between the ages of:
   a. 55 and 65
   b. 65 and 75
   c. 35 and 45
   d. 45 and 55

6. Women who do not enter menarche by age 16 are said to have:
   a. Primary Dysmenorrhea
   b. Secondary Dysmenorrhea
   c. Primary Amenorrhea
   d. Secondary Amenorrhea

7. Which part of the breast produces milk after a baby is born?
   a. Areola
   b. Mammary Glands
   c. Lobes
   d. Alveoli Glands

8. Between puberty and menopause, the average woman releases how many ova?
   a. 40
   b. 400
   c. 4,000
   d. 40,000

SHORT RESPONSE

1. Your younger sister is about to visit the gynecologist for her first exam. What can you tell her to expect?

2. At the visit, her doctor tells her about cycle-stopping contraceptives. What concerns would you share with her?

3. What preventive measures can women take to avoid toxic shock syndrome?

4. Explain the role of the fallopian tubes during the process of fertilization.

5. Describe the steps involved in a genital self-exam.

Answers: 1. c; 2. a; 3. d; 4. a; 5. d; 6. c; 7. d; 8. b.

Remember to check www.thethinkspot.com for additional information, downloadable flashcards, and other helpful resources.

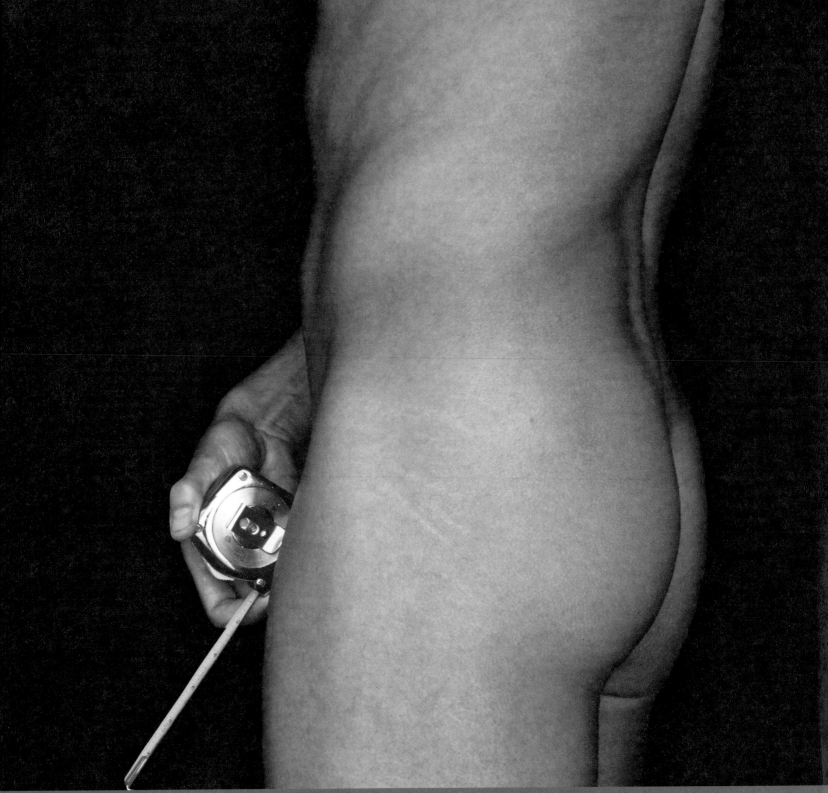

MALE SEXUAL

And Reproductive Anatomy and Physiology

HOW DO THE VARIOUS MALE SEXUAL
AND REPRODUCTIVE STRUCTURES
FUNCTION?

WHAT ARE THE CAUSES AND EFFECTS OF
ANABOLIC-ANDROGENIC STEROID USE
AMONG BOYS AND MEN?

WHAT ARE THE SIGNS AND TREATMENTS FOR
MALE REPRODUCTIVE DISEASES AND
CONDITIONS?

WHAT FORMS OF PREVENTIVE AND SELF-CARE
STRATEGIES ARE AVAILABLE TO MEN?

I'm probably

like most of the people in this class—I've had some type of "sex education" since I was in about the fifth grade. But I've always been frustrated, because it seems like women get all of the attention, like, their bodies are so complex that there's so much more discussion about them. Men just get kind of skipped over.

But I think men get skipped over because I don't really think that guys are that difficult to understand, I mean as far as sex is concerned. Pretty much the male sexual anatomy and physiology is all about the penis.

And I guess that's my point: Male sexuality is all about the penis. Think about it . . . everything centers on the penis, from sexual pleasure to reproduction to even sexually transmitted diseases. Is it any wonder that guys feel like they don't measure up— literally? In muscle-bound America, bigger is always better.

I want the truth—does penis size matter to women? Hell, you can't even go to the Gap any more or any other store without seeing the male [mannequins] sporting a huge package [genitals] and perfectly carved pecs. The message of what women want is pretty loud and clear.

So this is what I want to know. Does penis size really matter? And what about circumcision? I've heard that guys who are cut don't have as much sexual pleasure as men who aren't cut—is this true? And what about the sensitivity of the penis—is it true that a woman's clitoris has twice the nerve endings as the head of the man's penis?

As I write this I have to laugh, because my questions prove my point—male sexuality is all about the penis.

Source: Author's files

CHAPTER **05**

Many people believe that a female's sexual and reproductive anatomy is more complex than that of a male. This may be because a woman's reproductive organs are all inside her body and her sexual organs are somewhat hidden, but a man's sexual anatomy is outside his body and visible. But as you will see in this chapter, while the male's body is not built to carry a baby, the sexual and reproductive anatomy is both complex and intricate.

In this chapter, we'll begin with the study of the various structures of the male sexual/reproductive anatomy. We'll then move to male sexual maturation and how these structures function during sexual arousal. We will also take an in-depth look at male sexual and reproductive health, including a discussion of the use of anabolic steroids. The content in this chapter will help you better understand the sexual and reproductive functions of the male genitalia, some cultural practices that affect the functioning of the male organs, and perhaps clear up some misconceptions related to males' sexual functioning. Knowing your body promotes your sexual and reproductive health and well-being—and your sexual enjoyment!

ANATOMY OF THE MALE SEXUAL AND REPRODUCTIVE SYSTEM

The role of the male reproductive system is to manufacture and maintain *sperm* and deliver the sperm to the female's uterus, where the egg then travels to the fallopian tubes to be fertilized (Marieb & Hoehn, 2007). In the pages that follow, we'll discuss the structures and functions of the male reproductive system: the penis, scrotum, testicles, the production and pathway of sperm, and the pelvic floor muscles that support these structures.

THE PENIS

The **penis**, or "tail," is the male organ designed to deliver the sperm to the female reproductive tract. Made of fibrous tissue and spongy tissue, the penis has an abundance of nerve endings and blood vessels and is supported by an underlying muscular structure.

V
V **A flaccid,** uncircumcised penis.
V

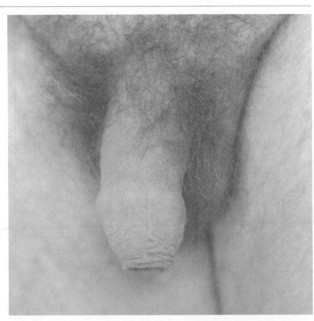

In humans, the penis is made of three parts: the **root**, which attaches to the wall of the abdomen; the body (length), or **shaft**, and the acorn-shaped head, or **glans penis**. The glans penis is covered by a loose layer of skin, which is referred to as the **foreskin**. The **urethra**, the tube that carries urine from the bladder to outside the body, is inside the penis. When a male is not sexually aroused, the penis is soft and limp, or *flaccid*, and the average length is about 3.5 inches (Harding & Golombok, 2002). The length of a flaccid penis does not correspond to the length of an erect penis—some smaller flaccid penises can lengthen more than larger flaccid penises (Chen et al., 2000; Harding & Golombok, 2002; Wessels, Lue, & McAnich, 1996). It is often said that erections are the "great equalizer" in penis size.

Inside the penis are three circular-shaped chambers of erectile tissue, or **corpora**, which run along the entire length of the penis. As Figure 5.1 illustrates, the two larger corpora, the **corpora cavernosa**, lie side by side inside of the penis and make up most of the penis (Marieb & Hoehn, 2007). The erectile tissue of the corpora cavernosa is like a sponge—it contains thousands of vacant spaces that fill with blood during *vasocongestion*. When these spaces fill with blood, the girth of the penis enlarges and becomes rigid, resulting in an **erection**. Under the

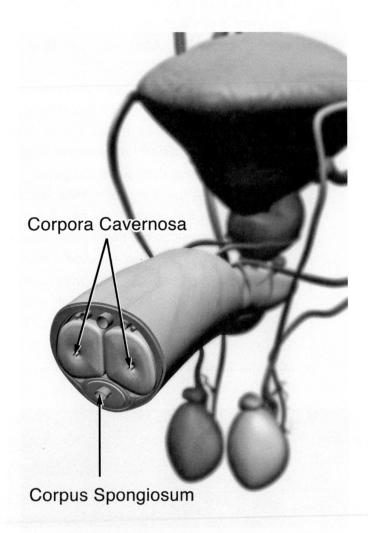

Corpora Cavernosa

Corpus Spongiosum

Figure 5.1 **The internal structures of the penis work together** to create sperm that can fertilize a woman's egg.

corpora cavernosa is a smaller chamber of erectile tissue, called the **corpus spongiosum**, or *spongy body* that also fills with blood and causes the penis to lengthen during sexual arousal. The penis is attached by the **cura**, or **roots**, which are a continuation of each corpus cavernosum of the penis; the cavernosa attach to the pubic arc. Although there are nerve endings in the penis shaft, the head of the penis is the most sensitive part (Yang & Bradley, 1998).

The Glans Penis

The glans penis (glans) is the tip, or head, of the penis. *Helmet* is the common slang term that is used to refer to the glans. The glans is often referred to as the "sensitivity tip" in males, because the 4,000 nerves found in it make the glans particularly sensitive to physical stimulation (Motofei & Rowland, 2005a, 2005b; Yang & Bradley, 1998).

The corpus spongiosum extends to form the cap of the glans penis; the two corpora cavernosa extend farther on the upper side of the penis than on the lower side of the penis, giving the rounded appearance to the glans (Yang & Bradley, 1998). At the tip of the glans is the **meatus**, the urethral opening through which urine and semen pass. At the base of the glans is the **coronal ridge**, a rim that separates the glans from the shaft. On the underside of the penis there is a Y-shaped region of skin that is attached to the glans; this is called the **frenulum**. Figure 5.2 illustrates these areas. Most men enjoy having not only the glans stimulated (either orally or by touch), but they particularly enjoy stimulation of the ridge and the frenulum.

The skin that covers the penis is loose, and it slides over the glans to form a cuff or a hood, similar to the clitoral hood found in females. All male babies are born with this cuff, which is called the *prepuce*.

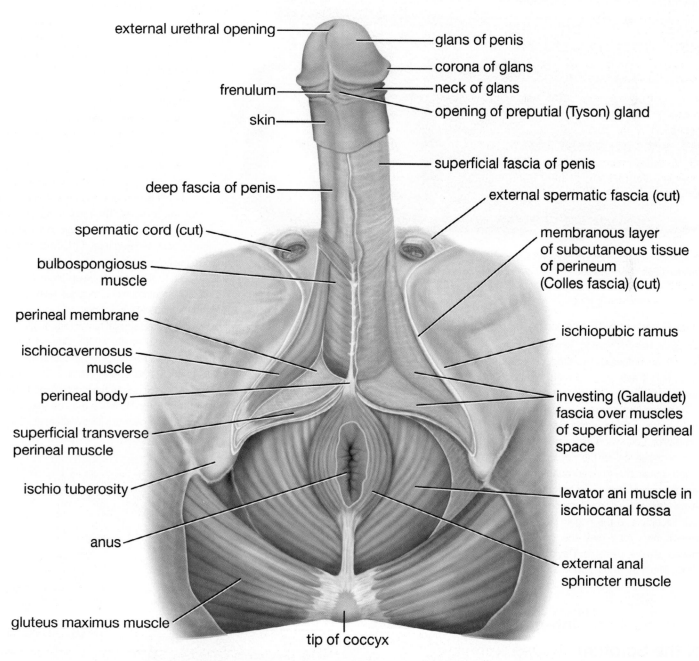

Figure 5.2 **The Underside of the Penis**

Figure 5.3 Functions of the Foreskin

12 Known Functions of the Foreskin

1. **To permit the development of the mucosal surface of the glans and inner surface**
2. **To protect the infant's glans from feces and ammonia in diapers**
3. **To protect the glans from friction and abrasion throughout life**
4. **To keep the glans moisturized and soft with emollient oils**
5. **To lubricate the glans**
6. **To coat the glans with a waxy protective substance**
7. **To provide sufficient skin to cover an erection by unfolding**
8. **To provide sexual pleasure during masturbation and foreplay**
9. **To serve as an aid to sexual penetration**
10. **To reduce friction and chafing during vaginal, oral, and anal intercourse**
11. **To serve as erogenous tissue**
12. **To contact and stimulate erogenous tissues in sexual partners**

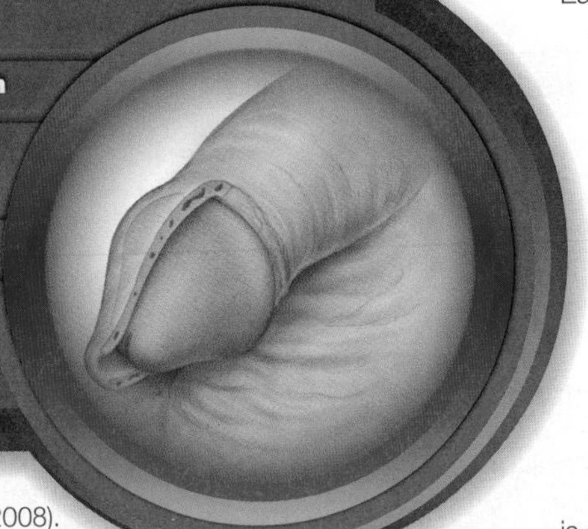

Source: Circumcision Information and Resource Pages. (2008). Retrieved February 15, 2009, from www.cirp.org.

The Prepuce (Foreskin)

The glans has a covering, which is referred to as the **prepuce**, or foreskin. When unfolded, the prepuce is large enough to cover the erect penis, and it acts as a "sheath" through which the penis glides during sexual intercourse (Fleiss, Hodges, & Van Howe, 1998).

The foreskin contains both an outer and inner layer that contain nerve endings that enhance a man's sexual pleasure and contribute to his erection (Taylor, Lockwood, & Taylor, 1996). Between these layers is an interface of tissue called the *ridged band*. In this interface skin, there are ridged, horseshoe-shaped bands, and each ridge contains sensory receptors, or **erogenous receptors**. During sexual intercourse or masturbation, not only are the erogenous receptors in the ridged bands stimulated, but the foreskin also rubs over the coronal ridge, producing intense sexual pleasure (Taylor, Lockwood, & Taylor, 1996). Thus, the most important erogenous areas of the penis are the sensations from the foreskin, the frenulum, and the glans. During various sexual activities, the foreskin slides up and down the shaft of the penis. When the penis is inside the vagina, mouth, or anus, the foreskin is drawn back, providing non-abrasive stimulation; on the outstroke the skin slides over the glans, completely engulfing it (Fleiss & Hodges, 2002). This sliding back and forth of the foreskin is known as the *gliding mechanism*. (See Figure 5.3 for other functions of the foreskin.)

THE SCROTUM

The **scrotum**, or *scrotal sac*, is a pouch of skin that is an extension of the lower abdomen and is located between the penis and the anus (see Figure 5.4) (Marieb & Hoehn, 2007). The tissue of the scrotum, rich in nerve endings and blood vessels, is homologous to the labia majora in females. Popular slang refers to the scrotum as *nut sack, coin purse, balls,* and *junk*. The scrotum has two separate compartments that house a single **testis**, or testicle. Each testicle is suspended within the sac by a **spermatic cord**, which can be felt through the skin. These spermatic cords consist of the *vas deferens* (the duct through which mature sperm travel), the *cremasteric muscles*, nerves, and blood vessels. The cremasteric muscles ensure and maintain sperm production by moving the testicles closer to the body when it is cold, and further away from the body when it is hot—it is the climate control center for the testicles. The ideal temperature in the scrotal sac is about four degrees lower than the normal body temperature. If the body temperature is cold, the cremasteric muscles tighten and draw the testicles closer to the body, to keep them warm. When the body is warm, the cremasteric muscles relax to bring the testicles further away from the already warm body.

Scrotal hyperthermia, or elevated scrotal temperature, affects testicular function and fertility (Thonneau et al., 1998). Several factors can cause scrotal hyperthermia, such as fever, hot tub or sauna use, or wearing tight underwear (Hjollund et al., 2002; Jung, Schill, & Schuppe, 2002; Saikhun et al., 1999). Recently, investigators have determined that men's use of laptop computers in the "laptop" position may be linked to statistically significant elevated scrotal temperature (Sheynkin et al., 2005). The

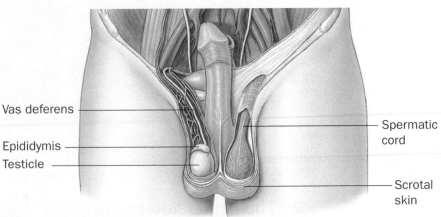

Figure 5.4 Internal Structures of the Scrotum The scrotum holds the testicles.

Vas deferens

Epididymis

Testicle

Spermatic cord

Scrotal skin

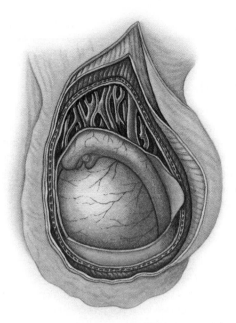

Figure 5.5 Internal Structures of the Testicle

researchers determined that the scrotal temperature increases because of the heat from the laptop computer and because of the sitting position necessary to balance the laptop—this position traps the scrotum tightly between the thighs.

THE TESTICLES

The two primary functions of the testes, or testicles, are to produce sperm (spermatozoa) and the male sex hormones, the androgens. These plum-size gonads (see Figure 5.5) are homologous to a woman's ovaries.

Toward the end of a baby's gestational development, the testicles move from the pelvic cavity and descend into the scrotal sac through a passageway in the groin. When one or both testicles fail to drop into the scrotum, the baby has a condition known as **cryptorchidism**, which means "hidden testis." Most infants with an undescended testicle do not need medical intervention because the condition usually corrects itself within the first year of life.

It is common for one testicle to hang lower than the other. One study found that 83 percent of the 502 men examined had a testicle that was lower than the other (Bogaert, 1997). The left testicle more commonly hangs lower than the right testicle due to a longer spermatic cord on that side (Chang et al., 1960).

Below, we'll examine the internal structures of the testes: the *seminiferous tubules*, the *epididymis*, and the *vas deferens*.

THE SEMINIFEROUS TUBULES

Inside each testicle are about 250 to 300 wedge-shaped lobes. Each lobe is packed with coiled channels, the **seminiferous tubules**. The two

>>> **Sperm and testosterone production happen inside the seminiferous tubules,** located in the lobes of the testicles.

primary functions of the testes, sperm and testosterone production, occur within the seminiferous tubules.

Some time after puberty in males, and well into old age, sperm production begins in the seminiferous tubules, the "sperm factories." **Interstitial cells**, or *Leydig cells*, lie in the soft connective tissue that surrounds the seminiferous tubules. These cells are the major producers of the masculinizing sex hormone, androgen (most importantly, testosterone) (Marieb & Hoehn, 2007).

THE EPIDIDYMIS

Each seminiferous tubule empties into a C-shaped structure that adheres to the top and back surfaces of each testis. The duct of the **epididymis**, which means "over the testes," is an intricate duct, approximately 20 feet long, that is tightly coiled (Marieb & Hoehn, 2007).

After sperm are produced in the seminiferous tubules, they enter the top (head) of the epididymis and begin to make their way through the duct. In this journey, the sperm move through a protein-rich fluid that nourishes and matures the sperm and aids in their mobility (Jones, 1999). The journey through the duct of the epididymis takes about 20 days (Marieb & Hoehn, 2007).

THE PATHWAY OF THE SPERM

In order for sperm to make it to the female reproductive tract, they must travel from the epididymis through the vas deferens, ejaculatory duct, and urethra, a pathway known as the **male duct system**.

THE VAS DEFERENS

When a man ejaculates, the muscles in the walls of the epididymis contract and expel sperm into the 18-inch-long **vas deferens** part of the spermatic cord. It joins with the *seminal vesicle* to form the short **ejaculatory duct**. There are two ejaculatory ducts (one on each side). The ends of the ejaculatory glands, which run through the prostate gland, open into the *urethra*.

The vas deferens is very close to the surface of the scrotum, and its thick muscular layers make it feel like a hard wire when it is squeezed between the fingers (Marieb & Hoehn, 2007). Because the vas deferens is easily accessible, physicians can tie off the ducts, thereby cutting off the

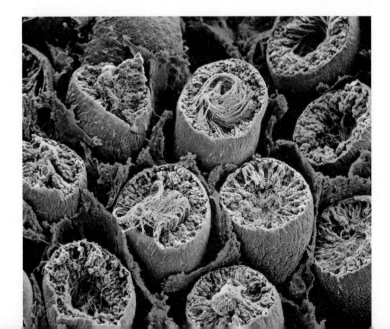

Daddy or Donor? The Call to Identify Sperm Donors as "Father"

In 1977, the first commercial sperm bank, California Cryobank, utilized sperm-freezing technology to preserve and bank sperm for human reproduction, thus launching the practice of *donor insemination*. Couples and individuals who require sperm for insemination make up most of the people who use sperm banks today. Most sperm donors are anonymous—the sperm bank cannot release the identifying information of the donor to the receiving couple or woman. The receiving couple/woman does receive limited donor information, such as his height, weight, and eye, hair, and skin color, education level, and IQ. Traditionally, the law has protected sperm donors from being held legally responsible for the children produced by their donations—they have not been responsible financially or otherwise. But all of that may be changing.

Should offspring of sperm donation be allowed to know the identity of their biological donor daddy?

YES!

According to the *Donor Sibling Registry (DSR)*, although parents may have signed a waiver of confidentiality and anonymity, the offspring of donor insemination did not, and those offspring have a right to know who their biological fathers are. Proponents of providing sperm donors' identities note that:

- Offspring have the right to know with whom they share genetic ties, such as half-siblings.

- Offspring retain the right to the support and care of *both parents*, no matter to what those parents have agreed.

- Men should not be excused of parental responsibility because they provided their sperm—and got paid for it.

- Offspring have a right to know their biological father's complete genetic and personal histories.

As the American Society for Reproductive Medicine notes, a greater understanding of and awareness of genetic and hereditary issues today make it necessary for children to know the identity of their biological parents (ASRM, 2008).

NO!

Gamete donation is important to the treatment of infertility. When anonymity of donors is not preserved by law, there are several deleterious outcomes:

- Gamete donors are less willing to participate, resulting in difficulty in recruiting sufficient numbers of donors to meet the necessary demand.

- This reduction in donors causes weaker regulation of the methods by which sperm are collected and stored. Eager to receive limited donations, sperm banks are more likely to skip necessary steps to ensure the health of the donors.

- Donors should not be forced, 15 to 18 years down the road, to be recognized as "father" to a biological child they know nothing about.

- When federal legislation prohibits anonymity, significant legal restraints are placed on the compensation of donors (for example, the more "desirable" sperm of a Jewish doctor cannot be compensated more highly than the sperm of a white grocery bagger).

As fertility specialists note, "The lack of anonymity has become a major stumbling block to sperm recruitment in some countries. There is concern that longer delays [will result] as donors become more reticent. [In countries where donor anonymity is not assured], there is serious concern over future donor gamete availability" (Brewaeys et al., 2005).

>>> WHAT DO YOU THINK?

1. Do the offspring of sperm donors have the inherent right to know the identities of their biological father and/or half-siblings?
2. Would you use sperm from a sperm bank to father one of your children? Why or why not?
3. In your opinion, what is the greatest benefit of knowing the identity of the sperm donor-father? What is the greatest harm?

Sources: American Society for Reproductive Medicine. (2008). Retrieved March 15, 2009, from www.asrm.org; Brewaeys, A., de Bruyn, J. L., Louwe, L. A., & Helmerhorts, F. M. (2005). Anonymous or identity-registered sperm donors? A study of Dutch recipients' choices. *Human Reproduction, 20*, 820–824; Donor Sibling Registry. (2008). *Redefining family*. Retrieved March 15, 2009, from www.donorsiblingregistry.com.

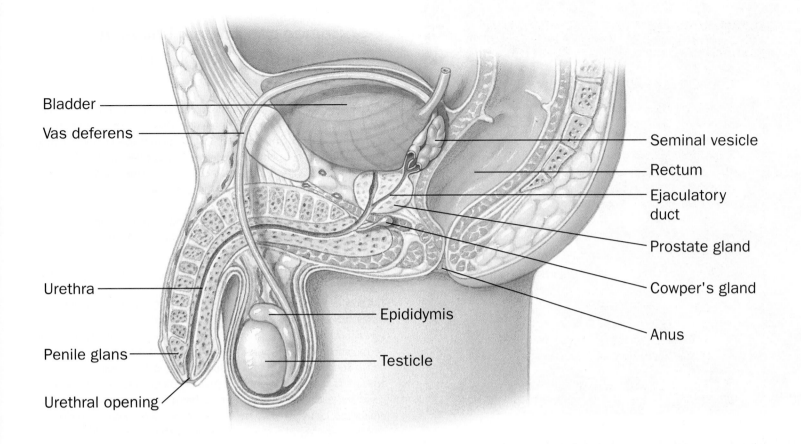

Figure 5.6 The Male Duct System

Bladder

Vas deferens

Urethra

Penile glans

Urethral opening

Seminal vesicle

Rectum

Ejaculatory duct

Prostate gland

Cowper's gland

Anus

Epididymis

Testicle

route of the sperm. This procedure, or a **vasectomy** (which means "cutting the vas"), is a means of male sterilization.

THE URETHRA

In males, the urethra serves not only the urinary system, but also the reproductive system by moving *semen* (sperm plus fluid from the accessory glands) to a woman's reproductive tract (Marieb & Hoehn, 2007).

A common question my students ask each semester is: Can a man unintentionally pee into a woman during sex? The answer is no. To prevent the semen from going the wrong way into the bladder, a tiny band of muscle that surrounds the opening of the urethra closes, making simultaneous urination and ejaculation impossible.

The accessory glands produce the bulk of semen (Marieb & Hoehn, 2007). These glands include the *seminal vesicles*, the *bulbourethral glands*, and the *prostate gland*.

THE SEMINAL VESICLES

A **seminal vesicle** is situated on the back of the surface of the bladder, on each side. This vesicle secretes *seminal fluid*, which is rich in fructose sugar, vitamin C, prostaglandins (fatty acids), and clotting agents that cause the sperm to gel. Secretions from the seminal vesicles make up about 60 to 70 percent of semen volume; about 30 to

40 percent of semen is prostate fluid, and less than 1 percent is sperm (Ndovi et al., 2006).

As we just saw, the ducts from each seminal vesicle join the vas deferens, forming the ejaculatory ducts. Referring to Figure 5.6, follow the pathway of the sperm. Until the sperm reach the seminal vesicles, they are propelled by tiny hair-like structures that line the inner walls of the epididymis and vas deferens. Once they reach the seminal vesicles, the secretions of these glands nourish and energize the sperm, enhancing their mobility and fertilizing capability (Marieb & Hoehn, 2007).

THE PROSTATE GLAND

Encircling the urethra and situated at the base of the penis, the main function of the **prostate gland** is to create a protein-rich, alkaline fluid that neutralizes the acidity of the vagina, prolonging the life span of sperm and aiding mobility (Anderson et al., 2006). The secretions from the prostate gland flow into the urethra, where the fluid then mixes in with the sperm and the fluid from the seminal vesicles, thus completing the seminal fluid. The prostate fluid is a thin, milky fluid that contains more nutrients and enzymes for the sperm.

The prostate gland is very sensitive to stimulation, and it can be a great source for sexual pleasure for men. Some men report they can stimulate the gland to orgasm, referring to it as the "male G-spot" (Ladas, Whipple, & Perry, 1982).

<<< Semen can contain between
40 million and 600 million sperm.

On average, most men ejaculate about one teaspoon of semen (Goldstein, 2007). Although ejaculate can contain between 40 million and 600 million sperm, it is normal for about 30 to 40 percent of the sperm to die. The amount of sperm in the semen is dependent on the *volume* of seminal fluid produced at ejaculation. Volumes consistently less that 1.5 milliliters (about one quarter of a teaspoon) are known as *hypospermia* (low sperm count), and volumes over 5.5 milliliters (over one teaspoon) are known as *hyperspermia*. It is astonishing to think that the quantity of sperm produced in one ejaculation would cover only the head of a pin!

MALE SEXUAL DEVELOPMENT

The changes in male puberty begin with **gonarche**, the enlargement of the testes, typically between the ages of 9 and 12, commonly the first physical sign of puberty in males (Marcell, 2006). Growth of fine, downy pubic hair begins about six months after gonarche, as does the enlargement of the penis. **Spermarche**, or sperm present in the ejaculate, begins about 12 to 18 months after the testes enlarge (Marcell, 2006). At some point between gonarche and spermarche, a male begins to experience **nocturnal emissions**, or *wet dreams*, as well as spontaneous erections during the daytime. Typically, mature sperm are not present in an adolescent's first ejaculate, but he should be considered capable of impregnating a female from the time of his first ejaculation (Marcell, 2006). Unlike females who experience their growth spurt at the start of puberty, male's growth usually takes place two to two and a half years after gonarche. Furthermore, the timing of males' sexual maturation varies by racial and ethnic groups. Among a national sample (Sun et al., 2002):

- *White males*: Genitalia development (growth of testes and enlargement of penis) begins at age 10.0, pubic hair at age 12.0

- *Latino American males*: Genitalia development begins at age 10.3, pubic hair at age 12.3

- *African American males*: Genitalia development begins at age 9.2, pubic hair at age 11.2

Researchers have found a number of reasons why there might be a difference in the onset of puberty for different racial/ethnic groups. Some bodies of science have found, for example, that the environmental effects of stress exert a physiological response that may bring about early puberty; thus, those who live in poverty or in neighborhoods where violence is prevalent are more likely to start puberty earlier than those who do not (Belsky et al., 1991; Goleman, 1991). Other research has discovered that a person's body mass composition is related to the onset of puberty— higher amounts of body fat are known to trigger

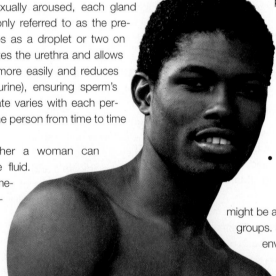

THE COWPER'S GLANDS

The **Cowper's glands**, or **bulbourethral glands**, are pea-sized glands that sit at the base of the penis and behind and on each side of the urethra. When a man becomes sexually aroused, each gland produces a clear, silky fluid, commonly referred to as the pre-ejaculate, or *precum*, which escapes as a droplet or two on the tip of the penis. The fluid lubricates the urethra and allows the seminal fluid to be discharged more easily and reduces the acidity of the urethra (due to urine), ensuring sperm's longevity. The amount of pre-ejaculate varies with each person, and it even varies within the same person from time to time (Goldstein, 2007).

Many students wonder whether a woman can get pregnant from the pre-ejaculate fluid. Although this fluid is not semen, it sometimes picks up sperm that are remaining in the urethral bulb from previous ejaculations, which is why the withdrawal method (see Chapter 13) of preventing pregnancy may not be effective (Goldstein, 2007).

SEMEN

The **semen** or **seminal fluid** ejaculated through the penis during sexual arousal comes from the various accessory glands along the male duct system. Only about 1 percent of the semen is comprised of sperm; the remaining fluid contains fructose (sugar), enzymes, amino acids, citric acids, and other substances.

<<< **Male maturation**
varies among different ethnicities.

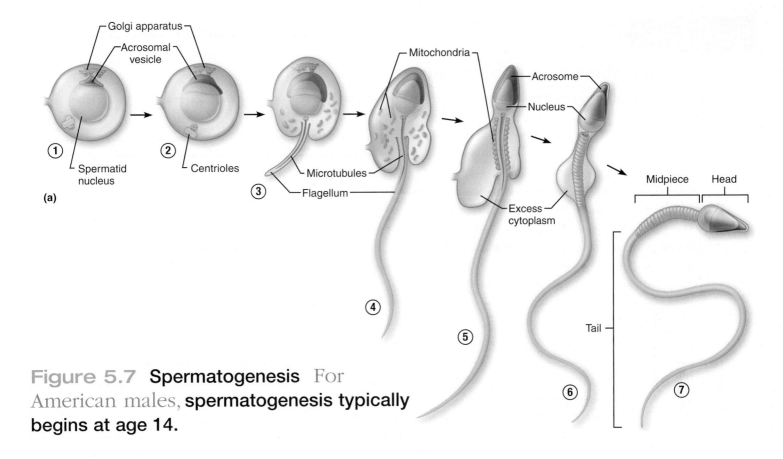

Figure 5.7 Spermatogenesis For American males, **spermatogenesis typically begins at age 14.**

puberty (Garcia-Mayor, et al., 1997). The increasing trends of childhood obesity in the United States may account for the earlier onset of puberty in low-income children, who are at risk for being fed inordinate amounts of fast food (Anspaugh & Ezell, 2006).

SPERMATOGENESIS

Spermatogenesis involves an elaborate process of cell differentiation and maturation of germ cells that are within the seminiferous tubules. Each tubule has a fluid-filled *lumen*, and a *seminiferous epithelium*, a wall made up of germ cells. The seminiferous epithelium also contains *Sertoli cells*, responsible for nourishing the germ cells. Spermatogenesis begins

around the age of 14 in U.S. males (Marieb & Hoehn, 2007) and involves several phases, which end in the formation of **spermatozoa**, or **sperm** (Holstein, Schulze, & Davidoff, 2003). Figure 5.7 illustrates these important phases of cell differentiation.

THE BRAIN AND TESTOSTERONE PRODUCTION

The distinct changes in the hypothalamus and pituitary direct the onset of puberty. These changes result in the increased release in *gonadotropin-releasing hormone* (GnRH). GnRH in turn stimulates increased production in luteinizing hormone (LH) and follicle-stimulating hormone (FSH). Just as with females, LH and FSH are responsible for the changes associated with sexual and physical development in puberty. In males, LH is responsible for the production of testosterone in the testes, and FSH stimulates the process of sperm production (Huhtaniemi & Poutanen, 2008).

The amount of testosterone and sperm that are produced by the testicles is a delicate balance of GnRH, LH and FSH, and testicular hormones (Marieb & Hoehn, 2007). The maturation of the interaction between the brain and the testes takes about three years from the onset of puberty. Once this intricate cycle is established, it remains through old age; however, testosterone production decreases as a function of age (Mooradian & Korenman, 2006). In Chapter 16, we'll further explore testosterone production in the aging male, as well as whether there is such a thing as male menopause. It's important to note, however, that a man of any age can experience a reduction in testosterone production due to illness, such as testicular cancer, or injury to the testicles (Morley, 2007; Pommerville & Zakus, 2006).

<<< **Testosterone production**

"Let's Talk About Sex, Baby" (Part 2)

Just as you did in the previous chapter, come back to this inventory and jot down your feelings and reactions to the topic content.

When it comes to studying male sexual and reproductive anatomy and physiology, I feel _____

_____.

When I look at the photos of men's sexual and reproductive anatomy, I feel _____

_____.

My religious/cultural upbringing makes studying the male body _____. This is because

_____.

Studying the male sexual and reproductive anatomy sexually arouses me. This makes me feel _____

_____.

Regarding the male sexual and reproductive anatomy, I have always wanted to know/ask _____

_____.

I think circumcision is _____.

The one question I have always wanted to ask about the male body is _____

_____.

The one question I have always wanted to ask about a male's sexual response is _____

_____.

The most important thing I hope to learn in this chapter is _____

_____.

PHYSIOLOGY OF THE MALE SEXUAL AND REPRODUCTIVE SYSTEM

Now that you have a solid understanding of the male sexual and reproductive anatomy (structures), we'll turn our attention to the two primary functions: *erection*, which allows the penis to enter the female's vagina, and *ejaculation*, which expels the male's gametes into the female reproductive tract.

ERECTION

A male erection is an intricate process that involves the coordination of his psychological, neurological, and cardiovascular systems. When a man is sexually aroused, nerve impulses travel through the spinal cord, to the pudendal nerve, and then to the nerve endings in the penis. The penis then relaxes and dilates, allowing about eight times more blood to flow into the spaces in the spongy corpora cavernosa. As more blood flows into the penis than out of the penis, an erection is achieved. When a man ejaculates, or when the sexual arousal ends, the penis returns to its flaccid state.

As a man ages, the angle of his erection changes. For instance, in their 20s, men typically have erection angles of about 90 degrees; by their 40s, the erection angle is about 45 degrees. The angle of the erect penis is determined by the size of the penis, as well as its attachment to the pubic arch by the roots and the **suspensory ligament**. The suspensory ligament holds the penis close to the pubic bone and supports it when it is erect. As men age, the suspensory ligament becomes stretched, thereby reducing the angle of the erection (Miner & Kuritzky, 2007). We discuss this, and other changes in erections, in Chapters 16.

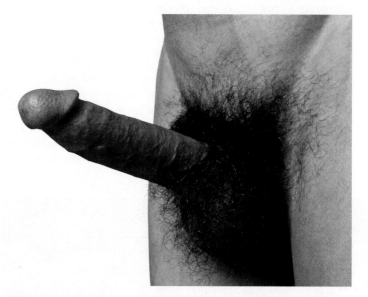

An erection allows the penis to enter the vagina.

EJACULATION

Ejaculation is the physiological process by which semen is expelled through the urethra outside the male's body (Clement et al., 2005). It involves two sequential processes: *emission* and *expulsion*.

The **emission phase** of the ejaculatory process involves the accumulation and deposit of seminal fluid from the ampullary vas deferens, the

Figure 5.8 Pelvic Floor Muscle Dysfunction Symptoms

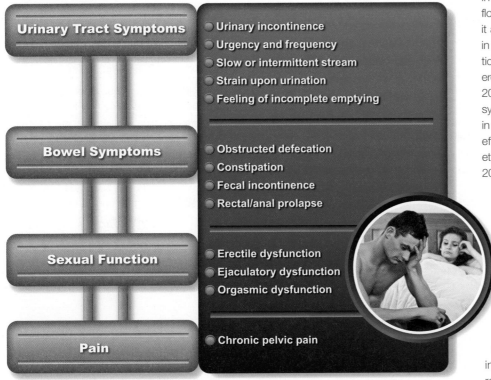

Urinary Tract Symptoms	○ Urinary incontinence ○ Urgency and frequency ○ Slow or intermittent stream ○ Strain upon urination ○ Feeling of incomplete emptying
Bowel Symptoms	○ Obstructed defecation ○ Constipation ○ Fecal incontinence ○ Rectal/anal prolapse
Sexual Function	○ Erectile dysfunction ○ Ejaculatory dysfunction ○ Orgasmic dysfunction
Pain	○ Chronic pelvic pain

Source: Based on Rosenbaum, T. Y. (2007)

seminal vesicles, and the prostate gland into the prostatic urethra (Waldinger et al., 2005). The emission phase of the ejaculatory response is under control of the *sympathetic nervous system*, which alerts the various systems in the body to provide the necessary energy.

During the **expulsion phase** of ejaculation, semen trapped in the urethral bulb is ejected through the urethra by a rapid series of strong, rhythmic contractions. These muscle contractions are accompanied by rapid heartbeat, elevated blood pressure, and an increased rate in breathing. Once the first contraction begins, a man cannot prevent ejaculation from taking place; this sensation is known as *ejaculation inevitability.* The expulsion of semen occurs in 10 to 15 muscle contractions.

Premature ejaculation occurs when a man ejaculates prior to the wishes of both sexual partners (Noble & Lakin, 2005), an intentionally broad definition to avoid specifying a precise duration for sexual relations. If, however, the man has little to no ejaculatory control in 50 percent of attempted sexual relations, treatment may be appropriate. Premature ejaculation occurs in all men at some point in their sexual lives; a prevalence rate of 30 percent is fairly consistent through all age categories of men (Busato & Galindo, 2004).

∧
∧ **The male** pelvic floor muscles.
∧

THE PERINEUM AND THE PELVIC FLOOR

In Chapter 4, you learned how important the pelvic floor muscles are in the sexual health in women, and it appears that the integrity of the pelvic floor muscles in men might also have an impact on their sexual functioning and issues such as premature ejaculation and erectile dysfunction (Piediferro et al., 2004; Rosenbaum, 2007). Figure 5.8 presents the various dysfunction symptoms associated with weak pelvic floor muscles in men. Pelvic floor exercises appear to be at least as effective as surgery and medications (Dorey et al., 2004; Hatzichristou et al., 2004; Morales et al., 2004; Van Kampen et al., 2003;).

Popular media today assert that improving pelvic floor muscle strength in men increases the ability to experience multiple orgasms. Those who support the multiple orgasm hypothesis suggest that if a man can control the genital contractions that occur just prior to ejaculation, he can experience several waves of these contractions ("orgasm") before he ejaculates.

Orgasm and ejaculation are two distinct events. The ability to separate the events involves the pelvic floor muscles. When a man reaches the "point of no return," it is thought that if he decreases his sexual stimulation by squeezing his pelvic floor muscles, he will gain control over his state of arousal and not crest over into ejaculation. He can do this repeatedly to delay ejaculation and experience many waves of orgasm as the genital contractions continue without ejaculation. Although pelvic floor exercises may be useful in preventing premature ejaculation, to date, no scientific studies support the finding of multiple orgasm experiences in men.

MALE KEGEL EXERCISES

Some research suggests that the muscular structures that underlie the male genitalia are weaker than that of women because men do not use these muscles other than during ejaculation (Sueppel, Kreder, & See, 2001). Men can exercise these muscles in the same manner in which women do:

- *Locate the pelvic floor muscles:* Imagine that you are trying to "start" and "stop" urination using the pelvic floor muscles. The penis and testicles will move up and down.

- *Tighten the muscles and hold for three to five seconds:* Tighten the muscles, then relax them; do five to seven exercises in one set. Do four sets a day to begin, gradually increasing to 15 sets a day.

Augmentative Phalloplasty

If bigger really is better when it comes to penis size, medical science has found a way to make that happen for men today. *Male enhancement procedures* are those in which penis size is enhanced, either through the use of certain exercises or surgery. **Augmentative phalloplasty** is a surgical procedure, performed by plastic or aesthetic surgeons, to enlarge the volume of the penis. The typical patient who seeks this surgery is a 33-year-old, well-educated, professional, married man with children (Panfilov, 2006).

About one-third to one-half of the penis is inside the male's body, attached by the roots to the pubic bone. Under the male pubic bone, at the base of the penis, is the *ligament fundiforme penis*. To increase the length of the penis, a surgeon cuts this ligament, leaving only the side strands of the ligament. These side strands of the ligament are left to provide stability to the penis during an erection. Releasing this ligament allows the penis to protrude on a straighter path, further out. Thus, after cutting this ligament the male penis is typically lengthened 3 to 5 centimeters (about 2 inches). It is important to note, however, that in a recent study that assessed phalloplasty procedures, over 70 percent of the men were dissatisfied with the results (Ralph & Christopher, 2007). Furthermore, this type of surgery carries the risk that a man may lose his erectile function altogether.

To increase the width or girth of the penis, a surgeon either uses silicon injections or fat tissue transplants from another part of the male's body, such as his inner thigh or buttock; the silicone or the fat tissue are injected into to the shaft of the penis. On average, the girth increases from 8.2 centimeters to about 11 centimeters (from about 3.25 inches to about 4.25 inches).

Considering the possible serious side effects that can result from augmentative phalloplasty, men should very carefully weigh the risks and benefits.

Sources: Panfilov, E. E. (2006); Ralph, D., & Christopher, N. (2007).

- *Incorporate short flexes:* After you notice that your pelvic floor muscles are becoming stronger, begin to incorporate a series of quick flexes (one-second contractions) into your exercise routine. Perform 30 quick flexes and then do one long contraction, holding it as long as you can. Repeat.

MALE SEXUAL ANATOMY AND THE 21ST-CENTURY

As with other topics in our study so far, men do not experience their sexuality in isolation but within the context of the culture in which they live. **Body image** refers to our own internal perceptions of our physical appearance—how we think our bodies look to other people. Central to how we perceive our body is the belief that there is a cultural "ideal" body size and shape. Failure to obtain this "ideal" can influence our attitudes, emotions, and behaviors—and our sexuality. Although research on women's body image has been ongoing for several decades, it has taken researchers longer to realize that guys have body issues, too.

ADONIS COMPLEX

Adonis was a Greek god who epitomized masculinity and male beauty: his body was a chiseled, muscular masterpiece. Today, the term **Adonis complex** is used to describe a collection of male body image problems that include body size and appearance (including the penis), compulsive exercising, steroid use, and eating disorders (Pope, Phillips, & Olivardia, 2000). Empirical evidence today suggests that this ideal lean, muscular body contributes to psychological distress in men (McArthur, Holbert, & Pena, 2005; Tager, Good, & Bauer Morrison, 2006).

It is perhaps this drive to achieve the Adonis ideal that has caused men of all ages, particularly in high school and college, to increase steroid and nutritional supplement use for the purposes of gaining muscles mass and improving strength. The use of these substances appears to be associated with weight preoccupation and body dissatisfaction (Field et al., 2005; Smolak, Murnen, & Thompson, 2005). Toward the end of this chapter, we'll take a thorough look at the use of anabolic-androgenic steroids and the effects of these substances on the male sexual and reproductive systems.

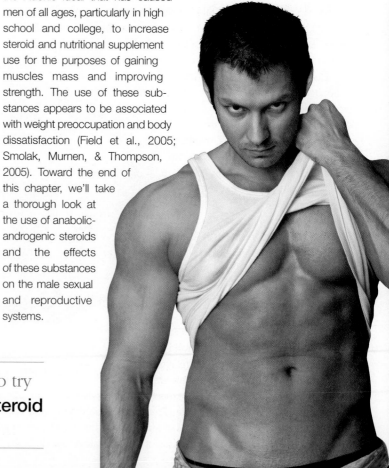

>>> The Adonis complex may prompt a male to try compulsive exercising, **eating disorders, and steroid use to improve his body image.**

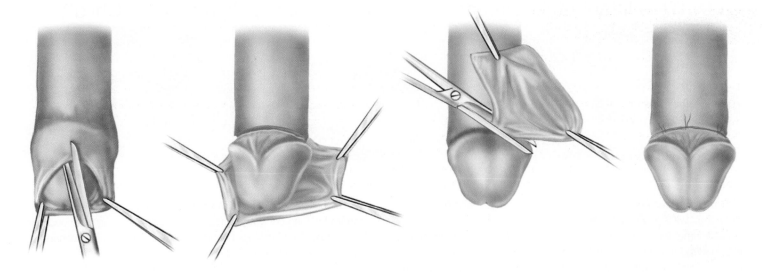

Figure 5.9 **Circumcision** There are many medical reasons circumcisions **are regularly performed on newborn American males.**

PENIS SIZE

It is said jokingly that the ruler was invented in 1675, because in 1674 someone needed an objective measurement of the length of his penis! Until about 20 years ago, penis size (either erect or non-erect) was not discussed, even in human anatomy textbooks (Panfilov, 2006). It's not surprising that men are concerned about penis size. All over the world, penis size symbolizes masculine power in every manifestation possible—socially, politically, economically, physically, reproductively, and, of course, sexually (Poulson-Bryant, 2006). Men who don't measure up—literally—wonder about their ability to sexually satisfy their partners.

Hangature is a 21st-century term that refers to "the amount or ability a [penis] has to hang" (Poulson-Bryant, 2006). A non-scientific nationwide poll found that only 55 percent of the men were satisfied with their penis size; 45 percent wished their penises were larger (Lever, Frederick, & Peplau, 2006). As the *Healthy Selves/Healthy Sex* feature box shows us, the insecurities men have about the size of their genitals are similar to the feelings women with smaller breasts experience (Panfilov, 2006),

leading some men to turn to surgical procedures to increase penis size. But, how do women feel about penis size? Does penis size matter to them? In the previously mentioned nationwide study, 85 percent of women *were satisfied* with the size of their partner's penis (Lever, Frederick, & Peplau, 2006). Another study revealed that for women, penis *width* is much more important that penis length (Eisenman, 2001). These findings show us that it's clear the majority of U.S. women who responded to research surveys don't care about the size of their partner's penis. If women mock their partners or leave them for having small- or modest-sized genitals, perhaps penis augmentation isn't what is needed. Instead, "What should be considered is a change of partners" (Panfilov, 2006, p. 184)!

CIRCUMCISION

Circumcision, which means "cutting around," is a surgical procedure in which some or all the foreskin is removed from the glans, exposing the end of the penis (see Figure 5.9). As Table 5.1 shows, the percentages

TABLE 5.1
Percent of Neonatal Circumcision Rates By Year and By Region of the United States

Source: National Center for Health Statistics (2007).

						Percent					
Year	**1980**	**1982**	**1984**	**1986**	**1988**	**1990**	**1992**	**1994**	**1996**	**2000**	**2005**
U.S.	64.7	62.5	62.4	59.4	58	59	60.7	62.1	60.2	62.4	57.3
Northeast	67.4	63.4	68.2	67.9	63.2	62.6	67.6	69.6	66.5	64.6	66.9
Midwest	75.9	75.9	75.1	71.8	72.7	76	78.2	80.1	80.9	81.4	78.7
South	56	57.3	58.3	57.5	53.8	57.1	62.7	64.7	63.6	63.9	58.7
West	61.8	54.3	49.4	43	45.2	42.4	37.5	34.2	36.3	37.3	31.5

OWN IT! Is Infant Male Circumcision an Abuse of the Rights of the Child?

Routine, non-therapeutic circumcision of newborn males and the ritual neonatal circumcision for religious reasons are widespread practices in the United States. Although the existing research shows that circumcision has medical benefits, such as reduced rates of penile cancer, the research also shows that when a circumcision is performed, a male loses a significant amount of sensitivity in his penis.

As you read the conflicting empirical evidence about circumcision, take time to consider the following questions:

1. Is infant male circumcision the equivalent of female genital mutilation? Why or why not?

2. Is infant male circumcision an abuse of the rights of the child? Why or why not? If you have a male child, will you have him circumcised after birth?

of neonatal circumcisions rise and fall, but they have steadily declined since the 1980s and vary by race.

Circumcision is routinely performed on slightly over 57 percent of all U.S. newborn males (National Center for Health Statistics, 2007). Circumcision is carried out on neonates for a number of reasons: decreased risk of urinary tract infections (UTIs), penile cancer and STIs, including HIV, as well as increased hygiene (Daling et al., 2005; Obermeyer, 2005; O'Farrel, Quigley, & Fox, 2005; Schoen, et al., 2000; Schoen, 2006a, 2006b; UNAIDS, 2007a, 2007b; UNAIDS/CAPRISA, 2007; Weiss et al., 2006; WHO, 2007; Williams et al., 2006;). Others practice circumcision for religious reasons.

The rates of circumcision vary widely. Worldwide, it is estimated that about 30 percent of men over the age of 15 are circumcised. Of these men, 68 percent are Muslim, about 1 percent are Jewish, and 17 percent are men in the United States who are not Muslim or Jewish (London School of Hygiene and Tropical Medicine, 2007). The practice is dependent on the cultural, social, religious, and biophysical reasons for which it is performed (Hankins, 2007). For instance, in some African and Pacific Islander traditions, the removal of the male foreskin is thought to turn boys to fully masculine males (Agberia, 2006).

THE PROCEDURE

For infant circumcision, physicians use local anesthesia to minimize the pain (Primary Children's Medical Center, 2004). In one procedure, a plastic bell-like structure is slid between the glans and the foreskin; the foreskin is then cut away with a surgical instrument. In a second type of procedure, the foreskin is held by clamps and cut away "freehand" then stitched around the coronal ridge.

THE RISKS AND POSSIBLE EFFECTS

The main risks or causes for concern are persistent bleeding, redness or swelling around the tip of the penis, infections, or the inability to urinate; the penis is lost or destroyed in about one in 1,000,000 circumcisions (Christakis et al., 2000; RACP, 2004). There may also be a link between neonatal male circumcision with a range of negative emotions (Anand & Scalzo, 2000; Boyle & Bensley, 2001; Boyle et al., 2002).

EFFECTS ON SEXUAL SATISFACTION

As Table 5.2 shows us, there is conflicting evidence on circumcision's effect on male sexual satisfaction. Although some research shows that women report a strong preference for circumcised over uncircumcised partners (Hankins, 2007; Williamson & Williamson, 1988), other studies report that women experience more vaginal dryness when the male partner is circumcised (Bensley & Boyle, 2003; O'Hara & O'Hara, 1999). Other research shows that circumcised men use less force in penetration, and that they thrust more gently with shorter strokes, thereby increasing their partner's comfort (Taves, 2002).

TABLE 5.2
Sexual Satisfaction Following Circumcision

Source: National Center for Health Statistics (2007).

Sexual Drive:	No difference between circumcised and uncircumcised men (Collins et al., 2002; Senkul et al., 2004)
Erectile Function:	No difference between circumcised and uncircumcised men (Collins et al., 2002; Masood et al., 2005; Senkul et al., 2004) Worse after circumcision (Fink, Carson, & DeVillis, 2002; Shen et al., 2004) Better after circumcision (Laumann, Masi, & Zuckerman, 1997; Richters et al., 2006)
Ejaculation:	No difference in ejaculation (Collins et al., 2002; Waldinger, 2005) Greater time to ejaculate after circumcision (Laumann, Masi, & Zuckerman, 1997; Shen et al., 2004; Senkul et al., 2004) Circumcised men more likely to ejaculate prematurely (Richters et al., 2006)
Penile Sensation:	Worse after circumcision (Fink, Carson, & DeVillis, 2002) Better after circumcision (Denniston, 2004; Masood et al., 2005; Richters et al., 2006)
Overall Satisfaction:	No difference between circumcised and uncircumcised men (Collins et al., 2002; Kigozi et al., 2008; Senkul et al., 2004) Better after circumcision (Fink, Carson, & DeVillis, 2002; Masood et al., 2005; Shen et al., 2004)

As the "Own It!" feature shows, although male circumcision is a routine procedure, its practice is now being called into question. At issue is the question as to whether male circumcision is a health issue or a human rights violation. In 2007, the Genital Mutilation Prohibition Act was proposed to the U.S. Congress. This bill suggests that routine circumcision of male newborns is equivalent to female genital mutilation because the same tissue is destroyed. Today, the decision to circumcise a male infant is a difficult one, as empirical evidence about its possible negative effects continues to emerge.

ANABOLIC-ANDROGENIC STEROID USE

Anabolic-androgenic steroids are synthetic (man-made) derivatives of testosterone (Kochakian & Yesalis, 2000). Today, *Arnolds*, *gym candy*, *juice*, *pumpers*, *stackers*, and *weight trainers* are the common street/slang terms used to describe steroids. In the 1930s, anabolic steroids were developed to help a number of medical conditions, such as *hypogonadism*, a condition in which the male's testes do not produce enough testosterone (see Chapter 3). Today, steroids are still used by the medical community to treat delayed puberty, certain types of erectile dysfunction, and "wasting" caused by HIV.

PERFORMANCE-ENHANCING DRUGS

Over time, anabolic steroids began to be used for purposes other than medical reasons, becoming known

>>> **A man injects himself with anabolic steroids** in an effort to make his body bigger.

as **performance-enhancing drugs** due to their popularity with elite athletes (such as bodybuilders, football players, track and field athletes, baseball players, and runners). Despite the reason for taking these drugs, the use of anabolic steroids for purposes of performance enhancement is illegal—and, some would argue, unethical.

Among college athletes, self-reported use of anabolic steroids is consistent among Division I through III colleges and universities (Yesalis & Bahrke, 2005). Among male college athletes, for instance, the average overall rate of anabolic steroids use is 14.7 percent (NCAA, 2001). At 29.3 percent, collegiate football players show the highest lifetime steroid use rates; male track and field college athletes report a use rate of 20.6 percent (NCAA, 2001).

EXTENT OF USE AMONG NON-ELITE ATHLETES

Over the past three decades, the level of steroid use has increased among non-athletes in an attempt to improve their appearance (Johnston, et al., 2004) and achieve the Adonis look (Yesalis & Bahrke, 2005). Of great concern to health professionals is that the use of anabolic steroids has trickled down from elite athletes to students.

Table 5.3 presents the results from the 2007 Monitoring the Future Study, a study that surveys eighth, 10th, and 12th grade students regarding their use of anabolic steroids and other drugs. As the data show us, 1.5 percent of eighth graders, 1.8 percent of 10th graders, and 2.2 percent of 12th graders reported using steroids at least once in their lifetimes (National Institute on Drug Abuse, 2007). It also appears that obtaining these drugs is relatively easy (Government Accountability Office, 2007;

TABLE 5.3
Percent of Students Reporting Steroid Use 2006–2007

Source: Monitoring the Future Study (2007).

	8th Grade		10th Grade		12th Grade	
	2006	2007	2006	2007	2006	2007
Past month	0.5	0.4	0.6	0.5	1.1	1.0
Past year	0.9	0.8	1.2	1.1	1.8	1.4
Lifetime	1.6	1.5	1.8	1.8	2.7	2.2

Figure 5.10 Percent of Students Reporting Lifetime Steroid Use 2001–2005

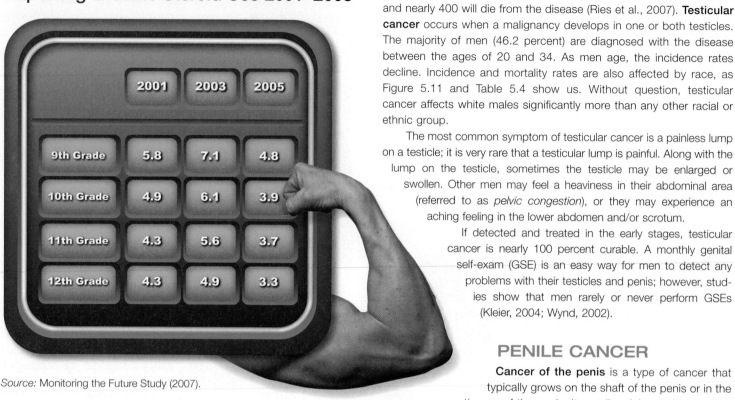

	2001	2003	2005
9th Grade	5.8	7.1	4.8
10th Grade	4.9	6.1	3.9
11th Grade	4.3	5.6	3.7
12th Grade	4.3	4.9	3.3

Source: Monitoring the Future Study (2007).

National Institute on Drug Abuse, 2007). The rates of steroid use among high schoolers peaked in 2003, but has declined since then (see Figure 5.10).

PHYSICAL, PHYSIOLOGICAL, AND PSYCHOLOGICAL EFFECTS

While anabolic steroids may improve athletes' performance (Bhasin et al., 1996) and decrease overall body fat (Herbst & Bhasin, 2004), there are short- and long-term health effects associated with the use of anabolic steroids. Although the effects vary, in general, the use of anabolic steroids in males has been shown to cause a number of negative physical side effects, such as erectile dysfunction; reduction in testicle size, testosterone production, sperm count and mobility; high blood pressure; increased breast size; and heart disease. There are also psychological effects associated with the use of anabolic steroids, including increased levels of irritability and aggression (see Yesalis & Bahrke, 2005 for a comprehensive review of the literature).

MALE SEXUAL AND REPRODUCTIVE HEALTH

Like women, men have reproductive health concerns that evolve and change throughout their life cycles. In the sections that follow, we will look at diseases and conditions that affect both the penis and the testicles.

TESTICULAR CANCER

Each year, nearly 8,000 men will be diagnosed with testicular cancer, and nearly 400 will die from the disease (Ries et al., 2007). **Testicular cancer** occurs when a malignancy develops in one or both testicles. The majority of men (46.2 percent) are diagnosed with the disease between the ages of 20 and 34. As men age, the incidence rates decline. Incidence and mortality rates are also affected by race, as Figure 5.11 and Table 5.4 show us. Without question, testicular cancer affects white males significantly more than any other racial or ethnic group.

The most common symptom of testicular cancer is a painless lump on a testicle; it is very rare that a testicular lump is painful. Along with the lump on the testicle, sometimes the testicle may be enlarged or swollen. Other men may feel a heaviness in their abdominal area (referred to as *pelvic congestion*), or they may experience an aching feeling in the lower abdomen and/or scrotum.

If detected and treated in the early stages, testicular cancer is nearly 100 percent curable. A monthly genital self-exam (GSE) is an easy way for men to detect any problems with their testicles and penis; however, studies show that men rarely or never perform GSEs (Kleier, 2004; Wynd, 2002).

PENILE CANCER

Cancer of the penis is a type of cancer that typically grows on the shaft of the penis or in the tissues of the penis. It usually originates in the glans and/or in the foreskin of the penis. Penile cancer accounts

Figure 5.11 Testicular Cancer Incidence Rates by Race

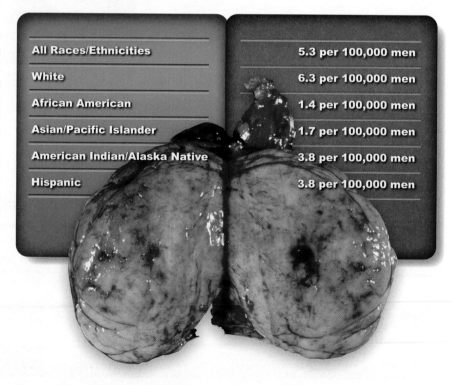

All Races/Ethnicities	5.3 per 100,000 men
White	6.3 per 100,000 men
African American	1.4 per 100,000 men
Asian/Pacific Islander	1.7 per 100,000 men
American Indian/Alaska Native	3.8 per 100,000 men
Hispanic	3.8 per 100,000 men

Source: National Cancer Institute (2007).

for about 0.4 to 0.6 percent of all cancers in the United States and Europe, but as high as 30 percent of all cancers diagnosed in men in developing countries due to poor hygienic practices (Brosman, 2006).

In the United States and Europe, the most common risk factors associated with penile cancer include HPV infection (human papillomavirus infection), smoking, smegma, phimosis, advanced age, and AIDS. Treatment options range from local excision of the malignancy, to either partial or total *penectomy* (removal of the penis). Chemotherapy and radiation treatments may also be used.

PRIAPISM

Named after the Greek god *Priapus*, who was given an enormous (yet useless) set of wooden genitals for attempting to rape a goddess, **priapism** refers to a medical emergency in which a male has an erection that lasts for four or more hours. The penis does not return to a flaccid state, even though stimulation is absent. Priapism is almost always due to neurological and/or vascular factors, such as among men with bleeding disorders, leukemia, and spinal cord injuries (Montague et al., 2003) and can be caused by medications used to treat erectile dysfunction (see Chapter 15), antidepressants, alcohol, and cocaine. Priapism constitutes a medical emergency because blood clots can form and damage blood vessels in the penis.

PEYRONIE DISEASE

Peyronie disease is caused by the growth of fibrous plaque (hard lumps) in the erectile tissues of the penis and is characterized by a curvature in the penis. The exact cause of Peyronie disease is not known, but some researchers believe that the plaque develops as the result of some sort of trauma, such as abnormal hitting or bending of the penis (National Kidney and Urologic Diseases Information Clearinghouse, 2005). This trauma causes bleeding that leads to the formation of a hardened scar that in turn results in curvature during erection (NKUDIC, 2005). Symptoms may also develop suddenly and with no known cause. Although Peyronie disease cannot be cured, there are a number of treatment options, such as oral vitamin E, steroids, radiation therapy, or surgery (Hauck et al., 2006; Hellstrom & Usta, 2003; Levine, 2003; Prieto Castro et al., 2003; Trost, Gur, & Hellstrom, 2007).

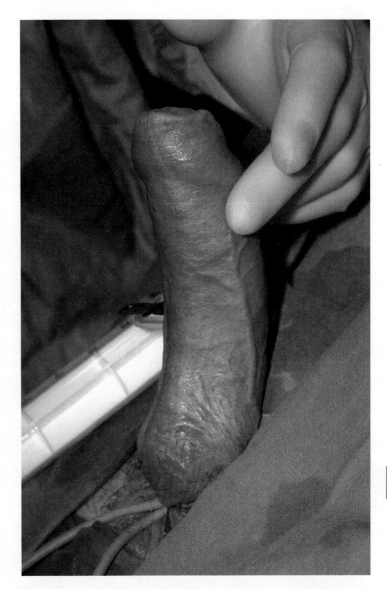

∧
∧ **Peyronie Disease** results in a curved
∧ erection.

TABLE 5.4
U.S. Testicular Cancer Mortality Rates By Race

Source: National Cancer Institute (2007).

All Races	0.3 per 100,000 men
White	0.3 per 100,000 men
African American	0.2 per 100,000 men
Asian/Pacific Islanders	0.1 per 100,000 men
American Indian/Alaska Native	(negligible)
Hispanic	0.2 per 100,000 men

Figure 5.12 Guide to Male Genital Health

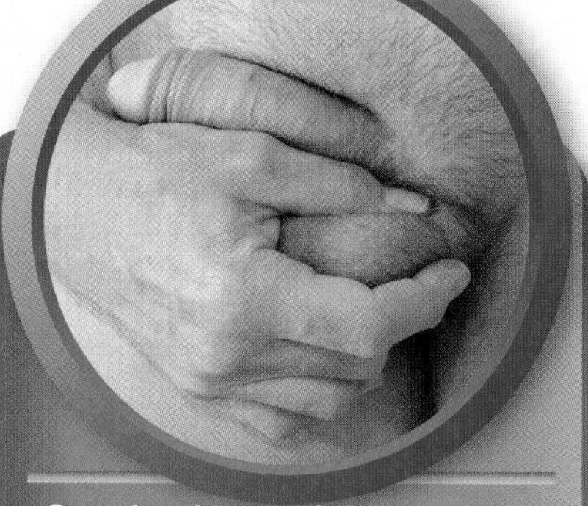

Begin here

Question		Possible Condition	Action
1. Do you have swelling or tenderness in scrotum?	YES	Go to question 9.	
2. Do you have a yellowish or greenish discharge from the tip of the penis?	YES	You may have an STI or an inflammation of the urethra.	See the doctor right away!
3. Do you have a burning sensation or pain when you urinate?	YES	You may have a bladder infection or an inflammation of the urethra.	See the doctor right away!
4. Do you have a painful, itchy rash; do you have small red bumps or blisters on your penis?	YES	You may have a bladder infection or an STI; you may have cancer.	See the doctor right away!
5. Do you have a painless sore on the shaft or glans of your penis?	YES	You may have an STI or a form of cancer.	See the doctor right away!
6. Do you have pain during intercourse?	YES	You may have balanitis.	See your doctor.
7. Do you have blood in your urine or semen, or pain when you ejaculate?	YES	You may have prostatitis.	See the doctor. Keep the area clean and dry and avoid skin lotions and creams.
8. Do you have pain during intercourse?	YES	This can be caused by a number of problems.	See your doctor whenever you have pain.
9. Is your scrotum very tender although no injury has occured?	YES	You may have epididymitis or testicular torsion.	THIS IS AN EMERGENCY! GO TO THE EMERGENCY ROOM RIGHT AWAY!
10. Do you have mild tenderness around the testicle?	YES	You may have a less severe form of epididymitis.	See your doctor.
11. Is there a hard, painless lump or knot in a testicle?	YES	You may have a noncancerous lump, or you may have testicular cancer.	See your doctor. Be vigilant in performing GSEs.
12. Is there a soft swelling in your scrotum on one or both sides?	YES	This can be caused by a number of reasons.	See your doctor to rule out any serious problems.
13. Is there a soft swelling above your testicle that gets aggravated with activity, lifting, or coughing?	YES	This could be a hernia.	See your doctor right away.

Source: American Academy of Family Physicians (2008).

BALANITIS

Balanitis occurs when the glans penis becomes inflamed and swollen. It is seen among all races and ethnicities, but it is twice as common in African American males and Hispanic males, perhaps due to the lower circumcision rates among these populations (Leber, 2006).

Smegma is a collection of secretions that are produced in the glands beneath the foreskin of the uncircumcised penis. If good hygiene is not practiced, smegma accumulates under the ridge of the glans, causing clumps of foul-smelling cheese-like material to form. Balanitis is most often caused by the buildup of smegma and/or other discharges from the penis.

The most common complication of balanitis is **phimosis**, the foreskin's inability to retract (move back and forth) from the glans. Balanitis without phimosis is treated with topical antibiotics and soaking the penis in warm water to cleanse it and the foreskin. Balanitis with phimosis is much more serious. If the foreskin adheres to the glans, surgical intervention may be necessary to loosen the foreskin.

EPIDIDYMITIS

There are also a number of conditions that can affect the testicles. **Epididymitis**, or *testicular infection*, is a medical condition that occurs due to inflammation or infection of the epididymis. *Urinary tract infections* are the most common bacterial cause of epididymitis, but in men under the age of 35, *chlamydia* and *gonorrhea* (STIs) are the most common cause (Chang, 2005). Among men over the age of 35 who practice anal sex, the most common cause is *coliform*, a bacterium that lives in the intestines.

Epididymitis is a serious medical condition that cannot be ignored or overlooked. If left untreated, the bacterial infection can cause sterility or the infection can spread into the bloodstream, becoming life threatening.

TESTICULAR TORSION

Testicular torsion occurs when the spermatic cord and testicle twist within the scrotum. It represents a true urologic emergency because when the spermatic cord twists, the blood vessels within the cord also twist, blocking blood flow to and from the testicle, resulting in the "death" of a testicle. This medical emergency therefore requires *immediate* treatment to save the testicle. If the condition is treated within six hours of onset of pain, the testicle can be saved 100 percent of the time; if treatment is delayed for 24 hours or more, there is no chance to save the testicle (Rupp, 2006).

SELF-CARE AND PREVENTION

During a GSE, men can check for all of the conditions we have discussed so far, such as Peyronie disease, balanitis, phimosis, epididymitis, and penile and testicular cancers. The American Cancer Society (ACS) recommends a genital exam by a physician as part of a man's routine health checkup.

GENITAL SELF-EXAM

The best time to do a genital self-exam (GSE) is right after a shower because the scrotal skin is more relaxed. Figure 5.12 presents a step-by-step guide to GSE for men. The general steps for GSE follow (Engender Health, 2003):

1) Naked, stand in front of a mirror. Visually check the penis. Is the glans tender or swollen? Are there any red or inflamed bumps or blisters on the scrotal skin or penis?

2) Using your fingers, examine each testicle. Place your index and middle fingers on the underside of the testicle, thumbs on top. Gently roll the testicle between your thumbs and fingers. Do you feel any lumps (about the size of a pea)? Is there any tenderness? Swelling? Heaviness?

3) Finish the exam by spreading the pubic hair to check the skin. Are there any new moles, growths, red bumps, or blisters?

PROSTATE HEALTH

At some point, most men will experience problems with their prostate, typically as the result of hormonal changes associated with aging. In Chapter 15, we'll take a thorough look at prostate cancer and other prostate problems. Here, we discuss *prostatitis*.

PROSTATITIS

Contained within the prostate gland are *acini*, pouch-like reservoirs that hold the prostatic fluid. **Prostatitis** involves the inflammation of the acini. This inflammation causes the prostate gland to swell, which in turn causes local pain.

Recent information suggests that regular exercise and stress management reduce prostate problems (NIH, 2003), as does avoiding high-fat and high-carbohydrate foods, alcohol, and caffeine. Vitamins B, C, and E also benefit prostate health (Cleveland Clinic, 2006).

SEXUAL LIFE EDUCATION

Well, you did it! The last three chapters of our study have detailed the complex development of the sexual and reproductive structures and the functions of these structures in women and men. Without question, the material covered in these chapters is perhaps some of the most rigorous material contained within this textbook, but understanding the interrelated, multifaceted biological aspects of your sexuality is a huge milestone in learning about "who" you are as a sexual being and "how" you function sexually.

The male college student in the opening vignette of this chapter raised an interesting point; in a lot of ways, male sexuality is "all about the penis," as it *is* central to a number of male physiological functions. Just as important to understanding men's overall sexual health is knowing about the pressing cultural ideals of the "perfect" male image. There is an emerging single standard of beauty for men today, a body that is nothing short of pure visual pleasure, including a circumcised penis that seems to be more "appealing" to look at. But at what cost to their physical and psychological health?

Without question, there is much more to sexual functioning than biology and culture alone. In the next chapter, we'll begin to look at the psychosocial domain of sexuality, or the interpersonal and intrapersonal aspects.

Summary

HOW DO THE VARIOUS MALE SEXUAL AND REPRODUCTIVE STRUCTURES FUNCTION? 82

• The role of the male sexual and reproductive system is to manufacture, maintain, and deliver sperm to the female's uterus, where it can fertilize the egg to conceive a child.

WHAT ARE THE CAUSES AND EFFECTS OF ANABOLIC-ANDROGENIC STEROID USE AMONG BOYS AND MEN? 95

• Physicians may prescribe anabolic-androgenic steroids to treat conditions like delayed puberty, certain types of erectile dysfunction or "wasting," caused by HIV. When boys and men use steroids to enhance their bodies or athletic skills, they use them to improve their muscle tone and to trim body fat.

• Steroid use can cause erectile dysfunction, decreased testicle size, testosterone production and sperm count, high blood pressure, increased breast size, and heart disease. It may also cause increased levels of irritability and aggression.

WHAT ARE THE SIGNS AND TREATMENTS FOR MALE REPRODUCTIVE DISEASES AND CONDITIONS? 96

• Male reproductive diseases and conditions include testicular and penile cancers, priapism, Peyronie disease, balanitis, smegma, phimosis, epididymitis, and testicular torsion. Signs can include any abnormalities, pain or discharge.

• Testicular and penile cancers can be treated with local excision, removal, chemotherapy, and radiation. While Peyronie disease cannot be cured, it can be treated with oral vitamin E, steroids, radiation therapy, and surgery. Balanitis, smegma, and phimosis can be treated with antibiotics, a warm-water soak, or surgery.

WHAT FORMS OF PREVENTIVE AND SELF-CARE STRATEGIES ARE AVAILABLE TO MEN? 99

• Men should conduct regular genital self-exams, usually after showering. They should check for any bumps or blisters, lumps, tenderness, swelling, heaviness, or moles. Like regular self-exams, it is a good preventive measure to have regular checkups with qualified physicians.

Key Terms

penis the male organ designed to deliver the sperm to the female reproductive tract 82

root part of the penis that attaches to the wall of the abdomen 82

shaft the body of the penis 82

glans penis the acorn-shaped head of the penis 82

foreskin the loose layer of skin that covers the glans penis 82

urethra tube that carries urine from the bladder to outside the body 82

corpora three circular shaped chambers of erectile tissue which run along the entire length of the penis 82

corpora cavernosa two larger corpora that fill with blood during vasocongestion 82

erection when the corpora cavernosa fill with blood and the girth of the penis enlarges and becomes rigid 82

corpus spongiosum smaller chamber of erectile tissue that causes the penis to lengthen during sexual arousal 83

crura (roots) continuations of the corpora cavernosa 83

meatus the urethral opening through which urine and semen pass 83

coronal ridge a rim that separates the glans from the shaft 83

frenulum the Y-shaped region of skin that is attached to the underside of the glans 83

prepuce foreskin 84

erogenous receptors sensory receptors found in the ridged band 84

scrotum pouch of skin that encases the testes 84

testis testicle 84

spermatic cord suspends testis into scrotal sac 84

cyptorchidism when one or both testicles fail to descend into the scrotum 85

seminiferous tubules coiled channels packed into lobes of the testicle 85

interstitial cells lie in the soft connective tissue that surrounds the seminiferous tubules 85

epididymis a tightly coiled duct that adheres to each testis 85

male duct system pathway of the sperm 85

vas deferens part of the spermatic cord through which sperm is expelled during ejaculation 85

ejaculatory duct the vas deferens and the seminal vesicle 85

vasectomy tying off the vas deferens cutting off the route of the sperm 87

seminal vesicle secretes seminal fluid 87

prostate gland creates a protein-rich, alkaline fluid that neutralizes the acidity of the vagina 87

Cowper's glands (bulbourethral glands) produce pre-ejaculate 88

semen (seminal fluid) fluid that contains sperm, fructose, enzymes, amino acids, citric acids and other substances 88

gonarche the enlargement of the testes 88

spermarche sperm present in the ejaculate 88

nocturnal emissions wet dreams 88

spermatogenesis cell differentiation and maturation of germ cells inside the seminiferous tubules 89

spermatozoa sperm 89

suspensory ligament holds the penis and supports it when erect *90*

ejaculation the physiological process by which semen is expelled through the urethra *90*

emission phase involves the accumulation and deposit of seminal fluid through the urethra outside the male's body *90*

expulsion phase semen trapped in the urethral bulb is ejected through the urethra *91*

premature ejaculation when a man ejaculates prior to the wishes of both sexual partners *91*

augmentative phalloplasty a surgical procedure to enlarge the volume of the penis *92*

body image our internal perceptions of our physical appearance *92*

Adonis complex a collection of male body image problems *92*

hangature ability a penis has to hang *93*

circumcision a surgical procedure in which some or all of the foreskin is removed from the glans *93*

anabolic-androgenic steroids synthetic derivatives of testosterone *95*

performance-enhancing drugs anabolic steroids used by elite athletes for purposes other than medical reasons *95*

testicular cancer malignancy in one or both testicles *96*

cancer of the penis grows on the shaft of the penis or in the tissues of the penis *96*

priapism an erection that lasts four or more hours *97*

Peyronie disease the growth of fibrous plaque in the erectile tissues of the penis *97*

balanitis occurs when the glans penis becomes inflamed and swollen *99*

smegma a collection of secretions that are produced in the glands beneath the foreskin of the uncircumcised penis *99*

phimosis the foreskin's inability to retract *99*

epididymitis inflammation or infection of the epididymis *99*

testicular torsion occurs when the spermatic cord and testicle twist within the scrotum *99*

prostatitis inflammation of the acini *99*

Sample Test Questions

MULTIPLE CHOICE

1. Recent research has identified what form of technology as a potential culprit in scrotal hyperthermia?
   a. Cell phones
   b. MP3 players
   c. Laptops
   d. GPS systems

2. Which of the following is NOT true regarding the vas deferens?
   a. It is involved in elective male sterilization procedures.
   b. It joins with the seminal vesicle.
   c. It is part of the spermatic cord.
   d. It is impossible to feel from the outside of the body.

3. The glands that produce pre-ejaculate are known as:
   a. Prostate
   b. Cowper
   c. Pituitary
   d. Seminal

4. The first stage of male puberty is typically:
   a. Spermarche
   b. Gonarche
   c. Growth spurt
   d. Pubic hair

5. What is the average age for the beginning of spermatogenesis in American males?
   a. 14
   b. 13
   c. 15
   d. 12

6. The _____ complex refers to a collection of male body image problems that can include excessive exercising, eating disorders, and steroid use.
   a. Zeus
   b. Adonis
   c. Prometheus
   d. Priapus

7. The condition in which a male has an erection that lasts for more than four hours is called:
   a. Balanitis
   b. Epididymitis
   c. Peyronie disease
   d. Priapism

8. The term *cryptorchidism* refers to:
   a. The insufficient production of FSH.
   b. The insufficient production of LH.
   c. A condition when one testicle hangs lower than the other.
   d. A condition when one or both testicles fail to descend into the scrotum.

SHORT RESPONSE

1. How can a man perform Kegel exercises?
2. Which hormones are involved in the production of testosterone and sperm by the testicles?
3. Using the information learned in this chapter, list three arguments **against** male circumcision.
4. A close friend, who is a star on the cross country team, has admitted to you in confidence that he uses steroids to enhance his performance. He claims it is "no big deal." What evidence from the chapter will you share with him?
5. Describe the steps involved in a male genital self-exam.

Answers: 1. c; 2. d; 3. b; 4. b; 5. a; 6. b; 7. d; 8. d

SEXUAL DEVELOPMENT
from Infancy through Early Adulthood

HOW DO SEXUAL SCRIPTS GUIDE SEXUAL ATTITUDES, BELIEFS, AND BEHAVIORS?

WHAT ARE THE BIOLOGICAL, COGNITIVE, PSYCHOSOCIAL, PSYCHOSEXUAL, AND SEXUAL CHANGES ASSOCIATED WITH LIFE COURSE CHANGES FROM INFANCY THROUGH EARLY ADULTHOOD?

WHAT WAYS HAVE THE SEXUAL EXPERIENCES OF TEENS CHANGED OVER TIME?

My husband

was working late, and I had to get my son and daughter to two different fields for T-ball and baseball practices, and each practice started at the same time. I was late getting home from work, so we were rushed getting out of the door and into the van . . . I was in a bad mood because I hate rushing around like that (and I was pretty mad at my husband because he couldn't help me out). I had dropped off my son at his practice, and I was making my way across town (speeding, actually) to my daughter's practice. And then it happened.

Out of nowhere, my 5-year-old daughter asked, "Mommy? When can I have nipples like you?"

"This cannot be happening right now!" I thought.

"Mommy. Did you hear me? I asked you when can I have nipples like you? Huh?" I heard her. I was trying to figure out how to answer her question.

"Well, honey, what do you mean?"

"I wanna have nipples like you. When can I have 'em?" Why is she so persistent?

"Honey, when you're a big girl like Mommy, you will have nipples like mine."

"But I want 'em now!"

"Sweetie, you can't have them now. Only big girls have nipples like Mommy's."

"But how come Aaron [her brother] has 'em? And Daddy? How come they have 'em and I can't have 'em too? It's not fair! When can I have nipples like everyone else, Mommy? When can I have 'em, Mom?"

I lost my temper and snapped, "When you're a big girl and need big nipples, you can have them! You have to wait your turn for your nipples like every other big girl does. You don't need big girl nipples right now, so you can't have them. And besides, Daddy and Aaron don't have big girl nipples!"

"Yes, they do, too!" she snapped back at me.

Everything was quiet for several seconds . . . until she said, "Show me your nipples, Mommy."

That was it! "All right little lady, this has gone on long enough! I don't want to hear another word until we get to the ball field, understand? And while we're at it, I don't want to hear another word about nipples, either!"

She looked at me, stunned and hurt, and said, "Mommy? Why are you so mad? Just smile and show me your nipples, Mommy."

At that moment I realized my daughter wasn't referring to nipples. She was referring to my *dimples*.

Source: Author's files

Even though kids seem to have an uncanny knack to ask sex questions at *the worst* possible time, they do so because of their unquenchable drive to know and understand every aspect of their worlds—including sex and sexuality. Your sexuality is a process that is in constant growth-motion, and it is continuously influenced by the multiple contexts that surround you. You don't *become* sexual at a certain point in your life span, but you *are continuously becoming* a sexual being.

In this chapter, we'll look at the significant biological, psychosocial, and sociocultural factors that contribute to—and eventually make up—a person's sexuality. Human sexuality encompasses much, much more than sexual equipment or physiology. Although we break each topic out separately for ease of study here, it is essential to remember the concept introduced in Chapter 1, that each realm of sexuality is intertwined. How our bodies develop, as well as how we experience these developments *intrapersonally* (within ourselves) and *interpersonally* (between people), are all integral parts of our sexuality equation.

In this chapter, after adding to our understanding of the sociocultural contributions to sexuality, we'll examine the biological, psychosocial, and psychosexual elements of sexuality from birth through early adulthood. Finally, we'll conclude with looking at ways that parents and caregivers, through verbal and nonverbal ways, can encourage healthy sexual development in children.

LEARNING TO BE SEXUAL

How do we ultimately arrive at what sex and sexuality mean to us? Studies show that people differ in the way they experience sex, sexual attitudes, and feelings, especially men and women (Baumeister & Tice, 2001; Okami & Shackelford, 2001; Wiederman, 2005). To explain these differences, John Gagnon and William Simon (1973) pioneered the idea that people *learn* how to be sexual as a function of being raised in a particular culture. They advanced the idea of *sexual scripts* as an explanation for how we internalize, or make a part of ourselves, our culture's unique expectations for sexual attitudes and behaviors.

SEXUAL SCRIPTS

Sexual scripts are shared, gender-specific social and cultural expectations that guide our beliefs, attitudes, and values about sex, such as our beliefs about appropriate sexual partners, sexual behaviors, and sexual conduct (Bowleg, Lucas, & Tschann, 2004). Just as there is no movie or play without a script, sexuality is also patterned and is not experienced without a sexual script.

Sexual scripts serve two functions. First, they provide us a framework for what is considered **normative** (expected) sexual behavior within a given culture. For instance, in the West, the frequency of sexual intercourse in married or committed couples ranges from less than once per week to twice per week, but in other

societies sexual intercourse is practiced one to three times per night (Ubillos, Paez, & Gonzalez, 2000). Second, sexual scripts provide a road map of sorts for us, giving directions as to how we should feel, think, and act in certain sexual situations (Wiederman, 2005). These messages write our sexual scripts and ultimately *prescribe* our sexuality.

Our sexual scripts determine, among other things (DeLamater & Hyde, 1998):

- With *whom* we can engage in sexual relations (age, relationship to self, gender).
- *How* we engage in sex (anal sex, oral sex, "legal" sexual positions).
- *How often* we engage in sexual relations (for example, it is expected that younger couples have sex more frequently than older couples).
- *When* we have sex (timing parameters such as age at first intercourse or when children are not present).
- *Where* we have sex (other than the bedroom).
- *Why* we have sexual relations (love, lust, anger, fun, play, boredom, jealousy).

Based on our individual upbringing, unique experiences, and our social scripts, we ultimately form our own unique sexual scripts (Bieneck & Scheinberger-Olwig, 2007). Figure 6.1 presents how our differences in upbringing influence our sexual scripts.

Gaining a complete understanding of sexuality development across the life span is an arduous task, and certainly, it cannot be accomplished in one chapter. Therefore, although the content in this chapter is from a primarily heterosexual developmental view, we expand upon this information in Chapter 7 to understand how different sexual orientations develop. In Chapter 8, we then build upon this

∧
∧ Sexual scripts **explain how we internalize our culture's**
∧ **unique expectations for sexual attitudes and behaviors. In Hispanic cultures, young girls and women often embrace marianismo, a Madonna-like purity.** This is symbolized in the religious practice of first communion.

Figure 6.1 Cultural Influences on Sexual Development In the United States today, there is more diversity in sexuality experiences than ever before. **This brief review provides a portrait of the global nature of our society today, and it illustrates how culture—specifically race,** ethnicity and religiosity —shapes our sexualities.

European Americans

- Ancestors from Europe or emigrated from Europe.
- Often refers to white caucasians.
- Emphasizes European geographical ancestral origins (The Ohio State University, 2006).
- Judeo-Christian traditions emphasize heterosexual partners in permanent, monogamous, committed partnerships.
- Married couples welcome children that result from the sexual union (Flaman, 2001).
- Overarching religious beliefs and values influence some sexuality attitudes, as well as laws and public policies (e.g. marriage laws that prohibit same-sex marriages; abortion laws).

Latino Americans

- Come from a number of different countries.
- Cultural traditions that influence sexual behaviors and attitudes include *familism* (emphasis is placed on the importance of family life), *machismo* (the essence of masculinity), and *marianismo* (the essence of femininity) (Noland, 2006).
- Familism: Because of the importance of family and family life, teens are expected to delay the onset of sexual activity (Spence, 2003).
- Machismo/marianismo: Traditional male/female gender roles are practiced (see Chapter 3), and these gender roles dictate men's and women's sexual scripts. These roles are the most important influence in the lives of Latinos (Romero et al., 2004), and affect such things as
  - contraceptive behavior
  - unprotected sex
  - sexual orientation (Feijoo, 2007; Gurman & Borzekowski, 2004; Villarruel & Rodriguez, 2003).

African Americans/African Caribbeans

- Diverse racial group.
- African Americans self-identify with African customs and rituals, or with their African ancestors who were brought involuntarily to the United States (Ogbu, 1990).
- African Caribbeans (Black Caribbeans) had ancestors who were involuntarily brought to Caribbean countries from Africa (Lewis & Kertzner, 2003).
- African Americans/Black Caribbeans commonly embrace spirituality, collectivism, emotional expressiveness, and interdependence in relationships (Williams, 2005).
- Embrace the importance of family, as well as traditional gender roles, such as females being submissive to males in their sexual relationships (Bowleg, Lucas, & Tschann, 2004). This prevailing cultural norm encourages women to assume a passive role in their sexual relationships.
- Men control sexual activities and whether contraception or condoms are used (Bowleg, Lucas, & Tschann, 2004).

Asian Americans

- Come to the United States from a number of countries; each Asian culture has a unique culture unto itself that accounts for vast cultural and ethnic differences.
- Generally conservative in sexual knowledge, attitudes, beliefs, and norms — it is a taboo topic (Meston et al., 1998; Okazaki, 2002); parents are hesitant to talk about sexuality or provide sexual information.
- Have their roots in collectivist cultures, which place greater influence on the family, rather than on the needs of the individual.
- Sexual behaviors and expressions outside marriage considered to be inappropriate; modesty and restrained sexuality are highly valued (Okazaki, 2002).
- Adolescents and college students are more likely than any other racial group
  - to be virgins
  - to have the highest median age of first intercourse
    - are less likely to engage in other sexual activities than their non-Asian counterparts (Meston et al., 1996; Okazaki, 2002; Upchurch et al., 1998).

Native Americans

- Native American refers to aboriginal peoples of the United States and their descendants. Unfortunately, there is a striking lack of empirical evidence about the sexuality of Native Americans. They are the most understudied ethnic group in the United States because of their relative cultural isolation (Hellerstedt et al., 2006).
- In traditional Native American societies, excessive sexuality was not condoned (Medicine, 2002).
- Native Americans embrace a collective identity and family, and that deeply embedded within their religious beliefs are tradition, respect, and reverence (Luan Fauteck Makes Marks, 2007).
- Native Americans are accepting of intersex individuals and homosexuality. *Two Spirit* refers to people who express both masculinity and femininity (Medicine, 2002). One tribe has created a social category for effeminate gay men — *winkte* — which translates to "wants to be like a woman" (Medicine, 2002).

Arab Americans

- Arab Americans have immigrated to the United States from 22 different Arab countries. Although nearly two-thirds of Arab Americans practice the Christian faith, about one-fourth practice the Muslim faith (Arab American Institute, 2007).
- For those who practice the Muslim faith (Islam), sexuality is strongly shaped by traditional gender roles, in which women raise and nurture the children, and men protect and provide for the family (Read, 2002).
- Within traditional Islam, a sex-positive religion, sexual pleasure is seen as an essential part of human life, and it is believed to be a foretaste of eternity; it is thought to be the right of every person (Boellstorff, 2005).
- Some Arab American women traditionally wear the hijab, or veil. According to Islam religious tenets, a woman's hair is to be covered since it is thought to be the very essence of her sensuality and sexuality (Zahedi, 2007).

We all experience intimacy differently in our intimate family and sexual relationships, largely as a result of how we related intimately within our families of origin. Over time, our experiences of intimacy change, and so do the meanings of intimacy. At this point in your personal and professional development:

1. How would you define intimacy? What types of intimacy are most important to you at this point in your life? What types of intimacy are least important to you?

2. Looking back over your life, what are the most significant cultural influences in your development of intimacy? The most significant ethnic influences?

3. If you were to choose five people who most influenced who you are as an intimate (either in positive or in negative ways), who would these people be and why?

content to understand why we're attracted to the people we are, along with dating and falling in love. In essence, these three chapters explain sexual development.

It is crucial to note at the outset that, although children are born with the biological capacity to develop their sexualities, their sexual development and sexual behaviors are significantly influenced by their social worlds (Thigpen, 2009). It is essential, therefore, to remember that a child's sexual development does not occur in an isolated fashion— sexual development is very much interrelated with all aspects of growth and development. For this reason, we'll look at each of these areas of development that occur in certain developmental stages and how they are intricately related to and directly influence sexual development.

DEVELOPING SEXUALLY IN INFANCY AND TODDLERHOOD: BIRTH TO TWO YEARS

Many people mistakenly believe that sexual development does not become an important aspect of a person's life until he or she reaches adolescence and his or her body begins to mature; however, this could not be further from the truth. The moment a baby is born, sexuality begins to take shape. As Alice Honig tells us, "Children learn about sexuality the way they learn about everything else—through words, actions, interactions, and relationships" (1998, p. 1).

PSYCHOSOCIAL DEVELOPMENT: LEARNING TO TRUST

Similar to a house that is built floor by floor, our ability to be intimate with another is built developmental stage by developmental stage.

Psychologist Erik Erikson provided a life span approach for psychosocial development. His **Eight Stages of Man** advanced the idea that our social and emotional development is a lifelong process, and that what happens or does not happen at one stage will eventually affect our psychosocial development during later stages of life. Figure 6.2 outlines Erikson's model, a *cradle-to-grave* approach to understanding individual psychosocial development.

The fundamental developmental task of infancy and toddlerhood is learning to *trust* or *mistrust* our parents or primary caregivers. During this time, if the baby is nurtured, loved, and receives affection, he or she will develop a sense of trust and security; if the baby's distress signals are ignored or neglected, the baby will become insecure and mistrustful of others. This is when the child's initial capacity for intimate and loving relationships begins to take shape—and the foundation for *current and future* intimacy, loving, and sexual relationships is formed.

PSYCHOSEXUAL DEVELOPMENT: DEVELOPING INTIMACY

Psychosexual development relates to the mental and emotional aspects of sexuality and sexual development. It is a blending of sorts of the sexual aspects of our personality with other psychological factors. Although there are no major physical sexual development milestones between birth and adolescence, psychosexual development clearly begins in infancy (Friedrich et al., 1991). Touching, cuddling, stroking, and snuggling babies helps them learn more about their bodies and also more about themselves. All types of appropriate touching further the baby's capacity to develop intimacy, as it strengthens the *parent–child bond*.

>>> Babies understand their worlds through their five senses (taste, touch, hearing, smell, and sight), and through movement, such as being able to roll over from tummy to back (Piaget, 1955). **As infants' nervous systems mature, as their vision improves, and as they attain more motor skills, they further their understanding of their environments, those around them and who care for them, and themselves.** The first year of life is a highly physical experience for infants (Boyd & Bee 2009).

Figure 6.2 Erikson's Theory of Psychosocial Development Influential psychologist Erik Erikson formulated the Eight Stages of Man developmental theory. **According to Erikson, a person is in a continuous state of development from the cradle to the grave.**

Stage	Age	Developmental Task
 **Trust vs. Mistrust**	Infancy 0–24 months	Child develops a belief that his/her caregivers will provide a secure and trustful environment.
 **Autonomy vs. Shame and Doubt**	Toddlerhood 2–4	Child develops a sense of independence and free will; feels shame if he/she doesn't use the free will appropriately.
 **Initiative vs. Guilt**	Early Childhood 4–6	"The Age of Acquiring": Child learns to explore his/her environment and acquires a newfound set of skills; feels a newfound sense of initiative and accomplishment.
 **Industry vs. Inferiority**	Middle Childhood 7–12	"The Age of Mastery": Child masters the skills acquired during early childhood.
 **Identity vs. Role Confusion**	Adolescence 13–21	Teen develops a sense of who he/she is in comparison to others (sense of "self"); develops a keen sense of expectations.
 **Intimacy vs. Isolation**	Young Adult 22–25	Develops ability to give and receive love; begins to consider long-term relationships, marriage, and parenting as realistic options.
 **Generativity vs. Stagnation**	Middle Adulthood 36–65	Develops interest in giving of themselves to younger generations by helping them lead meaningful lives and by caring for them.
 **Integrity vs. Despair**	Older Adulthood 65+	Desires to find meaningful and personal gratification with the life that has been lived.

SEXUAL BEHAVIORS: TOUCHING

Children's sexual behaviors vary greatly depending on their culture, their parents' values and beliefs about sex, and individual differences among children (Janssen, 2002; Martinson, 1994; Okami, 1991; Weis, 1997). Although even newborns are physiologically capable of feeling sexual pleasure, it is very important to understand that children's sexual behaviors are not motivated by *erotic* stimuli and that their sexual behaviors are not erotic in nature; that is, the behaviors are purely physiological in nature, with no feelings of anticipation of sexual activity attached (Honig, 1998; Martinson, 1994; Okami, 1991).

A newborn baby is not a purposeful being—he or she cannot do anything on purpose. Rather, the baby's actions are reflexive. Thus, it is not uncommon for male babies to sometimes have erections while breastfeeding or while having a diaper changed. Similarly, it is not unusual for a baby girl to experience vaginal lubrication or a clitoral erection while being cared for (Casteels et al., 2004; Yang et al., 2005). Although these physiological responses are normative, many parents mistakenly believe the behaviors are associated with sex and they subsequently "freak" out. Be sure, there is no cause for alarm.

GENITAL SELF-STIMULATION

Babies explore their bodies as a way of knowing themselves, and the genitals are certainly no exception. Self-stimulation or fondling of the genitals (**masturbation**), is also common during infancy and toddlerhood (Martinson, 1994). Although there is great variance among children, this sexual behavior appears to cut across all cultural and ethnic boundaries (Weis, 1997).

Some parents are quite uncomfortable with masturbation by infants and children. Many parents overreact and scold their children if they fondle themselves, or they are quick to move the child's hand away from the genitals. Scolding, however, sends messages to children that what they are doing is wrong and shameful (Martinson, 1994). More positive responses that contribute to a child's overall sexual development would be to react in such ways that instill confidence in the child, such as using the appropriate name for the body part ("penis," "scrotum," or "vulva") or kissing the baby's hands (Bullough & Bullough, 1994).

Although parents in the United States may be uncomfortable with masturbation by infants and children, other cultures practice what is referred to as transgenerational gender reference. **Transgenerational gender reference** is the practice of parents or caregivers who engage in masturbating or *fellating* (orally stimulating) infants to calm them (Weis, 1997; Janssen, 2002). Parents who engage in genital stimulation of their infants do not assign sexual meaning to these behaviors; to them, it's simply another measure to comfort and quiet their babies. You may be asking yourself, "Isn't this sexual abuse?" Yes—if the behaviors are considered within the various contexts of Western culture. But if we remember the concepts of Bronfenbrenner's ecological model, it's easier for us to see that culture assigns what are and what are not appropriate behaviors. In these particular cultures, the behaviors are seen as comforting measures— not remotely sexual in nature or purpose.

Figure 6.3 **What to Tell Children About Sex**

Age	Developmental Issues	What Children May Ask	Suggested Responses
3–5 years	Short attention spans	• What is that? (referring to specific body parts) • What do mommies do? • What do daddies do? • Where do babies come from?	Focus on the roles of family members, the development of a positive self-image, and an understanding that living things grow, reproduce, and die.
5–8 years	Curiosity about how the body works	• Where was I before I was born? • How does my mommy get a baby? • Did I come from an egg?	Sexuality education can include information on plant and animal reproduction, gender similarities and differences, growth and development, and self-esteem.
9–12 years	Curiosity about their bodies; interest in opposite sex and reproduction.	• How does the reproductive system work? • Why do some girls have larger breasts than others? • Do boys menstruate? • Why don't some women have babies?	Focus on biological topics such as the endocrine system, menstruation, masturbation and wet dreams, sexual intercourse, birth control, abortion, self-esteem, and interpersonal relationships.
12–14 years	Concern and confusion about physical changes • Body shape • Body control • Reproduction • Penis development • Breast development • Menstruation • Voice	• How can you keep yourself looking attractive? • Should your parents know if you're going steady? • Why are some people homosexual? • Does a girl ever have a wet dream? • Does sexual intercourse hurt? • Why do people get married?	Focus on increasing knowledge of contraception, intimate sexual behavior (why people do what they do), dating, and variations in sexual behaviors (homosexuality, transvestism, transsexualism).
15–17 years	Increased interest in sexual topics; curiosity about relationships, families, reproduction, sexual activity; dating	• What is prostitution? • What do girls really want in a good date? • How far should you go on a date? • Is it good to have sexual intercourse before marriage? • Why is sex considered a dirty word?	Share information on birth control, abortion, dating, premarital sexual behavior, communication, marriage patterns, sexual myths, moral decisions, parenthood, sexuality research, sexual dysfunction, and the history of sexuality.

>>> **During early childhood, the physical changes are not nearly as dramatic as those seen during the first two years of life.** The major changes are not seen as much in physical growth as they are in locomotor and fine motor skills (Boyd & Bee, 2009). **Cognitively, a child expands his/her understanding of the world.** They become very good at using symbols for thinking and communicating and use a lot of pretend in their play (Piaget, 1955).

DEVELOPING SEXUALLY IN EARLY CHILDHOOD: TWO TO SIX YEARS

In all areas of life span development, children develop by leaps and bounds between the ages of two and six—the period of **early childhood**. Figure 6.3 provides suggestions on what to tell children about sex.

PSYCHOSOCIAL DEVELOPMENT: GAINING AUTONOMY AND INITIATIVE

Erik Erikson believed that children develop both *autonomy* and *initiative* in their social/emotional capacities. **Autonomy** refers to a person's desire to self-rule. **Initiative** refers to a person's sense of purpose or resourcefulness. In most children, these capacities develop during the preschool years, particularly around the ages of two and three. As the opening vignette humorously illustrated, children become increasingly more curious about the world, and this curiosity extends to their bodies. Autonomy and initiative are important to the foundation of intimacy and psychosexual development, because they allow children to explore their environments with confidence and to relate to others, both essential qualities to satisfying interpersonal and sexual relationships down the road (Welch, 2007).

There is no aspect of a child's life that is as important as his or her family, because our parents are our first teachers of love, intimacy, gender, and sexuality, and they teach us to conform to cultural and societal rules and norms (Boyd & Bee, 2009; Harvard Family Research Project, 2006).

Based on her observations of parent–child interactions, Diana Baumrind believed that there are two specific dimensions of childrearing: parental warmth or responsiveness/affection toward the child, and parent control or how demanding or restrictive the parents are toward their child. In examining these two dimensions, Baumrind (1991) identified various **parenting styles**, which are presented for you in Table 6.1. The

TABLE 6.1
Parenting Styles

Baumrind believed that there were two specific dimensions of childrearing: parental warmth or responsiveness/affection toward the child, and parent control or how demanding or restrictive the parents are toward their child. In examining these two dimensions, Baumrind (1991) identified four parenting styles:

	Warmth/Responsiveness	Control
Uninvolved Parenting	Low levels • detached from or reject children	Low levels • uninterested in children's lives; can be neglectful
Permissive Parenting ("Indulgent" Parents)	High levels • warmth, affection, responsiveness • adequate to high levels of communication	Low levels • demands, control of behavior • children "self-regulated"
Authoritarian Parenting Type of parenting style is characterized by rigid rules of behavior	Low levels • responsiveness to needs • little warmth	High levels • demanding and controlling • expect obedience • rigid rules • "power" a key player
Authoritative Parenting Parents use a balance of power and reason.	High levels • responsiveness to needs • warm • encourage communication	High levels • demand certain behaviors but flexible • clear boundaries • do not use withdrawal of love or shame • children expected to follow rules; yet autonomous • balance of power and reason

109

Sexual Development from Infancy through Early Adulthood

manner in which parents interact with and guide their children influences children's ability to love, to be loved by another, and to form close, intimate bonds with others—the very bonds that will allow children to someday enter into love relationships of their own (Harvard Family Research Project, 2006). It is important to keep in mind, however, that parenting is a reflection of a person's social and cultural contexts.

For example, research shows that African American and Asian American parents tend to use *authoritarian* parenting styles, while whites and Hispanics tend to adopt *authoritative* parenting styles (Cheah & Rubin, 2004; Steinberg and others, 1991). Researchers suggest that Asian American parents may raise their children with the authoritarian parenting styles because they believe it helps to maintain their cultural identity; African American parents may do so because they are "keenly aware of the degree to which social forces such as racism may impede their children's achievements . . . they believe that adopting this parenting style will enhance their children's potential for success" (Boyd & Bee, 2009, p. 22).

As children's sense of autonomy heightens during the preschool years, this drive for independence also affects their relationships with peers (Prager, 1995, 1998). This research also indicates that young children are capable of expressing sensitivity and empathy in peer interactions; these abilities are key

<<< Although some parents are reluctant to do so, **research shows that teaching children the proper terminology for body parts—** including sex parts **—decreases children's shame and embarrassment about sex.**

elements in intimate and sexual relationships later in life. As one researcher concludes, "*These interactions serve as a basis for relationships that develop in the next stages of life*" (Cardillo, 2005, p. 3, italics mine).

PSYCHOSEXUAL DEVELOPMENT: LEARNING TO CATEGORIZE

By about the age of three, a child can keenly identify himself or herself as male or female (Skelton & Hall, 2001). New cognitive skills acquired during the early childhood years now give children the ability to categorize objects, so they can now categorize people in such a way that all girls are "mommies" and all boys are "daddies." These categorization skills further shape a child's *gender schemas*, which in turn solidify a child's gender identity and deepen a child's understanding of culturally driven *gender roles*.

TABLE 6.2
Frequency of Sexual Behaviors in Early Childhood

Source: Adapted from Friedrich et al. (1991)

Children engage in all types of sexual behaviors. This table presents types of sexual behaviors seen in boys and girls during early childhood (ages 2–6), as well as the frequency that the behaviors occur.

Behavior	Percent of Occurrence	
	Boys	**Girls**
Masturbates with hand	22.6	16.9
Shows sex parts to adults	25.8	17.9
Interested in opposite sex	21.0	20.6
Tries to look at people undressing	33.9	33.3
Touches breasts	43.5	48.4
Kisses non-family children	41.1	55.2
Kisses non-family adults	41.1	52.4
Undresses in front of others	49.6	61.9
Scratches crotch	58.1	67.9
Boy only/girl only toys	63.3	71.4
Walks around nude	47.7	65.4
Walks around in underwear	54.5	75.0

By about the age of three, children use the terminology that their parents or caregivers have taught them to describe their sexual anatomy (Bushnell & Lucas, 2004). When polled, most parents (about 67 percent) indicated that they teach their children the correct anatomical words; however, this is not always the case (Bushnell & Lucas, 2004). Some people may think that using the proper words to label body parts is sexual in nature, but there is no reason why correct terminology shouldn't be taught or used. By labeling body parts correctly, children learn to use the words without shame or embarrassment (Bushnell & Lucas, 2004).

SEXUAL BEHAVIORS: ENGAGING IN SEXUAL PLAY

Research suggests that sexual behaviors and **sex play** in young children are very common. When children play "doctor," for example, they explore their curiosity about body parts, which is simply an extension of the natural curiosity children have about the world and their surroundings. Table 6.2 presents the frequency of sexual behaviors commonly observed in early childhood. As you can see, sexual behaviors range from kissing to asking to engage in sex acts with another person (Friedrich et al., 1998; Sandnabba et al., 2003).

These findings raise interesting questions for us: What are age-appropriate sexual behaviors for young children? When should these behaviors give rise to concern? Table 6.3 classifies childhood sexual behaviors along a continuum, from normative and healthy to problematic. Generally speaking, behaviors that do not result in fear, shame, or anxiety are considered to be healthy and age appropriate (Johnson, 1991).

>>> Playing doctor gives children a chance **to explore their curiosity about body parts.**

Also characteristic of this level is a balance between sexual curiosity with their curiosity about other aspects of their world. We'll explore non-normative sexual behaviors, as well as the effects of childhood sexual abuse on sexuality development in Chapter 17.

DEVELOPING SEXUALLY IN MIDDLE CHILDHOOD: SEVEN TO ELEVEN YEARS

The changes that take place in middle childhood, between the ages of seven and 11, are perhaps not visible to others, but significant growth within the brain prompts changes in thinking and relationship skills.

During middle childhood, or **prepubescence**, significant physical growth occurs. By the end of this age range, girls are typically well ahead of boys

TABLE 6.3
Classification of Childhood Sexual Behaviors

Source: Johnson, T. (1991)

Classification of sexual behaviors helps professionals, as well as parents, make distinctions among children's sexual behaviors.

Group I: Children in this group engage in natural and healthy sexual play. Sex play is fun and spontaneous, and friends participate voluntarily. Sex play does not result in fear, shame, or anxiety. Children touch other children or look at others' bodies as a way of exploring their worlds; they exhibit a normal curiosity about the human body and sex. Play scenarios often involve sexual exploration as a means to understand this part of their world. The child's interest in sexuality is not greater than that of other children's. Their desire to learn about sex is balanced with their desire to learn about other aspects of their environment.

Group II: Children in this group engage in more sexual behaviors than those in Group I. Often, they feel anxious, guilty, or ashamed about their sexual curiosities and behaviors. Children may excessively masturbate, talk about sex, or act overtly sexual around children and adults. These behaviors may point to a child's confusion about sex and sexuality; it may indicate that the child has been exposed to sexually explicit materials; or the child has been inappropriately touched by another person.

Group III: All children in this group have been sexually or physically abused. In general, children often participate in all aspects of adult sexual behavior, but with a willing child partner. They are mistrustful of adults, since adults have betrayed them. Children are secretive about their sexual behaviors, but they show no anxiety. Often, they are unemotional about their sexual play.

Group IV: Children in this group are sexually aggressive and will coerce others into sexual acts. Their behaviors are often acts of molestation and abuse, because their partners are not willing participants. Often, these children have been sexually abused in the past. They have little to no impulse control, and they typically have a range of other behavior problems.

Is Honesty the Best Approach for Parents When It Comes to Talking to Their Children About Sex?

As children grow up and their sexual identities and behaviors develop, American parents often dread the questions with which they are faced and the responsibility to impart delicate information to their offspring. Talking about sex makes many uncomfortable, but as children begin to explore at increasingly younger ages, appropriate information is necessary. Is honesty the best approach for parents when it comes to talking to their children about sex?

YES!

Regardless of whether or not parents speak to their children about sex, as their sons and daughters get older, they will become curious and begin to experiment.

- Without a firm understanding of sexual behaviors, children are susceptible to finding misleading information on their own, from sources like friends and the Internet. Misinformation combined with curiosity can lead to poor judgment that can result in sexually transmitted infections (STIs) and unwanted pregnancy.

- Using examples in the media as a catalyst for a discussion about sex makes the conversation seem less personal and direct. This can make both parties more comfortable talking about issues that are potentially embarrassing.

- Keeping an open flow of information on both ends can facilitate an easier discussion. If parents are honest about their discomfort talking about such topics, kids will respect that their parents are human too. In turn, they'll be more likely to approach their parents with questions and concerns, especially if both sides remain open and non-judgmental (Levkoff, 2007).

In addition to keeping children correctly informed and knowledgeable about sexuality, an honest flow of information between parents and kids can result in a better understanding of one's body and a decreased sense of shame.

NO!

Although many feel that an abstinence-only approach to sex education ignores the reality of teen sex, several recent studies support that focus.

- A more comprehensive approach to sex education in the United States concurred with an increase in teenage sexual activity, as well as some of the negative consequences of it. Teen pregnancy rose 23 percent from 1972 to 1990.

- Opting for an abstinence-only angle on sex could potentially delay the age at which kids decide to become sexually active. The number of sexually active high school students having sex decreased from 54.1 percent in 1991 to 45 percent in 2001, coinciding with an increase in abstinence-only sex education, according to the CDC Youth Risk Behavior Survey.

- Premature sexual activity can be indicative of a larger problem for many teenagers, particularly girls. Elayne Bennett's "Best Friends" program finds that addressing outside issues, like self-esteem and a sense of efficacy, can lower the rates of irresponsible decision making when it comes to sex for at-risk teens (Hymowitz, 2003).

Abstinence is the only surefire birth control, and emphasizing it may be what many parents opt to do.

>>> **WHAT DO YOU THINK?**

1. What is an appropriate age for parents to speak to their children about sex? Did your parents talk to you about it? How old were you? Do you wish you had been older or younger?

2. How do you think a discussion about sex between parents and children impacts the kids' attitudes toward themselves and toward others?

3. If you plan on having children, how will you approach it?

in their growth (Eveleth & Tanner, 1990; Marshall & Tanner, 1970). Of course, there are wide variations in growth patterns. Children of racial and ethnic heritages typically reach adult height and other physical maturities more quickly than white children (Ozretich & Bowman, 2001). As you learned in the previous chapter, recent research suggests this early maturation is the interactive result of social forces (such as sexualizing children at younger ages), and biological forces (such as childhood obesity).

PUBERTY

Outward signs of the sexual maturation process are evidenced as early as second or third grade, about the ages of nine or 10. For instance, **breast buds** are visible in girls, and sparse pubic and underarm hair develops about six months later (Anspaugh & Ezell, 2006). These **secondary sexual characteristics** may appear as early as second grade in girls and are often accompanied by growth spurts in height and weight. The genitals also continue to develop.

Physicians use the *Tanner Genitalia Development Scale* (see Table 6.4) to determine whether a child's physical sexual development is normative (Harrison, 2003). Some girls will have their first menstruation during the middle childhood years. Boys, too, undergo the development of secondary sexual characteristics, although they are

typically about two years behind girls (Anspaugh & Ezell, 2006). In boys, the first sign of physical sexual maturation is an increase in the size of the testes.

PSYCHOSOCIAL DEVELOPMENT: FORMING INDUSTRY

Middle childhood presents a tremendous opportunity for social and emotional growth. The initiation and formation of peer groups increases, as does the significance of these relationships to the child's developing sense of self. With a new sense of **industry** (Erikson's fourth stage of psychosocial development), children feel they can master just about anything, and friends help nurture this sense of mastery.

PSYCHOSEXUAL DEVELOPMENT: DEVELOPING INTIMATE BONDS WITH PEERS

During the school years, children show a strong preference for peers of their same sex; within these *homosocial* friendship groups, gender socialization intensifies. These peer groups are referred to as "two cultures of childhood," because boys' groups are large, competitive, and hierarchical, with

TABLE 6.4
Tanner Genitalia Development Scale

Sources: Adapted from Marshall & Tanner (1969, 1970).

Physicians assess puberty development and its variations by using the five-stage developmental established by physicians Tanner and Marshall. For girls, pubertal development is measured by breast size and pubic hair distribution; boys' puberty development is measured by the development of the external genitalia and pubic hair distribution.

	Girls				Boys		
Stage	Breasts	Pubic Hair	Other	Stage	Genitalia	Pubic Hair	Other
1	• Prepubertal, elevation of milk ducts	• Prepubertal	—	1	• Prepubertal; Testes < 1.0 inches	• Prepubertal	—
2	• Breast bud appears under enlarged areola • Enlarged areola	• Sparse growth along labia	• Clitoris enlarges; • Labia becomes pigmented; • Uterus enlarges	2	• Thinning/ reddening of scrotum; • Testes 1.0– 1.28 inches	• Sparse growth of slightly pigmented hair at base of penis	• Decrease in total body fat
3	• Breast tissue grows beyond areola	• Hair is coarser, curled, pigmented; spreads across *pubes*	• Underarm hair • Acne	3	• Growth of penis, especially in length; • Testes 1.32– 1.6 inches	• Thicker, curlier hair spreads to *mons pubis*	• Gynecomastia • Voice break • Muscle mass increases
4	• Projection of areola/enlarged ducts form breast mound	• Adult-type hair, not spread to thigh	• Menarche • Regular menses	4	• Growth of penis and glans; darkening of scrotum; • Testes 1.64– 1.8 inches	• Adult-type hair, not spread to thighs	• Underarm hair • Voice changes • Acne
5	• Adult breast contour/shape	• Adult-type hair, spread to thigh	• Adult genitalia	5	• Adult genitalia	• Adult-type hair, spread to thighs	• Facial hair • Muscle mass continues to increase

<<< During the school years, children acquire huge gains in their cognitive abilities—**the faulty logic in early childhood develops into sound reasoning, and children begin to compare themselves to others (Ozretch & Bowman, 2001).** They are now also capable of understanding complex interrelationships—**including relationships between people (Piaget, 1955).**

frequent displays of strength, while girls' peer groups are smaller, with intimate conversation and an emphasis on group cohesion (Maccoby, 1998).

The formation of peers is a multistep process. A classic study of friendship development (Table 6.5) found that as children grow through childhood and enter the early years of adolescence, their dependence on their parents for intimacy lessens and they turn to "chumships" for support (Dunphy, 1963). These friendships provide tremendous support to a preteen's budding sense of self, and provide youth a "safety net" that allows them to practice and rehearse their new relational and sex roles.

By about age 11, most children have a basic understanding of the human reproduction process, and they also know the proper terminology for their sex parts. It's important to note that although most children do know the proper names for their sexual anatomy, they more often use slang words when discussing their body parts (such as "nut sack," or "junk" instead of testicles) or the acts of sex (such as "jerking off" instead of masturbation).

SEXUAL BEHAVIORS: EXPERIENCING SEXUALITY FOR PLEASURE

It's necessary to understand the types of sexual behaviors that occur during preadolescence, because today they are precursors to early sexual intercourse or early oral sex—risky behaviors among youth that may lead to early pregnancy and STIs (O'Donnell et al., 2006).

TABLE 6.5
Stages of Friendship Development

Source: Dunphy, D. C. (1963).

In a classic study about the formation of childhood friendships, D. C. Dunphy (1963) discovered the following stages of friendship development.

Stage One: Pre-Crowd	**Kindergarten through Fifth Grade** Isolated, same-sex peer groups exist in form of *cliques*—small groups of four to nine members; spontaneous, shared activities provide opportunities for interpersonal relating. Boys join larger groups and enjoy doing activities together; girls form smaller, intimate groups.
Stage Two: Beginning of the Crowd	**Sixth through Eighth Grade** Same-sex peer groups transition to *crowds,*consisting of 10 or more members. Crowd activities include after-school dances or sports activities; give preadolescents a chance to practice opposite sex interactions.
Stage Three: Crowd in Transition	**Ninth Grade through High School** Peer groups are in transition through high school. Smaller cliques are formed within larger crowd. Pairing off of boy/girl couples drives crowd to transition.
Stage Four: Fully Developed Crowd	**End of High School through College** Composed entirely of opposite-sex cliques. These friendships/cliques last only long enough for members to become fully socialized into gender roles needed for adult relationships.
Stage Five: Crowd Disintegration	**Through Early Adulthood** As adolescents mature into adults and take on adult responsibilities and jobs, crowd-friendships disintegrate. Support of friends often replaced by intimate partner; consequently, friendship groups become more loosely associated. Over time, intimate partner becomes "best friend," though adults still hang on to one or two close friends.

Although children begin to experiment more with masturbation during the school years, few parents want to discuss the issue (Weinstein & Rosen, 2006). As the data show in Table 6.6, boys touch their genitals more frequently than do girls, but masturbation is a common sexual behavior in boys and girls during this developmental period (Friedrich, et al., 1991, 1998).

In an effort to better understand those sexual behaviors that lead to unintended pregnancies, STIs, and other problems associated with very early sexual encounters, adolescent sexuality researchers assessed the sexual behaviors of urban African American/Black Caribbean, mixed-race, and Latino youth (O'Donnell et al., 2006). Among these sixth graders, O'Donnell discovered that a statistically significant percentage of the youth had already

- engaged in heterosexual kissing (43.6 percent).
- kissed and hugged a heterosexual partner for a long time (34.8 percent).
- had a girlfriend or a boyfriend (59.9 percent).

The researchers' primary concern with these early sexual behaviors is that these behaviors are all precursors to early sexual intercourse (before age 13).

Privacy becomes a major issue to children in grade school (Friedrich et al., 1998, 1991). Although their sexual curiosity begins to grow, they simultaneously become less likely to undress in front of others, touch their sex parts in public, or even kiss non-family adults. Although this shift to privacy may be due to the desire for autonomy during this developmental stage, some researchers believe that children in Western societies become more private in their sexual expressions because they have begun to internalize the social mores and sexual scripts of a sexually repressive culture (Haroian, 2000).

First sexual attraction usually begins in middle childhood, around age 10 (Harrison, 2003), and may be toward the same sex because children in this age range have peer groups that are homosocial (DeLamater & Friedrich, 2002). Does this mean that the child is gay or lesbian? Perhaps, but in all likelihood, no. It is normative, healthy behavior for children, as a means of exploring and understanding their environments and themselves, to experiment sexually with their same-sex peers.

To date, scant research exists that explores the racial and ethnic influences on childhood sexual development, although we do have a

TABLE 6.6
Frequency of Sexual Behaviors in Middle Childhood

Source: Adapted from Friedrich et al. (1991).

Children engage in all types of sexual behaviors. This table presents types of sexual behaviors seen in boys and girls during middle childhood (ages seven–12), as well as the frequency the behaviors occur.

Behavior	Percent of Occurrence	
	Boys	Girls
Talks flirtatiously	2.9	14.9
Pretends to be opposite sex	2.9	8.0
Masturbates with hand	11.2	8.6
Uses sexual words	19.9	12.1
Looks at nude pictures	27.2	18.4
Touches sex parts in public	15.5	2.9
Interested in opposite sex	19.9	32.8
Tries to look at people undressing	27.7	14.9
Kisses non-family adults	18.9	26.4
Sits with crotch exposed	15.5	29.9
Undresses in front of others	21.4	23.0
Touches sex parts at home	36.4	18.4
Scratches crotch	40.8	34.5
Boy only/girl only toys	30.6	42.5
Walks around nude	20.6	12.0
Shy about undressing	50.0	52.0
Walks around in underwear	44.1	16.0

>>> Sexual behaviors that occur during preadolescence **can be precursors to early sexual intercourse or oral sex.**

general understanding of the overarching influences on sexual beliefs and attitudes, discussed earlier. As a result, much of the existing sexual development research focuses on white, middle-class children. New research, however, explored childhood sexual behaviors among two- to 12-year-old African Americans (Thigpen, 2009). Research findings suggest that, similar to white children, African American children display a broad range of sexual behaviors (such as self-stimulation, voyeuristic behaviors, and exhibitionistic behaviors). The author noted that the significance of race in this study is twofold:

1. There is an increased frequency of sexual behaviors (both public and private) noted for 10- to 12-year-olds (male and female). This is inconsistent with research that found that as children become older, their sexual behaviors become covert.

2. There is a low incidence of masturbatory behavior (about 15 percent). The author notes that this may be because masturbation is less commonly practiced among heterosexual African American adults (Laumann et al., 1994; Sterk-Elifson, 1994); these attitudes are passed on to children.

These findings suggest that much more attention to identifying contextual factors that shape and direct childhood sexual development, as well as understanding racial and ethnic norms, is needed.

There is an encouraging downward trend in the number of students who report having sex before the age of 13 (O'Donnell et al., 2006). African American/Black Caribbean and Latino youth, however, remain at the highest risk for early sexual intercourse. Data from the Youth Risk Behavior Surveillance System (2009) indicate that slightly over 16 percent of the African American/Black Caribbean and 8 percent of Hispanic students surveyed reported they had sexual intercourse for the first time before the age of 13; this is in comparison to about 4 percent of white youth of the same age (Centers for Disease Control and Prevention, 2009).

Among all racial and ethnic groups, to the extent that children and adolescents experience parental involvement and communication, and to the extent that youth hold the sexual attitude that it is socially acceptable to delay sexual intercourse, they are more likely to remain virgins throughout high school (Lindley, Joshi, & Vincent, 2007).

Even more significant changes occur in the adolescent developmental period.

DEVELOPING SEXUALLY IN ADOLESCENCE: 12 to 18 YEARS

Adolescent sex and sexuality are of great interest to social science researchers and demographers, because often the behaviors put adolescents at risk for a number of health concerns, such as unwanted pregnancies, violence, and STIs (O'Donnell et al., 2006). In the sections that follow, we'll take a close look at the multiple factors that affect adolescent sexual development.

The adolescent period of human growth and development is a time of many transitions for the teen. According to adolescent intimacy research, the development of intimacy revolves around the biological,

cognitive, and psychosocial/sexual changes that occur through adolescence (Openshaw, 2004). These transitions create a change in teens' *need* for intimacy. The following key points highlight research findings about adolescent psychosocial changes (Huebner, 2000).

ESTABLISHING AN IDENTITY

Central to the adolescent's social and emotional development is the concept of **identity formation** (Erikson, 1963). The questions "Who am I?" and "Why am I on earth?" occupy an adolescent's thoughts, and during the adolescent development period, teens incorporate the beliefs, values, and opinions of influential others (parents, peers, teachers) into their own identity. At the same time, adolescents begin the process of **individuation**—that is, forming an identity that is separate from that of their parents. This developmental process of individuation affects sexual development, because as teens open up and disclose with their peers, it helps them clarify their own thoughts and emotions, and also helps them better define their own uniqueness and a sense of "who" they are as intimate, sexual persons (German, 2002).

For developing teens, establishing autonomy refers to not only establishing a sense of independence, but also becoming a self-governing person within the context of interpersonal and sexual relationships. Adolescents begin to take responsibility for their actions and decisions that affect them, and, in many cases, those around them.

Perhaps more than at any other time in our life course development, friends are most important during adolescence. Through friendships we learn to be open and honest, and we learn to self-disclose and to trust. These are all foundational relational skills necessary for satisfying sexual relationships. As we progress through adolescence and approach early adulthood, our friendships move from same-sex group interactions, to mixed-sex interactions, to coupling or pairing off, to eventually having only a select, few friends. For example, preadolescents spend about an hour or less per week interacting with the opposite sex, but by the 12th grade, boys spend about five hours a week with the other sex; girls spend about 10 hours per week with boys (Richards et al., 1998).

As the shifts in gender preference occur, other discrepancies between males and females emerge, and these are presented in Table 6.7. Researchers believe that the differences found between male and female friendship experiences are due to socialization patterns (Johnson & Aires,

The Influence of Parents on Sexual Scripts

Our parents and caregivers significantly affect the development of our sexual scripts. Think back to your childhood and adolescence to the ways in which your upbringing shaped who you are as a sexual person today.

Generally speaking, my parent(s) did/did not display their sexual feelings toward one another in front of me. Examples of this are:

_____

_____.

As a child, if I asked my parent(s) about sex or sexual parts of the human body, they _____

_____.

As a teenager, I could/could not ask my parents about such things as birth control, abortion, dating, or premarital sex. This made me feel

_____

_____.

I was/was not raised with religious beliefs. This impacted my sexual scripts in the following ways: _____

_____.

When I asked my parent(s) where babies come from, they told me _____

_____.

As a child, I remember asking my parents about _____. Their reaction was _____.

If I were to sum up my parents' attitudes about sexuality education, I would say _____

_____.

If I could change anything about my sexual development in childhood and adolescence, it would be _____.
This is because _____.
The person who had the greatest influence on my sexual development was _____. This is because

_____.

If I have children, I will/will not be open about sex and sexuality with my children because _____.

_____.

TABLE 6.7
Differences between Male and Female Friendships

Maccoby notes the unique differences between typical boys' and girls' peer groups (1998):

Boys' Peer Groups	Girls' Peer Groups
• large, competitive, and hierarchical	• smaller groups than boys'
• one or two boys at the top of the pecking order	• intense, intimate conversation dominates time together
• rough-and-tumble	• emphasis on group cohesion rather than competition
• aggressive play dominates their time together	• each member tries to promote own agenda, but each girl also tries to be "nice" to the others
• frequent displays of strength	
• sex jokes popular	
• sexual innuendoes abound	
• sexual materials, such as *Playboy* magazine or X-rated DVDs from a parent or a sibling's room, shared	
• condoms from a parent's dresser drawer introduced	

1983; Kuttler, LaGreca, & Prinstein, 1999). As you saw in Chapter 3, male socialization tends to emphasize the establishment and maintenance of achievement, whereas female socialization tends to emphasize the importance of the establishment and maintenance of interpersonal relationships. All of these experiences shape our sexual scripts.

THE INFLUENCE OF PARENTS

Although parents rarely provide the type and accuracy of sexuality information and education that school health programs do, they still influence their children in critical ways. For instance, several bodies of research suggest that adolescent sexual initiation is delayed if parents monitor and supervise their activities; there is also a decrease in sexual risk behavior (Capaldi, Crosby, & Stoolmiller, 1996; Luster & Small, 1994; Romer et al., 1994). Warm and responsive parenting styles are also associated with delayed sexual initiation in adolescents, as well as a decrease in the likelihood that teens will engage in frequent sexual intercourse when they do become sexually active (Jaccard, Dittus, & Gordon, 2000; Miller, Forehand, & Kotchick, 1999; Resnick et al., 1997). When parents disapprove of adolescent sexual activity, teens are less likely to engage in sexual behaviors, and if they do become sexually active, they tend to have fewer sex partners (Jaccard, Dittus, & Gordon, 2000).

Interestingly, verbal communication between parents and adolescents appears to have little or no effect on whether a teen decides to initiate sexual activity (Kaiser Family Foundation, 2004). Research has shown this is due to several reasons:

- Sexual communication is infrequent and limited, and includes only certain family members, such as between mothers and daughters (Rosenthal & Feldman, 1999).

- Parents have incomplete or inaccurate information (Eisenberg et al., 2004).

- Communication about sex often doesn't happen until after the teen has become sexually active (Eisenberg et al., 2004).

- Parents and teens don't agree on what should and should not be discussed (Shtarkshall, Santelli, & Hirsch, 2007).

There are also racial and ethnic differences in how parents communicate about sex with their teens. Research reveals that Hispanic and African American/Black Caribbean teens have the closest relationships with their mothers, and black teen girls are the most comfortable discussing sexual topics; sexual communication is lower among Hispanics and black groups than in white groups (Somers, 2006).

As family life educators, sexuality educators, social workers, sociologists, and psychologists continue their sexuality research efforts, we will come to learn more about adolescent sexuality development and subgroup differences, and we will ultimately be able to devise approaches that best equip and empower teens to make healthy choices.

PSYCHOSEXUAL DEVELOPMENT: INCREASING THE CAPACITY FOR INTIMATE RELATIONSHIPS

As the adolescent experiences the changes in cognition and thought processes, his or her *need for intimacy* changes. As they individuate, find their own identity, and are given more freedom, their *capacity to have intimate and sexual relationships* changes. This, too, is seen in the formation and maintenance of peer relationships. And as they undergo the physiological changes associated with puberty, they have a new way in which to *be intimate* with others.

Romantic relationships become increasingly important to the lives of adolescents, and they fulfill a number of adolescents' needs (Furman, 2002). For example, while 10th graders rely primarily on close friends for emotional support, by 12th grade, romantic partners become a major source of support (Furman & Buhrmester, 1992). Romantic relationships also contribute to a person's identify formation, the development of peer relationships, the transition to adulthood, and the development of sexuality (Furman, 2002). These relationships, however, do not fulfill the same functions that adult romantic relationships do. For instance, although adults turn to one another for caregiving and emotional support, adolescents still turn to their peers—not the romantic partner—for such support (Furman, 2002). Although these develop over time, the need for affiliation with another and sexual needs are met first in adolescent romantic relationships.

These changes in identity and intimacy create new ways in which teens can experience their sexuality.

SEXUAL BEHAVIORS: EXPERIENCING A WIDE RANGE IN ATTITUDES AND BEHAVIORS

Young people today are engaging in sexual behaviors, and their attitudes about sexuality and sexual expression are becoming increasingly open-minded.

<<< As changes in cognition and thought processes occur during adolescence, so does the need for intimacy.

Figure 6.4 Percentage of High School Students Who Ever Had Sexual Intercourse, by Race

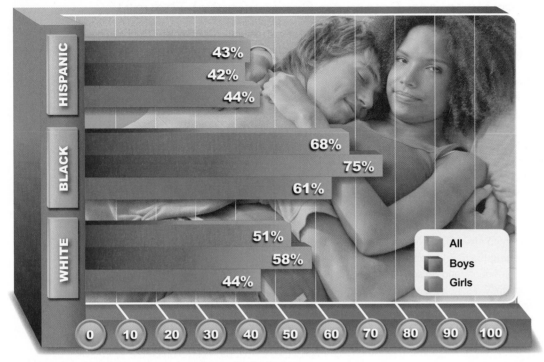

HISPANIC
- 43%
- 42%
- 44%

BLACK
- 68%
- 75%
- 61%

WHITE
- 51%
- 58%
- 44%

Legend:
- All
- Boys
- Girls

0 10 20 30 40 50 60 70 80 90 100

Source: Centers for Disease Control and Prevention (2008a).

Since the 1990s, the number of teenagers who are sexually active has fluctuated only slightly. In 2007, 35 percent of high school students reported being currently sexually active (Centers for Disease Control and Prevention, 2008a). Of course, there are gender and racial/ethnic differences, both in the percentages of high school students having had sexual intercourse, and using birth control, as illustrated in Figures 6.4 and 6.5.

The likelihood of being sexually active increases by about 11 percentage points each year (Centers for Disease Control and Prevention, 2008a):

- 20.1 percent of ninth graders have had sexual intercourse.
- 30.6 percent of 10th graders have had sexual intercourse.
- 41.8 percent of 11th graders have had sexual intercourse.
- 52.6 percent of 12th graders have had sexual intercourse.

In 2007, nearly one-half (48 percent) of all teens ages 15 to 19 had ever had sexual intercourse, and about 15 percent have had sex with at least four persons (Centers for Disease Control and Prevention, 2008a).

During the teenage years, oral sex is more common than sexual intercourse. Among teenagers, oral sex is common because many teens consider it to be more socially acceptable than vaginal sex (Halpern-Felsher et al., 2005; Lindberg, Jones, & Santelli, 2008). The numbers of teens having oral sex appear to support this notion. A nationwide study of 2,271 teens found that more teens had engaged in oral sex than vaginal sex (55 percent versus 50 percent). Although oral and vaginal sex tend to go hand-

in-hand, more than one-fourth of virgins reported engaging in oral sex (Lindberg, Jones, & Santelli, 2008). Generally speaking, white teens tend to engage in oral sex more than Latino, black, and Asian teens do (Rosenbaum, 2009).

Some researchers believe that the high percentages of teens having oral sex are a result of the increase in the number of teens who are pledging to remain virgins until marriage, because they believe it is a "safe" alternative to the dangers associated with intercourse (Bruckner & Bearman, 2005; Halpern-Felsher et al., 2005; Rosenbaum, 2009). In fact, some teens are unaware of *any* health risks associated with oral sex (Halpern-Felsher et al., 2005; Hoff, Greene, & Davis, 2003). They also believe they are still "technical virgins" if they have had oral sex, but not vaginal intercourse. Adolescents also experiment with anal sex. One study showed that approximately 11 percent had engaged in anal sex with someone of the opposite sex (Lindberg, Jones, & Santelli, 2008).

We discuss *hooking up* (casual sex) at length a bit later in this chapter. Here it's important to know that there is an increasing trend among preteens and adolescents to engage in recreational—not relational—sex (Wallace, 2008). To date, no studies have assessed just how many adolescents engage in hooking up, or the regularity with which it takes place. But as one high schooler noted, "Sex with a friend, sex with a stranger, sex in private, sex in public; it all boils down to just having fun. It's no big deal" (Wallace, 2008). Or is it?

Figure 6.5 Percentage of Sexually Active Students Who Reported Using Birth Control, by Race

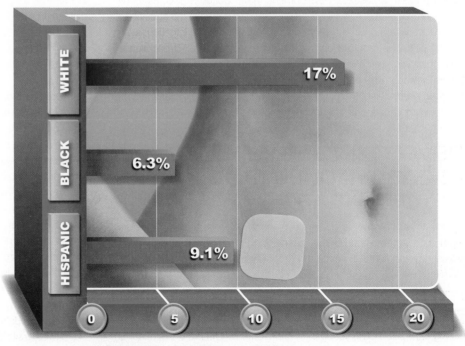

WHITE
- 17%

BLACK
- 6.3%

HISPANIC
- 9.1%

0 5 10 15 20

Source: Centers for Disease Control and Prevention (2008a).

Biological and Cognitive Development: Emerging Consequential Thought

When do we reach "adulthood?" By the time most of us complete high school, our biological sexual maturation is complete. Our brain development, however, is not yet complete—and this continuing brain development affects our psychosocial and psychosexual development in early adulthood.

The brain follows a "use it or lose it" policy with regard to neurons, the nerve cells in the brain. As we age, brain development in early adulthood occurs through synaptic pruning (Sylwester, 2007). **Synaptic pruning** is the process by which the weaker neurons that are not used are weeded out, or pruned back. This process results in a more efficient brain cortex and produces a more extensively connected, highly communicative cortex.

The **prefrontal lobe** of the brain plays a key role in the development and regulation of our social behaviors (Sylwester, 2007). The prefrontal lobe is oftentimes referred to as the "executive" center of the brain, because it is here that capabilities such as advanced abstract thought, planning, reasoning, decision-making, problem solving, judgment, moral reasoning, and impulse control are initiated. It is also the area of the brain where higher emotions, such as empathy and altruism, are managed (Sylwester, 2007).

These changes in brain maturation also now allow a young adult to "try on" or imagine themselves engaging in a certain activity, to analyze a list of if-this-then-that outcomes, imagine themselves in each possible outcome, and come to a decision whether to engage in the activity (Baird & Fugelsang, 2004). This ability to imagine alternative outcomes and understand the consequences of the outcomes is referred to as **counterfactual thinking/reasoning** (Baird & Fugelsang, 2004).

What are the implications of counterfactual thought and reasoning for sexuality? Because children and young adolescents lack the necessary developmental changes in the brain, they are incapable of thinking about different behavioral alternatives and outcomes—and this may be why adolescents are more likely than adults to engage in sexual risk-taking behaviors, such as having sex without a condom or having multiple sexual partners (Baird & Fugelsang, 2004; Baird et al., 2005). This emerging research may indicate that, in order for sexuality education programs to be more effective in improving pregnancy and STI rates among adolescents, creators of sexuality and health curricula need to consider ways in which to help teens better determine possible outcomes of their sexual and lifestyle behaviors, since their brain maturation perhaps limits their ability to do so.

The teen birth rate in the United States rose in 2006 for the first time since its downward trend began in 1991. Between 2005 and 2006, the birth rate among teens rose 3 percent over all. The largest increases were seen among African American/Black Caribbean teens (5 percent), followed by a 4 percent rate increase among American Indian/Alaska Native teens, a 3 percent rate increase among white teens, and a 2 percent rate increase among Hispanics (Centers for Disease Control and Prevention, 2008b).

Sexually transmitted infections (STIs) also pose a threat to an adolescent's health and sexual development. In the United States, as many as 26 percent — one in four — of adolescent girls between the ages of 14 and 19 are infected with at least one sexually transmitted infection; even among girls who reported only one lifetime partner, the STI prevalence was nearly 21 percent (Centers for Disease Control and Prevention, 2008b). African American/Black Caribbean teen girls were most severely affected; nearly half of them were infected with an STI. We'll examine STIs and their consequences at length in Chapter 14.

DEVELOPING SEXUALLY IN EARLY ADULTHOOD: 19 TO 35 YEARS

By the time most of us complete high school, our biological sexual maturation is complete. For this reason, our primary focus of early adult sexual development will be the psychosocial/psychosexual realm.

PSYCHOSOCIAL DEVELOPMENT: ESTABLISHING DEEPER FRIENDSHIPS

During early adulthood, young men and women find themselves accepting both the rewards and challenges of independence and the responsi-

bility that accompanies autonomy. Along with this independence, young adults begin to examine those qualities they find desirable in a life partner or spouse and begin to contemplate the commitment of marital and life-partnering relationships. The notion of bearing children also becomes more appealing and more realistic for many.

Social and emotional development during early adulthood is marked with the formation of deeper intimacy in interpersonal relationships. These intimate relations differ from childhood and adolescent friendships in that they involve a greater level of mutuality, respect, reciprocity, and self-sacrifice. Erikson (1950) suggested that these intimate relationships are essential to healthy development and without such, developing adults are at risk for an isolation-filled life. The relationships that we are born into, are surrounded by, and surround ourselves with ultimately shape our sexual selves.

Despite the fact that the United States is rich in cultural diversity, scant research exists that examines the influences of culture and/or ethnicity on friendship formation.

In a recent study of the formation of late adolescent/early adulthood friendships, researcher Caryn Dolich (2005) examined three cultures in an attempt to determine whether cultural differences affect males' and females' friendships. Dolich found that within all three cultures, females reported higher ratings of the importance of intimacy and companionship than did males. Additionally, females discussed personal and daily events/trivial issues more frequently than males did. Consistent with prior research (Johnson & Aires, 1983), females in Dolich's study developed more intimate and personal relationships than males did. Unlike the results found in previous research, the males in Dolich's study reported that they discuss with some frequency such things as intimacy, family relationships, dating, and sex with opposite-sex friends.

A University of Michigan study found that college students reported that their interracial/ethnic friendships were positive, and that these

Figure 6.6 Positive Feelings Toward Different Races: First Year in College Compared to Fourth Year in College

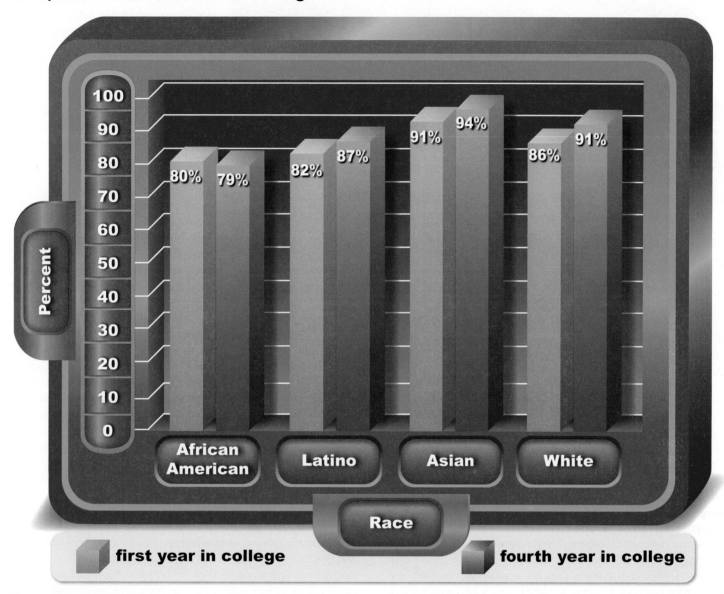

Source: Gurin (1999).

friendships increased in number throughout their four years of college (Gurin, 1999). Figure 6.6 denotes the percentages of college students who grew to be even more positive about these relationships over their four-year college experience.

SEXUAL BEHAVIORS: DOING "IT"

Is everyone doing it on college campuses? The National College Health Assessment (NCHA, 2008) provides us insight into the sexual practices of young adults.

In general, nearly one-half (about 47 percent) of college students report that they have had sex with at least one partner, and about one-half indicate that they have had vaginal sex at least once in the past 30 days. There are gender differences in sexual activity (NCHA, 2008):

- *one sexual partner:* 42 percent (males), 48.8 percent (females).

- *two sexual partners:* 10.6 percent (males), 11.0 percent (females).

- *three sexual partners:* 6.5 percent (males), 5.4 percent (females).

- *four or more sexual partners:* 9.9 percent (males), 5.4 percent (females).

Young adults today experience a wide range of sexual behaviors.

Today, researchers and sexuality educators are also concerned about a sexual practice that often leads to unsafe or unwanted sex: hooking up.

HOOKING UP

Hooking up refers to physical interactions (usually sexual) with the absence of commitment or affection. As one of my students described it, "It's awesome—there are literally no expectations from each other, no strings attached."

Today on college campuses, students are frequently opting to hook up, and college fraternities, sororities, and dorms commonly host "hooking up" parties, as do popular spring break destination hotels and resorts (England & Thomas, 2007; Wallace, 2008). With as many as 40 percent of college students reporting that they have hooked up, the latest trend in sexual behaviors involves sexual encounters and includes anything from kissing, to mutual masturbation, to oral sex, to sexual intercourse (Glenn & Marquardt, 2001). Researchers found a distinction between whites and

Figure 6.7 Sexual Acts in College Hookups

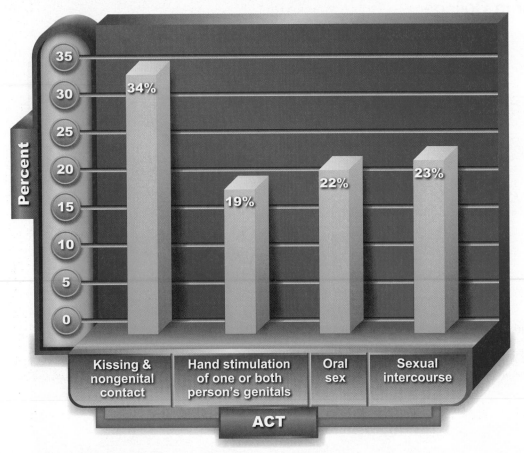

Source: England & Thomas (2007).

blacks when describing hooking up. When white college women describe hooking up, there is always a clear sexual connotation to the term. On the other hand, black college women describe hooking up as ranging from getting someone's phone number, to meeting up with someone after class, to going on a date, to a sexual fling (Glenn & Marquardt, 2001).

How often do hookups know one another? There are random hookups, in which the students who get together do not know one another before they hook up (about 14 percent) (England & Thomas, 2007). Over half of those who reported a recent hookup indicated that they had previously hooked up with the same person. A **friend with benefits** or **booty call** are terms used to describe a person who has regular sex with another, but does not relate to that person as a boyfriend or a girlfriend.

In a recent study of West Coast college students, researchers found that nearly half of all hookups start at a party or hanging out at a bar or a dorm, and about 25 percent of those who have hooked up had one to four hookups. About 20 percent experienced five to 10 hookups, and over one-third had hooked up more than 10 times (England & Thomas, 2007).

Figure 6.7 depicts the percentages of those college students who participated in certain sexual acts in their hookup encounters (such as kissing, touching, mutual masturbation, oral sex, and sexual intercourse). As you can see, the numbers are fairly evenly distributed among the different categories of sexual behaviors. Also, hooking up usually follows quite a bit of drinking (England & Thomas, 2007). College students indicated that drinking allows them to do things they were too self-conscious to do while sober, and young women indicate that drinking allows them to be more sexual and sexually free than while sober (England & Thomas, 2007; Glenn & Marquardt, 2001). A few of the college students reported that alcohol played a role in their going further sexually than they normally would, as the following discussion about spring break shows us.

Is hooking up a negative experience in the lives of young adults? Perhaps a concern on a developmental level is that hooking up experiences do not allow adults in a transition phase of their lives to learn how to form and maintain mature, committed relationships. More common than not, long-term committed relationships do not result from hookups, although some college students indicate they became a committed couple after several hookup encounters.

<<< Each year during spring break, popular destinations report significant increases in the number of deaths, rapes, and sexual assaults—**all related to drinking.**

^^^^ Many young women **feel that drinking allows them to be** more sexually free than while sober.

SPRING BREAK AND SEX

Alcohol and sex are a dangerous combination for college women. In a recent study of 644 college women, the American Medical Association found (AMA, 2006):

- 83 percent drank every night while on spring break, or had friends who did.

- 74 percent believed that drinking is an excuse to engage in outrageous behaviors.

- 86 percent believed that these outrageous behaviors contributed to dangerous behaviors by males toward females.

- 57 percent agreed that being sexually promiscuous was a way to fit in with the crowd.

- 92 percent said that it was very easy to obtain alcohol.

- 59 percent knew friends who had sex with more than one partner during spring break.

- Three out of every five respondents had friends who had unprotected sex during spring break.

- One in five women regretted the sexual activity they engaged in during spring break.

- 12 percent felt forced to have sex.

The combination of alcohol and sex is treacherous. Each year during spring break, popular destinations report significant increases in the numbers of deaths, rapes, and sexual assaults—all related to drinking.

The AMA contends that universities and colleges need to offer spring break alternatives that do not include alcohol.

SEXUAL LIFE EDUCATION

Parents and students often ask me when "sexuality education" should begin with their children. The simple answer to this is, "When children ask questions." And this is why it is so important to have an understanding of the ages and stages of sexual development across a person's life span. When children ask their parents or caregivers questions about sex—no matter how bad the timing is, as was shown in the opening vignette—they notice every nuance of the adults' expressions and reactions. Does the parent respond with embarrassment? Fear? Anxiety? Anger? Or, instead, does the parent respond with ease, and with patience and understanding, addressing the questions in a matter-of-fact, natural way?

You have discovered in this chapter that your sexuality consists of far more than body parts and how they work. Sexuality is a complicated tapestry that is woven together from the biological, cognitive, psychosocial, and psychosexual developments you experienced from the moment you were born; to understand who you are as a sexual person *now*, you need to understand those factors in your *past* that shaped your sexuality. Your past development and experiences since birth are also the very foundations of your sexual scripts today: The totality of your sexuality is a one-of-a-kind compilation of your individual developmental and relationship experiences, your unique individual expectations, and the cultural expectations that surround you.

06

Summary

HOW DO SEXUAL SCRIPTS GUIDE SEXUAL ATTITUDES, BELIEFS, AND BEHAVIORS? 104

- Sexual scripts provide a framework for normal sexual attitudes, beliefs, and behaviors, within a given culture. They give us direction on how to think, feel, and act when we find ourselves in sexual situations.
- Additionally, sexual scripts determine the age and gender of our sexual partners, the sexual positions we will engage in, how often we have sex, where we have sex, why we have sex, as well as many other factors.

WHAT ARE THE BIOLOGICAL, COGNITIVE, PSYCHOSOCIAL, PSYCHOSEXUAL, AND SEXUAL CHANGES ASSOCIATED WITH LIFE COURSE STAGES FROM INFANCY THROUGH EARLY ADULTHOOD? 106

- During infancy and toddlerhood, the child's initial capacity for intimate and loving relationships begins to take shape. Touching, cuddling, stroking, and snuggling babies further their capacity for intimacy. While even newborns are physiologically capable of feeling sexual pleasure, children's sexual behaviors are not erotic but are purely physiological in nature.

- From ages seven to 12, children become discriminating about their sexual behaviors, and the need for privacy intensifies. By the end of middle childhood, nearly all children have developed a very strong sense of their gender identity. Masturbation is a common sexual behavior in boys and girls.
- From ages 13 to 15, adolescents begin the process of individuation, forming an identity that is separate from that of their parents. Adolescents begin to take responsibility for their actions and decisions. As hormones come into play, the body again becomes a primary focus for the individual. Sexuality and sexual feelings become a preoccupation.
- From age 16 and up, hormonal balance is achieved, and the changing body is incorporated into the adolescent's sense of self. Sexual gratification is achieved through masturbation or partner sex.

IN WHAT WAYS HAVE THE SEXUAL EXPERIENCES OF TEENS CHANGED OVER TIME? 116

- Between 1950 and 2000, there was a steady decline in negative attitudes about sex before marriage, an increase in premarital sexual behavior and a difference in the nature of these sexual encounters (number of partners, likelihood to use birth control, etc.).

Key Terms

sexual scripts shared, gender-specific social and cultural expectations that guide our beliefs, attitudes and values about sex *104*

normative expected *104*

Eight Stages of Man psychologist Erik Erikson's idea that our social and emotional development is a lifelong process, what happens or does not happen at one stage will affect our psychosocial development during later stages of life *107*

masturbation self-stimulation or fondling of the genitals *108*

transgenerational gender reference the practice of parents or caregivers who engage in masturbating or fellating infants to calm them *108*

early childhood the period of a child's life between the ages of two and six *109*

autonomy a person's desire to self-rule *109*

initiative a person's sense of purpose or resourcefulness *109*

parenting styles the manner in which parents interact with and guide their children *109*

sex play sexual behaviors among young children *111*

prepubescence the time during middle childhood in which significant physical growth occurs *111*

breast buds one of the initial outward signs of sexual maturation in girls *113*

secondary sexual characteristics outward signs of the sexual maturation process *113*

industry Erikson's fourth stage of psychosocial development in which children feel they can master just about anything *113*

identity formation the time in which teens incorporate the beliefs, values, and opinions of parents, peers, and teachers into their own identity *116*

individuation forming an identity that is separate from that of their parents *116*

synaptic pruning the process by which the weaker neurons that are not used are weeded out, or pruned back *120*

prefrontal lobe the "executive" center of the brain, where capabilities such as advanced abstract thought, planning, reasoning, decision making, problem solving, judgment, moral reasoning, and impulse control are initiated *120*

counterfactual thinking/reasoning the ability to imagine alternative outcomes and understand the consequences of the outcomes *120*

friend with benefits (booty call) terms used to describe a person who has regular sex with another, but does not relate to that person as a boyfriend or a girlfriend *122*

Sample Test Questions

MULTIPLE CHOICE

1. Sexual scripts can determine the following:
   a. How we dress
   b. How we engage in sex
   c. How often we engage in sex
   d. All of the above

2. The theorist who followed a *cradle-to-grave* approach to development was:
   a. Piaget
   b. Dunphy
   c. Erikson
   d. All of the above

3. During which stage of life does a person develop a sense of trust or mistrust?
   a. Infancy
   b. Early childhood
   c. Adolescence
   d. Middle adulthood

4. A child who feels anxiety, guilt, or shame about sexual curiosities and behaviors belongs in which classification of childhood sexual behaviors?
   a. Group I
   b. Group II
   c. Group III
   d. Group IV

5. Early sexual behaviors among adolescents can put them at risk for the following:
   a. Sexually transmitted infections
   b. Unwanted pregnancy
   c. Violence
   d. All of the above

6. Individuation is the process of:
   a. Forming an identity that is separate from that of one's parents
   b. Forming an identity that is separate from that of one's friends
   c. Forming an identity that is separate from that of one's siblings
   d. None of the above

7. More so than female friendships, male friendships are characterized by:
   a. Reciprocity
   b. Sharing of problems
   c. Emotional attachment
   d. Discussion of sports and activities

8. Which of the following is TRUE regarding "hooking up?"
   a. White women use the term more loosely than black women.
   b. Alcohol does not appear to play a significant role in the practice.
   c. The absence of commitment or affection is a defining feature.
   d. All of the above are true.

SHORT RESPONSE

1. What role do parents play in teaching sexual scripts?

2. Your college president is doing some groundwork research in hopes of planning a spring break retreat option for students on campus next year. List three main research findings of which you think he or she should be aware as he or she explores his or her options.

3. Assume you are a pediatrician. The parents of two children, ages 4 and 8, have questions about what is "normal" sexual development and behavior at these ages. What do you tell them?

4. According to Erikson, when is the critical period of trust and intimacy development and what happens if there are complications at this stage?

5. Which research findings regarding oral sex among teens do you think the most alarming and why?

Answers: 1. d; 2. c; 3. a; 4. b; 5. d; 6. a; 7. d; 8. c

Remember to check www.thethinkspot.com **for additional information, downloadable flashcards, and other helpful resources.**

SEXUAL ORIENTATION
Development: Gay, Straight, or Bisexual?

WHAT IS SEXUAL ORIENTATION?
WHAT DETERMINES OUR SEXUAL ORIENTATION?
WHAT ARE SOME EXPERIENCES HOMOSEXUAL PEOPLE MAY HAVE THROUGHOUT THEIR LIVES?

So many

things about "gender" hit home for me. This is difficult for me to talk about. From an early age I can remember having lingering [sexual] thoughts toward other men. The majority of my family is Amish (we are Mennonite), so these feelings for other men are simply unacceptable to my family and to me on so many levels.

I'm not a playing-football-scoping-girls-scratching-myself kind of guy. I was a very sensitive kid who was not very athletic. I had many friends, but still felt very alone. My "secret" feelings led me to go through several severe bouts of depression in middle and high school. I tried so hard to overcome these feelings toward men, but it just seemed as though I could not. I know you're reading this thinking, "OK, this sounds more like struggles with sexual orientation than with gender." Don't you see? Both are intricately connected. Even if I were not attracted to men, I would still not be accepted by this society, because although my outward appearance says "male," my behaviors, expressions, gestures, and the like say "not-so-male."

I have gone through a lot emotionally and have found myself very bitter at times with God for not changing my feelings or helping me be more of a guy's guy. Suicidal at times, I have gone through a lot to get to the point where I am today. But the tremendous pain as a child and as an adolescent has made me a stronger person, I believe. It has been a very long road for me, but I'm thankful for every minute. I can see God's footprints in my life and the "why" question is answered more and more when I look at the person I've become. The pieces of the puzzle [of my life] all fit together now. At the surface, it's hard to understand as each piece is being put into place. But when I stand back and look at my life collectively, I can see how every piece is intricately put into place by Someone greater than me. God made me who I am—sensitive, compassionate, and caring. Though I'm not considered a "male" in today's society, I am a male.

Source: Author's files

CHAPTER 07

WHAT IS SEXUAL ORIENTATION?

We tend to live in an either/or society, and sexuality is no exception; someone is either gay or straight, male or female. The reality is, we live in a world of continuums, and sexual orientation is no exception to this—it is not simply an either/or concept or experience.

Often, when people think about sexual orientation, they frame it in the context of with whom someone prefers to have sex. But in reality, sexual orientation encompasses so much more. **Sexual orientation** includes the emotional, physical, sexual, and romantic (love/intimacy) attraction a person feels toward a specific gender (or genders). Certainly, sexual orientation isn't just about sex.

Who are you attracted to—men or women? Or both? If you are **heterosexual** (straight), you are attracted to someone of the opposite sex. If you are **homosexual** (gay), then you prefer someone of the same sex (the term *lesbian* refers to homosexual women; the term *gay* refers to homosexual men, but it is also the umbrella term for homosexual), and if you are **bisexual** (bi), then you are attracted to both men and women. Although it sounds simple, sexual orientation is much more complicated than checking a box on a census form: As with nearly every other area of intimate and relationship life, people don't fit into neat, tidy categories.

As you learned in Chapter 3, **transgender** is an umbrella term used to refer to someone whose behavior and/or appearance is not consistent

> ∧∧∧ If you are bisexual, **then you are attracted to both men and women.**

with their biologically assigned sex. Transgender, however, does not necessarily have to do with sexual orientation. Someone who is transgender may be gay, straight, or bi.

GAYDAR: KNOWING BY SEEING?

We seem to have a need to categorize people. Evolution theory would suggest that this is because we want to determine someone's sexual orientation so we can evaluate our prospects for a mate or perhaps our potential competition for mates. **Gaydar**, combining the words *gay* and *radar*, is the popular slang term that refers to a person's intuition or ability to discern another person's sexual orientation. There is an increasing amount of research that suggests gaydar is a real phenomenon.

Two studies determined that undergraduate students, both gay and straight, were able to correctly identify a man's sexual orientation by looking at a photograph for less than one second (Rule & Ambady, 2008; Rule, Ambady, & Hallett, 2009). Study participants looked only at facial features; hair was removed from the images so

> <<< **"Gaydar"** is a slang term used to describe the **ability to discern** another person's **sexual orientation.**

that participants were not biased by hairstyle or other aspects of self-presentation. Interestingly, the participants didn't realize that they were guessing correctly.

How is it that someone can correctly guess another person's sexual orientation at first glance? Cheryl Nicholas (2004) found evidence that eye gaze may be one of the primary contributors to gaydar. Other research has suggested that gaydar is actually an informally learned skill on the part of gays and lesbians (Wollery, 2007). It may be that gay people are motivated to identify other people who are gay because of the social isolation that they may experience, as well as the basic human need to associate with others who are like them (Shelp, 2002). Consequently, as society becomes more accepting of homosexuality and individuals become more open about their sexual orientations, gaydar may become less necessary. Although there is mounting evidence supporting the idea of gaydar, it is important to remember that there is no sure way to tell if someone is gay by sight alone—the only sure way to know for sure if someone is gay is if he or she tells you.

CLASSIFYING SEXUAL ORIENTATION: WHO IS GAY? STRAIGHT? BI?

In the early part of the 20th century, Magnus Hirschfeld was the first sexologist to advance the idea that sexual orientation and gender are not two distinct categories that differ widely from each other, but rather, exist on a continuum (see Chapter 2). Alfred Kinsey (1948) later reemphasized this point when he observed, "Males do not represent two discrete populations, heterosexual and homosexual. The world is not to be divided into sheep and goats. . . . The living world is a continuum in each and every one of its aspects."

As seen in Figure 7.1, Kinsey developed his seven-point **Kinsey Sexual Orientation Scale**, to illustrate the idea that sexual orientation is experienced on a continuum.

He placed *exclusively heterosexual* on one end, *exclusively homosexual* on the other end, and *equally heterosexual/homosexual* in the middle. Kinsey believed that his scale would assess both the behavioral (sexual behaviors) and the psychological (such as romance and love) dimensions of sexual orientation.

But think for a moment how important the psychological dimension might be in determining sexual orientation. If we just focus on behavior, how would we classify someone who has never engaged in any sexual activity at all? Let's look at Brad as an example.

Brad is a 19-year-old male who is very much attracted to other males and is not sexually interested in women. He identifies himself as gay, yet he has never had a relationship with or engaged in sexual activity with another man. Is Brad gay or straight? If you base your answer strictly on Brad's *behavior*, you might say that he is straight; this is because in our society we commonly assume heterosexuality is the norm. But by doing so, you are missing the *psychological* dimensions of attraction, as well as his self-identification as gay. These are both crucial aspects of Brad's sexual orientation. If you consider these, you might conclude that Brad is gay. This example illustrates the complexity of defining sexual orientation.

Recognizing the limitations of examining behavior and attraction together on one continuum, subsequent research expanded Kinsey's scale and placed behavior and attraction on two separate dimensions (Bell & Weinberg, 1978). Research with this expanded scale found that about one-third of those studied rated themselves exclusively homosexual in behavior, but not necessarily in attraction. This gave further support to the idea that sexual orientation is more complex than behavior alone.

The move to two dimensions was an improvement in trying to capture the complexity of sexual orientation, but sexual orientation grids were still met with much criticism from sexologists. As a result, Dr. Fritz Klein developed the **Klein Sexual Orientation Grid (KSOG)**,

| Exclusively heterosexual | Predominantly heterosexual, incidental homosexual | Predominantly heterosexual, more than incidental homosexual | Equally heterosexual and homosexual | Predominantly homosexual, more than incidental heterosexual | Predominantly homosexual, incidental homosexual | Exclusively homosexual |

Figure 7.1 Kinsey Sexual Orientation Scale Alfred Kinsey's seven-point **Sexual Orientation Scale** illustrates the idea that **sexual orientation is experienced on a continuum.**

seen in Figure 7.2. This grid includes seven dimensions of sexual orientation, and it captures the idea that sexual orientation is not only on a continuum, but that a person's place on the continuum may change over time (Horowitz, Weis, & Laflin, 2001). In other words, Klein believed that sexual orientation is a dynamic, ever-changing state. Consequently, people rate themselves on the seven dimensions for the past, the present, and the ideal.

Recent scholarship reveals that women's sexual orientation is not necessarily a stable trait, but instead is quite fluid over time (Diamond, 2008). The author notes that while there may be a biological basis for sexual orientation, biology doesn't provide the "last word" on sexual attraction and experiences for women. Diamond maintains that women's sexual orientations are situation dependent; that is to say, at times a heterosexual woman may be attracted to her same-sex best friend, or a lesbian woman may wish to date a man at some point in time. So common are these experi-

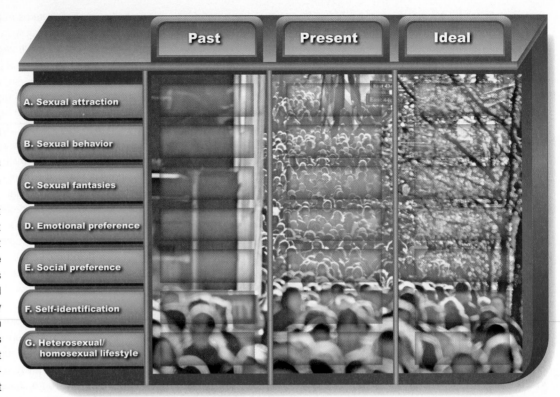

Figure 7.2 **Klein Sexual Orientation Grid** Who is **gay, straight,** or **bi?**

ences, notes the author, that it has given rise to new terminology to describe the phenomenon, such as *heteroflexibility*, *has-bian* (former lesbian), and *LUG—lesbian until graduation*.

Eli Coleman (1987) reviewed assessments of sexual orientation and proposed yet another model that included nine dimensions. The more dimensions measured the better, right? Well, not always! Sometimes, trying to measure too much can be confusing and burdensome, as proved in Coleman's research. The dimensions were so similar that it was difficult for some people to untangle the dimensions.

Assessing sexual orientation is an area of ongoing research. Although there are still unanswered questions, it seems clear that sexual orientation is not a simple either/or, but instead a matter of degree (Haslom, 1997). There is still debate regarding the best way to assess sexual orientation; most scholars do agree that sexual orientation is complex and that trying to reduce it to labels is an oversimplification.

THE U.S. POPULATION: WHAT DO THE NUMBERS SAY?

Now that you see how difficult it is to define and measure sexual orientation, you perhaps understand how difficult it is to actually know how many people in the United States identify themselves as gay, lesbian, or bisexual. Other reasons also make it difficult to establish the demographics of sexual orientation:

- Most studies rely on self-reported data—people are more likely to report having same-sex sexual experiences and attractions than they are to report that they are gay, lesbian, or bisexual.

- Studies tend to pose two different types of questions—one set of questions explores experiences and attractions, and the other examines behaviors.

- Samples are not always representative—studies rely on volunteers who agree to talk about their sex lives, and these voices may not necessarily represent the general population.

If we take all of these factors into consideration, we can see how the number of those with same-sex desires may be larger than those who act on those desires, and how this number may be larger than the class of people who actually *identify* as gay/lesbian/bisexual (Black et al., 2000).

In the 1940s, Kinsey's research indicated that between 2 and 4 percent of the population was homosexual. This number has been widely criticized, yet more recent surveys have yielded similar numbers. Analyses from the National Survey of Family Growth find that slightly over 4 percent of men and women ages 18 to 45 identify themselves as gay, lesbian, or bisexual—approximately 8.8 million Americans (Gates, 2006). This figure appears to be supported by recent polling: During the U.S. presidential election in 2008, exit polls showed self-identified gay, lesbian, and bisexual voters at 4 percent of the voting population. As our previous discussion just showed us, however, *how* homosexuality is measured plays a large role in determining how many people report that they are gay. Consequently, rather than definitive numbers, all we have are estimates when trying to answer the question "How many people are homosexual?" Modern survey results from around the world give us some insight into the global incidences and prevalence of homosexuality. These are presented in Table 7.1.

But what determines our sexual orientation? Are we just born that way, or is it a learned behavior? Do our parents influence our sexual orientation? Determining the cause of sexual orientation is just as complex as defining sexual orientation; the fact that it is a continuum rather than discrete categories points to the idea that there are multiple contributing factors.

OWN IT! What Is Your Sexual Orientation?

Sexual orientation is a personal topic, and it is likely that this chapter touches on some aspects of sexual orientation and identity that resonate with you emotionally. Understanding these reactions and exploring how you relate to your own sexual orientation and respond to that of others is important. Take the time now to assess your own sexual orientation using the Kinsey scale and the KSOG.

Take a moment to respond to the following questions:

1. Do you think that the various measures of sexual orientation accurately capture your own sexual orientation? Which

measure do you think is best for you? Do you think that you might answer differently if a researcher were asking you to complete the measurement?

2. Are there still dimensions of sexual orientation that are not captured in any of these scales?

3. What do these measures of sexual orientation contribute? Why are they important?

NATURE OR NURTURE? WHAT DETERMINES OUR SEXUAL ORIENTATION?

Why is it important to know the origins of homosexuality? Recent research reveals that to what people attribute the cause of homosexuality determines their level of support for homosexuality (Haider-Markel & Josyln, 2008). If, for example, research reveals a biological basis (such as genetics) for sexual orientation, this finding helps shape societal attitudes toward acceptance, rather than hostility.

In essence, there are two types of theories that seek to describe the origins of homosexuality. **Essentialist** theories maintain that homosexuality is an inborn, innate trait, likely due to biological or developmental processes. **Constructionist** theories suggest that homosexuality develops over time, most likely due to social forces. Let's begin by first looking at essentialist theories, the biological theories of homosexuality.

BIOLOGICAL THEORIES: IS SEXUAL ORIENTATION INBORN?

Biological theorists—*essentialists*—suggest that sexual orientation is the result of physiological influences. These influences can be differences in the brain, or due to genetics, hormones, and unique physical traits.

In 1991, Simon LeVay conducted the very first study of homosexual biological uniqueness when he compared the brain's hypothalamus of gay men to that of straight men and women (France, 2007). The hypothalamus is a small region at the base of the brain that is responsible for a variety of our more primal urges (such as hunger and thirst), including our sex drives. Specifically, LeVay looked at a particular part of the hypothalamus called the INAH 3. LeVay's research discovered that this part of the hypothalamus was more than twice the size in straight men as it was in homosexual men (LeVay, 1991). Further, the INAH 3 in homosexual men was the same size as in heterosexual women. Based on LeVay's findings, the media were quick to promote the idea that he discovered a biological cause for homosexuality: a "gay brain" or a "gay center" in the brain.

LeVay's research has come under fire by the scientific community due to many research methodology concerns (Lancaster, 2003). He was particularly criticized because he only studied 41 cadavers (19 of which were *presumed* to be gay), which he chose because all of the subjects had died due to complications of AIDS. Critics claim that medical treatments for AIDS can change the tissues in the brain and alter the size of the hypothalamus (Lancaster, 2003). LeVay himself noted when he first presented his findings, with caution, that this was a possibility.

Examining the brains of both HIV-positive and HIV-negative individuals, William Byne and his colleagues (2001) found similar differences in the INAH 3, though not as large. The difference in the size

TABLE 7.1
Global Demographics of Sexual Orientation

Sources: Canadian Community Health Survey (2003); Melbye & Biggar (1992); ACSF (1992); Durex Global Sex Survey (2003); The Observer (2005).

Country	Self-Identified As Gay or Lesbian	Reporting Same-Sex Attraction or Sexual Experiences
Australia	2.0–3.0%	20.0%
Canada	1.0%	—
Denmark	—	2.7%
France	—	4.1% men 12.6% women
Norway	—	12.0%
United Kingdom	6.0%	6.1% men

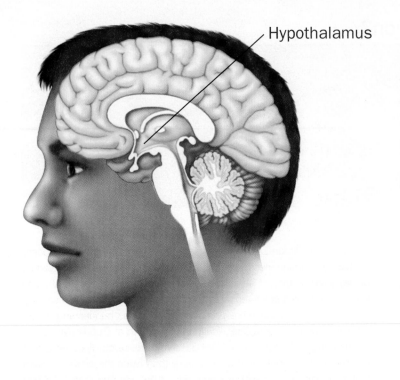

Hypothalamus

<<< The hypothalamus is responsible **for a variety of primal urges,** including our sex drives.

Thus, the higher rate of homosexuality observed in identical twins suggests that other factors outside the environment likely affect sexual orientation.

Still other researchers suggest that since biological siblings share the same mother—and hence, at one time shared the same womb—hormonal influences on sexual orientation may be the result of birth order.

BIRTH ORDER

Birth order has been championed as a strong influence on a number of personality traits, as well as sexual orientation. The **fraternal birth order hypothesis** suggests that some women may develop antibodies each time they carry a male fetus, which immunizes them against male antigens, and the placenta cells that remain in the uterine lining influence subsequent pregnancies. As these male antibodies increase in the pregnant woman's bloodstream with each subsequent male fetus, they may affect the brain of the fetus and cause it to differentiate as more female, although its biological sex is male (Blanchard & Lippa, 2008; Ridley, 2003). This research tries to biologically explain why gay men have more older brothers than older sisters, as other research has shown (Blanchard, 2004; Bogaert, 2006; Bogaert, Blanchard, & Crosthwait, 2007; Camperio-Ciani et al., 2004; Ridley, 2003; Cantor et al., 2002). In short, these multiple research studies show that the more older brothers a man has, the more likely it is he will be gay. To date, homosexuality and birth order are only linked to males—similar findings have not been seen in female birth order and lesbians (Blanchard, 2004).

For a gay man, having an older brother may be significant only if a man is right-handed (Bogaert, Blanchard, & Crosthwait, 2007). This ties the birth order theory to a *physiological* theory, which recognizes that neural characteristics that develop early may correlate to other characteristics an individual has, such as homosexuality.

could be due to how they were measured. In addition, Byne replicated LeVay's study with rams; these rams consistently showed exclusive sexual preference for other rams when they were given a choice between rams and ewes (Roselli et al., 2004). Of course, rams are not humans, but these results add to a growing body of research that suggests that there is a biological explanation for sexual orientation across species, including humans.

GENETICS

Another essentialist theory, the *genetic theory* of homosexuality, suggests that sexual orientation is largely in our genes and that we are born gay or straight. For decades, scientists have studied twins to determine whether genetics causes differences in such things as personality, obesity, and academic abilities (Boyd & Bee, 2009). In 1952, Franz Kallman initiated twin studies looking at genetics as an explanation of homosexuality; researchers have been building upon these foundations ever since.

Because twins share genetic material, they provide us insight into the genetic origins of homosexuality. The result of one egg and one sperm, *identical* twins share 100 percent of genetic material; *fraternal* twins share about 50 percent (because they come from two eggs and two sperm). If the expression of homosexuality in identical twins is significantly more frequent than in fraternal twins, the comparisons can reveal a potential presence of a homosexual gene.

Bailey and Pillard's research (1993) demonstrated that among gays and lesbians, slightly over one-half of identical male twins were both gay, compared to about one-fourth of fraternal male twins. In a study of females, 48 percent of identical female twins were both lesbians, compared to 16 percent of fraternal female twins (Bailey et al., 1993). These studies show us that the more similar siblings are in genetic makeup, the more likely they are to have similar sexual orientations. Of course, we also have to consider that often twins—particularly identical twins—tend to be emotionally closer than other siblings, so it is likely that they share similar experiences (Boyd & Bee, 2009). Given this, it's difficult to determine how much of the similarity (concordance) in sexual orientation is due to genetics, or to environmental influences, such as parenting. However, if parenting were a notable influence, we would expect to see the same rates of concordance in sexual orientation in both identical and fraternal twins.

∧
∧ **Studies on identical twins** can help
∧ provide information about the role genetics may play **in determining someone's sexual orientation.**

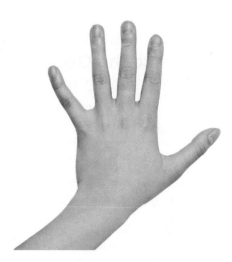

^^^ Which one will be gay?

>>> Studies show that lesbian women more commonly display a male pattern, **where the ring finger is longer than the index finger.**

PHYSIOLOGY

A number of studies have attempted to show that differences in physiological traits (such as facial hair and handedness) may point to sexual orientation. For example, about one-fourth of gay men have a counter-clockwise hair pattern; in the general population it is 8 percent (Lippa, 2003). A significant amount of research on finger-length patterns demonstrates that lesbian women more commonly display a male pattern where the ring finger is longer than the index finger, and gay men more commonly display a female pattern, in which either the index finger is longer or the fingers are the same size (Hall & Schaeff, 2008; McFadden et al., 2005). Also, gay men, similar to straight women, have increased density of finger print

ridges on the thumb and the pinkie of left hand (Hall & Kimura, 1994). Although this finding is less well established, taken together with other research that has shown physiological differences, we begin to see a trend that clearly indicates to some researchers that there are certain physiological traits related to sexual orientation.

Although biological (nature) theories offer promise in helping to determine the origins of sexual orientation, the exact nature as to how or why these differences exist is still unclear. So, while there is a growing body of work that supports a biological theory of sexual orientation as the primary influence, it is also important to look at how a person's environment (nurture) may interact with his or her biology to influence variations in sexual orientation. Let's turn our attention to development theories.

DEVELOPMENTAL THEORIES: DOES UPBRINGING MAKE A DIFFERENCE?

Rather than view biological forces as the origin of homosexuality, developmental theories are constructionist and suggest that how a person is raised, in combination with other social forces, shapes sexual orientation. Many people often wonder: Is homosexuality a learned behavior?

Behaviorist theories would suggest that sexual orientation is a *learned behavior* brought about over time due to the rewarding of some behaviors, and the punishing of others. These theories are *constructionist* theories, because they maintain that sexual orientation is a product of a person's environment. Therefore, it is not inborn; it is constructed.

According to behaviorism, *conditioning*, or reinforcement, plays a key role in the development of emotional responses to stimuli. *Positive reinforcements* make it likely that the behavior will be repeated, while *punishment reinforcements* elicit responses that bring painful or undesirable consequences (though this doesn't necessarily stop the behavior). *Extinction* means that the responses are not reinforced in any way, so they are not likely to be repeated.

For example, homosexuality is more likely to result if homosexual behaviors (attraction to a person of the same sex) are reinforced by the environment (e.g., through parents, the media, school, peers, and past/present relationships). On the other hand, it is less likely that homosexuality will result if there are negative or punishing reinforcements in the environment (e.g., through a church, mosque, or temple).

Many researchers have undertaken studies to determine whether sexual orientation is a learned behavior in Western cultures (Storms, 1980, 1981; Van Wyk & Geist, 1984). As you saw in Chapter 6, most children have same-sex friends and typically don't have mixed-sex peer groups until they reach adolescence. Storms (1981) hypothesized that those who mature early (prior to the age of 12) tend to have same-sex friend environments and thus identify with and sexually experiment with same-sex peers;

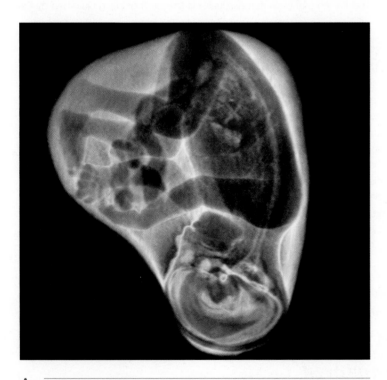

^^^ The **neurohormonal theory** suggests that being exposed to increased levels of opposite-sex hormones while in the womb **directs the brain to develop as if the fetus were the opposite sex.**

>>> According to Freud, **all boys experience the Oedipus complex,** a psychosexual stage in which they view their fathers as competition for the love of their mothers.

he believed that in early maturing males, emerging erotic feelings would likely be focused on other males. This supposition is referred to as **peer group interaction** influences. Other studies have not supported Storms' findings. For instance, in one study, the researchers looked at a preliterate New Guinea tribe, the Sambia, who encourage preadolescent homosexual activity (Stoller & Herdt, 1985). They discovered that most of the young men, regardless of the early homosexual encouragement, developed heterosexual orientations (Stoller & Herdt, 1985).

Some research suggests that modeling experiences in childhood or adolescence (such as, being masturbated by a same- or opposite-sex partner) predict partner preference and sexual orientation in adulthood (Van Wyk & Geist, 1984). This research asserts that, based on early sexual experiences, a person forms expectations. If the experience was pleasurable and sexually rewarding, the behavior is reinforced and cognitively encoded; the same cognitive imprinting holds true if it was a negative experience. According to this line of thinking, early, positive same-sex experiences hold predictive power for later same-sex sexual orientation; early, negative experiences with the opposite sex (such as, a young girl who is sexually molested by a man) are powerful predictors for later same-sex attraction, because these individuals avoid the painful memories (Van Wyk & Geist, 1984).

FREUD'S PSYCHOANALYTIC VIEW: SEXUAL ENERGY EXPLAINS IT

Sigmund Freud's theory asserted that children are sexual creatures born with *psychic energy*. According to Freud, to understand childhood development—and sexuality—we need to "follow the energy." As babies develop into children, then adolescents, then young adults, Freud believed the psychic energy is directed to first one area of the body, then another, and then another.

Freud believed all human beings are innately bisexual, and that they become heterosexual or homosexual as a result of their experiences with their parents (Freud, 1905). He believed that all boys and girls experience an **Oedipus complex**, a psychosexual stage in which they regard their fathers as someone who is competing with them for the love of their mothers. Freud maintained that male homosexuality is the result of being disturbed by the

Healthy Selves / Healthy Sex

Reparative Therapy

As we have moved away from a disease paradigm of homosexuality that was rooted in psychoanalytic theories, we have stopped trying to "cure" people of homosexuality and instead we now focus more on adjustment that centers on the social stigma of being gay or lesbian. Recently the American Psychological Association (APA) adopted a resolution stating that "mental health professionals should avoid telling clients that they can change their sexual orientation through therapy or other treatments" (APA, 2009). This conclusion was based on the findings on a special task force that conducted a rigorous review of the scientific literature on the subject.

Their report was in response to a growing movement of those who claim that they can change one's sexual orientation using reparative therapy. Reparative therapy, also called conversion, ex-gay, or reorientation therapies, is a form of orthodox therapy used to try to eradicate a homosexual person's desire for an intimate same-sex relationship. In the United States, the majority of reparative therapy programs are religious ministries and not clinical practices that can be held accountable by professional associations, licensing boards, or state departments of health (Cianciotto & Cahill, 2006).

Most claims of successful reorientation have been published on reparative therapy programs' Web sites or in the mass media and they are most often self-published (i.e., no peer review). Here are a few questions to ask yourself when you see claims of successful reorientation:

- For those who did change, how do we know that they would not have changed their sexual orientation without some form of therapy?

- What about the many people who have been harmed by reparative therapies?

- Why is it important for gay men and lesbians to become heterosexual in the first place? Does the real problem lie in their sexual orientations or in society's hostility toward people who are homosexual or bisexual?

Even if these studies did not suffer from a multitude of methodological flaws, their claims at changing people's sexual orientation are still misleading. It is important to view these results with a critical eye.

Sources: APA Task Force on Appropriate Therapeutic Responses to Sexual Orientation. (2009). Report of the Task Force on Appropriate Therapeutic Responses to Sexual Orientation. Washington, DC: American Psychological Association.
Cianciotto, J., & Cahill, S. (2006). Youth in the crosshairs: The third wave of ex-gay activism. New York: National Gay and Lesbian Task Force Policy Institute.

sight of female genitalia due to *castration anxiety*; the homosexual female is similarly threatened by the sight of male genitalia (Mills, 1990). A female, Freud thought, vies for the erotic attention of her father. She becomes angry and feels inferior when she discovers she does not have a penis, which Freud referred to as **penis envy**. She experiences intense disappointment with her father (her love object), and subsequently rejects him—and all men—and substitutes women for her love objects (Mills, 1990). Freud thus believed that all homosexuality was the result of unresolved Oedipus conflicts in childhood. Nevertheless, Freud agreed with others (as Havelock Ellis's views were discussed in Chapter 2) that a homosexual orientation shouldn't be viewed as a form of pathology or an abnormal behavior.

Although people have engaged in homosexual behaviors for centuries, **our current definition of homosexuality came into** existence sometime in the 19th century.

∨ ∨ ∨
∨ ∨

EVELYN HOOKER: HOMOSEXUALITY IS NOT A MENTAL ILLNESS

In 1973, the American Psychological Association (APA) declassified homosexuality as a mental health illness (APA, 2009). This was due in part to the work of Evelyn Hooker, who studied gays and lesbians who were functioning "normally" in society (they were not psychiatric patients). Up until this point, many of the prevailing theories about homosexuality were based on the observations of therapists and psychiatrists who relied on their observations of their clients who were homosexual. In other words, they had no experiences or interactions with gays or lesbians who were not under the care of a psychiatrist.

Hooker administered several psychological tests to heterosexual and homosexual males. She then had two independent experts, unaware of each subject's sexual orientations, evaluate the men's responses. When asked to classify the men as either homosexual or heterosexual based on their results from the tests, the two experts were unable to distinguish between the two groups. Hooker concluded that homosexuality is not inherently associated with psychopathology.

Hooker's work is important, because it marked the beginning of the end of psychoanalysis, behaviorism, and other development theories as the primary theories of sexual orientation. To some extent, psychoanalytic and behaviorist theories are still discussed today and some people still try to "treat" homosexuality with aversion therapy and even shock treatment, but this is not the position of most mainstream family life educators, sociologists, psychologists, therapists, or clinicians.

SOCIOLOGICAL THEORIES: IS HOMOSEXUALITY THE RESULT OF SOCIAL FORCES?

Most early sexuality research was based on Freud's concepts (Hogben & Dyrne, 1998). In the 1950s, however, early sociological theories began to suggest that instead of having a psychodynamic drive to have sex, we learn our culture's way of thinking about sexuality, and then we model and enact it (Rotter, 1954). **Sociological** theories emphasize the idea that sexual orientation is constructed based on society's expectations—it is a product of a given culture at a given time. For example, although people have engaged in homosexual behaviors for

centuries, homosexuality as we know it today (enduring emotional, romantic, and sexual attraction to someone; community membership) did not come into existence until sometime during the 19th century (Kirkpatrick, 2000). In other words, today homosexuality defines a person's *identity*, rather than just an activity in which they engage.

Queer theory, which emerged in 1991, gives attention to the social construction of "normal" and "deviant" forms of behavior, particularly sexual activities and identities (Green, 2007). This theory suggests that all sexualities are constructs created by certain social forces and institutions, such as science (biology), religion, and politics. As a result, given the ever-changing nature of our society, the construct of sexuality and sexual orientation is fluid and also subject to change. For example, though gaining increasing acceptance today in the United States, the concept of legal marriages for gays and lesbians was virtually nonexistent just 30 years ago. Almost always, these social constructs of sexuality fall into either/or categories—homosexual or heterosexual; male or female; normal or abnormal; moral or immoral (Foucault, 1976, 1984, 1992).

As we conclude our discussion about the theoretical explanations of sexual orientation, we must keep in mind that given the complexities of sexual orientation, no one theory can provide *the* answer; rather, it is more likely that an interaction of two (or more) theories are at play. Multiple contexts interact to shape a person's sexual orientation.

Similar to gender, there are a number of ways that social and interpersonal factors influence sexual orientation, which are shown in Figure 7.3. As the figure shows us, our sexual orientation

Figure 7.3 Bronfenbrenner's Ecological Model Sexual orientation can be influenced by multiple facets in our environments.

is influenced by the multiple contexts of society that surround us, from our home, school, and peers, to broader social forces such as the media, religious institutions, educational programs, and government policies. Without question, our sexual orientation does not develop in isolation!

Although variances in sexual orientation are becoming more accepted in certain Western cultures and in certain areas of the United States (see Figure 7.4), that is not to say that homosexuals, bisexuals, and transgenderists don't confront prejudice from society. In the section that follows, we'll examine the experiences of gays and lesbians throughout the life cycle.

HOMOSEXUAL EXPERIENCES THROUGHOUT THE LIFE CYCLE

Our society is heterosexual in nature. **Heterosexism** is discrimination or prejudice against lesbians, gays, bisexuals, and transgenders by heterosexual people. Heterosexism is similar to other "isms," such as racism and ageism, in that it is a belief system that denigrates and stigmatizes. Think about the following examples of heterosexism in our culture and other cultures around the world: Gays and lesbians cannot

Figure 7.4   Lesbian, Gay, Bisexual, and Transgender-Related Laws by Country

LGBT rights in country	Homosexual acts legal?	Same-sex marriage	Same-sex adoption	Allow gays to openly serve in military?	Anti-discrimination laws for homosexuality?
Egypt 	Public morals laws used against LGBT people; prison up to three years	No	No	No	No
Central African Republic	Yes	No	--	--	Unknown
South Africa	Yes (since 1994)	Yes (since 2006)	Yes (since 2002)	Yes	Yes
Canada	Yes	Yes (since 2005)	Yes	Yes	Yes
Mexico	Yes	No	Only single gays may adopt, not gay couples	No	Yes, but vague
USA	Yes	Yes, in only a few states	Varies by state	No, adopts "don't ask, don't tell" policy	Yes, but only 20 states have such legislation
Brazil 	Yes	No	Yes	No	No
Colombia	Yes	No	Only single gays may adopt, not gay couples	Yes	Yes
Iraq	Yes (since 2003)	Unknown	Unknown	Unknown	Unknown
Israel	Yes	Yes	Yes	Yes	Yes
Saudi Arabia	No (punishable by prison or by death)	No	No	No	No
India	Yes (since 2009)	No	No	Only in Delhi	Unknown
China 	Yes (since 1997)	No	No	No	No

be open about their sexuality if they serve in the military; many gays and lesbians are discriminated against in the workplace, such as not being granted benefits for their same-sex partners; the media (magazines, TV, movies) generally feature heterosexual relationships and exclude homosexual relationships. Can you think of other examples? This heterosexism in society is paramount in affecting the lives of gays, lesbians, and bisexual throughout their life spans and affects the timing of coming out.

It's important to remember that we can't generalize growing up and coming out to all gays; everyone has his or her own unique experiences over the course of his or her life. Yet, research does point to some pat-terns in gay experiences and, certainly, gays and lesbians face unique challenges. The following sections examine the life courses of gays and lesbians: identity development, coming out, and confronting the stigma that comes with being gay in our society.

GROWING UP GAY, LESBIAN, OR BISEXUAL

When asked to reflect on their childhood, many gays and lesbians report engaging in a variety of types of play that often crossed traditional gender lines, which is referred to as **gender bending**. Research shows that there

LGBT rights in country	Homosexual acts legal?	Same-sex marriage	Same-sex adoption	Allow gays to openly serve in military?	Anti-discrimination laws for homosexuality?
Japan	Yes	No	Unknown	Yes	Yes
Denmark	Yes	No	Yes	Yes	Yes
Ireland	Yes	No	Only single gays may adopt, not gay couples	Yes	Yes
Sweden	Yes	Yes	Yes	Yes	Yes
United Kingdom	Yes	No	Yes	Yes	Yes
Belgium	Yes	Yes	Yes	Yes	Yes
France	Yes	No	Only single gays may adopt, not gay couples	Yes	Yes
Netherlands	Yes	Yes	Yes	Yes	Yes
Austria	Yes	No	No	Yes	Yes
Germany	Yes	No	Single gays may adopt or a partner may adopt the other partner's children	Yes	Yes
Switzerland	Yes	No	Only single gays may adopt, not gay couples	Yes	Yes
Italy	Yes	No	No	Yes	Yes
Portugal	Yes	Yes	Yes	Yes	Yes
Spain	Yes	Yes	Yes	Yes	Yes
Australia	Yes	No	Yes	Yes	Yes

<<< Gender bending refers to **types of play** that cross traditional gender lines.

is a strong relationship between gender role nonconformity and homosexuality (Rieger et al., 2008). In other words, as children, gay men and lesbians often do not adhere to strict gender roles. On average, gay men tend to be somewhat more feminine, and lesbians somewhat more masculine, compared with heterosexual people of their own sex (Lippa, 2005). This gender role nonconformity is linked to homosexuality and lends support for a biological cause of homosexuality. However, there is not a *causal* link here: There is no evidence to suggest that cross-gender play (such as boys playing with dolls, girls playing with trucks) causes someone to be gay. Yet, this nontraditional play may result in teasing and feelings of alienation while growing up. These feelings of difference and not fitting in generally don't go away, but rather are amplified throughout the middle childhood and teenage years.

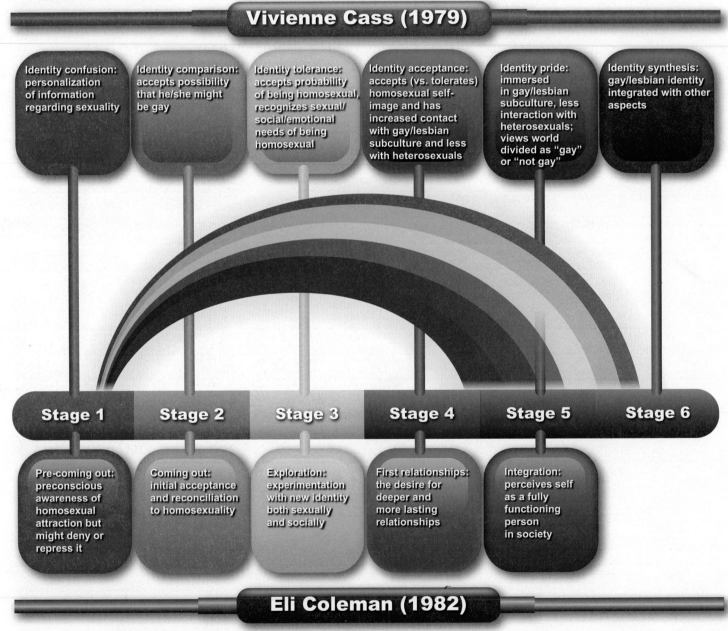

Vivienne Cass (1979)

Identity confusion: personalization of information regarding sexuality

Identity comparison: accepts possibility that he/she might be gay

Identity tolerance: accepts probability of being homosexual, recognizes sexual/social/emotional needs of being homosexual

Identity acceptance: accepts (vs. tolerates) homosexual self-image and has increased contact with gay/lesbian subculture and less with heterosexuals

Identity pride: immersed in gay/lesbian subculture, less interaction with heterosexuals; views world divided as "gay" or "not gay"

Identity synthesis: gay/lesbian identity integrated with other aspects

Stage 1   Stage 2   Stage 3   Stage 4   Stage 5   Stage 6

Pre-coming out: preconscious awareness of homosexual attraction but might deny or repress it

Coming out: initial acceptance and reconciliation to homosexuality

Exploration: experimentation with new identity both sexually and socially

First relationships: the desire for deeper and more lasting relationships

Integration: perceives self as a fully functioning person in society

Eli Coleman (1982)

Figure 7.5 Models of Identity Development Both models of identity development end in integration between one's identity and one's environment.

COMING OUT

The term **coming out** (of the gay closet) refers to the lifelong process of the development of a positive gay identity.

Several models of coming out and sexual identity development have been constructed. Vivienne Cass's model (1979) is still widely used today and includes six stages: *identity confusion*, *identity comparison*, *identity tolerance*, *identity acceptance*, *identity pride*, and *identity synthesis*. Eli Coleman (1982) offered a similar model with five stages: *pre-coming out*, *coming out*, *exploration*, *first relationships*, and *integration*. These models are presented in Figure 7.5. The important thing to note is that coming out is not a one-time event, such as telling parents or peers; instead, it's a process that unfolds over time, and it runs along a continuum. And in the final stage of each model, integration concludes the process. (As you're beginning to see, when it comes to sex and sexuality, everything is on a continuum!)

Although slightly different, each model promotes similar ideas about sexual identity formation and the corresponding coming out that occurs with this identity formation. As with anything, it's important to remember that sexual identity development is an individual process, and everyone (gay or straight) goes through this process in his or her own way and on his or her own timetable. As Figure 7.6 shows us, coming out involves three basic experiences: 1) opening up to oneself about the possibility of being gay (this can be thought of as coming out to oneself); 2) coming out to others; and 3) living openly as a gay, lesbian, bisexual, or transgender.

You may ask, "What is the fear of coming out?" Although there is individual variance, possible fears may include (Human Rights Campaign, 2006):

- Rejection; change in relationships
- Harassment; abuse
- Being disowned by the family
- Being thrown out of one's house
- Loss of place in religious community
- Loss of financial support
- Loss of job
- Physical violence
- Feelings of vulnerability

Given some of the fears and the reality of the consequences of coming out for many people, why might gay, lesbian, and bisexual people want to come out at all? Many want to end the hiding game and stop wasting the energy that it takes to hide a major part of their personality (Coleman, 1982). Coming out allows gays, lesbians, and bisexuals to feel whole around other people, to feel closer to those to whom they come out, to have integrity, and to make a statement that "Gay is OK" (Human Rights Campaign, 2006). A recent study of over 2,000 gay men, for example, found that younger gays recognized their attraction to other men, told others they were gay, and took part in the gay community at earlier ages than in the past (Drasin et al., 2008). These findings support the idea that the coming out process is beginning at earlier ages because of greater social acceptance of homosexuality. Although there is a growing number of organizations within high schools and colleges that support gay youth (See Table 7.2 on page 140), particularly within urban areas, there is still a need for more support systems for gay and lesbian youth (Drasin et al., 2008).

What other support mechanisms are in place to support young people during the coming out process? More and more young people use the Internet as a source of information and support, particularly during the early stages of coming out (Bond, Hefner, & Drogos, 2009). But although using the Internet can alleviate feelings of isolation, it might replace face-to-face communication and support. Bradley Bond and colleagues (2009) found that people who relied heavily on the Internet communicated less with their families regarding the coming out process.

Opening up to oneself about the possibility of being gay.

Coming out to others.

Living openly as gay, lesbian, bisexual, or transgender.

Figure 7.6 The Coming Out Process Coming out involves three **basic experiences**.

Coming Out Together as a Couple

John and Wyatt have been together as a couple for 10 years and for five of those, they have been "married." That is, they had a ceremony in which they committed themselves to each other because the state in which they live does not allow same-sex marriages. John came out to his family while he was still in high school, so they know all about John and Wyatt's relationship. Wyatt has not come out to his family—they think that John and Wyatt are just roommates and friends. John is starting to find it difficult not being able to be open about his relationship with Wyatt's family—he feels like Wyatt is ashamed of what he is and their relationship.

His side: You really think that they are clueless, that they don't have any idea that you are gay and that you and I are a couple? What are you afraid of? Do you think that they won't love you anymore, or that they won't want us to visit or come around on the holidays? I have known your family for as long as we have been together and love them as if they were my own. I feel guilty for lying to them, and I know how stressed you get every time we see them because you are afraid we are

going to be "outed." Maybe we could start by just telling your parents and your sister and see how they respond.

His side: Maybe they do already know or at least suspect that I am gay and that we are a couple, but what if they don't or they are simply in denial because they can't deal with the idea that their son might be gay? Even if they are OK with it, I am afraid that they will be hurt because I have kept this from them for so long. Maybe they would even hold it against you. You know how much I care about you, but you also know how much I have struggled with my sexual orientation. Can't we just keep things the way they are?

Your side: What would you do if you were in this same situation? What if you were good friends with a same-sex couple who was going through something similar—how would you advise them?

1. Do you think John is right that Wyatt's family probably knows already?

2. Can you think of a similar situation that a heterosexual couple would have to deal with?

3. Have you ever had a "big" secret you kept from your family?

THE EFFECTS OF STIGMA

As the opening vignette illustrated, being gay in a heterosexual world can cause a lot of inner turmoil for some. Although being gay does not cause someone to commit suicide or to use drugs or alcohol to excess, suicide and substance abuse rates are higher among gay, lesbian, and bisexual

youth than among straight youth. The *stigma*—the shame and disgrace attached to something regarded as socially unacceptable—of being gay and sexual prejudice often causes suicidal and other self-defeating behaviors in non-heterosexual youth and young adults.

There are many factors that seem to affect suicidal thoughts and substance use and abuse among gays and lesbians, such as levels of

TABLE 7.2
Lesbian, Gay, Bisexual, and Transgender Organizations

- National Gay and Lesbian Task Force (NGLTF)
  "NGLTF is the national progressive organization working for the civil rights of gay, lesbian, bisexual, and transgendered people, with the vision and commitment to building a powerful political movement."

- Human Rights Campaign (HRC)
  "HRC is a bipartisan organization that works to advance equality based on sexual orientation and gender expression and identity, to ensure that gay, lesbian, bisexual, and transgender Americans can be open, honest, and safe at home, at work, and in the community."

- Parents, Families, and Friends of Lesbians and Gays (PFLAG)
  "PFLAG promotes the health and well-being of gay, lesbian, bisexual, and transgendered persons, their families and friends through: support, to cope with an adverse society; education, to enlighten an ill-informed public; and advocacy, to end discrimination and to secure equal civil rights." PFLAG "provides opportunity for dialogue about sexual orientation and gender identity, and acts to create a society that is healthy and respectful of human diversity."

- Gay and Lesbian Alliance Against Defamation (GLAAD)
  "The GLAAD is dedicated to promoting and ensuring fair, accurate and inclusive representation of people and events in the media as a means of eliminating homophobia and discrimination based on gender identity and sexual orientation."

- Gay, Lesbian, and Straight Education Network (GLSEN)
  "The GLSEN strives to assure that each member of every school community is valued and respected regardless of sexual orientation or gender identity/expression."

- Web Active
  "WebActive is a site designed to offer progressive activists an up-to-date resource on the World Wide Web to find other organizations and individuals with similar values and interests. WebActive is a project of RealNetworks, Inc."

- Gay Vote
  Links to sites that that "offer ways for LGTB voters to get involved."

^
^ A hostile environment toward gay youth **may lead to suicidal behaviors.**
^

support. For example, one researcher found that being out around people in a support network resulted in lower distress regarding sexual identity (Wright & Perry, 2006). However, gay, lesbian, and bisexual youth do report higher rates of substance use compared with straight youth. In an analysis of 18 published studies, Michael Marshal and colleagues (2008) found that the odds for substance use among gay, lesbian, and bisexual youth may be as much as 190 percent higher than for straight youth.

The data are not so clear when it comes to suicide. Stephen Halpert (2002) reviewed more than 100 studies of gay youth and suicide. He determined that gay male youth are at increased risk for suicidal thoughts and suicide attempts and may actually engage in more suicidal behaviors. It is not clear, however, whether gay male youth actually complete suicide more often than straight youth. Another body of research that explored suicide attempts among sexual-minority male youth found that there are certain factors that increased risk of suicide attempts: an early age of first male sex, a large number of male partners, and permissive attitudes regarding unsafe sex (Savin-Williams & Ream, 2003). It appears that if young people are out and are comfortable with their sexual identity, they are not more likely than straight youth to engage in suicidal thoughts and behaviors (Savin-Williams, 2005).

There is as much diversity among gay, lesbian, and bisexual youth as there is among heterosexual youth. We can't assume that just because someone is gay that they are going to engage in self-defeating behaviors—there is nothing inherent in being gay that increases suicide or drug and alcohol abuse. Rather, the factors associated with a hostile environment can lead to these behaviors in some (not all) gay, lesbian, and bisexual youth.

Contrary to persistent myths, research shows that gay and lesbian individuals can form strong intimate partnerships and have high-quality, functional relationships (Peplau & Fingerhut, 2007). Although there are many unique challenges, in many regards, gay and lesbian relationships do not differ significantly from homosexuals in formation, satisfaction, or sexuality. The following sections explore aspects of homosexual relationships.

REAL LIFE, REAL ISSUES: PARTNERING, FALLING IN LOVE, AND SEXUALITY

Regardless of our sexual orientation, dating and forming relationships are important developmental tasks, because these relationships pave the way for long-term, committed partnerships.

<<< Many gay couples experience **long-term committed relationships.**

Although adolescence can be a stressful experience for everyone, there are additional stressors and barriers for gay and lesbian youth. Along with feelings of insecurity in their own sexual identity, barriers may include lack of support for same-sex relationships, fear of harassment from friends, and difficulty in finding a same-sex partner (Savin-Williams, 2005). These barriers can impair self-esteem and contribute to feelings of isolation and loneliness.

A review of a number of research studies into homosexual attraction and mate selection experiences found that gay men and lesbians tend to value the same things in a partner as heterosexuals, such as shared interests and similar religious beliefs (Peplau & Fingerhut, 2007). Additionally, gay men and lesbians meet potential partners in the same way heterosexuals do—at work, in bars, or at social events. (In Chapter 8, we'll examine at length same-sex attraction and dating scripts). One difference in relationship formation is that gays and lesbians are more likely to start the relationship as friends; if they break up, they are more likely to remain friends. However, the boundary between friendship and romantic partner sometimes poses a problem, because it is difficult to know if someone is a friend or a potential romantic partner (Peplau & Fingerhut, 2007).

Regardless of how relationships form, many gay couples experience long-term committed partnerships (Peplau & Fingerhut, 2007). It is natural that these couples want to legally recognize this relationship. It has only been in recent years that the idea of legal marriage has become a reality for some same-sex couples. We explore same-sex marriage and civil commitments at length in Chapter 10, but in the section that follows we briefly examine gay and lesbian marital satisfaction.

SAME-SEX MARRIAGE AND COMMITTED PARTNERSHIPS: MARITAL SATISFACTION AND HAPPINESS

Research has long shown that people who are married tend to be happier and healthier. Investigators recently tested this idea with heterosexual and homosexual couples in a variety of relationship situations (Wienke & Hill, 2009). Overall, people who are in romantic relationships, regardless of sexual orientation, are happier than those who are single. In particular, partnered homosexuals are happier and healthier than singles (either gay or straight). However, heterosexual married couples still report the highest levels of marital happiness.

In a similar study that compared gay men, lesbians, straight men, and straight women, all in committed relationships, all held similarly positive views of their relationship (Roisman et al., 2008). Overall, the researchers found no differences between gay couples and straight couples in terms of relationship quality and interactions with each other (except that lesbians had the most positive interaction patterns). The research findings of these two studies emphasize the importance of *relationship status* (partnered vs. single), more so than sexual orientation, in determining happiness. Chapter 10 provides an in-depth description of the sexual satisfaction of married gay and lesbian couples, and in Chapter 16, we'll take a look at the experiences of older gays and lesbians.

GAY AND LESBIAN PARENTING

Although the number of planned families by gay men and lesbian women has been steadily growing in recent years, little research has been undertaken to understand the motivations of gays and lesbians to become parents (Bos, van Balen, & van den Boom, 2004). Although the existing research concerning the perceived value of children and the appeal of parenthood certainly applies to homosexual parents as well to heterosexual parents, some have tried to determine whether gays and lesbians have additional, different motivations to become parents (Benkov, 1994; Flaks et al., 1995).

The emergence of planned gay fatherhood and lesbian motherhood is indicative of broad social change that is taking place in our society and societies around the world. Regardless of their sexual orientation, people are questioning existing parenting norms and are finding ways to create families (Berkowitz & Marsiglio, 2007). Examining the experiences of gay men and lesbians gives us an important opportunity to accept them as part of the parenting mainstream.

Despite the increasing numbers of parenting gays and lesbians, research demonstrates that some heterosexual adults hold negative attitudes toward them as parents. For instance, some people are concerned that gay male parents are more likely to sexually abuse their children than straight parents are. Research shows, however, that gay men are no more likely to do so than heterosexual men

Only recently has legal marriage become a possibility for same-sex couples **like Ellen DeGeneres and Portia de Rossi.**

are, and that girls are at far greater risk to be abused by their heterosexual fathers than their gay fathers (Jenny, Roesler, & Poyer, 1994). Gay and lesbian parents are also more likely to be well educated and affluent, in comparison to heterosexual parents (Patterson, 1996). Other benefits have been documented for children of lesbian parents: They learn respect, empathy, and acceptance of diversity and are more assertive in challenging traditional gender roles in their relationships (Allen, 1997; Savin-Williams & Esterberg, 2000). More recent research indicated that there are few differences between adolescents living with same-sex parents and those living with heterosexual parents (Wainwright & Patterson, 2006).

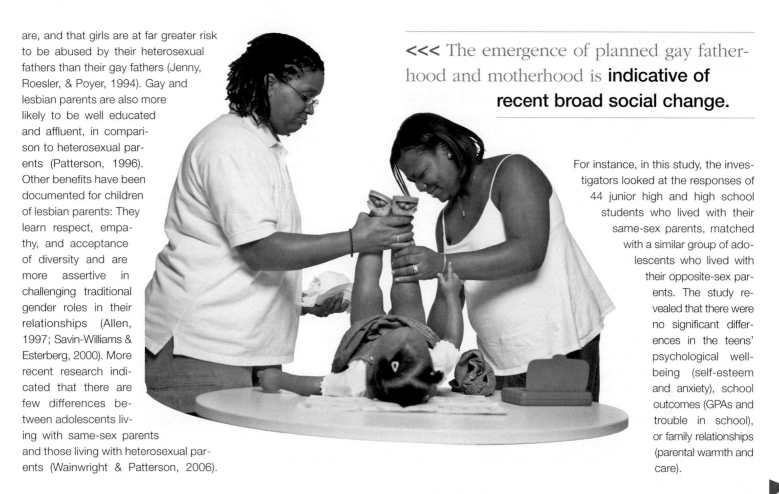

<<< The emergence of planned gay fatherhood and motherhood is **indicative of recent broad social change.**

For instance, in this study, the investigators looked at the responses of 44 junior high and high school students who lived with their same-sex parents, matched with a similar group of adolescents who lived with their opposite-sex parents. The study revealed that there were no significant differences in the teens' psychological well-being (self-esteem and anxiety), school outcomes (GPAs and trouble in school), or family relationships (parental warmth and care).

sex talk

Whether you are gay or straight, it is helpful to explore your attitudes and feelings toward homosexuality and to share those feelings and attitudes with your partner. This could also be helpful as you talk to your children about sexual orientation.

I was _____ years old when I first became aware of my sexual orientation.

I have had _____ same-sex/opposite sex sexual experiences.

Your same-sex/opposite sexual experiences make me feel _____.

I score _____ on Kinsey's continuum of sexual orientation.

I would define my sexual orientation as _____.

I feel _____ about my sexual orientation.

According to my beliefs and the research that I have read, _____ contributes the most in determining homosexuality.

My level of sexual prejudice is _____ because _____.

I feel _____ toward others who are gay or lesbian.

When it comes to same-sex couples marrying, I believe _____.

People, regardless of their sexual orientation _____ allowed to adopt children because _____.

My religion says that homosexuality is _____.

The messages that I received about sexual orientation when I was growing up were _____.

If I had a child who was gay or lesbian, I would _____.

I can try to reduce heterosexism in my environment by _____.

Should Gay Couples Be Allowed to Legally Adopt?

There are approximately half a million children in the United States who are in foster care, and of those, approximately 100,000 are waiting to be adopted. Three states (Florida, Mississippi, and Utah) restrict gay, lesbian, or bisexual individuals or couples from adopting and several other states have pending legislation that would ban LGBT people from adopting. In some cases, states are simply banning adoption for anyone who is not married. Although there are loopholes in adoption laws in many states that allow same-sex couples to legally adopt, whether or not they are able to varies from state to state, and in some cases, states are working to close these loopholes so that LGBT couples cannot adopt. Of course, this usually means that other non-married couples also cannot adopt. Only four states—Vermont, New Jersey, Massachusetts, and California—permit same-sex couple adoption. Should same-sex couples be allowed to legally adopt?

YES!

- Supporters of LGBT adoption suggest that many children are in need of homes and claim that since parenting ability is unrelated to sexual orientation, the law should allow them to adopt children.

- Older children and those with special needs are especially hard to place. Children who fit this category are in foster homes, while gay and lesbian parents who want to adopt them are available to provide permanent and secure homes.

- Numerous studies on LGBT parenting have concluded that lesbian mothers do not differ from heterosexual mothers in parenting ability and, while fewer studies exist on gay men and parenting, research suggests gay men may be similar in parenting ability to heterosexual men.

- The American Psychological Association has supported adoption by same-sex couples, citing social prejudice as harming the psychological health of lesbians and gays while noting there is no evidence that their parenting causes harm.

- The American Medical Association has issued a similar position supporting same-sex adoption, stating that while there is little evidence against the practice, lack of formal recognition can cause health care disparities for children of same-sex parents.

- Most children in the United States do not live with two married parents. In fact, according to the 2000 census, only 24 percent of homes were composed of a married mother and father with children living at home. In fact, scientific studies have shown that children who grow up in one- or two-parent gay or lesbian households fare just as well emotionally and socially as children whose parents are heterosexual. Studies have shown that children are more influenced by their interactions with their parents than by their sexual orientation.

- There is no legal basis for why gays and lesbians should be denied the right to adopt children.

NO!

- Opponents of LGBT adoption suggest that the greater prevalence of depression, promiscuity, domestic violence, and suicide among homosexuals might affect children or that the absence of male or female role models could cause maladjustment.

- They argue that research that shows no harmful effect related to having same-sex parents fails to distinguish between the parenting of a gay couple's biological children and the parenting of adopted children who are unrelated to them.

- Some opponents argue that children of gay and lesbian parents will be subject to harassment and ridicule.

- Proper child development requires that children have daily access to the different and complementary ways mothers and fathers parent. Same-sex caregivers cannot provide both the unique father-love and mother-love that children need.

- Research on various family structures calls into question the health of same-sex families for children.

>>> WHAT DO YOU THINK?

1. Should there be a federal law that prevents same-sex couples from adopting? Why or why not?
2. Is it better for children to remain in foster care rather than be adopted by same-sex parents?
3. Can we legally justify not allowing same-sex couples to adopt? In other words, based on the U.S. Constitution, can we justify allowing one group of people to adopt, but not another?

Sources: Gates, G. J., Lee Badgett, M. V., Macomber, J. E., & Chambers, K. C. (2007). Adoption and Foster Care by Gay and Lesbian Parents in the United States. Retrieved September 1, 2009, from http://www.law.ucla.edu/WilliamsInstitute/publications/FinalAdoptionReport.pdf Focus on the Family, Social Issues, Marriage and Family, Adoption, Talking Points. Retrieved September 1, 2009, from http://www.focusonthefamily.com/socialissues/marriage_and_family/adoption/talking_points.aspx

>>> The Matthew Shepard **Local Law Enforcement Hate Crimes Prevention Act** (LLEHCPA) was passed in 2009, giving the Justice Department power to investigate and prosecute crimes motivated by bias; it provides the department, rather than state authorities, jurisdiction over violent hate crimes. **Types of bias contained in the act include a person's actual or perceived race, religion, national origin, gender, sexual orientation, gender identity, or disability.**

Though much more research needs to take place in this area of family living, to date, the empirical evidence seems to indicate that children of gay and lesbian parents do not experience physical, emotional, psychological, or developmental disadvantages. As with any child, it appears to be the *quality of the parent–child relationship* that is the most important to a child's health and well-being—*not* the parents' sexual orientations or genders (Wainwright & Patterson, 2006).

Although opinion polls over the last several decades have shown a decrease in the number of Americans who think homosexuality is "always wrong" along with an increase of those who believe that homosexuality is an "acceptable" alternative lifestyle, many gays and lesbians still experience discrimination based on their sexual orientation (General Social Science Survey & Gallup polls).

IT'S NOT A JOKE: HATE CRIMES AGAINST GAYS, LESBIANS, BISEXUALS, AND TRANSGENDER PEOPLE

Homophobia refers to individual antigay attitudes and behaviors, but **sexual prejudice** is a more appropriate term because it encompasses prejudice against all types of sexual orientation including homosexuality, bisexuality, or heterosexuality (Herek, 2009). As we saw in our earlier discussion, homophobia and sexual prejudice are social phenomena that are rooted in the culture—not just in an individual.

In a recent study that utilized a representative sample of 662 gays, lesbians, and bisexuals, Gregory Herek (2009) examined the prevalence of victimization based on sexual orientation. Twenty percent of participants had experienced a personal or property crime, 10 percent had experienced housing or employment discrimination, and almost half had experienced verbal harassment. Overall, gay men were more likely to be the victims of personal and property crimes and of harassment than lesbians or bisexuals were.

Hate crimes are crimes motivated by prejudice against a social group, such as gays and lesbians. **Gay bashing** involves verbal and/or emotional denigration or physical violence against gays and lesbians. Enacted in 1990, the **Hate Crimes Statistics Act (HCSA)** requires the U.S. Justice Department to acquire data on crimes that "manifest prejudice based on race, religion, sexual orientation, or ethnicity" from law enforcement agencies across the country and to publish these statistics every year. This was a first-of-its-kind action on the part of the federal government to recognize and record acts of violence against people because of their sexual orientation. In 2007, the FBI recorded nearly 9,000 hate crime offenses; 16.2 percent of these crimes were motivated by a negative sexual orientation bias. Although a step in the right direction, the HCSA is still voluntary; some jurisdictions still do not report hate crimes. It is also thought that many hate crimes go unreported because of fear and stigmatization (Human Rights Campaign, 2009).

SEXUAL LIFE EDUCATION

Will we ever know the origins of sexual orientation? As with so many other aspects of sex and sexuality, sexual orientation is complex; there is no clear-cut biological evidence, and science does not offer conclusive developmental and sociological explanations as to what determines a person's sexual orientation. Therefore, rather than focus attention on the nature/nurture debate (another either/or situation), it's best to understand sexual orientation as the result of *both* biology and environment. Developmental factors, combined with genetic information, contribute to the development and experiences of homosexuality and bisexuality.

There is much more to learn about the experiences of homosexuality, and we'll discover more as we continue our study. Here, it's important to reinforce that homosexuality and bisexuality are not just about sex any more than heterosexuality is just about sex. The sexual behaviors of gays, lesbians, and bisexuals don't define sexual orientation—rather, a person's emotional and romantic responses do.

Summary

WHAT **IS SEXUAL ORIENTATION?**
128

- Sexual orientation isn't just about sex—it includes the emotional, physical, sexual, and romantic attraction a person feels toward a specific gender or genders.
- Those who are homosexual are attracted to people of the same sex. Those who are heterosexual are attracted to people of the opposite sex. Those who are bisexual are attracted to both sexes.

WHAT **DETERMINES SEXUAL ORIENTATION?** 131

- Essentialist theories maintain that there is a biological basis for sexual orientation. Research has found a slight size difference in the hypothalamus of homosexual and heterosexual men, and twin studies have shown that identical twins are more likely to share the same sexual orientation than fraternal twins are. Neurohormonal theory and research on birth order suggest that biological factors can influence sexual orientation even while a child is still developing in the womb.

- Constructionist theories argue that sexual orientation is a learned behavior reinforced by a child's environment throughout his or her life. Modeling experiences can affect expectations, leading a person to develop an orientation based on outside influences.
- Queer theory is a sociological model that proposes that sexual orientation is constructed based on society's expectations. Proponents assert that this orientation is a product of a given culture at a given time, and our views on homosexuality or heterosexuality now are not the same as they were 200 years ago.

WHAT **ARE SOME EXPERIENCES HOMOSEXUAL PEOPLE MAY HAVE THROUGHOUT THEIR LIVES?** 136

- Homosexual individuals may experience general discrimination against their sexual orientation, known as heterosexism. They may also be subject to hate crimes by sexually prejudiced people.
- Many homosexual people recall experiences of gender bending in their childhood. All must face a process of coming out, in which they begin their development of a positive sexual identity.

Key Terms

sexual orientation the emotional physical, sexual and romantic (love/intimacy) attraction a person feels toward a specific gender (or genders) 128

heterosexual straight 128

homosexual gay or same sex 128

bisexual being attracted to both men and women 128

transgender an umbrella term used to refer to someone whose behavior and/or appearance is not consistent with their biologically assigned sex 128

gaydar popular slang term that refers to a person's intuition or ability to discern another person's sexual orientation 128

Kinsey Sexual Orientation Scale illustration of Kinsey's idea that sexual orientation is experienced on a continuum 129

Klein Sexual Orientation Grid (KSOG) grid that includes seven dimensions of sexual orientation, and it captures the idea that sexual orientation is not only on a continuum, but that a person's place on the continuum may change over time 129

essentialist descriptive of a theory that maintains that homosexuality is an inborn, innate trait, likely due to biological or developmental processes 131

constructionist descriptive of a theory that suggests that homosexuality develops over time, most likely due to social forces 131

fraternal birth order hypothesis hypothesis that suggests that some women may develop antibodies each time they carry a male fetus 132

neurohormonal theory theory that suggests that being exposed to increased levels of opposite-sex hormones while in the womb directs the brain to develop as if the fetus were the opposite sex 133

behaviorist descriptive of theories that suggest that sexual orientation is a learned behavior brought about over time due to the rewarding of some behaviors and the punishing of others 133

peer group interaction theory theory that those who mature early (prior to the age of 12) tend to have same-sex friend environments and thus identify with and sexually experiment with same-sex peers; in early maturing males, emerging erotic feelings would likely be focused on other males 134

Oedipus complex a psychosexual stage in which the child regards the father as someone who is competing for the love of the mother 134

penis envy state in which a female child becomes angry and feels inferior when she discovers she does not have a penis 135

sociological descriptive of theories that emphasize the idea that sexual orientation is constructed based on society's expectations; it is a product of a given culture at a given time 135

queer theory the theory that suggests that all sexualities are constructs created by certain social forces and institutions, such as science (biology), religion and politics, so they are dynamic 135

heterosexism discrimination or prejudice against lesbians, gays, bisexuals and transgenders by heterosexual people 136

gender bending a variety of types of play that often cross traditional gender lines 137

coming out identifying oneself as gay to friends and family; part of sexual identity development 139

homophobia individual antigay attitudes and behaviors 145

sexual prejudice prejudice against all types of sexual orientation including homosexuality, bisexuality or heterosexuality 145

hate crimes crimes motivated by prejudice against a social group 145

gay bashing verbal and/or emotional denigration or physical violence against gays and lesbians *145*

Hate Crimes Statistics Act (HCSA) enacted in 1990, this requires the U.S. Justice Department to acquire data on crimes which "manifest prejudice based on race, religion, sexual orientation, or ethnicity" from law enforcement agencies across the country, and to publish these statistics every year *145*

Local Law Enforcement Hate Crimes Prevention Act (LLEHCPA) law passed in 2009, giving the Justice Department power to investigate and prosecute crimes motivated by bias; it provides the Justice Department (rather than state authorities) jurisdiction over violent hate crimes. Types of bias contained in the act include a person's actual or perceived race, color, religion, national origin, gender, sexual orientation, gender identity, or disability *145*

Sample Test Questions

MULTIPLE CHOICE

1. Sexual orientation encompasses:
   a. With whom we choose to have sex
   b. To whom we are romantically attracted
   c. Neither a nor b
   d. Both a and b

2. What does the slang term "gaydar" mean?
   a. The ability to discern another person's sexual orientation
   b. A derogatory term used to describe a gay man
   c. The inner turmoil a person may experience before he or she comes out
   d. Someone who is bisexual

3. Dr. Fritz Klein argued that:
   a. A person must be either gay or straight
   b. Everyone is bisexual
   c. One's sexual orientation is in a constant state of change
   d. Someone's sexual orientation is determined by his/her environment

4. Which theory about sexual orientation is NOT considered an essentialist theory?
   a. Simon LeVay's theory that the hypothalamuses of gay and straight men differ
   b. The similar genetic makeup that gay identical twins share is evidence that sexual orientation is a product of someone's nature
   c. Sexual orientation is determined by which behaviors are rewarded or punished throughout a person's life.
   d. Fraternal birth order hypothesis that suggests that different antibodies a woman carries may result in the types of antigens to which her fetuses are exposed

5. Gender bending means:
   a. Cross dressing
   b. Types of play that cross traditional gender lines
   c. Dating someone of the same sex
   d. Considering oneself to be transgender

6. Which stage is NOT part of Eli Coleman's model of sexual identity?
   a. identity tolerance
   b. pre-coming out
   c. exploration
   d. integration

7. Which statement is generally true about gays and lesbians?
   a. Gays and lesbians are less likely than heterosexual people to remain friends after a breakup
   b. Gays and lesbians do not typically desire relationships as much as heterosexuals do
   c. Gays and lesbians only have short-term relationships when compared to heterosexuals
   d. Gays and lesbians meet potential partners in the same way heterosexuals do

8. The number of planned families by homosexual people has:
   a. Declined in recent years
   b. Grown in recent years
   c. Remained the same in recent years
   d. Gone up and down in recent years

SHORT RESPONSE

1. What do you believe is the most important factor in determining someone's sexual orientation? Is it a factor that is considered nature or nurture?

2. Your younger brother comes to you and tells you in confidence he thinks he might be gay, but is afraid to tell your parents. What do you tell him?

3. Describe the differences between Kinsey's Sexual Orientation Scale and the concept that everyone must be either gay or straight.

4. Do you think homosexual couples should be allowed to marry and adopt? Why or why not?

5. Have you ever experienced an instance of sexual prejudice? How did you respond?

Answers: 1. d; 2. a; 3. c; 4. c; 5. b; 6. a; 7. d; 8. b

Remember to check www.thethinkspot.com **for additional information, downloadable flashcards, and other helpful resources.**

THINK READINGS

SCIENCE DAILY

Love May Be A Lateralized Brain Function, Like Speech; Links Seen To Stalking, Suicide, Clinical Depression, Even Autism

> A neuroscientist is someone who specializes in the study of the brain.

> An anthropologist is someone who studies the origin, the behaviors, and the physical, social, and cultural development of people.

> There are many regions in the brain where rewards and motivations are processed, one of which is the hippocampus. Using brain imagery devices (an MRI) to measure neural responses, the researchers were able to determine that romantic love is associated with increased brain activity in the reward/motivation centers of the brain. The researchers believe this activity in the brain drives us to pursue a love interest. In other words, love is not a feeling or an emotion; it's a biological state.

ScienceDaily (June 7, 2005)—BETHESDA, Md. (May 31, 2005)—You just can't tell where you might find love these days. A team led by a neuroscientist, an anthropologist and a social psychologist found love-related neurophysiological systems inside a magnetic resonance imaging machine. They detected quantifiable love responses in the brains of 17 young men and women who each described themselves as being newly and madly in love.

The multidisciplinary team found that early, intense romantic love may have more to do with motivation, reward and "drive" aspects of human behavior than with the emotions or sex drive. Brain systems were activated that humans share with other mammals. So the researchers think "early-stage romantic love is possibly a developed form of a mammalian drive to pursue preferred mates, and that it has an important influence on social behaviors that have reproductive and genetic consequences."

Diverse emotions occur, but reward response primary

"It's a stark reminder that the mind truly is in the brain," noted Lucy L. Brown of the Albert Einstein College of Medicine. "We humans are built to experience magical feelings like love, but our findings don't diminish the magic in any way. In fact, for some, it enhances the experience. Our research also helps to explain why a person in love feels 'driven' to win their beloved, amidst a whole constellation of other feelings."

The study, entitled "Reward, motivation and emotion systems associated with early-stage intense romantic love," is available online and will be in the July issue of the Journal of Neurophysiology, published by the American Physiological Society. The research was conducted by Arthur Aron, Helen E. Fisher, Debra J. Mashek, Greg Strong, Hai-Fang Li and Lucy L. Brown. Aron, Fisher and Brown contributed equally.

"Most of the participants in our study clearly showed emotional responses," noted Arthur Aron of the State University of New York-Stony Brook, "but we found no consistent emotional pattern. Instead, all of our subjects showed activity in reward and motivation regions. To emotion researchers like me, this is pretty exciting because it's the first physiological data to confirm a connection between romantic love and motivation networks in the brain.

"As it turns out, romantic love is probably best characterized as a motivation or goal-oriented state that leads to various specific emotions, such as euphoria or anxiety," Aron noted. "With this view, it becomes clearer why the lover expresses such an imperative to pursue his or her beloved and protect the relationship."

Sexual arousal 'very different'; confirmation of questionnaire methods

Aron added: "Our participants who measured very high on a self report questionnaire of romantic love also showed strong activity in a particular brain region—results that dramatically increase our confidence that self-report questionnaires can actually measure brain activity."

Aron also noted that the research answered the "historic question of whether love and sex are the same, or different, or whether romantic passion is just warmed over sexual arousal." He said, "Our findings show that the brain areas activated when someone looks at a photo of their beloved only partially overlap with the brain regions associated with sexual arousal. Sex and romantic love involve quite different brain systems."

fMRI confirms major predictions, yields "remarkable implications"; autism link

Aron reported that, using functional magnetic resonance imaging (fMRI) and other measurements, he and his colleagues found support for their two major predictions: (1) early stage, intense romantic love is associated with subcortical reward regions rich with dopamine; and (2) romantic love engages brain systems associated with motivation to acquire a reward.

Brown explains some of these findings, commenting that "when our participants looked at a photo of his/her beloved, specific activation occurred in the right ventral tegmental area (VTA) and dorsal caudate body. These regions were significant compared to two control conditions, providing strong evidence that these brain areas, which are associated with the motivation to win rewards, are central to the experience of being in love."

Brown noted that "an important concept is that the caudate probably integrates huge amounts of information, everything from one's early personal memories to one's personal notions of beauty. Then, this brain region (and related regions of the basal ganglia) helps to direct one's actions toward attaining one's goals. For neuroscientists," she said, "these findings about the diverse regional functions of the basal ganglia in humans have remarkable implications."

"Our data even may be relevant to some forms of autism," Brown added. "Some people with autism don't understand or experience any sort of emotional attachment or romantic love. I would speculate that autism involves an atypical development of the midbrain and basal ganglia reward systems. This makes sense, too, because other symptoms of autism include repetitive thoughts and movements, characteristics of basal ganglia function. "

Surprise discovery: romance is on the right, 'attractiveness' to the left

Another important discovery, Brown said, was that "to our surprise, the activation regions associated with intense romantic love were mostly on the right side of the brain, while the activation regions associated with facial attractiveness were mostly on the left.

"We didn't predict such a striking lateralization," Brown reported. "It is well known that speech is largely a left-sided cortical function. But our data indicate that lateralization also occurs in lower parts of the brain. Moreover, different kinds of rewards (in this case, the "rush" of romantic love, compared with the pleasing experience of looking at a pretty or handsome face) is also lateralized. These results give us a lot to think about how the normal human brain learns and remembers and functions in general," Brown added.

Love physiology changes over time; 'Romantic love more powerful than sex'

Another breakthrough, Brown noted, was that "we found several brain areas where the strength of neural activity changed with the length of the romance. Everyone knows that relationships are dynamic over time, but we are beginning to track what happens in the brain as a love relationship matures."

Helen E. Fisher, a research anthropologist at Rutgers University, New Jersey, noted that not only did the brain change as romantic love endured, but that some of these changes were in regions associated with pair-bonding in prairie voles. The fMRI images showed more activity in the ventral pallidum portion of the basal ganglia in people with longer romantic relationships. It's in this region where receptors for the hormone vasopressin are critical for vole pairbonding, or attachment.

"Humans have evolved three distinct but interrelated brain systems for mating and reproduction—the sex drive, romantic love, and attachment to a long term partner," Fisher said, "and our results suggest how feelings of romantic love might change into feelings of attachment. Our results support what people have always assumed—that romantic love is one of the most powerful of all human experiences. It is definitely more powerful than the sex drive."

Depression, murder/suicide, demonstrate strength of romantic drive

For instance, Fisher point out, "If someone rejects your sexual overtures, you don't harm yourself or the other person. But rejected men and women in societies around the world sometimes kill themselves or someone else. In fact, studies indicate that some 40% of people who are rejected in love slip into clinical depression. Our study may also suggest some of the underlying physiology of stalking behavior," she added.

Fisher noted that their study, which took barely an hour for each participant but many years for the researchers to process and interpret the data, also found a "fascinating continuity between human romantic love and the physiological expressions of attraction in other animals. Other scientists," she said, "have reported that expressions of attraction in a female prairie vole are associated with a 50% increase in dopamine activity in a brain region related to regions where we found activity. These and other data indicate that all mammals may feel attraction to specific partners, and that some of the same brain systems are involved."

Study explains second half of Darwin's puzzle, sexual selection & 'eyes of the beholder'

"Darwin and many of his intellectual descendants have studied the myriad physiological ornaments that one sex of a species have evolved to attract members of the opposite sex, like the peacock's fancy tail feathers that attract the peahen," Fisher noted. "But no one has studied what happened in the brain of the viewer, the individual that becomes attracted to these traits. Our study indicates what happens in the brain of the viewer as he

or she becomes physiologically attracted to these traits."

She added, "This brain system probably evolved for an important reason—to drive our forebears to focus their courtship energy on specific individuals, thereby conserving precious mating time and energy. Perhaps," she hypothesized, "even love-at-first-sight is a basic mammalian response that developed in other animals and our ancestors inherited in order to speed up the mating process."

Einstein's Brown concluded, "Our results suggest that romantic love does not use a functionally specialized brain system. It may be produced, instead, by a constellation of neural systems that converge onto widespread regions of the caudate where there is a flexible combinatorial map representing and integrating many motivating stimuli.

"This passion may be an excellent example of how a complex human behavioral state is processed. Moreover, taken together, our results and those of Andreas Bartels and Semir Zeki, who studied men and women in longer love relationships, show similar cortical, VTA and caudate activation patterns, suggesting that these regions are consistently and critically involved in this aspect of human reproduction and social behavior, romantic love."

###

Source and funding

The study, "Reward, motivation and emotion systems associated with early-stage intense romantic love," is available online and will be in the July issue of the Journal of Neurophysiology, published by the American Physiological Society.

Research was conducted by Arthur Aron, Debra J. Mashek and Greg Strong, Dept. of Psychology, State University of New York at Stony Brook; Helen E. Fisher, Dept. of Anthropology, Rutgers University, New Brunswick, New Jersey; Hai-Fang Li, SUNY Stony Brook Dept. of Radiology; and Lucy L. Brown, Departments of Neurology and Neuroscience, Albert Einstein College of Medicine, Yeshiva University, Bronx, New York.

Aron, Fisher and Brown contributed equally. Mashek is now at the Dept. of Psychology, George Mason University, Fairfax, Virginia.

Research was supported in part by a grant from the National Science Foundation (Aron).

Is love a left brain/right brain phenomenon? According to this body of research, when we are attracted to someone, the left brain is at work, but when we experience feelings of love, such as elation and obsessive thinking about the lover, the right brain is at work. The right brain, then, is what is responsible for the mating energy we focus on that one person. It is a drive, an instinct that arises from primitive parts of the brain. A powerful stimulant, dopamine is also released in the brain. As the researchers note, romance is a chemical high, and that is why the one takes a place of prominence.

How might this finding explain why the feelings associated with love may change over time? Have you ever experienced intense feelings of love, then have them fade into feelings of security? If so, did you wonder if you "fell out of love" because the feelings weren't as intense as they once were?

Source: Journal of Neurophysiology 94: 3270337, 2005; Reprinted with permission of the American Physiological Society (APS). For further information please contact Donna Krupa at DKrupa@The-APS.org

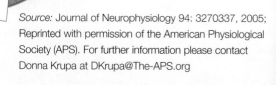

THE PATH TO COMMITMENT

Attraction, Dating, and the Experiences of Love

WHAT ARE THE INTERPERSONAL ATTRACTION THEORIES?
WHAT MAKES UP THE PATH TO COMMITMENT?
WHAT IS LOVE, ACTUALLY?

I am a

heterosexual female in the 21st century. I pride myself on the fact that I take people at more than face value, that I appreciate human beings for their character rather than their looks. Why do I find myself making conversations with physically attractive males while blowing off [others]?

Why does my head whip around when I see a man in a Porsche? Why do my male friends all have the same prerequisites for the perfect female despite race and ethnicity [differences]: perky breasts, slim waist, and full hips? Despite most people's lofty notions of equality, and beauty being in the eye of the beholder, we are all susceptible to certain physical and material traits that make some human beings more "desirable" than others.

Source: Fernandez, D. (2002).

151

CHAPTER 08

Love holds a central place in peoples' lives, and it is perhaps one of the most prevalent things to occupy people's thoughts (Bergner, 2000). But what is love, actually? How do we get there? And do we all take similar paths?

Dating, courtship, and partnering practices map out different courses to marriage and other lifelong couple relationships, such as civil unions between gays or lesbians, so it's important to understand these processes. In Chapter 10, we'll take a look at singlehood, cohabitation, marriage, and divorce. But first we need to explore why we are attracted to some people and not to others and how we fall in love.

In this chapter, we'll examine the theories and realities associated with interpersonal attraction, dating, mate selection, and the experiences of love and loving. Just like the college student in the opening vignette, we ask, "Why are we attracted to one person and not another? If we're straight, do we choose intimate partners differently than if we're gay or bisexual?"

"FRISKY BUSINESS": INTERPERSONAL ATTRACTION THEORIES

Whether we are referring to a technologically advanced society or to a tribal culture, all societies have certain beliefs and expectations about selecting a mate (Erber & Erber, 2001). Although we cannot answer here the age-old question, "How do I know if he/she is the right one for me?" we can investigate how and why we have been socialized to think the way we do about certain physical characteristics and qualities in those to whom we are attracted.

EVOLUTIONARY THEORY: THE EVOLUTION OF PHYSICAL ATTRACTION

Charles Darwin (1809–1882) became famous for his theories about evolution and **natural selection**, the belief that nature selects the

best-adapted varieties of species to survive and reproduce. **Sexual selection** refers to the struggles between individuals of one sex (generally males) for the possession of the other sex (Abraham, 2005). It occurs when members of one sex compete among themselves for opportunities to mate because the pool of potential mating candidates is limited. The "winners" out-reproduce the other competitors and natural selection occurs. Sexual selection also occurs when a sex chooses to mate with a specific person (or people), because some people are more preferable to mate with than others. The **evolutionary theory** for mate selection suggests that we choose mates for the sole purpose of maximizing and enhancing our reproductive efforts, ensuring reproductive success and the success of the species and society (Needham, 1999; Singh, 2004, 2002; Sprecher, Sullivan, & Hatfield, 1994; Symons, 1979).

Mate selection evolutionist-based theories maintain that there are two specific biological goals—one for *male sexual selection* and one for *female sexual selection*—that must be achieved when selecting a mate.

WHAT MEN WANT: REPRODUCTIVE PROMISE

The primary evolutionary goal of males is the need to impregnate as many women as possible (Needham, 1999). According to evolutionists, *men are concerned with quantity*—mating is a numbers game, and the more mates the better to ensure numerous offspring are produced. Mate selection research findings conclude that this is perhaps why men engage in more casual sex than women do and why men have more sexual partners across their life spans than women do (Schmitt & Buss, 2001; Schmitt et al., 2001). When seeking mates, then, men will select women who possess certain **fertility cues**, such as youth and curves (full breasts, small waist, curvy hips), because men associate these traits with successful fertility (Feingold, 1992).

WHAT WOMEN WANT: PROTECTORS AND PROVIDERS

Because childbearing (pregnancy, labor, birth, and breastfeeding) is risky for women, Darwin reasoned that women are more selective when it comes to finding a mate. A man produces millions of sperm each day and therefore has seemingly limitless supplies of his genetic material, but the female is very limited in her ability to reproduce: Women are concerned with the *quality of the children* they produce. Consequently, they look for someone who can contribute not only positive genetic traits and characteristics, but they also tend to seek a mate who possesses **protector/provider cues**, such as intelligence, physical strength, industry (a hard worker) and ambition (Feingold, 1992; Buss & Schmitt, 1993; Buss, 1994).

<<< **Charles Darwin (1809–1882)** is famous for his belief that nature selects the best-adapted species—**including humans—to reproduce.**

Who Determines Society's "Ideal Body" Standard—Men or Women?

Who determines society's "ideal body" standard—men or women? One researcher tried to answer this question by doing his own content analysis of *Vogue* magazine models (to assess the female standard of ideal body shape), *Playboy* centerfold models (to assess the male standard of ideal body shape), and Miss America winners (a sort of catch-all to assess both female and male standards of ideal body shape) (Barber, 1998). He posed two questions:

- Is a male's standard of women's attractiveness curvier than the female's standard?

- Do women or men determine the "ideal body" standard?

According to Barber (p. 3), "American women's standard for female bodily attractiveness differs greatly from that of men." From 1978 to 1986, the *Vogue* models' bust lines were significantly smaller than the *Playboy* models' bust lines or the winners of the Miss America beauty pageant. In fact, the *Vogue* standard for physical attractiveness did not predict the *Playboy* or Miss America standard of "ideal" body shape. Barber's analysis also determined that the bust-to-waist ratios for *Playboy* models and Miss America winners were not significantly different. Barber subsequently concluded from this research that the female body standard, over time, has converged with the male ideal body standard, which entail curves.

Wondering how students today would respond to Barber's research questions and findings, I posed them to my marriage and family class. Here are the students' responses:

Her Side: "I just don't get it. I mean, as women, we are bombarded day after day after day with images in print and electronic media that tell us we are never thin enough. We're urged to purge, we're urged to get rid of curves—and now we find out that men actually *like* curves? If that's the case, then why is a woman over a size six considered 'fat?' Why do women's magazines constantly insist on pushing their impossible-to-achieve version of 'beautiful' on us?"

"Why should *men* get to decide the standard of beauty?!"

His Side: "But I don't think that the images in *Playboy* are fair to women, either. That magazine sends the message that all women have to be perfectly proportioned to be attractive and beautiful, and that's not true. I think if you asked most guys they would say that women are attractive if they are healthy."

"Hey, don't blame the guys! Every man knows that women don't dress to please men; they dress and diet to please other women!"

Your Side: From your casual observations,

1. Do you think men or women determine the ideal body standard for women in today's society?

2. From looking at women's magazine covers, what is the woman's ideal body standard? From looking at men's magazine covers, what is the male's ideal body standard for women? Do you agree with the images that are advertised as "ideal"?

3. Do you think the ideal body standard for women will change over time?

Source: Based on Barber, N. (1998).

When it comes to body shape and size, women find average-size men more attractive than muscular men (Cunningham, 1986). Personality traits and behavior characteristics are also important factors for women in choosing a marriage mate. Characteristics such as kindness, warmth, openness and commitment are key influences in women's selection of a mate (Buss & Angleitner, 1989; Doosje, Rojahn, & Fischer, 1999; Hatfield & Sprecher, 1995; Li, Bailey, Kenrick, & Linsenmeier, 2002, among many others). Recent research indicates that women rate emotional stability and the commitment to marriage and family (*family orientation*) more highly than men do (Oda, 2001; Waynforth, 2001).

Now that you have an understanding of why men and women are attracted to certain physical traits and certain personality characteristics, let's turn our attention to two other theoretical frameworks that seek to explain why we choose the marriage mate or lifelong partner

that we do. Next we examine the social exchange theory and the filter theory of mate selection.

SOCIAL EXCHANGE THEORY: THE REWARDS AND COSTS OF ATTRACTION

Let's suppose you exchanged phone numbers with someone you met at a bar, and a few days later your cell phone rings—with that certain person's number showing on the caller ID. At the first ring, a scenario like the one that follows may play out in your mind (or even aloud!):

Phone: Ring!

You: Who could that possibly be? Don't they know I've got a chem test in an hour?

OWN IT! What Makes Your Head Whip Around?

Charles Darwin reasoned that men and women select mates based on certain interpersonal attraction cues that ensure successful reproduction of the human species.

From your experiences with dating, hooking up, or partnering, respond to the following questions:

1. Without giving it much thought, quickly jot down 10 things that attract you to another person. On your list, are there those things

that the evolutionary theory asserts that draw us to another person, such as a person's appearance or the ability to provide or protect? What surprises you the most about your list?

2. Have you ever given much thought to why you're attracted to one person and not to another? Have you ever *wanted* to be attracted to another, but found that something was missing? If so, what was that "something"?

Phone: Ring!!

You [glancing at caller ID]: Wow! It's so-and-so from the bar! Do I answer the phone or not? Was I only interested in him/her because I had a few too many to drink? Or do I really want to invest the time in getting to know this person? (You weigh the rewards of answering the phone. You weigh the costs. You perceive that answering the phone may result in greater benefits or rewards than not answering the phone. You answer the phone.)

This example illustrates the essence of the social exchange theory. Very broadly stated, the **social exchange theory** centers on the exchange of people's resources, and it asserts that individuals are thought to act out of self-interest in ways to make the most of the resources they possess. It also helps explain what motivates individuals to act (White & Klein, 2008).

Seen in Figure 8.1, Susan Sprecher (1998) outlines the key concepts of the social exchange theory. **Rewards** are the benefits (the payback or compensations) that are exchanged in social relationships (Boss et al., 1993). A reward is *anything* considered beneficial to an individual (White & Klein, 2008). As long as the perceived rewards are greater than the perceived costs of a given behavior, the behavior will continue. A **cost** increases the likelihood or probability that a person will *not* take part in a given behavior (Boss et al., 1993). For example, an unmarried woman may cohabit with her alcoholic, abusive partner. Although her partner gets drunk and physically abuses her (the *costs*), she may consider his paycheck, her home, and her financial security (the perceived *rewards*) to be greater than the costs of his drinking and abusive behavior. If there is no reward that results from a behavior, the individual will act in a way that will result in the least cost. For instance, although there may be no rewards in staying in the abusive relationship, if she tries to leave the relationship, he may harm her. She may therefore conclude that staying in the cohabiting relationship is the least costly to her.

You may think, "Wait a minute! How do you know what I consider rewarding or what I consider costly?" Precisely! Let's suppose that you are in a new relationship, and you view the increased time you spend together as a couple as rewarding. Your partner, on the other hand, may feel like he or she has less time, less freedom, and less independence because of the increased time spent together as a couple, and he or she sees the time commitment as a cost. Thus, when examining intimate and sexual relationships, we need to have an understanding of the significance or importance (the weight) that *each* person assigns to each reward and to each cost.

FILTER THEORY OF MATE SELECTION

Have you ever wondered how certain people come together as marriage or lifelong partners, even though their personality traits are polar opposites? The **filter theory of mate selection** may provide an explanation; it suggests that when looking for mates, we use a filtering mechanism that helps us sort out a potential mate from the vast **pool of candidates**, or eligible partners. Figure 8.2 illustrates the variables we use to filter potential mates include propinquity, homogamy, heterogamy, physical attraction, and reciprocity.

Each of us has our own ideal of what we find physically attractive in a potential mate, and we filter potential mates based on these culturally socialized internalized standards of physical attractiveness. Unlike evolution theory, filter theory isn't necessarily as concerned with *why* or *how* we are attracted to someone as it is with the notion that we just *are*—and physical attraction is one filtering mechanism. Regardless of sexual orientation, men are more likely than women to emphasize the importance of their partner's physical attraction; women, regardless of sexual orientation, assign greater importance to personality characteristics (Peplau & Spalding, 2000).

When all is said and done and we have exhausted all propinquity, social and physical attractiveness filters, we look at what someone can offer us that we cannot find in anyone else. Ultimately, whomever we choose must reflect a mutual, reciprocal commitment to the relationship in order for a mate to be considered "the one." Although this theory doesn't have much to do with developing a love relationship, it does help explain how and why we're attracted to one person and not another.

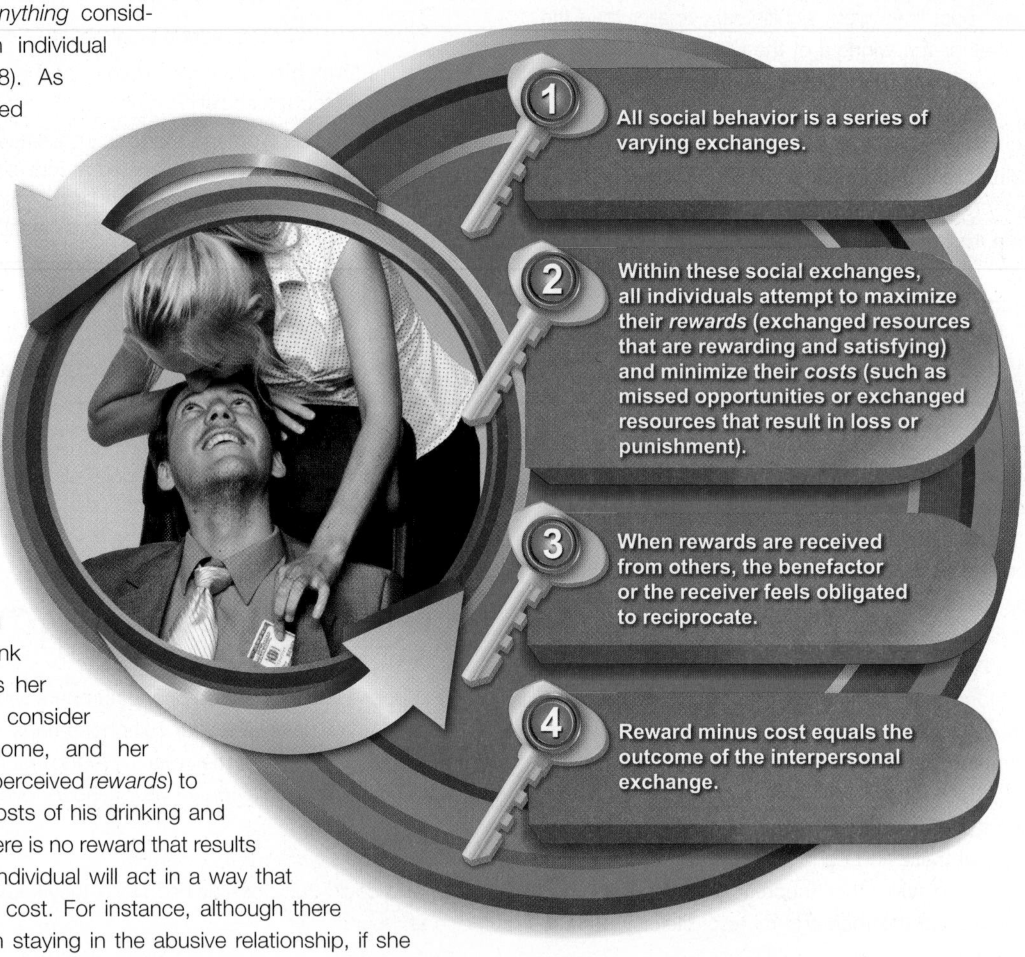

1. All social behavior is a series of varying exchanges.

2. Within these social exchanges, all individuals attempt to maximize their *rewards* (exchanged resources that are rewarding and satisfying) and minimize their *costs* (such as missed opportunities or exchanged resources that result in loss or punishment).

3. When rewards are received from others, the benefactor or the receiver feels obligated to reciprocate.

4. Reward minus cost equals the outcome of the interpersonal exchange.

Figure 8.1 Key Concepts of Social Exchange Theory Although we probably don't exchange money back and forth when we choose a mate, **we are calculating the rewards and costs of getting into a relationship with that particular person.**

Propinquity

This refers to *geographic closeness.* Simply stated, you can't get to know someone or interact with someone if you are not in the same general location.

Homogamy

We tend to marry someone with whom we share things in common. This refers to partnering with someone who is similar to you in ethnic and racial background, religious upbringing, age, education level, political ideology, socioeconomic status, and values and beliefs.

Exogamy

This means that we must marry outside of a particular group. In the United States, for example, we cannot marry a sibling or a first cousin. **Endogamy** refers to the notion that certain groups marry within that same group, such as Muslims marrying Muslims or Indians marrying Indians.

Heterogamy

This refers to partners who are of different races, religions, and ethnicities. It also refers to partners of different ages. In today's diverse society, more and more people are choosing heterogamous lifelong partners.

Figure 8.2 Mate Selection Filters

Although endogamy is still the prevailing norm in mate selection across cultures, today interracial, **interethnic, and interfaith relationships are becoming increasingly common.**

Now that we have looked at the various theories of how and why we select a particular mate over another, let's examine the pathway to committed relationships that may or may not result in marriage.

THE PATH TO COMMITMENT

Though the customs and rituals may vary across racial, cultural, ethnic, economic, and religious boundaries, people come together to form **pair bonds**, or couples. For example, Wodaabe nomad men of Niger participate in a males-only beauty pageant in which they parade before unmarried women who select their lovers from the parading pageant "contestants." The men spend countless hours painting elaborate patterns on their bodies in the hope of turning a young woman's eye. Although Western civilization's interpersonal attraction rituals may pale in comparison to other global mate selection customs, all serve the same purpose—to form a bond that will lead to marriage.

>>> Spending countless hours decorating their bodies with elaborate patterns, the Wodaabe men of Niger **participate in a beauty pageant in hopes of getting the attention of unmarried women.**

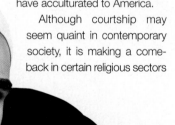

COURTSHIP: MARRIAGE IS THE GOAL

Although not all Americans follow the same path to marriage or committed partner relationships, when asked what causes young adults and adolescents the most stress, issues concerning dating and mate selection are at the top of the list (Myers, 2000). In a culturally, ethnically, and religiously diverse nation such as the United States, the path to commitment varies greatly. Not all of us will be in a committed relationship, nor will all of us marry. Here, our purpose is to explore how couples go from being attracted to one another, to loving one another, to committing themselves to relationships.

Courting and **courtship** are the practices that are socially prescribed forms of conduct that guide men and women toward matrimony (Kass, 1997). Although the practices and rituals associated with couple formation have changed dramatically in Western societies over the past 60 years, there are still people who adhere today to the practices of courting and courtship. For example, in Japan, there is a type of courtship called *omiai*, which is formal courting with the intention of pursuing a marriage partner. This is still commonly practiced among Japanese and Japanese Americans who have acculturated to America.

Although courtship may seem quaint in contemporary society, it is making a comeback in certain religious sectors of the United States. In Islamic and Islamic-American cultures, for example, premarital, one-on-one intimate relationships with the opposite sex are routinely forbidden; with a few exceptions, these cultures are sexually segregated (Kaya, 2009). Although couples may meet socially under some circumstances, often women will not agree to meet a man socially unless she thinks she may potentially fall in love with him (Kaya, 2009). One researcher puts forth the idea that this may be why the practice of Internet chatting is popular among Muslim women, because they are able to socially interact with men without social consequences, such as condemnation and ostracism (Wheeler, 2006).

According to the tenets of Islam, the choice of a marriage partner is considered to be one of life's most important decisions (Joseph & Najmabadi, 2006), and this decision should not be taken lightly or left to hormones to decide. When a young adult is ready to marry, the decision is made with his or her family's involvement. In Islamic cultures, the process of courtship is viewed as an assurance that the marriage will be a strong, enduring relationship because it draws upon others' wisdom and guidance, not on the erotic or romantic feelings of young adults (Joseph & Najmabadi, 2006).

In other mainstream religious denominations, the concept of courtship is seen as a way to teach lifelong commitment. As prominent religious commentator James Dobson (2005) notes, "[Dating teaches young adults] to go from one relationship to another. Wouldn't they then be more inclined later to bail out on a marriage partner when bored or frustrated?" Some religious contemporaries maintain that courtship charts the course for a committed marital relationship with the probable husband or wife. The customs and rituals of courting help the couple navigate the complexities of physical attraction, sexual attraction, falling in love, and committing to a lifelong partnership (Cere, 2001).

THE DATING GAME

In contemporary Western societies, **dating** is an occasion in which people get together socially for any number of reasons, such as "hanging out," pursuing a relationship to determine whether the partner is a potential partner for a lifelong relationship ("going out"), or getting together sexually with no strings attached ("hooking up" and "friends with benefits").

<<< Courtship is making somewhat of a comeback among some groups in the United States, **but in Muslim cultures, courting is actually the socially approved form of mate selection.**

>>> What do your dating scripts include? Do you prefer to go out with a group of people so you can get to know your dating partner, or do you prefer to be alone? **Who influenced your dating scripts the most?**

The primary distinction between dating and courting is that courtship is viewed as preparation for and anticipation of marriage. Dating, on the other hand, is considered more recreational and fun. It's a way for people to get to know each other and determine whether there are commonalities beyond their initial physical attraction that might lead to a committed relationship, such as marriage. Dating also provides a range of supportive functions in healthy social development (Shulman & Kipnis, 2001; Zimmer-Gembeck, Siebenbruner, & Collins, 2001). When we go out on dates, we tend to follow culturally determined dating scripts.

DATING SCRIPTS

According to **script theory**, each of us uses *scripts* that help us to organize the information in our environments. Scripts typically provide information about expected actions; they help us predict the behaviors of people and help guide our decisions about how to act and interact with others (Klinkenberg & Rose, 1994). In essence, scripts are internalized guidelines, or a "how-to" manual for social behavior. These are referred to as **dating scripts**, and these models guide our dating interactions.

HETEROSEXUAL DATING SCRIPTS

For a number of years, social scientists have examined the behaviors of dating couples. These studies are important, because they help us better understand how relationships develop and are maintained. For example, past studies have revealed that the man is the initiator of the date, the planner, and the one who pays for the date, while the woman is the one who nurtures the conversation during the date (Laner & Ventrone, 1998; Levinger, 1982; Rose & Frieze, 1989, 1993). But do college students today still adhere to these stereotypical dating scripts?

In a study of 182 college students, investigators looked at men and women's dating scripts for a "typical date" (Bartoli & Clark, 2006). The study participants were given dating scenes and were asked to report what activities and events usually took place on a typical date in these scenes. Figure 8.3 shows us dating scripts of first-year college students. Traditional gender roles were present; women were the sexual "gatekeepers," limiting sexual activity, and men had higher expectations for sexual activities other than intercourse than women did. Overall, the study found that if the dating scenario was "typical," men and women held similar dating scripts or expectations.

Of course, not all dating couples are heterosexual couples. This leads to some interesting questions. For example, because our cultures socialize all of us to follow certain dating scripts—scripts that assume heterosexual coupling—what dating scripts do gay men and lesbian couples follow? And how do they come by them?

SAME-SEX DATING SCRIPTS

There are few studies that address relationship initiation and formation among homosexual couples. What we do know,

Source: Bartoli & Clark (2006).

Figure 8.3 Scripted Events for a Typical Date Movies are often chosen as an activity **for a typical date.**

>>> Dating script templates for gays and lesbians contain some scripts that are traditionally adopted by straight couples, but they also venture from traditional gender roles. **If you are gay or lesbian, what or who influenced your dating scripts the most?**

however, is that gays and lesbians incorporate some traditional gender roles in their dating scripts; they also appear to have more opportunities to develop their own unique, interpersonal scripts than heterosexuals do. For example, just as with straight men, gay men are likely to stress the physical and sexual attraction to their dating partners over the emotional aspects early in relationships (Sergios & Cody, 1985). Similarly, lesbians, like heterosexual women, tend to emphasize personality traits in their partners, rather than sexual attraction (Deaux & Hanna, 1984). But unlike straight women, emotional intimacy is a valued aspect of lesbian dating (Klinkenberg & Rose, 1994). They engage in deep levels of self-disclosure and emotional sharing on their first dates, and they are much more likely to establish a close friendship with someone before dating them (Zand & Rose, 1992).

In a study that looked at dating scripts of 96 gays and lesbians, the researchers examined hypothetical versus actual dating scripts; the results are presented in Table 8.1. (Klinkenberg & Rose, 1994). These findings are very interesting, because they show us that the cultural/interpersonal dating scripts for same-sex partners mirror those of heterosexual partners. It appears that when it comes to going out on a date, it doesn't necessarily matter if we're gay or straight—we tend to follow culturally determined dating scripts regardless of our sexual orientation.

Contemporary dating can take the form of more traditional dating that eventually leads to cohabitation or marriage, or it can take more casual forms, such as Internet dating and hooking up (see Chapter 6 for the hooking up discussion).

TABLE 8.1
Scripts for Hypothetical and Actual First Dates for Gay Men and Lesbians

Source: Klinkenberg, D., & Rose, S. (1994).

Hypothetical Date		Actual Date	
Gay Men	**Lesbians**	**Gay Men**	**Lesbians**
Discuss plans	Discuss plans	Discussed plans	Discussed plans
Groom/dress	Tell friends about date	Were nervous	Were nervous
Prepare (clean apartment)	Groom/dress	Groomed/dressed	Groomed/dressed
Meet date at location	Meet date at location	Picked up date	Prepared (cleaned apartment)
Get to know by talking	Leave for another location	Left for another location	Picked up date
Talk/laugh/joke	Get to know by talking	Evaluated date	Got to know date
Go to movie/show	Talk/laugh/joke	Went to movie/show	Talked/laughed/joked
Eat/drink (non-alcohol)	Go to a movie/show	Ate/drank (non-alcohol) Went to movie	Ate/drank (non-alcohol)
Initiate physical contact	Initiate physical contact	Drank alcohol	Had positive feelings
Make out	Make plans for another date	Made out	Kissed/hugged
Make plans for another date	Kiss/hug goodnight Go home	Had sex	Took date home Stayed over
Go home	Take date home	Made plans for another date	Went home

>>> Instead of bars or fraternity and sorority parties, students today often opt for Internet chatrooms to meet eligible mates. **Have you ever met someone on the Internet and agreed to meet in person? What are some advantages to this contemporary way of meeting someone?**

ONLINE DATING

Internet chatrooms are quickly replacing bars as a place for meeting available singles. Organizations such as Match.com, eHarmony.com, and Facebook.com, provide people a virtual space in which they can place personal ads and photos. People can engage in synchronous communication (such as IMing), or asynchronous communication (like e-mail). Today, many Skype (Web cam) to enhance their interactions. These online sites generate opportunities to initially interact with someone, and then move to face-to-face relationships if they desire to pursue the friendship or relationship. These electronic liaisons allow people to remain anonymous or to fully self-disclose personal information. Today, some sites are getting the entire family involved in the matchmaking process. The social networking site, Engage.com, invites family and friends to engage in choosing potential partners for their loved ones (Barraket & Henry-Waring, 2008).

A $1 billion dollar industry in the United States, there are currently about 3 million registered online dating users; in 2006, one in 10 Internet users indicated having gone to a Web site to meet people online, and nearly one-third of all American adults say they know someone who has used a dating Web site (Madden & Lenhart, 2006). In one survey of more than 4,500 Internet users, respondents aged 18 to 24 indicated that they met an average of 10 dating partners in online chatrooms (Hollander, 2003). People engage in various dating-related activities online; individuals use the Internet in a number of ways, from flirting to breaking up. However, it is important to take precautions when Internet dating. Safety tips are outlined in Figure 8.4.

Recent research reveals some benefits to online dating, some of which challenge our existing understanding of relationship formation. For example, earlier we discussed the importance of geographic closeness in selecting a potential mate. With online dating, physical proximity is de-emphasized as a necessary feature of relationship formation—individuals are free to interact with people across the globe (Barraket & Henry-Waring, 2008).

Another benefit of Internet dating is that it frees people to meet others outside their existing social networks (Barraket & Henry-Waring, 2008). As one 25-year-old male observed,

It elevates you out of your social circle, and you're sort of broadcast to a broad bunch of people, and if you're fairly open-ended in your profile, and not so descriptive about what you do or don't do, then you get the opportunity to meet lots of different people that you would never know (p. 157).

For some, being able to go beyond their current social network allows them the freedom to explore and express their sexuality in different ways, or to experience deeper levels of self-disclosure (it's easier for some people to disclose over the Internet than it is for face-to-face disclosure). For others, the increased freedom gives them

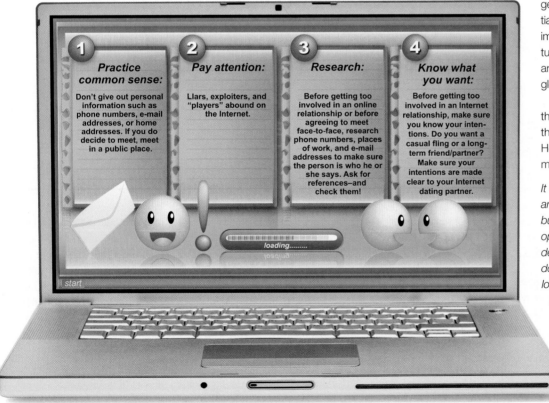

Figure 8.4 Internet Dating Safety To minimize risk to a person's safety and well-being, **some guidelines to Internet dating have been proposed.**

sexual (life) now

Is Love the Basis for Marriage?

Is love a prerequisite for marital bliss and happiness? While people from *collectivist cultures* may marry someone based on what is considered to be good for the entire group, people from *individualistic cultures*, like the United States, typically marry someone who fulfills their personal, individual goals, such as being in love. Is love the basis for marriage?

YES!

Marriage and family therapist Henry Grunebaum (2003) notes that "love" contains unique characteristics that are unlike any other emotion or feeling experienced by human beings and that true love rarely occurs. People consider love a precious and enduring experience, and the elements needed to foster an enduring relationship of any kind are needed to foster a strong, enduring love relationship: intimacy, communication, kindness, and an active interest in the other person. Grunebaum points out that loveless marriages are difficult to repair. In his clinical experience, "When romantic love is lost, it is almost always gone for good."

NO!

Marriage and family therapist Joseph Silverman (2003) contends that the feelings associated with love are mainly nervousness associated with the excited feelings produced by the chemicals in the brain when we are attracted to another person. When in this excited state, couples make lifelong commitments to one another and set themselves up for disappointment. According to Silverman, there are problems with linking love as a basis for marriage:

- People overestimate the significance of the importance of love, and they feel deprived or empty if the excitement wanes. Other aspects of the relationship, such as compatibility, sharing experiences, or similar family goals are equally important as feelings of love.

- According to Silverman, there is no such thing as a "perfect partner"; anyone who is reasonably tolerant and flexible can successfully marry nearly anyone.

- The most important relationship in any person's life, marriage cannot fulfill every desire of both partners.

In Silverman's view, "not every marriage has to be violins and roses." Marriages of convenience and marriages in which love does not exist have a place all the same.

>>> **WHAT DO YOU THINK?**
1. Do you agree with Grunebaum's statement that romantic love occurs rarely? Why or why not?
2. Do you agree with Silverman's statement that a person can successfully marry nearly anyone? Why or why not?
3. Is love a prerequisite for marriage for you?

Sources: Grunebaum, H. (2003) & Silverman, J. S. (2003).

---

the opportunity to take chances on relationships they might not venture to try in their "real" lives, because if the relationship doesn't work out they don't have to see them every day. One female noted,

I think the fact that you never have to see them again is wonderful. You know, if it's friends or work or whatever, and it doesn't work out, then you've got all the awkwardness . . . that carries into your life (Barraket & Henry-Waring, 2008, p. 157).

Others indicate that being able to have high levels of control over the "pace and place" of electronic communication is a benefit (Barraket & Henry-Waring, 2008). What may be surprising to some people is that online dating etiquette seems to mimic off-line dating norms; traditional gendered patterns of interaction are practiced in online dating, with male users "making the first move" in contacting their prospective partners online (Barraket & Henry-Waring, 2008).

Of course, there is a hazardous side to online dating. While you may be looking for love or for fun, the person on the other end of the mouse may be looking for a quick sexual encounter or may have even more dangerous intentions in mind (Madden & Lenhart, 2006). For example, in 2005, 17-year-old coed Taylor Behl formed an Internet relationship with a 38-year-old man who portrayed himself on the Internet as a photographic artist. After meeting the man face to face and having a brief sexual encounter with him, she tried to end the relationship. She was murdered a short time later.

Others are at risk for cyberstalking. **Cyberstalking** is the use of information technology (such as the Internet or cell phones) to harass others. A number of cyberstalking factors have been identified (Bocij, 2004):

- **False accusations:** Some harass people by attempting to damage the reputations of their victims. They do this by posting false information or by setting up their own Web sites or blogs for this purpose.

I Can't Help Falling in Love: The Science of Love

What is love, actually? What is the basis of the giddy, walking-on-air feelings we experience when we fall in love? Recent advances in science may reveal the answer.

The initial feelings of love don't have much to do with romance, but instead have more to do with functions of the brain. Chemicals called neurotransmitters carry information between brain neurons across areas of the brain. When we begin to fall in love, the "high" we experience is the result of the release of these neurotransmitters. When two people are attracted to one another, the brain becomes flooded with a gush of neurotransmitters that mimic *amphetamines* (commonly referred to as "uppers"). The neurotransmitter culprits are *dopamine*, which makes us feel good; *norepinephrine*, which causes pounding hearts and racing pulses; and PEA (*phenylethylamine*), which causes feelings of excitement and euphoria. Because chocolate contains PEA, it has long been rumored to promote infatuation between lovers (however, it is probably more the result of the large amounts of caffeine and sugar found in chocolate).

The neurotransmitters then signal the *pituitary gland*, located in the region of the brain known as the hypothalamus, to release a multitude of hormones that rapidly flood the bloodstream. The sex glands, in turn, release even more hormones. It is the combination of the flood of neurotransmitters in the brain and the subsequent release of the hormones into the bloodstream that allow new lovers to make love all night or talk for hours on end. When these chemicals are produced over a period of time, people interpret the physical sensations as "falling in love." Love, actually, is a cocktail of neurochemicals.

Source: Based on Aron, A., Mashek, D. J., Fisher, H. E., Li, H., & Brown, L. L. (2005).

- **Attempts to gather information about the victim:** Some cyberstalkers advertise for information or hire a private detective. Often, they try to track the victims' IP addresses in an attempt to gather more information.

- **Encouraging others to harass the victim:** Often, cyberstalkers enlist others by claiming the victim has harmed the stalker or his or her family. This is referred to as *false victimization*.

- **Attacks on data and equipment:** Some try to damage a victim's computer by sending viruses.

- **Arranging to meet:** Adolescents and young adults are at a particularly high risk of having cyberstalkers try to set up face-to-face meetings.

To minimize risk to a person's safety and well-being, some guidelines have been proposed. If approached with caution and care, Internet dating is another alternative to meeting people of like interests.

The ways in which people come together to form intimate couple bonds have changed significantly in the United States. From the centuries-old practice of courtship under the watchful eye of a parent to today's Internet dating and hooking up, couples have always found ways to be intimate with one another. Now let's look at the experiences of love and loving.

WHAT IS LOVE, ACTUALLY?

I "love" buttered movie popcorn. I "love" the prairie. I really "love" collegiate football. I "love" my husband and my children, family, and friends. I "love" teaching. This crazy little thing called love has been assigned over 20 definitions in the dictionary, and includes such descriptions as fondness, devotion, and having a weakness for something. A problem with these definitions still remains, though: We can "have a weakness for" pizza; we can be "fond of" pizza; we may even be "devoted to" or "adore" pizza! In today's society, we tend to use the word *love*

when we really mean we *prefer* something or *enjoy* something or *like* to be in someone's company.

Over the years, numerous theorists have provided explanations about the components and characteristics of love (Fehr, 1988; Hatfield & Sprecher, 1986; Hazan & Shaver, 1987; Hendrick & Hendrick, 1986; Lee, 1988; Tennov, 1979, among many others). It's impossible to address each of these theories here; because of this, our goal is to gain a basic understanding of those components that make up what we call "love." One researcher found a way to help us to understand the different types of love we might experience in relationships.

LEE'S SIX TYPES OF LOVE STYLES

The Greeks solved the problem of using only one word—love—for perhaps the most complex emotion known to humankind. John Alan Lee (1973) conceptualized love in a manner similar to that of the Greeks. He proposed six different love styles.

- **Eros:** Eros refers to a type of sensual or sexual love. **Erotic lovers** are passionate and romantic and seek passionately expressive lovers. They thrive on the tantalizing nature of love and sex. They have an "ideal mate" in their mind's eye and believe there is only one

<<< Love is a very difficult relational process to define and to describe **because it is experienced in so many different ways.**

"true love" in the world for them. Sexual activity usually occurs early on in the relationship, and the sex is hot, passionate, exciting, and insatiable all at once. Once sexual activity takes place, the eros lover is usually monogamous.

- **Ludus:** This love is playful, flirtatious, carefree, and casual. **Ludic lovers** don't care as much about commitment as they do about playing the sport or the game of love. Variety is the spice of life—the more partners, the better. Because ludic lovers don't share intimacy, love with a ludic person is fun and easy-going, nonchalant and uncon-cerned about tomorrow.

- **Storge:** Storge (pronounced STOR-gay) love can best be conceptualized as friend-ship love, or a type of affectionate love between companions. **Storgic lovers** typically come to love each other over time, as op-posed to the instantaneous type of love found with eros lovers.

- **Manic:** Jealousy, envy, protectiveness, and exclu-sivity are the hallmark traits of **manic lovers**. Manic love is frenzied, agitated, hectic, and chaotic. The highs are very high, the lows are very low—making the relationship very much a roller coaster ride of emotions. When a love relationship ends, a manic lover has diffi-culty thinking of anyone or anything else except the lost love.

- **Pragma:** Practicality and logic guide the *pragmatic* lover. With **pragma** love, the costs and benefits associated with love are care-fully weighed and considered before entering into a relationship. If the "perfect mate" items on the pragmatic lover's list are fulfilled—suitability of education, family background, socioeconomic status, religion, and so on—the love candidate has a good chance of becoming a mate or life partner.

- **Agape:** Agape love is a selfless, enduring, other-centered type of love. The term *agape* refers to unconditional, willful, "I-love-you-because-I-choose-to" kind of love. It is a love type that provides intrinsic (rewarding in and of itself) satisfaction, with no reciprocity expected or demanded. Inherent to agape love is patience, kind-ness, and permanence.

>>> Passionate love is a wildly powerful emotion that is fueled, in part, by chemicals in the brain and by hormones. **The intense sexual attraction and the all-consuming desire for the other person typically isn't the kind of love that long-term relation-ships are made of.**

∧
∧
∧
∧ Companionate love is a deep, tender, emotionally mature attachment shared between two people. **It grows slowly, gradually over time, and accepts all the shortcomings and faults of each partner.**

But does everyone the world over experience love the same way? Not necessarily. For example, some research has found that love typologies that involve "strong emotional feelings," such as *mania*, *eros*, and *agape*, are nearly free of cultural influences; across cultures, people tend to experience these love typologies in very similar ways. Those love typologies that involved "strict social rules," such as *pragma*, *storge*, and *ludus*, are quite dependent on cultural values.

PASSIONATE LOVE AND COMPANIONATE LOVE

Passionate love is a wildly powerful emotion that is expe-rienced as intense longing for the selected love object, along with profound sexual arousal and confused feelings (Hatfield et al., 1988). Passionate love can either be a blissful experi-ence if the love is reciprocated or a painful experience if the love is ignored. Other research found that passionate love involves a mix of intense emotional and phys-ical characteristics, such as a pounding heart, a choking sensation in the throat, sweating palms, and/or a constricting sensation in the chest (Rice, 1993). The emotional manifestations include idealizing the roman-tic partner, intense sexual attraction, a surge of self-confidence, adora-tion of the love interest, and an all-consuming, selfless desire to promote the well-being of the partner (Rice, 1993).

For some couples, family, friends, academics, sports, work, and every-thing else that used to be important lose their priority in life. Family and friends may disapprove of the relationship because they are being neg-lected and ignored by the couple. In fact, if parents, family, and friends voice concern about the exclusivity of the relationship, it is perhaps an indication that the relationship is not "real love." In short, it's the lovestruck stuff that the relationships on reality TV dating shows are made of—but not what long-lasting marriages are made of.

The Passionate Love Scale

Think of the person whom you love most passionately right now. If you are not in love, please think of the last person you loved. If you have never been in love, think of the person you came closest to caring for in that way. Try to describe the way you felt when your feelings were most intense. Answers range from (1) *Not at all true* to (9) *Definitely true*.

	Not at all true								Definitely true
I would feel deep despair if _____ left me.	1	2	3	4	5	6	7	8	9
Sometimes I feel I can't control my thoughts; they are obsessively on _____.	1	2	3	4	5	6	7	8	9
I feel happy when I'm doing something to make _____ happy.	1	2	3	4	5	6	7	8	9
I would rather be with _____ than anyone else.	1	2	3	4	5	6	7	8	9
I'd get jealous if I thought _____ was falling in love with someone else.	1	2	3	4	5	6	7	8	9
I yearn to know all about _____.	1	2	3	4	5	6	7	8	9
I have an endless appetite for affection from _____.	1	2	3	4	5	6	7	8	9
For me, _____ is the perfect romantic partner.	1	2	3	4	5	6	7	8	9
I sense my body responding when _____ touches me.	1	2	3	4	5	6	7	8	9
_____ always seems to be on my mind.	1	2	3	4	5	6	7	8	9
I want _____ to know me—my thoughts, fears, and my hopes.	1	2	3	4	5	6	7	8	9
I eagerly look for signs indicating _____'s desire for me.	1	2	3	4	5	6	7	8	9
I possess a powerful attraction for _____.	1	2	3	4	5	6	7	8	9
I get extremely depressed when things don't go right in my relationship with _____.	1	2	3	4	5	6	7	8	9

Passionate Love Scale Scores

Extremely Passionate: 106–135 points *You are wildly and recklessly in love!*

Passionate: 86–105 points *You are passionate, but with reduced intensity.*

Average: 66–85 points *You have occasional bursts of passion.*

Cool: 45–65 points *Your passion is lukewarm and infrequent.*

Extremely cool: 15–44 points *Sorry, baby, but the thrill is gone.*

Sources: Hatfield, E., & Sprecher, S. (1986); Fehr, B. (1988); Hendrick, C., & Hendrick, C. (1989).

This type of situation occurs as the result of a physical attraction. Although physical attraction is an important element in emotionally mature love relationships, it is not one of the *primary* factors in relationship satisfaction and longevity. With passionate love, there are relatively few factors beyond the physical traits that attract us to the other; such attraction doesn't lead to loving someone else, but only loving or being attracted to a certain part of the person. As the attraction to a particular trait begins to wane, so too does the "love."

There's love . . . and there's love that lasts. It's not uncommon for relationships to move from the have-to-be-intimate-24-hours-a-day phase (passionate love) to a phase of love that is less dominated by lust. If the love remained at the sexually and emotionally charged state, we would be too worn out to accomplish much else! If love is to endure, it must at some point be combined with or transition into a calmer, more tender, more affectionate type of love. **Companionate love** refers to deep, tender, mature, affectionate attachment bonds shared between two people; companionate love may or may not include feelings of physical arousal.

While passionate love happens quickly, companionate love grows gradually over time—it develops between partners who have known each other long enough to have acknowledged and accepted all of the failings, faults, shortcomings, oddities and quirks of each partner—and still *like* the partner. Passionate love relationships typically do not want to devote the time necessary to build up rewards, because the very nature of these relationships contradicts spending time on anything beyond the physical.

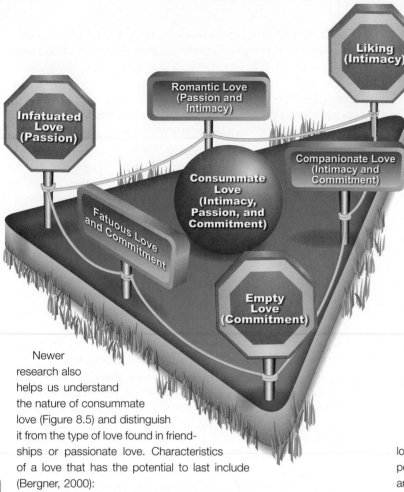

Figure 8.5 Sternberg's Triangle of Love Theory According to Sternberg, love is composed of different combinations of the **three components of love—intimacy, passion, and commitment.**

- **Intimacy/inclusion:** This means that we give our love object the central place in our lives, both physically and emotionally. The beloved is the primary confidant and "soul mate." Great care is taken to avoid anything that would drive the couple apart.

- **Commitment:** The researcher describes this component as an "ever-fixed mark" that does not change, despite circumstances.

- **Exclusivity:** The intimacy, sexuality, and commitment are reserved for the love interest alone.

- **Understanding:** This implies that lovers grasp the truest sense of who their love partner is—their world view, values, goals, vulnerabilities, and so forth.

Because of the investment required to promote the well-being of a love partner, a mutual love relationship often holds great importance in peoples' lives (Bergner, 2000). This body of work also notes that there are barriers that prevent some people from experiencing lasting love relationships. These are presented in Table 8.2.

Unfortunately, there is also a negative side of love.

Newer research also helps us understand the nature of consummate love (Figure 8.5) and distinguish it from the type of love found in friendships or passionate love. Characteristics of a love that has the potential to last include (Bergner, 2000):

- **Investment in the well-being of the beloved:** To be "in love" with someone requires that the needs, desires and wants of the love object are placed above our own and that acts on the behalf of the wellbeing of the beloved; it also involves avoiding anything that hurts him or her.

- **Appreciation/admiration:** This characteristic involves appreciation and respect, as well as accepting the person just as he or she is without expectation or requirement of change.

- **Sexual desire:** Love often involves the desire to touch and to be touched, to hold and to be held.

THE NEGATIVE SIDES OF LOVE: JEALOUSY AND STALKING

Jealousy is an emotional reaction to the perception that a valued relationship is endangered and may be taken over by a rival (DeSteno, Valdesolo, & Bartlett, 2006; Knox, Breed, & Zusman, 2007). This perceived threat can be real or imaginary. Jealousy is typically aroused when one person believes

TABLE 8.2
Barriers to Love

Source: Bergner, R. M. (2000).

There are several barriers to being able to love another person.

Inability to understand and treat persons as persons: Some people have an inability to recognize how others think and feel, and they are insensitive and/or indifferent to other peoples' rights; there are some individuals who are severely restricted in their abilities to treat people with respect and kindness.
Inability to understand and appreciate love itself: Often, people hold misconceptions about love, such as understanding love as a feeling or strong affection, rather than as a relationship in which each love partner values the status of the other.
Preemptive needs and motives: Sometimes, a person has individual or personal needs that interfere with or make it difficult to meet the needs of another unselfishly. This is one of the most common barriers to love.
Hypercritical tendencies: Some people have a tendency to be extremely critical of others. This prevents them from fully loving and accepting another.
Ineligibility for love: Sometimes, people perceive that they possess undesirable qualities, are physically unattractive, lack personal appeal, or are sexually inadequate. Because they believe they are disqualified to be a love interest, they act in ways to make sure they are not selected as a lover.

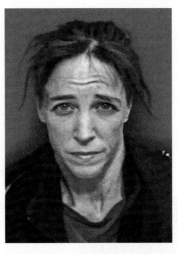

> Referred to by the media as "Astronut," NASA astronaut Lisa Nowak stalked her romantic rival for months. **So obsessed was Nowak, she drove from Texas to Florida wearing adult diapers so she wouldn't have to stop along the way.**

that someone is getting what the person wishes to have for himself or herself, such as attention, love or affection. It is an emotion that can manifest in several ways, including anger, fear, pain, betrayal, anxiety, sadness, paranoia, depression, feelings of powerlessness or inadequacy (Brehm, 1992).

The central emotion behind jealousy is *fear*—fear of change, fear about the future of the relationship, fear of abandonment or fear of losing power in the relationship. At the very least, jealousy causes hurt feelings; at its worst, it can result in intimate partner violence (see Chapter 17) or lead to a murderous rage (White, 1981). Jealousy was a likely contributing factor in about 40 percent of female homicides in 2000 (Knox, Breed, & Zusman, 2007; U.S. Department of Justice, 2003).

There are a number of factors that determine how we experience jealousy, such as family of origin experiences, past relationship experiences, sexual attitudes and beliefs, and gender role attitudes (Russell & Harton, 2005). Jealousy is a complex emotion that has many sides to it, which makes it difficult for scientists to measure.

Stalking is the obsessive following, observing or contacting of another person, or the obsessive attempt to engage in any of these activities. It can be done in person, or online. The U.S. Department of Justice (2007) shows us that:

- Each year, over 1 million women and over 370,000 men are stalked.

- One in 12 women and one in 45 men will be stalked in their lifetime.

- Most victims know their stalker.

- 81 percent of women who are stalked have also been physically assaulted by that person.

- The average duration of stalking is 1.8 years, and two-thirds of stalkers attempt to contact their victims at least daily, using many methods.

Stalking can also be a problem on college campuses, with three in 10 college women reporting emotional, psychological, or physical harm from being stalked; 80 percent knew their stalker. In 2007, over one half of stalked women took some type of self-protective measure, and 11 percent had to relocate. More than one-fourth of stalking victims lost time from work as a result of emotional turmoil caused by stalking (U.S. Department of Justice, 2007).

Stalking exists in many forms, and sometimes victims don't even realize that it is happening because it can be subtle. Online and offline stalking are federal crimes under the laws of all 50 states. It is also considered a crime in Canada, Japan and the United Kingdom.

BREAKING UP

The nature of relationships is that pain is always possible because someone said or did something—or didn't say or do something. Sometimes we let the hurt stay under the surface and allow it to fester. This unresolved conflict almost always becomes the "background" of the relationship, and it's always present no matter how hard we try to make the relationship work (Gottman, 1994a, 1994b, 1999; Gottman & Gottman, 2007). Other times, it seems as though all we do is fight with our partner, over big things, small things, and things that don't really matter at all. Breaking up becomes almost inevitable.

There are a number of relational transgressions that can cause pain. Generally speaking, **relational transgressions** are hurtful words or actions that communicate a devaluation of the partner or the relationship (Bachman & Guerrero, 2006). Some examples of relational transgressions include deceit, unfaithfulness, criticism, blaming, and betrayals of self-disclosure (Bachman & Guerrero, 2006). At the very least, these hurtful comments or actions may increase uncertainty about the relationship and may create temporary problems for the couple. For many, the ultimate consequence of relational transgressions is a breakup. Although some people do stay in relationships and work out even the most serious violations of trust (Roloff, Soule, & Carey, 2001), people who are deeply hurt by their partner's actions are likely to dissolve the relationship (Vangelisti & Young, 2000).

Breaking up is tough for most people, and it is associated with a number of negative physical and emotional responses, from anxiety and depression, to loneliness, to the suppression of the immune system due to stress (Davis, Shaver, & Vernon, 2003). In a study of nearly 5,300 participants (mostly in their teens and 20s), the researchers observed a range of reactions to breaking up; these are presented in Table 8.3.

TABLE 8.3
Distress/Protest Reactions to Breaking Up

Source: Davis, D., Shaver, P. R., & Vernon, M. L. (2003).

Type of Reaction

Distress reactions
Physical/emotional distress
Lost interest in sex
Self-blame
Guilt
Partner blame

Protest reactions
Want/try to get back together
Sexual arousal
Anger/hostility/revenge
Physically hurt
Preoccupation
Exploration/interference

As the table shows us, there are two types of breakup reactions: *distress* and *protest*. **Distress reactions** include such things as physical and emotional pain, loss of interest in sex and guilt. **Protest reactions** are behaviors and feelings that attempt to reestablish the relationship, such as trying to re-involve the ex-partner in sexual relations (Davis, Shaver, & Vernon, 2003). The researchers also found that those who did not initiate the breakup felt a lost sense of identity and were more likely to jump immediately into a replacement relationship. Some also turned to alcohol and/or drugs to help them cope with the breakup.

Sometimes, the end of a relationship means that we'll go through a period of mourning and loss. There appear to be three phases that follow the end of a relationship, particularly in breakups that involve college students: 1) *experiencing a loss*, which includes emotionally processing the loss and realizing its implications; 2) *pulling apart*, which involves separating emotionally, physically and symbolically from the partner; and 3) *moving beyond*, which encompasses not only a reduction in distress, but an ability to grow from the experiences (Hebert & Popadiuk, 2008). College students in this study went from devastation ("This wasn't a breakup—it was a smash up") to coping ("I'm sad, but I'm trying to use my sadness in the most constructive ways possible; I'm letting it motivate me to do better in school and go to the gym"), to healing and resolution ("Breaking up is the best divorce you can have before you get married. You learn *a lot* from it").

There are a number of ways to cope with a breakup, such as taking time to examine what really happened and why; thinking through things thoroughly, but not excessively; dealing effectively with the hate phase (talking to friends or writing your feelings down in a journal); staying active; and making a conscious decision to let go of the hatred and realizing that harboring hate only hurts you, not your ex. If after a breakup you find that your sleeping and eating patterns are changing, that you can't focus, that you have low energy or are irritable, or if you feel a continuous, general sense of sadness, it's best to talk to a health care professional on campus. Being single doesn't mean you have to be alone.

∧
∧ Breaking up is almost always hard to do! **For most**
∧ **of us, it's hard to repair a relationship if our partner has hurt us deeply.**

THE CONNECTION BETWEEN LOVE AND SEX: IS SEX BETTER IF WE LOVE OUR PARTNER?

Certainly we can love someone without experiencing sex, and certainly we can experience sex without loving the sexual partner. Is there a connection between love and sex?

New research suggests that being in love is what actually drives someone to want to have sex with his or her love object. Neuroscientist Arthur Aron and his colleagues (2005) used brain scans to study the brains of men and women who were "newly" or "madly" in love. The researchers wanted to answer the historic question of whether love and sex are really the same thing and if the feelings we have in our early love relationships are, in actuality, just warmed-over feelings of sexual arousal. The researchers found that passionate love is a highly motivated, goal-oriented state, and this state is what makes us want to pursue sex with our lovers and to protect our lovers and the relationship. According to this research, passionate love is more powerful than the human sex drive.

Love can be an important motivational force for the participation in sexual activities (Kaestle & Tucker-Halpern, 2007; Aron et al., 2005). But is sex actually better if we love our partners?

How we experience sex, and the sense of enjoyment or satisfaction we get from sex is highly personal (Davidson, Darling, & Norton, 1995). But a wide body of empirical evidence indicates that there is an association between sexual satisfaction and relationship satisfaction (Aron et al., 2005; Bartels & Zeki, 2000; Christopher & Sprecher, 2000; Kaestle & Tucker-Halpern, 2007; Regan, 2000, among many). For example, one study of college-age dating couples found that men and women who are most sexually satisfied tend to also report high levels of love and commitment, whereas couples who report lower levels of sexual satisfaction are more likely to report lower levels of love and commitment (Sprecher, 2002). The most recent investigation of 6,421 young adults, ages 18 to 26, revealed that study participants who were in love reported higher levels of sexual satisfaction (Kaestle & Tucker-Halpern, 2007). Study respondents who reported high levels of love for their partners and who reported that their

>>> "But I love you, baby. I really, really love you." Be careful—**while he may be sincere in his expression of love, he may be just trying to get some.**

partners felt high levels of love for them, engaged in a greater variety of sexual activities than those who reported lower levels of love. Overall, the research findings supported the researchers' notion that higher levels of love are associated with greater sexual variety within the relationship, leading to higher levels of relationship satisfaction.

ARE THERE DIFFERENCES IN HOW MEN AND WOMEN VIEW LOVE AND SEX?

There is some evidence that it is easier for men to have sex with little or no emotional attachment or commitment to the sex partner than it is for women; it is also easier for men to have sex just for pleasure than it is for women (Buss, 1999). There is also research that indicates men are more likely than women to want sex early on in the relationship (perhaps within hours!) (Knox, Sturidivant, & Zusman, 2001). Interestingly, although men are more likely to engage in sex without an emotional attachment to their partner, they tend to express their love first and have higher levels of romantic beliefs than do women (Sharp & Ganong, 2000).

A recent study of 147 college undergraduates showed that men are significantly more likely than females to say "I love you" sooner in the relationship—but they have a sexual agenda for doing so (Brantley, Knox, & Zusman, 2002). In this study, the researchers wanted to understand the timing and meaning of saying "I love you" to a new partner. Analysis of their findings showed two interesting results:

- Men tend to say "I love you" first: Men reported that in relationships where both partners mutually loved each other, men disclosed their love first.

- Men tend to say "I love you" for sex: If men thought that saying "I love you" would increase the chance that their partners would have sex with them, they did so.

This study clearly showed that within this study sample, men used love to get sex. As the researchers note, "Students now have empirical verification that hearing 'I love you' may mean little more than 'I am saying this because I hope you will have sex with me'" (Knox & Zusman, 2002).

SEXUAL LIFE EDUCATION

This is an ambitious chapter, and we've covered a lot of ground as we explored different theories that attempt to explain how and why we are attracted to some people, and not to others, as well as different paths to committed relationships, such as dating and courtship. Relationally, as a society we are living in uncharted and unprecedented times. How did we move from the tradition of courting under the eye of a parent, to free-for-all, ephemeral sexual relationships? If we look at the past 50 or 60 years, the way people develop interpersonal partnerships has undergone extraordinary changes, from parent-directed and parent-approved courtship with the intention of marriage, to Internet dating. We wonder what other types of changes might be in store.

And although all cultures define and experience love differently, as Bergner's research helped us see, love that lasts requires that we invest ourselves wholly and fully to our individual partners, and that we appreciate and accept them for who they are. Sternberg's triangle theory perhaps helps us best understand that the three elements of love—passion, intimacy and commitment—are the stuff that lasting life partnerships are made of—what real love is made of.

Summary

WHAT ARE THE INTERPERSONAL ATTRACTION THEORIES? 152

- Evolutionary theory proposes that we choose mates based on the probability of reproductive success. Males inherently seek a large quantity of sexual partners to pass on their genes, while women prefer to be more selective due to the strain of childbearing.
- Social exchange theory suggests that individuals are motivated by self-interest to make the most out of the resources they possess. In relationships, people act in ways that maximize the benefits and minimize the costs.
- The filter theory of mate selection claims that we each use variables such as propinquity and heterogamy to select potential mates from the pool of eligible candidates.

WHAT MAKES UP THE PATH TO COMMITMENT? 155

- In some societies, traditional courtship practices are used to steer a couple toward the commitment of marriage. The decision to wed is not taken lightly and is usually decided by the entire family. In more Western societies, dating is used in place of courtship. Dating is more recreational and not necessarily seen as leading to marriage.

- Both heterosexual and homosexual couples use similar dating scripts to help guide their decisions and behaviors during romantic socialization.

WHAT IS LOVE, ACTUALLY? 161

- According to John Alan Lee, six different love styles exist: eros, ludus, manic, storge, pragma, and agape. Another theory focuses on passionate and companionate love; passionate love is based on sexual arousal and physical attraction to a partner, while companionate love stems from deep feelings of attachment and friendship.
- Breakups usually result from relational transgressions, and can lead to distress or protest reactions.
- Research of sexual relations has shown that higher levels of love between partners lead to increased sexual pleasure and variety. Men are more likely than women to have sex purely for pleasure and to initiate it early on in a relationship. While men tend to experience and express romantic feelings before women do, a majority also claim that they profess false feelings of love to initiate physical relations.

Key Terms

natural selection theory that nature selects the best-adapted varieties of species to survive and reproduce *152*

sexual selection process in which members of one sex compete among themselves for opportunities to mate when the pool of potential mating candidates is limited; the "winners" out-reproduce the other competitors and natural selection occurs *152*

evolutionary theory theory that human beings choose mates for the sole purpose of maximizing and enhancing our reproductive efforts, ensuring reproductive success and the success of the species and society *152*

fertility cues traits associated with successful fertility, such as full breasts, small waist, and curvy hips *152*

protector/provider cues cues that indicate that a man will be a good protector/provider, such as intelligence, physical strength, industriousness, and ambition *152*

social exchange theory theory that centers on the exchange of people's resources and asserts that individuals are thought to act out of self-interest to make the most of the resources they possess *154*

rewards benefits, such as payback or compensations, that are exchanged in social relationships *154*

cost a debit that increases the likelihood or probability that a person will not take part in a given behavior *154*

filter theory of mate selection theory that suggests that when looking for mates, we use a filtering mechanism that helps us sort out a potential mate from the vast pool of candidates *154*

pool of candidates potential array of eligible partners *154*

pair bonds couples *155*

courting and **courtship** the practices that are socially prescribed forms of conduct that guide men and women toward matrimony *156*

dating an occasion in which people get together socially for any number of reasons, such as "hanging out," pursuing a relationship to determine whether the partner is a potential partner for a lifelong relationship, or getting together sexually with no strings attached *156*

script theory each of us uses scripts that help us organize the information in our environments *157*

dating scripts internalized guidelines, or a "how-to" manual for social behavior *157*

cyberstalking the use of information technology (such as the Internet or cell phones) to harass others *160*

eros a type of sensual or sexual love *161*

erotic lovers passionate and romantic lovers who seek passionately expressive lovers *161*

ludic lovers playful, flirtatious, carefree, and casual lovers who don't care as much about commitment as they do about playing the sport or the game of love *162*

storge friendship love, or a type of affectionate love between companions *162*

storgic lovers lovers who typically come to love each other over time (compared to erotic lovers) *162*

manic lovers lovers who exhibit jealousy, envy, protectiveness, and exclusivity *162*

pragma a love in which the costs and benefits associated are carefully weighed and considered before entering into a relationship *162*

agape love a selfless, enduring, other-centered type of love *162*

passionate love a wildly powerful emotion that is experienced as intense longing for the selected love object, along with profound sexual arousal and confused feelings   *162*

companionate love deep, tender, mature, affectionate attachment bonds shared between two people that may or may not include feelings of physical arousal   *163*

jealousy an emotional reaction to the perception that a valued relationship is endangered and may be taken over by a rival   *164*

stalking the obsessive following, observing, or contacting of another person, or the obsessive attempt to engage in any of these activities   *165*

relational transgressions hurtful words or actions that communicate a devaluation of the partner or the relationship and include deceit,

unfaithfulness, criticism, blaming, and betrayals of self-disclosure   *165*

distress reactions breakup reactions that include physical and emotional pain, loss of interest in sex, and guilt   *166*

protest reactions behaviors and feelings that attempt to reestablish the relationship, such as trying to re-involve the ex-partner in sexual relations   *166*

Sample Test Questions

MULTIPLE CHOICE

1. Choosing mates based on reproductive purposes is the foundation of which interpersonal attraction theory?
   a. Social exchange theory
   b. Filter theory of mate selection
   c. Evolutionary theory
   d. None of the above

2. Courtship includes:
   a. Family involvement
   b. One-on-one premarital relationships
   c. Dating without the intention of marrying
   d. All of the above

3. Regarding dating scripts, homosexual women have which of the following in common with heterosexual women?
   a. Emotional intimacy is a valued aspect when dating.
   b. First dates feature deep levels of self-disclosure and emotional sharing.
   c. A close friendship is likely to be established before dating begins.
   d. They tend to emphasize personality traits in their partners over sexual attraction.

4. False victimization in cyberstalking is when:
   a. The cyberstalker claims the victim has harmed the stalker or his or her family.
   b. The cyberstalker tracks the victim's IP address in an attempt to gain more information.
   c. The cyberstalker attempts to damage the reputation of the victim.
   d. The cyberstalker sends a virus to the victim's computer.

5. Which neurochemical is NOT one of the ones that mimics amphetamines when two people are attracted to one another?
   a. Dopamine
   b. Testosterone
   c. Phenylethylamine
   d. Norepinephrine

6. Storge love is:
   a. Passionate and sexual love
   b. Friendship and affectionate love
   c. Flirtatious and casual love
   d. Frenzied and chaotic love

7. According to Sternberg, commitment and intimacy comprise which type of love?
   a. Companionate love
   b. Empty love
   c. Passionate love
   d. Consummate love

8. Which of the following can be considered a relational transgression?
   a. Criticism
   b. Deceit
   c. Blaming
   d. All of the above

SHORT RESPONSE

1. Which interpersonal attraction theory do you feel best describes the way you have selected your mates thus far? Why?

2. How much influence have your parents had over whom you date and for what purposes? If you were to have children, how much influence would you want to have?

3. Using Sternberg's classifications of love, which types have you experienced?

4. Have you ever agreed to meet someone you met over the Internet in person? How do you prefer to find potential partners?

5. Explain the difference between courtship and dating.

Remember to check www.thethinkspot.com **for additional information, downloadable flashcards, and other helpful resources.**

COMMUNICATION:
Enriching Intimate Relationships

<<< *"If you can't talk to
someone about having
sex, you shouldn't be doing it."*

Q

I'm 19

and I've been with my boyfriend for almost nine months, and we talk about sex ... a lot. But it wasn't easy at first. Here's my horror story.

One night we were fooling around. He was about to go down on me, and I just started bawling my eyes out. He FREAKED out! (Wouldn't you?) He had no idea what to do or what was wrong. He told me maybe it would be a good idea for us to get dressed. He spent about an hour trying to calm me down before I actually told him what I was thinking about.

I don't know why I became such an emotional wreck right at that moment. But I think it was because we had never talked about sex, and all of a sudden we were about to do it. Every time the conversation had come up before, I changed the subject or avoided it. Once I finally confessed my fears and how I was feeling, we had a long talk ... now it's really easy to talk about just about anything related to sex. Had I just been up-front in the first place in the earlier months of our relationship, that situation would never have happened. So, basically, the moral of my story is, just talk about it. If you can't talk to someone about having sex, you shouldn't be doing it.

Source: Author's files (Internet Blog)

CHAPTER **09**

At one time or another in our relationships, all of us have probably either said or heard:

- "That's not what I said!"
- "You never listen to me!"
- "Let me finish!"

Why is it that so many of us have such difficulty conveying what we *mean*? Why is it that our mates, family members, or friends sometimes have such difficulty in accurately receiving the messages we send? How does the psychosocial/psychosexual realm of sexuality (see Figure 9.1) come into play?

It is important for you to build an understanding of communication in intimate relationships because solid communication patterns, skills, and behaviors are the necessary foundation of any satisfying intimate or sexual relationship, as well as every aspect of relational life. First, we need to have an understanding of what communication is. Then we'll examine factors that influence sexual communication, such as differences in gender and sexual orientation. We'll then explore two key aspects of communication, intimacy, and attachment. We'll conclude with an exploration of sexual communication and couples' sex talk through different relationship stages.

> ∧
> ∧ All communication is multigenerational
> ∧ and cultural. **When we communicate with others, we draw on the ways we have learned from our families.**

Psychosocial/ Psychosexual

- Intimacy development
- Experiences of love and loving
- Body image
- Self-concept and self-worth
- Gender identity
- Feelings associated with sexual trauma
- Feelings and emotions associated with sexual orientation
- Interpersonal relationships
- Sexual attitudes
- Sexual decision making and communication skills

Figure 9.1 The Psychosocial/ Psychosexual Domain Communication has a direct effect **on the psychosocial/ psychosexual realm of sexuality.**

TYPES OF COMMUNICATION

Communication, the process of making and sharing meanings, influences the quality and content of your relationships and makes your own relationships different from anyone else's (Galvin, Bylund, & Brommel, 2008). The culture in which you are raised also has a significant influence on the way you communicate. You learned in Chapter 6 that as we grow and develop from infancy, each of us internalizes *sexual scripts* that define what a given society or culture considers normative and expected sexual behavior. Whether we do it consciously or not, each of us relies on our culturally defined sexual scripts to tell us what to do and how to act when we have sex (Greene & Faulkner, 2005). These scripts also influence our sex talk, or our sexual communication.

Sexual communication between partners is equally critical to the identity of a couple's relationship (Vohs & Baumeister, 2004). Within **sexual communication**, members of couples talk about their sexual lives with one another (Holmberg & Blair, 2009). This may include such things as their likes and dislikes, secrets, fears, fantasies, sexual satisfaction or dissatisfaction, desires, wants, needs, and so forth. Through sexual communication, couples deepen their levels of intimacy (Vohs & Baumeister, 2004). Sexual communication is not a separate form of communication; instead, it is an *extension* of the couple's day-to-day communication. Past research has discovered that heterosexual women tend to engage in higher levels of sexual communication than heterosexual men do (Byers & Demmons, 1999; Catania, 1998; Greene & Faulkner, 2005). However, a recent study of 423 gay and straight men and women found that sexual communication was nearly identical between partners in mixed-sex and same-sex relationships (Holmberg & Blair, 2009).

When we discuss marital and family communication, we are referring not just to the talk that takes place among couples, but to the entire array of communication transactions.

VERBAL COMMUNICATION

The role of communication receives a lot of attention when talking about intimate relationships, and for good reason: the presence or absence of effective communication skills plays a key part in whether a relationship succeeds or fails (Gottman, 1999; Gottman et al., 2002). **Verbal** forms of **communication** refer to exchanges of thoughts, messages, or information through the spoken word. It includes the content and substance of the words being spoken, the tone and the expression, as well as the structure and organization of the words. All verbal communication takes place within the context of a specific environment. It is the language we speak. Despite the information communicators exchange, though, exclamations of "You don't understand!" and "That's not what I mean!" often echo throughout our relationships.

Barbara Okun (2002) examined verbal communication skills as they relate to relationship satisfaction. She noted that the majority of the problems found in intimate relationships stemmed from ineffective communication. Okun observed that when couples sought professional help with their verbal communication inadequacies, these couples consistently had trouble recognizing and communicating their problems or concerns to the spousal partner.

William Shadish and colleagues (1993) believe that the reason troubled couples rarely have positive outcomes is because each member of the couple lacks effective communication skills.

There are four fundamental verbal communication processes or skills; these are summarized in Figure 9.2 on page 174. These skills range from conveying our messages accurately to how we process social information we receive from our environment. But when people communicate, they also use behaviors other than words to express and exchange their thoughts, feelings, and information. This is referred to as *nonverbal communication*.

NONVERBAL COMMUNICATION

Nonverbal communication occurs with or without the spoken word. It includes facial expressions, motions of the body, eye contact, patterns of touch, expressive movements, hand gestures, spatial arrangements in the physical environ-

> **<<< Sexual communication is private talk that allows couples to share their sexual wants and dislikes.** It can help build trust and foster a closer sense of intimacy.

OWN IT! The Slang of Sex

Research shows that men and women use different terms to describe their sexual anatomies and to describe different aspects of their sexual experiences and relationships. Men, for instance, tend to use **power sexual slang**, or "dirty" and aggressive words, when discussing or describing sex, such as "f___ing," and/or their or their partner's bodies, such as the word "cock." Conversely, women not only discuss sex less frequently than men do, but they tend to use **cute sexual slang**, or euphemisms, when they talk about sex, such as "making love," and/or describe body parts, such as the term "va-jay-jay." Given these differences, it's important for couples to develop a common sexual vocabulary that is unique and personal to them, especially to find idioms for genitalia, sexual rituals, and routines. By cocreating and jointly sharing these expressions, couples create shared meanings within their sexual relationships.

1. When men talk about sex or sexual anatomy, do you find their terms to be rough, unromantic, or demeaning? Why or why not?

2. When women talk about sex or sexual anatomy, do you find their terms to be too cutesy, immature, or clinical? Why or why not?

3. Up to this point in your relationship, has your sexual communication been subverted because you do not use the same sexual slang as your partner does? In your sexual communication, do you and your partner share the same meanings?

Sources: Cornog (1986); Sanders & Robinson (1979); Simkins & Rinck (1982).

Figure 9.2 Verbal Communication Processes There are four fundamental verbal communication processes/skills **that affect how we send and receive messages (Burleson, 1992).**

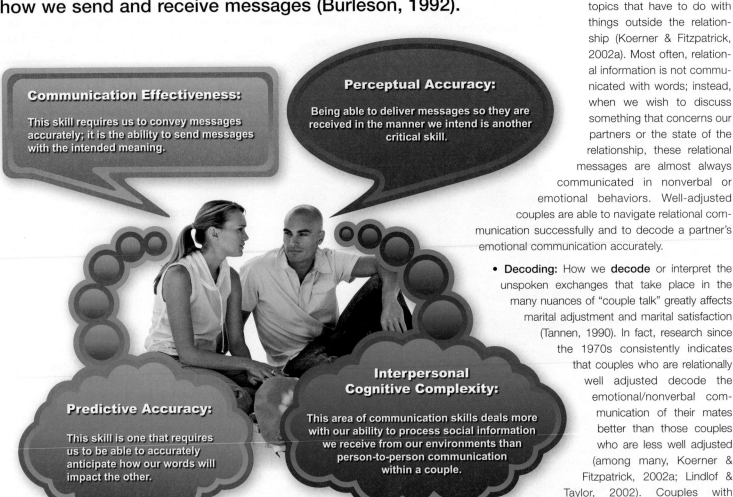

Communication Effectiveness:

This skill requires us to convey messages accurately; it is the ability to send messages with the intended meaning.

Perceptual Accuracy:

Being able to deliver messages so they are received in the manner we intend is another critical skill.

Predictive Accuracy:

This skill is one that requires us to be able to accurately anticipate how our words will impact the other.

Interpersonal Cognitive Complexity:

This area of communication skills deals more with our ability to process social information we receive from our environments than person-to-person communication within a couple.

the relationship; these differ from **nonrelational messages**, or those issues or topics that have to do with things outside the relationship (Koerner & Fitzpatrick, 2002a). Most often, relational information is not communicated with words; instead, when we wish to discuss something that concerns our partners or the state of the relationship, these relational messages are almost always communicated in nonverbal or emotional behaviors. Well-adjusted couples are able to navigate relational communication successfully and to decode a partner's emotional communication accurately.

• **Decoding:** How we **decode** or interpret the unspoken exchanges that take place in the many nuances of "couple talk" greatly affects marital adjustment and marital satisfaction (Tannen, 1990). In fact, research since the 1970s consistently indicates that couples who are relationally well adjusted decode the emotional/nonverbal communication of their mates better than those couples who are less well adjusted (among many, Koerner & Fitzpatrick, 2002a; Lindlof & Taylor, 2002). Couples with stronger relationships are better able to read each other's nonverbal behaviors than are those with weaker relationships.

Being able to recognize (decode) messages so we can recognize whether emotional communication is due to relational or nonrelational factors is crucial for overall relationship satisfaction (Koerner &

ment, and displayed emotions. Emotions provide invaluable information as we attempt to interpret the messages conveyed by the sender (Galvin, Bylund, & Brummel, 2008). The physical gestures and movements that convey our emotions are most often referred to as **nonverbal communication** or **emotional communication** (Senecal, Murad, & Hess, 2003). Although we all may have difficulty in accurately interpreting the meaning of words that we hear, interpreting nonverbal/emotional communication can present an even greater challenge. There are a number of ways to convey emotional communication.

• **Relational and Nonrelational Messages:** Relational messages refer to messages that have something to do with the partner or

>>> We validate our partner and send affirming messages through verbal and nonverbal communication.

∧
∧
∧ Which man is gay? Which man is straight? **Does their body language provide any clues?**

Fitzpatrick, 2002a). The danger lies in how we decode messages. There are times we may *think* a partner's behavior concerns the relationship, when, in fact, it does not. If we decode the nonverbal information as something that pertains to the relationship—if we *personalize* it—when it does not, these misinterpretations over time can lead to the dissolution of the couple.

NONVERBAL COMMUNICATION AND SEXUAL ORIENTATION

Does sexual orientation influence nonverbal communication behaviors? Interpersonal communication researchers commonly look at four types of nonverbal communications that occur between couples:

- *Self-touch*: touching one's face, rearranging one's hair, scratching the eyebrow or earlobe.
- *Body posture*: men often use relaxed, wide-stretched postures, such as legs open and widely spread knees, whereas women typically use less space and are mostly closed (Hall, Coats, & Smith LeBeau, 2005).
- *Body orientation*: how closely a person sits to another person, or at what angle a body is positioned.
- *Eye gaze*: women almost always look at others more often and more intensely than men do.

A recent observational study with heterosexual and homosexual participants indicated that when a homosexual is involved in a pair interaction (whether intimate or social), distinct differences are observed in the

>>> **"You don't understand!"** Are men and women on the same page when it comes to communication?

four areas of nonverbal communication (Knöfler & Imhof, 2007). For example, the open male body position was observed in heterosexual couples. In contrast, in mixed (heterosexual and homosexual) and homosexual pairs, neutral body positions (such as arms resting on a chair or legs crossed) were more prominent. Furthermore, homosexual couples almost exclusively used full face-to-face orientation when they interacted, whereas heterosexual couples did not. The researchers conclude that this research yields valuable insight into the nonverbal communication patterns of gays and lesbians. Contrary to popular opinion, which maintains that each partner in a homosexual relationship adopts "male" and "female" roles, the researchers did not find that homosexuals mimic behavior patterns of the opposite sex when interacting as couples. Rather, they adopt neutral postures and behaviors (Knöfler & Imhof, 2007).

Miscommunication or a lack of communication causes frustrations and misunderstandings in all forms of human interactions, especially in intimate and sexual relationships. Some researchers argue that these frustrations would be greatly minimized if we understood the differences between how men and women acquire and share language meanings.

COMMUNICATION BETWEEN MEN AND WOMEN

You learned in Chapter 3 that as we grow up, we are taught how to be a "boy" or a "girl," or a "man" or a "woman" in a number of different ways. We receive countless messages from society on a daily basis that reinforce these *gender cues*. It's no different with communication; we are taught, by examples in our environment, how to communicate as a boy and how to communicate as a girl. And as we have seen so far in our study, we then carry these patterns of communicating and relating into our future relationships.

According to Dorothy Tannen (1990), boys and girls grow up and learn entirely different—yet equally valid—communication meanings and symbols. Tannen asserts that men and women are so different in how

they communicate and interpret relational messages that their communication is akin to differences we might expect to see between people from different cultures. Tannen therefore refers to the communication differences as *genderlects*, or *cross-sex* communication styles (Tannen, 1990, p. 42). She proposed that these gender differences can lead to problems, misunderstandings, and tensions in all kinds of communication between men and women.

MEN'S COMMUNICATION: OFFERING ADVICE

In all human behavior and communication, there are two levels of meaning that are conveyed. First, there is the **message**, which is the obvious meaning of the communication. The second level of meaning is what Tannen refers to as the metamessage. A **metamessage** is the underlying context in which the communication takes place; it is the information about the relationship between the parties communicating and the attitudes toward each other. Tannen's gender difference linguistic research shows that men attune to the metamessage of *helping* and *fixing problems*; the underlying context of men's communication is to be a problem solver and an advice giver (Tannen, 1990). Tannen asserted that men's communication behaviors are focused on control and dominance, and that this is why men are problem solvers in dialogues with women.

Tannen (1990) also suggested that when men are confronted with **trouble talk**, or talking about emotional and relationship problems, they are much more likely than women to give advice, tell jokes, change the subject, or remain silent (to avoid emotional expression). Tannen believes that when men engage in trouble talk and women offer sympathy to them, men feel that they are being looked down upon, lowered in status, or being spoken to condescendingly (Michaud & Warner, 1997).

WOMEN'S COMMUNICATION: CONNECTING WITH OTHERS

According to Tannen's research, women attune to the metamessage of *empathy* and *understanding*. In trouble talk, women tend to express sympathy for and care about the situation; this shows that they align with or show solidarity with the other person openly. When women communicate, they desire to connect with others, build relationships, give support, and show cooperation (Tannen, 1990).

AND HEREIN LIES THE PROBLEM

When we communicate, there are a number of possible emotional responses when receiving messages, and we often expect the same emotional response that we would give in a similar situation (Michaud & Warner, 1997). For instance, when a woman conveys sympathy in trouble talk, she anticipates that she will receive sympathy in response to her trouble talk (Michaud & Warner, 1997; Edwards & Hamilton, 2004). When a man gives advice or suggestions for solving a problem, he expects that he will receive advice in response to his trouble talk. But when he offers *advice* when she is expecting *sympathy*, she feels that her feelings are invalidated or that her problems are being trivialized. When she offers *sympathy* when he needs or wants *advice*, he feels that she is putting him down (Michaud & Warner, 1997). She may feel that his joking is making fun of her situation; he may feel that her comforting is treating him like a child. Thus, it is not the *words* that are the underlying source of communication differences between men and women; it is the tendency for women and men to *interpret messages in systematically different ways* that is at issue (Edwards & Hamilton, 2004).

Tannen (1990) advances the idea that if men and women stop blaming one another for their communication difficulties, differences, and frustrations, and instead begin to communicate across gender cultures, then marriages and other intimate relationships would become stronger and more durable. Once men and women enhance their understanding of gender differences in communication, they are less likely to say to their intimate partner, "You don't understand!"

One recent study showed that there was no evidence that men were more unresponsive than women when talking to friends about

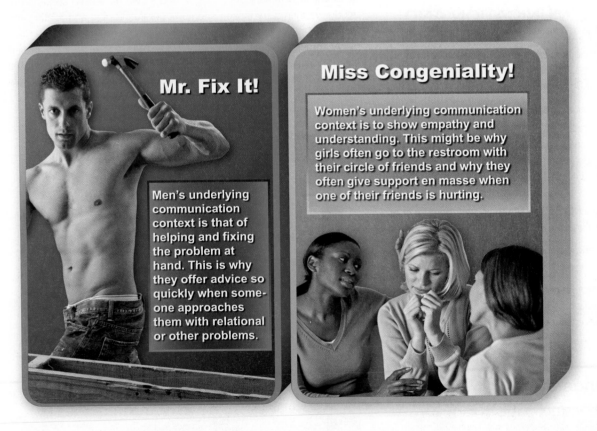

Mr. Fix It!

Men's underlying communication context is that of helping and fixing the problem at hand. This is why they offer advice so quickly when someone approaches them with relational or other problems.

Miss Congeniality!

Women's underlying communication context is to show empathy and understanding. This might be why girls often go to the restroom with their circle of friends and why they often give support en masse when one of their friends is hurting.

Figure 9.3 Underlying Communication Contexts

The Faker

pretends to listen but does not. Their minds wander in and out of the conversation, but they may nod their head or smile as if they are listening.

The Interrupter

is more concerned about his/her own thoughts and feelings than with those of others. They seldom allow the other person to finish, or they immediately respond without pausing for much reflection or consideration of what the other has said.

The Intellectual Listener

attends only to the actual spoken words rather than listening relationally. They ignore nonverbal communication cues and approach the conversation in a rational, logical way, rather than rely on feelings or emotions.

The Self-Conscious Listener

is more concerned with his/her own status and impressing someone than with the thoughts, ideas, or feelings of the other. Because this person is trying to impress the communication partner, the self-conscious listener is already forming their reply.

The Judge and Jury Listener

judges the ideas and behaviors of others. In doing so, they do not hear what the other is saying. Oftentimes these listeners let the other know how wrong or incorrect their thoughts and feelings are.

Figure 9.4 Poor Listening Having trouble listening?

problems; in fact, they did not differ in their expressions of sympathy or minimize the other's problems (MacGeorge et al., 2004). Another study found that the use of humor by men is a means of support for distressed friends, not a *lack* of support as Tannen asserted (Bippus, 2000). Indeed, as one study concluded,

"Both men and women view the provision of support as a central element of close personal relationships; both value the supportive communication skills of their friends, lovers, and family members; both make similar judgments about what counts as sensitive, helpful support; and both respond quite similarly to various support efforts." (MacGeorge et al., 2004, p. 172)

To better understand the nature of sexual relationships, we must also have a solid understanding of why we need to relate to others. In the section that follows, we'll explore the process of intimacy, as well as the obstacles to the development of intimacy.

INTIMACY: ENRICHING YOUR RELATIONSHIP AND SEXUAL BOND

Intimacy refers to the need to have relationships in our lives, and this is a universal, innate drive (Erber & Erber, 2001). This drive for interpersonal relations is thought to fulfill important psychological needs (Clinebell & Clinebell, 1970).

FULFILLING PSYCHOLOGICAL NEEDS

Empirical investigation in the 1970s, 1980s, and much of the 1990s virtually ignored the concept of relationship intimacy as a contributor to psychological need fulfillment. Researchers sought to determine whether the presumed links between need fulfillment and intimacy would promote a

Human nature requires that each of us desires to be emotionally close and connected to another person.

better understanding of the link between couple intimacy and individual well-being (Prager & Buhrmester, 1998). They found that through the course of frequent, intimate communication in which partners' communications consist of a positive tone, daily personal sharing with the partner, listening, and understanding, the *couple* meets *individual* psychological needs. Other bodies of research substantiate that high levels of intimacy in relationships enhance the psychological, physical, and relational well-being of each partner, as well as lower the risk for divorce or relationship deterioration (Firestone & Firestone, 2004; Hasserbrauck & Feher, 2002; Schneller & Arditti, 2004).

When people form close relationships, five essential psychological needs are met that cannot be met in other forms of impersonal human contact (Weiss, 1969):

(1) *Intimacy* is the need that drives us to share our innermost feelings.

(2) *Social integration* needs are the innate needs that make us desire to be a part of a social group or the need to belong.

(3) The need to *nurture and to be nurtured* is best met when we have someone in our life to take care of and to take care of us.

(4) There will be times in our lives when we need *assistance* from others. Interpersonal relationships provide this assistance.

(5) Having a significant other in our life *reassures* us that we have worth and that we are wanted, needed, and loved.

Through our intimate relationships, our basic psychological needs and our basic relationship needs are met. These healthy intimate relationships, in turn, contribute to the overall well-being of each partner (Kirby, Baucom, & Peterman, 2005).

Intimacy is experienced differently from relationship to relationship. Its meaning varies not only from couple to couple, but over time as well. Regardless of how couples experience intimacy in their relationships, intimacy is a necessary component in meaningful relationships.

THE ROLE OF INTIMACY IN RELATIONSHIPS

Though the aspects of intimacy may vary from one person to another, intimacy in committed relationships can best be thought of as an *emotional attachment* to another person (Openshaw, 1998). Intimacy can be thought of as a three-prong process that involves: 1) disclosing things that are personal and private to ourselves; 2) experiencing positive feelings about ourselves and the other person(s) involved in the relationship; and 3) having interpersonal interactions that serve to advance or reflect partners' understanding of each other (Prager, 1995).

But, intimacy is not a static or unchanging aspect of a relationship. As we get to know another person and as we begin to talk about our thoughts and feelings, personal sharing often leads to deepened levels of trust. This trust, in turn, facilitates greater self-disclosure and greater sharing of personal vulnerabilities, which further deepens the level of trust (Heller & Wood, 1998) and strengthens the intimate bonds that families share.

sex talk

Intimacy Inventory

High levels of intimacy in personal relationships are associated with positive mental health and emotional well-being for couples and families. As you have learned, establishing and maintaining intimacy require nurturing attention to the relationship. Take time to examine your individual intimacy needs by completing the intimacy inventory below.

When we are emotionally close, I feel _____.

I would describe our intellectual closeness as _____.

As far as intimacy in our relationship is concerned, I am most satisfied when _____.

I am least comfortable about our relationship when _____.

When you express your emotions and feelings, it makes me _____.

When you express physical closeness, it makes me _____.

Spiritual closeness is _____.

When I experience intimacy with you, I feel _____.

When I am with you, my individuality is _____.

Intimacy leads to good feelings and bad feelings. Knowing this makes me feel _____.

Some people resist intimacy. This makes me think _____.

When I reveal my innermost thoughts, feelings, emotions, and fears, I expect _____.

When my partner/friend reveals his or her innermost thoughts, feelings, emotions, and fears, it makes me _____.

Intimately relating with another carries with it a risk of rejection. The possibility of rejection makes me feel _____.

In general, I am/am not trusting of others. This makes me _____.

If I were to sum up the role of intimacy in my life, I would characterize it as _____.

CHARACTERISTICS OF INTIMACY

What constitutes intimate relationships? One researcher describes eight components that comprise intimacy, including how couples manage conflict, how they express affection and share feelings and emotions, the degree to which the relationship is valued, whether a couple communicates sexual needs and wants and if those needs are met, if each member of the couple has maintained an *individual* identity, how each partner relates to the other, the amount both members of the couple share their personal thoughts and feelings, and the degree of autonomy from families of origin (Waring, 1984). Some research supports these dimensions of intimacy (Hook et al., 2003; Mackey, Diemer, & O'Brien, 2000; Peven & Shulman, 1999); other research identifies spirituality and shared religious faith to be the foundation of all other components of intimacy (Heller & Wood, 2000; Morgan & Kuykendall, 2000).

Because we each have different needs and capacities for intimacy, we may find that our need for intimacy is not the same as that of our partner or significant other. Such differences may lead to significant levels of relationship discord. In the next section, we examine common obstacles to developing relationship intimacy.

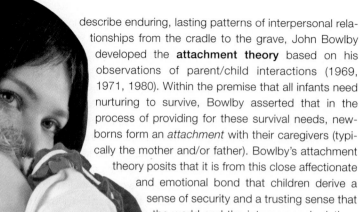

^^^ Theorist John Bowlby believed that when care-givers provide for the needs of their infants, children form a close, enduring emotional bond with them—an attachment bond. **So significant are these early experiences that researchers believe that they impact all of our present and future interpersonal relationships.**

FEAR OF INTIMACY

Intimacy with another requires that we unmask ourselves and thus become vulnerable. In doing so, many people have a fear of intimacy. The Glendon Association (2005) notes that fear in personal relationships sets up barriers to becoming truly intimate with another person. In fact, most of what goes wrong in an intimate relationship comes from fear. We bring these fears into our relationships from our family experiences, and we become guarded to avoid becoming hurt (Glendon Association, 2005).

Many people may not even be aware that they possess intimacy fears. The sources of intimacy fears are varied, and fears may manifest themselves in a number of ways, including fears of failure, vulnerability, rejection, emotional smothering, sex, potential loss, risk-taking, responsibility, emotions, and abandonment (Firestone & Catlett, 2000).

The development of our capacity and ability for intimacy takes place in the context of early emotional relationships, particularly within our family of origin. In the next section, we take a closer look at the emotional bond that significantly affects our ability to give and receive intimacy throughout our lives, or attachment.

ATTACHMENT: AN EMOTIONAL BOND

Attachment is best described as an emotional bond that ties or binds the child to the parent or primary caregiver (Bowlby, 1988). To describe enduring, lasting patterns of interpersonal relationships from the cradle to the grave, John Bowlby developed the **attachment theory** based on his observations of parent/child interactions (1969, 1971, 1980). Within the premise that all infants need nurturing to survive, Bowlby asserted that in the process of providing for these survival needs, new-borns form an *attachment* with their caregivers (typically the mother and/or father). Bowlby's attachment theory posits that it is from this close affectionate and emotional bond that children derive a sense of security and a trusting sense that the world and the interpersonal relationships we encounter along the way are safe.

Because of the importance of these early human relationships, Bowlby, along with researcher Mary Ainsworth and her associates, asserted that the attachment behaviors that take place throughout infancy ultimately direct, shape, and mold our personalities. Consequently, these behaviors significantly impact the interpersonal attachment relationships we experience later on as children, adolescents, and adults (Ainsworth et al., 1978). Some researchers believe that attachment may begin even earlier. They suggest that the bonds actually begin during pregnancy, well before birth takes place (Klaus, Kennell, & Klaus, 1995). Although all researchers may not agree on the exact time attachment occurs, they do agree that the ability to form and experience an emotional attachment to caregivers in the earliest days of life is, in effect, a predictor of an individual's ability to form interpersonal and intimate relationships in the future.

ATTACHMENT TYPES

One study in particular is quite helpful in our quest to gain insight into the development of our ability to love others. Based on Ainsworth and colleagues' (1978) descriptive categories of attachment styles observed in infants, psychologists Cindy Hazan and Phillip Shaver's (1987) research supports the notion that patterns of attachment early in life influence adult intimate relationships. In their examination of adult interpersonal relationships conceptualized as an attachment process, Hazan and Shaver classified adult love relationships:

- *Secure attachment types* Secure adults, like securely attached infants, have little difficulty seeking or maintaining closeness (physical, sexual, emotional, and affectionate) with another person. They don't fear being abandoned or losing their partner. Secure adults allow others to get close to them and to depend on them. These adults report enduring, happy, warm, trusting relationships that promote self-esteem.

- *Avoidant attachment types* Avoidant types report that they seldom find "real" love/intimacy. Hazan and Shaver describe these adults as being uncomfortable when too emotionally or physically close to another person. Avoidant attachment types show discomfort with intimacy and are hesitant to trust others (Feeney & Noller, 1990). They find it difficult to allow themselves to depend on others. Avoidant types commonly report that they experienced separation from their mothers (emotional and/or physical separation).

- *Anxious/ambivalent attachment types* Insecurity is the hallmark of this adult attachment type. When an adult shows this type of attachment, the question is not *if* a romantic partner leaves them, but *when*. With the constant fear or worry that the partner isn't really in love with them, anxious/ambivalent adults cling to their partner and push for commitment (Feeney & Noller, 1990), and in doing so, often push the partner completely out of the picture. Poor attachment in adulthood can prohibit people from getting too emotionally close to attachment figures, causing them to withdraw and pull away before they are rejected (Pickover, 2002).

ATTACHMENT AND ITS SIGNIFICANCE TO SEXUAL RELATIONSHIPS

Using the same concepts and principles associated with attachment to more fully understand the concept of adult experiences of intimacy, researchers have gathered an abundance of empirical evidence that speaks to the importance and significance of the quality of attachment during infancy and the subsequent impact of this attachment quality to relationships later in life, throughout childhood, adolescence, and adulthood (among many, Elliot & Reis, 2003; Furukaw et al., 1999; Markeiwicz, Doyle, & Brendgen, 2001). For example, not only do securely attached individuals report that they experience more intimacy in their relationships, but they also indicate that their relationships are characterized by higher levels of commitment, trust, warmth, and support than are avoidant/anxious attachment types' relationships (for a review, see Shaver & Mikulincer, 2006a). Conversely, avoidant/anxious individuals, more so than securely attached types, often initiate breakups in fear of becoming *too* attached or dependent upon their love interests (for a review, see Strachman & Impett, 2009).

The understanding of attachment is significant to our study of sexuality and sexual relationships because attachment types are closely associated with our sexual goals, attitudes, and behaviors, as well as how we function sexually (Davis, Shaver, & Vernon, 2004; Shaver & Mikulincer, 2006b; Strachman & Impett, 2009). Among those securely attached adults, for example, sexual behaviors almost always take place within committed romantic relationships (such as dating, cohabiting, civil unions, or marriage) (see Birnbaum et al., 2006). Securely attached individuals also report fewer one-night stands than insecurely (those high in anxiety or avoidance) attached people; these people report a greater number of sexual partners and more short-term relationships (Bogaert & Sadava, 2002). Securely attached adults also indicate that they have positive sex scripts, and they report higher levels of comfort with sexual exploration, as well as greater

>>> **Because of attachment disorders, some people need to re-learn how to relate to others.** They are and may always be high-need people in their relationships because of a fear of being abandoned.

pleasure from sexual touch than their insecurely attached counterparts (Cyranowski & Andersen, 1998; Hazan, Zeifman, & Middleton, 1994).

Attachment anxiety individuals, because of their need to avoid disapproval and/or rejection, are more likely than securely attached people to engage in sexual behaviors to reassure themselves that their partners care about them (Schachner & Shaver, 2004). This is an important factor to consider, because sometimes those who are anxiously attached consent to and engage in sexual activities they do not want because of their approval-seeking needs (Impett & Peplau, 2002). Other research has demonstrated that insecurely attached individuals are less likely to engage in sexual communication than securely attached people are. This lack of communication lowers overall relationship satisfaction (Birnbaum et al., 2006).

The empirical evidence is clear: Our experiences with early attachment relationships to our primary caregivers become the foundation upon which all future adult intimate relationships are built, including our sexual relationships.

SEXUAL COMMUNICATION

Although empirical studies repeatedly show that sexual satisfaction is a key factor in overall relationship satisfaction, it's interesting to observe that there has not been much research in the realm of sexual communication (Sprecher & Cate, 2004). Despite this gap in the empirical literature, there are aspects specific to sexual communication that can enrich a couple's relational and sexual lives.

SELF-DISCLOSURE

Self-disclosure is voluntarily sharing things that are personal or private to us with someone else. Self-disclosure requires a high degree of trust, which Galvin and her associates (2008) refer to as **emotional safety**. In general, self-disclosure

- increases as relational intimacy increases.
- increases when doing so is rewarded or responded to positively.
- tends to be reciprocal (mutual).
- increases relational satisfaction; relational satisfaction appears to be greatest when moderate levels of disclosure take place.

Women tend to disclose more personal and intimate information about themselves than men do (Bank & Hansford, 2000; Dindia & Allen, 1992). Married men self-disclose less frequently to their male friends than married women do to their female friends (Omarzu, 2000). More recent research found that in first encounters of college-aged men and women, self-disclosure was nearly equal. Interestingly, if a man or a woman were attractive and possessed other positive attributes, the partner in the interaction self-disclosed more than if the partner were not as attractive (Noland, 2006).

So far, our study has shown us that culture plays a significant role in shaping our sexual scripts. Earlier in this book, we explored the concept of *machismo*, an attitude common in Latino cultures wherein men exhibit their masculinity and virility. One study found that machismo affects sexual self-disclosure in Latino heterosexual couples by influencing what can and cannot be said (women had more restrictions on what they were able to express) or preventing any sexual communication at all. As one respondent noted, "When there is a lot of machismo, there is no communication" (Noland, 2006).

> ^^^^ **When we share our deepest thoughts, fears, hopes, dreams, and goals with our partners, we increase relationship intimacy.** Do you struggle with opening up to someone, or does it come easily to you? Why do you think this is?

Other research has attempted to determine how the social identity of a culture—whether the culture is collectivist or individualistic—influences the degree to which people disclose and express attributes about themselves (Markus & Kitayama, 1991). People in individualistic (independent) cultures such as those of the United States and Western European countries tend to express and talk about their unique and best attributes, whereas people in collectivist (interdependent) cultures such as Japan, Africa, and southern European cultures tend to de-emphasize and are more inhibited about talking about themselves and their attributes.

SEXUAL SELF-DISCLOSURE: SEXUAL ASSERTIVENESS

The willingness and ability to communicate our sexual likes and dislikes or to talk about sexual behaviors is referred to as **sexual assertiveness** (Greene & Faulkner, 2005). Specifically, sexual assertiveness refers to the ability to (Morokoff et al., 1997):

- initiate sexual activity.
- refuse unwanted sexual activity.
- talk about sexual likes and dislikes (before, during, and after sexual interactions).
- discuss contraceptive use.
- negotiate safer-sex behaviors.
- discuss a partner's sexual history.

Although alien to many couples, sexual assertiveness serves vital functions in a couple's relationship. First, it increases the pleasure of sexual interactions for couples (Sprecher & Cate, 2004). During lovemaking, for example, simple dialogues such as, "Where do you want me to touch you?" or "Does this feel good?" or "Is this a good pace?" all serve to enhance each partner's pleasure.

Sexual assertiveness also serves the vital function of increasing relationship and sexual satisfaction (Byers & Demmons, 1999; Christopher & Sprecher, 2000; Cupach & Comstock, 1990; MacNeil & Byers, 2005; Metts & Spitzberg, 1996; Wheeless & Parsons, 1995). One study of

<<< **Sexual self-disclosure refers to a number of ways in which we tell our partner what we want and don't want in our sexual relationship.** Not only does this increase our sexual and relationship satisfaction, but it also protects our sexual health and well-being.

college students found that couples who were sexually assertive self-disclosed about issues such as certain sexual likes (such as oral sex) and behaviors (such as contraceptive use) were more comfortable with talking about a wider range of sexual topics together than couples who were not sexually assertive (Greene & Faulkner, 2005).

SEXUAL CONFLICT AND DISCREPANCIES

Consider a scenario that takes place on college campuses or college bars on a regular basis: A man and a woman are engaging in conversation and she briefly places her hand on his knee. This is a difficult situation to interpret, because only she knows the meaning she is ascribing to her behavior. To be sure, miscues and misinterpretations can lead to sexual conflict and discrepancies between partners. **Sexual conflict**, or problems arising from a lack of successful sexual communication, is common in dating relationships, permeating a number of areas, including who initiates sex and how often, how sexual initiations are received, the ability to communicate sexual likes and dislikes, and discrepancies in sexual desires (Sprecher & Cate, 2004).

In general, there are two different types of sexual conflict. With **general conflict**, the source of conflict is not specific to a particular sexual issue (Sprecher & Cate, 2004). For instance, a couple can be experiencing financial difficulties, in-law problems, or other family-related problems, such as the stressors associated with childrearing. Nonetheless, because of the interconnected nature of relational life, non-sexual issues can easily spill over into the couple's sexual life.

Content-specific sexual conflict are problems specific to sexual issues within the couple's relationship. This type of conflict is commonly found in **partner discrepancies** that include areas of sexuality, such as attitudes, values, beliefs, desire, preferences, response, and health. Generally speaking, the more discrepancies partners have in the sexual realm of their relationship, the greater the conflict will be; the fewer discrepancies partners have, the greater their sexual satisfaction will be (Sprecher & Cate, 2004). Sometimes, conflict-specific sexual conflict escalates into more serious issues, such as coercion, violence, rape, and questions about sexual consent. The *Healthy Selves/Healthy Sex* feature box explores sexual consent at length.

SEX TALK: COMMUNICATING DIFFERENTLY OVER TIME

In most relationships, it takes time before couples can establish a climate in which they feel comfortable talking about their sexual relationship and expressing their desires, likes, and dislikes (Brinley, 2000). Remember, sexual fulfillment and communication begin with the quality of the nonsexual areas of the couple's relationship.

Healthy Selves / Healthy Sex

Sexual Consent

Generally speaking, college students have a firm understanding of what **sexual consent** means, but some gender differences are evident. For instance, women, more so than men, stress the importance of consent more than men do, and they prefer more explicit ways of obtaining it, such as by firmly saying "yes" or "no" (Humphreys, 2004). On the other hand, men tend to assume that consent has been given; they will assume "yes" until verbally told "no" (Humphreys, 2007).

Since sex without consent is legally considered rape or sexual assault, it is imperative that each partner consents to each sexual encounter. Precisely what is sexual consent? The Minnesota Criminal Code (2008) provides the definition, "Sexual consent means words or overt actions by a person indicating a freely given present agreement to perform a particular sexual act with the actor."

According to this legal definition, sexual consent:

- *Does not* mean a person failed to resist. Consent is not the absence of "no." Instead, it is "yes, yes, yes!"

- *Is active.* Until a partner overtly says "yes" by words and/or actions, non-consent is implied.

- *Is in the present.* This means the answer is "yes" *for this particular sexual encounter*. It doesn't matter that the partner said "yes" yesterday or this morning.

- *Is freely given.* This means there is no threat, no fear, no intimidation, and no coercion of any kind.

- *Applies to a particular sexual act.* Consent to one act (oral sex) doesn't mean you have permission for another act (anal or vaginal intercourse).

Further, it is important to keep in mind that a person who is incapacitated or physically impaired cannot consent to a sexual act. This includes:

- If the sexual partner is drunk.

- If the sexual partner is drugged.

- If the sexual partner has passed out or is asleep.

As couples establish a relationship history and can anticipate the sequence of sexual activities, their private couple meanings and sexual slang help guide sexual consent; over time, couples do not seek sexual consent because it is assumed. If a member of the couple doesn't violate the trust established in sexual encounters, each partner can confidently rely on his or her partner to not violate that trust and to ask for consent to introduce new sexual acts.

Sources: Humphreys, T. P. (2004, 2007).

Is she flirting? Does she want him? Or is she just engaging in casual conversation? **Misinterpretations of verbal and nonverbal sexual communication often lead to sexual conflict.**

IS HE FLIRTING?

Because of the symbolic nature of interpersonal communication, there is great potential for imperfect sexual communication and episodes for miscues, as the opening vignette to this chapter illustrated. For instance, some research suggests that men tend to overestimate women's sexual intentions conveyed in nonverbal flirting communication (Henningsen, 2004) because they perceive women's friendly behaviors as sexual in nature (Henningsen, Henningsen, & Valde, 2006). In most cases, it seems men and women *do* mutually interpret sexual communication cues (such as flirting) and continue "on the same page" with their interactions (Metts & Spitzberg, 1996). Because early phases of sexual intimacy in a couple's relationship are restricted to their cultural sex scripts (Metts & Cupach, 1989), it is necessary that couples work together through the multiple processes of sexual communication to develop their own couple sex script, relational culture, and private couple meanings. Although it does take time, it also deepens the trust and intimacy levels in the relationship, making the time invested worthwhile.

SEXUAL COMMUNICATION IN ESTABLISHED RELATIONSHIPS

Over time, as members of a couple discover what is sexually pleasing and what they enjoy, and what is not pleasing and what they do not enjoy, they develop sexual vocabularies that are unique to them. This unique vocabulary, their sexual communication, ultimately shapes and defines their relationship.

A quick glance at popular magazines would suggest that "dirty talk" is an essential part of a couple's healthy sexual communication. But is it necessary? Does it enhance sexual relationships? To understand why "sexy" or "dirty talk" works for some couples but not for others, we need to explore two more concepts related to sexual communication:

- **Expressive communication** refers to conveying messages to another person by gesturing, speaking, or writing (Demchak, Rickard, & Elquist, 2001). Meaning can be added to expressive communication by using nonverbal communication and vocal inflection.

SEXUAL COMMUNICATION IN THE EARLY STAGES OF A RELATIONSHIP

In the early stages of any intimate relationship, our sexual scripts guide our initial interactions (Metts & Spitzberg, 1996). But after these initial interactions, what factors influence the sexuality that is (or is not) conveyed?

Cognitive valence theory (CVT) is a model that explains why a person increases or decreases his or her intimacy behaviors in response to another person's behaviors (close conversational distance, forward lean, relaxed body, positive vocal cues, and body language) (Manusov, 2005). According to CVT, in any interaction with another person, we go through a series of perceptual and cognitive processes and allow these processes to determine our response—our next "move"—to the other person's behavior (Henningsen, Henningsen, & Valde, 2006). With *perceptual* processes, individuals must first notice that the other person has changed his or her current level of intimacy before responding to sexual or intimate nuances. With *cognitive* processes, or **appropriateness judgments**, a person assesses whether increasing his or her intimate behaviors is appropriate for *situational*, *relational*, or *cultural* reasons. If we deem the intimacy behaviors of another person to be situationally, relationally, and/or culturally appropriate, CVT predicts that we will respond by reciprocating intimacy (Anderson, 1998).

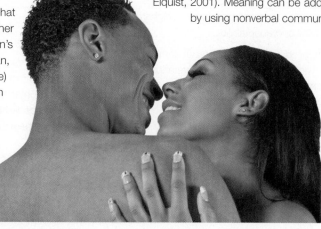

Sometimes it's embarrassing or difficult to talk about sex or our sexuality, especially for younger couples. Over time, however, sexual communication deepens the trust and intimacy shared between partners.

- **Receptive communication** refers to what a listener receives from his or her communication partner and what the listener understands from the communication process (Demchak Rickard, & Elquist, 2001).

Sexual communication will enhance and enrich a couple's relationship only to the extent that the communication is mutually positive and rewarding (Metts & Cupach, 1989). Because of the shared, reciprocal nature of sexual communication and its impact on sexual and relationship satisfaction, couples need to negotiate ways to communicate that make sex enjoyable for each partner—dirty talk or not.

sexual life now

Interracial Intimacy

Throughout history, racist fears such as "racial impurity" led to regulations that banned interracial sexual and marital relationships (romantic or marriage partners who are of differing races). For example, South Africa, Canada, Australia, and the United States all had laws against miscegenation. **Miscegenation** refers to those of different races, ethnicities, or religions who produce children together. In 1967, the United States Supreme Court ruled in *Loving v. Virginia* that state statutes preventing relationships and marriages between persons solely on the basis of race were unconstitutional. Not all states were quick to abolish their anti-miscegenation laws; however it wasn't until 2000 that Alabama removed its bans on interracial marriage. As of 2005, no countries have laws that ban interracial intimate partnering.

To be sure, interracial dating, intimate partnering, and marriage are on the rise in U.S. culture. For example, according to the Population Reference Bureau (2005), the rates of interracial partnering have more than quadrupled between 1970 and 1995, from 65,000 interracial marriages to nearly 400,000. Indeed, the cultural climate surrounding interracial coupling has changed since the *Loving* case. Given the increase in the numbers of couples choosing to date or marry outside their race or ethnicity, it is important to consider whether these relationships promote family health and well-being.

YES!

Interracial families possess many strengths, according to Burrello (2005), including:

- *The richness of living in culturally diverse neighborhoods.* Interracial couples tend to live in diverse communities. Living in such communities teaches children and others that races can successfully coexist.

- *The preservation of customs, rituals, and languages of both cultures represented in the family home.* Children are privileged to experience all sides of their multiple heritages. Additionally, couples and children in interracial families are often bilingual or multilingual.

- *The first-hand experience of understanding diversity.* Children of interracial couples experience the benefits of learning about diversity first-hand. Burrello notes that interracial couples and children have a higher capacity for flexibility and adaptability.

- *The acceptance of differences.* Interracial families tend to exhibit more patience and understanding about others' differences. They tend to exhibit less prejudice than children from monoracial families.

NO!

Some opponents to interracial dating, marriage, and parenting believe that those who date or marry outside their race or ethnicity are betraying their families, as well as abandoning their cultural heritage. In a recent study that examined interracial couples, the researcher found social and psychological implications associated with interracial intimacy (Killian, 2001). These include:

- *Reduced social support.* Killian's study found instances of resistance and avoidance from family, friends, and the community. Many of the couples in Killian's study limited their contact with their family and friends to preserve their emotional well-being. They also reported an extensive disruption or loss in their family support networks.

- *Social resistance.* Several interracial couples reported overt experiences of racism. These include subtle cues of avoidance while in public, exclusion from conversations, people staring, and discrimination in housing.

- *Silenced family histories.* Creating a couple identity from two distinct ethnic/cultural backgrounds proved difficult for the interracial couples in Killian's study. Couples found they needed to reach compromise in everything from the foods they ate to family rules and rituals.

>>> WHAT DO YOU THINK?

1. Do you approve of interracial dating and/or marriage? Have you dated someone of a different race? If not, would you? Why or why not?

2. After reviewing the above studies, what do you think is most positive about interracial dating or marriage? The most negative?

3. If you chose to marry someone from a race other than your own, would your family approve or disapprove? Why or why not?

Sources: Burrello, K. N. (2005). What are the strengths of interracial families? *Diversity Dating Organization.* Retrieved January 1, 2010, from www.diversitydtg.com/articles/interracial families.htm; Killian, K. D. (2001). Reconstituting racial histories and identities: The narratives of interracial couples. *Journal of Marital and Family Therapy, 27*(1), 27–42; Lee, S. M., & Edmonston, B. (2005). New Marriages, New Families: U.S. racial and Hispanic intermarriage. *Population Bulletin, 60*(2).

SEXUAL LIFE EDUCATION

Intimacy does not always come easily to everyone. In fact, most of the time, establishing and maintaining intimacy with another requires hard work because it is a process that unfolds and changes over time. As you take that step that brings you to reveal, share, and disclose your innermost thoughts and feelings about every area of your relationship as you lower the barriers and allow another person to really know you, you begin the processes of intimacy, and relational and sexual communication. This intimacy and communication not only allows you to know and understand your partner, but also helps you to be known and to be understood by your partner as well.

All too often in our society today, sex talk is portrayed in the media as perfectly timed one-liners that always result in sexual arousal of each partner. But as you've learned, sexual communication isn't about talking dirty to your partner or saying the "right" words to excite your

<<< **Establishing and maintaining intimate relationships requires mutual self-disclosure and mutual sharing in all areas of relating—** emotionally, intellectually, physically, and spiritually. It also requires time.

partner sexually. Our study in this chapter has shown us that sexual communication can be that, but it is also much more than that. It's about who we are, all day long, that we bring to our sexual lives; sexual communication is an extension of every other aspect of our relational lives. Without question, it is an area of sexuality that requires a commitment to nurturing and maintaining, but something that ultimately enhances sex.

▶▶▶ TAKING SIDES

Why Are Men So Analytical? Why Do Women Talk So Much?

Do men and women speak different languages? There have been many attempts over the years to determine and explain the differences in communication between men and women. The debate centers on biological or genetic influences and environmental or socialization influences.

For example, Moir and Jessel (1991) contend that the areas of the brain that are essential to communication are programmed in the early stages of pregnancy by the presence or the absence of testosterone. According to their work, male and female brains are structured differently and thus process information differently. Moir and Jessel claim the innate, biological differences appear to be:

High-Testosterone People (Male Brains) Prefer:	Low-Testosterone People (Female Brains) Prefer:
Things	People
Facts, logic	Feelings, senses
Power/status	Relationships
Winning	Sharing
Analyzing	"Knowing"
Assertion	Cooperation
Intellectual understanding	Empathizing
Sex	Intimacy
Thinking	Feeling
Reports/information	Rapports/bonding

Differences in communication are also due to our socialization and environmental experiences. As you learned in Chapter 3, each society and culture has different expectations for boys and girls, and, as a result,

people react differently to the genders. For example, girls are allowed and expected to cry, and boys are not. Whether communication differences between the genders are due to genetics or socialization, these contrasting language practices can create discord and become fertile ground for conflict.

Her Side: Sometimes, he seems so distant, so insensitive. He doesn't want to talk about *real* things, like how he's feeling about something or what he thinks about a certain topic. If I share a problem with him, he immediately has a solution for the problem or has a suggestion about how to "fix" it. He doesn't try to understand my *feelings*.

His Side: *Everything* is an important topic to her, and she shares every detail—what her friend said (or didn't say) to her, the conversation she had with her mother, the new outfit she found at the mall. And she always wants to talk about our relationship. If I don't want to talk about it, she gets offended and will say something like, "You see, our relationship *is* in trouble!" It's very confusing and frustrating to me.

Your Side: In your opinion, do you think there are gender differences in men's and women's communication styles? In making your decision, consider the following questions:

1. Have you ever experienced any difficulty in communicating with the opposite gender?

2. Do you agree with Moir and Jessel's research that suggests that the male and female brains are wired differently in the womb and that these differences contribute to communication differences? Do you agree or disagree with the "male brain" and "female brain" lists the researchers compiled? What led you to your conclusion?

3. In your opinion, are the differences in communication between the genders determined genetically, or are they due to the influences of socialization?

Source: Based on Moir, A., & Jessel, D. (1991).

Summary

WHAT IS COMMUNICATION? 172

- Communication is the process of making and sharing meanings, and it influences the quality and content of your relationships, making them different from anyone else's. Each person's culture and upbringing affects how he or she communicates.
- Different types of communication include sexual, verbal, and nonverbal communication. Often the ways men and women communicate proves to be fundamentally different.

WHAT ROLE DOES INTIMACY PLAY IN A RELATIONSHIP? 177

- Intimacy is the innate, universal need that humans possess to have relationships in their lives, and it fulfills important psychological needs. It encompasses the emotional attachment one person has to another. Intimacy is not static, and it changes over time.
- Intimacy involves disclosing things that are personal and private to ourselves, experiencing positive feelings about ourselves and the other person involved in the relationship, and having interpersonal interactions that serve to advance or reflect the partners' understanding of each other.

HOW DOES ATTACHMENT AFFECT OUR RELATIONSHIPS THROUGHOUT OUR LIVES? 179

- According to John Bowlby, attachment is the emotional bond between a child and his or her caregiver. From this relationship, children develop a sense of security and trust in future interpersonal relationships.
- The three attachment types are secure attachment types, avoidant attachment types, and anxious/ambivalent attachment types. A person's attachment type can have a profound impact on his or her sexual life and relationships.

WHAT ARE THE DIFFERENT ASPECTS OF SEXUAL COMMUNICATION? 181

- Sexual communication includes self-disclosure, sexual self-disclosure and sexual assertiveness, sexual consent, and sexual conflict. As a couple gets to know each other, sexual communication changes over time.

Key Terms

communication the process of making and sharing meanings *172*

sexual communication members of a couple talk about their sexual life with each other *172*

power sexual slang "dirty" and aggressive words used to describe aspects of sexuality *173*

cute sexual slang euphemisms used to describe aspects of sexuality *173*

verbal communication use of the spoken word to exchange thoughts, messages, or information *173*

emotional communication using physical gestures and movements that convey our emotions *174*

relational messages messages that have something to do with the partner or the relationship *174*

nonrelational messages messages about issues or topics that have to do with things outside the relationship *174*

decode to interpret *174*

message the obvious meaning of a communication *176*

metamessage the underlying context in which a communication takes place; the information about the relationship between the parties communicating and the attitudes toward each other *176*

trouble talk communication about emotional and relationship problems *176*

intimacy the need to have relationships in our lives, which is a universal, innate drive *177*

attachment an emotional bond that ties or binds the child to the parent or primary caregiver *179*

attachment theory in the process of providing for survival needs, newborns form an attachment with their caregivers; this bond provides a sense of security, a trusting sense that the world and future interpersonal relationships are safe *179*

self-disclosure the voluntary sharing of things that are personal or private to us with someone else *181*

emotional safety a high degree of trust *181*

sexual assertiveness the willingness and ability to communicate our sexual likes and dislikes or to talk about sexual behaviors *181*

sexual consent words or overt actions by a person indicating a freely given present agreement to perform a particular sexual act with the actor, according to the Minnesota Criminal Code of 2008 *182*

general conflict the source of conflict is not specific to a particular sexual issue *182*

sexual conflict problems arising from a lack of successful sexual communication *182*

content-specific sexual conflict problems specific to sexual issues within the couple's relationship *182*

partner discrepancies differences between partners in areas of sexuality, such as attitudes, values, beliefs, desires, preferences, responses, and health *182*

cognitive valence theory (CVT) a theory that explains why a person increases or decreases his or her intimacy behaviors in response to another person's behaviors *183*

appropriateness judgments cognitive processes in which a person assesses whether increasing their intimate behaviors is appropriate for situational, relational, or cultural reasons *183*

expressive communication the conveying of messages to another person by gesturing, speaking, or writing *183*

receptive communication the messages a listener receives from his or her communication partner and what the listener understands from the communication process *183*

miscegenation the act of reproducing members of different races, ethnicities, or religions who produce children together *184*

Sample Test Questions

MULTIPLE CHOICE

1. When describing aspects of sexuality, men tend to use:
   a. Cute sexual slang
   b. Power sexual slang
   c. Dirty talk slang
   d. None of the above

2. Eye contact is an example of:
   a. Verbal communication
   b. Sexual communication
   c. Nonverbal communication
   d. Sexual assertiveness

3. Which metamessage are men most likely to attune to when encountering trouble talk?
   a. Making jokes
   b. Providing empathy and understanding
   c. Helping and fixing problems
   d. Avoiding trouble talk entirely

4. Intimacy can best be described as:
   a. An emotional attachment
   b. Sexual intercourse
   c. Self-disclosure
   d. Emotional well-being

5. Those adults who find it difficult to allow themselves to depend on others are likely:
   a. Secure attachment types
   b. Anxious attachment types
   c. Ambivalent attachment types
   d. Avoidant attachment types

6. Which cultural attitude can be linked to a lack of communication?
   a. Marianismo
   b. Machismo
   c. Individualistic
   d. None of the above

7. According to Sternberg, commitment and intimacy comprise which type of love?
   a. Companionate love
   b. Empty love
   c. Passionate love
   d. Consummate love

8. Sexual consent is NOT:
   a. The absence of "no"
   b. Active
   c. In the present
   d. Freely given

SHORT RESPONSE

1. Using your family of origin, how was intimacy encouraged or discouraged while you were growing up?

2. Describe cognitive valence theory.

3. List three benefits of sexual assertiveness.

4. How can intimacy improve one's life?

5. Your close friend has begun to date someone of a different race, but his family doesn't approve, and he asks for your advice. What would you tell him?

Answers: 1. b; 2. c; 3. c; 4. a; 5. d; 6. b; 7. a; 8. a

Remember to check www.thethinkspot.com **for additional information, downloadable flashcards, and other helpful resources.**

ADULT RELATIONSHIPS
Singlehood, Cohabitation, and Marriage

I'm a

senior in college and just about all of my friends who are in serious relationships live with their boyfriends or girlfriends. So when my fiancé asked me if I wanted to move in with him, I didn't give it a second thought. I mean, it's so common today and it just seemed like the logical next step in our relationship. Our wedding was planned for the summer after we were going to graduate from college, so it made sense that we would already have our finances pooled together and our apartment all set up, so we could start graduate school in the fall.

Now, I'm not a prude by any means. But after we had lived together for a couple of months, this enormous guilt just swallowed me! I was raised in a super religious home, and I knew my parents would absolutely flip out if they found out I was living with him. After a while, it really started to come between us. One Saturday we had a super-long talk and out of nowhere we decided to get married—right then and there. On Monday we got a marriage license, and on Thursday we drove to the county seat and got married in front of a justice of the peace. No one, other than our witnesses, knows! We'll still go ahead with our wedding this summer. In the meantime, if my folks find out I'm living with [him], at least I can tell them that we're legally married!

I know that cohabitation works for a lot of people, but it just didn't feel right or work for me. Am I the only one who feels this way? Why did a piece of paper make such a difference in my relationship?

Source: Author's files

CHAPTER **10**

When I was a college student in the 1970s in the midst of the sexual revolution, living with someone before marriage was referred to as "shacking up" or "living in sin." This terminology reflected the cultural attitudes about living together instead of, or prior to, marriage. Although a few of my friends cohabited before they married, the practice was taboo and largely forbidden because of the social prohibitions against it during the 1970s. As you'll see in the discussions that follow, this relationship type/living arrangement is common in Western cultures today. But as the young woman illustrates for us in the opening vignette, there are still complexities associated with cohabiting despite its common practice.

In our examination of sex, sexuality, and sexual life, we must consider singlehood and relationships such as cohabitation and marriage. It is also important to study adult relationships because today's trends represent a sociological and structural change in how people experience their sexuality. In the 1970s, a discussion such as this would have probably focused on married couples, but because of societal changes today, we must also give consideration to singles, cohabiters, married couples, gays, and lesbians.

Before we examine marriage, we will first discuss being single, which is an increasing trend among America's young adults. We will then look at cohabitation in a variety of contexts, such as factors that affect who live together, as well as cohabitation among gays and lesbians. We'll then explore sexual and relationship satisfaction within marriages. Our study of sex in adult relationships concludes with a look at infidelity.

BEING SINGLE

In cultures around the world, marriage is assumed to be the next stage in a person's life after adolescence and early adulthood. But not everyone who dates necessarily has marriage on his or her mind. Western culture is seeing increasing numbers of single people, and singlehood is becoming a popular trend among the young and old as well. This trend is due, in part, to the *individualistic* nature of American society; that is, individual needs and wants, such as self-fulfillment, educational attainment, and the fulfillment of career goals, are promoted over the *collective* needs of the society (Ambert, 2009). Noted relationship researcher and author Dr. Anne-Marie Ambert observes that today's individualistic cultures encourage individuals to be happy and fulfilled, which contributes to the trend of singlehood. This current trend in the large and increasing numbers of singles is also partly because numbers of young adults are delaying marriage. Today, the average age of marriage for men is 27.5 years, and for women it is 25.5 years (Smock, Casper, & Wyse, 2008). Figure 10.1 shows the average age of marriage for men and women from 1890 to 2008. As you can see, the age at which people marry fluctuates over time; these fluctuations mirror society's attitudes toward marriage and singlehood.

Historically, U.S. culture viewed singlehood as a transitional stage that preceded marriage and parenting—being single was not viewed as a lifestyle that adults purposely chose, but as a stepping stone to the eventual, expected adult roles of spouse and parent. Although 90 to 95 percent of adults eventually marry (Smock, Casper, & Wyse, 2008), there is an increasing number of adults who are single in contemporary society.

Figure 10.1 Average Ages of Marriage for Men and Women, 1890–2008

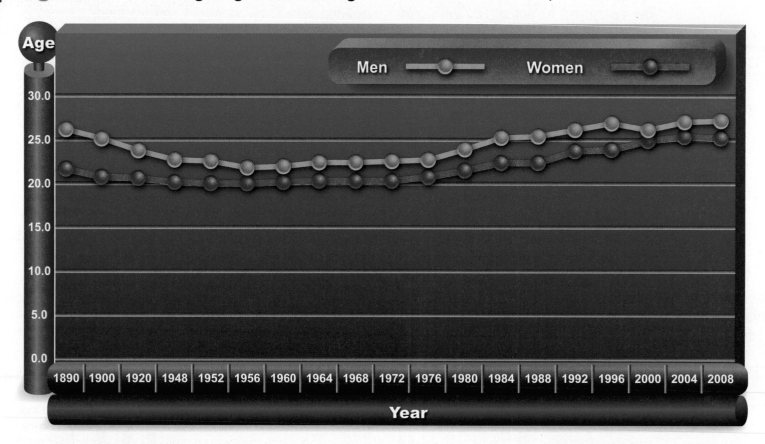

Source: U.S. Census Bureau (2008).

Figure 10.2 Stein's Types of Singlehood

In 2006, for example, single men and women headed nearly 56 million U.S. family households, slightly over one-half (U.S. Census Bureau, 2006a). By comparison, the number of households of married couples stood at slightly more than 55 million, or about 50 percent of all U.S. households (U.S. Census Bureau, 2006a). These trends are significant, because they represent a dramatic shift from the year 2000, when married couples made up over 52 percent of American households.

The experience of being single is not universal. Singles are a complex and diverse group, and there are differences in how people experience singlehood.

TYPES OF SINGLEHOOD

Peter Stein (1981) developed various categories of singlehood, shown in Figure 10.2. This typology shows us that being single is a fluid, dynamic

state. There will always be people who are single for a certain period of time, and there will always be people who remain single throughout their lives, either by choice or by circumstance (1981).

Most of us at some point in our lives, will find ourselves single, whether it's because we haven't found Mr. or Ms. Right, because we just ended a relationship, or because a spouse has died. Being single means that someone is not married; however, not all unmarried people have the same experience.

NEVER-MARRIED SINGLES

Never-married singles are those individuals who have not married, may or may not live alone, and may or may not have an intimate partner. Never-married people may be gay or straight, young or old, cohabiters or live-alones.

Figure 10.3   Racial/Ethnic Trends in Singlehood

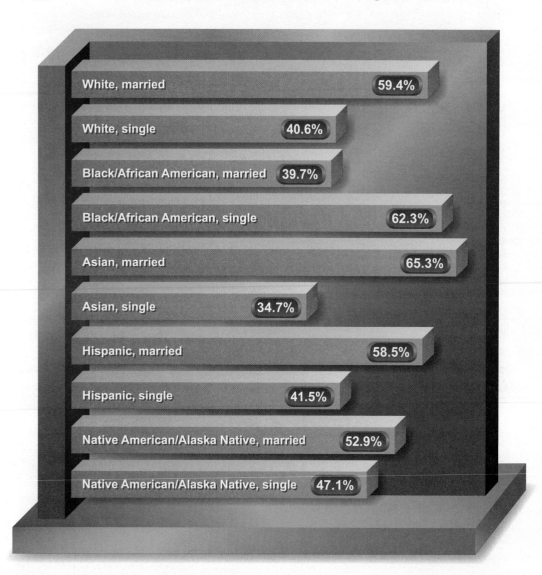

White, married	59.4%
White, single	40.6%
Black/African American, married	39.7%
Black/African American, single	62.3%
Asian, married	65.3%
Asian, single	34.7%
Hispanic, married	58.5%
Hispanic, single	41.5%
Native American/Alaska Native, married	52.9%
Native American/Alaska Native, single	47.1%

Source: National Center for Health Statistics (2008).

There are different racial/ethnic trends among never-marrieds. As Figure 10.3 shows us, nearly two-thirds of African Americans/Black Caribbeans are not married; this racial group has the highest percentage of not-married singles (National Center for Health Statistics, 2008). What accounts for this trend? Some research has found that non-marriage among African American/Black Caribbean men and women is often due to economic instability and the stressors associated with low incomes and poverty (Coontz & Folbre, 2002). Another study indicates that black women may choose not to marry if a man doesn't have an adequate income or if marrying him places an additional economic burden upon her family (Edin, 2000).

Note also that among Native Americans/Alaska Natives, the percentage of those who are married is similar to those who are unmarried. Asian Americans experience the highest percentage of marriage with over two-thirds who are married, and this group has the lowest rate of non-married singles.

What is the reason for the increasing number of singles in America? The trend toward delaying marriage has emerged over several decades as financial and social forces, such as the global economic crisis and skyrocketing unemployment rates, have made it more difficult for those in their 20s to start lives independent of their parents (Campbell, 2002; Waite & Joyner, 2001). In the past, society frowned on those who delayed marriage or chose singlehood. After all, taking on spousal and parenting roles was expected and considered to be *the* only appropriate gender roles for both men and women (Campbell, 2002). Today, however, being single is more socially acceptable than it was in the past, particularly if a young adult is pursuing higher education or career goals. Other social factors, such as society's acceptance of premarital or nonmarital sexual behavior and nonmarital cohabitation, also contribute to the increasing number of never-married singles (Waite & Joyner, 2001).

Demographers speculate that other social factors are also at work. Today, there are more highly educated women, and they face a smaller pool of eligible, highly educated men of comparable age to marry. In addition, there are more relationship and career choices open to women today than in decades past; women no longer depend on men for their financial and/or relationship security (Smock, Casper, & Wyse, 2008).

OWN IT! Single and Loving It?

Although being single may be perfectly acceptable and comfortable for some 20-somethings, they still may have a tough time explaining to their parents (for the umpteenth time) that they are quite content with their single status and that they're in no hurry to tie the knot. Others may struggle with being single because they've come to believe that they need a partner to be truly happy in life.

Are you single and loving it, or single and loathing it?

1. *If you are single and loving it*: If your parents constantly ask you about your dating status, do you ever make up an imaginary partner, just to quiet their concerns? If so, how did that tactic work?

2. *If you are single and loathing it*: What is it about your single status that concerns you the most? Have you ever found yourself falling in love, just so you could be "in love"?

It is also increasingly common for young adults to remain financially dependent upon their family of origin longer than young adults did in the past (Barrett, 1999; Campbell, 2002). If parents and other caregivers continue to help with college expenses and living expenses, it is financially advantageous for a young adult to remain single.

Existing research seems to indicate that singlehood is a positive, satisfying experience for many, not a lonely, isolated experience.

URBAN TRIBES

Given that the traditional social institutions of marriage and family are presumed to provide social and emotional support, an interesting question arises when considering the increasing number of never-marrieds. Who becomes the primary institution or system of support between the years of living in a family of origin and a family of choice?

An **urban tribe** is a mixed-gender circle of friends (typically in their 20s and 30s) who are the primary social support system for singles (Waters, 2004). The term was first coined in 1985 by French sociologist, Michel Maffesoli (1996). According to Maffesoli, urban tribes are common in metropolitan areas where microgroups of people who share common interests (such as similar worldviews) bond together.

Similar to the peer groups portrayed in popular television shows such as *How I Met Your Mother*, urban tribes are redefining family and commitment. Typically, urban tribes begin as a group of friends who socialize together every now and then, but over a period of five years or so, each individual within the tribe assumes certain roles, much like in a family. Similar also to families, urban tribes share rituals, such as holiday celebrations, stories, and, over time, histories. Urban tribe members feel a mutual obligation to support each other and to care for one another. Today it appears that these circles of friends are becoming substitutes for spouses (Waters, 2004). In today's complex society, these emerging support systems allow marriage to wait. Because these friendships are

emotionally satisfying—and sometimes sexually satisfying, as hookups are not uncommon among these urban friendships—young adults do not feel the need to rush into marriage (Waters, 2004).

GAY AND LESBIAN NEVER-MARRIEDS

Because gay men and lesbians do not have the legal privileges of marriage in all states, many view them as never-married singles. In June 2009, however, the Obama administration determined that same-sex couples would be categorized as married in the 2010 national census.

Other recent changes make it somewhat easier to ascertain people's living arrangements in the United States. For example, unlike the decennial (every 10 years) census, which aims to count every person in the United States, census demographers are now beginning to use data from the *American Community Survey (ACS)* to assess various family structures. Unlike the U.S. Census, the ACS is an ongoing survey that is conducted every year, and it samples about 2.5 percent of the total U.S. population. By 2010, it will replace the decades-old census long form.

The 2005 ACS (the first to be conducted nationwide), sampled about 1.5 million households in the United States. Dr. Gary Gates of UCLA (2006) analyzed the data and found that:

- About 4.1 percent of U.S. adults (approximately 9 million) identify as a sexual minority (gay, lesbian, or bisexual).

- The number of same-sex couples who lived together as intimate partners in the U.S. grew from 600,000 in 2000 to 777,000 in 2005. This growth represents an increase of more than 30 percent.

- 53 percent of same-sex couples were gay men, and 47 percent of same-sex couples were lesbian women.

- Although increases of 41 to 81 percent in same-sex couples were seen in all 50 states, and California, Florida, New York, Texas, Illinois, and the District of Columbia have the largest sexual minority populations. As such, these states have the largest numbers of same-sex couples.

How do we explain these increases between 2000 and 2005? Gates suggests that the magnitude of growth in same-sex couples documented in the ACS is probably due to the fact that more gay and lesbian couples are reporting their relationships to U.S. demographers (Gates, 2006). He also suggests that today's same-sex couples may be more willing to come out of the closet because there is a decline in the stigma attached to homosexuality or that some same-sex couples are taking a stand against anti-gay

<<< Who needs marriage?
Increasing numbers of young adults today lean on their circle of friends–their urban tribes–to meet their emotional, physical, and sometimes, sexual, needs.

Figure 10.4 Gay and Lesbian Never-Marrieds, 2000–2005

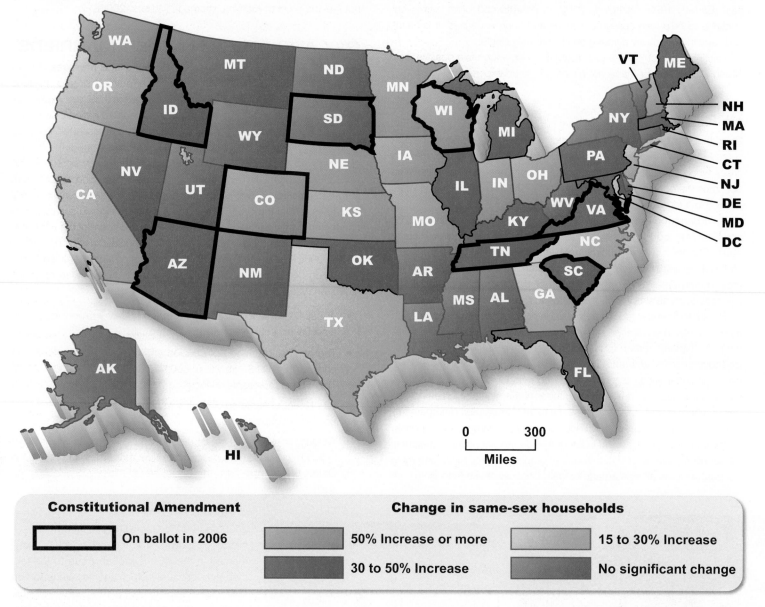

Constitutional Amendment

☐ On ballot in 2006

Change in same-sex households

■ 50% Increase or more

■ 30 to 50% Increase

■ 15 to 30% Increase

■ No significant change

Source: University of California (2010).

groups. Figure 10.4 illustrates which states had the greatest increases in same-sex households.

Although we have this information, empirical science on the experiences of gay and lesbian singles is relatively new, so the research is still virtually silent about LGBT singlehood and relational status (Hostetler, 2009). An important question to consider is are gays and lesbians involuntarily single because of the restricted marriage laws in the United States? Or are they single by choice?

To date, limited studies exist that address singlehood among lesbians, but one study indicates that among older lesbian women (ages 55 and beyond), study participants lived alone involuntarily (Kehoe, 1986). Hostetler (2001, 2004) has researched the lives of single gay men and found that singlehood is often a voluntary state for them. These men tend to have higher income levels, high levels of psychological well-being, and good social support from friends and family. A recent study of 94 gay men (over the age of 35) discovered that nearly 65 percent of the study participants were single by choice, while 35 percent were involuntarily single (Hostetler, 2009). The findings of the study suggest that voluntary

singlehood was a *gradually* adopted lifestyle for gay men. As the researcher notes,

> "As [the gay man] comes to see himself as happily and perhaps permanently partnerless, he adjusts his goals and perhaps even his desires to bring them into line with the reality that *not* being single in the future is an increasingly unlikely scenario" (Hostetler, 2009, p. 521).

DIVORCED SINGLES

A small percentage of America's singles are divorced men and women. Although divorce rates escalated in the 1970s and remained high through the 1990s, they appear to have stabilized somewhat (Heaton, 2002). Figure 10.5 illustrates for us that there are gender differences seen in divorced singles, and there are also racial and ethnic differences. For our discussion here, it is important to understand that most divorced people will experience life as a single person at least for some period of time following the end of their marriages.

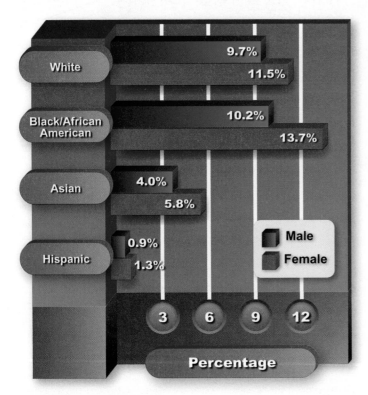

> ∧
> ∧ Are gays and lesbians involuntarily
> ∧ single because of the restricted laws in
> the United States? **Or are they single
> by choice?**

THE WIDOWED

Women are much more likely to outlive their husbands than men are to outlive their wives. There is a greater percentage of single *widows* (women) than single *widowers* (men), among all races. In addition to their shorter life expectancies, men are also more likely than women to remarry after the death of a spouse, thus reducing the numbers of

Figure 10.5 Divorced Singles

Race	Male	Female
White	9.7%	11.5%
Black/African American	10.2%	13.7%
Asian	4.0%	5.8%
Hispanic	0.9%	1.3%

Source: U.S. Census Bureau (2006).

single widowers (Lemme, 2005). Additionally, retirement pensions and Social Security benefits allow older adults to live independently for longer periods of time (Lemme, 2005).

As the current trends in singlehood show us, marriage in the United States today exerts less influence than it used to in how adults experience their intimate relationships.

NONMARITAL COHABITATION: LIVING TOGETHER

Cohabitation is a term used to describe the living arrangements of unmarried, intimate partners who typically have a sexual relationship, and such relationships often resemble marriages. A cohabiting relationship can be a short-term arrangement or a long-term union with the shared economic and parenting responsibilities found in marriage (Trask & Koivunen, 2006). A **common law marriage** is a relationship between cohabiting heterosexual partners without a legal marriage ceremony; however, the couple presents themselves as husband and wife. After the couple has been living together for a certain length of time (the time varies by state), they are considered legally wed. In Canada, cohabitation is referred to as *common-law status*.

Cohabiters can be straight or gay, never-before-married, or divorced-and-now-single. They can be young parents or 68-year-old widows and widowers. Studying cohabitation is important to our understanding of sex and sexuality, because this social phenomenon corresponds to a dramatic shift in the social and demographic behaviors through which intimate and sexual relationships, as well as families, are formed, organized, and dissolved (Wu, 2007).

Cohabiting before marriage (or instead of marriage) is now *the* prevailing living arrangement of intimate partners, the step that follows serious dating. In fact, data show that there were 5.5 million unmarried

> ∧
> ∧ A cohabiting relationship can be a
> ∧ short-term arrangement or a long-term
> union **with the shared responsibilities
> found in marriage.**

heterosexual partner households (over 11 million people) in the year 2006 (U.S. Census Bureau, 2006b). When gay couples are included in the numbers of those cohabiting, the figure increases to nearly 6 million unmarried partner households (Simmons & O'Connell, 2003).

CHARACTERISTICS OF COHABITATION

Consider the following trends of nonmarital cohabitation in the United States (Black, Sanders, & Taylor, 2007; Kennedy & Bumpass, 2007):

- Almost half of adults in the 20s and 30s live together before marriage.

- For 70 percent of young adults, cohabitation comes before marriage.

- Of the cohabiting couples that recently married, 58 percent lived with their partner before marriage; 14 percent had also lived with someone else other than the person they married.

- Among self-identified gays and lesbians nationwide, cohabiting estimates for gay men and lesbians are about 50 and 63 percent, respectively.

There are several factors that contribute to whether a person chooses to live with an intimate partner and forgo the traditional path of marriage. The rates of cohabitation vary between populations in different regions of the United States, along with religion, age, race, social class, and levels of educational attainment.

FACTORS THAT AFFECT COHABITATION

As presented in Figure 10.6, nonmarital cohabitation is higher in the Northeast than it is in the South or the Midwest (Simmons & O'Connell, 2003). In states in which religion is a predominant part of the culture (such as the Church of Latter-Day Saints in Utah, and throughout the

Figure 10.6 Percentages of Persons of the Opposite Sex Sharing Living Quarters across Regions of the United States

Hundreds of thousands of unmarried opposite-sex couples live together in the seven states where cohabitation is illegal:

9.4%	8.0%	7.9%	7.5%	7.5%	7.2%	7.1%
336,506	32,933	170,307	41,143	118,242	130,147	10,216
Florida	West Virginia	Michigan	Mississippi	Virginia	North Carolina	North Dakota

Percentage of coupled households with opposite-sex unmarried partners, by state:

- 10.4%–13.5%
- 8.6%–10.3%
- 6.9%–8.5%
- 4.4%–6.8%

Source: U.S. Census Bureau (2003).

<<< Do adults view cohabitation as an alternative to being single or as a substitute for marriage? **In the U.S., about 1 million adults live with a cohabiting partner.** Research shows that cohabitation among older adults provides a key source of emotional support for them, **protection of their financial assets, and the security of having a regular sex partner (Brown, Lee, & Bulanda, 2006).**

Bible Belt, or the South and the Midwest), cohabitation rates are lower. Nearly 45 percent of those who cohabit before marriage claim no religious affiliation, whereas those who attend church or other religious services on a weekly basis are twice as likely to not cohabit before marriage (Jones, 2002).

The Pew Research Center is a nonpartisan "fact tank" that provides information on the issues, attitudes, and trends that shape the United States and the world. Their recent random telephone survey of more than 2,000 respondents in the United States queried whether living together without getting married or before marriage is a good thing for society, a bad thing, or a new

	Ever Cohabited %
Wanted to be sure/Trial relationship	21
Timing not right for marriage/Too young	15
Convenience/Easier/Just wanted to	12
Financial reasons/Cut costs/No money or time for wedding	10
Misgivings about marriage	9
Planned to marry at a later time	8
Love and compatibility	5
Had children together/pregnant	3
Didn't know better	2
Legally couldn't marry	1
Easier to change if it didn't work out/No legal battles	1
Other	16
Don't know	6

Figure 10.7 Why Did You Decide to Live Together Rather than Marry?

Source: Pew Research Center (2007).

trend that doesn't make much difference (Pew Research Center, 2007). Their survey revealed a number of differences in attitudes about cohabitation.

For example, those who attend church or temple frequently (weekly or more) tend to believe that living together in lieu of marriage is a bad thing for society, whereas those who attend church or temple less frequently (monthly or less) tend to look more favorably on cohabitation. Similarly, those who hold more moderate or liberal political beliefs tend to view cohabitation more favorably than those who do not. Figure 10.7 illustrates the many reasons people have for cohabiting.

In general, women who cohabit tend to be younger than cohabiting men. For college-aged students, 24 percent of the women and 16 percent of the men are under age 25 (Fields, 2004). However, college students do not represent the largest group of cohabiters; rather, most unmarried partners are in their 30s and 40s (Simmons & O'Connell, 2003). About

>>> Births to cohabiting couples are a common occurrence.

three-fourths of cohabiting women expect to marry their partners, but only about one-third of those living together eventually marry (Trask & Koivunen, 2006).

Race is also a key factor in cohabitation, and it is especially common among lower-income minority groups such as blacks and Hispanics (Brown, Van Hook, & Glick, 2005). Figure 10.8 illustrates the rates of nonmarital cohabitation by race. As you can see, African Americans and Native American/Alaska Natives have nearly equal rates of cohabitation; Asian Americans have the lowest rate of nonmarital cohabitation (Simmons & O'Connell, 2003). Further, as depicted in Figure 10.9, among Hispanics, blacks, and whites, the birth of a couple's first child occurred during cohabitation in anywhere from 12 to 32 percent of couples (Centers for Disease Control and Prevention, 2008). Marriage is a more likely outcome of cohabiting relationships for whites than it is for blacks and Hispanics, and if a pregnancy occurs during the cohabiting period, whites are much more likely to marry than blacks and Hispanics are (Manning & Jones, 2006).

Employment also plays a key role in whether a cohabiting couple eventually marries. Research focusing on marriage among cohabiters indicates that cohabiting couples who have greater economic resources are more likely to marry if they have a child while living together rather than remain simply cohabiting partners (Osborne, 2005). Research also finds that often cohabiters desire marriage, but they delay or forgo it until they become

Figure 10.8 Rates of Cohabitation by Race

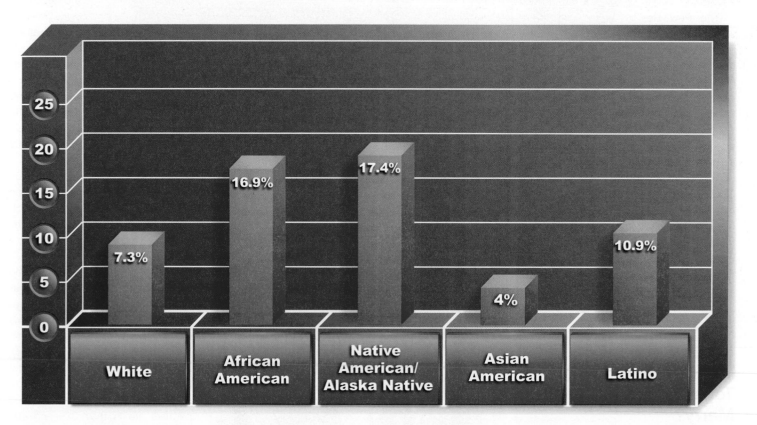

Source: Simmons & O'Connell (2003).

Figure 10.9 Percentage of Parents Who Were Married or Cohabitating at the Birth of Their First Child, by Race/Ethnicity and Sex

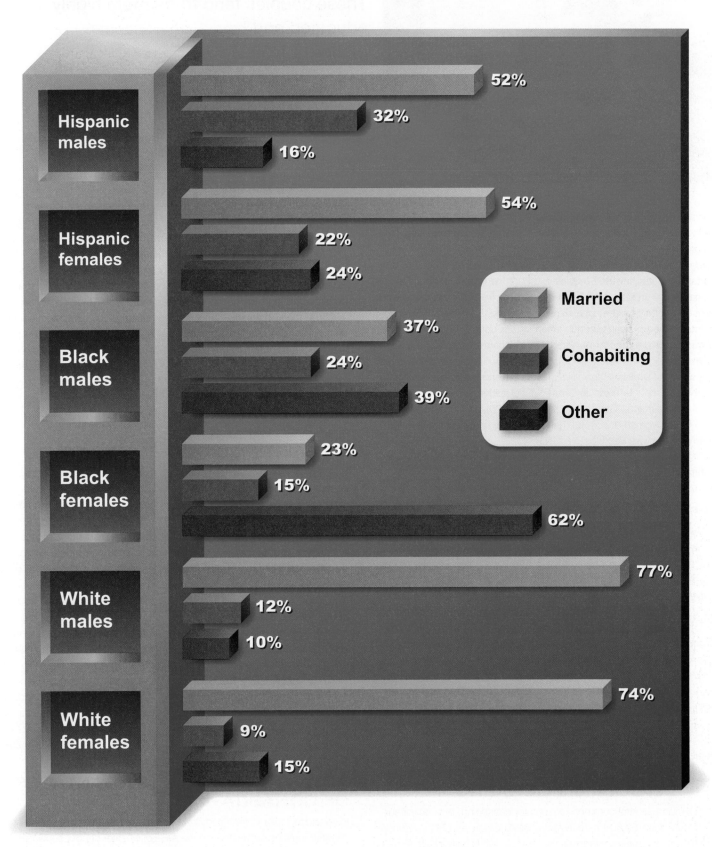

Source: Centers for Disease Control and Prevention (2006).

<<< About half of gay couples cohabit. These couples tend to be more highly educated and have higher incomes compared to those gay men who do not cohabit.

- Increased intimacy
- Less complication in dissolution of relationship if it doesn't work out
- "Testing" compatibility
- Trial marriage

financially stable (Gibson-Davis, Edin, & McLanahan, 2005; Smock, Manning, & Porter, 2005). Among blacks, if both partners are working, they are more likely to marry; however, among white couples, if a woman is not working, the couple is less likely to wed (Manning & Jones, 2006). It is very important to note, however, that even though nonmarital cohabitation is seen among all groups, it still continues to be a trend among those who are economically disadvantaged (Smock, Manning, & Porter, 2005).

Among Puerto Ricans, cohabitation unions usually begin informally, and these relationships are unlikely to be legalized through marriage (Brown, Van Hook, & Glick, 2005). However, unlike blacks and whites who cohabit, Puerto Ricans' live-together relationships are similar to their married counterparts in terms of education, employment, and childbearing (Brown, Van Hook, & Glick, 2005). In one study, most Puerto Rican women described their cohabiting relationships as a form of marriage (Brown, Van Hook, & Glick, 2005).

All of these findings are important, because they help us see how cohabitation varies among different racial groups.

COHABITATION AMONG GAY MEN AND LESBIANS

The availability of social science data concerning cohabitation experiences of gay men and lesbians is quite limited. Earlier we noted that the prevalence of cohabiting is about 63 percent for lesbian couples, and about 50 percent for gay men (Black, Sanders, & Taylor, 2007). Other demographic characteristics reveal that gay male cohabiters are more likely to be white, more highly educated, and less likely to have children in their household compared to nonpartnered gay men (Black, Sanders, & Taylor, 2007). Lesbians in cohabiting relationships tend to be older (about age 39), are more likely to be white and to have been in a prior legal heterosexual marriage, more likely to have children in their household, and more highly educated than nonpartnered lesbians (Black, Sanders, & Taylor, 2007).

Are cohabiting relationships *substitutes* for marriage or viewed among the couples as a *trial* marriage? And what reasons do couples give for cohabiting?

WHY DO COUPLES COHABIT?

Couples report several common reasons for cohabiting. In a recent survey of more than 50,000 respondents, David Olson and his colleague found these contemporary reasons that couples live together before marriage (Olson & Olson-Sigg, 2007):

- Economic advantages
- Time together

Pew Research Center (2007) data gives us further insight into why couples live together before marriage or in lieu of marriage. Nearly one-fourth of the survey respondents who cohabited did so to test the relationship and to make sure that the partner is the right one.

There is much ambiguity with cohabiting relationships. As the researchers note, there are really no defining moments that signal the beginning or end of the cohabiting arrangements (Manning & Smock, 2003). In many instances, there is a gradual transition, with most couples drifting in and out of these arrangements. The researchers contend that living together before marriage does not appear to be a substitute marriage (a long-term commitment between intimate partners that does not involve legal marriage), or a trial marriage (living together to see what marriage would be like). Cohabitation, instead, is seen as an alternative to being single.

COHABITING COUPLES AND SEX

Surprisingly, scant attention has been given to the sexual and relational aspects of this couple type. Blumstein and Schwartz's 1983 study of American couple types is perhaps the most extensive study to date.

In their research, the authors found differences in sexual expression between cohabiting and married couples. The findings suggest that cohabiting couples were likely to have sexual intercourse more frequently than married couples (three times per week compared to once per week) and were not only more likely to have sex outside the cohabiting relationship, but were also less secretive than married couples about the outside sexual activities. In cohabiting relationships, the female was more likely to initiate sexual acts than the married women were. Men in cohabiting relationships tended to be more committed to the relationship if the partner was "attractive."

In a recent study that examined sexual satisfaction in premarital cohabitating relationships, Sprecher (2002) found that the respondents indicated overall sexual satisfaction within the cohabiting relationship and that sexual satisfaction was also positively correlated with relationship satisfaction, love for the partner, and level of commitment to the relationship.

ADVANTAGES AND DISADVANTAGES OF COHABITATION

In certain regions of the United States, there are few more hotly or intensely debated topics in family life than the issue of whether or not couples should cohabit before marriage. Aside from whether cohabitation is a moral life choice is the issue of whether cohabitation is an advantageous or disadvantageous choice for couples. Does cohabitation work? Figure 10.10 presents the advantages and disadvantages of cohabitation.

Advantages of Cohabitation

Our study so far has shown us that non-marital cohabitation is an increasingly common living arrangement for intimate partners both in the United States and other cultures. Given the current trends in living together, many are curious as to what advantages are associated with cohabiting. The literature is virtually silent on the potential positive outcomes associated with cohabiting, but what little empirical evidence that does exist suggests that couples do experience a few advantages if they cohabit before or instead of marriage:

- Couples who cohabit have more personal autonomy than those who are married (Bernhardt, 2004).

- Cohabiters have more personal individual freedom than married partners do (Waite & Gallagher, 2001).

- Those who live together have more individual financial freedom than married partners do (Waite & Gallagher, 2001).

- Cohabiters have greater gender equity, less traditional gender roles, and share household chores more than married couples do (Bernhardt, 2004).

- Couples who cohabit have greater flexibility in their commitments to their relationships (Bernhardt, 2004).

Given the unique, individualized nature of intimate relationships, some might argue that these points are disadvantages, rather than advantages, of nonmarital cohabitation.

Disadvantages of Cohabitation

While there is little information available regarding the advantages of cohabitation, the research is consistently clear regarding its disadvantages; cohabitation before marriage or in place of marriage is by and large a negative relationship experience. Specifically:

- Cohabitation before marriage correlates with higher relationship dissatisfaction and higher risk of divorce in the event of marriage (among many others, Bramlett & Mosher, 2002).

- Couples who live together have the lowest level of premarital satisfaction when compared to other living arrangements (Olson & Olson-Sigg, 2007).

- Marriages preceded by cohabitation are more likely to end in divorce (among many others, Waite & Gallagher, 2001).

- Married couples that cohabited before marriage have poorer communication skills in discussing problems than those couples who did not live together (Cohan & Kleinbaum, 2000).

- Cohabiting couples are less sexually committed and are not as faithful to their partners as married partners are (Waite & Gallagher, 2001).

- Cohabitation before marriage carries with it an increased risk of violence against women and children (see especially Fagan & Hanks, 1997). In cohabiting relationships, there is more verbal aggression, anger, and attempts to control the partner's feelings than exists in married relationships (Cohan & Kleinbaum, 2002).

- Cohabiting women report twice the rate of abuse than do married women (Bumpass & Lu, 2000). Chapter 17 provides an in-depth look at family violence.

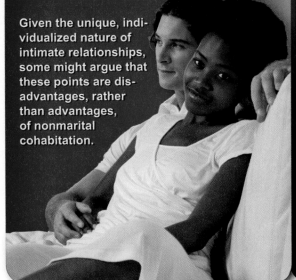

Figure 10.10 Advantages and Disadvantages of Cohabitation

Upon reviewing these aspects, you may be asking yourself, "If cohabitation is thought of as a trial marriage for some, why are such negative consequences associated with this living arrangement?" David Olson notes,

"One explanation is that while the basis for marriage is a strong ethnic of commitment, cohabiting couples are much more oriented toward their own personal autonomy and are more willing to terminate the relationship. It is easy to speculate that once this *low-commitment/high autonomy pattern* of relating is learned, it becomes hard to change. Cohabitation reflects uncertainty" (Olson & Olson-Sigg, 2007, p. 3).

To answer the question posed earlier, "Does cohabitation work?", the answer from empirical research suggests that no, it does not.

Despite the increasing numbers of singles today, despite the noticeable trend of couples delaying marriage for longer periods of time, and despite the increased trends in nonmarital cohabitation, most Americans still marry at least once in their lifetime.

THE EXPERIENCES OF MARRIAGE

In the United States alone, each month, upward of 168,000 couples wed, vowing to love, honor, and respect their chosen life mates until death parts them (National Vital Statistics Reports, 2006).

The following are recognized (though perhaps at varying levels) by all states:

- The right to visit a spouse in the hospital

- The right to make medical decisions on behalf of a spouse in the event that he or she is unable to do so

- The right to joint custody of children

- The right to privileged and confidential communication between the husband the wife

- The right to rear children in a manner the couple deems appropriate (i.e., religious training, education, discipline)

- The right to terminate a marriage according to the laws of the state

Federal and state legislation also provide additional legal benefits to married couples:

- Lower federal income tax rates

- Social Security and Medicare benefits

- Health insurance benefits that cover spouses

- Lower home and auto insurance rates

- Legal protection from domestic violence and abuse

- State-specific inheritance and death benefits for spouses

- The rights associated with the Federal Family Medical Leave Act

- State-specific rights afforded in instances of divorce

Figure 10.11 **The Importance of Legal Marriage**

Figure 10.12 Why Did You Get Married Rather than Live Together?

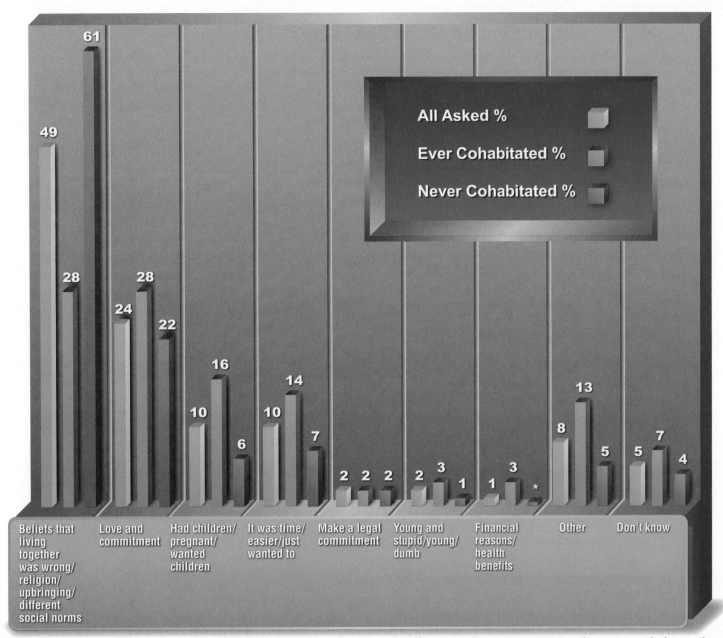

Legend:
- All Asked %
- Ever Cohabitated %
- Never Cohabitated %

Category	All Asked %	Ever Cohabitated %	Never Cohabitated %
Beliefs that living together was wrong/religion/upbringing/different social norms	49	28	61
Love and commitment	24	28	22
Had children/pregnant/wanted children	10	16	6
It was time/easier/just wanted to	10	14	7
Make a legal commitment	2	2	2
Young and stupid/young/dumb	2	3	1
Financial reasons/health benefits	1	3	*
Other	8	13	5
Don't know	5	7	4

Note: Responses total to more than 100% because respondents could offer more than one answer to the open-ended questions.

Source: Pew Research Center (2007).

The relevance of marriage is rapidly changing in contemporary society, making it less clear-cut than at any other point in history. For instance, in a Pew Research Center (2007) random polling of more than 2,000 individuals, less than half indicated that if a man and a woman plan to spend the rest of their lives together as a couple, there are many reasons it is still important that they legally marry (see Figure 10.11). Note that there are age, religious, and racial/ethnic differences in the opinions on the importance of marriage.

Those of us who choose to marry have specific reasons why we choose to marry the person we do. There is a common desire, however, in our Western, individualistic culture; we tend to marry for reasons that benefit ourselves, rather than for reasons that benefit the society at large,

which is usually the case in collectivist cultures (Ambert, 2009). Research in Western cultures has found, for example, that the top reason people cite for marrying is to signify a lifelong commitment to someone they love (Australian Relationships Survey, 2006).

However, this reason is not the only response to why people wed. People today get married for reasons of commitment, security, and personal belief systems. The Pew Research Center's recent findings suggest that the main reasons people get married are for mutual happiness and commitment, as well as bearing and raising children (Pew Research Center, 2007). As the data from this survey show us in Figure 10.12, what people consider to be the main reasons for getting married varies.

Should Same-Sex Couples Be Allowed to Marry?

If marriage is a civil union, is it also a civil right? Across the nation, same-sex couples are challenging long-held marriage laws that only sanction (legally recognize) marriage between heterosexuals. Human rights advocates believe that gay and lesbian couples, as U.S. citizens, should have the same rights and privileges as heterosexual couples, including the right to legally marry the person they choose, regardless of the partner's sex. Those who oppose same-sex marriages believe that marriage is a social institution that should be protected and that allowing same-sex couples to marry would further erode the family.

YES!

The Human Rights Campaign (HRC) is America's largest civil rights activist organization that works to achieve gay, lesbian, bisexual, and transgender equality and end discrimination. According to the HRC (2004), giving gay and lesbian couples the legal right to marry enhances and strengthens the social institution of marriage and the American family. They contend that same-sex marriages address the true, diverse needs of today's families, and if gay and lesbian married couples shared the same rights and privileges enjoyed by married heterosexual couples, families would benefit. Further, denying same-sex couples the right to marry denies them certain rights, which include:

- *Hospital visitation:* Same-sex couples do not have the automatic right to visit their partners or to make medical decisions for them, as heterosexual couples do.

- *Health insurance:* If health care coverage is provided by an employer for a gay/lesbian partner, the employee must pay taxes on the value of the insurance.

- *Family leave:* Gay and lesbian partners are not entitled to unpaid leave from their jobs to care for an ill spouse.

- *Pensions:* Same-sex couples cannot receive pension benefits.

- *Nursing homes:* Gay and lesbian aging partners cannot live together in retirement or long-term care facilities.

NO!

According to Peter Sprigg of the conservative activist organization, the Family Research Council (2004), legal marital unions between homosexual couples will have negative consequences on the institutions of marriage and family. Specifically, Sprigg contends that:

- *Gays and lesbians are not denied the right to marry.* The right to marry extends to *individuals,* not to *couples.* Every individual is free to marry within certain parameters.

- *Same-sex marriage would change the concept of marriage and family.* If gay and lesbian couples were allowed to marry, they would be able to more easily adopt children, perpetuating the negative consequences of growing up without a mother *and* a father.

- *Same-sex couples can easily have the rights of married heterosexual couples.* By simple legal documents, such as a will or a medical power of attorney, same-sex couples can provide for their partner after a loved one's death or care for them while they are ill.

>>> **WHAT DO YOU THINK?**

1. Is marriage a *civil* right, or is it a *human* right?
2. If you were to summarize the basis of the HRC's position, what would it be? What is the basis of Sprigg's argument? Do you agree with one position more than the other? Why?
3. What are the advantages to the institutions of marriage and the family by allowing gays and lesbians to marry? What are the disadvantages?

Sources: Human Rights Campaign Foundation. (2004). Answers to questions about marriage equality (pp. 164–172); Sprigg, P. (2004). Questions and answers: What's wrong with letting same-sex couples "marry"? (pp. 173–179). In E. Schroeder (Ed.), *Taking sides: Clashing views on controversial issues in family and personal.*

SEXUAL ORIENTATION AND MARRIAGE LAWS

The legislation that addresses same-sex couples' rights to marry changes quickly, and it can be difficult to keep up with it! Here are some quick facts about same-sex marriages (as of this writing):

- *Issues marriage licenses to same-sex couples:* Massachusetts, Connecticut, Iowa, Vermont, and New Hampshire

- *Recognizes same-sex marriages that take place in other states:* Rhode Island, New York, and Washington, D.C.

- *Allows civil unions that provide state-level spousal rights to same-sex couples:* Connecticut, Vermont, New Jersey, and New Hampshire

- *Provides some state-level spousal rights to unmarried same-sex couples:* Hawaii, Maine, Washington, D.C., Washington, and Maryland

Despite these changes, though, the fight to legalize same-sex marriages is proving arduous: In July 2004, the U.S. Senate blocked a measure to amend the Constitution to allow a ban on same-sex marriages.

Beyond the legal responsibilities and requirements associated with the act of marriage, there are certain rights, privileges, and benefits of marriage, too. These rights and benefits are what distinguish the marital union from any other intimate pair bond relationship, such as cohabitation or civil unions between same-sex couples.

THE RIGHTS AND PRIVILEGES OF MARRIAGE

The U.S. government grants each state the ability to determine the rights, privileges, benefits, and responsibilities associated with marriage. These state-generated and regulated laws specifically define the privileges of marriage. These privileges may or may not be applicable in other states.

Suppose that because of your academic path, you reside in a different state than your "home" state. During the summer months, you and your fiancé marry in your home state, and then return to school in a different state. Perhaps the state in which you marry has different marriage and family laws than the state in which you later reside. Once you move to another state, your marriage is subject to the laws of the state that you now live in.

Healthy Selves / Healthy Sex

Before You Say "I Do"

In Western cultures, most people marry because they are in love. Having realistic expectations about marriage—what each partner expects of a spouse and the marital relationship—significantly affects overall marital satisfaction and happiness. Because each partner comes into a marriage with different family-of-origin experiences and models, couples often have different goals and expectations. By discussing these expectations before they trip down the marriage aisle, couples have a chance to align their ideas and attitudes about what marriage will and won't be. Discussing expectations about marriages also gives couples the opportunity to strengthen their communication skills, a key component in successful marriages.

Before you say "I do," there are many issues to consider. First, you should consider *why* (other than being in love) you want to get married. The aim of this discussion is for each partner to fully understand and appreciate each person's reasons for marrying.

As you consider your reasons for getting married, check off each that applies to you.

- Because it's the next logical step in our relationship.
- Because I want to show my commitment to him/her.
- I'm tired of being single.
- I want more independence in my life.
- My religion mandates marriage before we can be sexually intimate with one another.
- I want security.
- I'm ready to have children.
- I need his or her friendship and companionship.
- I'm not getting any younger.
- I'm a single parent and I want two parents in my child's life.

1. Did you and your partner come to a general agreement on the reasons why you want to marry? Are your expectations for marriage realistic in comparison to your partner's expectations?

2. Do you see significant discrepancies in your reasons for marrying? If there are some, do you believe these are potential trouble spots in your marriage?

Source: Quilliam, S. (2005). *Staying together: From crisis to deeper commitment.* London: Vermillion.

<<< Is it possible to have a great sexual relationship **without a great marriage and vice versa?**

The most relevant example that illustrates the impact of state-by-state regulation of marriage is the cases of same-sex couples who marry and then move to a different state. For example, although the residents of Massachusetts may approve of same-sex marriages, the residents of a more conservative state might not. Because marriage and family laws are entrusted in the hands of individual states, same-sex marriages most likely will not be recognized in other states.

This has far-reaching ramifications with regards to rights and privileges allowed for married couples. The **Defense of Marriage Act (DOMA)** allows states to choose whether they recognize same-sex marriages as legal unions. This legislation, signed by President Clinton in 1996, forbids federal recognition of same-sex marriages (such as Medicare benefits, Social Security benefits, and income tax benefits that are extended to married couples) (Eskridge & Hunter, 1997). Currently, 38 states recognize DOMA legislation.

SEXUAL RELATIONSHIP SATISFACTION AND MARITAL SATISFACTION

What makes a great sex life? Is it possible to have a great marriage without a great sexual relationship? Is it possible to have a great sexual relationship without a caring, committed, rich marital partnership?

As early as the 1960s, researchers explored the roles of sexual satisfaction as a contributor to overall marital satisfaction. According to Kelli-Ann Lawrance and her colleague (2005), sexual satisfaction in long-term heterosexual relationships depends on the partners' perceptions of the relationship. These perceptions include expectations,

hopes, desires, and anticipation. All of us enter into relationships with such perceptions and expectations, whether they are spoken or unspoken, realistic or unrealistic.

In a study that examined sexual practices in the United States, one body of research found that, overall, married couples are enjoying sex (Laumann et al., 1994). The majority of individuals, around 88 percent, indicated that their sexual relationships were either extremely or very physically pleasing, and these relationships tended to be high in physical affection. Of all couple types who responded to the survey, including married people, cohabitants, and gay men and lesbians, monogamous married couples reported the highest levels of sexual satisfaction. An abundance of other research also indicates that married couples have high levels of sexual satisfaction within their marital relationships (among many others, Edwards & Booth, 1994; Haavio-Mannila & Kontula, 1997; Janus & Janus, 1993; Lawrance & Byers, 1995; Purnine, Carey, & Jorgensen, 1994). In one recent study, the researchers discovered that the quality of the couple's intimate communication, particularly self-disclosure, leads to greater relationship satisfaction, which, in turn, leads to greater sexual satisfaction (MacNeil & Byers, 2005).

Researchers have also explored how sexual scripts influence marital relationships and sexual satisfaction. Susan Sprecher (2002) found that among women, increased relationship satisfaction leads to increased sexual satisfaction, and among men, increased sexual satisfaction leads to increased relationship satisfaction. Sprecher attributed her findings to the fact that women's sex scripts socialize them to enjoy sex only in committed, fulfilling relationships, whereas men's sex scripts socialize them to be motivated by sex. Other recent research confirmed Sprecher's ideas about sex scripts and relationship/sexual satisfaction in marriages (Byers, 2005; Vohs, Cantonese, & Baumeister, 2004).

In a rare study that sought to determine sexual and relationship satisfaction of married couples in mainland China, researchers found that Chinese men and women are moderately satisfied with their marital sexual relationships (Renaud, Byers, & Pan, 1997). The more affection and sexual behavior that exists in the relationship, the greater the sexual and marital relationship satisfaction is. These conclusions are consistent with American and Canadian research in which husbands' and wives' ratings of

∧
∧
∧ **"You want sex all the time!"**

sexual satisfaction are associated with increased marital relationship satisfaction (Henderson-King & Veroff, 1994; Lawrance & Byers, 2005; Oggins et al., 1993; Schenk, Pfrang, & Rausche, 1983; Young et al., 2000).

So, what makes great marital lives and great sex lives? Perhaps Hunt sums it up best:

> "The husband and wife who have a free and intensely pleasurable sexual relationship are much more likely to be emotionally close than the husband and wife who do not, and the close marriage is more likely to involve a genuinely liberated marital sex than the distant one" (1974, p. 232).

SEXUAL FREQUENCY IN MARRIAGE RELATIONSHIPS

In a nonscientific global sex survey funded by Durex, the largest condom manufacturer in the world, statisticians found that, worldwide, married couples have sex an average of 127 times a year (about 10 times per month). Americans were low on the frequency list, at 98 times per year (about eight times per month) (Durex, 2007). The countries with the lowest frequency of sex were Japan (37 times per year), Malaysia (62 times per year), and China (69 times per year). Approximately 4 percent of Americans claimed to have sex every day.

We do know from research that age is often negatively associated with sexual frequency and sexual satisfaction. Married couples tend to have sex less frequently and to feel less sexually satisfied as they age; this finding is also true among Chinese societies (Chevret et al., 2004; Mazur et al., 2002; Guo & Huang, 2005).

Many partners involved in intimate relationships expect that their emotional connections and sexual behaviors be restricted to their relationship (Banfield & McCabe, 2001). But what happens when one partner (or both) oversteps the expectations of monogamy and exclusivity?

CHEATING: SEX OUTSIDE THE RELATIONSHIP

Infidelity, or cheating, is a breach of faith that occurs when there is a violation of the couple's mutually agreed-upon rules or boundaries of a relationship. Often, infidelity is referred to as *extramarital affairs* or *extramarital experiences*. Extramarital experiences can occur when one marital partner ventures outside the relationship and becomes emotionally and/or sexually involved with another person. What constitutes an act of infidelity varies between and within cultures, as well as within individual relationships. Almost always,

<<< **Caught with his pants down?**
In 2009, 15 women went to the media with claims that they had had ongoing affairs with married golf legend Tiger Woods.

these types of extramarital experiences result in a breakdown of trust within the relationship. When one partner ventures outside the relationship without the other's knowledge or permission, it is said to be an *involuntary extramarital experience*.

INVOLUNTARY EXPERIENCES

Intimate relationships (dating, cohabiting, gay/lesbian, or marriages) involve behaviors and emotions that are generally expected to be restricted to the relationship. When any behavior oversteps the expectations of exclusivity and expectations of monogamy, it is considered to be an **extra relationship involvement (ERI)** (Banfield & McCabe, 2001). There are three types of ERI, shown in Table 10.1 (Thompson, 1984). **Extramarital sex (EMS)** occurs when a married person has a sexual relationship with anyone other than his or her spouse. Just as with ERI, there are different types of EMS. These include (Clayton, 1997):

- *Clandestine:* The participating members do not believe either of their spouses (if the partner is married) knows about the sexual relationship, nor do they believe their spouse(s) would approve.

- *Ambiguous:* In these relationships, the nonparticipating spouse may know about the EMS but cannot prove it; the nonparticipating

---

TABLE 10.1
Types of Extra Relationship Involvement

- *Sexual ERI:* This type of behavior involves a wide range of behaviors, from flirting, to mutual masturbation, to oral and anal sex, to sexual intercourse.

- *Emotional ERI:* Emotional extra relationship involvement also includes a range of behaviors and includes a close friendship (with much self-disclosure) to being "in love."

- *Combination of Sexual and Emotional ERI:* As the term implies, in this category a person can engage in a wide variety of behaviors that encompasses both emotional and sexual areas of a relationship.

spouse may choose to tolerate it rather than seek divorce; the non-participating spouse may have at one time condoned the EMS but later disapproved; or he or she may tolerate the EMS but does not want details.

- *Consensual:* The nonparticipating spouse both knows and approves of the EMS; each spouse may have a consensual relationship outside the boundaries of marriage.

It is very difficult to acquire data on just how many spouses cheat on their partners, and what data are available are probably outdated. One study suggested that nearly 40 percent of married men and 20 percent of married women have been involved in ERI/EMS at least once during their marriage (Laumann et al., 1994). A more recent study had similar findings: Approximately 44 percent of men and 24 percent of women had at least one ERI/EMS experience in their marriages (Banfield & McCabe, 2001).

Given the devastating effect cheating has on marital relationships and the difficulty in repairing marriages that have been impacted by extramarital relationships (Oppenheimer, 2007), why do people cheat on their spouses?

WHY DO PEOPLE CHEAT?

Research has revealed a number of factors that are associated with an increased risk of engaging in ERI/EMS; these are shown in Figure 10.13.

Past research claimed that men and women have different ideas about sex and love. For instance, one study found that men believe women must be in love to have sex, and women think that men may have sex without being in love (Harris & Christenfeld, 1996). Other research has similarly found that women do not tend to become sexually involved in the absence of emotional commitment (love), but men can (Townsend, 1995). This research is interesting, because it suggests that women may be more likely to engage in emotional ERI, whereas men are more likely to engage in EMS. This leads us to another important question. Is an Internet relationship "cheating"?

sex talk

Adult Relationships

The way society views adult relationships today is constantly changing. Think about what different forms of relationships mean to you.

Being single makes me feel _____

_____.

When I am in a relationship, I feel _____

_____.

I plan/do not plan to get married one day because _____

_____.

I would/would not cohabit with someone before marrying him/her because _____

_____.

The best advantage to cohabitation is _____

_____.

The worst disadvantage to cohabitation is _____

_____.

My parents' relationship makes me view marriage as _____

_____.

Marriage is/is not necessary for a satisfying sexual relationship because _____

_____.

A satisfying sexual relationship is/is not important for a successful marriage because _____

_____.

Cheating is/is not acceptable when _____

_____.

If my partner cheated on me, I would feel _____

_____.

Gender: Men are more likely to have extramarital relationships than women are (Atkins, Jacobson, & Baucom, 2001).

Age: Younger married people experience higher rates of extramarital activity than older married people (Kimuna & Kjamba, 2005).

Personality traits: Some personality traits such as narcissism and low levels of conscientiousness are associated with cheating (Atkins et al. 2001).

Marital satisfaction: Lower levels of relationship satisfaction are linked to increased rates of extramarital behaviors for both men and women (Wiederman, 1997).

Length of marriage: The longer the duration of the marriage, the less likely a man or a woman is to cheat on their spouse (Liu, 2000).

Opportunity: Some people have more opportunities to cheat, such as jobs that take them away from their spouses (Atkins et al. 2001).

Figure 10.13 **Factors in People Cheating** Why do people cheat? **Research reveals a number of factors that increase a person's risk of engaging in ERI/EMS.**

>>> **Actors Will Smith and Jada Pinkett Smith have a pact** that either of them can have sex with a third party so long as the other gives permission.

ARE INTERNET RELATIONSHIPS "CHEATING"?

This is a common question that many students ask. In some respects, it is a difficult question to answer, because it is difficult to determine the meaning people attach to these relationships—is it just for fun because an Internet user is bored? Is it for sexual pleasure/gratification? Is it "innocent" flirting?

In a study of more than 500 online users, researchers found several themes in online relationships (Wildermuth & Vogl-Bauer, 2007). When it came to the question of whether online relationships constitute extramarital affairs, views were mixed among study participants. Several indicated that they participated in Internet affairs because they were unhappy in their real-life marriages; they stressed that their preexisting marriage problems caused them to seek an affair. Other participants noted that the online affairs were just as painful a betrayal as in real-life affairs, and just as devastating. One participant noted,

> "The effect on a husband when he discovers his wife has been having cyber-sex is sheer hell. I now have a deep distrust of my wife and a feeling of constant paranoia. The effects on my marriage [of her online affair] have been disastrous." (Wildermuth & Vogl-Bauer, 2007, p. 219)

Extramarital affairs or sexual relationships outside committed relationships cause much emotional pain, devastation, and torment for the victimized partner, and they include reactions such as rage, feelings of shame, depression, overwhelming powerlessness, and abandonment, along with a prolonged disruption in daily functioning (Gordon, Baucom, & Snyder, 2004). So traumatic are the effects of extramarital affairs, marriage therapist Douglas Snyder (2004) maintains that sexual infidelity is the most difficult relationship issue to treat.

VOLUNTARY EXTRAMARITAL EXPERIENCES

Is there a middle ground between monogamy and infidelity? Despite our deeply ingrained socialization toward monogamy, there are a number of non-monogamous relationships that are currently practiced.

Open marriage is a marriage relationship in which the husband and wife have no reservations about one another being sexually involved with other people. There are two types of open marriages. In the first type, married partners are open to sex outside the boundaries of their marriage, but neither party discusses the matter; it's accepted if it happens. In the second type, spouses are explicitly open to sex outside the marriage, and both married partners have agreed to it.

A common form of a non-monogamous relationship that is practiced among heterosexual couples is **swinging**, in which couples are romantically and emotionally committed to their marriage partners but enjoy having recreational sex with others. Swinging is all about sex, and it's usually considered a social activity. With swinging, couples typically spell out specific rules about who can have sex with whom. With swinging, no emotional involvement or commitment is permitted.

Polyamory refers to a relationship orientation that practices having more than one loving, intimate, committed relationship at a time. Polyamory is practiced with the full knowledge and consent of everyone involved, unlike cheating, in which deception and betrayal are involved, and often polyamory members live together in the same household (Cook, 2005). People who practice polyamory are referred to as **polyamorous**, or **polys**, and they reject Western culture's norm that sexual and relational exclusivity are necessary for long-term loving relationships

Marriage Models

We frequently carry interaction patterns and behaviors from our family of origin to our family of choice when we marry. Sometimes, continuing these behaviors is a deliberate choice; other times, we may not want to interact in ways similar to our parents, but because these patterns are so deeply ingrained in our way of thinking, we carry them into our own marriages. When contemplating marriage, couples must consider the marriage models in their lives and how these have shaped their own attitudes and ideas about marriage.

Her Side: For the most part, the marriage models in my life have been quite positive. My parents have been married for over 25 years, and today they are still warm and affectionate toward each other. My grandparents were married for over 50 years before my grandma died. My parents frequently talk things over, and many times it seems as though they communicate without saying a single word to each other. Of course, they've argued, and quite passionately at times. But I always get the feeling that they really *enjoy* being married. Divorce? No way. Our religion really frowns upon divorce. I have a feeling that if they had a bad marriage, they would stay married because of their religious beliefs. I've never given it much thought, but as I look across my family background, there is no divorce in the family tree. I've always wanted a marriage like my parents have. To me, theirs is an "ideal" marriage. I am concerned, because I feel that my fiancé's parents' marriage is empty, and that it is void of the positives I see in my marriage models.

His Side: My parents' marriage is sometimes good, sometimes bad. I suppose this is how *all* marriages are. Unlike my fiancée's parents, my parents are more independent in their marriage; they do things together, but they are just as content doing things separately from one another. And unlike her family, my family typically doesn't interact a lot with extended family. For example, we seldom have family reunions or celebrate holidays together with them. Yes, there is divorce in our family tree. My fiancée is concerned about this. She thinks that since it has been an acceptable way of handling marital distress in my family background (my sister recently divorced), it might be easier for me to divorce her if things don't work out. It would be fruitless for me to argue that the marriage models in my life have not influenced me. I believe that it is my *choice* to adopt their behaviors or not, and that I will not necessarily repeat these behaviors in my own marriage.

Your Side: In your opinion, how will this couple's marriage models influence their marriage? In your decision, consider the following questions:

1. In what ways does each of these partners' marriage models differ? Specifically, what are her marriage model influences? What are his marriage model influences?

2. Do you foresee any potential marital distress ahead for this couple? Why? What areas of their marriage may have difficulty, and why did you choose these specific areas?

3. In your opinion, what things should this couple focus on before they wed?

and relationship satisfaction. Most often, these relationships are built upon trust, loyalty, and negotiation, and they reject jealousy and possessiveness (Echlin, 2003).

There are challenges that polys face. For instance, because Western cultures embrace monogamy, people who practice polyamory report that they face discrimination by mainstream society, from their families, their friends, and their employers (Davidson, 2002). They also fear that Child Protective Services or Child Welfare will take their children away if their non-monogamous lifestyles are discovered (Cook, 2005). Unlike marriage, there is no legal protection in property law should the relationships dissolve; parenting and child custody issues also become significantly more complicated if the relationship dissolves (Davidson, 2002).

Sweeping changes are occurring in the sexual and relationship landscape. Only time will tell if they will be embraced and accepted by monogamy-only societies or whether these cultures will continue to endorse marriage as the only socially sanctioned intimate pair bond.

SEXUAL LIFE EDUCATION

This is the point where much of what you've studied so far comes together. Your experiences of gender, communication, love, intimacy, sexual development, and dating eventually contribute to whether you enter into a lifelong, committed relationship (be it cohabitation, a same-sex union, or marriage), and with whom you choose to share your life. Each of you has unique, individual experiences, and you will probably some day merge with another person whose experiences are vastly different.

No two couples experience a lifelong partnership the same way, because these experiences are affected by our experiences within our families of origin, as well as by our racial, ethnic, cultural, and religious backgrounds. Many of you will some day vow to stick by your partner for "better or worse." Whichever type of partnership you enter, keep in mind that wedding and commitment ceremony promises speak to the either/ors in life; either things will be good or they will be bad; either someone will be healthy or someone will be sick; either the bills will be paid, or they won't. But as you will discover, an intimate partnership isn't just about the good days or the bad days. It's about all the days in between. Some days just *are*; they're not good, they're not bad, they're not great, they're not horrible. They just *are*. And that's when it's important to remember what you've learned in your study so far, that life with an intimate partner is all about change over time.

Hard work? Without a doubt!

Summary

HOW IS THE TREND OF SINGLE-HOOD GROWING TODAY? 190

- Every person will be single at one point in his or her life, and for most, singlehood will not be a static state of being. As young adults come to depend on their friends to satisfy familial needs, the age at which people first get married is increasing, as is singlehood, as a trend.
- Singles can include people who have never been married, gays and lesbians who are not legally able to get married, divorced singles, and widows and widowers.

WHY DO COUPLES COHABIT?

195

- As not getting married becomes an increasingly socially acceptable option, many couples choose to live together without getting married for various amounts of time, sometimes sharing the responsibilities that typically come with marriage.
- The reasons people have for cohabiting are many, ranging from viewing it as a trial marriage to doing it for financial reasons. Whatever the reasons, there are both upsides and downsides to cohabiting.

WHAT ARE THE EXPERIENCES OF MARRIAGE? 202

- Each couple's marriage is unique, but legal marriage provides people with rights and privileges that are denied unmarried couples and gay and lesbian couples who are not legally recognized as married. Marital satisfaction and sexual relationships often impact one another.

WHY DO PEOPLE CHEAT?

207

- Different people have different definitions of cheating, but if one party is unaware of the other's extra-relationship experience, it can often end in feelings of betrayal and a disintegration of the relationship. Extra relationship involvement can be physical, emotional, or both.
- Some couples choose to allow extra relationship involvement, and they have agreed upon boundaries. Polyamory is when a relationship includes more than two committed parties at a time.

Key Terms

never-married singles individuals who have not married, may or may not live alone, and may or may not have an intimate partner   *191*

urban tribe a mixed-gender circle of friends (typically in their 20s and 30s) who are the primary social support system for singles   *193*

cohabitation the living arrangements of unmarried, intimate partners who typically have a sexual relationship; such relationships often resemble a marriage   *195*

common law marriage a relationship between cohabiting heterosexual partners, but without a legal marriage ceremony   *195*

Defense of Marriage Act (DOMA) 1996 law that allows states to choose whether they recognize same-sex marriages as legal unions   *206*

infidelity cheating within an intimate relationship   *207*

extra relationship involvement (ERI) any behavior that oversteps the expectations of exclusivity and expectations of monogamy; there are three types   *207*

extramarital sex a sexual relationship with a person other than one's spouse   *207*

open marriage a marriage relationship in which the husband and wife have no reservations about one another being sexually involved with other people   *210*

swinging non-monogamous relationship in which couples are romantically and emotionally committed to their marriage partners, but enjoy having recreational sex with others   *210*

polyamory a relationship orientation that practices having more than one loving, intimate, committed relationship at a time; practiced with the full knowledge and consent of everyone involved, polyamory members often live together in the same household   *210*

polyamorous, or **polys** people who practice polyamory   *210*

Sample Test Questions

MULTIPLE CHOICE

1. Which characteristic of American culture contributes to a rise in singlehood?
   a. Collectivism
   b. Capitalism
   c. Individualism
   d. None of the above

2. A nun is an example of a/an:
   a. Involuntary temporary single.
   b. Involuntary permanent single.
   c. Voluntary temporary single.
   d. Voluntary permanent single.

3. Which aspect of cohabitation is NOT considered a disadvantage?
   a. Couples who cohabit have greater flexibility in their commitments to their relationships.
   b. Cohabiting couples are less sexually committed and are not as faithful to their partners as married partners are.
   c. Married couples that cohabited before marriage have poorer communication skills in discussing problems than those couples who did not live together.
   d. Couples who live together have the lowest level of premarital satisfaction when compared to other living arrangements.

4. Not being able to legally get married does not prohibit gay and lesbian couples from:
   a. Living together in a nursing home.
   b. Having automatic hospital visitation.
   c. Cohabiting.
   d. Receiving pension benefits.

5. The Defense of Marriage Act:
   a. Does not allow legal same-sex marriages.
   b. Allows states to choose whether they recognize same-sex marriages as legal unions.
   c. Encourages states to recognize same-sex marriages as legal unions.
   d. Allows federal recognition of same-sex marriages.

6. According to Susan Sprecher, women's sex scripts socialize them to enjoy sex only when:
   a. They are motivated by sex.
   b. They are not in a committed, fulfilling relationship.
   c. They are in a committed, fulfilling relationship.
   d. None of the above

7. A close friendship with much self-disclosure with a person outside of one's relationship is an example of:
   a. Sexual ERI.
   b. Emotional ERI.
   c. Physical ERI.
   d. Sexual and emotional ERI.

8. Which of the following is NOT true regarding open marriages?
   a. Both married partners do not have to be open to sex outside the relationship.
   b. Married partners can be open to sex outside the relationship, but not discuss it.
   c. Married partners are explicitly open to sex outside the relationship.
   d. Swinging can be a part of an open marriage.

SHORT RESPONSE

1. Should gay and lesbian couples be allowed to legally marry? Why or why not?
2. Have you cohabited? If so, what were the advantages and disadvantages for you? If not, would you and why or why not?
3. How have the marriage models in your life influenced you?
4. What constitutes cheating to you?
5. Do you plan to get married? Why or why not?

Answers: 1. c; 2. d; 3. a; 4. c; 5. b; 6. c; 7. b; 8. a

Remember to check www.thethinkspot.com **for additional information, downloadable flashcards, and other helpful resources.**

THINK READINGS

THE NEW YORK TIMES

Divorce, It Seems, Can Make You Ill

By TARA PARKER-POPE

Published: August 3, 2009

Married people tend to be healthier than single people. But what happens when a marriage ends?

New research shows that when married people become single again, whether by divorce or a spouse's death, they experience much more than an emotional loss. Often they suffer a decline in physical health from which they never fully recover, even if they remarry.

And in terms of health, it's not better to have married and lost than never to have married at all. Middle-age people who never married have fewer chronic health problems than those who were divorced or widowed.

The findings, from a national study of 8,652 men and women in their 50s and early 60s, suggest that the physical stress of marital loss continues long after the emotional wounds have healed. While this does not mean that people should stay married at all costs, it does show that marital history is an important indicator of health, and that the newly single need to be especially vigilant about stress management and exercise, even if they remarry.

"When your spouse is getting sick and about to die or your marriage is getting bad and about to die, your stress levels go up," said Linda Waite, a sociology professor at the University of Chicago and an author of the study, which appears in the September issue of The Journal of Health and Social Behavior. "You're not sleeping well, your diet gets worse, you can't exercise, you can't see your friends. It's a whole package of awful events."

The health benefits of marriage, documented by a wealth of research, appear to stem from several factors. Married people tend to be better off financially and can share in a spouse's employer health benefits. And wives, in particular, act as gatekeepers for a husband's health, scheduling appointments and noticing changes that may signal a health problem. Spouses can offer logistical support, like taking care of children while a partner exercises or shuttling a partner to and from the doctor's office.

But in the latest study, researchers sought to gauge the health effects of divorce, widowhood and remarriage in a large cohort of people over time.

Among the 8,652 people studied, more than half were still married to their first spouse. About 40 percent had been divorced or widowed; about half of that group were remarried by the time of the study. About 4 percent had never married.

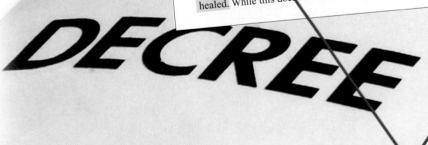

The study found that people who were divorced and remarried had worse health than never-divorced adults. They also discovered the same health consequences in those who lost a spouse to death. What situations could cause these physical and psychological health declines?

In this sense, a **gatekeeper** is a person who monitors and oversees the actions of another or others.

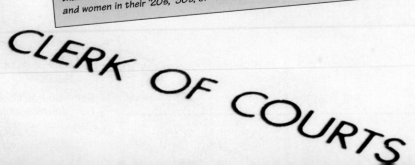

The study found that divorced or widowed people have 20 percent more chronic health conditions (heart disease, diabetes, or cancer) than married people. Might the results of the study differ if men and women in their '20s, '30s, or '40s were studied? How and why?

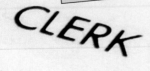

Over all, men and women who had experienced divorce or the death of a spouse reported about 20 percent more chronic health problems like heart disease, diabetes and cancer, compared with those who had been continuously married. Previously married people were also more likely to have mobility problems, like difficulty climbing stairs or walking a meaningful distance.

While remarrying led to some improvement in health, the study showed that most married people who became single never fully recovered from the physical declines associated with marital loss. Compared with those who had been continuously married, people in second marriages had 12 percent more chronic health problems and 19 percent more mobility problems. A second marriage did appear to heal emotional wounds: remarried people had only slightly more depressive symptoms than those continuously married.

The study does not prove that the loss of a marriage causes health problems, only that the two are associated. It may be that people who don't exercise, eat poorly and can't manage stress are also more likely to divorce. Still, researchers note that because the effect is seen in both divorced and widowed people, the data strongly suggest a causal relationship.

One reason may be changes at the cellular level during times of high stress. In an Ohio State University study, scientists analyzed blood samples of people undergoing the stress of caring for a loved one with Alzheimer's disease. The research focused on telomeres, which insulate and protect the ends of chromosomes; with aging, telomeres shorten and the activity of a related enzyme also declines.

Compared with a control group, the Alzheimer's caregivers showed telomere patterns associated with a four- to eight-year shortening of life span. Dr. Waite said the stress of divorce or widowhood might take a similar toll, leading to chronic health and mobility problems.

None of this suggests that spouses should stay in a bad marriage for the sake of health. Marital troubles can lead to physical ones, too.

In a series of experiments, scientists at Ohio State studied the relationship between marital strife and immune response, as measured by the time it takes for a wound to heal. The researchers recruited married couples who submitted to a small suction device that left eight tiny blisters on the arm. The couples then engaged in different types of discussions—sometimes positive and supportive, at other times focused on a topic of conflict.

After a marital conflict, the wounds took a full day longer to heal. Among couples who exhibited high levels of hostility, the wound healing took two days longer than with those who showed less animosity.

"I would argue that if you can't fix a marriage you're better off out of it," said Janice Kiecolt-Glaser, an Ohio State scientist who is an author of much of the research. "With a divorce you're disrupting your life, but a long-term acrimonious marriage also is very bad."

Some previous studies indicate that a person's immune system response is weakened because of marital strife and stress. The authors of this study suggest that the impacts of marriage, divorce, and remarriage on health are correlated with how certain illnesses develop and heal over time. Have you ever found that you become ill quicker and more frequently when you're under large amounts of stress?

The authors of the study, Linda Waite and Mary Elizabeth Hughes, note that people enter adulthood (and marriage) with a certain "stock" of health. According to the researchers, experiences in marriage—loss and gain, negative and positive—either take away or add to this stock. They also suggest that once lost, the stock cannot be replenished. At this point in time, what is your physical health stock? Your emotional health stock? Do these findings suggest that young adults should enter into a marriage physically healthy?

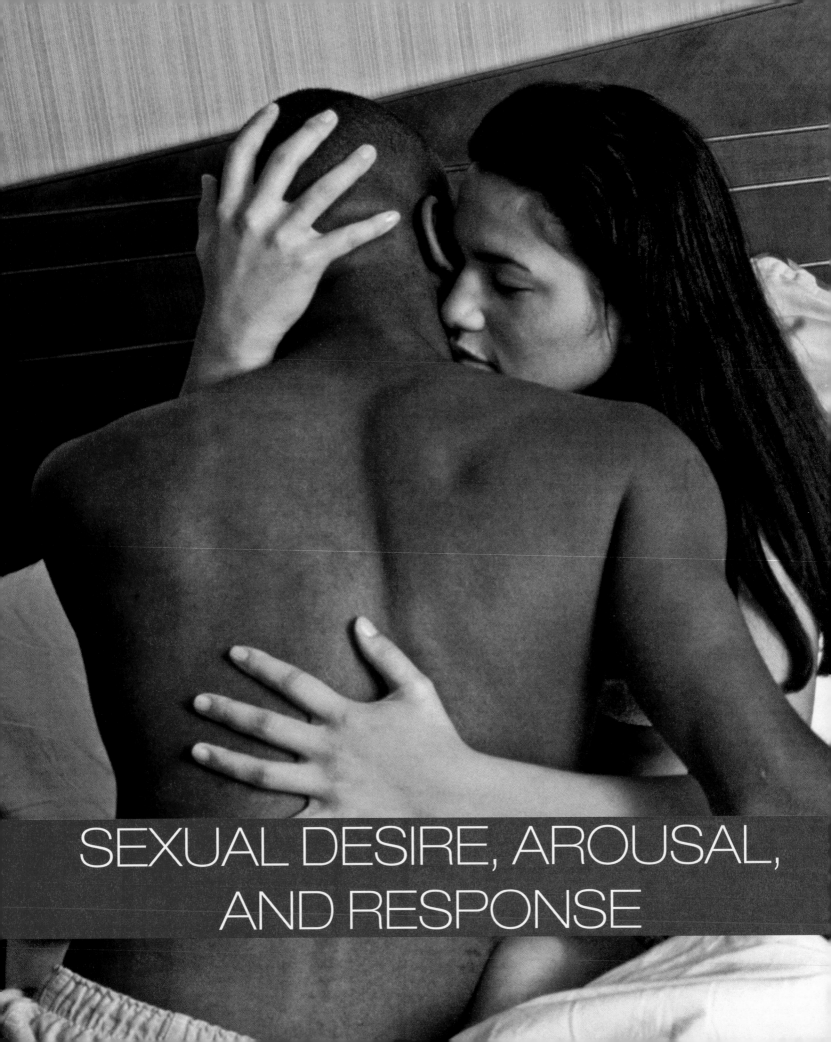

SEXUAL DESIRE, AROUSAL,
AND RESPONSE

<<< *Human sexuality is about more than sex parts and physiology.*

WHAT FACTORS INTO HUMAN SEXUAL RESPONSE?

WHAT KINDS OF SOLITARY SEXUAL EXPERIENCES ARE THERE?

HOW IS SEXUALITY EXPERIENCED WITH OTHERS?

WHAT CAUSES SEXUAL DIFFICULTIES, AND HOW CAN THEY BE TREATED?

I don't

understand why sometimes I don't feel like having sex, like why I'd rather have a bowl of popcorn and watch a DVD than make love to my boyfriend. That scares me because I'm in my early 20s—and if I don't want sex *now*, what on earth will it be like when I'm older? You have to admit that's a scary thought! I don't understand why sometimes I just kind of lay there and think, "God, is this almost over?" and other times I can't get enough of him. I don't understand why I'm always on the verge of an orgasm but just can't ever seem to have one—or if I have, I don't know because I don't really understand what one is or what it even feels like! I'm hoping that as I get older, it will be just as easy for me to have an orgasm as it is for him, but then I wonder if women can ever really be as sexually satisfied as guys are. Ever? And why is it that if my head isn't in the right place or if I'm worried about things, sex is more of a chore than a fun experience? Sometimes, I feel so out of it when I'm having sex that it's tough to let go and "enjoy the ride" as my boyfriend says.

So, you asked what questions I have about sexual response. My questions aren't about body parts, but about all of these other things that I just don't understand!

Source: Author's files

There is little denying that human sexuality encompasses more than sex parts or physiology. So far in our study of sexuality, you have discovered that biological and cultural influences shape who you are as a sexual being—your *sexual scripts*—from your earliest days of life and well into old age. The three realms of sexuality (see Chapter 1) are intricately intertwined and interrelated, and sexuality is not a homogenized or generic experience because of the continuous influences of the multiple contexts that surround us. The same holds true for how you experience sexual arousal and response; no two people will necessarily experience sexual arousal and response the same way because of unique biological, psychosocial/psychosexual, and cultural influences. Despite these differences, however, sexologists and researchers have discovered that women and men do experience certain common physiological and psychological responses during sexual behavior.

Teaching and writing about sex in the 21st century sometimes poses a dilemma. On the one hand, sex and open expressions of sexuality are commonplace in Western cultures today. Yet on the other hand, a woman often doesn't understand or accept her body, a man often feels that he doesn't measure up to her sexual expectations (or to his own), and the act of sex becomes a proving ground. Although images of sexuality barrage today's young men and women, oftentimes they are not taught how or why their bodies respond to sexual stimulation.

There is never enough time to answer all the questions my students have about sex. "Why is it that my boyfriend can become sexually excited so much faster than I can?" and "Why can I orgasm when I masturbate but not with my fiancé?" And, as the woman in the opening vignette asks, why is sex sometimes thrilling and other times dull?

In this chapter, we'll examine human sexual desire, arousal, and response. Understanding these processes allows us to not only comprehend *how* our bodies work, but *why* we respond the way we do. It also allows us to appreciate how and why our partners respond the way they do. Knowing our bodies not only increases our sexual pleasure and satisfaction, but also enhances our sexual relationships and our overall relationship satisfaction.

IN THE MOOD: THE NATURE OF SEXUAL DESIRE AND AROUSAL

What does it mean to have "sexual desire" or to "sexually desire" someone? Does it mean we have strong, sometimes uncontrollable, urges to have a sexual encounter, such as an inborn drive? Does it disappear when a sex act ends (Giles, 2004)? First, let's explore what it really means when we say, "I want you" or "I gotta have you" to an intimate partner.

SEXUAL DESIRE

Sexual desire is typically thought of as a conscious, purposeful act (Everaerd, 2006). Most researchers and theorists define **sexual desire** as the wish, drive, or motivation to engage in sexual activities, or the anticipation of sexual pleasure in the future (Clayton et al., 2006; Impett et al., 2008). It can be strong, such as an all-consuming urgency to engage in sexual behaviors with someone, or it can be less obvious, such as giving someone a flirtatious look (Giles, 2004). In essence, sexual desire can involve any potential rewards and positive emotional experiences that motivate us; it varies from person to person and from culture to culture (Gabel, 2006).

Sexual desire is not the same thing as *physiological*, or genital, sexual arousal, although this can certainly be a component for some people. For instance, we can engage in a sexual behavior, but that doesn't necessarily mean we desired or wanted it, and the absence of sexual activity doesn't necessarily reflect a lack of desire (Regan, 1999).

Healthy Selves / Healthy Sex

Body Image: In and Out of the Bedroom

When we become preoccupied with the appearance of our bodies outside the bedroom, these concerns ultimately end up in the bedroom. Because sexual arousal and response require attention and focus, when we focus on how our bodies *look*, rather than what we are *experiencing*, we are less able to let our guards down and fully experience sexual pleasure and sexually pleasuring our partner.

For healthy relationships–and great sex–redefine what sex is all about!

- *Get real:* Sexy is as sexy does! *You* define what body type is sexy and appealing to your partner, *not* media images. Your partner probably wouldn't be with you in bed in the first place if he or she didn't see something about you that was appealing.

- *Let it happen:* You can't force great sex, especially if you're overly concerned about how you look during the act. Just let sex happen. Focus on what feels good and all the different sensations going on in your body.

- *Let go:* Get rid of those inhibitions by giving yourself permission to enjoy sex fully. When you truly let go, it's tough to think about what your thighs must look like in a particular position.

- *Connect, communicate, and trust:* When you focus on emotionally connecting and communicating during sex, you feel safe and secure—and you'll realize the shape of your body has nothing to do with these other feelings.

- *Be adventurous:* Explore, explore, explore. This attitude shifts the focus to each other's bodies, and in doing so, you begin to see how fun sex really can be, and that it's not all about looks.

Sources: Sanches, D. T., & Kiefer, A. K. (2008). Body concerns in and out of the bedroom: Implications for sexual pleasure and problems. Retrieved October 20, 2004, from www.disanche@rutgers.edu; Ma, L. (2004). How to have great sex. *Psychology Today,* March 8, 2004.

So, on one level, sexual desire is *cognitive* (such as sexual wishes, thoughts, desires, or daydreams), and on another level, it can be *physical* (genital arousal). Sexual desire is also thought to be a *psychosexual* experience, and as Figure 11.1 illustrates, every one of our senses gets involved.

Sexual desire is commonly referred to as **libido**, the term coined by Sigmund Freud to describe a person's inborn sexual drives and his or her sexual instincts, that person's *psychosexual energy*, or *psychic energy*. Freud thought that this psychosexual energy is present at birth and is directed to certain areas of the body, like the mouth and the oral pleasures of sucking in the early years of life (see Chapter 7).

Our study of sexual desire and libido does not focus on the psychoanalytic theories of Freud and Carl Jung; nonetheless, these theorists played a pivotal role in sexologists' earlier understandings of how and why we behave sexually in the ways we do. The broader point to consider here is that sexual desire is defined in a number of ways by a number of different researchers and theorists, like Freud and Jung. Despite these differing definitions, the underlying psychosexual premise is that sexual desire is an inborn need or biological drive—we need to have sex!

But this raises another question: Are there differences between men and women's sexual needs? The college student in the opening vignette posed an interesting question. Why is it that sometimes she can't get enough sex, and why is it that she's sometimes bored with sex, even

Sight

We can become sexually aroused by what we see. Brain activity in certain regions increases, as do testosterone levels when men view sexually explicit materials (Arnow et al., 2002; Stoleru et al., 1999). It was previously thought that women were not visually stimulated by erotic images, but recent research suggests that women experience measurable arousal when watching filmed erotica (Kinsey, Pomeroy, & Martin, 1948; Kinsey, Pomeroy, Martin, & Gebhard, 1953; Laan, Everaerd, & Evers, 1996; Murnen & Stockton, 1997). Some women deny arousal when they are studied, but some researchers think this is because women are offended by particular types of pornography in which women are degraded or treated insensitively (Koukounas & McCabe, 1997; Striar & Bartlik, 2000).

Smell

Smell can also influence what we find arousing, and what we don't. Sex pheromones convey species-specific information among males and indicate availability for breeding among females. Contrary to the claims of popular culture, although humans do secrete pheromones, there is no evidence yet to link these secretions to sexual attraction and arousal; human pheromones are not sexual attractants (Kohl, 2002).

Taste & Sound

Other sensory input includes taste and hearing. The mouth (including the lips, tongue, and cheeks) can be intensely aroused when stimulated through *soul kissing*, *deep kissing*, and *French kissing*. Some people find sex talk and other sounds extremely arousing, while others find them to be a turnoff. One research study discovered that saying or hearing "I love you" after orgasm intensifies the sexual experience (Haffner & Schwartz, 1998).

Figure 11.1 **Senses and Sexual Arousal**

while she's doing it? She also wondered if she'll ever be as interested in sex as her male partner is. There are a number of research studies that give us insight into the differences between the sexual desires of men and women.

MEN'S SEXUAL DESIRE

Do men have higher sex drives than women? Several studies suggest that men have more interest in sex than women do (for a comprehensive review, see Impett et al., 2008). Men, more so than women:

- Think about sex (Laumann et al., 1994).

- Report having more sexual fantasies (Beck, Bozman, & Qualtrough, 1991).

- Have stronger sexual desire (Leitenberg & Henning, 1995).

- Want sex more frequently (Sprecher & Regan, 1996).

- Emphasize sexual pleasure and sexual intercourse when describing sexual desire (Regan & Berscheid, 1999).

There is a substantial amount of empirical evidence that indicates that sexual desire is, to varying degrees, testosterone-dependent (Regan, 1999). Testosterone is also associated with sexual desire in women.

WOMEN'S SEXUAL DESIRE

In general, women have lower levels of sexual desire than men do (Impett et al., 2008). An abundance of scientific studies suggest that when women have sex, they, more so than men,

- Emphasize the interpersonal, not physical, aspects of the relationship, such as goals for the relationship, love, and intimacy (Peplau, 2003).

- Engage in sex to enhance relationship commitment (Basson, 2002).

- Have sex to express love for their mates (Impett, Peplau, & Gable, 2005).

Interestingly, an increase in testosterone in women is associated with an increase in sexual interest and desire (Regan, 1999). Recall from our

sexual life now

Aphrodisiacs: Do They Really Enhance Sexual Desire and Arousal?

From foods like chilies to rare objects like rhinoceros horns (hence the term, *horny*, used to describe strong sexual desire), people all over the world look for **aphrodisiacs**, which are believed to boost sexual desire and/or increase a person's capacity to engage in sexual activities. But do aphrodisiacs really enhance sexual desire and arousal?

Some agents have been found to increase libido, such as:

- *Testosterone:* Sex drive and sexual response in both men and women have been clearly linked to levels of sex hormones, particularly testosterone.

- *Yohimbine:* The sap from the bark of this West African tree has been shown to induce intense sexual arousal in rats. There has been some indication it acts as a true aphrodisiac in some men with erectile disorders and in postmenopausal women.

- *PEA:* A chemical called *phenylethylamine (PEA),* found in chocolate, is thought to increase sexual arousal and attraction.

To date, the Federal Drug Administration (FDA) has not approved any product or agent as an effective aphrodisiac. The FDA:

- Declares that there is no scientific proof that aphrodisiacs, sold over the counter or over the Internet, work.

- Cautions that many purported aphrodisiacs are potentially unsafe and should be used with great caution.

- Cautions lovers to stay away from alcohol, opiates (heroin, morphine, methadone), cocaine, tranquilizers, amphetamines, nicotine, and marijuana, because these agents severely *reduce* libido and performance, not enhance them.

In summary, although aphrodisiac research may be creating some very happy lab rats, there is little evidence to suggest that humans will experience the same effects.

>>> WHAT DO YOU THINK?

1. Have you ever tried a substance (including a food) to alter your typical patterns of sexual arousal and response? What was the effect?
2. If a proven aphrodisiac were on the market at a reasonable cost, would you use it? Would you use it every so often, or would you use it with every sexual encounter? What negatives could be associated with using an aphrodisiac with every sexual experience?

Sources: Harndwerk, B. (2006). Effectiveness often in the eye of the beholder. *National Geographic News,* February 14, 2006; Ernst, E., & Pittler, M. (1998). Yohimbine for erectile dysfunction: A systematic review and meta-analysis of randomized clinical trials. *Journal of Urology, 159,* 433–436; Meston, C. (2000). The psychophysiological assessment of female sexual function. *Journal of Sex Education and Therapy, 25,* 6–16.

study in Chapter 4 that the sex hormones, *estrogens*, are feminizing hormones that are largely secreted by the ovaries. It was once believed that higher levels of estrogens were necessary for sexual desire in women, but today we know that estrogens appear to have little influence on sexual desire in women (Regan, 1999). Researchers have discovered that when women are given testosterone as a substitute for low levels of estrogen (as in the case of hormone replacement therapy, visited in Chapter 16), they notice a significant increase in sexual desire (Sherwin, 1985, 1988).

Like all other areas of sexuality, sexual desire is a process that undergoes change over time. It's a subjective experience based on biological and societal influences. As such, we can experience sexual desire as an all-consuming "gotta have it, baby" drive, and we can experience it as a way to grow and develop intimacy with a partner. Every healthy person is able to respond to sexual desire. This is known as *sexual arousal and response*.

SEXUAL AROUSAL AND RESPONSE

Sexual arousal is the stimulation of sexual desire in preparation for sexual behaviors. It is a state of heightened physiological and emotional activity that produces changes in the human body in response to one or more of our physical senses. For instance, a woman may be sexually aroused by her partner's certain scent, or her partner may be aroused by a certain sound that she makes. When we are aroused, we experience sexual pleasure. **Sexual pleasure** is the positive feelings that arise from sexual arousal (Rye & Meaney, 2007). Some argue that sex *is* pleasure (Abramson & Pinkerton, 1995).

Sexual arousal often occurs in the form of foreplay. **Foreplay** refers to the acts at the beginning of a sexual encounter that serve to build sexual arousal. It can be preparation for sexual intercourse or it can be an act in and of itself for sexual pleasure and arousal. It can include the acts of kissing, touching, stroking, licking, slapping, tickling, and massaging. Foreplay often involves mutual masturbation and oral sex (discussed later).

Foreplay is of substantial significance for both men and women, both psychologically and physically (Griffitt & Hatfield, 1985). Many will agree that what often makes sex so pleasurable and desirable is the ways in which it deepens the shared intimacy, trust, care, love, closeness, and warmth in the couple, which are communicated verbally and nonverbally through foreplay. Psychologically, foreplay allows couples to lay their responsibilities and concern aside to focus solely on one another. Some sexologists refer to it as a *transitional period* (Griffitt & Hatfield, 1985). It allows couples to leave the stressors of their daily lives and enter intimacy, to relax, and to become vulnerable.

Physically, foreplay enhances sexual arousal and excitement and is often the means by which a woman experiences orgasm. It is also the time during which most couples experiment and become creative with techniques, positions, and other sexual behaviors (Rye & Meaney, 2007). For example, some couples use **sex toys** (devices to enhance sexual arousal and pleasure), or **erotica** (sexually explicit books or media). Other couples may engage in role-playing or *sadomasochism (S&M)*, which typically includes the use of other elements, such as gags, handcuffs, or leather clothing (Rye & Meaney, 2007).

sex talk

What Sexually Excites You?

Part of understanding who you are as a sexual person is becoming familiar with what increases your sexual desire, arousal, and response. Take a moment to respond to the following statements.

I am most often in the mood for sex when _____.

I am least often in the mood for sex when _____.

The most sensitive parts of my body are (this may or may not include genitals) _____
_____.

The least sensitive parts of my body are _____.

In general, I am most sexually aroused by _____.

When I think of my partner exploring every inch of my unclothed body, it makes me feel _____.
This is because _____.

When I think of exploring every inch of my partner's unclothed body, it makes me feel _____.
This is because _____.

The one thing I wish my partner would do to increase my sexual desire is to _____.

The one thing my partner does that decreases my sexual desire is when he or she _____.

The five places I want to be touched the most include my _____.

When someone suggests that I view erotic materials to increase my sexual desire and arousal, it makes me feel _____.
This is because _____.

When someone suggests that I stimulate myself to better understand my body, it makes me _____.
This is because _____.

I would describe my sex drive as _____. Compared to others, my sex drive is
_____.

To enhance my sexual desire and arousal, I wish I knew more about _____.

The couple's pursuit of sexual arousal and pleasure through foreplay ultimately allows them to show and experience who they are as sexual people. It often begins with stimulation of erogenous zones.

EROGENOUS ZONES

Of all the human senses, our sense of touch is the dominant sexual sense and is most often responsible for sexual arousal (Ferris et al., 2004). **Erogenous zones** are the areas of the body that are most sensitive to the touch of a sex partner; they are sometimes referred to as *love producing zones*. Typically, erogenous zones are areas that have rich, dense populations of nerve endings; this is what makes them so sensitive to touch and so "turned on" when we become sexually aroused.

But sexual arousal is much more complex than a simple formula such as touching this spot + this spot + this way = score! To enjoy sex to the fullest and to provide the greatest pleasure to our partner, we should take time to explore every inch of our lover's body, so we know what provides the most pleasure to him or her; we should also know which areas our partners *don't* want to be touched, and why. We should also become familiar with how our own bodies respond to touch. It's important to recognize our unique sexual arousal patterns and erogenous zones, because they serve as our *sensual maps*.

Our individual sexual arousal patterns are much like our fingerprints, unique, complex, and one-of-a-kind. Although sexual desire refers to the interest to engage in sexual behaviors, and sexual arousal refers to the arousal of sexual desire in preparation for sexual behaviors, **sexual response** refers to the specific physiological and emotional changes and responses that lead to and follow orgasm. Although this response is never exactly the same in any two people (or even in the same person on different occasions or in different circumstances), all men and women share its basic physiological pattern. Different researchers have constructed various models that specify these changes.

HUMAN SEXUAL RESPONSE PROCESSES

In Chapter 2 we learned about Masters and Johnson, who scientifically measured human sexual response in men and women. They determined that women and men experience four distinct, linear phases of sexual response: *excitement*, *plateau*, *orgasm*, and *resolution*.

MASTERS AND JOHNSON

Presented for us in Figures 11.2 and 11.3, we can see the similarities and differences in men and women's sexual response patterns. For example, in the excitement phase, both men and women experience **vasocongestion**, which refers to the genitals filling with blood; in women, this occurs in the labia and the clitoris, and in men, the penis. Both may experience a **sex flush**, which is a reddening of the flesh caused by increased blood flow. **Myotonia**, the involuntary head-to-toe muscle tension

> ˄
> ˄ **Primary erogenous zones** include the
> ˄ genitals, buttocks, anus, perineum, navel, inner surfaces of the thighs, the breasts and/or nipples, neck, mouth, ears, armpits, and the soles of the feet. **Secondary erogenous zones** are those areas of the body that become eroticized over the course of sexual encounters, such as the inside of the elbow.

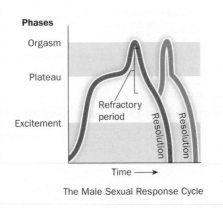

The Male Sexual Response Cycle

(a)

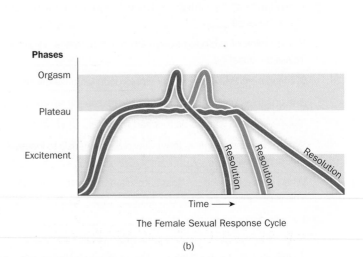

The Female Sexual Response Cycle

(b)

Figure 11.2 Masters and Johnson's Sexual Response Graph

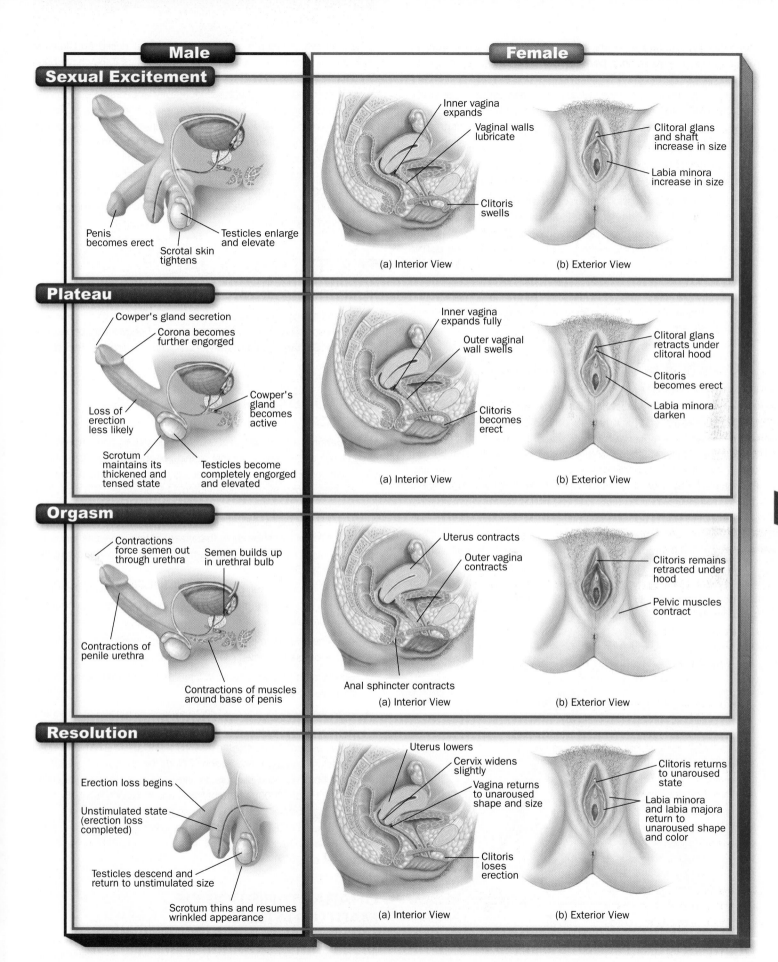

Figure 11.3 Masters and Johnson's Phases of Sexual Response

("toe-curling"), also begins. During the resolution phase, unlike women, men experience a **refractory period**, when they are physically incapable of achieving erections. In looking over these phases of sexual response, it is important to recall what you learned earlier in our study, that physiologically, men and women are more similar than dissimilar. For example, because the tissue of his penis is the counterpart of her clitoris, what feels good to him may also feel good to his female partner.

KAPLAN'S THREE-STAGE MODEL

Helen Singer Kaplan's sexual response model contains three stages: *desire*, *excitement*, and *orgasm* (see Figure 11.4). She believed that sexual difficulties fall into one of these three categories. What distinguishes Kaplan's model is that she replaced the excitement phase with *desire* as a distinct phase of sexual response.

A problem with both of these stage models is that some women do not always move progressively and sequentially through the phases of these models. Thus, a new model of female sexuality has been introduced.

WOMEN'S SEXUAL RESPONSE: HIGHLY CONTEXTUAL

The earlier models of sexual arousal and response ignore the highly contextual nature of women's sexuality, such as the importance women attach to emotional intimacy, sexual stimuli, and relationship satisfaction (Basson, 2001, 2005). According to recent research, women engage in sexual activities for a number of reasons, not simply because they have an inborn drive to do so (Basson, 2001, 2005, 2006). These reasons include the desire for increased emotional closeness, increasing her own well-being and self-image, such as feeling attractive, loved, and/or wanted (Cain et al., 2003). Thus, *these* factors are what propel a woman to participate in sexual activity, *not* an innate sexual drive or urge. Once she is sexually aroused, then sexual desire emerges. Finally, some research suggests that the goal of sexual activity for women is personal satisfaction, not orgasmic release (Basson, 2005).

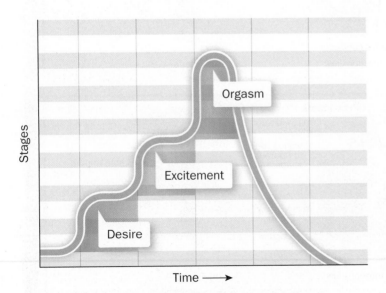

Figure 11.4 **Kaplan's Sexual Response Model**

Commonly, women experience high sexual desire and interest when they first enter a new relationship, or perhaps if they have been separated from their partner for a period of time. However, this sexual hunger and need for frequent sexual activity appears to decrease in long-term relationships, both heterosexual and homosexual (Leiblum, 2002). A woman's initial sexual appetite, within the context of a certain relationship, is replaced by a desire for increased *emotional closeness* and *intimacy* (Basson, 2005). This new focus takes us toward a model of *triggered* desire that accompanies sexual arousal. Figure 11.5 presents this model. This model helps to explain why the college woman in the opening vignette experiences differing levels of sexual desire, arousal, and response.

SOLITARY SEXUAL EXPERIENCES

Sex doesn't always take place within the context of a relationship or with another person. Sex encompasses many other behaviors beyond sexual intercourse. **Solitary sexual behaviors** include *masturbation* and *sexual fantasies*.

MASTURBATION: A PERSONAL CHOICE

Masturbation is the stimulation of one's own genitals by hand movements or by friction of the genitals against clothing or objects (such as a pillow). When one person masturbates another, it is called **mutual masturbation**.

Despite former stigmas (see Figure 11.6 on pages 226 and 227), researchers, health care providers, and clinicians recognize masturbation as a safe sexual activity (Pinkerton et al., 2002). In addition, substantial bodies of evidence show that masturbation serves as a positive sexual behavior. For example, masturbation (for a complete review, see Gerressu et al., 2008):

- Serves as a way for people to become familiar with their own bodies, as well as the bodies of their partners (Zamboni & Crawford, 2002).

- Is an effective treatment for premature ejaculation in men and orgasmic disorders in women (Heiman & LoPiccolo, 1988).

- Serves as a way for people in later life to fulfill their sexual needs (Kontula & Haavio-Mannila, 2002).

- Provides a way for aging adults to express intimacy and closeness (Ginsberg, Pomerantz, & Kramer-Feeley, 2005).

Other research found that the reasons young adults and middle-aged adults masturbate vary. These reasons include the ability to release sexual tension, to obtain physical pleasure, to relax, and to get to sleep (Laumann et al., 1994; Ellison, 2000). Masturbation is not necessarily a substitute for partner sex; a number of studies have shown that it is a part of a wide range of sexual behaviors, regardless of whether a person has a sexual partner (Dekker & Schmidt, 2002; Kontula & Haavio-Mannila, 2002; Pinkerton et al., 2002).

CHARACTERISTICS OF MASTURBATION

A recent landmark study that examined the sexual attitudes and practices of over 11,000 adults (ages 16 to 44) provides us greater insight into not only the frequency of masturbation among men and women

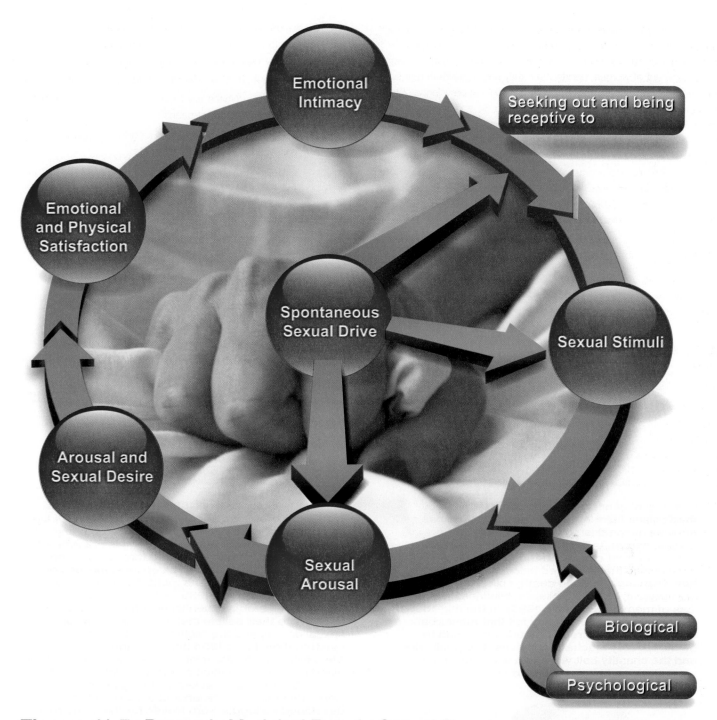

Figure 11.5 **Basson's Model of Female Sexual Response** Rosemary Basson's non-linear model of female sexual response **considers contextual factors.**

OWN IT! Female Orgasm 101

No, it's not true that women take longer to reach orgasm than men, that there is something wrong with a woman if she doesn't have an orgasm, that she can only have an orgasm through vaginal intercourse, that she fakes most of her orgasms, or that every orgasm is an earth-moving experience.

1. What are some other things you've heard about female orgasms? Do you believe these are myths or facts? Why?

2. Do you think orgasms should happen with every single sexual encounter with a partner? Why or why not?

3. If you or your partner has an orgasm, do you think you have "achieved" something, or attained the "ultimate" sexual experience? Why or why not?

(see Table 11.1), but also into other factors that are associated with masturbation, such as education and religious beliefs (Gerressu et al., 2008). Masturbation is a prevalent sexual activity: 95 percent of men and slightly over 71 percent of women reported that they had masturbated at some point in their lives (Gerressu et al., 2008). The highest prevalence of masturbation was found among those aged 25 to 34 and was particularly high among divorced and single men. This finding is comparable to findings in previous studies (such as Oliver & Hyde, 1993). Among women, cohabiting, single, and divorced women were more likely to report masturbation than married women; men and women who had children reported masturbation less frequently than those who were childless. Table 11.2 on page 228 outlines the demographic variables associated with masturbation, which include (Gerressu et al., 2008):

- *Socioeconomic status (SES):* People who have higher incomes masturbate more frequently than people with lower incomes.

- *Education:* A high prevalence of masturbation is reported among those with higher educational achievement.

- *Religiosity:* Those who adhere to religious beliefs are less likely to masturbate than those who do not, particularly among women.

- *Race/Ethnicity:* Whites are more likely to masturbate than African Americans or Black Caribbeans.

- *Duration of partnership:* People in long-term relationships of at least 10 years are least likely to masturbate.

Finally, this research revealed that for men, masturbation is a substitution for vaginal sex, but for women the practice is a part of their overall sexual fulfillment.

Another area of solitary sexual behaviors that has long been of interest to sex researchers is *sexual fantasies*, an area of sexuality that deals with our thoughts.

1700s

1800s

1700s and 1800s

Self-sexual genital stimulation was damned by theologians Saint Augustine and Saint Thomas Aquinas as the flesh out of control and a sin against nature. In the 1700s, masturbation was at the forefront of sexual study, because of such claims that it caused baldness, wrinkles, bleeding lungs, sudden death, epilepsy, convulsions, insanity, epilepsy, blindness, and loss of memory (Stephen, 1995). In the mid-1800s, certain segments of society felt that masturbation was such a widespread practice that it had to be stopped by mechanical means. The penile ring and the chastity belt were two such devices that were designed to curb masturbation.

Victorian Era (1837–1901)

During the Victorian era (1837–1901), self-sex was thought to present a serious danger to the individual, and believed to be detrimental to individuals' overall health. The predominant thinking of this era promoted the notion that semen circulated through the body just like blood, and, just like blood loss, the loss of semen through any means made a person seriously weak and ill (Mooney, 1985; Sokolow, 1983). During this time in history, influential health advocates began to promote their beliefs that a proper diet would curb sexual desire, and the "self-abuse" caused by masturbation. In his 1834 book, *Lecture to Young Men*, Sylvester Graham introduced the idea that eating bland foods would inhibit sexual arousal—hence the birth of the graham cracker. Not long after, John Henry Kellogg, a physician and disciple of Graham, developed Kellogg's Corn Flakes for the same reason (Mooney, 1985; Sokolow, 1983). The Victorians' fear of "self-pollution" also resulted in a book, *Treatment of Masturbation* (Sturgis, 1900), which recommended that boys' foreskins be pierced with safety pins—with the intent that as a boy's penis swelled (due to sexual excitement), excruciating pain would result.

Figure 11.6 **History of Masturbation** Today, masturbation is recognized as a safe sexual activity, **but that wasn't always the case.**

TABLE 11.1
Last Occasion of Masturbation by Gender

Source: Gerressu et al., 2008

Last occasion of masturbation	Men %	Women %	Last occasion of masturbation	Men %	Women %
Last seven days	51.7	17.8	Between one year and five years ago	4.6	7.7
Between seven days and four weeks ago	21.3	19.0	Longer than five years ago	4.5	6.5
Between four weeks and six months ago	8.3	13.7	Ever	95.0	71.2
Between six months and one year ago	4.3	6.5	Never	5.4	28.2

1900s　　　　　　　　　　　　　　　　　　　　　　　**2000s**

Mid-20th Century

In the mid-20th century, folklore gave way to science on views of masturbation. For instance, Alfred Kinsey's empirical sexual behavior studies in the 1940s and 1950s provided insight into the frequency of masturbation in adult populations (Kinsey, Pomeroy, & Martin, 1948; Kinsey, Pomeroy, Martin, & Gebhard, 1953). Kinsey's surveys revealed that 90 percent of men had masturbated, and that more than 50 percent of women had done so. The findings for women were particularly surprising, because it was a time when masturbation was not a socially approved of behavior—particularly for women.

1990s

Fast forward to the 1990s, when not only was masturbation accepted, it became the topic of television shows, such as an episode of *Seinfeld* in which there was a contest among the main characters to see who could refrain from masturbating the longest and remain the "master of [his/her] domain." Yet despite its widespread discussion in pop culture, in the 1990s, then U.S. Surgeon General, Joycelyn Elders was forced to resign when she declared that masturbation should be taught in school sex education classes.

TABLE 11.2
Selected Demographic Factors Associated with Reporting Masturbation in the Last Four Weeks by Gender

Source: Gerressu et al. (2008).

Factor	Men %	Women %	Factor	Men %	Women %
Age			**Ethnicity**		
16–24	72.6	33.9	White	74.7	37.4
25–34	76.9	38.8	Black Caribbean	53.6	32.6
35–44	69.2	36.5	Black African	42.5	21.1
			Indian	49.5	32.5
Marital Status			Pakistani	52.7	10.0
Married	68.5	33.7	Other	60.1	33.1
Cohabiting	70.8	40.4			
Previously married	83.8	39.2	**Religiosity**		
Single, never married	77.9	38.9	No	73.7	37.6
			Yes	66.1	31.7
Children					
No	77.8	43.4			
Yes	67.5	32.7			

FANTASIZING ABOUT SEX

Sexual fantasies are the most common fantasy or daydream in which people engage, and it can be a healthy aspect of sexuality for men and women (Byrne, 1977; Strassberg & Lockerd, 1998). Studying sexual fantasies not only helps us understand human sexual behavior, but it helps us at an individual level to better understand "who" we are as sexual beings. Sexual fantasies are private, so we are free to imagine anything we like (such as having sex with a same-sex partner or experimenting with different sexual positions), without experiencing embarrassment or rejection (Dubois, 1997). Our fantasies therefore provide us great insight into our private and unique sexual scripts (Gagnon & Simon, 1973).

Most researchers define **sexual fantasies** as sexual thoughts and images created in our minds that help provide an outlet to sexual feelings we have. Sexual fantasies are the most common form of human sexual experience and can range from a fleeting thought to an intentional act (Ellis & Symons, 1990; Renaud & Byers, 2001). In the few studies that include gay or lesbian participants, researchers discovered that the fantasies of homosexuals are similar in content to those of heterosexuals (Masters & Johnson, 1979; Price, Allensworth, & Hillman, 1985). Not all people appraise them in positive ways, however. For instance, in one research study of 160 conservative Christians, nearly one-half of the respondents indicated that they believed their sexual fantasies were

>>> Masturbation—male, female, and mutual— is as much about self-discovery as it is about sexual pleasure.

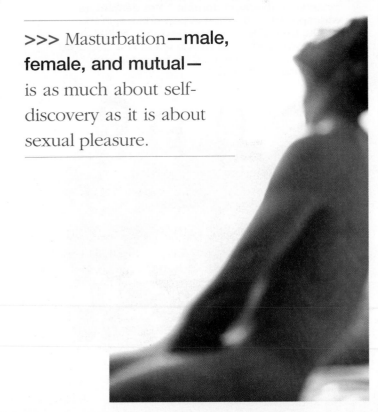

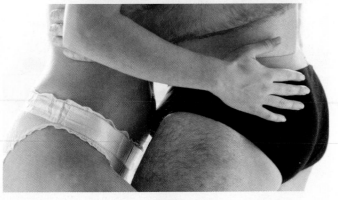

Figure 11.7 Sexual Fantasies In most cases, the sexual fantasies of men and women tend to be fundamentally different.

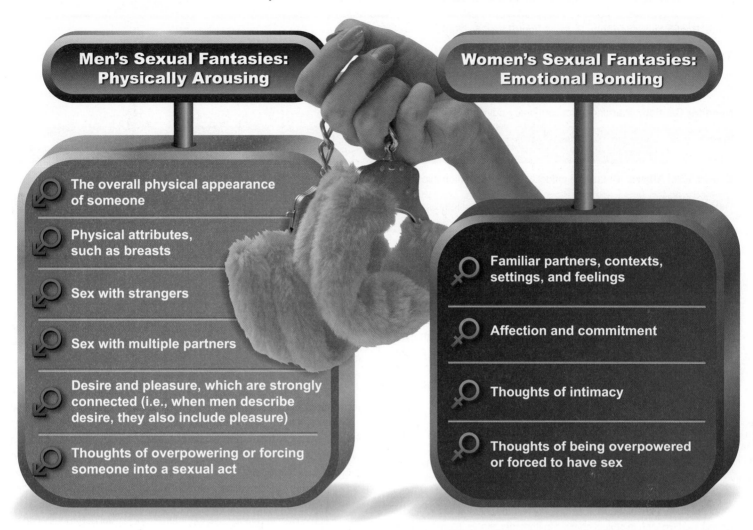

Men's Sexual Fantasies: Physically Arousing

- The overall physical appearance of someone
- Physical attributes, such as breasts
- Sex with strangers
- Sex with multiple partners
- Desire and pleasure, which are strongly connected (i.e., when men describe desire, they also include pleasure)
- Thoughts of overpowering or forcing someone into a sexual act

Women's Sexual Fantasies: Emotional Bonding

- Familiar partners, contexts, settings, and feelings
- Affection and commitment
- Thoughts of intimacy
- Thoughts of being overpowered or forced to have sex

"morally flawed or unacceptable" (Gil, 1990). A number of people also report that they feel guilty and/or embarrassed about their sexual fantasies (Davidson & Hoffman, 1986; Knoth, Boyd, & Singer, 1988).

There are themes in sexual fantasies, such as intimacy and sexual variety; however, there are sex differences in sexual fantasy.

MEN'S SEXUAL FANTASIES: PHYSICALLY AROUSING

Men have about twice as many sexual fantasies as women do, and this finding is common globally (among many, Iwawaki & Wilson, 1983; Jones & Barlow, 1987). In general, men's sexual fantasies include detailed sexual acts, sexual organs, and plenty of visual imagery (Follingstad & Kimbrell, 1986). Men are also more likely than women to view others as the *objects* of their sexual desires, and they tend to focus on action and achievement (Ellis & Symons, 1990; Dubois, 1997). Men's sexual fantasies are said to be *explicit* because they commonly stress overt sexual details. Figure 11.7 shows men's common sexual fantasies.

WOMEN'S SEXUAL FANTASIES: EMOTIONAL BONDING

Women are more likely to become emotionally—not necessarily physically—aroused by their sexual fantasies, and the fantasy content tends to

emphasize tenderness (Knoth, Boyd, & Singer, 1988). Thus, women's sexual fantasies are classified as *implicit*, because they only imply sexual details in a general context (Ellis & Symons, 1990). In essence, women's sexual fantasies are less frequent than men's, and they are contextual, emotive, intimate, and passive, as illustrated in Figure 11.7 (Ellis & Symons, 1990). And, while men view others as sexual recipients in their fantasies, women tend to view *themselves* as the recipients of fantasized sexual behaviors (Dubois, 1997).

TYPING AND DOING: SEX ON THE INTERNET

Visiting the Web for sex-related materials is a common occurrence: an estimated one-half of all Internet traffic is related to sex sites (McNair, 2002). In the United States, 13 percent of Web site visits are to sex sites, and about 80 percent of all Arabic Internet users go to sex sites (Kettmann, 2001; *The Economist*, 2007). A study of undergraduate college students found that nearly one-half of the study participants had viewed sexually explicit materials online (Goodson, McCormick, & Evans, 2001). By comparison, a study of 10,000 Norwegians revealed that only about one-third of the male and female users had accessed sex-related Web sites (Træen & Nilson, 2006). There is no question that the Internet has brought a new dimension and a new culture to the experiences of sex and sexuality, because it provides a

TABLE 11.3
Themes in Online Relationships

Source: Based on Wildermuth, S. M., & Vogl-Bauer, S. (2007).

Theme	Percentage of Occurrence
Intensity of Emotion: The ability of the online environment to elicit emotional reactions.	87%
Need for Caution: Warnings and cautionary advice about online romances.	46%
Power of Linguistic Connections: Positive and negative implications of the nonphysical nature of online relationships.	43%
Extramarital Affairs: Relational infidelity in online relationships.	27%
Response from Social Networks: Concerns from online romance participant's off-line social network.	25%

domain in which people are sexually aroused and a place in which they can imagine and carry out sexual fantasies by engaging in "computer sex."

Cybersex, or **net sex**, is defined as erotic interactions that take place through rich, detailed Internet discussion that results in sexual arousal, is sometimes accompanied by masturbation, and often leads to orgasm (Blair, 1998; Ross & Kauth, 2002). In the past, sexual fantasies were a private, solitary affair, but now they can be carried out with a mutual partner through the Internet. Today, any person can fantasize and experiment with his or her sexual fantasies, desires, and all types of sexual behaviors in a relatively anonymous environment (Ross, 2005).

ONLINE SEXUAL ACTIVITY

Online sexual activity (OSA) refers to the use of the Internet for any activity that involves sexuality for the purposes of recreation, entertainment, exploration, education, and/or seeking out sexual or romantic partners (Cooper & Griffin-Shelley, 2002). Activities can include looking at erotic pictures; participating in sexual chat via instant messenger, blogging, Web discussion boards; exchanging sexually explicit images of oneself via Web cam; exchanging sexually explicit e-mails; and sharing fantasies (Boies, 2002). As you can see in Table 11.3, the themes of OSAs vary, and some activities are more visually oriented, while others are more interactive and communicative (Daneback, Cooper, & Mansson, 2004). But are there differences in OSA behaviors between men and women?

SEX DIFFERENCES IN OSA

In the past, research discovered that men held more permissive/progressive attitudes about erotic materials, but today that gap is significantly narrowing. For example, in one U.S. online poll of 9,000 adults, the investigators found that about 86 percent of men reported accessing sex sites online, and that nearly 60 percent of women also had (Cooper, 2000). There are, however, differences in what men view and what women view.

- *Men and OSA:* In general, men are more interested in visually oriented OSA. This is referred to as *non-directed*, or "just looking," OSA. Men also tend to play more online sex-related games than women do (Boies, 2002).

- *Women and OSA:* Women are much more likely than men to engage in interactive, or *directed*, sex activities, such as erotic chatting, instant messaging, and posting on discussion boards, and they prefer these venues to visually explicit ones (Cooper, 2000; Ferree, 2003).

It's clear that the use of the Internet is a new domain of sexuality, but are there downsides to its use?

THE NEGATIVES OF OSA

There can be serious downsides to cybersex, and some claim that the impacts of sex-seeking behaviors on the Internet are highly addictive (Corley, 2003). For instance, one study that followed Internet users' behaviors found that accessing sexual materials online was linked to compulsive computer use after one year (van den Eijnden et al., 2008). If a person views sex-related sites for more than 11 hours per week, that person has a **cybersex compulsion** (Cooper, Delmonico, & Burg, 2000). This compulsion is thought to occur in about 2 to 8 percent of people who access erotic materials on the Web; however, single gay/lesbian adults and bisexuals are more likely to admit to compulsive levels of sex-seeking on the Internet than straight adults (Albright, 2008; Cooper, Delmonico, & Burg, 2000).

People who frequently use the Internet for sexual communication or stimulation also run the risk of becoming isolated, neglecting work and other duties, and allowing online life to become a substitute for off-line life (Daneback, Cooper, & Mansson, 2004; Turkle, 1995). Other studies show that OSA leads to depression, anxiety (fear of others finding out), and problems in relationships with real-life partners (Philaretou, Maoufouz, & Allen, 2005). These activities may also lead to divorce, because some partners view cybersex as sexual and emotional cheating (Orzack, 2004; Schneider, 2002; Whitty, 2003). Finally, new research suggests that males are more critical of their partners' bodies as a result of viewing sexual images online; females feel more pressure to engage in the types of sex acts they view online (Albright, 2008).

Although there is virtually no empirical evidence regarding the benefits of OSA for individuals or couples, some studies are slowly beginning to emerge. Sex therapists have long used explicit sexual materials to help stimulate the sex lives of couples who are struggling, and using OSA might have similar benefits. Engaging in OSA as a couple may serve as visual and sexual stimulation, as well as a relational stimulant (Albright, 2008; Philaretou, Maoufouz, & Allen, 2005). Studies are underway to determine whether viewing erotic Web-camming with other couples works as a way to enhance couples' sexual relationships in which boredom is a problem (Albright, 2008).

Exploring OSA is important because it shows us how sexuality and the experiences of sex change over time and how they are influenced by culture and society.

Figure 11.8 **Cunnilingus** One partner usually kisses, licks, or sucks his or her partner's clitoris and labia; this is often accompanied by manual stimulation, such as with fingers, a vibrator, or other sex toys. **He or she will sometimes penetrate the partner's vagina with the tongue, mimicking the thrusting motions of the penis in the vagina.**

SEX WITH OTHERS

Adults engage in a wide array of sexual behaviors with their partners, whether they are in love or are hooking up, whether they are straight or gay. Keep in mind that the following discussion in no way captures all types of sexual techniques or expressions, and that not everyone feels comfortable with each activity. **Sexual acts** are generally described by the positions the participants use.

ORAL-GENITAL SEXUAL BEHAVIOR

Oral-genital sexual behavior, or **oral sex**, involves the contact between the lips, mouth, tongue (and possibly teeth) of one partner and the genitals of the other. **Cunnilingus** (see Figure 11.8) involves the erotic stimulation of the woman's external sex organs; **fellatio** (see Figure 11.9) is the oral stimulation of the male's external sex organs. Oral-genital sex is practiced by all couples types, and recent national survey data from the United States reveal that the number of people who have oral sex has increased since the 1990s; over 80 percent of people ages 15 to 44 have engaged in this sexual behavior (Aral et al., 2005; Mosher, Chandra, &

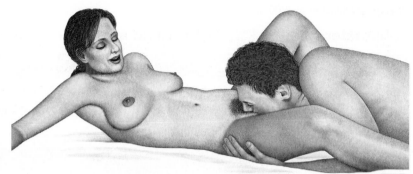

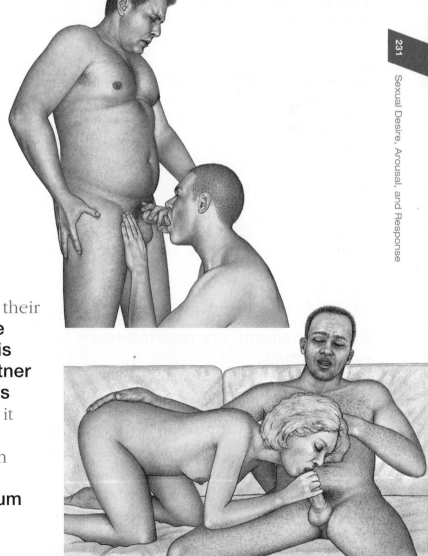

Figure 11.9 **Fellatio** Most people focus their stimulation on the glans of the penis. **While stroking or grasping the shaft of the penis and gently squeezing the scrotum, a partner will usually kiss, lick, or suck on the glans and sometimes the shaft.** Some men find it particularly exciting to have their partners "stroke" the entire penis in an up-and-down motion with their mouths. **Men also enjoy stimulation of the underside of the scrotum and/or perineum.**

TABLE 11.4
Percentages of Heterosexual Anal and Oral Sex, by Demographic Characteristics and General Sexual Behavior, in Women Aged 15–44 Years

Source: Leichliter et al. (2007).

Characteristic	Ever had anal sex	Ever received oral sex	Ever gave oral sex
All women	30.0	78.9	75.8
Race			
White (non-Hispanic)	34.4	84.8	84.3
Hispanic	22.7	64.2	60.7
Black (non-Hispanic)	21.9	73.6	57.4
Age			
15–19	10.9	49.6	43.6
20–24	29.6	80.3	76.3
25–34	35.4	86.5	83.3
35–44	34.0	84.8	83.5
Marital status			
Never married, not cohabiting	20.0	63.6	57.4
Married	32.2	86.6	86.4
Cohabiting	41.6	87.8	82.4
Formerly married, not cohabiting	45.2	89.7	86.6
Non-monogamous			
No	32.6	95.2	89.4
Yes	49.4	95.2	89.4

Jones, 2005; Gilbart et al., 2006). Table 11.4 shows that there are racial, ethnic, and gender differences in the experiences of oral sex. These numbers are important, because they speak to the commonality of oral sex, as well as to how effective genital stimulation is for producing sexual arousal and/or orgasm.

ANAL INTERCOURSE/EROTICISM

Anal intercourse is the sexual activity of the male placing his penis into his partner's anus and rectum; **anal eroticism** can include anal intercourse, as well as oral stimulation of the anus (*rimming*), manually stroking the outside of the anus, and inserting one or more fingers into the anus. Stimulating the anus is very erotic for most people, because the area contains a vast supply of nerve endings.

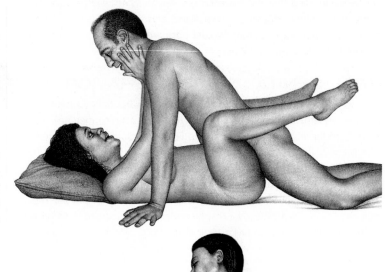

Figure 11.10 Face-to-Face Coitus
Some positions are referred to as *face-to-face.* In these positions, either the man or the woman is above their partner, or "on top." **Many couples prefer face-to-face positions because it is easier to make eye contact, kiss, look at a partner's body, and to communicate with other forms of verbal and nonverbal expressions.**

Figure 11.11 **Rear-Entry and Side-Lying Positions** With *rear-entry* positions, the man enters his partner's vagina from behind. The pressure or slapping of a woman's buttocks against him is enjoyable and stimulating for him; **she can also push back against him, deepening his thrust.** Additionally, his hands are free to caress her and stimulate her clitoris, facilitating her orgasm. **A side-lying position is particularly comfortable for pregnant women, or for a person who is ill.**

Many people incorrectly believe that anal stimulation is practiced only by homosexual men. In actuality, data from a recent U.S. study of more than 12,000 men and women, ages 15 to 44, reveal that nearly one-third of those surveyed indicated they had engaged in anal sex (Leichliter et al., 2007); additionally, one in 10 female and male adolescents have engaged in heterosexual anal sex. In Great Britain, one-fourth of those surveyed reported they had had heterosexual anal sex (Gilbart et al., 2006). Table 11.4 shows that there are racial and ethnic differences in the experiences of anal sex, with whites engaging in it more often than Hispanics or blacks. Partner status also plays a role in whether couples engage in anal sex.

THE WAYS OF HETEROSEXUAL SEX

A remarkably simple act for most men and women, **coitus** is the process in which the penis is inserted into the vagina, thereby joining the male and female genitals (Griffitt & Hatfield, 1985). Although the possibilities are virtually endless, Figures 11.10 and 11.11 illustrate the most common **coital positions** that heterosexual couples use when having penile-vaginal sexual intercourse.

As we have discovered throughout our study together, sex is about more than perfected techniques or sexual positions. Instead, it is an opportunity to share physical and emotional closeness, to desire and to be desired, and to give and to receive pleasure.

THE WAYS OF HOMOSEXUAL SEX

It is important to keep in mind that while homosexuality refers to the sexual behaviors shared between two people of the same sex, for many it also encompasses other relationship characteristics, such as commitment, love, romance, conflict, and relationship satisfaction.

LESBIAN SEXUAL ACTIVITIES

The research on sexual satisfaction and sexual orientations is complex and gives us mixed results. For example, in two studies that explored

sexual satisfaction, little or no differences in sexual satisfaction were found among gay, lesbian, heterosexual cohabitants, and heterosexual married couples; in fact, results indicate far more similarities than differences (Holmberg & Blair, 2009; Kurdek, 2004). Other studies, however, demonstrate that lesbian couples engage in sexual intercourse less frequently than heterosexual married women (Kurdek, 2004; Lever, 1995). In general, although lesbians report less frequent sex than do gay couples or heterosexual couples, they do express physical intimacy in other ways, such as cuddling and kissing (Diamant, Lever, & Schuster, 2000; Kurdek, 2006). Some sex researchers note that among lesbians, enduring emotional connections and loving a partner heighten sexual satisfaction (Garza-Mercer, Christensen, & Doss, 2006).

Common sexual behaviors among lesbians include genital stimulation and tribadism. **Tribadism** (or *tribbing*, or *scissoring*) is a form of mutual masturbation in which a woman rubs her vulva against her partner's body for sexual stimulation (Winks & Semans, 2002).

GAY SEXUAL ACTIVITIES

Studies show us that gay men who are single, dating, or in a relationship report average to above-average sexual satisfaction, and that in comparison to heterosexual men, have the highest frequencies of sex and report higher levels of sexual desire (Baumeister, Catanese, & Vohs, 2001; Holmberg & Blair, 2009; Rosser et al., 1991). Similar to lesbian couples and heterosexual couples, gay men also engage in foreplay activities with their intimate partners, and they also experiment with a variety of sexual positions. Virtually any sexual position can be adapted for use by gay men, but common to gay sexual behaviors are oral sex, anal sex, and interfemoral intercourse (see Figure 11.12). **Interfemoral intercourse** (or *rubbins*) involves the practice of masturbating by moving the penis between the upper thighs of a partner.

We have seen how, when stimulated psychologically, emotionally, and/or physically, we respond with feelings of pleasure—but not everyone does. Having too little sexual desire and being unable to achieve orgasm are just two of the sexual difficulties people can experience. In the next section we will explore sexual difficulties.

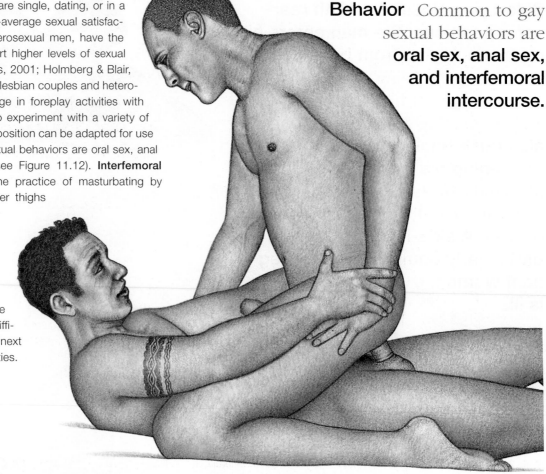

Figure 11.12 Gay Sexual Behavior Common to gay sexual behaviors are **oral sex, anal sex, and interfemoral intercourse.**

EXPERIENCING SEXUAL DIFFICULTIES

Sexual difficulties can be agonizing and can negatively affect relationships. Broadly speaking, **sexual dysfunction** is the inability to enjoy sex fully. Sexual dysfunction can begin early in a person's life, or it may gradually develop after a person has previously experienced satisfying and pleasurable sex. For convenience and ease of study, we'll organize our discussion into two categories, women and men.

SEXUAL DYSFUNCTIONS IN WOMEN

Sexual dysfunctions in women are common occurrences, affecting 48 percent of women, to one degree or another (Connell, 2005). Female sexual difficulties include inadequate or unsatisfactory sexual functioning in desire, arousal, and/or orgasm. Table 11.5 summarizes the American Psychiatric Association's (APA) descriptions of these disorders. In general, there are two types of desire disorders: hypoactive sexual desire (HSD) and sexual aversion. **Hypoactive sexual desire (HSD)** is a disorder that is characterized by a persistent absence of sexual desire, sexual thoughts, and/or motivation for becoming sexually aroused (American Psychiatric Association, 2000).

Having too little sexual desire is the most common sexual issue that women encounter, commonly accompanied by low levels of sexual excitement and infrequent orgasms (Basson, 2006; Elnashar et al., 2006; Laumann et al., 2005; Matthiesen & Wenn, 2004; Mercer et al., 2003). Desire difficulties may be connected to interpersonal and contextual factors (emotional well-being, relationship quality), personal psychological factors (daily life distractions, past experiences), and biological factors (medication, hormone imbalances, depression) (Basson, 2005, 2006).

Sexual aversion disorder (SAD) is characterized not only by a lack of sexual desire, but it also includes disgust, fear, and revulsion at the thought of genital contact with a partner (APA, 2000). The causes of SAD are complex and multifaceted, but are often due to interpersonal problems, such as conflict and discontent, and past traumatic experiences, such as rape, molestation, abuse, or incest (Butcher, 1999). In Chapter 17, we'll explore SAD at length as we explore issues that arise when sex is used as a weapon.

SEXUAL AROUSAL DISORDERS

Female sexual arousal disorder (FSAD) is characterized by absent or very noticeable reduced feelings of sexual arousal, sexual excitement, and pleasure from any type of stimulation (APA, 2000). It often also includes problems with desire and orgasm (Sanders, Graham, & Milhausen, 2008). Lack of, or reduced, lubrication and vasocongestion are also associated with FSAD (Basson, 2005). Recent clinical trials have attempted to determine whether estrogen and/or testosterone can assist women who experience FSAD, and the results are promising (Buster et al., 2005; Simon et al., 2005).

<<< To better determine whether we or our partners are experiencing a sexual desire disorder, it is important to become familiar with our "normal" levels of sexual desire. **We can then compare our "normal" levels with situations that may cause us to lose interest in sex. Given time and attention, low sexual desire is often reversible.**

ORGASM DISORDERS

Anorgasmia is a persistent delay or absence of orgasm after a normal sexual excitement phase (APA, 2000). In heterosexual encounters, women experience orgasm at lower rates than men. For example, one study found that 69 percent of the female respondents had an orgasm during their most recent sexual encounter, compared to 95 percent of males (Richters et al., 2006).

TABLE 11.5
Definitions of Female Sexual Dysfunction

Sources: American Psychiatric Association (2000); American Urological Association Foundation (2008).

APA Definition	AUA Foundation Definition
Hypoactive sexual desire disorder Characterized by persistent/recurrent deficiency or absence of sexual fantasies and desire for sexual activity. Judgment of deficiency is made by the clinician, taking into account factors that affect sexual functioning (such as age).	*Sexual desire/interest disorder* Characterized by absent or diminished feelings of sexual interest or desire, absent sexual thoughts or fantasies, and a lack of responsive desire. Scarce or absent motivation to become sexually aroused. Lack of interest goes beyond normal lessening with age.
Lack of subjective arousal No DSM-IV definition addresses the lack of subjective arousal.	*Combined arousal disorder* Characterized by absent or markedly reduced feelings of sexual arousal (excitement and pleasure) from any type of stimulation; absent/impaired genital sexual arousal (such as no lubrication).
	Subjective arousal disorder Characterized by absent or markedly reduced feelings of sexual arousal (excitement and pleasure) from any type of stimulation; lubrication and other signs of response present.
Female sexual arousal disorder Characterized by persistent/recurrent inability to attain/maintain adequate lubrication and/or swelling response of excitement through completion of sexual activity.	*Genital arousal disorder* Characterized by absent/impaired genital sexual arousal (lubrication, reduced sexual sensations when genitals are caressed). Subjective excitement still occurs from nongenital sexual stimuli.
Female orgasmic disorder Characterized by persistent/recurrent delay or absence of orgasm after normal sexual excitement phase.	*Orgasmic disorder* Characterized by lack of orgasm, diminished intensity of orgasm sensations, or delay of orgasm from any kind of stimulation, despite self-reported high sexual arousal or excitement.

> > > Cross-cultural studies discovered that Asian women who live in their country of origin report high levels of sexual satisfaction and very low levels of sexual dysfunction (Liu & Ng, 1995). **When they move to Western cultures and adopt the attitudes of the culture, they report higher levels of dysfunction (Brotto et al., 2005).** These findings suggest that *cultural expectations* shape what a person deems to be sexual function/dysfunction—not the sexual difficulty per se.

Why is it that so many women have difficulties with orgasm? A number of factors are known to influence orgasmic response in women, such as upbringing, attitudes, religion, anxiety, and previous sexually traumatic experiences (Anderson & Cyranowski, 1995; Davidson & Darling, 1989). Is it possible that sexual satisfaction and orgasmic response/consistency are two different things?

Suiming Pan's (1993) study of Chinese women found that 54 percent experienced low orgasmic response, yet felt that this was perfectly fine and acceptable. In fact, 11 percent of the women surveyed felt that their orgasmic responses were too high! Although this study illustrates possible differences in how women

view their sexuality, it also indicates that there is a difference between *goal-oriented* sexual activity ("achieving," "reaching," "attaining" orgasmic response) and *pleasure-oriented* sexual activity ("I may not be having an orgasm, but this feels really good, and I'm having a great time!").

SEXUAL PAIN DISORDERS

There are two primary types of sexual pain disorders in women: dyspareunia and vaginismus. **Dyspareunia** is recurrent genital pain caused by sexual activity; the pain can be superficial or deep. *Superficial* dyspareunia occurs in or around the vaginal entrance. Symptoms include pain around the vulva, itching, burning, or stinging. *Deep* dyspareunia is pain that results from deep thrusting during intercourse; the pain may be the result of pelvic inflammatory disease (Chapter 14), surgery, endometriosis, tumors, irritable bowel syndrome, urinary tract infection, or ovarian cysts (Sadovsky, 2000).

Vaginismus (see Table 11.6) occurs as the result of an involuntary spasm of the muscles around the lower one-third of the vagina. For many women, vaginismus comes as a surprise, with unexplained tightness making it difficult (or impossible) for entry into the vagina during manual stimulation or intercourse. Pain results from the tightening of the muscles around the vagina.

There are a number of physical causes associated with vaginismus, such as a pelvic infection or scarring of the vaginal opening due to injury, childbirth, or surgery. In most instances, however, the cause of vaginismus is a combination of physical and nonphysical triggers that cause the body to anticipate pain and to unconsciously tighten the vaginal muscles. Nonphysical causes of vaginismus include any number of fears, anxieties, partner issues, traumatic events, or past childhood experiences that can contribute to painful sex. Because of the multiple contexts of sexuality that influence our experiences, a woman and her partner should

be careful not to assume there is something wrong if sexual difficulties occur (Basson, 2005).

SEXUAL DYSFUNCTIONS IN MEN

Male sexual dysfunction is one of the most common health problems that affect men (Parmet, 2004). Just as with women, male sexual difficulties can be caused by physical problems, psychological problems, or a combination of both. According to the American Association of Clinical Endocrinologists (AACE, 2003), there are several types of male sexual dysfunction: low libido, erectile dysfunction, premature ejaculation, delayed or inhibited orgasm, physical abnormalities of the penis, or a combination of these factors.

Scant research addresses **low libido**, or sexual desire/interest in men. In many ways, low sexual desire may be one of the more difficult sexual problems a man can experience, because it contradicts the cultural beliefs that men are always supposed to be ready for sex or that they always want it. Recall from Chapter 5 that a man's sexual function is linked to the amount of testosterone he produces (AACE, 2003). Low libido can also be caused by relationship problems, stress/anxiety, depression, medical illnesses, or the use of certain drugs, such as antidepressants and

TABLE 11.6
Physical and Nonphysical Causes of Vaginismus

Source: Vaginismus.com

Physical Causes of Vaginismus

Medical Conditions	Urinary tract infections, yeast infections, STIs, endometriosis, genital or pelvic tumors, cysts, cancer, pelvic inflammatory disease, vaginal prolapse.
Childbirth	Pain from normal or difficult vaginal deliveries and/or complications, C-section, miscarriage.
Age-Related Changes	Perimenopause, menopause, hormonal changes, vaginal dryness, inadequate lubrication.
Temporary Discomfort	Resulting from insufficient foreplay, inadequate lubrication.
Pelvic Trauma	Pelvic surgery, difficult pelvic exam.
Abuse	Physical attack, rape, sexual/physical abuse or assault (any of these can be past or present).
Medications	Side effects may cause pelvic pain.

Nonphysical Causes of Vaginismus

Fears	Anticipation of intercourse pain, not being completely physically healed after pelvic trauma (i.e., childbirth), being "torn" (tissue damage), getting pregnant, concern that a pelvic problem may reoccur.
Anxiety or Stress	General anxiety, performance pressures, previous unpleasant sexual experiences, negativity toward sex, guilt, emotional traumas (past or present), other unhealthy sexual emotions.
Partner Issues	Abuse, emotional detachment, fear of commitment, distrust, anxiety about being vulnerable, losing control.
Traumatic Events	Past emotional/sexual abuse, witness of violence or abuse, repressed memories.
Childhood Experiences	Overly rigid parenting, unbalanced religious teaching ("Sex is sinful"), exposure to shocking sexual imagery, inadequate sexual education.
No Cause	Sometimes there is no identifiable cause (physical or nonphysical).

"He wants it all the time, at least three times a week." "I hardly want it at all, only three times a week."

A common theme runs through American families today–too many demands, too many pressures, and too little time for couples to connect and feel like a real part of each other's lives. Often, hectic lives lead to hectic relationships, and rather than talk about hurt feelings and pent-up sexual frustrations, both members of the couple roll over in bed away from each other, and the hurt intensifies.

Her Side: It's not that I don't love him. I do love him, and I know he tries so hard to make me happy. It's just that I'm *so tired* all the time. With my job, the kids, and all of their activities, plus all the things that need to be done around the house all the time, I'm just too tired to have sex. And I don't think he even notices what I do in a day, or that I even exist until he wants to have sex. Plus, I don't get a whole lot out of it. I mean, it's great for him, but I never feel like he's in it for me. He just doesn't understand that I can't get in the mood as quickly as he can, and then he gets upset because he thinks I don't need him like he needs me.

It's just not worth the trouble; I'm tired of not feeling satisfied, and he's tired of my pushing him away.

His Side: I try to be understanding. I mean, I know it's hard for her to have to be a "single parent" all the time with my work schedule and all. I know it's not fair for her to have to do everything for the kids and around the house, plus her job, but I wish she would understand the tremendous pressure I feel at work, and the pressure to succeed and give her the things she deserves. I feel like I give her so much! Not just material things—I'm constantly trying to surprise her with romantic things I know she likes, but she thinks I'm doing those things just so we can have sex. These things aren't just to get her in the mood. I really do want her to be happy. But when we have sex, she just seems so distant. I never know if she's enjoying it or not.

Your Side: Typical of many relationships today, this couple's sex life is beginning to suffer the effects of too much to do in too little time. In your opinion,

1. What are three main issues that are affecting this couple?
2. If you were a marriage and family therapist or counselor, what would you recommend for this couple?

---

blood pressure medications. Problems with partners are also a factor in low libido (Marano, 2003). As men age, testosterone levels decrease by about 1.2 percent each year; these decreases may be associated with erectile dysfunction (AACE, 2003).

ERECTILE DYSFUNCTION

Often referred to as *impotence*, **erectile dysfunction (ED)** is the inability of a man to develop and/or maintain a firm erection long enough to have satisfactory sex. This problem can occur at any age, and most men experience it from time to time. It is thought to be a concern if it persists over a period of three months (Parmet, 2004).

Erectile dysfunction is the most common sexual problem for men, affecting more than 18 million men in the United States over the age of 20 (Selvin, Burnett, & Platz, 2007). A recent study of 3,400 heterosexual and gay men found that from one-third to nearly one-half of the study participants experienced ED at least occasionally (Bancroft et al., 2005).

ED becomes increasingly prevalent with age; at age 40, about 40 percent of men experience some type of ED; this rate increases to nearly 70 percent by age 70 (Feldman et al., 2000). Because most men experience ED as a function of aging, we'll explore treatment options at length in Chapter 16.

RAPID EJACULATION

Rapid ejaculation (RE), also referred to as *premature ejaculation*, is ejaculation that occurs before, upon, or shortly after penetration with minimal sexual stimulation (American Urological Association, 2008). **Primary RE** typically occurs in younger men and lessens with age; **secondary RE** has a later onset and is often associated with ED (Bancroft et al., 2005).

Rapid ejaculation is the most common sexual dysfunction among men. For instance, data indicate that in the United States, about one-fourth of men ages 18 to 59 have RE (American Urological Association, 2008). Shown in Table 11.7, RE occurs more frequently among heterosexual men than it does among gay men, but it increases with age among gay men

TABLE 11.7

Frequency of rapid ejaculation (RE) in the gay and heterosexual samples ("Have you ever had a problem ejaculating too quickly?")

Source: Bancroft et al. (2005).

	Number	Never	Occasionally	Less than half the time	Most of the time
Gay Men	1,196	57.3%	33.3%	4.9%	4.5%
Heterosexual Men	1,558	43.9%	43.1%	5.8%	7.1%

^
^ **Not all sexual problems require medical attention, but any problem that persists for**
^ **more than a few weeks is worth a visit to a health care provider, counselor, or sex**
therapist. Sometimes, couples just need to learn or relearn different ways of thinking about
and having sex (Basson, 2005).

(Bancroft et al., 2005). Among heterosexual men, RE is associated with anxiety and being in an exclusive relationship.

TREATMENT FOR SEXUAL DIFFICULTIES: THERE IS HELP

If the sexual problem is caused by a medical or physical problem, a physician or health care provider can outline a specific treatment plan, which may include *hormone replacement therapy (HRT)*, vaginal lubricants, topical estrogen, and clitoral therapy (a device that draws blood to the clitoris, aiding lubrication and arousal), and Viagra for men (see Chapter 16).

After physical causes have been ruled out, many couples seek advice and/or treatment from a certified sex therapist; some also use sex therapy in conjunction with physical treatments. **Sex therapy** is a specialty in the area of psychological counseling that is often used when individuals and/or couples have experienced sexual trauma, infidelities, or other sexual concerns and difficulties. Sex therapy is referred to as *solution-focused* therapy. This means that the sex therapist, together with the couple or individual, actively helps to clearly define the issues that are causing the problems, to devise a plan to work on the various issues, and to resolve them.

Just as with any other area of intimate and marital relationships, the benefits of working toward solutions for sexual difficulties are well worth the time and effort it takes to enjoy satisfying, rewarding sexual relationships.

SEXUAL LIFE EDUCATION

Throughout this discussion, we have explored how and why we experience sexual desire, arousal, and pleasure, and we have also taken a close look at the nature of human sexual response. It is very important to understand how our bodies function and how our partners' bodies function, because this knowledge really does help us experience our sexuality to its fullest.

We've learned about real sex in this chapter. Real sex isn't about perfectly timed orgasms between two perfect bodies. Instead, real sex means that sometimes you just don't feel like having sex. It means sometimes being interrupted. It means that sometimes you can't get aroused. It means lowering inhibitions through every one of the human senses so partners can emotionally and physically experience the other. It means allowing sex to change through the experiences of pregnancy, age, and trauma. And finally, real sex means that the "hot spots" are there because *you* put them there.

Summary

WHAT FACTORS INTO HUMAN SEXUAL RESPONSE? 218

• The sexual desires of men and women differ, and therefore various factors contribute to sexual arousal and response. The five senses play a major part in sexual arousal, as do the body's multiple erogenous zones.

• Researchers such as Masters and Johnson, Kaplan, and Basson have worked to determine the human sexual response processes. According to Basson, the female sexual response is contextual, rather than linear, as previously thought by Masters and Johnson, and Kaplan.

WHAT KINDS OF SOLITARY EXPERIENCES ARE THERE? 224

• Though often stigmatized throughout history, masturbation is a common means for self-discovery and sexual pleasure. Sexual fantasies are common and prevalent in the thoughts of most people, but men's typically focus on the physically arousing, while women's often focus on emotional bonding.

HOW IS SEXUALITY EXPERIENCED WITH OTHERS? 231

• As the Internet becomes an increasingly dominant force in today's society, it also becomes a part of our sexuality. From looking at erotic images to having online relationships, online sexual activities are common.

• Sexual activities and positions are many, for heterosexual couples and homosexual couples as well. Sex with others can include mutual masturbation, oral-genital sexual behavior, anal stimulation, and vaginal sex.

WHAT CAUSES SEXUAL DIFFICULTIES, AND HOW CAN THEY BE TREATED? 234

• Broadly stated, sexual dysfunction is any time sexual activity is less than satisfying. Women can suffer from sexual arousal, orgasm, and sexual pain disorders, while men can suffer from erectile dysfunction and rapid ejaculation. Any time a sexual difficulty is persistent, a person should seek help from a health care provider or a sex therapist because most dysfunctions are easily treatable.

Key Terms

sexual desire the wish, drive, or motivation to engage in sexual activities 218

libido a person's inborn sexual drives and sexual instincts 219

aphrodisiac food or drink believed to boost sexual desire 220

sexual arousal the stimulation of sexual desire in preparation for sexual behaviors 221

sexual pleasure positive feelings induced by sexual arousal 221

foreplay acts at the beginning of a sexual encounter to build sexual arousal 221

sex toys devices to enhance sexual arousal and pleasure 221

erotica sexually explicit books or media 221

primary erogenous zones genitals, buttocks, anus, perineum, navel, inner surfaces of the thighs, the breasts and/or nipples, neck, the mouth, the ears, armpits, and the soles of the feet 222

secondary erogenous zones the areas of the body that become eroticized over the course of sexual encounters such as the inside of the elbow 222

erogenous zones the areas of the body that are most sensitive to touch of 222

sexual response the specific physiological and emotional changes and responses that lead to and follow orgasm 222

vasocongestion the filling of blood in the genitals for during the excitement phase 222

sex flush a reddening of the flesh caused by increased blood flow 222

myotonia involuntary head-to-toe muscle tension 222

refractory period point during the resolution phase in which men cannot physically achieve an erection 224

solitary sexual behaviors sexual behavior without a partner 224

masturbation stimulation of one's own genitals by hand movements or by friction of the genitals against clothing or objects 224

mutual masturbation type of masturbation in which one person masturbates another 224

sexual fantasies the sexual thoughts and images created in our minds 228

cybersex, or **net sex** erotic interactions that take place through rich, detailed Internet discussion that results in sexual arousal 230

online sexual activity (OSA) any activity using the Internet that involves sexuality for the purposes of recreation, entertainment, explo-

ration, education, and/or seeking out sexual or romantic partners 230

cybersex compulsion viewing sex-related sites for more than 11 hours per week 230

sexual acts descriptions of positions that participants use 231

oral sex sex act that involves the contact between the lips, mouth, tongue (and possibly teeth) of one partner and the genitals of the other 231

cunnilingus form of oral sex that involves the erotic stimulation of the woman's external sex organs 231

fellatio oral stimulation of the male's external sex organs 231

anal intercourse sexual activity of the male placing his penis into his partner's anus and rectum 232

anal eroticism anal intercourse and oral stimulation of the anus, manually stroking the outside of the anus 232

coitus the process in which the penis is inserted into the vagina 233

coital positions positions that heterosexual couples use when having penile-vaginal sexual intercourse 233

tribadism a form of mutual masturbation in which a woman rubs her vulva against her partner's body for sexual stimulation *233*

interfemoral intercourse the practice of masturbating by moving the penis between the upper thighs of a partner *234*

sexual dysfunction the inability to enjoy sex fully *234*

hypoactive sexual desire a disorder that is characterized by a persistent absence of sexual desire, sexual thoughts, and/or motivation for becoming sexually aroused *234*

sexual aversion disorder (SAD) disorder characterized not only by a lack of sexual desire, but also includes disgust, fear, and revulsion at the thought of genital contact with a partner *234*

female sexual arousal disorder (FSAD) disorder characterized by absent or very noticeable reduced feelings of sexual arousal, sexual excitement, and pleasure from any type of stimulation *234*

anorgasmia a persistent delay or absence of orgasm after a normal sexual excitement phase *235*

dyspareunia a sexual pain disorder in women, a recurrent genital pain caused by sexual activity *236*

vaginismus a sexual pain disorder in women that is the result of an involuntary spasm of the muscles around the lower one-third of the vagina *237*

low libido low level of sexual desire/interest *237*

erectile dysfunction (ED) the inability of a man to develop and/or maintain a firm erection long enough to have satisfactory sex *238*

rapid ejaculation (RE) ejaculation that occurs before, upon, or shortly after penetration with minimal sexual stimulation *238*

primary RE RE that typically occurs in younger men and lessens with age *238*

secondary RE RE that has a later onset and is often associated with ED *238*

sex therapy a specialty in the area of psychological counseling that is often used when individuals and/or couples have experienced sexual trauma, infidelities, or other sexual concerns and difficulties *239*

Sample Test Questions

MULTIPLE CHOICE

1. Which Freudian term is used for sexual desire?
   a. Id
   b. Libido
   c. Ego
   d. Superego

2. Which hormone is closely associated with high sexual desire?
   a. Estrogen
   b. Testosterone
   c. Progestin
   d. Dopamine

3. Which term is used for oral-genital sex performed on a woman?
   a. Fellatio
   b. Cunnilingus
   c. Tribadism
   d. Interfemoral intercourse

4. Which sexual dysfunction is recurrent genital pain caused by sexual activity?
   a. Vaginismus
   b. Dyspareunia
   c. Anorgasmia
   d. Endometriosis

5. Which researcher developed a model of sexual response that is not linear?
   a. Basson
   b. Masters
   c. Kaplan
   d. Johnson

6. Which male sexual dysfunction typically occurs in younger men and lessens with age?
   a. Erectile dysfunction
   b. Low libido
   c. Primary rapid ejaculation
   d. Secondary rapid ejaculation

7. Which result is NOT a downside of online sexual activity?
   a. Unrealistic expectations of partners' bodies
   b. Cybersex compulsion
   c. The ability to anonymously explore one's sexuality
   d. Problems in real-life relationships

8. Which cause of vaginismus is nonphysical?
   a. Inadequate lubrication
   b. Performance pressure
   c. Hormonal changes
   d. Pelvic surgery

SHORT RESPONSE

1. How does each of the five senses contribute to sexual arousal and response?

2. Explain the differences between primary erogenous zones and secondary erogenous zones.

3. Discuss Masters and Johnson's, Kaplan's, and Basson's models of sexual response. What are the differences? Which one do you feel is most accurate?

4. Do you believe masturbation and sexual fantasies are acceptable or not? Why do you feel this way?

5. Describe the different treatments available for different sexual dysfunctions in both men and women.

Answers: 1. b; 2. b; 3. b; 4. b; 5. a; 6. c; 7. c; 8. b

Remember to check www.thethinkspot.com **for additional information, downloadable flashcards, and other helpful resources.**

THE CHOICES
And Challenges of Childbearing

Q

WHO IS HAVING BABIES?

HOW DO WE REPRODUCE AND WHAT CHANGES OCCUR DURING PREGNANCY?

WHAT HAPPENS DURING LABOR AND BIRTH?

WHAT ARE SOME UNEXPECTED OUTCOMES AND HOW DO PEOPLE DEAL WITH THEM?

You asked

for questions I have about pregnancy, labor, and birth. Since I just found out about three weeks ago that [she's] pregnant, here's my list of questions.

- Are her food cravings for real, or is this all in her head?
- She has to pee every hour, it seems. Why is this, and does it ever get better?
- What is the cause of morning sickness?
- Why is she so tired all the time?
- She complains a lot about headaches. Are these for real, or just caused by the stress of going to school, working, and being pregnant all at the same time?
- Will I ever be able to touch her boobs again?

- Isn't it just better for her to have a C-section so she doesn't have to go through the pain of labor?
- Is it really OK to have sex? I have to admit that the thought of having sex with her when her belly gets huge kind of freaks me out.

I was pretty freaked out when we found out she was pregnant. It's not like we planned it. I'm worried about becoming a dad and everything, but all I'm really worried about is her; I just want to make sure she's OK, and that what she's going through is to be expected.

Source: Author's files

Pregnancy always intrigued me and newborns always took me captive. So, it didn't come as a surprise to anyone who knew me when I became a maternal specialist and a **doula**, a professional provider of labor support (emotional, physical, and informational) to women and their companions. Many years and countless births later, I am still intrigued with the mystery of how a single-celled zygote develops in the mother's womb into a 10 trillion-celled person.

The birth of a baby is life altering. In this chapter, we take a look at the current childbearing trends in America, how we reproduce, the physical and emotional changes associated with pregnancy, and the processes of labor and birth. We'll conclude our discussion by looking at unexpected outcomes in pregnancy and childbirth.

CHILDBEARING TRENDS: WHO'S HAVING BABIES?

Who's having babies, and how old are America's parents? Each year, the population in the United States increases by the addition of slightly more than 4 million babies (Centers for Disease Control and Prevention, 2005). Figure 12.1 illustrates America's birth rates by age group. By tracking the **crude birth rate** from year to year, as well as the **fertility rates**, demographers are able to see certain childbearing trends, such as the age of birth mothers. And in the United States, significant changes are being seen in childbearing trends, especially among the nation's adolescents.

TRENDS AMONG TEENAGERS

In the next 12 months, 1 million teenagers will become pregnant, and nearly 500,000 will give birth—about one every minute (The Alan Guttmacher Institute, 2008). Making up one-fourth of all unintended pregnancies each year in the United States, adolescent birth rates continue to remain higher than similar birth rates in other Western or developed countries. Adolescent birth and abortion rates are twice as high as those found in Great Britain and Canada, and five times higher than those rates found in Sweden and France (The Alan Guttmacher Institute, 2008).

∧
∧ The one-child policy in China, a
∧ practice that encourages late marriages and late childbirths, and mandates only one child per couple in urban areas, **is a cultural norm that accounts for China's and Taiwan's low fertility rates.**

TABLE 12.1
Teen Birth Rates by Race, 1980–2006

Source: Centers for Disease Control and Prevention, National Center for Health Statistics. National Vital Statistics Report, 56(7), December 5, 2007.

Age	1980	1985	1990	2000	2002	2004	2006
All Races 15–19 years	53.0	51.0	59.9	47.7	43.0	41.2	41.9
White 15–19 years	41.2	–	50.8	43.2	39.4	37.8	–
African American 15–19 years	97.8	95.4	112.8	77.4	66.6	62.9	63.7
American Indian 15–19 years	82.2	79.2	81.1	58.3	53.8	52.5	54.7
Asian/Pacific Islander 15–19 years	26.2	23.8	26.4	20.5	18.3	17.4	16.7
Hispanic 15–19 years	82.2	–	100.3	87.8	83.4	82.6	83.0

Figure 12.1 Birth Rates Among All Age Groups, 2004

Source: Centers for Disease Control and Prevention. (2005). Births: Preliminary data for 2004. *National Vital Statistics Report, 54*(8). www.cdc.gov/nchs/data/nvsr/nvsr54/nvsr54_08.pdf.

In 2004, the birth rate for teenage mothers reached a historic low, with 41.2 births per 1,000 women aged 15 to 19; this reflected a decrease of 33 percent since 1991 (Centers for Disease Control and Prevention, 2005). But in 2006, the teenager birth rate in the United States rose among teens aged 15 to 19 (Centers for Disease Control and

Brianne Mackey, 17, participated in a "pregnancy pact," in Massachusetts, where a group of teens all agreed to become pregnant within the same year. **What can organizations do to prevent situations like this in the future?**

∨ ∨ ∨

Prevention, 2008). The largest increases were seen among African American/Black Caribbean teens who experienced an increase of 5 percent. Hispanic teens saw a 2 percent rate increase, white teens experienced a 3 percent rate increase, and American Indian/Alaska Native teens had a 4 percent increase (Centers for Disease Control and Prevention, 2008). Although it is too early to determine whether these data indicate that a new trend in teen childbearing is on the horizon, it is concerning to see these notable changes after 15 years of decreasing childbearing trends. Table 12.1 shows the birth rates to teens among racial groups. After a drop-off in the early 2000s, the rate of pregnancy among America's teens is increasing (National Center for Health Statistics, 2007).

In our study of sex, sexuality, and intimate relationships, it is important to understand the incidences of teen pregnancy because births to teen moms are linked to a host of critical issues: poverty, overall child health and well-being, births to unmarried women, responsible fatherhood, sexuality and health concerns, education/school failure, child abuse and neglect, and other risky behaviors, such as drug and alcohol use and abuse, and crime (National Campaign to Prevent Teen Pregnancy, 2008). A range of potential problems is associated with teen pregnancy; these are presented in Table 12.2.

In 2007, then-U.S. Presidential candidate, Senator Barack Obama introduced a bill to try to reduce teen pregnancies in minority communities. The *Communities of Color Teen Pregnancy Prevention Act of 2007* seeks to strengthen community-based intervention efforts for teen pregnancy services and to establish a comprehensive national database to provide culturally and linguistically sensitive information on teen pregnancy reduction. Obama noted, "We must develop innovative approaches to strengthen our community support networks and services to educate our teens about pregnancy and provide them with every chance to succeed in school and beyond."

TABLE 12.2
Impacts of Teen Pregnancy on the Mom

Teen parents and their babies start out with many disadvantages. When the head of the family is an adolescent girl, both the teen parent and her child are at increased risk for medical, psychological, developmental, and social/emotional problems.

- **Medical/Psychological** The medical risks for adolescent mothers and their babies are significant, especially for younger adolescent mothers (10- to 14-year-olds). For example, their risk of dying during labor and birth is two to four times higher for women at age 17 than it is for women who have children in their 20s (The Alan Guttmacher Institute, 2004).

- **Developmental** Research consistently shows that adolescent mothers struggle when trying to form and maintain stable interpersonal relationships and family life (Lehrman, 2001; Larson, 2004; Quinlivan et al., 2004). Many of these teen parents continue their dependence on family members rather than shifting to more independence and autonomy (Hanson, 1992).

- **Socioeconomic** About half of all teen moms and more than three-fourths of all unmarried teenage mothers receive welfare within five years of the birth of their first baby; about 80 percent of teen parents eventually depend on welfare for their economic support (Klerman, 2004; The Alan Guttmacher Institute, 2004). Teenage moms are also more likely to drop out of high school than their nonpregnant peers.

TRENDS AMONG UNMARRIED PARENTS

In 2006, a record 38.5 percent of all United States births were nonmarital births (Solomon-Fears, 2008). Births to unmarried partners can be first births or subsequent births; they can occur to a woman who has never married, as well as to divorced or widowed women. Further, a woman may have had one or more children within marriage and other births outside marriage. And, because U.S. demographers do not consider gay or lesbian partnerships "marriages," births to these couples are also considered "nonmarital" births.

There are a number of factors associated with the unprecedented rates of births that occur outside marriage. These include (Solomon-Fears, 2008):

- Marriage postponement; there is an increase in the median age at first marriage

- Childfree movement; there is decreased childbearing among married couples

- Increased divorce rates

- Increased numbers of cohabiting couples

- Increased sexual activity outside marriage

- Improper use/lack of use of contraceptive methods

- Participation in risky behaviors that often lead to sex, such as alcohol and drug use

When considering all of these factors, the trend of births to unmarried partners may very well continue and may even further increase.

Compared with children born to parents outside of any union (such as births to teenage mothers and fathers), children born to cohabiting parents are at an economic advantage (Acs & Nelson, 2002). This is because cohabiting parents, unlike adolescent parents, are more likely to have dual incomes, and because mothers who cohabit are more likely to be older and have attained a level of higher education (Acs & Nelson, 2002). Childbearing among cohabiters, however, results in more overall negative outcomes for children compared to children born to married parents: Children born to cohabiting parents may be economically disadvantaged and have poorer cognitive outcomes, as well as poorer social/emotional and health outcomes (Brown, 2004; Manning, Giordano, & Longmore, 2006). Negative consequences for children born to cohabiting parents are presented in Table 12.3. The sociological trends of unmarried childbearing, coupled with these research findings, suggest the need for

>>> Births to older women are on the rise; **model and actress Brooke Shields gave birth to her two children at ages 37 and 40.**

TABLE 12.3
Negative Consequences of Nonmarital Childbearing

There are a number of negative consequences associated with births that occur outside marriage.

- **Consequences for women:** Having a birth outside marriage is associated with reduced rates of subsequent marriage and a higher risk of subsequent poverty and receipt of welfare (Lichter, Graefe, & Brown, 2003).

- **Consequences for men:** Fathering children prior to marriage is associated with lower rates of subsequent marriage and lower rates of education and full-time employment (Nock, 1998).

- **Consequences for children:** Children born to unmarried parents have a greater chance of being poor and growing up in poverty (Acs & Nelson, 2002; Haveman, Wolfe, & Pence, 2001; Moore, Jekielek, & Emig, 2002). Overall, children have lower educational attainment and are at greater risk of experiencing limited father involvement and unstable family structures than children who have married parents (Manning, Smock, & Majudmar, 2004; Mincieli et al., 2007; Moore, Jekielek, & Emig, 2002). This family instability is associated with lower levels of cognitive growth and social/emotional well-being (Brown, 2006; Cavanagh & Huston, 2006; Heard, 2007; Osborne & McLanahan, 2007).

prevention efforts targeted to young adults to help them avoid unintended pregnancy and childbearing (Kirby, 2008).

PREGNANCY AT DIFFERENT AGES

In 2006, among women aged 20 to 24, the birth rate dipped to an all-time low, with 92.8 births per 1,000 women (U.S. Census Bureau, 2008). In line with historical trends, in 2006, among women aged 25 to 29, the birth rate was the highest of any age group, with 104.6 births per 1,000 women. These data tend to support the idea that women in their 20s are in their peak childbearing years.

Births to older women are also on the rise. Among women aged 30 to 34, for example, the birth rate was 95.5; among women aged 35 to 39, the birth rate was 45.4; and among women in their 40s, the birth rate was 10.0 (Centers for Disease Control and Prevention, 2005). However, in 2006 there was a decline of births to women in their 30s and 40s.

Childbearing trends have been changing throughout the 20th and into the 21st centuries. As the data show, many women are delaying childbearing, perhaps due to education and career opportunities or perhaps due to relationship circumstances.

Now that you have an understanding of who's having babies in America, let's look at the process of reproduction. Most of the time, this occurs naturally; other times, nature needs assistance by medical means.

HOW WE REPRODUCE

The dynamic process of human life begins with the union of the sperm provided by the male and an ovum provided by the female. Fertilization of the ovum is a complex process that involves a delicate balance of male and female hormones, excellent timing, and a little bit of luck.

FERTILIZATION

During heterosexual intercourse, millions of mature sperm are ejaculated into the vagina. In the subsequent 24 to 72 hours, sperm begin their remarkable journey through the cervix, through the uterus, and into each of the fallopian tubes. Only about 200 of the original 100 million-plus sperm reach the ovum, which is usually located in the upper third of the fallopian tube after it is released from the ovary during the process of ovulation.

Once the sperm reach the mature ovum, they connect themselves to its outer layer. As this occurs, the egg has a series of contractions that pull the sperm into it. Once a sperm penetrates the egg, *fertilization* has occurred. The outer layer of the egg hardens, making it impossible for another sperm to penetrate it. The product of fertilization is a single-celled *zygote* (see Chapter 3).

CONCEPTION

There are three phases of prenatal development: the germinal period, the embryonic period, and the fetal period. The **germinal period** begins with the fusion of the sperm and the ovum in the fallopian tube and ends after the **conceptus** (the fertilized ovum) has been successfully implanted in the blood- and nutrient-rich lining of the uterus. As the zygote undergoes cellular changes, it makes its way through the fallopian tube to the uterus. This five- to seven-inch journey takes approximately 10 to 14 days, during which the zygote develops into a ball of cells, called a **blastocyst**. Once the blastocyst reaches the uterus, it implants in the endometrium, the lining that was prepared to nourish the product of fertilization. Implantation signifies that **conception** has occurred.

For most couples, the process of fertilization and conception works as it is supposed to. But for other couples, becoming pregnant represents grueling work and becomes a difficult and heart-wrenching challenge.

WHEN CONCEPTION FAILS: INFERTILITY

In the United States today, approximately 7 million women have an impaired ability to become pregnant (Centers for Disease Control and Prevention, 2009). **Sterility** refers to the absolute inability to reproduce,

either because the woman has no uterus or ovaries, or the male has no testes or sperm production. No amount of medical intervention can help a sterile person reproduce. **Infertility** is the inability to conceive a baby after trying for a period of one year.

Approximately one-third of the problems associated with infertility are due to women's reproductive systems (American Society of Reproductive Medicine, 2008). Problems with ovulation (see Chapter 4) are responsible for most female infertility. Lack of ovulation may be due to *hormonal imbalances*, which refers to a decline in or an absence of the hormones estrogen and progesterone, which are necessary for pregnancy. Other causes for infertility may be a pituitary gland tumor (quite rare), or lifestyle habits such as poor nutrition (as in the case of anorexia or bulimia), stress, or even intense athletic training (ASRM, 2008). Once a woman reaches the age of 35, her ovaries' ability to produce eggs diminishes.

Even when women successfully ovulate, the fertilized ovum may have difficulty reaching the uterus due to blocked or scarred fallopian tubes. This disorder, called **pelvic inflammatory disease (PID)**, is primarily caused by untreated sexually transmitted infections (for a full discussion about the serious effects of PID, see Chapter 14). PID renders 150,000 women per year infertile, making it the leading cause of infertility in young women (Centers for Disease Control and Prevention, 2009). **Endometriosis**, a disease characterized by the buildup or migration of uterine tissue to other parts of the body (such as the ovaries or fallopian tubes), may also prevent the fertilized ovum from traveling through the fallopian tube to the uterus or may prevent the fertilized ovum from becoming embedded in the uterine lining.

About one-third of fertility difficulties are due to male reproductive problems (ASRM, 2008). There are two primary forms of infertility in men: **azoospermia**, which means that no sperm cells are produced, and **oligospermia**, which means that few sperm cells are produced. Sometimes, these conditions are the result of a genetic disease, such as cystic fibrosis, and sometimes, they are the result of poor reproductive health. To produce an adequate number (at least 20 million sperm per milliliter of semen), the male must be healthy and lead a healthy lifestyle.

TREATING INFERTILITY

There are a variety of treatment options available, ranging from medication (fertility drugs to enhance ovulation) to surgery. Less invasive medical treatments include fertility drugs and donor insemination, often referred to as artificial insemination. In women, fertility drugs increase egg production. When fertility drugs are used, sometimes more than one egg is produced, leading to multiple births. **Artificial insemination**, a popular fertility treatment used by both heterosexual and homosexual couples, is the medical process in which donor sperm is placed into the woman's vagina, cervix, or uterus by a syringe. Sperm are collected (through masturbation of the donor) and stored by medical facilities called **sperm banks**. Sperm donors are typically paid $30 to $50 per specimen; a vial of sperm from a sperm bank costs anywhere from $150 to $3,000 (ASRM, 2008). If these treatment options fail, there are other more invasive (and more costly) treatment options, such as using an egg

>>> Boxers or briefs? Although folklore suggests men should wear boxers rather than briefs **to promote the production of healthy sperm, to date, no empirical evidence has been found to support such claims.**

from a female donor (see Chapter 3). These options are presented in Table 12.4.

THE PSYCHOLOGICAL IMPACT OF INFERTILITY

Infertility is often distressing, frustrating, and depressing. Hoping, longing, and wishing month after month after month for a positive pregnancy test only to find out that the efforts failed again constitutes a real crisis for couples. The stress on finances and on the marriage can lead to a breakdown of the couple's relationship. Fortunately, many support groups and infertility counseling organizations exist to help infertile women and couples navigate through the physical and emotional challenges infertility brings. Groups such as the National Infertility Association and the International Council on Infertility Information Dissemination offer psychological, psychosocial, and informational support for those experiencing infertility.

THE CHANGES THROUGH PREGNANCY

From the moment the egg is fertilized, throughout the approximate 260 to 280 days of pregnancy, a woman's body is in a continuous state of change and growth. The changes are so dramatic that an obstetrician colleague of mine once noted, "The pregnant body almost constitutes a third sex." Although everyone recognizes the enlarged, expanded abdomen of child-bearing, other physiological changes take place that are not visible.

Discussed at length in Chapter 4, the uterus is a pear-shaped organ that houses the fetus. During pregnancy, muscle fibers of the uterus become thicker and lengthen to accommodate the growing fetus, and it becomes capable of holding 500 to 1,000 times the volume of its non-pregnant state. The ligaments that support the weight of the uterus stretch, causing much of the discomfort associated with pregnancy.

The **placenta** and **umbilical cord** are the life-support systems between the fetus and the mother. Typically attached to the upper portion of the mother's uterus, the placenta weighs about two pounds by the time the baby has reached full term. It provides critical functions, such as transporting oxygen between the mother and baby, and passing mothers' immunities to the baby (Welch, 2004).

Everything travels back and forth between the mother and baby via the umbilical cord. About three feet long, it is composed of two arteries and one vein. The two arteries carry the blood from the baby to the placenta, which

> ∧∧∧ **Pictured here, the placenta** is about the size of a large dinner plate.

> ∧∧∧ Although everyone recognizes the ever-expanding abdomen of a pregnant woman, **other drastic physiological changes are taking place as well.**

rids it of carbon dioxide and other waste materials and provides oxygen, returning the blood back to the baby. The cord is without nerves, so there is no pain caused for either the mother or the baby when the cord is cut.

Inside the uterus, the **amniotic sac** is a tough membrane that holds the fetus, placenta, umbilical cord, and amniotic fluid. About the thickness

TABLE 12.4
Treating Infertility

Assisted reproductive technology (ART) are treatment options that involve fertilization through the hands-on manipulation of the woman's ova and the male's sperm. In 2006, more than 50,000 babies were born in the United States as a result of ART (ASRM, 2008).

- **In vitro fertilization (IVF)** For infertile couples in which a woman has blocked or absent fallopian tubes, or where a man has a low sperm count, IVF is typically used to help the couple conceive. IVF is a process whereby a woman's eggs are surgically removed from her ovary and mixed with a man's sperm in a laboratory culture dish. After about 40 hours in the culture dish, the eggs are examined to see if they were fertilized, and if they were, to see if cell division is taking place. If the balls of cells appear to be growing at a normal rate, the eggs (embryos) are placed within the uterus. This process bypasses the fallopian tubes. The average cost of IVF is $12,400 per attempt (ASRM, 2008).

- **Gamete intrafallopian transfer (GIFT)** This involves manually manipulating the sperm and eggs, but instead of fertilizing the eggs in a dish, the unfertilized eggs and the male's sperm are placed in the woman's fallopian tubes. This is designed to foster natural fertilization within the woman's fallopian tubes. The average cost of GIFT is about $10,000 per attempt (ASRM, 2008).

- **Zygote intrafallopian transfer (ZIFT)** The man's sperm fertilizes the woman's eggs in a laboratory. The fertilized eggs are placed immediately in the woman's fallopian tubes, rather than in her uterus (as in IVF), allowing the conceptus to travel naturally to the uterus and implant. The average cost of ZIFT is $10,000 per attempt (ASRM, 2008).

- **Surrogacy** Men or women may desire to have a biological child, but for medical or other reasons (as in the case of gay men) they may not be able to do so. IVF is performed, but the embryos are implanted into a surrogate mother who carries the pregnancy to term. Upon birth, the baby is given to the biological parents.

of the skin between the thumb and forefinger, the membrane ruptures when labor begins, or the mother's "water breaks." The amniotic fluid is comprised of the baby's urine, amniotic cells, secretions from the baby's lungs, and the baby's sloughed-off skin cells. Replaced every three to four hours, the baby swallows the fluid and excretes it as urine.

Over the course of approximately nine months, many changes take place physically and emotionally within the mother, as well as in her relationship with her partner, if she has one. In the following section, we'll study the changes in the mother, her intimate relationship, and the baby.

PREGNANCY TRIMESTERS

The **first trimester** covers the first 12 weeks of pregnancy, the **second trimester** covers weeks 13 through 26, and the **third trimester** covers weeks 27 through 40. A pregnancy that is carried from 37 to 40 weeks is considered full term; any baby born before the 37th week of pregnancy is considered **pre-term** and may be prone to respiratory and other difficulties.

Throughout the trimesters, both the mother and the growing baby undergo specific week-by-week changes. For our purposes here, we discuss the growth and development that take place in the baby (see Figure 12.2) and the changes taking place simultaneously within the mother's body.

Figure 12.2 Fetus Development

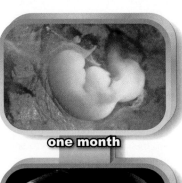

one month

three months

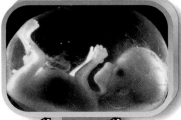

five months

seven months

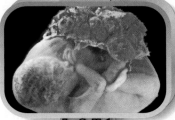

nearly full-term

The Fetus at 0–12 Weeks

At about four weeks, the embryo embeds in the uterine lining. It is about one-quarter of an inch long; at about seven weeks, it is an inch or less in length and begins to look recognizably human. With eyes, nose, arms, a digestive system, and a beating heart, the embryo is over 10,000 times its size as a zygote just a few short weeks ago. At about nine weeks, the embryo reaches the status of *fetus*, a Latin word meaning "young one" or "offspring." At the end of the third month, or 12 weeks, the fetus is about three inches long and weighs about three ounces. The fingers and toes are differentiated and the sex is distinguishable. By the end of the first trimester, the once-zygote is completely formed with all of the anatomical structures and organs formed and functioning at some level. The fetus, at this point, can move its arms and legs, curl its toes and open and close its mouth. Now, it needs only to mature and to grow.

The Fetus at 13–28 Weeks

By the sixth month of pregnancy, the fetus is about 12 to 14 inches long and weighs about 1.5 pounds. The skeleton begins to harden, and toenails and fingernails are visible. The skin is covered with a white waxy coating called *vernix*. This coating provides a lubricant for the baby's skin and will slough off as the baby approaches the 37th and 40th weeks of pregnancy. If the baby is born before the 24th week of pregnancy, the chances of survival are slim; some babies do survive, but there is a strong possibility that development will be impaired or delayed.

The Fetus at 29–40 Weeks

By the eighth month of pregnancy, the baby's brain and nervous system are nearly fully developed. At 32 weeks, the fatty layer of tissue under his skin is complete, and his eyes, which have been sealed closed early in the pregnancy, are now open. His living quarters are becoming too cramped for sweeping movements or side-to-side rolls, but his jabs, pokes, and kicks provide reassurance to the mother. The fine, downy hair on the baby's skin disappears, as does the vernix.

sexual life now

Freebirthing: Freedom of Choice or Dangerous Consequences?

There are a number of birth setting options (see Figure 12.3), but **freebirthing**, or **unassisted childbirth (UC)**, refers to the process of intentionally giving birth (typically in the home) without the guidance of a midwife, physician, or other medical professional. Freebirth is also referred to as *DIY (do-it-yourself) birth*, *unhindered birth*, and *couple's birth*. Many moms-to-be also forgo prenatal care. The National Center for Health Statistics (2005) reports that about 1 percent of the nation's annual birth total were freebirths by choice. Freebirth is different from traditional home births, because home birthing involves the expertise of a medical professional.

Women and couples who opt for freebirth often adhere to the beliefs that birthing is a natural function of the female body, not a medical one, and that women have given birth for thousands of years without medical assistance. But given the possibility of complications with any labor and delivery, should women have the right to give birth without medical assistance?

YES!

Laura Shanley is the author of the book, *Unassisted Childbirth* (1993), and has helped popularize the freebirthing underground movement in Western culture. Shanley, who has no formal obstetrics training, gave birth to five of her children at home, unassisted; one child died a few hours after birth. Shanley notes that birthing options are a woman's right, because:

- Birth is not a medical condition or a medical emergency and should not be treated as such.

- Most common medical interventions (such as an IV, or an epidural for pain relief) cause more harm than good and often result in unnecessary C-sections.

- The mother has the right to experience the intuitive, natural progression of her individual birth and the right to give birth in an undisturbed setting.

- Birth is an intimate, sexual, and orgasmic experience; privacy is of the utmost importance to ensure the erotic dimension of birth.

- Freebirth increases the mother's ability to bond with her infant, because she is required to take full responsibility for the welfare of her child.

NO!

Because of the increase in the number of unassisted childbirths and the growth of this underground movement, several national medical societies have issued strong statements opposing the practice, indicating that unassisted childbirth is "courting danger" (Society of Obstetricians and Gynaecologists of Canada, 2007). To date, the Society of Obstetricians and Gynaecologists of Canada (SOGC), the American College of Obstetrics and Gynecologists (ACOG), the Royal Australian and New Zealand College of Obstetricians and Gynaecologists, the Royal College of Midwives, and the American College of Nurse-Midwives urge pregnant women to avoid freebirth because of the risks associated with the practice:

- Unassisted childbirth is linked to substantially higher rates of maternal and neonatal deaths.

- Each year, more than 500,000 women worldwide die from childbirth complications in parts of the world where prenatal and obstetric care is unavailable (SOGC, 2007).

- When a complication occurs during childbearing (such as the sudden decrease of available oxygen to the baby or cardiac problems with the mother), death of the mother or fetus can occur within a matter of minutes without the expertise of trained medical professionals.

In the United States and the United Kingdom, mothers who engage in unassisted childbirth may face legal repercussions; if something happens to the mother or the baby in a planned freebirth, the birth mother, partner, family members, or friends may face criminal charges (Discovery Health Channel, 2008). In some instances, social services or Child Protective Services becomes involved because of the perceived disregard for the baby's safety.

>>> WHAT DO YOU THINK?
1. Is freebirth a woman's healthy choice, or is it a reckless choice? What are your reasons?
2. What do you find appealing about freebirth? What scares you about freebirth?
3. Would you or your partner ever consider having an unassisted childbirth? Why or why not?

The First Trimester (0 to 12 weeks)
Baby

The first trimester of pregnancy is characterized by rapid cell differentiation and growth of the embryo. Termed the **critical period** of human development, this is when *all* the baby's anatomical structures and organs are formed and begin to function at a rudimentary level. Recall from Chapter 3 that the developing fetus is extremely susceptible to environmental influences, or *teratogens*. Exposure to teratogens can cause major anatomical abnormalities, including heart defects, limb defects, brain and central nervous system defects, abnormalities in the external genitalia, and a cleft or

Figure 12.3 Types of Birth Settings

Where we give birth and who cares for us during pregnancy, labor, and delivery significantly affects the overall birth experience. Today, there are a number of birth setting options available. Women and their partners are encouraged to seek a provider that offers consistent, safe, and effective care, and to select an environment that enhances individual wishes for birth experiences. Care providers and birth settings should provide abundant support, comfort, and information.

Hospital Birth

The most common setting in the United States, births are typically supervised by obstetric nurses or midwives, and/or physicians (OB/GYN or family physician). Interventions, such as IV for hydration, fetal monitoring, episiotomy, bed confinement, and limited food intake may be used routinely. Today, hospital rooms often resemble comfortable bedrooms or birth centers—but this does not mean that the *hospital birth model* (often referred to as the *medical birth model*) supports an intervention-free birth. Hospital birthing models vary widely, however, and pregnant women and their partners are encouraged to choose a hospital that best suits their needs and wishes. Hospital birth settings are best for high-risk pregnancies or newborns who are at risk for developing complications. If the baby is healthy and the birth was without complications, most women and their babies leave the hospital within 48 hours following birth.

Birthing Center

Free-standing birthing centers are not widely available in the U.S. These facilities are not within a hospital, and are typically not associated with a hospital. Prenatal care and care throughout labor and birth are usually provided by a nurse midwife; often, there is a physician available if complications arise. Care is reflective of the *midwifery model*, which adheres to the belief that birth is a natural, physiological process. Continuous physical, emotional, and informational support is provided throughout labor and birth. Interventions, such as IV fluids, constant fetal monitoring, and episiotomies are not routinely used. Women are encouraged to listen to their bodies, to move freely, to use a number of birth positions, and to eat if they feel hungry. Birth centers are not equipped to provide certain types of pain management. If an emergency arises, ambulance transport to a hospital is required. If all is well, moms and babies are typically discharged within 12 hours of birth.

Home Births

Home births resemble birthing center births in a number of ways. Care is often provided by a nurse midwife, who adheres to the midwifery model of childbirth. Women who choose this birth setting often do so because of the individualized, personal birth experience. As with birth centers, home births do not provide pain medication options; if there is an emergency, transport to a hospital is necessary.

open palate. It is therefore essential for women of childbearing age, who know that one day they may want to become pregnant, to understand the potential risks that lifestyle habits (such as smoking and drinking) pose to their unborn child. During weeks 8 through 12, the embryo undergoes rapid growth, and during critical periods, teratogens may cause major anomalies.

Mother

Some of the first signs that indicate to a woman that she may be pregnant include cessation of her menstrual cycle, a feeling of fatigue, full breasts due to increased blood supply, and for some, moments of nausea and vomiting (Marieb & Hoehn, 2010). By the time these **presumptive signs** of pregnancy occur, much of the critical period of human development has already passed.

Couple

Due mostly to the hormonal changes that occur, in the early weeks of a pregnancy a woman's emotions are often unstable, resulting in mood swings, and it is not uncommon for her to feel depressed. Even if the pregnancy was planned and hoped for, she may cry, often for no apparent reason. Frequently, these emotional changes are unsettling for her partner, and he or she may feel inadequate or incapable of meeting the pregnant woman's

needs. It is not uncommon for both partners to be concerned about the family's finances and the additional costs associated with rearing a child.

Studies that explore couple relationships during pregnancy are rare, but in one study, the researcher found that couple relationships are more stable than unstable during pregnancy, despite the hormonal changes that take place in the woman (Richardson, 1981). The researcher also found that overall, women rate their relationships with their partners as more satisfactory than unsatisfactory during pregnancy. Studies have found that a pregnant woman is particularly sensitive to her partner's negative attitude/mood, and these cause depressive symptoms in her (Buehlman, Gottman, & Katz, 1992). These depressive symptoms are thought to lead to increased levels of conflict in a couple's relationship (Salmela-Aro et al., 2006). Another study found that pregnancy could result in decreased levels of closeness and communication in couples, which leads to increased conflict (Florsheim et al., 2003).

As you have seen in our study so far, human sexuality is reactive to our daily circumstances, and a couple's sex life changes as they encounter altered circumstances—certainly pregnancy is a time of "altered" circumstances! Couples are often concerned that having sex during the early weeks of pregnancy may harm the baby or the mother, but these concerns are typically unwarranted. Unless her physician indicates otherwise, sexual

251

The Choices and Challenges of Childbearing

activity is permissible throughout pregnancy. However, the pregnant woman may not be in the mood for any kind of touch because she is reacting to the changes in her body. Couples need to keep in mind that the woman is not rejecting her *partner*, just the *thought of or act of sex*. It's best for a partner to follow the pregnant woman's lead about sex throughout pregnancy.

The Second Trimester (13 to 26 weeks)
Baby

The second trimester begins in the fourth month of pregnancy, or at about 13 weeks. The growth of the fetus causes the mother's uterus to expand, giving her the appearance of being pregnant. Although the fetus has been moving for quite some time, the mother has not yet felt the movements because of the fetus' size. Fetal movement, referred to as **quickening**, is most often felt around the 20th week of pregnancy (Marieb & Hoehn, 2010). By about the end of the fourth month of pregnancy, the larger fetus makes its presence known by jabbing, poking, kicking, stretching, hiccupping, and occasionally rolling side to side. The fetus also begins to develop hair and eyebrows, and on its body appears a soft, downy hair called **lanugo**. The fetus begins to suck and swallow the amniotic fluid in which it is surrounded.

Mother

The second trimester is often the most enjoyable period of pregnancy for many women, although it is also a period when some realities are setting in. The discomfort of early pregnancy, such as nausea, vomiting, and fatigue, begin to lessen, and because the threat of miscarriage is reduced, women begin to enjoy the experience.

Common physical changes include a steady weight gain of about one-half to one pound per week, though individual variations do occur. It is expected that women gain 25 to 35 pounds during pregnancy (American College of Obstetrics and Gynecology, 2009). Some women, particularly brunettes of all races/ethnicities, will notice what is called the *mask of pregnancy*, which is simply increased pigmentation along the jaw line. The nipples/areolas change to a deeper, darker color, and the mother may get what is referred to as the *mother line*, a dark vertical line that runs from the pubic area to the navel.

Couple

The second trimester brings changes in the woman's emotions, too. Although most women understand that weight gain is a normal and necessary part of pregnancy, some women, particularly those who struggle with eating disorders, may become dismayed at their ever-increasing weight. Although most women feel attractive and sexy during pregnancy, some feel awkward and unappealing. Most women indicate that this is a time of great sexual pleasure.

The Third Trimester (27 to 40 weeks)
Baby

The third trimester begins in the seventh month of pregnancy. This is characteristically the period of the most rapid fetal growth. During the seventh month, the baby begins to develop fatty tissue under the skin, and at a length of 15 inches, it weighs about 2.5 pounds. If born now, the baby has a chance at survival, although it is unlikely that a baby would be able to maintain an adequate oxygen supply on its own. Babies born before the

Figure 12.4 Labor and Birth Stage 1 of labor is divided into 3 phases, early, active, and transition. Stage 2 begins with pushing.

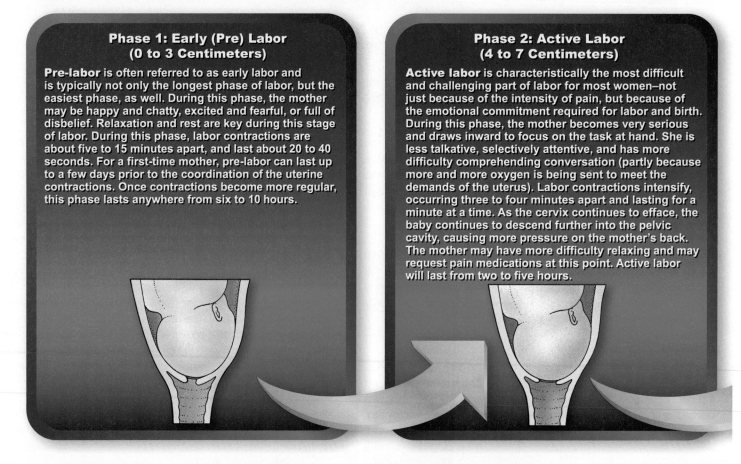

**Phase 1: Early (Pre) Labor
(0 to 3 Centimeters)**

Pre-labor is often referred to as early labor and is typically not only the longest phase of labor, but the easiest phase, as well. During this phase, the mother may be happy and chatty, excited and fearful, or full of disbelief. Relaxation and rest are key during this stage of labor. During this phase, labor contractions are about five to 15 minutes apart, and last about 20 to 40 seconds. For a first-time mother, pre-labor can last up to a few days prior to the coordination of the uterine contractions. Once contractions become more regular, this phase lasts anywhere from six to 10 hours.

**Phase 2: Active Labor
(4 to 7 Centimeters)**

Active labor is characteristically the most difficult and challenging part of labor for most women—not just because of the intensity of pain, but because of the emotional commitment required for labor and birth. During this phase, the mother becomes very serious and draws inward to focus on the task at hand. She is less talkative, selectively attentive, and has more difficulty comprehending conversation (partly because more and more oxygen is being sent to meet the demands of the uterus). Labor contractions intensify, occurring three to four minutes apart and lasting for a minute at a time. As the cervix continues to efface, the baby continues to descend further into the pelvic cavity, causing more pressure on the mother's back. The mother may have more difficulty relaxing and may request pain medications at this point. Active labor will last from two to five hours.

36th week typically lack the smooth surface coating of the lungs that allow them to freely expand and fill with air. If a woman enters into labor prematurely, every effort is made to stop the labor through a variety of medications. Every day that can be added to life inside the womb increases the baby's chances of survival and allows the respiratory system to develop more fully. At 32 weeks, the baby is about 17 inches long and weighs over four pounds. By about week 36, the baby will gain one to two pounds per week, and at full term will weigh 6 to 10 pounds (or more), and reach a length of 20 to 23 inches.

After 266 to 280 days, the once single-celled zygote has matured into a 10 trillion-celled baby and has matured sufficiently to survive outside the confines of the mother's protective womb.

Mother

By the end of pregnancy, breathing becomes increasingly difficult; the expanding uterus interferes with the movement of the diaphragm and lung function changes because of hormonal influences. With the 25- to 35-pound weight gain and the increasing energy demands of her growing baby, the mother experiences increasing fatigue. The enlarged uterus displaces the mother's stomach upward, often causing heartburn. The weight of the growing uterus and the added weight of the baby cause pressure on her bladder, resulting in frequent trips to the bathroom. A persistent backache is the result of the growing baby. Physiological changes take place in the ligaments that support the uterus in preparation for labor and birth, which also causes achiness in the pelvic area. The woman's breasts undergo hormonally influenced changes in preparation to nourish her child. Her breasts begin to feel full, and bluish veins appear under their surface. *Colostrum*, a nutrient-rich precursor to breast milk, is secreted from the nipples. **Braxton-Hicks contractions** begin quite early in pregnancy, but

<<< Pregnancy can be a time of great sexual pleasure **for many women.**

usually aren't noticed (sometimes not noticed at all) until after mid-pregnancy. Almost imperceptible at first, these "practice" contractions increase in number (and perhaps intensity), but are not actual labor. Unlike actual labor, Braxton-Hicks contractions generally don't grow consistently longer, stronger, and closer together.

Couple

As the big day nears, there are multiple relational and emotional changes. By the ninth month, many women feel overwhelmed and, frankly, tired of being pregnant! Many women and their partners may lose interest in sex, not only because of exhaustion, but also because finding a comfortable sexual position is at times an exercise in futility and hilarity. Birth partners may be afraid that sex at this point in the pregnancy might harm the mother or the baby. Worries about labor and birth become very real and very intense for mothers and their partners; women may worry that they will not be able to tolerate the pain or that they will appear foolish, and the birth partners may worry that they will not be able to meet their partners' physical and emotional needs during the birth process. It is not uncommon for birth partners to worry that the mother will turn to someone else for support; they worry that they will be inadequate. Sometimes, a woman may feel that the baby is taking over not only her body, but her entire being. Sometimes, a birth partner feels that she is no longer interested in him or her, and that she will turn all of her attention to the baby.

Phase 3: Transition (8 to 10 Centimeters)

With contractions occurring every two to three minutes and lasting from 60 to 90 seconds, **transition** presents the most physically and emotionally challenging phase of childbearing. The mother becomes irritable, hypersensitive, and emotionally overwrought. She may panic, be unpredictable, lose any hint of inhibition, and her needs may change quite suddenly. Many women feel terribly out of control during transition and need tremendous emotional and physical support from their birth partner. As the mother's focus continues to turn inward, she may become unaware of her surroundings. The descent of the baby causes severe lower backache, and the mother often has a strong, irresistible urge to bear down or move her bowels. Many women experience "the shakes," become flushed, and feel sleepy. The good news is that this phase only lasts from about five to 25 contractions.

Phase 4: Pushing and Delivery

Although the journey through the vagina is only about 5 inches, it may take a first-time mother approximately two hours to push her baby out. During the uterine contraction, as the mother is bearing down, the force of the contraction holds the baby down on the mother's perineum, helping it to stretch. As the intensity of the contraction lessens, the baby retreats upwards. The mother may feel overwhelmed with the sensations she is feeling in her body (bursting or a splitting sensation with the baby's descent), but once pushing efforts become coordinated, most women feel as though they are now active participants in the birth, rather than engaging in an act of passive surrender to the contractions. When the baby's head *crowns* or is visible, the baby will no longer retract after a contraction. The second stage of labor ends with the delivery of the baby.

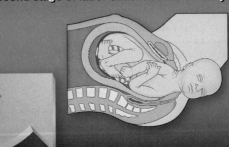

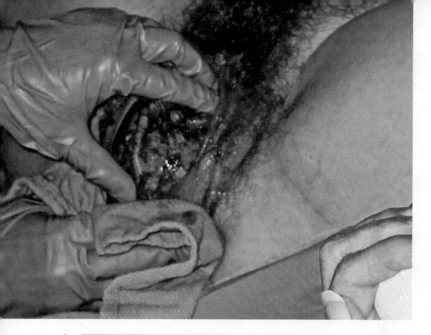

>
> Once the baby's head crowns, **the baby**
> **will no longer retract after a contraction.**

Finally, the fibrous muscle layers of the uterus begin to tighten. Initially uncoordinated, these rhythmic uterine contractions become longer in duration, stronger in intensity, and closer together. This signifies that labor has begun and soon birth will occur.

LABOR AND BIRTH

Several theories exist that explain what may trigger the onset of **labor** (see Figure 12.4), the rhythmic uterine contractions that help expel the baby, but no one knows for certain why a woman enters labor when she does. Does the fetus somehow transmit a hormonal signal that it is ready for birth? Does the placenta emit a signal that it can no longer sustain the growing baby? Does the pituitary gland play the central role? What medical science does tell us is that the body produces chemicals called **prostaglandins** (usually at the end of pregnancy) that aid in the softening of the cervix (Marieb & Hoehn, 2010). Although the exact reason may remain a mystery in medical science, a woman's body does provide clues that the birth of her child is approaching.

UNDERSTANDING LABOR

The question students always have is, "How will I know when labor is really real?" With true labor, the contractions always become longer, stronger, and closer together; with "false" or practice labor, the frequency and intensity of contractions don't noticeably change. Labor is divided into four stages, and each stage has one or more phases.

Stage 1: Labor

The cervix **effaces** (becomes thinner) and it **dilates** (opens). Before a woman can begin to push, the cervix must dilate to an opening of 10 centimeters, or about 4 inches. Typically about the thickness of the space between your eyebrows, and about as firm as the tip of your nose, the cervix thins to about the thickness of the small piece of skin between your thumb and forefinger; by the time the baby is born, it is as soft as the inside of your cheek. This stage is divided into three phases: *early* (0 to 3 centimeters), *active* (4 to 7 centimeters), and *transition* (8 to 10 centimeters). In early labor, contractions may be as far as 20 minutes apart and last for just a few seconds; by the transition stage, contractions occur as frequently as every 90 seconds to two minutes, and last for as long as 90 seconds. In early labor, the uterus is about as hard as the tip of your nose; in active labor, it becomes as hard as your chin; by transition, it feels as hard as your forehead. Stage 1 is complete when a woman is dilated to 10 centimeters; at this time, she begins to push.

Stage 2: Pushing and Delivery

Although the journey through the vagina is only about 5 inches, it may take a first-time mother approximately two hours to push her baby out. During the uterine contraction, as the mother is bearing down, the force of the contraction holds the baby down on the mother's perineum, helping it to stretch. As the intensity of the contraction lessens, the baby retreats upward. The mother may feel overwhelmed with the sensations she is feeling in her body (bursting or a splitting sensation with the baby's descent), but once pushing efforts become coordinated, most women feel as though they are now active participants in the birth, rather than engaging in an act of passive surrender to the contractions. When the baby's head **crowns** or is visible, the baby will no longer retract after a contraction. The second stage of labor ends with the delivery of the baby. Some physicians perform episiotomies to hasten delivery. The **episiotomy** (see Figure 12.5) is a surgical cut made in the perineum. This is one of the most hotly debated practices in obstetrics. Widely and routinely practiced, the episiotomy is touted to speed delivery and thereby lessen the chance of decreased oxygen to the baby. They are also performed to avoid tears into the rectum that may occur during delivery. The most often cited reason for the use of episiotomy is that a clean, surgical cut is more easily repaired than a jagged tear, implying that all women tear during the second stage. Research, however, consistently indicates this is not the case (Gass, Dunn, & Stys, 1986; Hofmeyr & Sonnedecker, 1987; Thacker & Banta, 1983; Thorp & Bowes, 1989).

Stage 3: Delivery of the Placenta

The birth of the placenta usually occurs within five to 30 minutes after the delivery of the baby. Immediately after the baby's birth, the placenta begins to separate from the uterine wall. Some health care providers let the placenta deliver on its own timetable; others give the umbilical cord a tug to expedite the process. To aid expulsion of the placenta (and to

OWN IT! Too Posh to Push?

Scheduled, elective cesarean section births are becoming a growing trend among both celebrities and mainstream moms. The reasons are many, but they range from picking their optimum date of delivery, to avoiding labor altogether, to giving birth as much as a month early to avoid getting stretch marks.

1. Should a woman have the right to determine the date of her baby's birth? Why or why not?

2. What potential dangers could be posed if the baby is delivered as much as a month early?

3. If given the choice, would you have a C-section to avoid labor? Why or why not?

Figure 12.5 The episiotomy is a surgical cut made in the perineum.

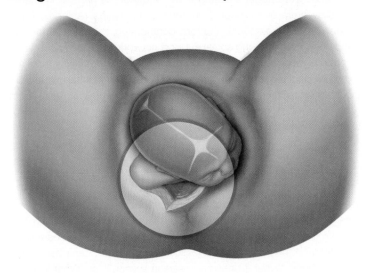

help minimize the risk of postpartum bleeding), women are encouraged to breastfeed as soon as possible.

Stage 4: Recovery

This stage is probably the least mentioned process of labor and birth, but is by no means less important. This stage encompasses the first two to three hours after birth through the first 24 months after labor and delivery. Because of the tremendous fluctuations that a woman's hormones undergo during the nine months of pregnancy, labor, and birth, it takes time for her body to return to its pre-pregnancy state. During this time, new mothers may experience **postpartum depression** due to hormonal fluctuations after giving birth, which may include a loss of appetite, crying spells, feelings of helplessness and hopelessness, inability to sleep, or fear of going near the baby. Any or all of these symptoms signify the immediate need to contact the health care provider.

Although the hours of labor are challenging, many couples experience great closeness and intimacy as they work together to bring their child into the world.

SEXUAL AND RELATIONSHIP LIFE AFTER CHILDBIRTH

As a childbirth educator, perhaps one of the most common questions I have been asked is, "How soon after childbirth can we have sex?"

SEXUAL LIFE AFTER GIVING BIRTH

According to the American College of Obstetrics and Gynecology (ACOG, (2009)), couples are encouraged to wait for six weeks before resuming intercourse. This waiting period allows episiotomies and vaginal tears time to heal, and it also allows time for the cervix to close and regain its barrier to infection. All women have a vaginal discharge made up of mucus, blood, and bits of tissue from the uterine lining from the site where the placenta was attached. This is referred to as **lochia**, and this discharge lasts nearly six weeks. A general rule of thumb is to wait to resume sexual intercourse until after the initial postpartum checkup; at this point, couples can also discuss birth control options available to them. Nevertheless, most couples resume sexual activity when they feel comfortable doing so.

Healthy Selves / Healthy Sex

The Breast Is Best: The Benefits of Breastfeeding

Without proper nutrition, babies cannot thrive and reach their physical and cognitive potentials (Gregory, 2005). In the 1950s, women were encouraged to bottle-feed formula to their babies because at the time it was thought that breastfeeding was obsolete (Feldman, 2010). But today, breastfeeding is considered an important health choice because there are many benefits of breast milk for babies and for moms (American Academy of Pediatrics, 2005):

- Breast milk contains hormones and disease-fighting antibodies that protect infants from germs, illness, and sudden infant death syndrome (also known as *crib death*).

- Breast milk changes over time to meet a baby's needs. It has balanced amounts of fat, sugar, water, and protein required for the baby's growth.

- In infants, breastfeeding is linked to a lower risk of ear infections, allergies, stomach viruses, respiratory infections, asthma, childhood obesity, Type 1 and Type 2 diabetes, and childhood leukemia.

- Breastfed babies have higher levels of adult intelligence than bottle-fed babies (Der, Batty, & Deary, 2006).

- In moms, breastfeeding is linked to lower risks of Type 2 diabetes, breast cancer, ovarian cancer, and postpartum depression.

Although a woman may not always successfully breastfeed her baby (due to health problems, such as HIV/AIDS or anatomical problems with her breasts), most of the time breastfeeding works as nature intended. Women should keep in mind that breastfeeding is a learned technique and is not something that immediately "clicks," both she and the baby learn from each other what works best for them. But the research continues to be clear: *Breast is best!*

Sources: American Academy of Pediatrics. (2005). Breastfeeding and the use of human milk: Policy statement. *Pediatrics, 115,* 496–506; Gregory, K. (2005). Update on nutrition for preterm and full-term infants. *Journal of Obstetrics and Gynecological Neonatal Nursing, 34,* 98–108; Feldman, R. K. (2010). *Discovering the life span* (3rd ed.). Boston: Pearson Education.

A recent study indicates that most couples resume sexual activity within six weeks of delivery, although women may not experience an orgasm until about three months after delivery (Connolly, Thorp, & Pahel, 2005). As one body of research confirmed, if both partners enjoy a rich sex life throughout pregnancy, they tend to evaluate their levels of tenderness and communication higher in the first six months after delivery (von Sydow, 1999).

Couples' sex lives typically undergo change after they become parents. In particular, sexual desire appears to be lower for mothers than it is for fathers in the first year after giving birth (Ahlborg, Dahlof, & Strandmark, 2000; Ahlborg, Lars-Gosta, & Hallberg, 2005). Apart from lower sexual desire, there are also physical changes in the experience of sex after childbirth. A study that examined 480 postpartum women found among new mothers that more than 50 percent experienced pain during first intercourse after delivery; this pain continued somewhat for six months (Barrett et al., 2000). A more recent study examined more than 500 women and their partners to evaluate which factors determined sexual activity and sexual relationship satisfaction one year after a first birth (Brummen et al., 2006). By three months after the birth of their babies, more than 80 percent of couples had had sex; by one year after birth, about 94 percent had. The most significant finding was that there was a predictive factor for no sexual intercourse one year following birth, women who were not sexually active when they were three months pregnant had an 11 times higher chance of not being sexually active one year after giving birth (Brummen et al., 2006).

RELATIONSHIP LIFE AFTER GIVING BIRTH

These changes, in turn, cause stress and tension between the couple and compound the transition to assume the new roles of parents. Two different Dutch studies of women and their partners through pregnancy and into the early months of parenthood found that problems don't just suddenly appear after the birth of a child; rather, marital and sexual dissatisfaction were present during pregnancy (Kluwer & Johnson, 2007; Salmela-Aro et al., 2006).

If new parents are able to communicate openly about their sexual desires and the stressors associated with becoming parents, and if they validate each other emotionally and sexually, they experience better adjustment—and have more sex (Ahlborg, Dahlof, &

Strandmark, 2000; Ahlborg, Lars-Gosta, & Hallberg, 2005). For example, a study of 820 postpartum couples found that by the time the babies were about six months old, most of the parents indicated that they were "very happy" in their relationships (Ahlborg, Lars-Gosta, & Hallberg, 2005). Factors contributing to their relationship happiness were a strong social support network and having someone to provide relief so the couple could spend some time away from the baby. Among those who indicated that they were unhappy, factors included economic problems, having a partner who was away from home too much, and frustration with the partner's lack of help or sharing responsibility.

UNEXPECTED OUTCOMES

In the many years that I taught childbirth education classes, expectant parents commonly expressed fears and worries about the health and well-being of their babies. It is common for most soon-to-be parents to think through the list of "what ifs," such as, "What if I can't handle the pain of labor?" "What if I need a cesarean section?" or "What if something is wrong with the baby?"

CESAREAN SECTIONS

A **cesarean section (C-section)** is a surgical incision that is made through the abdomen and the uterus to deliver the fetus. In 1970, the percentage of women who gave birth by cesarean section was 5.5 percent (Centers for Disease Control and Prevention, 2005). Today, nearly one-third (31.8 percent) of all children in the United States are born by cesarean section (Centers for Disease Control and Prevention, 2008). As Figure 12.6 shows us, this rate has climbed by more than 50 percent in the last 10 years.

How high a cesarean section rate is too high? The World Health Organization (WHO) noted, "There is no justification for any region to have a rate higher than 10–15 percent" (WHO, 1985). Although the rate of births by cesarean section is on the increase, and all may not be medically necessary, there are medical indications for the procedure; these are presented in Table 12.5.

As in all areas of health care, it is essential that childbearing women and their partners take a proactive stance in every aspect of prenatal care, from routine monthly doctor visits through the labor and birth process. Holistic childbirth educators recognize that birth is not just a physical event, but a social, emotional, and spiritual event as well.

To avoid unnecessary medical interventions, it is imperative that pregnant women and their partners know their rights, which are presented in

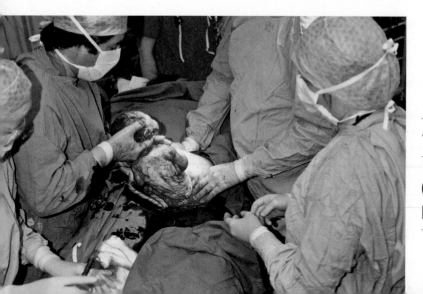

<<< Nearly one-third of all children in the United States are **born by cesarean section (Centers for Disease Control and Prevention, 2008).**

Figure 12.6 Cesarean Section Rates Since 1989

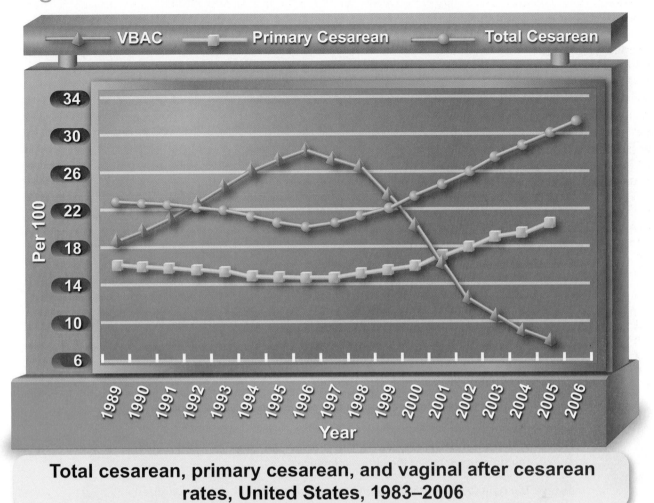

Total cesarean, primary cesarean, and vaginal after cesarean rates, United States, 1983–2006

Source: U.S. National Center for Health Statistics (2008). Birth data. www.cdc.gov/nchs/births.htm

Table 12.5
Medical Reasons for Cesarean Births

Although the rate of births by cesarean section is on the increase, and although all may not be medically necessary, there are medical indications for the procedure:

- *Cephalopelvic disproportion (CPD).* This condition occurs when the size, shape, or position of the baby's head prevents it from passing through the mother's pelvis.

- *Breech presentation.* This refers to when the part nearest the cervical opening is the buttocks, feet, or knees instead of the head.

- *Abrupted placenta.* This condition occurs when the placenta partially or completely prematurely separates from the uterine lining.

- *Placenta previa.* This occurs when the placenta is abnormally implanted low in the uterus and completely or partially blocks the cervical opening, rather than implanted in the upper quadrant.

- *Prolapsed cord.* This occurs when the umbilical cord comes ahead of the baby.

- *Maternal disease.* They include high blood pressure, diabetes, STIs, HIV/AIDS, and heart disease. In some cases, such as with high blood pressure or diabetes, the cesarean section is performed if a vaginal delivery is considered too dangerous for the mother. If the mother has an STI or HIV/AIDS, a cesarean section is performed to prevent the transmission of the infection to the unborn baby during the birth process.

- *Fetal distress.* This occurs when there are decelerations in the fetal heart tones due to decreased oxygen supply to the baby.

Figure 12.7 Pregnant Patient's Bill of Rights

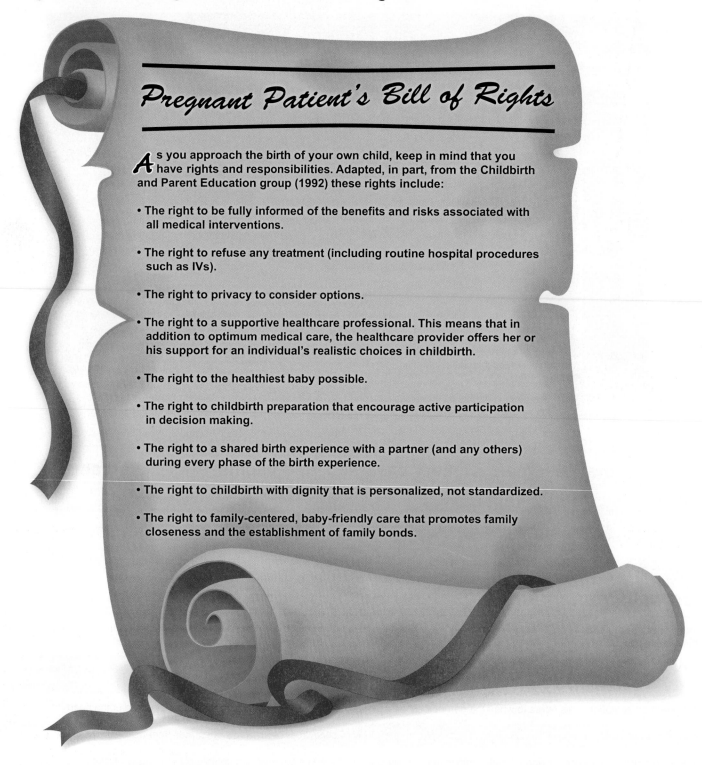

Pregnant Patient's Bill of Rights

As you approach the birth of your own child, keep in mind that you have rights and responsibilities. Adapted, in part, from the Childbirth and Parent Education group (1992) these rights include:

- The right to be fully informed of the benefits and risks associated with all medical interventions.

- The right to refuse any treatment (including routine hospital procedures such as IVs).

- The right to privacy to consider options.

- The right to a supportive healthcare professional. This means that in addition to optimum medical care, the healthcare provider offers her or his support for an individual's realistic choices in childbirth.

- The right to the healthiest baby possible.

- The right to childbirth preparation that encourage active participation in decision making.

- The right to a shared birth experience with a partner (and any others) during every phase of the birth experience.

- The right to childbirth with dignity that is personalized, not standardized.

- The right to family-centered, baby-friendly care that promotes family closeness and the establishment of family bonds.

Figure 12.7. When interventions (such as a cesarean birth) are suggested, pregnant women and their partners should ask (Haire, 1977):

- *Why* do I need it?

- *How* will it help my baby and me?

- *What* are the side effects or risks?

- What could be done *instead*?

- What will happen if I *don't* have it?

Childbirth preparation classes help mothers and their partners not only know what to expect during the birth process, but also understand the available options. If a childbearing woman doesn't know her options, she doesn't have any.

THE PHYSICALLY CHALLENGED BABY

Although we all long for a healthy baby, not all of us will have the perfect "Gerber" baby. Birth defects and anomalies can range from barely noticeable to life-threatening to fatal. No matter how severe the defect,

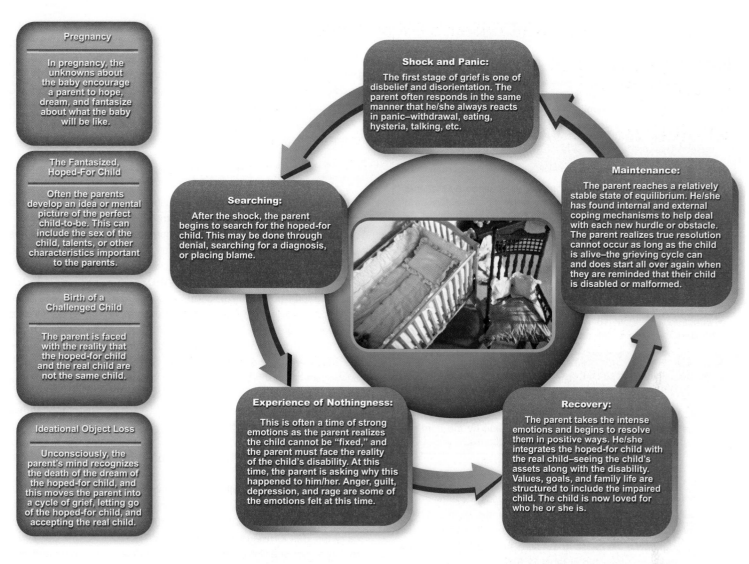

Pregnancy

In pregnancy, the unknowns about the baby encourage a parent to hope, dream, and fantasize about what the baby will be like.

The Fantasized, Hoped-For Child

Often the parents develop an idea or mental picture of the perfect child-to-be. This can include the sex of the child, talents, or other characteristics important to the parents.

Birth of a Challenged Child

The parent is faced with the reality that the hoped-for child and the real child are not the same child.

Ideational Object Loss

Unconsciously, the parent's mind recognizes the death of the dream of the hoped-for child, and this moves the parent into a cycle of grief, letting go of the hoped-for child, and accepting the real child.

Shock and Panic:
The first stage of grief is one of disbelief and disorientation. The parent often responds in the same manner that he/she always reacts in panic—withdrawal, eating, hysteria, talking, etc.

Searching:
After the shock, the parent begins to search for the hoped-for child. This may be done through denial, searching for a diagnosis, or placing blame.

Maintenance:
The parent reaches a relatively stable state of equilibrium. He/she has found internal and external coping mechanisms to help deal with each new hurdle or obstacle. The parent realizes true resolution cannot occur as long as the child is alive—the grieving cycle can and does start all over again when they are reminded that their child is disabled or malformed.

Experience of Nothingness:
This is often a time of strong emotions as the parent realizes the child cannot be "fixed," and the parent must face the reality of the child's disability. At this time, the parent is asking why this happened to him/her. Anger, guilt, depression, and rage are some of the emotions felt at this time.

Recovery:
The parent takes the intense emotions and begins to resolve them in positive ways. He/she integrates the hoped-for child with the real child—seeing the child's assets along with the disability. Values, goals, and family life are structured to include the impaired child. The child is now loved for who he or she is.

Figure 12.8 Loss and Grief Cycle for Parents of Physically Challenged Children
When parents lose a child to death, or when they have a baby born with birth defects they experience a cycle of grief and loss.

parents of infants with birth defects and physically challenged babies mourn the loss of the healthy child they imagined they'd deliver. The *loss and grief cycle* (see Figure 12.8) shows us common patterns of grief that parents of physically challenged babies experience (Figard & Figard, 1992). As you can see, the grief isn't a one-time event, but instead is something that is experienced, at varying levels, throughout the life of the child.

PREGNANCY LOSS

Many pregnancies proceed without many complications, but the most common loss in the first month of pregnancy is miscarriage. Any loss of a fetus or embryo before the 20th week of pregnancy is termed a **spontaneous abortion**, or **miscarriage** (Marieb & Hoehn, 2007). *Early miscarriage* occurs with the loss of a fetus before the 12th week of pregnancy; *late miscarriage* occurs with the loss of a fetus between the 12th and 20th weeks of pregnancy. Approximately 20 percent to 30 percent of pregnant women experience some type of bleeding or cramping during the first 20 weeks of pregnancy; of those, about half

of the pregnancies result in pregnancy loss (Porter et al., 2008). About 85 percent of all miscarriages take place before the first 12 weeks of pregnancy; these pregnancy losses usually take place because of abnormalities in the embryo or fetus. In two-thirds of these miscarriages, the pregnancy loss can be linked to the mother's health or lifestyle, and in one-third, no cause is known (Porter et al., 2008). Known causes of miscarriage include abnormalities in the embryo or fetus resulting from illnesses or disorders such as diabetes, infections, injury, hypothyroidism, or from lifestyle choices such as using cocaine, especially crack (Merck Medical Manual, 2003).

STILLBIRTH

Stillbirth is a tragic and heart-wrenching loss. Even though society at large may not recognize the emotional and physical impact of any pregnancy loss, the impact on the parents is life altering. **Stillbirth** refers to the death of a fetus after the 20th week of pregnancy and occurs in approximately one in every 160 (ACOG, 2009). Only about 14 percent of the fetuses die during the labor and birth process; the remaining die

TABLE 12.6
Known Causes of Stillbirth

There are a number of known causes of stillbirth. Sometimes, more than one of these causes contributes to the baby's death.

- *Birth defects.* About 15 to 20 percent have one or more birth defects due to chromosomal disorders or environmental causes (such as the effects of teratogens).

- *Placenta problems.* About 25 percent are caused by *placental abruption*, where the placenta peels partly or completely away from the uterus. This results in heavy bleeding; the baby will die from lack of oxygen.

- *Poor fetal growth.* About 40 percent have poor growth patterns in the womb and are too small to survive within the womb. Women who smoke and/or have high blood pressure are at increased risk for stillbirth.

- *Infections.* In about 10 to 25 percent, infections involving the mother, the fetus, or the placenta cause fetal death.

- *Chronic health conditions.* About 10 percent are related to chronic health conditions of the mother, such as high blood pressure, diabetes, and kidney disease.

- *Umbilical cord accidents.* Knots in the cord, abnormal placement of the cord into the placenta, or strangulation by the cord are rare, occurring in about 2 to 4 percent of stillbirths.

before labor has begun (ACOG, 2009). In developing countries or less economically advantaged countries, the stillbirth rates are much higher, because medical care is not as readily available. In up to half of all cases, tests cannot determine the cause of the stillbirth (Reddy, 2007). Known causes of stillbirth are presented in Table 12.6.

The loss of an embryo or fetus at any stage in the pregnancy is devastating. A stillbirth is particularly crushing, however, because most often women have experienced fetal movement, and many women indicate the emotional and physical bond with the baby intensifies once fetal movement takes place. Women are keenly aware of every flutter, poke, kick, and jab the baby makes, and when the fetal movement stops, the mother becomes aware that something is wrong. When a mother reports the cessation of movement to her physician, an ultrasound is performed to detect cardiac movement, or a heartbeat. If there is no cardiac movement, the baby is no longer alive.

Some women will choose to carry the baby and let labor begin naturally; most prefer to have labor *induced*, or started by artificial methods. Although at first glance it may seem cruel to allow a woman to endure the pain of labor to deliver a stillborn baby, it is essential for the woman to preserve her capacity for future childbearing and to minimize any possible complications (ACOG, 2009). The other alternative is to have the fetus delivered by cesarean birth. As with any surgical procedure, a cesarean birth carries with it added risk to the mother's health such as complications from the anesthesia, postoperative infection, and permanent scar tissue that forms near her reproductive organs. Even though cesarean birth rates are soaring, vaginal birth is still the safest method of delivery with the shortest and least painful physical recovery.

Many women find the labor and birth experiences of stillborns to be rewarding and satisfying. Despite the fact that the woman and her partner did not receive the outcome they had hoped for, the birth

process is a time of quiet reflection and recognition that the baby was, is, and will always be a significant part of their lives and in the lives of their family. Although it may seem morbid, after the birth of the baby, physicians encourage parents and family to hold, bathe, dress, cuddle, and sing to their infant to bond with the baby. Parents and families of stillborn babies are typically given several hours to bond with the baby because this bonding experience is crucial in their grieving and mourning.

NEONATAL DEATH

Premature birth (before 37 weeks gestation) is a cause or contributor to neonatal death, accounting for approximately 20 percent of all neonatal deaths (March of Dimes, 2009). As you learned earlier in this chapter, the earlier a baby is born, the greater difficulty he or she will have surviving because the baby's organs (particularly the lungs) are not yet fully developed. **Respiratory distress syndrome (RDS)**, a lung disease caused by immature lung development, claims about 1,200 babies a year in the United States (March of Dimes, 2009). Furthermore, babies born before 30 weeks also have a high risk of developing brain bleeds, which can result in death or permanent damage. For example, babies born before the 23rd week have a 90 percent to 95 percent death rate; only about 50 percent of babies born at 24 weeks will survive, and 80 percent of babies born at 26 weeks survive (March of Dimes, 2009).

When a baby dies within the first 28 days of life, **neonatal death** is said to occur. The most common cause of neonatal death is birth defects (March of Dimes, 2009), accounting for approximately 25 percent of neonatal deaths in the United States. About one in every 125 babies is born with a heart defect.

In instances of stillbirth and neonatal death, greeting the baby also means saying goodbye. Although parting with anyone we love is devastating, parents who suffer the prenatal or postnatal loss of a baby carry the loss for the rest of their lives. Whether or not the baby ever took a breath, the life had meaning and significance to the parents and their families. The intense, overwhelming feelings of grief are simply an affirmation that the baby's life was real. Moving through the grief and mourning to a place of healing takes time. Sometimes, outside resources are necessary to help parents cope with their devastating loss. In time, the loss is integrated into their marriages, their relationships, and their lives.

Unexpected outcomes are just that—something we do not anticipate. When preparing for the birth of a baby, I strongly encourage you to make your own "what if" list. Although we certainly cannot anticipate every possible result associated with pregnancy and childbirth, coming to terms with the fact that sometimes the pregnancy and childbirth experience doesn't yield our desired outcomes is an essential and necessary step in becoming a parent.

SEXUAL LIFE EDUCATION

When I practiced as a doula, I was in a sense a "protector" of the birth memory. I wasn't there to make decisions; I was there to be a voice for the laboring woman and her partner. But as with any other aspect of personal health and well-being, the pregnant woman and her partner need to have a fundamental knowledge of pregnancy, labor, and birth so they can work in partnership with their health care team. Knowing, understanding, and accepting the rights and responsibilities as a pregnant woman/partner sets the stage for a family-centered birth experience that provides a sense of satisfaction and achievement.

My List of "What Ifs"

When preparing for childbirth, most books and childbirth preparation classes skim over or ignore altogether the possibility that things won't go perfectly in birth. Take time to reflect on the following.

What if I find out I'm pregnant and I'm not ready to be a parent? _____
_____.

What if my partner isn't ready to be a parent? _____
_____.

The things that most excite me about pregnancy are _____
_____.

The things that most frighten me about pregnancy are _____
_____.

My vision of an ideal birth is _____.

If I want a nonmedicated birth and have to use pain medications, I would feel _____
_____.

If I discover that I am infertile, I would _____
_____.

I do/do not want to breastfeed. If I felt pressure that goes against my beliefs, I would_____
_____.

If for some reason I couldn't breastfeed, I would feel _____. This is because _____
_____.

If my baby were stillborn, I would/would not want to see or hold him/her. I feel this way because _____
_____.

If my baby were born with birth defects, I would feel _____
_____.

▶▶▶ TAKING SIDES

Childbearing and Intimate Partner Violence

For many women, pregnancy is not a time of joy; in fact, for 324,000 women each year, pregnancy is the most dangerous time of their lives because of the violence they suffer at the hands of their intimate partners. Intimate partner violence includes physical, emotional, and sexual abuse (see Chapter 15). Murder by an intimate partner is the most common cause of death among pregnant women (Family Violence Prevention, 2006).

Her Side: My fiancé is not violent. He's just feeling really insecure about our relationship, worried that the baby is going to take up so much of my time that I won't have anything left for him. He's very moody right now, and he does get in my face and yell a lot, but that's my fault; I'm so moody and teary right now because of all these hormones, and he doesn't know how to react to that. He has pushed me a couple of times, and he has hit me, but that was only one time. He was never like this before I got pregnant, so I'm sure this is all just temporary. Once the baby gets here, he'll be fine.

His Side: This is not my fault! I may have pushed her around a couple of times, but it's only because I was drunk. I won't go so far as to say she deserved it, but she did keep the fight going until I just lost it. I don't see what the big deal is.

Your Side: There are signs that intimate partner violence is taking place in this couple's relationship, although some of them might be subtle.

1. What are the signs of intimate partner violence?

2. If you were this woman's health care provider, what would you recommend she do?

3. Why do you believe that pregnancy is such a dangerous time for women? Why does violence escalate?

Summary

WHO IS HAVING BABIES?   244

• Although teen pregnancies have generally been on a decline since the early '90s, pregnancy among adolescents continues to be a problem in the United States. Pregnancies among unmarried couples are on the rise as are pregnancies among older women. Overall, women in their late 20s represent the age group with the highest birthrate, but delaying childbirth is an increasing trend.

HOW DO WE REPRODUCE AND WHAT CHANGES OCCUR DURING PREGNANCY?   247

• The fertilization of a woman's egg occurs when a man's sperm enters a woman through sexual intercourse. Not all couples are able to reproduce, but there are various forms of infertility treatments available for people who want to get pregnant.

• Everyone is familiar with the growing shape of a woman's pregnant belly, but as a pregnancy proceeds throughout each trimester, changes in the mother's body, the baby, and within the couple's relationship occur, making those nine months an emotional and unique time.

WHAT HAPPENS DURING LABOR AND BIRTH?   254

• When it is time for an expecting mother to have her baby, she will go into labor, experience pushing and delivery, the delivery of the placenta, and recovery. Each of these four stages is made up of multiple stages as well. Giving birth is a life-changing experience and a person's sexual and relationship life will also be affected.

WHAT ARE SOME UNEXPECTED OUTCOMES AND HOW DO PEOPLE DEAL WITH THEM?   256

• Even though expecting parents will be hoping for a normal delivery without complications, sometimes medical reasons make it necessary for the mother to undergo a cesarean section, whereby a baby is delivered through a surgical incision made in the abdomen.

• There are a number of reasons a woman may not deliver a healthy baby. Genetic and environmental factors can result in a physically challenged baby. Miscarriages and stillbirth are other unexpected outcomes that can be a part of pregnancy. Once the baby is born, if he or she dies within the first month, it is considered a neonatal death.

Key Terms

doula a professional provider of labor support to women and their companions *244*

crude birth rate the number of childbirths per 1,000 women per year *244*

fertility rate the average number of live births per woman in a given population per year *244*

germinal period period that begins with the fusion of the sperm and the ovum and ends after the fertilized ovum has been successfully implanted in the uterus *247*

conceptus the fertilized ovum *247*

blastocyst the ball of cells that develop after a 5- to 7-inch journey that takes approximately 10 to 14 days *247*

conception part of prenatal development that ends after the ovum is fertilized, develops into a blastocyst, and implants in the endometrium *247*

sterility the absolute inability to reproduce *247*

infertility the inability to conceive a baby after trying for a period of one year *247*

pelvic inflammatory disease (PID) disorder primarily caused by untreated sexually transmitted infections that renders 150,000 women per year infertile *247*

endometriosis a disease characterized by the buildup or migration of uterine tissue to other parts of the body, such as the ovaries or fallopian tubes *247*

azoospermia primary form of infertility in men in which no sperm cells are produced *247*

oligospermia primary form of infertility in men in which few sperm cells are produced *247*

artificial insemination fertility treatment in which donor sperm is placed into the woman's vagina, cervix, or uterus by a syringe *247*

sperm banks medical facilities for the purpose of collecting sperm *247*

assisted reproductive technology (ART) treatment options that involve fertilization through the hands-on manipulation of the ova and sperm *248*

in vitro fertilization (IVF) process whereby a woman's eggs are surgically removed from her ovary and mixed with a man's sperm in a laboratory culture dish, examined for fertilization, and then replaced in the uterus *248*

gamete intrafallopian transfer (GIFT) process by which the unfertilized eggs and the male's sperm are placed in the woman's fallopian tubes *248*

zygote intrafallopian transfer (ZIFT) process by which fertilized eggs are placed immediately in the woman's fallopian tubes, allowing the conceptus to travel naturally to the uterus and implant *248*

surrogate mother woman who is used as a vessel to carry a baby to term for biological parents *248*

placenta part of the life support system between the fetus and the mother; typically attached to the upper portion of the mother's uterus; provides critical functions, such as transporting oxygen between the mother and baby, and passing the mother's immunity to the baby *248*

umbilical cord the fetus' lifeline in which everything travels from the mother to the baby (and vice versa) via the blood in the umbilical cord *248*

amniotic sac a tough membrane within the uterus that holds the fetus, placenta/umbilical cord, and the amniotic fluid *248*

first trimester the first 12 weeks of pregnancy *249*

second trimester weeks 13 through 26 of pregnancy *249*

third trimester weeks 27 through 40 of pregnancy *249*

pre-term describing a baby born before the 37th week of pregnancy *249*

critical period the time when all the baby's anatomical structures and organs are formed and begin to function at a rudimentary level *250*

freebirthing childbirth, or **unassisted childbirth (UC)** the process of intentionally giving birth without the guidance of a medical professional *250*

presumptive signs signs that indicate to a woman that she may be pregnant; cessation of her menstrual cycle, a feeling of fatigue, full breasts due to increased blood supply, and for some, moments of nausea and vomiting *251*

quickening fetal movement, starting in the fourth month of pregnancy *252*

lanugo a soft, downy hair that covers a fetus' body *252*

Braxton-Hicks contractions "practice" contractions that increase in number (and perhaps intensity), but are not actual labor *253*

labor rhythmic uterine contractions that help expel the baby from a mother's uterus *254*

prostaglandins chemicals that aid in the softening of the cervix before labor *254*

efface to become thinner *254*

dilate to open *254*

crown to become visible *254*

episiotomy a surgical cut made in the perineum *254*

postpartum depression hormonal fluctuations after giving birth *255*

lochia vaginal discharge made up of mucus, blood, and bits of tissue from the uterine lining *255*

cesarean section (C-section) surgical incision that is made through the abdomen and the uterus to deliver the fetus *256*

spontaneous abortion, or **miscarriage** the loss of a fetus or embryo before the 20th week of pregnancy *259*

stillbirth the death of a fetus after the 20th week of pregnancy, and occurs in approximately one in every 160 *259*

respiratory distress syndrome (RDS) a lung disease caused by immature lung development *260*

neonatal death when a baby dies within the first 28 days of life *260*

Sample Test Questions

MULTIPLE CHOICE

1. Since the early 1990s, teen birth rates in the United States have generally:
   a. Declined
   b. Increased
   c. Gone up and down
   d. Remained stable

2. Which age group of women has the highest birth rate?
   a. 15–19
   b. 20–24
   c. 25–29
   d. 30–34

3. Which disorder that renders women infertile is primarily caused by untreated STIs?
   a. Endometriosis
   b. Pituitary gland tumor
   c. Gonorrhea
   d. Pelvic inflammatory disease

4. Which infertility treatment involves cultivating embryos in a laboratory culture dish for 40 hours?
   a. Artificial insemination
   b. Gamete intrafallopian transfer
   c. In vitro fertilization
   d. Zygote intrafallopian transfer

5. Freebirth is:
   a. Giving birth without the assistance of a medical professional
   b. Giving birth in a tub of water
   c. Giving birth in a hospital
   d. Giving birth with a midwife in a birthing center

6. Which surgical procedure is performed in order to expedite delivery?
   a. Cesarean section
   b. Artificial insemination
   c. Episiotomy
   d. Surrogacy

7. Which condition occurs when the placenta is abnormally low in the uterus?
   a. Abrupted placenta
   b. Breech presentation
   c. Prolapsed cord
   d. Placenta previa

8. Which cause of stillbirth is the rarest?
   a. Inadequate lubrication
   b. Performance pressure
   c. Hormonal changes
   d. Pelvic surgery

SHORT RESPONSE

1. Explain the difference between sterility and infertility.

2. Describe what an expecting mother experiences in each trimester.

3. Your teenage sister thinks she might be pregnant. What facts and statistics would you tell her to consider?

4. Explain why pregnancy can sometimes have a negative impact on a couple's relationship.

5. Would you consider planning a cesarean section for yourself or for your partner rather than having a vaginal delivery? Why or why not?

Answers: 1. a; 2. c; 3. d; 4. c; 5. a; 6. c; 7. d; 8. c

Remember to check www.thethinkspot.com **for additional information, downloadable flashcards, and other helpful resources.**

BOSTON HERALD

Sterilized for Being Poor?

By CONSTANTINO DIAZ-DURAN

Published: January 3, 2010

When a Welfare-collecting mother of nine was allegedly sterilized against her will, she was shocked by the outpouring of public support—for the doctors who did it.

When Tessa Savicki checked into Baystate Medical Center on December 18, 2006, for a Caesarean section, she didn't know it was the last baby she would ever give birth to. Lying in the O.R. with her daughter at her side, the morning after she had delivered a healthy baby boy, she claims she overheard her surgeons make two cryptic remarks. "I heard the doctor on the left side say 'left one's done,'" she says, "then the doctor on the right side says, 'right one's done.' I just looked at my daughter because, honestly, I didn't know what they were talking about."

What she now thinks they were talking about was a tubal ligation. When Savicki's C-section was over, instead of being fitted for the IUD she says she had asked for, her doctors tied her tubes, leaving her sterile for life. She is now suing the attending physicians and the Springfield, Massachusetts, hospital, which told her last May that it cannot find any consent form for the sterilization procedure.

She filed her lawsuit on December 15.

"How long before we are paying for all her babies' kids?" asked one commenter. "Sterilize the whole family—I'll pay."

"Honestly, it's so hard to even explain how you feel," she says, referring to the moment the nurse told her what happened. "You are shocked, you're upset, you're disgusted."

But Savicki isn't the only one who's disgusted. When her story was recounted in the Boston Herald last week, the public response to her plight was immediate and vicious. That's because Savicki is an unmarried mother of nine who collects Welfare from the state. The two stories about the incident on BostonHerald.com have generated more than 1,000 comments each, the vast majority of them hostile toward Savicki. "Those doctors were true heroes. I knew she was a state-checkcollecting waste of space," reads one. "How long before we are paying for all her babies' kids?" asks another. "Sterilize the whole family—I'll pay." And: "We should sterile [sic] all the people on Public assistance for more than 2 yrs."

"It's been nasty," says Savicki, who's received dozens of angry texts and Facebook messages from strangers since the story broke. "I've been called a slut, a whore—they say I'm pathetic." She says they've even gone after her children. "They're saying my kids are crumb munchers, that they are bastards, that they should sterilize my kids so they don't pay for my grandchildren."

With millions relying on government assistance, Savicki is being portrayed as a "Welfare queen" for the new decade, the public face of that alleged army of women who mooch off the state and pop out babies with impunity. Such stories helped turn the tide of public opinion against federal Welfare in the 1990s, putting an end to the system that had been in place since the Depression, in which the poor were given federal benefits—for life, if need be—without regard to personal circumstances.

But Savicki says she's not the woman she's being accused of. "People are under the impression that I had nine kids with nine different daddies," she says, "and that is not true. I had four kids with my previous partner. He passed away in May, of cancer, and that man worked until the week he died, paying child support and taking care of his kids." As for her current partner, Angel Flores Tirado, she says

---

Forced sterilization is the process of permanently ending someone's ability to reproduce through surgical techniques without their consent. This occurs around the world, including in the U.S. In other parts of the world, the practice is done for population control.

A **tubal ligation** is a surgical procedure that requires anesthesia. In this process, the woman's fallopian tubes are cut or fused, permanently disrupting the sperm's pathway to the egg, making fertilization impossible. The **IUD** is a device placed inside the woman's uterus. A health care provider can do this procedure in a clinic. It does not require surgery or anesthesia (and therefore carries less risks), and can be easily removed if a woman wishes to become pregnant.

In the United States, every medical procedure requires the patient to give informed consent. **Informed consent** means that a patient agrees to undergo a medical or surgical treatment or to participate in an experiment after all of the risks involved are explained. By signing this consent form, patients not only acknowledge that they agree to the procedure, they also acknowledge that the risks were explained, and they accept this. Informed consent protects both the health care provider and the patient.

they've been together for 10 years and have three children. According to Savicki, "Angel has a full-time job. He works day and night, and he supports his kids." She says Tirado "wanted another boy, and that's gone. I can't." Now she worries he'll leave her because she can't bear more children. "I mean, that could actually mess up things, because if it gets to the point where he really wants it—which he better not, because he better love me to stay with me—it could jeopardize my relationship."

But all this self-defense is academic, says Savicki's lawyer, Max Borten, a former obstetrician. "The real issue here," he says, "is who has the right to determine who gets sterilization. The patient? The doctor? A hospital committee? A state committee?" The obvious answer, says Professor Linda Fentiman of Pace University School of Law, is the patient. Fentiman says federal law requires written consent, signed 30 days prior to the procedure—a waiting period put in place in the 1970s because of so-called Mississippi Appendectomies, the involuntary sterilizations imposed mainly upon poor, black women in the early- and mid-20th century.

Despite these safeguards, compulsory sterilization isn't a thing of the distant past. Though it's technically illegal, the state of Oregon sterilized wayward teenage girls as recently as 1981. Three years ago, California proposed elective sterilization for women who gave birth in state prisons—which, considering these women's disempowered position, was widely seen as not really "elective" at all. And

last year, Nadya "Octomom" Suleman's story sparked an onslaught of earnest demands for her to be forcibly sterilized. Could popular support for compulsory sterilization make a comeback?

Louisiana state Rep. John LaBruzzo raised eyebrows last year when he presented a plan to offer women who are on Welfare $1,000 to have their tubes tied. Giving the idea more than a whiff of *Bell Curve* mentality, however, was the fact that his proposal included tax incentives for people with college degrees and higher incomes to have more kids. LaBruzzo's office did not return a call for comment.

Professor Fentiman says there is probably nothing inherently unconstitutional about LaBruzzo's plan, but she says she believes it is a reflection of what she calls a "closet eugenics feeling in the United States." She points out that "the fact that [Savicki] is poor and living on state assistance raises a lot of issues for some who think poor people shouldn't have the same rights to reproduce as everybody else." Borten, who has received his share of hate mail stemming from the Herald articles, agrees. "When you read the comments and the attacks on her and on me," he says, "it just blows your mind, because you see how ingrained the bigotry is against poor people." Borten is careful not to accuse Savicki's doctors of tying her tubes for ideological reasons, and a spokeswoman for the hospital refused to comment on the matter.

Fentiman also points to an apparent paradox in what she

believes is the ideology of those who are attacking Savicki. "I think it is ironic," she says, "that, I would guess, many of the people who would be for compulsory sterilization would also be those who are fervently—what they call themselves—pro-life. But what ties it together, I think, is the lack of respect for women's reproductive autonomy." Fentiman sees this disdain for women's rights as pervasive in medicine. "The history of the medical profession and the way it disregards women's rights is quite extraordinary... It's so paternalistic."

Still, Savicki's personal past is a sticking point. She had her first two children while she was still a teenager and never finished high school. (She says she plans to get her GED next month.) And she has a history of litigation—in 2001, she sued CVS for selling her an expired spermicide. Nevertheless, she says she believes that how many children she has is no one's business but hers, and she defends the job she has done as a mother. "I'm trying to teach [my children] the right way to be," she says. "I tell them they need to go out there and get a good education, get a job, take care of their family. I'm trying, and I'm not doing that bad of a job."

When all is said and done, however, what she truly feels is that it's not our place to question how many children she has. "Does it really matter how many kids I have? They sterilized me without my permission, and here in the United States you have your rights," she says. "No one can tell you to do anything."

If someone is a welfare recipient, should there be limits placed on how many children the mother has? Who decides, and how should that decision be made? Do you favor or oppose forced sterilization for welfare moms? If so, what is the "maximum" number of children welfare recipients should be allowed to have?

Eugenics, which means "well born," refers to the practice of or belief in the possibility of improving the qualities of the human race by discouraging reproduction by persons having genetic defects or presumed to have inheritable "undesirable" traits.

Is reproductive freedom a basic human right? Is there any situation in which someone should be permanently sterilized without their permission? How do contemporary issues, such as women who give birth in prison, healthcare reform, illegal immigration, stem cell research, and human cloning factor into your decision?

PREVENTING PREGNANCY:

Contraceptives and Abortion

<<< There are a variety of condoms to choose from.

WHAT ARE THE DIFFERENT WAYS TO PREVENT PREGNANCY AND PROTECT YOUR SEXUAL HEALTH?
WHAT ARE THE PERMANENT CONTRACEPTIVE METHODS?
WHAT OPTIONS ARE THERE WHEN CONTRACEPTION FAILS?

I've known

since about seventh grade that a guy should use a condom every time—but what they don't tell you is where to get them or how embarrassing it is to have to go buy them. I didn't know much about them, and I had no clue who to ask. There's no way I was going to ask my friends about birth control; I could have never lived that down!

I made my way to Wal-Mart at about 11:30 on a weeknight, hoping that no one would be around, and I'd already decided that I was going to go through self-checkout. I found the condom aisle, and just stood there. Who the hell knew there were that many condoms to choose from? I just grabbed the first box I saw and got out of there as fast as I could.

I'm not gonna lie; I practiced putting one on [while I masturbated] probably four or five times before that Friday night. I wish I could say it made it easier to put one on when "the" time came, but it's a lot different putting one on in the backseat of a car with her watching than it is at home! Now, using condoms is pretty much second nature. I still don't like to buy them, though.

Dear Dr. Welch, have you considered putting a jar of free condoms on your desk so students can grab a handful when they come into your office hours? That would make my life a lot less complicated.

Source: Author's files

CHAPTER **13**

PREVENTING PREGNANCY AND PROTECTING YOUR SEXUAL HEALTH

When it comes to having sex, the stakes can be pretty high. The rate of unintended pregnancies in the United States is higher than the world average. Each year, almost one-half of all pregnancies (about 3 million) in the United States are unintended; this rate has not changed since 1994 (Finer & Henshaw, 2006; Trussell et al., 2009). Of these, approximately one-third occur in women between the ages of 18 and 25. Today, half of all sexually active people acquire a sexually transmitted infection (STI) by the age of 25 (Planned Parenthood, 2009).

Everyone has different needs, values, and beliefs, so there are many factors that go into deciding what type of birth control or contraception works best for you. But one factor, *knowledge*, is critically important. Knowing what types of birth control and contraception are available, the benefits and risks associated with each method, and the effectiveness rates help you minimize the risks associated with sexual behaviors. But just as importantly, this knowledge equips you with the tools to make informed decisions and choices, tools to help you protect your sexual health. As with many other areas of sexuality, if you don't know your options, you don't really have any.

In this chapter, we'll explore each contraceptive method available to you today: the barrier, hormone, intrauterine, fertility awareness, withdrawal, and permanent methods. We also look at abstinence. As we conclude the chapter, we'll examine a difficult decision faced by many women today—abortion.

CONTRACEPTIVE BEHAVIOR

Often, the terms "birth control" and "contraception" are used interchangeably, but there is a difference between the two. **Birth control** is any action, method, or practice that controls the number of children born by preventing or reducing the likelihood of conception. **Contraception** prevents the fertilization of the ovum by the sperm (American College of Obstetrics and Gynecology, 2009). The term contraception is also commonly used to refer to methods that prevent implantation of a fertilized egg. Regardless, there are many methods to choose from, as illustrated in Figure 13.1. Although contraception is used as a way to prevent having children, it is also used by couples as a family planning method so they can determine the number of children they have, as well as the time between children. Some women use certain contraceptive methods (such as the birth control pill) for reasons other than preventing pregnancy, such as management of menstrual difficulties and pain (Disease Management, 2008).

Contraceptive behavior refers to how women and men utilize methods to prevent pregnancy, and this behavior is multidimensional. In a recent report on unplanned pregnancies in emerging adulthood, the researcher discovered that there are different facets of contraceptive behavior (Jaccard, 2009). Contraceptive behavior refers to more than just remembering to take a birth control pill every day; all components are necessary to prevent unplanned pregnancies.

There are many family and other social factors that influence a person's feelings about contraception, and these affect the choices we make. Think about, for example, how your parents may have influenced your contraceptive attitudes and behaviors. Did they promote abstinence, or did they discuss various contraceptive options with you? Both? Or neither? What about your friends? Have you had sexuality education in school? Do you adhere to your church, temple, or mosque's attitudes and beliefs about contraception? As you can see, contraceptive behavior encompasses much more than the act of using a condom every time.

CONTRACEPTIVES: THEN AND NOW

The methods of birth control and contraception have changed considerably over time, as you can see in Figure 13.2. From tree bark, to cow dung mixed with honey, to cabbage and onions, even thousands of years ago, people were quite creative in the methods they invented in attempt to prevent pregnancy. Past and present methods work in a number of ways for pregnancy prevention. They may (ACOG, 2009):

- Block the sperm from reaching the egg in the fallopian tube.

- Kill or damage sperm.

- Keep eggs from being released each month (prevent ovulation).

- Change the lining of the uterus so the fertilized egg does not attach to it.

- Thicken the mucus in the cervix so sperm cannot easily pass through it.

Today, women and their partners have a number of options from which to choose to delay or avoid pregnancy and to prevent STIs; the forms and methods are wide and varied, as are the effectiveness rates and complications.

Figure 13.1 College Students and Birth Control

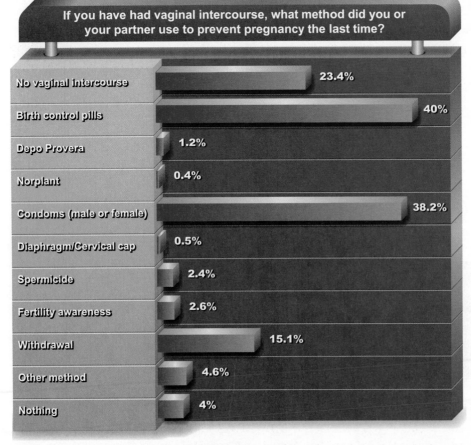

If you have had vaginal intercourse, what method did you or your partner use to prevent pregnancy the last time?

Method	Percentage
No vaginal intercourse	23.4%
Birth control pills	40%
Depo Provera	1.2%
Norplant	0.4%
Condoms (male or female)	38.2%
Diaphragm/Cervical cap	0.5%
Spermicide	2.4%
Fertility awareness	2.6%
Withdrawal	15.1%
Other method	4.6%
Nothing	4%

Source: National College Health Assessment (2008).

Contraceptive choice, accuracy, consistency, and switching are all important aspects of contraceptive behavior. The decision we make in regards to each can increase or decrease the chances of an unintended pregnancy. Take a moment to think about the following questions:

1. On a scale of 1 to 10, with 10 being high, what would you say is your risk for an unplanned pregnancy? Guys, what would you say is your risk for getting someone pregnant?

2. Why do you use the contraceptive that you do? If you are not sexually active, what method would you use and why?

3. How do you know that you are using or would use your chosen method correctly?

Ancient Society–Biblical Days

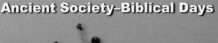

Coitus interruptus

1350–1200 BCE

Sheath of linen to cover penis

Ancient Greeks

First to determine that male and female union can result in pregnancy

Ancient Barrier Methods

A **pessary** is something inserted into the vagina to kill sperm and/or block its passage through the cervix. Ancient pessaries included acacia tree and honey, olive oil and cabbage, peppermint oil and soft wool, sea sponges, and plugs of cloth soaked in brandy.

Abortion: Ancient Times–1800s

Abortion was one of the earliest and most common birth control methods. Herbal abortion potions that have been around for thousands of years include paste of mashed ants, lavender, marjoram, parsley, and thyme, root of worm fern, opium and ginger, and sitting over a pot of steamed onions.

1800s

1775: First vasectomy
1834: First female sterilization
1838: First cervical cap
1840: Process of ovulation understood; condoms available in U.S.
1868: First type of IUD
1870s: Comstock laws define contraceptive information as "obscene," making it difficult to obtain condoms
1882: First type of diaphragm; first birth control clinic opens in Germany

Early 1900s

Female condoms commercially available

1907: Mandatory sterilization of those "at risk" for passing on hereditary conditions
1909: U.S. production of IUD
1916: Margaret Sanger opens first U.S. birth control clinic
1930: Sanger helps overturn Comstock laws

Mid-1900s

1950: Contraception by injection
1960s: First morning-after pill
1960: First birth control pill approved by FDA and publicly available
1961: Estrogen-only pills available
1967: Contraceptive implants
1969: Minipill available in Britain

Late 1900s/Early 2000s

1972: Abortion legal in U.S.
1974: Depo Provera available
1983: Combination (estrogen/progestin) available
1992: Polyurethane female condoms produced
1995: Norplant released
1996: IUD with hormones produced
2000s: Menstrual suppression becomes popular
2000: Abortion pill available
2002: NuvaRing available

Figure 13.2 History of Contraceptives With the exception of the birth control pill introduced in the 1960s, there are no new contraceptive methods—**all of the techniques we have available to us today were practiced in the ancient world.**

Figure 13.3 Choosing a Method That's Right for You When considering sexual activity, **it's important to consider methods of protection against unwanted pregnancy** and to think about you and your partner's individual needs and circumstances.

Barrier Contraceptive Methods
Barrier contraceptive methods provide a chemical or physical barrier between the sperm and the ovum. These methods are often not invasive and will usually not affect lifelong fertility. They are typically inexpensive and available over the counter (OTC) without a doctor's prescription.

Method	Pros	Cons	Failure Rate (rated by the FDA)
Condom	Available OTC; inexpensive; STI protection	Lack of sensitivity; interruption of "the moment"	11%
Female Condom	Available OTC; STI protection	Cumbersome; interruption of "the moment"	21%
Diaphragm	Can be inserted hours before sex; does not impede sensitivity	Available only by prescription; often messy; no STI protection	17%*
Cervical Cap	Can be used for multiple acts of sex; convenience	Available only by prescription; often messy; no STI protection	17–23%*
Cervical Shield	Can be used for multiple acts of sex; convenience	Available only by prescription; often messy; no STI protection	15%*
Contraceptive Sponge	Can be used for multiple acts of sex; available OTC	Messy (requires spermicide); possible health side effects; no STI protection	14–28%*
Intrauterine Device (IUD)	Can remain in place for 10 years; very convenient	Must be inserted by a health care professional; no STI protection	<1%
Spermicides	Inexpensive; available OTC	Messy; no STI protection; not as reliable when used alone	20–50%

*when used with spermicide

Hormonal Contraceptive Methods
Hormonal methods of birth control use artificial hormones to prevent ovulation as well as thicken the cervical mucus, which inhibits sperm from traveling into the uterus. Because each method uses the same basic principle, the pros and cons of each method are similar. The convenience of hormonal methods makes them very desirable, but because the hormones essentially alter the body's chemistry, side effects are common. Hormonal methods are used by women.

Method	Usage	Failure Rate (rated by the FDA)
Birth Control Pills	One pill taken every day for a cycle of 21, 28, or 91 days	1–2%
Minipills (POPs)	One pill taken at the same time every day for 28 days	2%
Contraceptive Patch	A patch is worn that releases hormones into the skin; patch is changed weekly	1–2%
Contraceptive Ring	A ring is inserted into the vagina that releases hormones; changed every month	1–2%
Contraceptive Injections (Depo Provera)	One injection of contraceptive hormones every three months	<1%
Hormone-Releasing IUDs	IUD that releases hormones into the uterus; replaced every five years	<1%
Morning-After Pill	High-dosage hormone pill; taken after sex to prevent fertilization or implantation	11–25%*

*Rated by the National Women's Health Information Center

Other Methods
Many couples faced with matters of personal preference and/or religious conviction may choose a birth control method that involves neither barriers nor chemicals.

Method	Usage	Failure Rate (rated by the FDA)
Natural Family Planning (Rhythm Method)	Woman's menstrual cycle is carefully monitored; sex during ovulation is restricted	>20%
Withdrawal	Penis is removed prior to ejaculation	4–19%
Sterilization	Reproductive ducts are blocked or severed (vasectomy for men, tubal ligation for women	<1%
Abstinence	Complete avoidance of all sexual activity	0%

Deciding which method is right for you often depends on individual needs and circumstances. There are several things to think about when choosing a method, and these are presented for you in Figure 13.3. It's best to discuss the pros and cons of each method with your health care provider, as well as your partner, so you can determine which method is best for your sexual health and circumstances. It's also important to consider the advantages and disadvantages of each method. The **failure rate** for each method is the number of women who become pregnant if 100 women used the method for one year. For example, approximately 85 of 100 women will become pregnant if they use no method at all; about 15 women of 100 will become pregnant using condoms (Planned Parenthood, 2009). The effectiveness rates for each contraceptive method are also presented in Figure 13.3. Which method do you think is best for you? For your partner?

sex talk

How to Talk to Your Partner about Contraception

It seems sometimes we find it easier to have sex than to talk about it, especially when it comes to discussing birth control. These statements might help you and your partner talk about birth control.

Birth control is important to me because _____.

Talking about birth control with my partner makes me feel _____.

Before I become a parent, I want to _____.

If we use contraception, it will _____ our sex life.

I do/do not use contraception *every time* I have sex. This is because _____
_____.

According to my religious beliefs, contraception is _____. This makes
me feel _____.

I don't want a contraceptive method that _____.

I prefer to use _____ contraceptive method because_____.

We can incorporate our contraceptive into our sex play by _____.

I would feel _____ about a pregnancy right now.

The most important things that I want in a contraceptive method are _____
_____.

To determine the best contraceptive method for us, we can _____.

I think that _____ should pay for our contraceptives.

My three biggest questions about contraception are: 1) _____;
2) _____; and 3) _____.

In general, there are three categories of contraceptives: barrier methods, hormone methods, and other methods. Unless otherwise noted, all data are from the American College of Obstetrics and Gynecology (2009).

BARRIER METHODS: PREVENTING SPERM FROM REACHING THE OVA

As the name implies, **barrier contraceptive methods** provide a chemical or physical barrier between the sperm and the ovum; sperm cannot reach the egg, and fertilization is thus prevented. These methods are typically not invasive (do not interfere with a woman's menstrual cycle) and will usually not affect lifelong fertility. They are inexpensive and available over the counter (OTC), without a doctor's prescription. To be effective, they must be used each and every time sexual intercourse occurs. We describe each barrier method in the sections that follow.

CONDOMS: "NO GLOVE, NO LOVE"

A **condom** is a thin sheath of latex, polyurethane, or animal intestine that is worn over an erect penis or inside the vagina during intercourse; it is used to prevent pregnancy and to protect against STIs. There are two main types of condoms, *male condoms* and *female condoms*. Male rubber condoms were first made available in the United States in 1850, making condoms one of the oldest forms of contraception (McLaren, 1990). Early condoms were referred to as *penis sheaths*. For example, Egyptians in 1350 BCE wrapped decorative linens over their penises. Over time, condoms were made out of animal skins or animal intestines.

Condoms prevent sperm from reaching the egg; when semen is released, it remains inside the condom. The male places a condom on his erect penis prior to vaginal or anal penetration. By preventing semen from entering the vagina, anus, or mouth, condoms also reduce the risk of STIs and HIV. To be effective, condoms must be used each and every time a person has sex. It must also be put on correctly. Condoms are more effective if they are used with a spermicide.

Social and family scientists have a great interest in examining birth control trends among high school and college students, because these trends give a comprehensive picture of students' overall health and well-being and allow campuses to enhance health promotion and prevention services. The *National College Health Assessment* is a survey that collects data regarding college students' sexual behaviors and other lifestyle habits (such as smoking and drinking). In 2008, more than 80,000 students responded to the survey. The trends indicate that students are not using a condom every time, which greatly increases their risk of unwanted pregnancy and STIs/HIV.

Available since 1994, a female condom is a thin, polyurethane pouch that fits inside the vagina prior to penile penetration; the condom has rings on either end. The outer ring fits over the labia, and the inner ring (at the closed end) holds the condom inside the vagina. Many women find the female condom difficult to insert, but making sure that the vagina is well lubricated helps insertion. One of its main advantages, however, is that it can be inserted up to eight hours before sex. A female condom should never be used simultaneously with a male condom, because both are more likely to break (Planned Parenthood, 2009). Figure 13.4 provides more information on the female condom and other female barrier methods.

DIAPHRAGMS

A **diaphragm** is a small, latex, dome-shaped cup that is inserted into the vagina. It covers the cervix and provides a barrier that prevents sperm from entering the uterus; a spring in the rim of the cup helps lock the diaphragm in place over the cervix. Diaphragms are always used in conjunction with a spermicide. It can be inserted up to six hours before sex; after sex, it must be left in place for at least six hours, but no longer than 24 hours. It should never be used during menstruation. Used with a spermicide, it is highly effective for pregnancy and STI and HIV prevention. Today, less than 1 percent of U.S. women use diaphragms (The Alan Guttmacher Institute, 2008).

A diaphragm can only be obtained by visiting a health care provider, because a doctor, midwife, or nurse practitioner must fit it to the individual woman. A diaphragm should *never* be borrowed from a friend. Women need to be refitted for a new diaphragm after giving birth, miscarriage, or abortion, and after gaining/losing more than 10 pounds, and the diaphragm should be replaced about every two years (Planned Parenthood, 2009). College students can visit their campus health center to be fitted for a diaphragm.

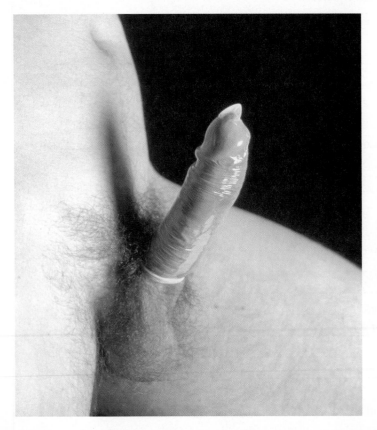

<<< Gradually roll the condom onto the penis, making sure to leave a half-inch space at the tip to allow room for the semen. Withdrawal must take place immediately after intercourse to prevent semen leakage. While the penis is still erect, grasp the condom at the base of the penis to prevent it from slipping off (Planned Parenthood, 2009).

Figure 13.4 Female Barrier Contraceptive Methods

Female Condom

A pouch that fits inside the vagina prior to penile penetration, the female condom has rings on both ends. The closed end holds the condom inside the vagina while the open end fits over the labia. A female condom should not be used simultaneously with a male condom, but it can be inserted up to eight hours prior to sex.

Gently insert the inner ring into the vagina. Feel the inner ring go up and move into place.

Place the index finger on the inside of the condom, and push the inner ring up as far as it will go. Be sure the sheath is not twisted. The outer ring should remain on the outside of the vagina.

Be sure the penis is inserted into condom, not next to it.

Diaphragm

Diaphragms must be fitted by a health care provider because they come in a variety of sizes. Women should practice how to insert and remove the diaphragm; the woman's partner can also insert it. Before insertion, spermicide must be applied around the rim and inside the dome. The woman should first prop up her leg, squat, sit on the toilet, or lie on her back. Then, the diaphragm is folded in half and inserted into the vagina, much like a tampon. Once inserted, the cervix should be completely covered by the rubber cap. After it is in place, a woman should not be aware of it; if she is, it is improperly inserted.

 Cream or jelly

Diaphragm

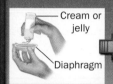

Apply spermicide to inside and around edge of diaphragm.

Squeeze edges to insert into vagina.

Be sure diaphragm is placed snugly against cervix.

Cervical Cap

The *FemCap* is a reusable silicone cap that fits snugly over the cervix. Spermicide is placed inside the cap; the cap is then inserted into the vagina in the same way that a diaphragm is. Once inserted, the cap is pressed onto the cervix. The cap provides protection for up to 48 hours, no matter how many times a woman has sex. Spermicide doesn't have to be reapplied for each act of sex.

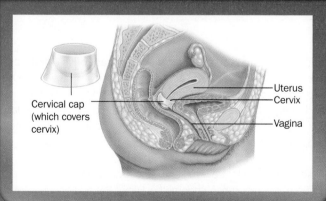

Cervical cap (which covers cervix)

Uterus
Cervix
Vagina

Sponge

The *Today* sponge is a 2-inch plastic foam disc that contains spermicide. Prior to vaginal insertion by the woman or her partner, the sponge is moistened with water, which allows it to expand; the water also activates the spermicide. After it is moistened, it is folded in half and inserted deep into the

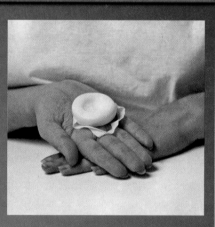

vagina. The sponge covers the cervix and provides a barrier so sperm cannot enter the uterus. Simultaneously, it absorbs sperm and releases a spermicide that immobilizes sperm. Intercourse can take place immediately after insertion and can occur as often as desired within 24 hours of insertion. It is not necessary to add more spermicide. The sponge is removed by grasping the attached cloth loop and pulling gently.

Contraceptive Use and Sexual Satisfaction

Of course, a very important aspect of contraceptive use, (one that does not get as much attention), is how it relates to our sexual pleasure or satisfaction. As sexuality educators, we often hear people say that condoms decrease sensitivity and spontaneity. Both of these are related to our sexual pleasure or enjoyment, which is the immediate, in-the-moment pleasure we feel when we are having sex. Sexual satisfaction is different in that it's more about our overall satisfaction with our sex lives. This includes factors such as sexual self-esteem and relationship satisfaction.

- A recent study conducted by The Kinsey Institute found that women who used condoms alone or in combination with a hormonal method reported decreased pleasure but higher levels of overall satisfaction. Women who used a hormonal method alone were less likely to report decreased pleasure, but they also reported lower levels of overall satisfaction than condom only and condom and hormonal methods combination. Combination users had the highest level of overall satisfaction. The researchers suggested that this may be because these women felt the most protected against unwanted pregnancies and STIs. For healthy selves and healthy sex, remember that we can experience sexual pleasure from sex acts other than intercourse.

- Think about your sexual pleasure and how your contraceptive choice affects it. Are you only focusing on intercourse?

- It may be that the belief that condoms will reduce pleasure makes you feel that it does. Think about where that belief comes from: experience or what others have told you? Try experimenting with different types of condoms.

- Take time to think about your sexual satisfaction and how it relates to your sexual pleasure. What role does you contraceptive choice play in that relationship?

Source: Higgins, J.A., Hoffman, S., Graham, C.A., & Sanders, S.A. (2008). Relationships between condoms, hormonal methods, and sexual pleasure and satisfaction: an exploratory analysis from the Women's Well-Being and Sexuality Study. *Sexual Health*, 5 (4): 321–330.

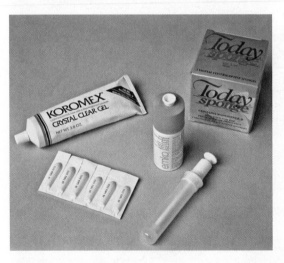

<<< A **spermicide** is a chemical contraceptive. **It works by killing sperm or by making them inactive. Before each act of sex, the spermicide is placed either directly into the vagina, or on the diaphragm or cap; suppositories need to be given time to melt before sex.** Today, researchers are studying the effects of some 60 new products, **microbicides**, which reduce the infection rate of viruses or bacteria. Although they are not available yet, they show a great deal of promise in protecting women against STIs and HIV (The AIDS Infonet, 2009).

THE CERVICAL CAP

As the name suggests, a **cervical cap** is a small, thin, cup-shaped device made of plastic or latex that is inserted into the vagina, fitting tightly over the cervix. Unlike the diaphragm, the cap is much smaller and stays in place by suction; it prevents the sperm from entering the cervical opening. It is used with a spermicidal cream or jelly, which deactivates sperm and is highly effective in preventing pregnancy and STIs and HIV. *FemCap* is the only brand of cervical cap available in the United States today.

HORMONE METHODS: PREVENTING OVULATION

As you remember from Chapter 4, estrogen and progesterone fluctuate throughout a woman's menstrual cycle, and orchestrate the maturation and release of an ovum. **Hormone contraceptive methods** use artificial hormones (estrogen and progesterone) to prevent ovulation; due to the addition of synthetic hormones in the body, the pituitary gland does not release hormones to signal the ovaries to release an egg. In addition, the increased levels of artificial estrogen mimic the estrogen levels of pregnancy; this, too, interrupts the process of ovulation. The hormones simultaneously thicken the cervical mucus, which inhibits sperm from traveling into the uterus and also reduce the buildup of the blood-rich endometrial lining, the nutrients necessary to sustain a pregnancy.

Each hormone method uses the same basic principle (the mode of delivery is usually the biggest difference), so the advantages and disadvantages of each method are similar. The convenience of hormonal methods makes them very desirable, but because the hormones essentially alter the body's chemistry, side effects are

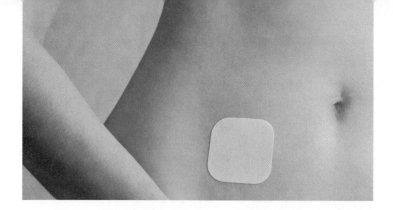

> The contraceptive **skin patch** is a 2-inch adhesive patch that a woman wears on her buttocks, chest, back, arm, or abdomen. **Like oral contraceptives, artificial estrogen and progesterone work in the bloodstream.**

> The **NuvaRing** is a flexible plastic ring that is placed monthly in the upper segment of the vagina. **About 2 inches in diameter, the ring slowly and continuously time-releases low doses of estrogen and progestin into the vaginal walls.**

common. Only women use hormonal methods, which come in several forms:

- Birth control pills
- Skin patch
- Vaginal ring
- Injections
- Implant

Hormonal methods prevent pregnancy, but offer no protection against STIs and HIV.

BIRTH CONTROL PILLS: "THE PILL"

Birth control pills, also known as **oral contraceptives**, are used by about 30 percent of women; it has been one of the most popular methods in the United States since 1982, particularly among white women (The Alan Guttmacher Institute, 2008). The pill is the method most widely used by women who are in their teens and 20s and by never-married women. If taken correctly, oral contraceptives are 95 percent effective in preventing pregnancy (Planned Parenthood, 2009). Missing one or more pills will decrease the effectiveness of your birth control, so if you forget to take it, be sure to ask your doctor or pharmacist how to proceed. Women who take oral contraceptives should be aware, however, that common drugs and herbs may interact with the pill and lower its effectiveness; these are presented in Table 13.1.

Table 13.1
Common Drugs and Herbs That May Interact with Birth Control Pills

Source: Hatcher, R. A. et al. (2004). *Contraceptive technology* (18th Rev. ed.). New York: Ardent Media.

Certain medications taken together may make the drugs less effective. Some over-the-counter (nonprescription) drugs, prescription medications, and herbal supplements may interact with the birth control pill. A drug interaction is any mechanism by which one drug may interact with the action(s) of another drug.

Drug	Interaction Effect
Prescription:	
Anti-Depressants (i.e., Adapin, Elavil, Prozac, Paxil)	Blood levels of anti-depressant increased
Antibiotics (i.e., Amoxicillin, Ampicillin, Adoxa, Erythromycin, E-mycin, Methenamine, Rifampin, Tetracyclines)	May decrease effectiveness of hormones from the pill, increasing risk of contraceptive failure
Anti-fungal (i.e., Grifulvin, Grisactin)	May cause spotting or breakthrough bleeding, a sign of contraceptive failure
Anti-seizure (i.e., Tegretal, Phenobarbital)	May decrease effectiveness of hormones from the pill
Over-the-counter (OTC):	
St. John's Wort (herbal supplement)	May decrease effectiveness of hormones from the pill
Orlistat (i.e., Alli)	Reduces absorption of oral contraceptives

Figure 13.5 Get the Facts: Birth Control Pills

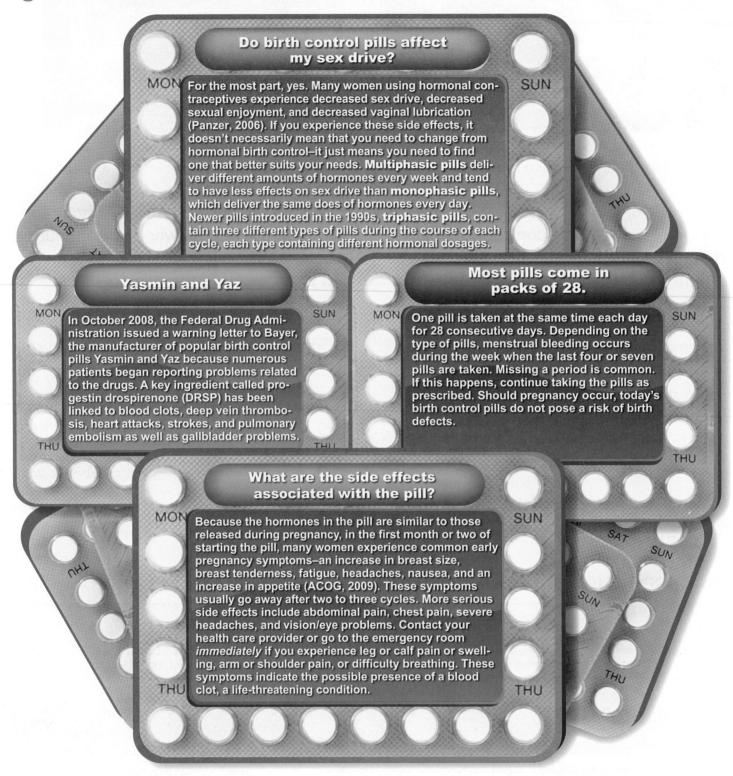

Do birth control pills affect my sex drive?

For the most part, yes. Many women using hormonal contraceptives experience decreased sex drive, decreased sexual enjoyment, and decreased vaginal lubrication (Panzer, 2006). If you experience these side effects, it doesn't necessarily mean that you need to change from hormonal birth control—it just means you need to find one that better suits your needs. **Multiphasic pills** deliver different amounts of hormones every week and tend to have less effects on sex drive than **monophasic pills**, which deliver the same does of hormones every day. Newer pills introduced in the 1990s, **triphasic pills**, contain three different types of pills during the course of each cycle, each type containing different hormonal dosages.

Yasmin and Yaz

In October 2008, the Federal Drug Administration issued a warning letter to Bayer, the manufacturer of popular birth control pills Yasmin and Yaz because numerous patients began reporting problems related to the drugs. A key ingredient called progestin drospirenone (DRSP) has been linked to blood clots, deep vein thrombosis, heart attacks, strokes, and pulmonary embolism as well as gallbladder problems.

Most pills come in packs of 28.

One pill is taken at the same time each day for 28 consecutive days. Depending on the type of pills, menstrual bleeding occurs during the week when the last four or seven pills are taken. Missing a period is common. If this happens, continue taking the pills as prescribed. Should pregnancy occur, today's birth control pills do not pose a risk of birth defects.

What are the side effects associated with the pill?

Because the hormones in the pill are similar to those released during pregnancy, in the first month or two of starting the pill, many women experience common early pregnancy symptoms—an increase in breast size, breast tenderness, fatigue, headaches, nausea, and an increase in appetite (ACOG, 2009). These symptoms usually go away after two to three cycles. More serious side effects include abdominal pain, chest pain, severe headaches, and vision/eye problems. Contact your health care provider or go to the emergency room *immediately* if you experience leg or calf pain or swelling, arm or shoulder pain, or difficulty breathing. These symptoms indicate the possible presence of a blood clot, a life-threatening condition.

Source: The Alan Guttmacher Institute (2008).

Figure 13.5 illustrates the many options and facets of birth control pills, and as Figure 13.6 shows us, there are racial/ethnic differences in teenagers who use the birth control pill. In ninth grade, about 9 percent of females use the pill; by 12th grade, slightly more than one-fourth do (Centers for Disease Control and Prevention, 2008).

There are two types of pills: the **combination pill**, which contains both estrogen and progestin, and the **progestin-only pill**, or **minipill** (this is a good choice for women who cannot take estrogen, such as women who have had/are at high risk for getting breast cancer, or women who are breastfeeding). The minipill can be used by women who smoke or who are breastfeeding, because they have fewer side effects than combination pills (Planned Parenthood, 2009). Combination pills also offer some health benefits to women, such as protection against ovarian and endometrial cancer (ACOG, 2009). Also, women who take either type of pill typically have shorter, lighter periods, less abdominal cramping, and fewer outbreaks of acne. The pill is also a good method to regulate menstrual periods and to

Figure 13.6 Percentage of Sexually Active High School Students Who Use Birth Control Pills, by Race

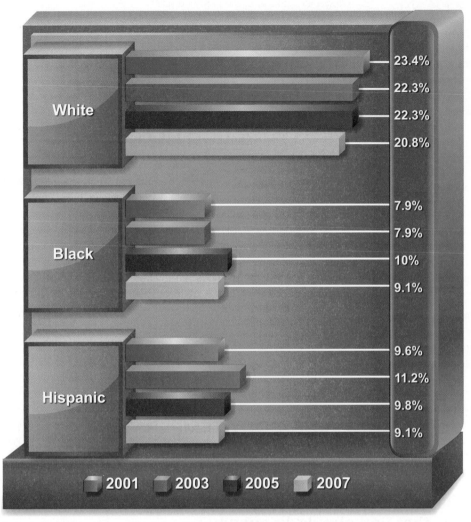

White
- 23.4%
- 22.3%
- 22.3%
- 20.8%

Black
- 7.9%
- 7.9%
- 10%
- 9.1%

Hispanic
- 9.6%
- 11.2%
- 9.8%
- 9.1%

■ 2001   ■ 2003   ■ 2005   ■ 2007

Source: Centers for Disease Control and Prevention (2008). *Surveillance Summaries, MMWR* 2007: 57 (No. 55-4), Table 65.

help alleviate symptoms associated with endometriosis, as well as a way in which to induce menstrual suppression (see Chapter 4).

Continuous-dose pills are taken for 84 consecutive days, with seven days off. This means that a woman will only have four periods in a year; some continuous-dose pills are taken year-round, which means a woman will not menstruate at all (see Chapter 4). A common side effect of continuous-dose pills is **breakthrough bleeding**, or bleeding at a time other than a period. This lessens over time, as the body adjusts to the constant levels of hormones.

Birth control pills are available by prescription only, so starting the pill requires a trip to the campus health center or to a health care provider. A month's supply of the pill usually costs between $15 and $50.

HORMONAL INJECTIONS

The most common contraceptive used by Hispanic and African American women of childbearing age (The Alan Guttmacher Institute, 2008) are **hormone injections**, which a health care provider administers every three months. Today, about 5 percent of U.S. women rely on hormone injections for pregnancy prevention, but poor and low-income women are more than twice as likely to rely on the three-month injectable than those in higher income brackets.

The "shot," injected into the woman's arm muscle or buttock, contains progesterone and is typically referred to as *Depo Provera*. It inhibits ovulation and also thickens cervical mucus. Weight gain may occur in some women, but women who use this method prefer it because they do not have to remember to take a pill every day. It is also a good contraceptive method for breastfeeding women. A woman's ability to become pregnant returns after the last dose is administered; however, because it takes about six to 18 months for the body to return to its "normal" state, women should plan ahead if they desire to conceive.

Because of the possibility of bone loss with prolonged use, the U.S. Food and Drug Administration (FDA) recommends that Depo Provera should not be used for more than two years unless other birth control methods are inadequate. There does not appear to be a link between Depo Provera and long-term skeletal health, so it can still be considered a viable birth control option (Kaunitz, 2005).

>>> A **contraceptive implant**, *Norplant*, is a single rod, about the size of a matchstick, that contains progestin. **Effective for three years, it prevents pregnancy by inhibiting ovulation, thickening cervical mucus, and thinning the endometrium.** Approximately 1 percent of U.S. women use implants to prevent pregnancy (The Alan Guttmacher Institute, 2008).

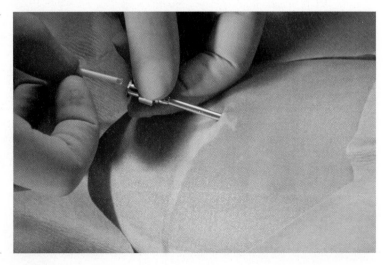

INTRAUTERINE METHODS: BLOCKING SPERM AND PREVENTING IMPLANTATION

An **intrauterine device (IUD)** is a small, T-shaped, plastic device that contains copper. It is inserted by a health care provider into the uterus (see Figure 13.7). An **intrauterine system (IUS)** resembles an IUD, but it also contains a synthetic sex hormone, progestin; this hormone is time-released directly into the uterus. The IUD is about 98 to 99.9 percent effective in preventing pregnancy, but offers no protection against STIs and HIV. About 2 percent of U.S. women use this contraceptive, particularly women over the age of 35 (The Alan Guttmacher Institute, 2008).

There are two types of intrauterine methods. Both types work by creating a mild infection in the uterus, which is thought to reduce sperm mobility. Trussell et al. (2009) delineate other differences between the two methods:

- **Hormonal IUS:** The small amount of progestin released thickens cervical mucus, blocking sperm from entering into the uterus; it also renders sperm less active, making it less likely for them to reach an egg in the fallopian tube. It thins the endometrium; if pregnancy does occur, a fertilized conceptus cannot attach in the uterus. The IUS must be replaced every five years.

- **Copper IUD:** This doesn't release hormones, but instead, copper. The copper prevents sperm from entering the cervix and also reduces sperm's ability to fertilize an egg. If pregnancy occurs, the copper prevents the conceptus from attaching to the uterine wall. The IUD must be replaced every 10 to 12 years.

Each IUD has a thin plastic thread attached to it, and this string helps women check its proper placement.

There are still many misconceptions about intrauterine methods, particularly surrounding its side effects, long-term fertility, and general safety. Both types available today have been found to be safe and effective contraceptive methods. Although side effects are rare, there can be complications. Some women who use the copper IUD may experience increased cramping and bleeding, but commonly menstrual periods stop altogether with use of the hormonal IUS.

In a review of studies on IUDs, researchers concluded that an IUD is a good contraceptive choice for young women and adolescents (Deans & Grimes, 2009). Because IUDs do not affect a woman's ability to get pregnant in the future, the fact that the IUD lasts five to 10 years is a plus.

THE SYMPTOTHERMAL METHOD: FERTILITY AWARENESS

Fertility awareness, often referred to as **natural family planning (NFP)**, does not rely on hormones or barrier devices; instead, these contraceptive methods rely on predicting ovulation and avoiding sexual intercourse during this fertile time frame. There are three primary fertility awareness methods that can help women and their partners predict ovulation: basal body temperature (BBT), the calendar method, and the mucus method. Together, these three methods are referred to as the **symptothermal method**. Success or failure of these methods largely hinges on a woman's ability to recognize her signs of ovulation and her ability to abstain from sex during ovulation. When used correctly, the symptothermal method is up to 98 percent effective in preventing pregnancy (ACOG, 2009). Women are not protected against STIs or HIV using these methods. Also referred to as *periodic abstinence*, about 4 percent of U.S. women practice fertility awareness (The Alan Guttmacher Institute, 2008).

BASAL BODY TEMPERATURE

Basal body temperature (BBT) is the lowest body temperature, attained while sleeping. Commonly, women have a lower BBT before ovulation and higher body temperatures after an egg has been released; this is known as a **biphasic pattern**. Because the rise in temperature is very slight (a degree or less), a BBT thermometer is used instead of a regular thermometer; daily temperatures are recorded on a BBT chart (see Figure 13.8). With practice, women may begin to see patterns in their monthly menstrual cycles. To avoid pregnancy, many women combine this method with the *calendar* method. With this, women chart their menstrual cycle on a calendar and are aware when they should typically ovulate (such as the 14th day in a 28-day cycle). Most women should avoid sexual intercourse during their *fertile* time, about a day before ovulation, the day of ovulation, and a day or two after ovulation (Weschler, 2002). Some women also use the *cervical mucus* method in combination with BBT. The calendar method, also called the rhythm method, involves

Figure 13.7 The Intrauterine Device There are various side effects, health risks, and precautions **that you should know when considering an intrauterine device as your form of birth control.**

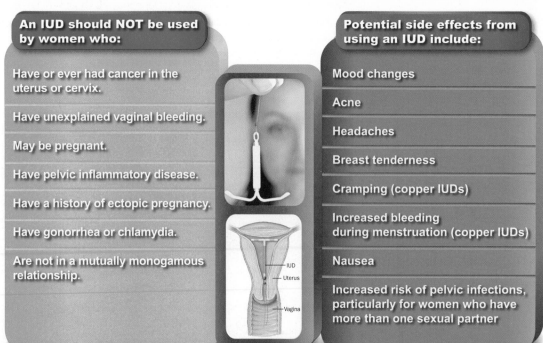

An IUD should NOT be used by women who:

Have or ever had cancer in the uterus or cervix.

Have unexplained vaginal bleeding.

May be pregnant.

Have pelvic inflammatory disease.

Have a history of ectopic pregnancy.

Have gonorrhea or chlamydia.

Are not in a mutually monogamous relationship.

Potential side effects from using an IUD include:

Mood changes

Acne

Headaches

Breast tenderness

Cramping (copper IUDs)

Increased bleeding during menstruation (copper IUDs)

Nausea

Increased risk of pelvic infections, particularly for women who have more than one sexual partner

sexual life now

Should a Pharmacist Be Able to Refuse to Fill a Prescription for Birth Control?

A few years ago there was much discussion about pharmacists who refused to fill medications for abortifacients and prescription contraceptives on the grounds that dispensing such medications violated their personal moral or religious beliefs. This has been referred to as the "pharmacy conscience clause," and it has been an issue that state legislators have been handling. Some pharmacists have refused to fill prescriptions for anyone, whereas others won't fill prescriptions for teenagers or unmarried women. The American Pharmacists Association's official policy is that a pharmacist has the right to refuse a prescription as long as he or she makes sure customers can get their medications some other way (APhA-ASP Report, 2006). However, some pharmacists have refused to refer their patients to other pharmacists. Should pharmacists be allowed to refuse to fill birth control prescriptions?

YES!

Supporters of pharmacists' rights see this as an expression of personal belief. They claim that theirs is a healing profession, and birth control does not heal a person. In fact, some have argued that birth control is just another form of abortion and that abortion ends a life.

NO!

Women's health advocates claim that refusing to fill a prescription violates a woman's reproductive rights. Although it may be the case that a women can go elsewhere to get her prescription filled, in many rural areas there are no alternatives or it is a great inconvenience because they may have to drive an hour or more to get to the next town. Some have asked, "Who decides what is next?" If a person believes AIDS or another illness is a punishment from God, would that pharmacist be allowed to withhold other medications?

>>> WHAT DO YOU THINK?

1. Should a pharmacist be allowed to refuse to fill a prescription for birth control because of personal beliefs? If so, should the pharmacist be required to refer to another pharmacist who will fill the prescription?
2. Are a woman's reproductive rights being violated if her prescription is not filled? Why or Why not?
3. How might we strike a balance between the pharmacist's rights and a woman's rights?

Sources: American Pharmacists Association Academy of Student Pharmacists Report of the Resolutions Committee: 2006 Proposed Resolutions and Background Statements. Retrieved August 16, 2009, from http://74.125.47.132/custom?q5cache:YpuxDJwf67QJ: www.pharmacist.com/students/meetings/annual/2006%2520Proposed%2520Resolutions%2520with%2520Background% 2520Statements.doc+right+to+refuse&cd=6&hl=en&ct=clnk&gl=us&client=google-coop-np; Guttmacher Institute State Policies In Brief: Refusing to Provide Health Services (August 1, 2009). Retrieved August 16, 2009, from http://www.guttmacher.org/statecenter/spibs/spib_RPHS.pdf.

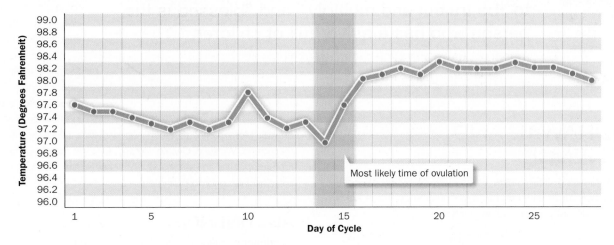

Figure 13.8 **Basal Body Temperature** Lower BBTs are the result of higher levels of estrogen that are present during the follicular (pre-ovulatory) phase of the menstrual cycle. After ovulation, higher levels of progesterone are released by the corpus luteum; this causes a rise in the BBT, typically seen the day after ovulation (Weschler, 2002).

Preventing Pregnancy: Contraceptives and Abortion

keeping track of the number of days in your menstrual cycle. After this has been recorded for a number of months, a formula can be used to determine which days of the month you are likely to be fertile.

CERVICAL MUCUS METHOD

The **mucus method**, sometimes referred to as the ovulation method or the Billings Method, is based on changes in cervical mucus that occur during the menstrual cycle. As you saw in Chapter 4, because of hormonal changes, the process of ovulation involves changes in a woman's cervical mucus—both in amount and in how it feels. Immediately after a woman's menstrual period ends, there is little or no mucus. These are "dry days," and for most women it is safe to have sex without concern of becoming pregnant (Weschler, 2002). Just before ovulation, the mucus becomes thin and watery; these are referred to as "slippery days," and to prevent pregnancy, sex should be avoided during this time. Ovulation commonly occurs the last day of thin and watery discharge (Weschler, 2002). Just like the BBT, mucus changes should be charted daily so women can better recognize their ovulation patterns over time. In addition to taking the BBT and assessing mucus changes, women may also be aware of other signs of ovulation, such as slight abdominal cramping.

> ∧∧∧ Jim Bob and Michelle Duggar of Tontitown, Arkansas, are parents of 19 children–and counting. **They are adherents to the Quiverfull Movement, a belief among some evangelical Protestant Christians, Catholics, and Mormons, that they are to adhere to the Bible when it says to "be fruitful and multiply," and "blessed is the person who has a quiver full of children."** They accept however many children they have (Campbell, 2003).

about 4 percent of the U.S. population (The Alan Guttmacher Institute, 2008), this contraceptive method involves the man withdrawing his penis from the vagina prior to ejaculation, thus preventing sperm from entering the vagina. In a review of research on contraceptive use, the researchers concluded that withdrawal as a contraceptive is more common than people report (Jones et al., 2009). This is because many people do not consider withdrawal an actual contraceptive method.

The effectiveness rate varies greatly, particularly because a man's ability to withdraw prior to ejaculation time varies greatly. If a man withdraws in time, every time, the effectiveness rate can be as high as 96 percent; realistically, about 18 percent of couples will become pregnant in a year by using withdrawal (Kost et al., 2008). Withdrawal is not recommended for adolescents or sexually inexperienced men because it takes considerable practice to be able to gain enough control to effectively pull out before ejaculation. In comparison to male condoms, withdrawal is only slightly less effective (Kost et al., 2008).

It was once thought that the pre-ejaculate, or *pre-cum* (see Chapter 5), contained viable sperm thereby reducing the effectiveness of with-

WITHDRAWAL AND ABSTINENCE

Natural family planning (NFP) refers to any use of fertility awareness methods to identify fertile times and to avoid pregnancy. There are two other NFP methods: withdrawal and abstinence.

WITHDRAWAL

Withdrawal, or **coitus interruptus**, is one of the oldest methods of birth control; it is more commonly known as *pulling out*. Practiced by

drawal. More recent research suggests that this may not be the case (Zukerman, Weiss, & Orvieto, 2003). However, there may be sperm left in the urethra after an ejaculation, and these sperm may be contained in the pre-ejaculate, prior to pulling out.

ABSTINENCE

Abstinence refers to the act of refraining from sexual intercourse. Outercourse (see Table 13.2) can be a satisfying alternative to intercourse. **Periodic abstinence**, a form of the symptothermal method, refers to abstaining from sexual intercourse during a woman's peak fer-

TABLE 13.2
Advantages and Disadvantages of Outercourse

Source: Planned Parenthood (2009). Retrieved February 3, 2010, from http://www.plannedparenthood.org/health-topics/birth-control/outercourse-4371.htm

As with any other form of sexual behavior, outercourse has both advantages and disadvantages. Before engaging in it, partners should openly discuss what outercourse means to them. Is it restricted to kissing and touching, or does it include mutual masturbation and oral sex?

Advantages:
- It's convenient and free
- It has no hormonal or medical side effects
- If semen and vaginal fluids aren't exchanged, it helps to prevent STIs
- It can increase trust and intimacy between partners
- Helps to make sex play last longer
- Helps people to better understand their bodies and their partners' bodies
- May help some women to have more satisfying orgasms
- May relieve "performance pressure" for men

Disadvantages:
- Sperm may come in contact with the vagina
- Outercourse may lead to intercourse without protection
- It may be harder to abstain from intercourse
- Touching a partner's genitals or anus during masturbation may lead to STIs

sion. **Outercourse** is sex play that keeps sperm out of the vagina to prevent pregnancy and may include mutual masturbation, oral, and anal sex, but does not include vaginal sex (Planned Parenthood, 2009). It is nearly 100 percent effective; however, pregnancy is possible if semen or pre-cum is spilled on the vulva and gets into the vagina. Unless body fluids are exchanged in oral and/or anal sex, outercourse also greatly reduces the risk of STIs/HIV (Planned Parenthood, 2009). As with abstinence, there is a risk with outercourse that a couple may have vaginal sex when they weren't intending to. It is important to be familiar with contraceptive options and to be prepared if this should occur.

All of the contraceptive methods we have discussed so far are reversible within a relatively short period of time. However, permanent methods of birth control include tubal ligation and vasectomy.

PERMANENT CONTRACEPTIVE METHODS: SURGICAL STERILIZATION

Other than abstinence, sterilization is the most effective contraceptive method. For both men and women, **sterilization** involves a surgical procedure that prevents either the egg or the sperm from reaching its intended destination.

FEMALE STERILIZATION

Tubal ligation (see Figure 13.9), commonly referred to as *tying the tubes*, is a surgical procedure in which the fallopian tubes are severed (such as by tying, banding, clipping, or cutting them) and sealed with an electric current; this prevents sperm from reaching an egg in the fallopian tube, and thus prevents fertilization. Some women have a tubal ligation after childbirth; this is referred to as *postpartum sterilization*. Other women opt to have their tubes tied during a cesarean birth; this eliminates the need for another surgical procedure. Recovery time varies, but most women are up and around in approximately two to five days. Common postoperative side effects include slight abdominal cramping, bloating, and minor changes in bowel habits.

Tubal ligation is effective immediately and has an effectiveness rate of 99 percent (Mayo Clinic, 2009). Because this is a permanent

tility time. Abstinence is 100 percent effective in preventing pregnancy and against STIs/HIV. People choose this method for a number of reasons, such as waiting until marriage to have sex, or for a short period of time, such as getting over a recent breakup. About 2 percent of U.S. adults surveyed indicate they adhere to abstinence (The Alan Guttmacher Institute, 2008).

Some people who are sexually abstinent, particularly teens and young adults, engage in outercourse as a means of sexual expres-

Figure 13.9 Tubal Litigation Tubal litigation is most frequently performed as an outpatient procedure. **Typically under local anesthesia, a physician makes a small incision in or near the woman's navel.** The physician then inserts a laparoscrope, a tube-like instrument that is inserted through the abdominal wall via the small incision. **Reduced pain, shorter recovery time, and the use of local anesthesia are some of the benefits associated with using a laparoscope.**

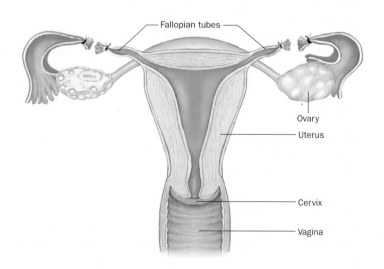

Fallopian tubes
Ovary
Uterus
Cervix
Vagina

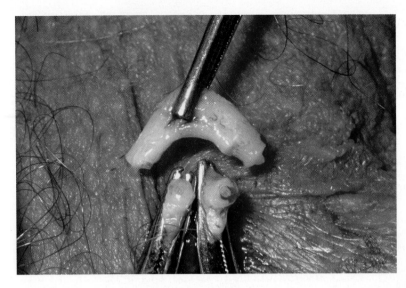
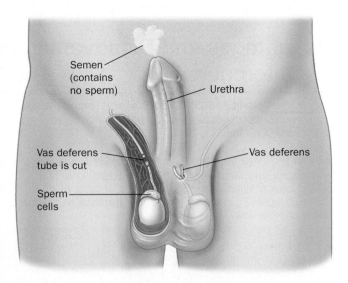

Figure 13.10 Vasectomy A vasectomy is typically performed by a urologist in the doctor's office or clinic, usually taking less than 30 minutes. **There are two types of procedures. In the traditional procedure, a doctor numbs the scrotum and then makes one or two small incisions into it to access the vas deferens.** The vasa are tied, cut, clipped, or sealed with an electric current. **With the no-scalpel technique, the vasa are cut in the same way, but a special tool is used to puncture the scrotum, reducing healing time and the risk of infection.** Most men experience an almost immediate recovery.

sterilization method, it is a major decision that should be made with care. Although reversing the procedure is possible, it is not always effective.

About 27 percent of U.S. women use this contraceptive method, and its popularity is second only to the pill (The Alan Guttmacher Institute, 2008). Women over age 35 and Hispanic and African American women most commonly rely on female sterilization.

Tubal ligation does not affect a woman's menstrual cycle, and it typically does not affect her sexual desire, arousal, and response. Some women, however, report reduced sexual functioning and desire (Costello et al., 2002). Researchers believe that reduced feelings of sexual arousal and response are most likely due to psychological factors associated with feeling regret for having the procedure and/or when their identity as women is strongly tied to the ability to have children. Some women report an increase in sexual arousal and desire; researchers attribute this increased interest is attributed to no longer fearing pregnancy (Costello et al., 2002).

MALE STERILIZATION

A **vasectomy** is an in-office medical procedure that removes all or part of the vas deferens, the ducts that transport sperm from the testes to the penis (see Figure 13.10). It works as a contraceptive method by preventing the release of sperm; once the vasa are cut, there is no pathway by which the sperm can reach the urethra.

It is an easier, less intrusive, and less expensive surgery than tubal ligation. Vasectomy also carries fewer possible complications, and has a

quicker recovery time; it has about the same effectiveness rate as the tubal ligation (nearly 100 percent). About 9 percent of the U.S. population uses this contraceptive method (The Alan Guttmacher Institute, 2008). Compared with white men, Hispanic and African American men are less likely to rely on vasectomy. Unlike a tubal ligation, a vasectomy is not effective right away, because some sperm may remain in the vas deferens; it typically takes two to three months for a vasectomy to be reliable. For this reason, couples should use an alternate contraceptive method until a *sperm count* (a laboratory procedure) verifies that there is no sperm in the ejaculate.

A vasectomy does not affect a man's hormone production or masculinity. The majority of men are satisfied with their vasectomy and experience no side effects. Occasionally, some men report genital pain of varying intensity; this is referred to as **post-vasectomy pain syndrome (PVPS).**

Today, couples have a wide range of contraceptive options available to them. Choosing a contraceptive that's right for you is dependent on many factors, such as how many sex partners you have. For example, if you're not in a monogamous relationship, you might want to consider a method that provides protection against STIs, in addition to pregnancy prevention. If you have sex frequently, birth control pills, used in tandem with a condom, may be a good option for you. As you move through your life, your contraceptive choices will probably change. If you want children in the near future, for example, you may opt for a method that's easily reversible. After you've had children, you may decide on a more permanent method. Because of your changing needs, it's important for you to familiarize yourself with the options available.

Figure 13.11 College Students and Emergency Contraception

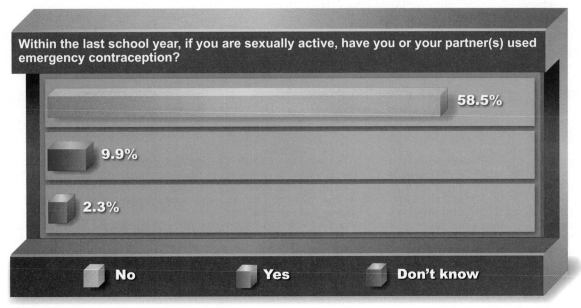

Within the last school year, if you are sexually active, have you or your partner(s) used emergency contraception?

- 58.5%
- 9.9%
- 2.3%

No   Yes   Don't know

Source: Based on National College Health Assessment (2008).

Sometimes, contraceptives fail and a woman becomes pregnant. When this happens, she can utilize emergency contraception or obtain an abortion.

EMERGENCY CONTRACEPTION

Emergency contraception (EC), also referred to as the **morning-after pill** or **Plan B**, is made of the same hormones found in birth control pills. There are several types of EC pills, but progestin-only (Plan B) and combined estrogen/progestin are the two most common. Plan B is the most effective (World Health Organization, 1998).

These hormones work by keeping a woman's ovaries from releasing an egg and also by thickening a woman's cervical mucus to keep sperm from joining an egg. The morning-after pill is *not* an abortion pill. As you'll see in our discussion a bit later, abortion pills empty the uterus of an already fertilized egg, but the morning-after pill prevents pregnancy by interrupting the release of an egg. If taken within 72 hours of an "oops!" sexual experience (the condom broke or slipped off, a woman forgets to take her birth control pill, he didn't pull out in time, etc.), EC reduces the risk of pregnancy by 89 percent (Planned Parenthood, 2009); the combination pill has an effectiveness rate of about 74 percent (Trussell et al., 2009). Although college students haven't typically been using EC (see Figure 13.11), it can be obtained by seeing a health care provider on campus or in your community.

>>> The most common side effect reported of emergency contraception pills (ECPs) has been nausea and vomiting. **Other common side effects include breast tenderness, abdominal pain, fatigue, headache, and dizziness.** These effects are generally over within 24 hours. **It is not uncommon for women who use ECPs to experience a temporary disruption of the menstrual cycle.**

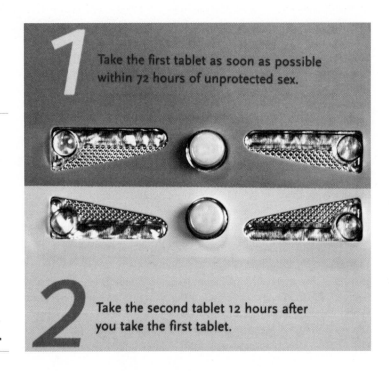

1 Take the first tablet as soon as possible within 72 hours of unprotected sex.

2 Take the second tablet 12 hours after you take the first tablet.

Figure 13.12 The practice of abortion dates back to ancient eras. Historical Timeline of Abortion.

5th Century	9th–18th Century	19th Century

Up to the 5th Century	5th–8th Century	9th–18th Century	Early 1800s	Mid-1800s
Techniques include strenuous labor and weightlifting, blood-letting, sitting on a heated coconut shell, mercury, pessaries, enemas, "abortion wine," and a copper needle to extract the embryo.	Techniques include sitting over a pot of steaming onions, applying firm pressure to the abdomen, obsessive exercise, and tightening a girdle above the abdomen.	Techniques include herbal plants like rue, Italian catnip, savory, sage, cyperus, hellebore, pennyroyal, and tansy. In the 18th century, abortion is allowed before fetal movement.	1821: Connecticut passes first law that outlaws using poison to induce abortion. 1840: First D&C is designed in France.	1861: U.K. outlaws abortion. 1869: Pope Pius IX declares abortion a mortal sin; anyone who has an abortion is to be excommunicated. Paper published about abortion services in Syracuse, N.Y.

In 1996, the FDA approved the use of the emergency contraceptive pill with a prescription, and in 2006, the FDA approved Plan B as an OTC medication for those aged 18 and older. In 2009, the age was reduced to 17. Some states require that EC services be made available to women who have been sexually assaulted; some have regulations that allow pharmacists to refuse to fill an EC prescription. Furthermore, some states have attempted to restrict access to EC by excluding it from state Medicaid family planning coverage (The Alan Guttmacher Institute, 2009).

Some women faced with an unwanted pregnancy opt to terminate the pregnancy through abortion.

▶▶▶ TAKING SIDES

What Birth Control Method Should a Couple Use Once They Have Finished Having Children?

John and Elizabeth have three healthy, happy children: Susan, 10, Jason, 7, and Kimberly, 2. John and Elizabeth are both in their late 30s; they are healthy and active. They had originally planned to have only two children; Kimberly was an unplanned pregnancy due to contraceptive failure; Elizabeth had been taking a birth control pill. Although they are living comfortably within their means with three children, one more would really change their standard of living. As a result, they are certain that they do not want to have any more children. They are trying to decide what birth control they should use and cannot seem to agree on what would be the best option for them.

Her side: I have been on the pill since I was 16 years old, and I am tired of it. Plus, I am worried about potential side effects, even though I know it is very unlikely, but why should I take the chance? And who's to say we won't have another "little surprise"? I could have my tubes tied, but there is the possibility of complications, it is more expensive, and I would need time to recover from the surgery. After having three children, two of which were C-sections, I am tired of being cut, stitched up, and put back together.

His side: So, you think I should get a vasectomy? Won't I just be shooting blanks and what if I can't, you know, perform anymore? I have heard that for some men there is a lot of pain afterward. I agree, maybe surgery isn't the best option. What if we want another kid one day? Maybe you could change to something so that you would not have to take a pill every day.

Your side: What would you do if you were a member of this couple? Or what if you were their doctor and they came to you for advice?

1. Are John's fears about a vasectomy valid?

2. Are there other options that John and Elizabeth should consider?

3. Is it fair for John to ask Elizabeth to continue to bear the responsibility for birth control?

Late 1800s

1873: Comstock law makes abortion and abortion-related services illegal.

1820–1900: Physicians in the American Medical Association work to outlaw abortions in the U.S.

First vacuum device created; used in China, Japan, and Soviet Union.

Early 1900s

1920: Abortions legal in Soviet Union.

1931: Mexico legalizes abortion in cases of rape.

1935: Iceland legalizes abortion.

1938: Legal in Sweden on a limited basis.

Mid-to Late 1900s

1961: California state legislature introduces abortion reform law.

1966: Mississippi is first U.S. state to allow abortion in rape cases.

1967: U.K. legalizes abortion.

1967-1970: States begin to loosen abortion laws.

1968: President Lyndon Johnson calls for repeal of U.S. abortion laws.

1969: Abortions lawful in Australia.

1970: Some U.S. states allow abortion on demand.

1973: U.S. Supreme Court, in *Roe v. Wade*, declares that all bans on abortion in the first trimester are unconstitutional; regulates abortion in second and third trimesters; court legalizes abortions in all trimesters for mental and physical health matters.

1979: China enacts one-child policy.

1988: France legalizes RU-486 abortion pill.

1994: U.S. Freedom of Access to Clinic Entrances Act forbids obstruction or use of force to block access to reproductive health services.

1999: U.S. Congress passes ban on partial birth abortion; President Bill Clinton vetoes the legislation.

Early 2000s

2000: RU-486 is approved by U.S. Food and Drug Administration.

2003: U.S. enacts Partial Birth Abortion Ban Act; President George W. Bush signs it into law.

2007: U.S. Supreme Court upholds Partial Birth Abortion Act.

ABORTION: A PERSONAL CHOICE

Abortion is the termination of a pregnancy (an embryo or fetus) by various means before the end of its natural term. A **therapeutic abortion** is an induced abortion to preserve the life of the mother; a *spontaneous abortion* is an abortion that occurs naturally, such as in the case of miscarriage or stillbirth (see Chapter 12).

As you can see in Figure 13.12, the practice of abortion dates back to ancient times when people used herbs, sharpened implements, and the application of abdominal pressure to induce abortions. Until about 1900, abortion was legal in the United States. It was made illegal because of physicians' concerns about the safety of abortions being performed by untrained midwives and "abortion providers." The thinking at the time was that if abortions were criminalized, women would stop obtaining them from unsafe providers and that those non-physicians who performed the procedures would stop or face criminal prosecution. Women continued to obtain abortions, but under even worse circumstances than existed before. Fast-forward to 1973, where abortion was legalized in the United States again.

ABORTION TRENDS

Today in the United States, nearly half of all pregnancies are unintended; four out of 10 of these are terminated by abortion (Jones et al., 2008). There are racial and ethnic differences of women who obtain abortions. Blacks and whites have nearly similar rates, but Hispanics have significantly lower rates. Lower abortion rates among Hispanics are attributed to this group's religious beliefs, which is predominantly Catholicism (Jones, Darroch, & Jenshaw, 2002). Since the legalization of abortion in 1973, about 50 million abortions have been performed (The Alan Guttmacher

Institute, 2008). Figure 13.13 illustrates a downward trend in abortions. This decline may be due to increased use of contraceptives or the increased trends in abstinence until marriage (Planned Parenthood, 2008).

In 2009, public opinion took a more conservative turn on abortion. Recently, two separate abortion opinion polls revealed that Americans' support for legal abortions in most cases has slipped (Pew Research Center, 2009; Gallup Poll, 2009). In 2008, for example, 53 percent of men polled indicated that abortion should be legal in most cases; today, 43 percent say it should be legal (Pew Research Center, 2009). Among mainline Protestants (such as Methodists and Presbyterians), support for abortion also steadily declined within a one-year time frame, from 69 percent to 54 percent.

There are two types of abortion: the abortion pill and in-clinic abortions. A woman or a couple has many decisions to make when considering abortion. A decision to terminate a pregnancy is a highly personal, individual one, and for most women, it is an agonizing one. Depending on her circumstances and how far along she is in her pregnancy, she may decide to use a medication that ends a first-trimester pregnancy.

THE ABORTION PILL (MEDICATION ABORTION)

The type of abortion provided depends on how far along a woman is in her pregnancy. In the United States, approximately 61 percent of all abortions are performed when a woman is nine weeks pregnant or less (see Figure 13.14). Generally speaking, the abortion pill can be used up to 63 days (nine weeks) after the first day of a woman's last menstrual period (ACOG, 2009). This nonsurgical, medication abortion involves three steps:

1. **The Abortion Pill (Mifepristone, or RU-486):** At the clinic, the health care provider gives the woman mifepristone in pill form; Methotrexate (MTX) is the injection form of this medication (the preferred procedure for up to seven weeks' gestation). The pill works by blocking the hormone progesterone; without this hormone, the lining of the uterus breaks down and pregnancy cannot continue. The woman is also given an antibiotic to prevent infection.

2. **Misoprostol:** The second pill is taken at the woman's convenience, up to three days after taking the abortion pill. This pill causes cramps and bleeding usually within a few hours of taking it. It causes the uterus to empty. It is common for a woman to have bleeding and cramping for up to four weeks after the abortion.

3. **Follow-up:** A follow-up appointment is made with the health care provider, to ensure that the abortion is complete and that the woman is well.

Women choose this option because it can be done early in the pregnancy and because it is very private. The abortion pill is safe for most women,

Figure 13.13   Number of Abortions per 1,000 Women Ages 15–44, by year (1973–2005)

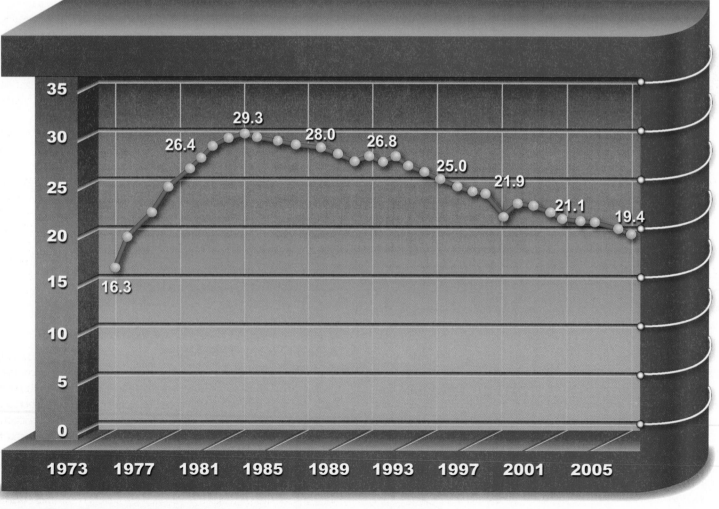

Source: The Alan Guttmacher Institute (2008).

>>> The abortion pill can be used **up to 63 days after the first day of a woman's last menstrual period (ACOG, 2009).**

but risks include allergic reactions, incomplete abortions, infections, and very heavy bleeding. If the abortion pill is ineffective, a woman must agree to a surgical abortion (American Pregnancy Association, 2009). Abortions performed this early pose virtually no long-term risks of infertility, ectopic pregnancy, miscarriage, or birth defects (Boonstra et al., 2006). Medical abortions are 95 to 97 percent effective.

IN-CLINIC ABORTION

There are several different kinds of abortions that are performed by health care providers within medical clinics or hospitals; the type of procedure performed largely depends upon how far along the woman is in her pregnancy. **In-clinic abortions** are typically performed when a woman is in her second or third trimester (The Alan Guttmacher Institute, 2008). Slightly more than 11 percent of abortions in the United States are provided when women are 13 to 21-plus weeks pregnant. Teens are more likely than adults to delay having an abortion until after 15 weeks of pregnancy (Strauss et al., 2007).

During these procedures, the woman is medicated with numbing medications, pain medications, or with types of sedation, to make her more comfortable. The uterus is emptied by **aspiration**, use of a suction device, or by D&C or D&E, the use of suction and other devices. In the third trimester, an **induction abortion** (commonly referred to as a *saline abortion*) is a rarely performed procedure in which saline (salt) water and potassium chloride are injected into the amniotic sac (causing fetal demise). Prostaglandins are inserted into the vagina (to soften the cervix), and *pitocin* (a synthetic hormone) is injected intravaneously; these medications induce uterine contractions to expel the fetus. **Dilation and extraction** is a surgical abortion procedure used to terminate a pregnancy after 21 weeks. It is often referred to as *intrauterine cranial decompression* or *partial birth abortion*.

There are risks associated with any medical procedure, and abortion is no exception. Risks for in-clinic abortions range from blood clots, injury to the cervix or other organs, to very heavy bleeding; death can occur, but this is a very rare complication. Abortions performed in the first trimester are virtually free of complications—less than 1 percent require further treatment for infection or other problems, and prior to eight weeks gestation, there is about one death per 1 million abortions (Boonstra et al., 2006). At 16 weeks, the death rate is one in 29,000 abortions, and one in 11,000 at 21 weeks or more.

FEELINGS AFTER AN ABORTION

Deciding to terminate a pregnancy is traumatic for most women, and it's not unusual for women to have a wide range of feelings after an abortion. Little empirical evidence exists that tracks the long-term emotional, physical, and psychological consequences of abortion procedures. Some organizations, such as Planned Parenthood, note that immediately after the abortion it is common for women to experience anger, regret, guilt, sadness, or depression; some feel relief (Planned Parenthood, 2008). Earlier research studies that explored whether women experienced depression, regret, anxiety, guilt, mental changes, and changes in emotional health suggested that there are few psychological effects in women who have undergone an abortion (Cohen & Roth, 1984; Major et al., 2000; Russo & Zierk, 1992).

Other studies, however, demonstrated that abortion is problematic, leading to prolonged grief, problems with intimacy and sexuality, and prolonged guilt (Angelo, 1994; Lewis, 1997; Williams, 2000). One recent study of postabortive women found that abortion is not a one-time experience; rather, abortion is a process that unfolds over time, and one that "may not be time limited in its effects and influences" (Trybulski, 2005, p. 573). Interviewing the women who had abortions at least 15 years before the study, the investigator discovered that emotional and psychological problems were intermittent over the years and were present sometimes years after the termination. All of the women interviewed knew how old their child would have been "today" had it not been aborted.

SEXUAL LIFE EDUCATION

Choosing a contraceptive method that is right for your lifestyle can be tough, especially if this topic is or has been off-limits in your family or in your community. And as the young college student told us in the opening vignette, purchasing birth control may prove an embarrassing experience. Unfortunately, teens and young adults sometimes forego using contraceptives because of this embarrassment. But being sexually active requires responsibility, both responsibility to yourself and responsibility to your partner(s). There are many options available to you today, and each option carries its own benefits and risks. It's well worth the time and effort to educate yourself about these various options, because there are few things that are as important as your sexual health and well-being.

Figure 13.14 Rates of Abortion Procedures, by Gestation

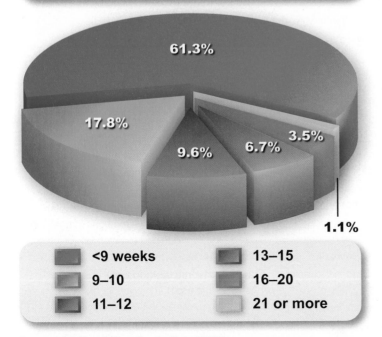

When women have abortions (in weeks from the last menstrual period)
Eighty-nine percent of abortions occur in the first 12 weeks of pregnancy, 2004.

61.3%
17.8%
9.6%
6.7%
3.5%
1.1%

- <9 weeks
- 9–10
- 11–12
- 13–15
- 16–20
- 21 or more

Source: The Alan Guttmacher Institute (2008).

Summary

WHAT ARE THE DIFFERENT WAYS TO PREVENT PREGNANCY AND PROTECT YOUR SEXUAL HEALTH? 268

• Contraception and birth control have been a part of human sexuality since ancient times. Barrier methods include condoms, diaphragms, the cervical cap, and the sponge. Hormonal methods include birth control pills, the vaginal ring, and hormonal injections and implants. There are also intrauterine methods.

• If a couple decides to take a natural approach to contraception, the woman can use the symptothermal method by being aware of her fertility by charting her menstrual cycle, basal body temperature, and cervical mucus changes. Withdrawal is another option, but the only method with a 100 percent effectiveness rate is abstinence.

WHAT ARE THE PERMANENT CONTRACEPTIVE METHODS? 281

• Once a person or couple are certain that they no longer wish to have children, there are permanent

surgical sterilization methods available for both women and men. Women can opt for tubal ligation, while men can have vasectomies.

WHAT OPTIONS ARE THERE WHEN CONTRACEPTION FAILS? 283

• If a condom breaks, a man neglects to pull out in time, or any contraceptive method fails in any other way, a woman can procure emergency contraception, or the morning-after pill, a high dose of hormones to prevent conception. If a pregnancy does occur, abortion is an available option, but it is a hard decision for many women to make.

Key Terms

birth control any action, method, or practice that controls the number of children born by preventing or reducing the likelihood of conception 268

contraception methods or devices that prevent the fertilization of the ovum by the sperm 268

contraceptive behavior how women and men utilize methods to prevent pregnancy 268

failure rate the number of women who become pregnant if 100 women used the method for one year 271

barrier contraceptive methods methods that provide a chemical or physical barrier between the sperm and the ovum 272

condom a thin sheath of latex, polyurethane, or animal intestine that is worn over an erect penis or inside the vagina during intercourse 272

diaphragm a small, latex, dome-shaped cup that is inserted into the vagina 272

cervical cap a small, thin, cup-shaped device made of plastic or latex that is inserted into the vagina, fitting tightly over the cervix 274

spermicide chemical contraceptive 274

microbicides a class of 60 chemical contraceptives that reduce the infection rate of viruses or bacteria 274

hormone contraceptive methods methods that use artificial hormones (estrogen and progesterone) to prevent ovulation 274

skin patch an adhesive patch that a woman wears on her buttocks, chest, back, arm, or abdomen and works the same way that oral contraceptives do 275

NuvaRing a flexible, plastic ring that is placed in the upper segment of the vagina 275

birth control pills, or **oral contraceptives** the contraceptive method most widely used by women who are in their teens and 20s and by never-married women 275

multiphasic pills birth control pills that deliver different amounts of hormones every week 276

monophasic pills birth control pills that deliver the same levels of hormones every day 276

triphasic pills birth control pills that contain three different types of pills 276

combination pill a type of birth control pill that contains both estrogen and progestin 277

progestin-only pill, or **minipill** a type of birth control pill that is a good choice for women who cannot take estrogen 277

continuous-dose pills birth control pills that are taken for 84 consecutive days, with seven days off 277

breakthrough bleeding bleeding at a time other than a period 277

contraceptive implant a single rod that contains progestin and is effective for three years 277

hormone injections a three-month injectable shot 277

intrauterine device (IUD) a small, T-shaped, plastic device that contains copper 278

intrauterine system (IUS) similar to an IUD, but also contains a synthetic sex hormone, progestin 278

fertility awareness, or **natural family planning (NFP)** contraceptive methods that rely on predicting ovulation and avoiding sexual intercourse during a fertile time frame 278

symptothermal method basal body temperature (BBT), the calendar method, and the mucus method of preventing pregnancy 278

basal body temperature (BBT) the lowest body temperature *278*

biphasic pattern pattern in which women have a lower BBT before ovulation and higher body temperatures after an egg has been released *278*

mucus method method of contraception based on changes in cervical mucus that occur during the menstrual cycle *280*

withdrawal, or **coitus interruptus** contraceptive method involving the man withdrawing his penis from the vagina prior to ejaculation *280*

Quiverfull movement movement among some evangelical Protestant Christians, Catholics, and Mormons to follow commands in the Bible—to "be fruitful and multiply," and "blessed is the person who has a quiver full of children" *280*

abstinence the act of refraining from sexual intercourse *280*

periodic abstinence abstaining from sexual intercourse during a woman's fertile time *280*

outercourse sex play that keeps sperm out of the vagina to prevent pregnancy *281*

sterilization a surgical procedure that prevents either the egg or the sperm from reaching its intended destination *281*

tubal ligation a surgical procedure in which the fallopian tubes are severed and sealed with an electric current *281*

vasectomy an in-office medical procedure that removes all or part of the vas deferens *282*

post-vasectomy pain syndrome (PVPs) genital pain of varying intensity following a vasectomy *282*

emergency contraception (EC), or **morning-after pill**, **Plan B** hormonal contraception that reduces the risk of pregnancy by 89 percent after a sexual experience *283*

abortion termination of a pregnancy before the end of its natural term *285*

therapeutic abortion an induced abortion to preserve the life of the mother *285*

abortion pill, or **mifepristone** pill form to induce medication abortion *286*

misoprostol pill taken to cause evacuation of uterus; second step of medication abortion *286*

in-clinic abortions abortion typically performed when a woman is in her second or third trimester *287*

aspiration suctioning of fetus from uterus *287*

D&C or **D&E** the use of suction and other devices *287*

induction abortion a rarely performed procedure in which saline water and potassium chloride are injected into the amniotic sac, causing fetal demise *287*

dilation and extraction (D&E) a surgical abortion procedure used to terminate a pregnancy after 21 weeks *287*

Sample Test Questions

MULTIPLE CHOICE

1. A condom is which type of contraceptive method?
   a. Hormonal
   b. Barrier
   c. Symptothermal
   d. Intrauterine

2. Spermicides work by:
   a. Creating a physical barrier between the sperm and the egg
   b. Altering a woman's hormones
   c. Rendering sperm inactive
   d. Altering a man's hormones

3. Which contraceptive method requires a fitting by a health care professional?
   a. Diaphragm
   b. Norplant
   c. Female condom
   d. Cervical cap

4. The minipill contains:
   a. Estrogen
   b. Estrogen and progestin
   c. Progestin
   d. Progestin and testosterone

5. An intrauterine system is different from an intrauterine device because it:
   a. Doesn't need to be inserted by a health care professional
   b. Contains copper
   c. Contains estrogen
   d. Contains progestin

6. Which method is NOT part of the symptothermal method?
   a. Basal body temperature
   b. Calendar
   c. Withdrawal
   d. Mucus

7. Which method is the most successful at preventing both pregnancy and the risk of STIs?
   a. Birth control pills
   b. Emergency contraception
   c. Sterilization
   d. Abstinence

8. When do the majority of women choose to have abortions?
   a. Less than 9 weeks after their periods
   b. 9–10 weeks after their periods
   c. 13–15 weeks after their periods
   d. 21 or more weeks after their periods

SHORT RESPONSE

1. Explain the difference between contraception and birth control.

2. What aspects of your life have influenced what type of contraception you have chosen to use or which type you will choose to use once you become sexually active?

3. Explain how the failure rate of a contraceptive method is determined.

4. Is it difficult for you to talk about contraceptives with your partner? Why or why not?

5. Should someone's contraceptive method of choice remain static or should it change through his or her life? Why?

Answers: 1. b; **2.** c; **3.** a; **4.** c; **5.** d; **6.** c; **7.** d; **8.** a

Remember to check www.thethinkspot.com **for additional information, downloadable flashcards, and other helpful resources.**

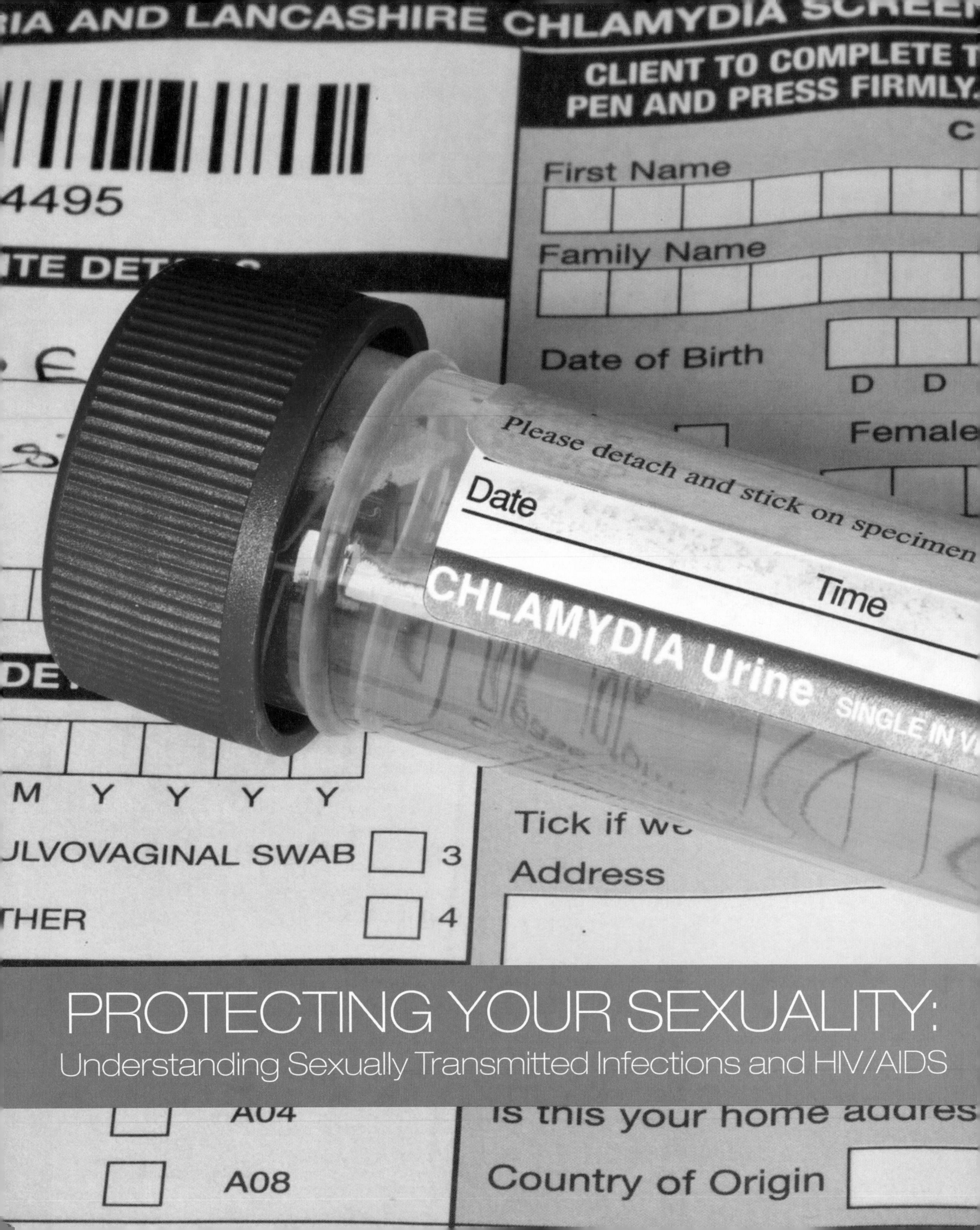

RIA AND LANCASHIRE CHLAMYDIA SCREEN

CLIENT TO COMPLETE T
PEN AND PRESS FIRMLY.

First Name

Family Name

Date of Birth

D D

Female

Please detach and stick on specimen

Date

Time

CHLAMYDIA Urine SINGLE IN VI

4495

TE DET

€

M Y Y Y Y

JLVOVAGINAL SWAB ☐ 3

THER ☐ 4

Tick if we

Address

PROTECTING YOUR SEXUALITY:
Understanding Sexually Transmitted Infections and HIV/AIDS

A04

Is this your home addres

A08

Country of Origin

WHAT KINDS OF SEXUALLY TRANSMITTED INFECTIONS ARE THERE AND HOW ARE THEY TRANSMITTED AND TREATED?

WHAT IMPACT HAVE HIV AND AIDS HAD ON THE WORLD?

HOW DO YOU TELL YOUR PARTNER ABOUT AN STI?

I have

always prided myself on making good decisions. All through high school, the only person I ever had sex with was my boyfriend. We dated for three years and didn't have sex until the third year of our relationship. But that all changed last month. James and I broke up soon after I left for college. I didn't think that I would date again for a long time, but a few weeks ago, I went to a party with some friends and I drank way too much. I met [this guy] and he seemed nice enough. You know how it goes . . . before I knew it, we hooked up. It's been about three months since I had sex with him, and now I have some weird things going on. I am so afraid that I have the clap or something. On the one hand, I don't think it's really that big a deal, because I could list at least 10 of my friends who have had an STD. But on the other hand, I know that I should get tested—but I'm just too damn embarrassed! God, how did I get myself into this mess? I know better, and should have done better.

Source: Author's files

CHAPTER **14**

Sexually transmitted infections and the HIV/AIDS epidemic are major threats to public health, both in the United States and abroad: one in four teenage girls in the United States has a sexually transmitted infection, and today 1.1 million people in the United States are living with HIV (Centers for Disease Control and Prevention, 2009a; Johnson-Mallard et al., 2007). Without swift intervention, public health experts and epidemiologists (scientists and doctors who study the causes and transmissions of diseases) predict dramatic increases in cases (Margolis et al., 2006).

In many ways, this chapter is a continuation of Chapter 13. In the previous chapter, we learned how to protect ourselves against unwanted pregnancies, and sexually transmitted infections and HIV/AIDS through the use of contraceptives, such as condoms and spermicidal creams. But in a survey of more than 80,000 college students, only 36 percent used a condom during vaginal intercourse, and only 28 percent used a condom during oral sex (NCHA, 2008). And, nearly three times as many students did not use a condom during anal intercourse (14 percent) compared to the people who did (5 percent). These trends are important, because they tell us that even though many students have had sexual and health education, and even though they know they *should* use a condom every time to protect themselves, they *do not*.

The purpose of this chapter is twofold. The information here is presented to increase your awareness of STIs and HIV/AIDS and also to increase your scientific understanding of how these infections affect your health and overall well-being. To accomplish this, we'll first take a look at the national and global epidemic of sexually transmitted infections and

Who has a sexually transmitted infection?

HIV/AIDS, paying particular attention to why women and people of racial/ethnic heritages are significantly more susceptible to these infections. We'll then explore bacterial and viral STIs, as well as HIV/AIDS—what they are, how we acquire them, and how they are treated. We'll then examine HIV/AIDS and the trends here in the United States and abroad. We'll conclude this chapter by looking at ways partners can communicate about their sexuality and sexually transmitted infections and, in doing so, how to enhance their sexual relationships.

So great are STI rates in the United States that they have been referred to as a "hidden epidemic," one with enormous health and economic consequences (Centers for Disease Control and Prevention, 2006; Montgomery, Gonzalez, & Montgomery, 2008). Sexually transmitted infections are a major health issue for people of all ages, but teenagers, young adults, and certain racial/ethnic groups are particularly vulnerable (Lindley et al., 2008). The Centers for Disease Control and Prevention (CDC) is taking several measures to curb the growing trends (see Table 14.1).

SEXUALLY TRANSMITTED INFECTIONS: THE EPIDEMIC

Sexually transmitted infections (STIs) are diseases that are transmitted between partners through sexual contact, such as vaginal intercourse, oral sex, nonpenetrative genital contact, or anal sex, and they remain one of our nation's greatest health challenges. In the past, STIs have been referred to as *sexually transmitted disease (STD)* and *venereal disease (VD)*. Within the past decade or so, public health officials have started to use the term *sexually transmitted infection*, because infection means that a germ, such as a virus, bacterium, or parasite, can lead to disease (Shafer & Moscicki, 2006).

Each year, state health departments are required to provide the Centers for Disease Control and Prevention with the number of STI cases diagnosed by health care providers. Syphilis, hepatitis B, gonorrhea, chancroid, chlamydia, human immunodeficiency virus (HIV), and acquired immune deficiency syndrome (AIDS) are required to be reported; other STIs, such as herpes, do not need to be reported (The Alan Guttmacher

---

TABLE 14.1
What is the CDC Doing To Reduce STIs?

Source: Centers for Disease Control and Prevention (2009c).

Actively seeking ways to fight STIs and HIV in minority communities remains one of the CDC's highest priorities. What's being done today?

- **Designing Prevention/Intervention Programs:** The CDC is developing culture-specific education and intervention programs.

- **Implementing Prevention/Intervention Programs:** The CDC is training providers to educate and work with high-risk minority groups.

- **Addressing Social/Structural Factors:** These studies assess why some people have hindered access to health care, and what can be done to increase care among disadvantaged groups.

- **Increasing Awareness:** The CDC is working with more than 200 racial/ethnic leaders to develop and implement actions that will reach all minorities with the tools and knowledge they need to protect themselves against STIs and HIV.

- **Increasing Testing:** In 2008, the CDC doubled its investment (to $70 million) to increase STI/HIV testing among minorities.

OWN IT! STI Risk

Anyone who is sexually active is at risk of an STI. How high is your risk? If you have multiple sex partners, engage in sexual intercourse without a condom, drink alcohol or use drugs prior to having sex, or fail to communicate with your partner, then you are at a greater risk for getting an STI. Reflect on the following questions as a way to help you assess your own risk for acquiring an STI and to think about ways that you can reduce your risk.

1. Do you drink alcohol or use drugs? If so, how do you think such substance use affects your decisions about sexual activity?

2. How likely are you to discuss STIs and condom use with a new sexual partner?

3. What are some techniques that you have used (or plan to use) to initiate conversation about safe sex with a partner?

Institute, 2008). This information is valuable, because it not only helps demographers and public health officials track the trends of these infections, but it also helps them better understand who is at greater risk of acquiring STIs and HIV, such as women and minority groups (CDC, 2009a).

Today, two-thirds of all STIs are found in young adults under the age of 25 (CDC, 2009a), and almost half of the 19 million diagnosed cases of STIs each year in the United States are among young adults aged 15 to 24 (CDC, 2009a); more than 65 million people in the U.S. currently have an STI (Montgomery, Gonzalez, & Montgomery, 2008). In the U.S. alone, medical costs associated with STIs are estimated at nearly $15 billion annually, and more than $8 billion is spent each year to diagnose and treat STIs. This does not include the costs associated with the treatment of HIV (American Social Health Association, 2009).

It is necessary to have an understanding of the trends, treatments, and prevention of common sexually transmitted infections. By gaining knowledge of STIs, young men and women can both protect their sexual and reproductive health, and they can better enjoy their sexuality. In addition to the burden on youth and young adults, women are also severely affected, because their physiology places them at a greater risk than men for the severe consequences of STIs (CDC, 2009a).

WOMEN AND STIS/HIV

Younger women are more biologically susceptible to STIs, particularly gonorrhea, chlamydia, and HIV, than older women and men are (Boskey, 2007). There are different layers of cells on the surface of the cervix. The cells facing the vagina, the *ectocervix*, are squamous (pronounced *s-kway-mus*) cells, and the passage from the vagina to the uterus, the *endocervix*, contains epithelial cells. The **transformation zone** (also known as the *squamocolumnar border*) is the space between these two cell types, and it is clearly established. Most cervical cancers start in this transformation zone, because these cells are most susceptible to disease and infection, particularly to chlamydia, gonorrhea, and human papillomavirus (HPV) (Boskey, 2007). They are also at risk for cervical dysplasia (see Table 14.2), a problem that does not affect men.

Some females are even more susceptible to STIs because of a condition known as cervical ectopy. Normal among teen girls, young women, pregnant women, and women who take the birth control pill, **cervical ectopy** is a condition in which the inner lining of the cervix (the epithelial cells) turns to the outer edge; this condition causes greater risk to infection by numerous STIs—especially to chlamydia, gonorrhea, and HPV—because these inner cells are thinner and more susceptible to

---

TABLE 14.2
What is Cervical Dysplasia and How Do You Get It?

- **Cervical dysplasia** is an abnormal growth of cells on the cervix, the lower part of the uterus that opens into the vagina. It is not cancer, but it can become cancer of the cervix if not treated.

- A common term for cervical dysplasia is **CIN (cervical intraepithelial neoplasia)**. CIN describes how much of the thickness of the lining of the cervix contains abnormal cells. Sufferers usually don't present with symptoms, but sometimes CIN causes bleeding during or after sex.

- Risk factors include having sexual intercourse before the age of 18, having more than two sex partners, smoking, having had genital warts, herpes, or HIV/AIDS, having unprotected sex with multiple partners, and not having enough folic acid in your diet.

- If you are female and sexually active, it is imperative that you have an exam by a health care provider who can screen you for CIN and other STIs. The ACOG recommends that cervical cancer screenings begin at age 21; screenings before age 21 should be avoided because it may lead to harmful evaluation and treatment (ACOG, 2009).

- It is very important to treat CIN to prevent it from becoming cervical cancer. CIN is diagnosed by a Pap test (see Chapter 4), and there are three different treatments, depending on how advanced the CIN is:
  - **Mild cervical dysplasia (CIN 1):** This often goes away without treatment. Women undergo another Pap test in four to six months as a follow-up.
  - **Moderate dysplasia (CIN 2):** The health care provider may freeze (referred to as *cryo*), burn, or use a laser to destroy the abnormal tissue; a LEEP (a thin wire loop attached to an electrical unit) may also be used. Each of these procedures may be performed in the doctor's office.
  - **Severe dysplasia (CIN 3, or carcinoma in situ):** Done in the operating room, the provider will do a **cone biopsy**, in which a cone-shaped piece of the cervix containing abnormal cells is removed. Cryo, laser, or LEEP may also be used.

Figure 14.1 Pregnancy & STIs How common are STIs in pregnant women in the United States, and what impacts do STIs have on the mother and child?

STIs in Pregnant Women

STI	Estimated Number of Pregnant Women
Bacterial vaginosis	1,080,000
Herpes simplex virus 2	880,000
Trichomoniasis	124,000
Chlamydia	100,000
Hepatitis B	16,000
Gonorrhea	13,200
HIV	6,400
Syphilis	<1,000

Source: Center for Disease Control and Prevention (2008).

The Effects of STIs (mom=red, baby=green)

Infection	Method of Transfer	Risks	Treatment
Gonorrhea	In birth canal during delivery	Ectopic pregnancy; PID	Antibiotics
		Premature birth; stillbirth; eye infections	Antibiotics in the eyes to prevent infections
Chlamydia	In birth canal during delivery	Ectopic pregnancy; PID	Antibiotics
		Pneumonia; eye infections; blindness	Antibiotics
Trichomoniasis	In birth canal during delivery	Possible fallopian tube damage	Antibiotics
		Premature birth; low birth weight	Antibiotics
Syphilis	Can cross placenta during pregnancy and in birth canal during delivery	Miscarriage	Antibiotics to prevent damage to the fetus
		Stillbirth; congenital syphilis, which can result in mental and physical problems	Antibiotics to prevent damage to the fetus
HPV	Rarely transfers during delivery	Can lead to genital cancer; warts in birth canal, which can lead to delivery complications	Topical treatments
		Warts can develop in baby's throat, which requires surgery	Topical treatments
Hepatitis B	In birth canal during delivery	Significant liver damage	
			No cure, but can be prevented with vaccinations
Herpes	Rarely crosses placenta	Severe outbreak in first trimester can cause miscarriages	Outbreaks can be treated with oral medications
		Fetus is at higher risk if herpes is contracted during pregnancy; can lead to neonatal herpes	
HIV	Can cross placenta during pregnancy; in the birth canal during delivery; through breastfeeding	Can develop into AIDS	Antiviral medications to reduce symptoms
		Can develop into AIDS	Treatment during pregnancy greatly reduces transmission to baby

Source: Based on American Pregnancy Association (2009).

infection and disease. Furthermore, young women have larger transformation zones, which also result in increased risk of infection by STIs (Boskey, 2007). As women age, the transformation zone becomes smaller, and cervical ectopy decreases; thus, older women are not as susceptible to STIs.

Pregnant women are at greater risk of acquiring STIs than those who are not pregnant; Figure 14.1 presents the number of pregnant women in the United States who are infected with specific STIs each year. When pregnant, the consequences of an STI can be even more serious for a woman and her baby. Figure 14.1 also shows us the risks of each STI for the mom and baby, as well as the method by which it is transferred to the baby and what treatment options are available. As you can see, risks can include ectopic pregnancy for mothers (which can lead to infertility), miscarriage, and significant damage to the liver (American Pregnancy Association, 2009; CDC, 2009a). Potential problems for the baby are even more severe, including premature birth, low birth weight, stillbirth, pneumonia, fetal infections, blindness, neurological damage, and mental retardation. If a pregnant woman is not in a monogamous relationship, or if she doesn't know her partner's STI status, she should always use condoms while engaging in sex.

STIs of all types affect women of minority races and ethnicities the most. For example, African American/Black Caribbean women are eight times more likely to have chlamydia than white women are; Alaskan Natives are five times more likely to acquire this STI (CDC, 2009b). Why are some groups are at a greater risk for STIs and HIV? Although no single cause explains why some groups are disproportionately affected, who acquires an STI is determined by certain social and economic factors, and these, in turn, facilitate transmission. The CDC (2009b) recently adopted the *social determinants of health (SDH)* approach as an explanation of causal pathways of STIs and HIV among different demographics.

RACE/ETHNICITY AND SEXUALLY TRANSMITTED INFECTIONS/HIV

The **social determinants of health (SDH)** approach advances the idea that there are certain characteristics that are systematically associated with social disadvantage and health disparities (Braveman, 2003); this approach helps us see why some groups are at greater risk for STIs and HIV/AIDS than others. Although we don't fully understand all the social forces that are at work, a general relationship between social factors and health is well established (Solar & Irwin, 2007). As our study throughout this text has shown us, our sexuality is a fluid process that is continuously shaped and orchestrated by cultural forces. Although we still don't quite understand how social forces cause the biological changes (such as an increased biological risk to STIs and HIV), the following factors are known to affect infection rates (Tugwell et al., 2007):

- *Poverty*: Some children raised in economically disadvantaged homes and neighborhoods are more likely to be drawn into behaviors such as illegal drug use and early sexual intercourse, which puts them at higher risk for STIs and HIV/AIDS (Black AIDS Institute, 2009).

- *Education level:* Some ethnic minorities raised in poverty are prone to dropping out of school, preventing them from gaining access to school-based sexuality and health education programming (CDC, 2007).

- *Socioeconomic background (SES):* Some cannot afford health insurance and cannot afford health care. This means they may not have access to STI testing and treatments (CDC, 2008).

Empirical studies suggest that these social inequalities are the "building blocks" of health inequalities (among many, Burrows & Gane, 2006; Tugwell et al., 2007). Recognizing the cultural forces that put some people at higher risk to acquiring STIs/HIV is important, because this knowledge helps us understand the social determinants of health, both in the United States and globally. It also speaks to the need to address and attack the problem on multiple levels (Lowndes & Fenton, 2004).

In our study that follows, we'll take a look at two broad categories of sexually transmitted illnesses: *bacterial infections*, and *viral infections*. Complications from STIs and parasitic infections also exist; these are described in Table 14.3. Throughout our discussion we will note certain demographic trends, such as differences in infection rates in men and women, and among racial and ethnic minorities. We must note these trends because they give us insight into the social contexts that surround the transmission of STIs (Lowndes & Fenton, 2004).

TABLE 14.3
Other Infections

- **Pelvic inflammatory disease (PID)** refers to any type of infection of the uterus, fallopian tubes, or other reproductive organs. It is generally caused by complications of an STI, most commonly gonorrhea and chlamydia. PID can lead to infertility or ectopic pregnancy. About 1 million women experience PID each year, and at least 100,000 become infertile every year because of it. It is most common in sexually active women of childbearing age, particularly women younger than 25. Women who douche, have multiple sex partners, or have sex with someone who has multiple sex partners are at an increased risk for PID. Some women experience few or no symptoms, while others experience abdominal pain, vaginal discharge, painful urination, fever, or vaginal bleeding. PID may go untreated for a long period of time because of mild and nonspecific symptoms. As it is left untreated, scar tissue continues to develop in the uterus and fallopian tubes, potentially contributing to infertility and ectopic pregnancy. When properly diagnosed, PID can be successfully treated with antibiotics.

- **Trichomoniasis**, sometimes called *trich* or *TV,* is a parasitic infection that can be acquired through sexual activity; symptoms may include a foul-smelling, green or yellow vaginal discharge, and vaginal burning or itching. It is treated with the antibiotic Flagyl.

- **Scabies** and **pubic lice** are ectoparasitic infections that are highly contagious. **Ectoparasitic infections** are STIs that are caused by parasites that live on the skin's surface. Both of these STIs are quite common. Symptoms often include itching and a rash. Medical treatment is necessary to get rid of these infections. For pubic lice, Kwell ointment is prescribed. An infected person applies the ointment and leaves it in place for about 12 hours; bed sheets, blankets, and all items of clothing should be machine washed in very hot water to kill the parasite. Topical creams are available for scabies. Just as with public lice, all bedding and clothing should be laundered.

Safer Sex

You can take actions to reduce the risk of getting an STI. These risk-reducing behaviors are referred to as *safer sex*. The only way to completely avoid the risk of getting an STI is to abstain from sexual behaviors. But here are some ideas for safer sex:

- *Be honest*. Assess your risk-taking behaviors, and be honest with yourself about them. Educate yourself on the various STIs, including how they are spread and what the symptoms are. Be honest with your partner!

- *Use a condom every time*. Condoms are one of the easiest and most effective ways to have safer sex.

- *Avoid alcohol and illicit drugs*. The use of too much alcohol or any amount of drugs often leads to high-risk sex.

- *Be vigilant*. If you have an STI, such as herpes, monitor your outbreaks.

Source: Planned Parenthood. Health Topics: Safer Sex ("Safe Sex"). Retrieved September 23, 2009, from http://www.plannedparenthood.org/health-topics/stds-hiv-safer-sex/safer-sex-4263.htm

BACTERIAL INFECTIONS

Caused by certain microorganisms (bacterium), **bacterial infections** can be treated with antibiotics. Bacterial STIs are widespread in developing countries, but their prevalence is declining somewhat in the United States (Donovan, 2004). Unless otherwise noted, all data references are from the Centers for Disease Control and Prevention (2009b).

GONORRHEA

Sometimes referred to as the *clap* or *drip*, **gonorrhea** is the second most common bacterial STI reported in the United States. On average, 700,000 people are diagnosed with it each year. Racial disparities in gonorrhea rates are severe: the rate among African Americans is 19 times greater than that of whites (663 cases per 100,000 for blacks, compared to 35 cases per 100,000 for whites), and in 2007, 70 percent of all gonorrhea cases occurred among blacks. Figure 14.2a shows how rates have remained relatively stable for the past 12 years, and Figure 14.2b presents the racial/ethnic differences in gonorrhea infections.

Gonorrhea is caused by a bacterium, *Neisseria gonorrhoeae*, that survives in the mucus membranes of the body, such as the eyes, throat, mouth, cervix, rectum, and urethra. It is transmitted through intercourse, oral sex, and anal sex, and it can also be transmitted from the mother to her baby during birth; ejaculation does not have to occur for gonorrhea to be transmitted or acquired. In most cases, there are no symptoms of gonorrhea: 80 percent of women and 10 percent of men with this STI show no symptoms. Most people do not know that they are infected, but they are still able to infect their sex partners. Infected males experience a

Figure 14.2a   Gonorrhea Rates per 100,000 Population by Sex, 2007

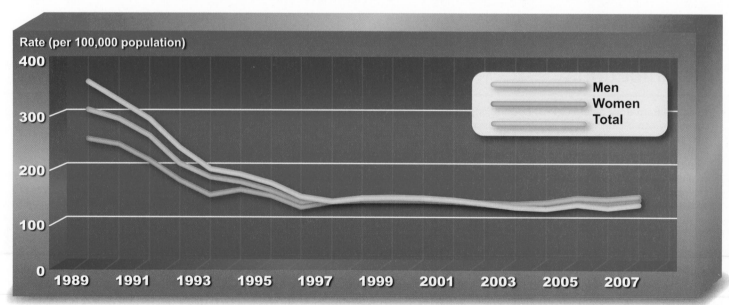

Source: Centers for Disease Control and Prevention (2009b).

Figure 14.2b Gonorrhea Rates per 100,000 Population by Race/Ethnicity, 2008

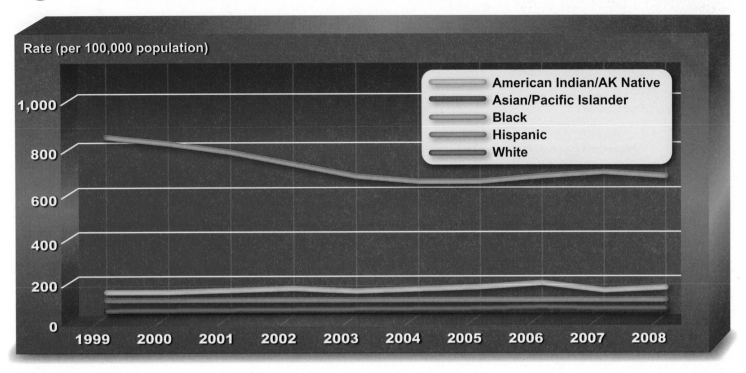

Source: Centers for Disease Control and Prevention (2009b).

foul-smelling, cloudy discharge from the penis, and painful or burning urination; some may have tender/painful testicles (referred to as epididymitis). Although uncommon, some women experience a yellow or green vaginal discharge or breakthrough bleeding between periods. Others may experience painful urination, which is often mistaken for a urinary tract or bladder infection. Rectal gonorrhea (transmitted through anal intercourse) may cause bloody stools and a pus discharge. If left untreated, the infection may spread to a woman's upper reproductive tract and cause pelvic inflammatory disease, or PID.

Infection is not limited to the vagina and the penis. For example, anal intercourse with an infected partner can lead to an anal infection that might be characterized by itching, soreness, discharge, or bleeding. Oral sex can lead to an infection in the throat. This may cause a sore throat, but usually does not cause any other symptoms. Health care professionals can test for gonorrhea with a urine or discharge sample collected with a cotton swab.

Because gonorrhea is a bacterial infection, it responds to tetracycline and/or cephalosporin antibiotics (such as rocephin or doxycycline). There is a wide range of antibiotics used today to treat gonorrhea; however, the disease is becoming more resistant to the standard treatments. Left untreated, this STI can cause PID in women, causing infertility.

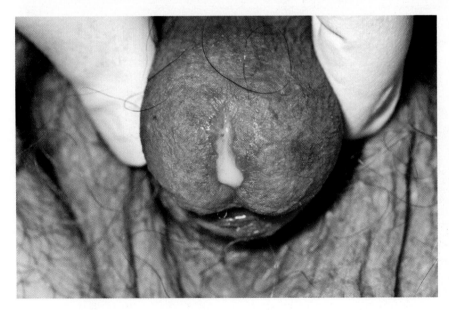

CHLAMYDIA

Chlamydia, commonly referred to as *clam chowder* and *chowder head*, is the most common bacterial STI reported in the United States, with over 1.1 million cases reported in 2007; however, demographers believe that the majority of chlamydia cases are unreported, with at least 2.8 million cases that went unreported in 2007. As with other STIs, racial and ethnic minorities are disproportionately affected,

<<< Men show more symptoms of gonorrhea than women, but it can take up to a month for symptoms to appear.

Figure 14.3a Chlamydia Rates per 100,000 Population by Sex, 2008

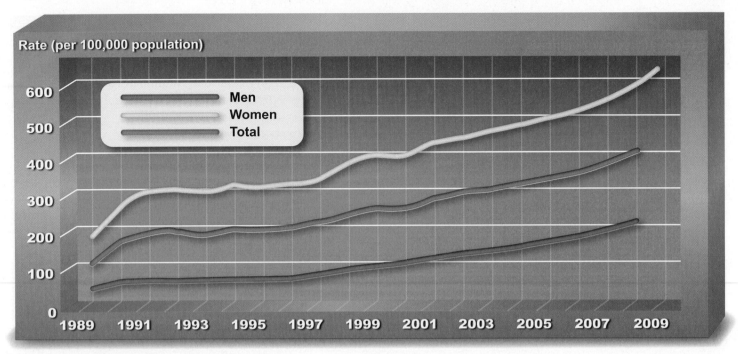

Source: Centers for Disease Control and Prevention (2009b).

and approximately one-half of all chlamydia cases occur among blacks. Figure 14.3a shows us that chlamydia infection rates have steadily increased over the past 20 years, and Figure 14.3b presents chlamydia rates by race/ethnicity. The disease is transmitted through oral sex, vaginal, and anal intercourse, and from a mother to her baby during birth. Worldwide, chlamydia is the most common STI (World Health Organization, 2009). Chlamydia is much more common in women than it is in men and is a particular concern for adolescent women ages 15 to 19 (Chiaradonna, 2008).

Three-fourths of women and half of men experience no symptoms of chlamydia. If symptoms do occur, they may begin as early as five to 10 days after infection; however, if symptoms occur, most experience

Figure 14.3b Chlamydia Rates per 100,000 Population by Race/Ethnicity, 2008

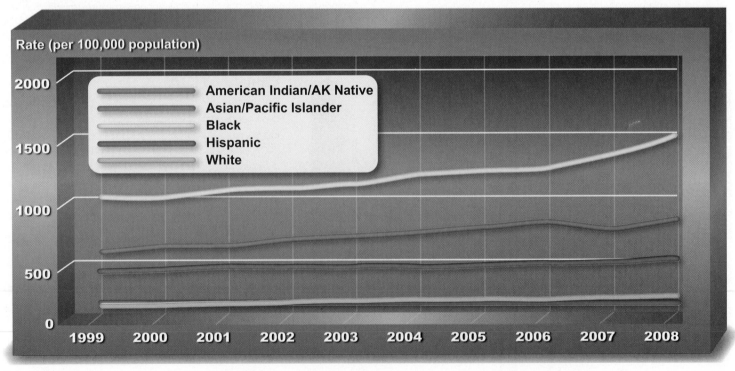

Source: Centers for Disease Control and Prevention (2009b).

Men: white/cloudy, watery discharge from the penis; burning sensation while passing urine.

If the infection occurs in the rectum (from anal sex), there are rarely symptoms. Finally, although rare, the infection can be transferred on fingers to the eyes.

Chlamydia is treatable with antibiotics. Commonly, the antibiotics are taken over the course of seven days. To avoid the risk of reinfection, both partners are typically treated and are advised to be tested again after treatment before they resume sexual activity. The CDC recommends annual screenings for *all* sexually active women, ages 20 to 25, and for any woman who has multiple sex partners.

If left untreated, chlamydia can have serious long-term consequences. In women, untreated infection can spread to the uterus and fallopian tubes, causing PID. Furthermore, infected women, when compared to uninfected women, have five times the risk of HIV infection if exposed to the virus (Chiaradonna, 2008). Long-term complications among men are much less common.

SYPHILIS

Syphilis, also referred to as *cock pox*, *pox*, or the *great imitator*, is a bacterial infection caused by the spirochete *Treponema pallidum*. It is spread through direct contact with a syphilis sore, which typically occurs on the external genitals, vagina, or anus. These sores can also develop on the lips, tongue, or mouth. This STI is transmitted through vaginal, oral, and anal sex, as well as from the mother to her unborn baby during birth. If a mother is untreated, her unborn baby has a 70 percent chance of being infected with syphilis during birth; over 40 percent of babies are stillborn if the mother is untreated. Syphilis

> ˄˄˄ If a child is infected with the mother's chlamydia, **it can ultimately result in blindness.**

them within one to three weeks after they have become infected (Johnsen, 2005). Symptoms can include:

Women: minor increase in vaginal discharge; bladder infection; frequent urination or burning while urinating; pain during sexual intercourse; bleeding during/after sex; mild lower abdominal cramping; irregular menstrual bleeding.

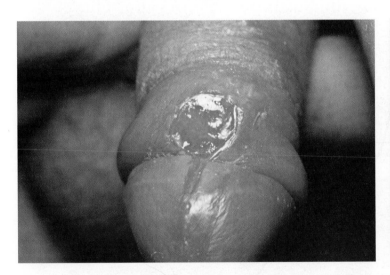

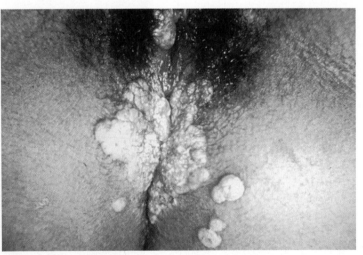

> ˄˄˄ A **chancroid** (SHAN-kroyd) sore is often mistaken for a syphilis chancre (pictured here on both male and female patients); however, the two are quite different in appearance and texture. **A chancroid often has softer edges, while a syphilis sore has hard edges. This type of STI is relatively rare in the United States; the majority of cases involve someone who has traveled to a foreign country, particularly to poor countries such as the Caribbean and Asia.** Uncircumcised men are at greater risk of acquiring chancroids than uncircumcised men, and it is associated with HIV transmission.

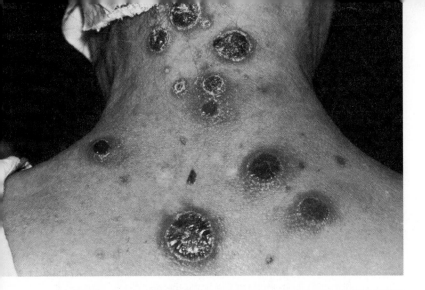

^ ^ ^ A rash over some or all of the body **is characteristic of the secondary stage of syphilis.**

rates (rates per 100,000) in the United States reveal the disparities in infection:

- African Americans/Black Caribbeans: 14.0

- Whites: 2.0

- Hispanics: 4.3

- Asians: 1.2

- American Indian/Alaska Native: 3.4

People with syphilis have been found to be more susceptible to infection with HIV.

There are three stages of syphilis:

1. During the **primary stage**, the first sore, or *chancre* (SHAN-ker), appears at the site of the infection. This usually occurs 10 days to three months after contact; the site of the infection is often internal and not visible to the eye. During this stage, there are no other symptoms.

2. Three to six weeks after the chancre appears, a rash develops over some or all of the body. This is called the **secondary stage**. During this stage, an infected person may also experience headaches, fever, fatigue, sore throat, and enlarged lymph nodes. These symptoms disappear without treatment.

3. Left untreated, syphilis goes into a **latent period**, where the infected person is no longer

contagious. During this stage, however, about one-third will experience damage to the heart, brain, eyes, bones, liver, kidneys, arteries, and nervous system. Untreated, this can result in mental illness, even death.

Can syphilis be treated? Yes. Even during the latent stage of the disease, patients can be treated and cured, although the damage that occurs is irreversible. The drug of choice since the 1940s is penicillin. As with other STIs, syphilis is best prevented through abstinence, sex within a monogamous relationship, or consistent and correct condom usage.

VIRAL INFECTIONS

Viral infections include herpes, human papillomavirus (HPV), viral hepatitis, and HIV (discussed later in the chapter). These diseases cannot be treated with antibiotics, although there are antiviral medications that help alleviate or lessen the symptoms. Unless otherwise noted, all data are gathered from the CDC (2009b).

HERPES

Herpes (see Figure 14.4) is caused when the *herpes simplex virus (HSV)* enters the body. After this virus enters the body, it has the capability of reproducing itself; it cannot be destroyed by antibiotics like bacterial infections can. Consequently, once a person becomes infected with a viral sexually transmitted infection, he or she will have it for life. When the viral infection occurs on or near the mouth and face, it is called *oral*

Can herpes be transmitted to another person even when no active symptoms are showing?

Herpes can be transmitted even when the infected partner doesn't have any symptoms. This is because of **viral shedding**, a process in which the virus is released between outbreaks of infected skin; this is why it's of the utmost necessity for infected partners to use a condom *every single time, for every kind of sex*. An infected person can also reinfect themselves on another part of their body. This is referred to as **autoinoculate**, or self-infecting.

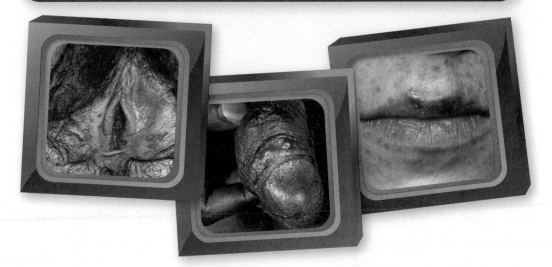

Figure 14.4 The Herpes Simplex Virus Oral herpes (HSV-1) and Genital herpes (HSV-2)

Should Gardasil be mandatory?

In 2006, the Federal Drug Administration approved Gardasil, a vaccine that targets two cancer-causing HPV strains that are responsible for 70 percent of cervical cancer; the vaccine also targets two other strains of HPV, which cause 90 percent of genital warts. The vaccine has a 90- to 100-percent effectiveness record, but this rate is dependent upon vaccination occurring before the girl becomes sexually active. The CDC recommends the vaccine for routine use on 11- and 12-year-old girls; they suggest it can be given to a girl as young as age 9. Should the vaccine be mandatory for young girls?

YES!

Dr. Arthur L. Caplan, Chairman, Department of Medical Ethics at the University of Pennsylvania, notes there are advantages associated with early, mandatory vaccination:

- Ensures that young girls who would otherwise not have access to the treatment (such as those who are part of minority groups) would receive it.

- Decreases health care disparities experienced by minority youth.

- Decreases cervical dysplasia and cervical cancer rates observed among adolescent females and young women.

NO!

There are still questions about the side effects and that it will promote sexual promiscuity in those who are vaccinated. Dr. Janice Shaw Crouse of Concerned Women for America cites a number of concerns:

- Some parents may shirk their responsibility to teach their daughters about making good sexual decisions, thereby reducing safer sex practices.

- Some girls may perceive this as a safety net for promiscuity.

- Although there is normally a period of months or even years of use before a vaccine is mandated, legislation to mandate the HPV vaccine was being considered even before it was readily available.

>>> WHAT DO YOU THINK?
1. Should the HPV vaccine be mandatory? Why or why not?
2. Will the vaccine lead to sexual promiscuity?
3. Would you have a daughter vaccinated? Why or why not?

Source: Caplan, A. (2007, May 11). At Issue: Will the HPV vaccine promote promiscuity? No. *CQ Researcher*, p. 425.

herpes, or **herpes simplex I (HSV-1)**; when it occurs on or near the genitals, it is called *genital herpes*, or **herpes simplex II (HSV-2)**. Each year, nearly 1 million people are infected with genital herpes, and nationwide, at least 45 million people over the age of 12 have had genital HSV; this represents one of five adolescents/adults. Today, about one in every four women has herpes, and one of eight men.

The virus is transmitted through touching, kissing, and vaginal, anal, or oral sex. Generally, transmission occurs from an infected partner who is not aware that he or she has the virus. Most people are not aware that they are infected with genital herpes. Those who have symptoms notice the development of a herpes sore, usually within two weeks after the person is infected. The blister-like sores will open, "weep," scab over, and heal within two to four weeks. It is important to note that most people will not develop these blisters, and if they do, the blisters may be so mild that they are mistaken for a bug bite or skin rash.

After the first outbreak or episode of genital herpes, most people will have four or five additional outbreaks within the first year. There is no cure for genital herpes. Usually, over a period of five or six years, the outbreaks of the sores become less frequent and weaker, gradually disappearing altogether. If a person experiences more than six outbreaks in a one-year period, there are prescription antiviral medications that can help reduce the frequency and the symptoms of the virus. These types of treatment are called *suppressive therapy*, because although they do not cure the infection, they alleviate the symptoms.

HUMAN PAPILLOMAVIRUS (HPV)

The **human papillomavirus (HPV)** infected 20 million people in 2007. Experts estimate that three out of four sexually active men and women will be infected with the HPV virus at some point. In its more severe form, *high risk* HPV can lead to certain cancers, such as cancer of the mouth, cervix, vagina, anus, and penis. Other types of the HPV virus, *low risk*, can cause genital warts. HPV is spread through vaginal, oral, and anal intercourse, as well as through skin-to-skin contact.

In most cases of HPV, there are no symptoms. The virus lives, undetected, in the skin or mucus membranes of the body. Sometimes, a symptom of the virus is the appearance of **genital warts**, which are soft, moist, pink/flesh-colored growths found on the vulva, vagina, anus, cervix, penis, scrotum, groin, or thigh. These warts may appear anywhere from six weeks to nine months after infection, or not at all. Most people are diagnosed upon visual examination of a wart or cluster of warts. Women are typically diagnosed by a Pap test, which is a routine cancer-screening tool.

HPV can be treated, but not cured. But because most of the cases of HPV are low-risk cases and go away by themselves, HPV is considered relatively harmless. To keep the warts from growing and multiplying, doctors have several treatment options, including:

- Chemical solutions that destroy the warts
- Removing the warts by freezing them with liquid nitrogen (*cryotherapy*)
- Removing the warts with surgery or lasers

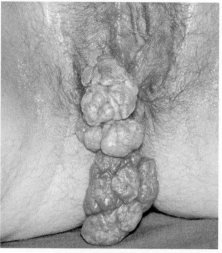

>>> Genital warts can indicate **low-risk human papillomavirus.**

There is now a vaccine that is highly effective against the types of genital HPV that cause most cases of cervical cancer and genital warts. The vaccine, *Gardasil*, is given in three shots over a six-month period. It is routinely recommended for 11- and 12-year-old girls and boys, and for girls and women ages 13 through 26 who have not yet been vaccinated; in 2009, the use of Gardasil was approved for boys and young men (FDA, 2009). If you are sexually active and have not yet had the vaccination, your health care provider on campus will be able to provide you with helpful information.

VIRAL HEPATITIS

In general, **viral hepatitis** refers to inflammation of the liver, causing impairments in liver function. There are three types of viral hepatitis:

- **Hepatitis A (HAV)** is spread through infected fecal matter that is found in water and in food. This type of hepatitis is usually transmitted when people do not wash their hands after using the bathroom.

Figure 14.5 Sex of Adults and Adolescents with HIV/AIDS, 2007

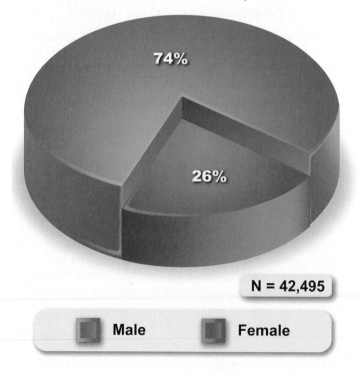

N = 42,495

Male   Female

Source: Centers for Disease Control and Prevention (2009a).

Figure 14.6 College Students Tested for HIV, 2008 Have you ever been tested for HIV infection?

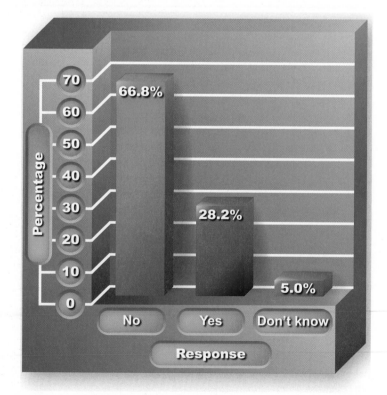

Source: Based on NCHA (2008)

- **Hepatitis B (HBV)** is transmitted through bodily fluids during sexual contact, such as through semen, vaginal fluids, saliva, blood, and urine.

- **Hepatitis C (HCV),** is typically spread through illegal drug use (infected needles) and unscreened blood transfusions.

Hepatitis B is the most common type of hepatitis. Each year in the United States, 78,000 people are infected with hepatitis B; about one in 20 Americans will become infected with HBV at some point during their lives. Because it is viral infection, it cannot be treated with antibiotics.

Understanding and protecting your sexual health is essential. Not only is it crucial to your overall health during your reproductive years, as well as having a child or avoiding an unwanted pregnancy, but it also affects the health of the next generation, the children you may bear. But the importance of sexual health goes beyond even that. It directly contributes to your intimate relationships in many areas, including sexual fulfillment, and the physical and emotional comfort and closeness you share with your partner. Generally speaking, abstinence is the best way to avoid getting an STI. Having sex with just one person you know and trust can help as well. Finally, using a condom correctly and consistently can go a long way toward preventing the transmission of an STI.

HIV AND AIDS

Every 9.5 minutes in the United States, someone becomes infected with the **human immunodeficiency virus (HIV)**, the typically sexually transmitted infection that leads to **acquired immune deficiency syndrome (AIDS)** (CDC, 2009c). At the end of 2007, an estimated 1.1 million persons in the United States were living with HIV/AIDS; nearly 43,000 new cases were diagnosed in adults, adolescents, and children (CDC, 2009a). As of 2007, more than a half million people in the United States have died from AIDS. And, as Figure 14.5 shows us, adult and adolescent males are disproportionately affected, accounting for nearly three-fourths of new diagnoses in 2007. Of these, 53 percent were men who have sex with men (MSM). Despite the threat that HIV poses, college students are not routinely tested for infection. Shown in Figure 14.6, the NCHA (2008) survey

of 80,000 college students indicates that nearly 67 percent of the study respondents have not been tested for HIV. Although not as prominent in the media today as it was 10 or 20 years ago (see Figure 14.7), one thing is certain; HIV/AIDS is no less of a concern now than it was then.

In this section, we'll first take a look at the biological processes associated with HIV/AIDS, as well as how they are diagnosed and treated. We'll then explore the national trends, paying particular attention to the racial and ethnic disparities. We'll conclude by looking at the global incidences of HIV/AIDS. Biologists Elaine Marieb and Katja Hoehn (2010) help us understand how HIV occurs.

Figure 14.7   The History of HIV/AIDS

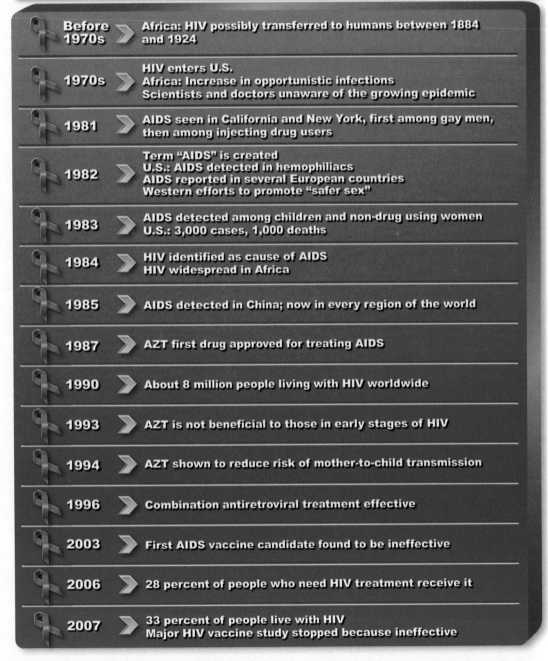

"The dominant feature of [the early history of HIV] was silence. During this period of silence, spread was unchecked by awareness or any prevention action" (Mann, 1989).

Before 1970s	Africa: HIV possibly transferred to humans between 1884 and 1924
1970s	HIV enters U.S. Africa: Increase in opportunistic infections Scientists and doctors unaware of the growing epidemic
1981	AIDS seen in California and New York, first among gay men, then among injecting drug users
1982	Term "AIDS" is created U.S.: AIDS detected in hemophiliacs AIDS reported in several European countries Western efforts to promote "safer sex"
1983	AIDS detected among children and non-drug using women U.S.: 3,000 cases, 1,000 deaths
1984	HIV identified as cause of AIDS HIV widespread in Africa
1985	AIDS detected in China; now in every region of the world
1987	AZT first drug approved for treating AIDS
1990	About 8 million people living with HIV worldwide
1993	AZT is not beneficial to those in early stages of HIV
1994	AZT shown to reduce risk of mother-to-child transmission
1996	Combination antiretroviral treatment effective
2003	First AIDS vaccine candidate found to be ineffective
2006	28 percent of people who need HIV treatment receive it
2007	33 percent of people live with HIV Major HIV vaccine study stopped because ineffective

Source: Based on information from AVERT.org

Figure 14.8a HIV Transmission and Diagnosis

How is HIV Transmitted?

There are three principle ways in which HIV is transmitted.

Sexual Contact

Sexual intercourse (vaginal and anal): HIV may infect the mucus membranes in the genitals and the rectum, or may enter through cuts and sores caused during intercourse (often unnoticed). *Unprotected vaginal and anal sex are high–risk practices.* Semen contains higher concentrations of the HIV virus than vaginal fluids do.

Oral sex (mouth-penis; mouth-vagina): The risk of HIV transmission through the throat, gums, and oral membranes is rather low, because the mouth is a hostile environment for HIV (contained in the semen, vaginal fluids, or blood). However, there are documented cases where HIV was transmitted orally.

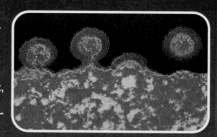

Blood

Blood contains the highest concentration of HIV. Therefore, any direct contact with blood puts a person at risk for contracting HIV.

Common methods of transfer through blood: Sharing injection needles; blood transfusions (although the risk has been greatly reduced due to efficient blood screenings today); and accidents in health care settings.

Mother to Baby

HIV can pass the placenta, thus it is possible for an HIV-infected mother to pass the virus directly before birth to the baby; it can also be transferred during delivery as the baby passes through the birth canal.

Breastmilk contains HIV, and is a viable means of transmission to infants.

HIV cannot be transmitted through saliva or tears.

How is HIV Diagnosed?

A person can have HIV for a long time and not know that they have it until they are tested. This is because the HIV infection doesn't have any immediate symptoms. If you are sexually active, it is essential that you are tested for HIV–early detection allows earlier treatment, before serious symptoms appear.

There are a number of HIV tests available today that can detect the virus within several weeks of infection. Screening tests typically look for HIV antibodies in the blood (not the virus itself).

Types of HIV Tests

Blood Test

This is the most common HIV test, and the blood sample is usually taken in a health care setting. The ELISA test is performed–if it is positive, then the Western blot test is done to confirm the result. Results may take up to two weeks.

Oral Fluid Test

This test checks for HIV antibodies in the oral fluids–a test pad is placed between the cheeks and the gums; the pad absorbs fluids in the mouth. Results may take up to two weeks.

Urine Test

ELISA and Western blot type tests have been developed to test for HIV in urine. This result may take a few days to two weeks.

Home Testing

As of 2009, the FDA has approved only one HIV home test kit, *Home Access* (although many others are on the market). After using a simple finger-prick process to collect a blood sample, the sample is smeared on a special paper in the kit; the paper with the sample is mailed to a lab, along with a personal identification number (PIN). To get results, the person calls the lab and gives them their PIN.

Quick Test

Since 2002, the FDA has approved quick tests (blood and oral swab) that yield results within 10 to 20 minutes. If the result is negative, no further testing is needed; if it is positive, a Western blot test is done (final results are received within two weeks).

Testing newborns

Because babies are born with their mothers' antibodies, any baby born to an HIV-infected mother will test positive for HIV antibodies. Therefore, certain blood tests are used to actually test for the HIV virus (not HIV antibodies).

Figure 14.8b HIV Infection Process

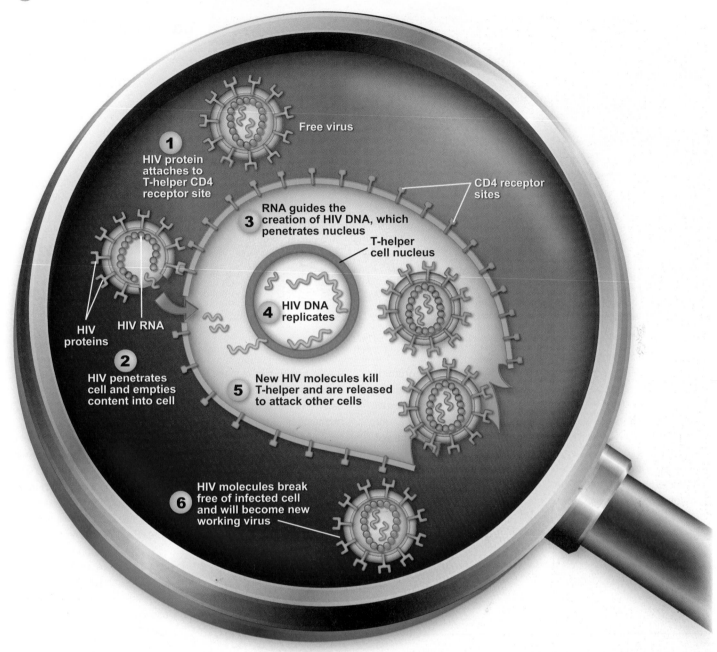

Free virus

1 HIV protein attaches to T-helper CD4 receptor site

CD4 receptor sites

3 RNA guides the creation of HIV DNA, which penetrates nucleus

T-helper cell nucleus

HIV proteins

HIV RNA

4 HIV DNA replicates

2 HIV penetrates cell and empties content into cell

5 New HIV molecules kill T-helper and are released to attack other cells

6 HIV molecules break free of infected cell and will become new working virus

HOW DOES HIV OCCUR?

The immune system protects the body from disease and infection. When a bacterium or a virus (a pathogen) enters the body, the immune system recognizes it as foreign material and alerts the immune response. Within hours of the pathogen's appearance in the body, immune system cells, **T-helper cells**, target the pathogen and attempt to destroy it. These T cells then activate a specialized group of white cells (our infection/disease-fighting blood cells), the *B cells*. These B cells produce antibodies that bind the virus or bacterium and immobilize it, preventing it from spreading throughout the body. The antibodies are specific for only one virus or bacterium; each time a new one enters the body, the process begins again for that specific pathogen.

Once the immune system is activated for a given virus or bacterium, *memory cells* are produced. These memory cells ensure that the next time the same pathogen enters the body, the immune system will elicit a quicker and stronger response. This is the process by which vaccinations (such as the Gardasil vaccination against genital HPV) provide protection against disease. By introducing the disease into the bloodstream, T-helper cells and B cells are activated, and a memory record of the pathogen is made; this results in lifelong immunity to that pathogen. To do their jobs effectively, T-helper cells must be mobile so they can connect with other immune cells; this is how they create their line of defense to fight disease.

Given this sophisticated immune response system, how does HIV invade the body? As Figures 14.8a and b illustrate, the human immunodeficiency virus (HIV) is unique because it specifically attacks the mobility of T-helper cells. New science has revealed that, unlike other viruses and bacterial infections, HIV makes a protein called *Nef*, which cripples T-helper cells and stops the cells' abilities to move (Stolp et al., 2009). Once immobile, the affected T cells can no longer fulfill their immune-providing function. In essence, the "whole immune system is turned topsy-turvey" (Marieb & Hoehn, 2010). Without the help of the immune system, HIV multiplies over and over in the body.

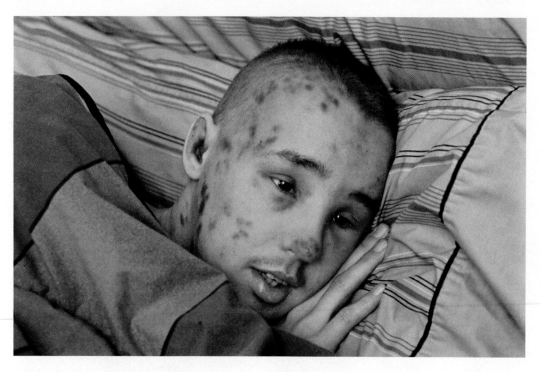

<<< Kaposi's sarcoma, **a cancer commonly found in AIDS patients,** is an example of an opportunistic infection.

Most people are **asymptomatic** (they exhibit no symptoms) as the virus multiplies itself. Symptoms only appear when the immune system collapses. The HIV-positive person who undergoes no treatment will typically exhibit AIDS within 10 years of acquiring HIV (Marieb & Hoehn, 2010). There are various methods for diagnosing HIV, and although traditional test methods (such as ELISA and the Western blot) require at least two weeks before test results could be obtained, a new test, the OraQuick Rapid HIV Antibody Test, can yield results within approximately 20 minutes. This test is almost always followed up with the ELISA and Western blot tests.

On the surface of each T-helper cell is a protein, the **CD4+ protein;** the CD4 has *receptor sites* that appear as little peg-like sticks on the surface of the T-helper cell. When HIV enters the body through sexual contact, the HIV pathogen attaches itself to the CD4 receptor site. HIV then enters the cell and empties its infectious material (RNA) into the cell body. The cell then converts the HIV RNA to DNA and enters the nucleus of the cell; once it is converted to DNA, it replicates itself and breaks free of the infected cell. It is now a new virus that travels to other T-helper cells of the body. It's important to note that because RNA is not very accurate, it frequently produces errors when it converts to DNA; because of this, as the DNA replicates in the body, each new generation of HIV differs slightly from the one before. These differences are referred to as **mutations,** explaining HIV's ever-changing resistance to drug therapies (Marieb & Hoehn, 2010).

When HIV has crucially depleted the population of T-helper cells, the body loses its ability to launch the immune response, resulting in immunodeficiency, or acquired immunodeficiency syndrome (AIDS). Once the immune system becomes suppressed, it becomes vulnerable to opportunistic infections. **Opportunistic infections,** which are described in Table 14.4, are infections that are caused by pathogens that don't normally affect someone with a healthy immune system. Because of their depressed or destroyed T-helper cells, people with HIV contract opportunistic infections more easily than those who are not infected. Figure 14.9 also shows the progression from HIV infection to AIDS. As you can see, it's not the HIV per se that leads to death in the infected person; rather, death is the result of complications due to opportunistic infections.

TABLE 14.4
Opportunistic Infections

Common opportunistic infections include:

- **Pneumocystis crinii pneumonia (PCP):** A rare type of pneumonia

- **Oral candidiasis:** A mouth infection caused by an excess growth of fungus

- **Toxoplasmosis:** A parasite infection that causes headaches, seizures, altered mental states, or coma

- **Cryptococcosis:** Affects the lungs or the central nervous system

- **Kaposi's sarcoma (KS):** The most common cancer that affects people who aren't treated; results in characteristic lesions (sores) around the ankle, foot, face, mouth, chest, or back

TREATMENT

There is no cure for HIV or AIDS. Today, the main type of treatment, **antiretroviral drugs (ARV),** is not a cure, but it does stop the virus from advancing to AIDS for many years. There are three broad classes of antiviral drugs (Marieb & Hoehn, 2010):

- *Reverse transcriptase inhibitors:* This class includes AZT and ddC, the first-generation HIV treatments, which inhibit the virus after it gains entry into the T-helper cells.

- *Protease inhibitors:* This includes saquinavir and ritonavir. These also inhibit the virus once it enters the T-helper cells.

- *Fusion inhibitors:* This new class of drugs, which includes enfuvirtide, prevents HIV from entering the T-helper cell in the first place.

Today, the most common type of treatment is **combination therapy,** where two or more drugs are taken at the same time. When a person takes a combination of three or more anti-HIV drugs, it is referred to as *highly active antiretroviral therapy (HAART).*

Once an HIV-infected person begins ARV treatment, its effectiveness is tracked through a viral load blood test. **Viral load** refers to the amount of HIV found in the bloodstream. If the viral load is high, it signifies that the T-helper cells are being quickly destroyed and that the ARV treatment is not effective. It takes as long as three to six months for the ARV to become effective in keeping down the viral load. In some people, the treatment is so effective, the viral load drops to undetectable.

It's important to keep in mind that ARV drugs only slow the replication of HIV—they don't stop it. As we just learned, HIV has the ability to mutate; although some of the virus is effectively attacked by drug treatments, other strains of HIV are not. This is referred to as *drug-resistant HIV*. This is why ARV treatment fails for some people. Once the strains become drug resistant, the viral load increases and the person eventually becomes ill with AIDS. Taking the drugs *exactly* as prescribed helps reduce the occurrence of drug-resistant HIV. Some physicians describe the combination therapy as delivering a one-two punch to the virus: It boosts the number of T-helper cells while simultaneously dropping the viral load and delaying drug resistance (Marieb & Hoehn, 2010).

Figure 14.9 The Realities of HIV

How HIV Progresses to AIDS

HIV infection generally exhibits four distinct stages. Over time, HIV leads to a severe reduction in the number of T-helper cells—this process typically takes several years.

STAGE 1: Primary HIV Infection

This stage lasts for a few weeks. Sometimes, though not frequently, initially infected people have flu-like symptoms, such as fever, a rash, muscle aches, and swollen lymph nodes and glands. For most people, it takes about three to six months for the HIV virus to be detected by lab testing. This is because it takes awhile for the HIV antibodies to build up–a process referred to as *seroconversion*. The timeframe during which HIV antibodies are not detectable is referred to as the *window period*. People can unknowingly pass on the HIV infection during this period of time.

STAGE 2: Clinically Asymptomatic Stage

Many people infected with HIV are symptom-free for an average of 10 years after initial infection. HIV antibodies are detectable in the blood, so lab tests will be positive for HIV.

STAGE 3: Symptomatic HIV Infection

Over time, HIV mutates as it replicates itself within the body; this leads to T-helper cell destruction. As the immune system weakens and fails, symptoms develop. The symptomatic stage is characterized by opportunistic infections and cancers that a healthy immune system could ward off. Infections can occur in almost every body system.

STAGE 4: Progression from HIV to AIDS

HIV progressively destroys the immune system, and as a result, opportunistic infections become more and more severe. In the U.S., someone may be diagnosed with AIDS if they have a very low T-helper cell count; in the U.K., AIDS is diagnosed if a person has had one or more severe opportunistic infections or cancers.

Is there a vaccine for HIV?

To date, no attempts at HIV vaccines have proved to be effective. However, recent advances in HIV research have allowed scientists to screen a range of substances that appear to block the actions of Nef. These are referred to as *molecule inhibitors*. Once researchers have a better understanding of how HIV shapes and forms on the surface of cells, they can identify the molecule inhibitors that work the best to combat HIV.

Source: AVERT (2010). *The different stages of HIV infection.* Retrieved February 4, 2010, from: www.avert.org/stages-hiv-aids.htm

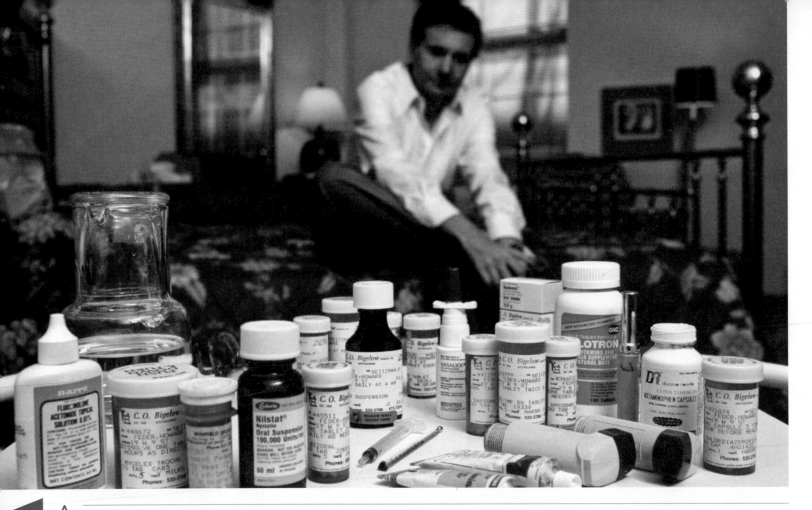

>>> Antiretroviral drugs can delay HIV **from advancing to AIDS.**

Although the process of understanding HIV and AIDS has been slow and fraught with delays due to global political agendas, today's scientists are encouraged that, with the discovery of the Nef protein, strides are being made in finding enzymes that work to block Nef's attacks on T-helper cells. With 33 million people worldwide currently infected with HIV—including some 2 million children—it is worth questioning what has taken so long (UNAIDS, 2008).

Now that you have an understanding of what HIV/AIDS is and how it is treated, let's take a brief look at those who are affected by it as we examine national and global incidences.

HIV AND AIDS IN THE UNITED STATES AND ABROAD

Within the United States in 2007, the largest proportion of HIV/AIDS diagnoses was among adult and adolescent men who have sex with men (CDC, 2009a). About 11,000 female adults and adolescents were diagnosed with HIV/AIDS during the same time frame; of these, more than 80 percent engaged in high-risk sexual contact (sexual contact with people known to have HIV or have a higher risk of contracting HIV due to injection drug use) (CDC, 2009a). Figure 14.10 shows at what age people are diagnosed in the U.S. As we saw earlier in this chapter, the SDH model helps explain the racial and

ethnic health disparities we see. Without question, these unequal distributions are evident in HIV/AIDS infection rates. As you look over the trends in the following sections, be mindful of the social forces, such as education levels, socioeconomic status, and poverty experiences, that might contribute to the higher incidences of HIV/AIDS among minority groups.

Figure 14.10 Age of People with HIV/AIDS Diagnosed in 2007 in the U.S.

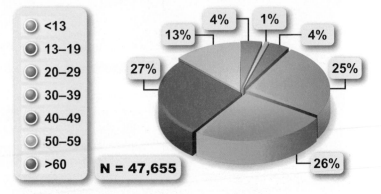

- <13
- 13–19
- 20–29
- 30–39
- 40–49
- 50–59
- >60

N = 47,655

4% 1%
13%   4%
27%   25%
26%

Source: Centers for Disease Control and Prevention (2009a).

HIV/AIDS AMONG AFRICAN AMERICANS/BLACK CARIBBEANS

Of all the new HIV/AIDS diagnoses in 2007, blacks accounted for 51 percent; today, they also account for nearly one-half of all people in the United States living with HIV/AIDS (CDC, 2009c). Although these diagnoses decreased in 2007, blacks still experience the highest incidence of HIV/AIDS than any other racial or ethnic group (see Figure 14.11). In 2007, 40 percent of those who died of AIDS-related complications were black. For African American/Black Caribbean women, the most common methods of transmission were high-risk heterosexual sexual contact and injection drug use. Among black men, the most common methods of transmission were MSM, injection drug use, and high-risk heterosexual sex. African American and Black Caribbeans face a number of risk factors (Black AIDS Institute, 2009; CDC, 2009c):

- Unprotected sex with multiple partners.
- Unaware of partner's sexual history or incorrectly assess partner's risk.
- Injection drug use.
- Unprotected sex under the influence of drugs and/or alcohol.
- Higher rates of STIs, which significantly increase HIV infection.
- Lack of awareness of HIV status (didn't know they were infected).
- Stigma associated with homosexual sex in black community.
- Socioeconomic issues, including poverty, limited access to high-quality health care, and less access to sexuality health education/prevention programs.

Because the African American community continues to be at the highest risk for STIs and HIV/AIDS (Black AIDS Institute, 2009; CDC, 2009c), in 2007 and 2008 the federal government intensified its efforts to accelerate funding to increase testing and to provide greater access to education programs for this racial group. Sexuality educators, public health officials, and public health organizations continue to urge U.S. political forces to address the deeper social factors, such as poverty, that place African Americans at risk, and perhaps obstruct access to prevention efforts.

HIV/AIDS AMONG HISPANICS/LATINOS

In 2007, Hispanics/Latinos accounted for 18 percent of the new HIV diagnoses and 19 percent of all new AIDS diagnoses (CDC, 2009d). Of all races and ethnicities, this group was the third most affected demographic. By the end of 2007, AIDS diagnoses among Hispanic/Latina women were five times that of white women. Among females, high-risk heterosexual sex and injection drug use were the common methods of transmission; among men, homosexual sex, injection drug use, and high-risk heterosexual sex were.

The CDC lists a number of cultural, socioeconomic, and health-related factors that contribute to the growing number of HIV/AIDS infections in Hispanics/Latinos. For example, Hispanic/Latinos born in Puerto Rico are more likely to contract HIV due to injection drug use, while homosexual sex is the primary means of infection among those born in Mexico or the United States (CDC, 2009d). Culture also plays a role in heterosexual sex, because Latina women are less likely to question their partners' condom use due to cultural beliefs and attitudes (Diaz, Ayala, & Beink, 2001). Also, many men avoid testing or treatment due to rigid

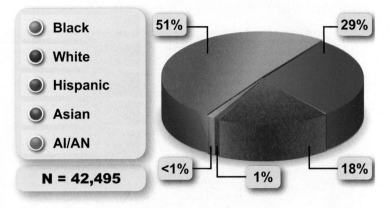

Figure 14.11 Race and Ethnicity of Persons Diagnosed with HIV/AIDS: 2007

- Black — 51%
- White — 29%
- Hispanic — 18%
- Asian — 1%
- AI/AN — <1%

N = 42,495

Source: Centers for Disease Control and Prevention (2009c).

gender roles and the cultural machismo norm. Finally, socioeconomic factors such as poverty, language barriers, unemployment, lack of formal education, and immigration status make access to prevention, testing, and care difficult (CDC, 2009d).

HIV/AIDS AMONG AMERICAN INDIANS/ALASKA NATIVES

In the United States, American Indians/Alaska Natives make up only about 1.5 percent of the total population (U.S. Census Bureau, 2008). Although they account for less than 1 percent of HIV/AIDS diagnoses (see Figure 14.11), when population size is taken into consideration, this ethnic group ranks third in HIV/AIDS diagnosis rates. The majority of newly diagnosed cases were among men who have male-to-male sexual contact. Other transmission categories include injection drug use (15 percent), and homosexual sex or injection drug use (13 percent).

Since the beginning of the epidemic in the 1980s, American Indians/Alaska Natives tend to survive for a shorter time than others do. For example, after nine years, about two-thirds of American Indians/Alaska Natives were alive, compared to three-fourths of whites and Hispanics. Demographers speculate that these lower survival rates are due to higher rates of STI infections and illicit drug use, poverty, and reduced access to HIV testing (U.S. Department of Health & Human Services, 2009). To be effective, HIV/AIDS prevention education and interventions must be culture-specific (CDC, 2009a). Because the American Indians/Alaska Natives population is made up of more than 500 federally recognized tribes, each tribe has its own culture, beliefs, and practices; this diversity makes it challenging to develop prevention programs.

HIV/AIDS AMONG ASIANS AND PACIFIC ISLANDERS

Among Asians and Pacific Islanders, the HIV/AIDS cases have steadily increased over the past few years; about 1 percent of this population accounts for the total number of HIV/AIDS diagnoses (National Institutes of Health, 2009). Of the newly diagnosed, 78 percent were

Figure 14.12 People Living with AIDS/HIV, Globally, 1990–2008. The number of people living with HIV has risen from around 8 million in 1990 to 33 million today, and is still growing. Around 67 percent of people living with HIV are in sub-Saharan Africa.

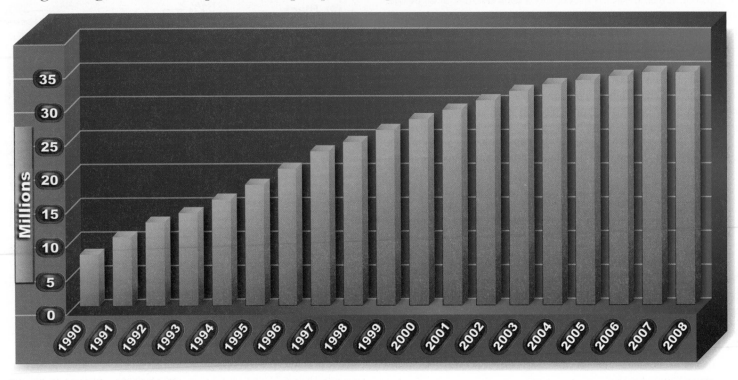

Source: www.avert.org/worldstats.htm

CHAPTER 14

men, 21 percent were women, and 1 percent were children (under the age of 13). MSM, high-risk heterosexual contact, and injection drug use are the primary means of transmission in this racial group; females are more likely to contract HIV/AIDS from high-risk heterosexual contact (80 percent).

Risk factors and barriers to prevention for this group include (CDC, 2009a):

- Unprotected sex among MSM, particularly in those aged 18 to 29 years.

- Unprotected heterosexual sex due to cultural taboos against discussing sexual topics, and power differentials between sexes (women having difficulty in getting partners to use condoms).

- The use of methamphetamines and alcohol, which are associated with unprotected anal intercourse.

- Low HIV testing rates.

Similar to American Indians/Alaska Natives, more than 1 million Asian Americans live at or below the federal poverty level, which contributes to poorer health outcomes and limited access to health services (National Institutes of Health, 2009).

<<< These orphans in Cameroon **are a few of the 11.6 million AIDS orphans in Africa.**

THE GLOBAL INCIDENCES OF HIV/AIDS

There is no question that HIV and AIDS affect the lives of adults, adolescents, and children in the United States. Sadly, no region of the world is untouched by its devastation, and Figure 14.12 shows us the global trends of HIV/AIDS. Consider these global statistics (UNAIDS/WHO, 2008):

- Africa has 11.6 million AIDS orphans.

- Worldwide, people under the age of 25 account for half of all new HIV infections.

- Nearly 10 million people are in need of life-saving drug therapies, but only 3 million receive them.

- Since 1988, more than 25 million people have died of AIDS.

- In 1990, 8 million people were living with HIV. Today, 33 million are, and the number continues to grow.

- Two-thirds of people living with HIV are in sub-Saharan Africa.

As you can see in Table 14.5, sub-Saharan Africa and Asia account for most of the adults and children living with HIV/AIDS in the world today. Despite recent advances to access of ARV drug therapies, 2 million people died from AIDS in 2007 (UNAIDS/WHO, 2008).

IS HONESTY ALWAYS THE BEST POLICY? TELLING YOUR PARTNER ABOUT AN STI

In Chapter 13, we learned about the methods to protect ourselves against sexually transmitted infections and HIV/AIDS. But there is one more critical component to keeping ourselves sexually healthy— *communication*. It's understandable that it is difficult to discuss STI history with a sexual partner, particularly if we've only recently met that partner, such as a hookup. In fact, one recent review of studies that examined self-disclosure of sexually transmitted infections found that it's easier for people to have sex than it is to talk about it (Montgomery, Gonzalez, & Montgomery, 2008). But to protect yourself against dangerous and potentially fatal sexually transmitted infections, partners must be willing to openly discuss their past sexual histories, their STI and HIV/AIDS status, and their drug use.

In general, people who disclose their STI/HIV status are younger, female, have high ethical and moral standards, have participated in disclosure intervention groups, and are in a *serodiscordant* relationship; that is, one person has HIV or an STI, and the other does not (Knight et al., 2005; Simoni et al., 2005; Swanson & Chenitz, 1993). According to

TABLE 14.5
People Living with HIV/AIDS, Worldwide

Regional Statistics for HIV & AIDS, End of 2008

Region	Adults & Children Living With HIV/AIDS	Adults & Children Newly Infected	Adult Prevalence*	Deaths of Adults & Children
Sub-Saharan Africa	22.4 million	1.9 million	5.2%	1.4 million
North Africa & Middle East	310,000	35,000	0.2%	20,000
South and South-East Asia	3.8 million	280,000	0.3%	270,000
East Asia	850,000	75,000	<0.1%	59,000
Oceania	59,000	3900	0.3%	2,000
Latin America	2.0 million	170,000	0.6%	77,000
Caribbean	240,000	20,000	1.0%	12,000
Eastern Europe & Central Asia	1.5 million	110,000	0.7%	87,000
North America	1.4 million	55,000	0.4%	25,000
Western & Central Europe	850,000	30,000	0.3%	13,000
Global Total	33.4 million	2.7 million	0.8%	2.0 million

* Proportion of adults aged 15–49 who were living with HIV/AIDS

During 2008 more than 2.5 million adults and children became infected with HIV (Human Immunodeficiency Virus), the virus that causes AIDS. By the end of the year, an estimated 33.4 million people worldwide were living with HIV/AIDS. The year also saw two million deaths from AIDS, despite recent improvements in access to antiretroviral treatment.

Notes: Adults are defined as men and women aged 15 or above, unless specified otherwise.

Children orphaned by AIDS are defined as people aged under 18 who are alive and have lost one or both parents to AIDS.

All the statistics on this page should be interpreted with caution because they are estimates.

∧
∧
∧   Even though some people are at a high risk for getting HIV **due to their lifestyle**
∧   **choices, they may not get tested for the infection because of the stigma associated**
with the disease. A stigma is a negative social label that identifies people or their
behaviors as deviant. **And behavior that is deemed deviant, such as men having sex**
with men or IV drug use, is *stigmatized*. Stigmatizing sexual behaviors makes some
people avoid testing, counseling, or treatment **because they are ashamed and**
embarrassed, and often they are afraid that others will reject them.

research, some people who don't disclose include some homosexuals, racial/ethnic minorities, and sex workers (for a review, see Montgomery, Gonzalez, & Montgomery, 2008).

Why don't people tell their partners? Some people indicate that they are afraid that having an STI or HIV makes them less sexually desirable, so they do not disclose that information (Darroch, Myers, & Cassell, 2003; Lindberg, Lewis-Spruill, & Crownover, 2006). Recent research indicates that, despite the substantial health risks associated with STIs and HIV, people often don't tell their sexual partners because of the stigma and shame associated with such a diagnoses (Foster & Byers, 2008; Mulholland & Van Wersch, 2007). **STI-related stigma** refers to a person's awareness that society negatively perceives sexually transmitted infections; **STI-related shame** refers to the internal negative feelings a person has as a result of the STI diagnosis (Fortenberry et al., 2002). Despite the initial embarrassment, shame, or guilt that may accompany an STI or HIV diagnosis, sexual partners owe it to each other to be upfront about their sexual histories and infection history. Although such self-disclosure can be difficult, it can also enhance the intimacy and communication couples share. Here are a few tips to help you get started.

TIMING IS EVERYTHING

Although there is never a perfect time to tell a partner something that is difficult to discuss, some times are better than others. Before you tell your partner, first be sure to gather information about your STI, HIV, or AIDS. Knowing the facts, such as by what means it can be transmitted to your partner and what treatment options are available, helps both partners work the STI into their lives, both sexually and personally. Also, be sure to plan ahead. It's best not to blurt it out in the middle of a passionate embrace or on the way to a romantic weekend! By planning ahead, you can also determine when each of you is better able to engage in such a difficult and private conversation. For example, one of my students wanted to tell her partner that earlier that day she had been diagnosed with chlamydia, but she decided to postpone the conversation to the next evening, when he didn't have a 13-hour day of classes and work.

PRACTICE MAKES PERFECT

Prepare a script, and practice it again and again, until you are comfortable with what you are going to say. Include such things as your diagnosis, what treatment the health care provider has recommended, how long you'll be following that treatment regimen, how this affects your sex life together, and safe sex options you have. Be straightforward, calm, and sincere. After you disclose to your partner, listen to him or her. Be prepared for an entire range of emotions (from each of you), from casual acceptance to anger. Don't assume that the worst will happen, because honesty is not only valued in mature relationships, but your partner should also appreciate how difficult it is to be honest about things like this.

ENGAGE IN A DIALOGUE

Expect questions and lots of them. How did you get it? Who did you get it from? Did you sleep with anyone else that I should know about? How long have you had it? Why weren't you more careful? How could you do this? You may not have all the answers to the questions, but the important thing is to try to put yourself in your partner's shoes; how would you feel if you were getting this information from your partner? It's helpful to give each other permission to experience feelings and emotions. It's also important to listen to the emotions behind the words, not the actual words spoken. In situations such as these, the emotion is almost always fear—fear of rejection, fear of losing the relationship, fear of failure, fear of the disease, and/or fear of others finding out.

Honest conversations about sex aren't always easy. But as you've seen in our study across this term, sexual health and well-being require responsibility to both ourselves and to our partners.

SEXUAL LIFE EDUCATION

In some respects, this is the most difficult information to teach in sexuality courses. Why? Because as your instructors, we recognize the fact that many students have been exposed to this content before, and as a result, far too often students become complacent and unreflective about the very real dangers associated with sexually transmitted infections and unsafe sex. The reality is, by age 24, at least one in three sexually active people will have contracted an STI at some point (Kaiser Foundation, 2009). If left untreated, it can have serious effects on your health, ranging from infertility due to PID, to cancer, to death.

The take-home message from this chapter? Abstinence is the only safe method to protect yourself from STIs, HIV, and AIDS. If you are sexually active, now is a good time to reexamine your boundaries or to set them if you've never done so. It's time to examine your genitals and your partner's (if you are comfortable doing so). It's also time to sit down and have an open, honest discussion with your partner about your sexual histories and the ways that you can protect your sexual health. This means telling each other about *every* person you've ever had sex with. If you have never done so, or haven't done so in a while, it's a good time to make an appointment with your health care provider. Most campus health facilities can provide STI testing, as well as free (or nearly free) condoms and options for birth control. Early detection of STIs and treatment are key.

Being sexually active carries with it responsibility to yourself and to your partner(s). Safeguarding your physical and emotional health is perhaps the greatest step you can take toward a fulfilling and enjoyable sex life.

---

sex talk

Sexual Histories and STIs

Talking with your partner is one of the most important STI prevention techniques. However, this can be a difficult conversation to have. Think through and insert your responses to the following statements. Your responses might help you initiate a conversation with your partner.

I feel _____ about talking about STIs with my partner.

When it comes to safer sex, I _____ .

The best time to talk about STIs is _____ .

The best place to have a conversation about STIs is _____ .

To help my partner feel more comfortable during the conversation, I can _____
_____ .

I _____ to share my sexual history with my partner because I am _____ .

When talking to my partner about my own sexual history, I need to be sure to share _____ and
_____ .

If I bring up the topic of STIs with my partner, he or she may _____ .

The best way for me to bring up the subject of STIs is to _____ .

If my partner and I decide to get tested, we can go _____ .

In assessing my risk for getting an STI, I would say I am _____ .

When I think of HIV/AIDS, I think _____ .

People who get STIs _____ .

14

Summary

WHAT KINDS OF SEXUALLY TRANSMITTED INFECTIONS ARE THERE AND HOW ARE THEY TRANSMITTED AND TREATED? 292

- Sexually transmitted infections and HIV/AIDS pose major treats to public health, and the female physiology makes women more susceptible to severe consequences if their STIs go untreated. STIs can be transmitted through skin-to-skin contact and via the exchange of bodily fluids.
- Bacterial infections include gonorrhea, chlamydia, and syphilis, while viral infections include herpes, HPV, and viral hepatitis. There are also parasitic infections like scabies, public lice, and trichomoniasis.

WHAT IMPACT HAVE HIV AND AIDS HAD ON THE WORLD? 303

- HIV, transmitted through sexual contact and blood, attacks the body's immune system, and when it goes untreated, it ultimately advances to AIDS, leaving a person susceptible to opportunistic infections that can ultimately be fatal. Because treatment for HIV/AIDS was not widely understood until the 1980s, it has become a global epidemic, taking major tolls on Africa.

HOW DO YOU TELL YOUR PARTNER ABOUT AN STI? 311

- Although talking about STIs can be uncomfortable and embarrassing, these conversations are essential to protect your own sexual health and the sexual well-being of others. Honesty is the best policy, and preparing yourself for a difficult conversation is the best way to approach it.

Key Terms

sexually transmitted infections (STIs) diseases that are transmitted between partners through sexual contact 292

cervical dysplasia an abnormal growth of cells on the cervix 293

CIN (cervical intraepithelial neoplasia) common term for cervical dysplasia 293

mild cervical dysplasia (CIN 1) CIN that goes away without treatment 293

moderate dysplasia (CIN 2) CIN that requires abnormal tissue to be destroyed 293

severe dysplasia (CIN3) CIN that requires a cone biopsy 293

cone biopsy a cone-shaped piece of the cervix containing abnormal cells is removed 293

transformation zone the space in the cervix between the squamous cells and the epithelial cells 293

cervical ectopy a condition in which the inner lining of the cervix turns to the outer edge 293

social determinants of health (SDH) the idea that there are characteristics that are systematically associated with social disadvantage and health disparities 295

pelvic inflammatory disease (PID) infection of the uterus, fallopian tubes, or other reproductive organs 295

trichomoniasis a parasitic infection that can be acquired through sexual activity 295

scabies highly contagious ectoparasitic infection 295

pubic lice highly contagious ectoparasitic infection 295

ectoparasitic infections STIs that are caused by parasites that live on the skin's surface 295

bacterial infections caused by certain microorganisms and can be treated with antibiotics 296

gonorrhea the second most common bacterial STI reported in the United States 296

chlamydia most common bacterial STI reported in the United States 297

chancroid sore often mistaken for a syphilis chancre 299

syphilis bacterial infection caused by the spirochete *Treponema pallidum* 299

primary stage when first chancre appears 300

secondary stage when a rash develops over some or all of the body 300

latent period when syphilis goes untreated; can vitally damage the body 300

viral infections diseases that cannot be treated with antibiotics 300

herpes caused when the herpes simplex virus enters the body 300

viral shedding process in which the virus is released between outbreaks of infected skin 300

autoinoculate self-infecting 300

herpes simplex I (HSV-1) oral herpes 301

herpes simplex II (HSV-2) genital herpes 301

human papillomavirus (HPV) can cause cancer or genital warts 301

genital warts soft, moist, pink/flesh-colored growths found on the genitals or anus 301

viral hepatitis inflammation of the liver 302

Hepatitis A (HAV) spread through infected fecal matter 302

Hepatitis B (HBV) transmitted through bodily fluids during sexual contact 303

Hepatitis C (HCV) typically spread through illegal drug use 303

human immunodeficiency virus (HIV) typically sexually transmitted infection that leads to AIDS 303

acquired immune deficiency syndrome (AIDS) disease caused by HIV that attacks the body's immune system *303*

T-helper cells immune system cells *305*

CD4+ protein protein on the surface of the T-helper cells *306*

mutations differences in each new generation of HIV *306*

asymptomatic exhibiting no symptoms *306*

pneumocystis crinii pneumonia (PCP) a rare type of pneumonia *306*

oral candidiasis a mouth infection caused by a growth of fungus *306*

toxoplasmosis parasite infection that causes headaches, seizures, altered mental states, or coma *306*

cryptococcosis infection that affects the lungs or central nervous system *306*

Kaposi's sarcoma (KS) common cancer that affects those who aren't treated *306*

opportunistic infections caused by pathogens that don't normally infect someone with a healthy immune system *306*

antiretroviral drugs (ARV) delays HIV from advancing to AIDS *306*

combination therapy two or more drugs taken at the same time *306*

viral load amount of HIV in the bloodstream *307*

STI-related stigma a person's awareness that society negatively perceives STIs *312*

STI-related shame the internal negative feelings a person has as the result of the STI diagnosis *312*

Sample Test Questions

MULTIPLE CHOICE

1. Which factor does NOT put you at a higher risk for STIs?
   a. Having sexual intercourse without a condom
   b. Being female
   c. Drinking alcohol or using drugs prior to having sex
   d. Having multiple sex partners

2. Which test detects cervical dysplasia in women?
   a. Blood test
   b. Pap test
   c. Urine test
   d. None of the above

3. Which condition is NOT an STI?
   a. HIV
   b. Pubic lice
   c. Pelvic inflammatory disease
   d. Trichomoniasis

4. Gonorrhea is treated with:
   a. Antibiotics
   b. Antiretroviral therapy
   c. It goes away on its own
   d. Topical creams

5. Genital warts are a symptom of:
   a. Herpes
   b. Syphilis
   c. HIV
   d. Human papillomavirus

6. Which opportunistic infection is parasitic?
   a. Pneumocystic crinii pneumonia
   b. Taxoplasmosis
   c. Oral candidiasis
   d. Cryptococcosis

7. Which region has experienced the most deaths as a result of HIV/AIDS?
   a. Sub-Saharan Africa
   b. North Africa and the Middle East
   c. North America
   d. Latin America

8. ARV works by:
   a. Increasing the viral load
   b. Destroying T-helper cells
   c. Decreasing the viral load
   d. Creating T-helper cells

SHORT RESPONSE

1. Explain the differences between parasitic, bacterial, and viral infections.

2. Describe the social determinants of health approach to explaining why certain groups are at a greater risk than others for contracting STIs.

3. What are the different stages of syphilis?

4. What is the difference between HSV-1 and HSV-2?

5. Explain how HIV attacks a person's immune system.

Answers: 1. b; 2. b; 3. c; 4. a; 5. d; 6. b; 7. a; 8. c

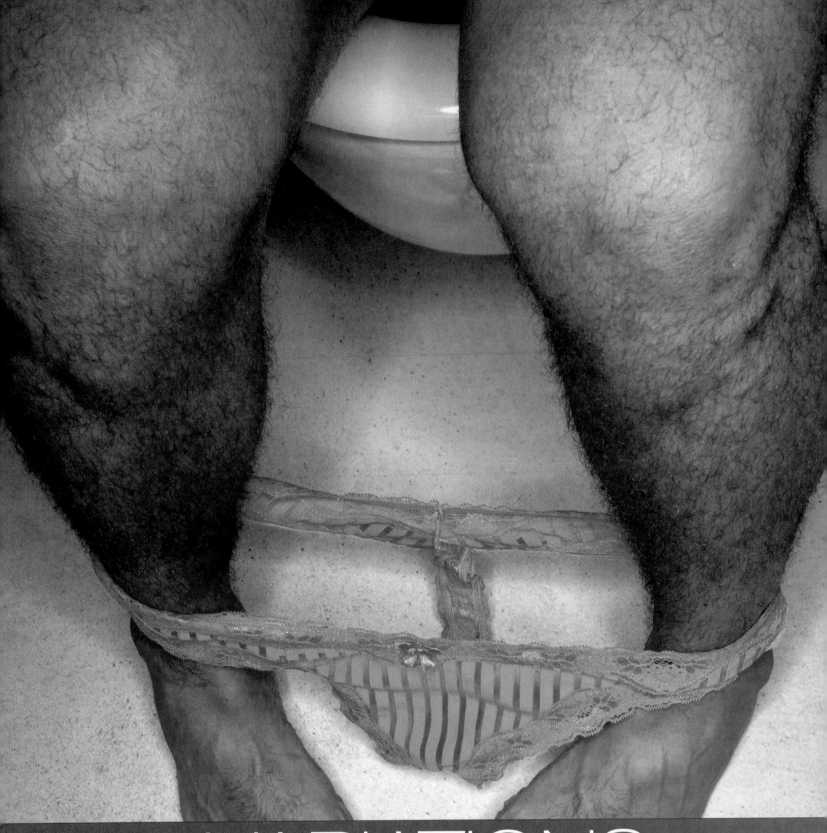

VARIATIONS

in Sexual Expression

WHAT ARE PARAPHILIAS, AND ARE THEY VARIANT OR DEVIANT?
HOW ARE PARAPHILIAS TREATED?
WHAT IS SEXUAL ADDICTION?

I think

it must have started when I was in junior high school or maybe even younger. I remember looking at the fliers in the Sunday paper with the women in their underwear and feeling aroused. Eventually, I started masturbating while looking at these advertisements and then progressed to lingerie catalogues. I was fine with that for a few years and really didn't think much about it.

The first time I used an actual piece of lingerie to masturbate with was in high school. I had a friend with an older sister, and one time I stayed the night. I went to the laundry room to get some chips (that's where they kept them), and I noticed a pair of her panties in a laundry basket and took them without really thinking about it. I could hardly wait to get home the next day to be alone with them—weird, I know.

I was fine with just that pair for a while, but then I wanted more, so I went to a store and bought some (I said they were a gift for my girlfriend), but it wasn't the same. I really needed underwear that had been worn—don't ask me why. So, I started stealing them from other friends' sisters, sometimes from laundry that was hanging out to dry, and occasionally I would go to laundromats and take a pair or two. I was careful not to take too many from any one place so that the women would think they had just lost a pair somehow. And I didn't keep more than a couple of pairs at any one time because I didn't want to get caught with a big stash of panties.

Now that I am in college, I am worried about being caught. I live in the dorms where there is a large laundry room and people leave their clothes unattended. I have taken a few [women's things], but there isn't much privacy here so the chances of someone finding out are pretty high. I know that I am not normal, but I am not sure what to do.

Source: Author's files

>>> The American Psychiatric Association publishes the *DSM-IV-TR*, **which provides diagnosis criteria for mental disorders.**

What sexually arouses you? In what kinds of sexual behaviors do you like to engage? Like the college student in the opening vignette, have you ever wondered if you are sexually "normal"?

As with many other aspects of sexuality, such as sexual orientation, how we sexually express ourselves is on a continuum. Defining something as normal or abnormal is difficult, because, as you will see in our study in this chapter, there is much variation in sexual expression. For example, sexual behaviors such as masturbation, oral sex, anal sex, and homosexuality were once considered abnormal and were classified as mental disorders (Moser & Kleinplatz, 2005). Yet, these behaviors are now part of the continuum of what is considered in many cultures to be healthy sexual expression. So rather than think about whether something is normal or not, it might be more helpful to think about whether it is healthy.

Psychologist/sexologist Lorraine Benuto (2009b) explains that although "normal" and "healthy" might be used interchangeably, they actually mean different things; *normal* refers to what is average, whereas *healthy* refers to what is adaptive. Behaviors can be adjusted in different situations or conditions. Up to this point in our study of sex and sexuality, we have focused our attention on normal, healthy sex. Here, we look more closely at sexual experiences that are not as common, and those that may be classified as abnormal. Behavior or behaviors that are *abnormal* are characterized by three components (Getzfeld, 2006):

1. The *frequency* with which it occurs: Is the behavior occupying someone's time, attention, and/or resources?

2. *Social acceptability*: Is the behavior considered to be normative within the culture?

3. *Problems* associated with the behavior: Is the behavior coercive or manipulative? Does it cause problems for me, my partner, or society? Is it compulsive? (Benuto, 2009b)

In this chapter, we'll first focus our attention on the many different types of paraphilias. Within this discussion, we'll examine the incidences of the behaviors, as well as the legality of each of these types of sexual acts. This discussion will help us better determine what types of sexual behaviors are normal and healthy and which are not. We'll then take a look at treatment options for certain paraphilias. We'll conclude this chapter by exploring the ranges of sexual frequency, as well as look at the seemingly growing trend in sexual addiction and sexually compulsive behaviors. Some of you may have been sexual victims, and this content may be troublesome for you. If you have experienced sexual victimization and this material is difficult for you to study, I encourage you to talk with your professor or instructor.

PARAPHILIAS: VARIANT OR DEVIANT?

Table 15.1 presents the possible causes of paraphilias, and, as you can see, there is no one answer that explains why or how someone becomes a paraphiliac. **Paraphilia** is a medical or psychological term that is used to describe sexual arousal caused by objects, situations, or individuals. The term also implies that this sexual arousal is not part of socially/culturally normative sexual stimulation and arousal; often, the behaviors cause distress or other problems for the **paraphiliac**, the person who engages in these behaviors (de Silva, 1999).

^
^ Necrophilia is a paraphilia **in which**
^ **someone has a sexual attraction to or intercourse with dead bodies.**

OWN IT! Are Your Sexual Turn-Ons "Normal"? Does it Matter?

We all have different things that physically attract us to someone. Likewise, there is a wide array of things that turn us on sexually. Some people like to be kissed in certain places, some like their partners to dress in particular ways, and some people become excited when having sex in particular places.

Take a few minutes to respond to the following:

1. Quickly write down the top three things that really "turn you on."

2. Where do you believe these come from? Why do these things arouse you? Are they learned behaviors?

3. How would you feel if you found out your desires were considered abnormal? What if your significant other or a friend recommended that you seek therapy?

TABLE 15.1
Possible Origins of Paraphilias

Source: Lee, J. K. et al. (2002).

- *Biological theories:* Some believe that testosterone increases the susceptibility of males to develop paraphilias.

- *Learning theories:* Some believe that paraphilia behaviors are learned and emotional, physical, and sexual abuse in childhood, and family dysfunction increase the risk of developing paraphilias.

- *Psychoanalytic theories:* These theorists believe that little boys' psychological separation from their mothers may cause them to grow up and form deviant desires.

- *Head trauma:* Some brain-injured men become exhibitionists after severe head traumas.

- *ADHD:* Some children with a history of attention-deficit/ hyperactivity disorder (ADHD) have multiple paraphilias as adults.

Paraphilias were first observed and identified by Krafft-Ebing (see Chapter 2) in 1886, and they have been considered a mental disorder since 1905 (Seligman & Hardenburg, 2000). The term **sexual deviance** encompasses paraphilias and is often extended to include sexual assault and rape (Williams et al., 2009). **Sexual variations** is also a term that is sometimes used to refer to paraphilia behaviors, because it is a more neutral term and does not imply that each of the behaviors is deviant or illegal (de Silva, 1999). The common thread in all of these definitions is that the behaviors focus on the unusual nature of the source of arousal (Feierman & Feierman, 2000).

Physicians, psychiatrists, psychologists, therapists, and clinicians use the *Diagnostic and Statistical Manual of Mental Disorders* to classify and diagnose paraphilias, defined as intense, recurring sexually arousing fantasies, urges, or behaviors that commonly involve non-human objects, the suffering or humiliation of the person or his or her partner, or children and other non-consenting persons (pp. 522–523). To qualify as a paraphilia, the behavior must also cause significant problems in the person's life, and symptoms must be present for at least six months. The severity of paraphilias is also on a continuum. For example, some people experience very mild disorders, perhaps just fantasies in the privacy of a person's own home, and others experience very severe cases, such as behavior that involves sex with children.

There are no racial/ethnic, sexual orientation, or socioeconomic boundaries; paraphil-

ias can occur in anyone. It is difficult to know the incidence and prevalence of paraphilias because of the social stigma attached. Because of this, much of the available data come from victims of abuse or incarcerated individuals (Wylie et al., 2008). We do know, however, that paraphilias are found almost exclusively in males (Ward, Laws, & Hudson, 2003). Onset tends to begin sometime early in puberty and it is fully developed by young adulthood (Ward, Laws, & Hudson, 2003). Often, there is an overlap of paraphilias, with multiple occurring in the same person simultaneously (Ward, Laws, & Hudson, 2003). Also, although paraphilias are present in other cultures, they are primarily a Western culture phenomenon (Bhugra, 2000). For example, in a review of the literature on cross-cultural variations in sexual expression, one researcher found that in sex-negative societies—societies that view sex as only for procreation and not recreation—fewer paraphilias are present (Bhugra, 2000). They are more prevalent in sex-positive societies, where sex is perceived as recreational.

Paraphilias certainly are not all similar; rather, they consist of a group of disorders that fall at different points on a continuum of social acceptability. For instance, **zoophilia** is an erotic attraction to or sexual contact with an animal (see Figure 15.1). They can be perceived as private

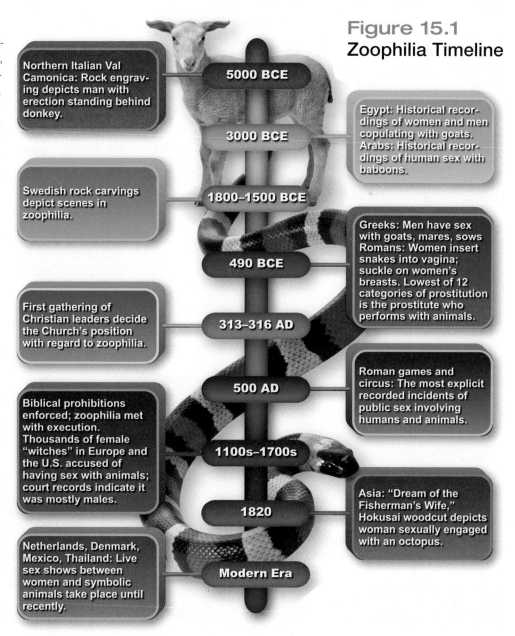

Figure 15.1
Zoophilia Timeline

5000 BCE — Northern Italian Val Camonica: Rock engraving depicts man with erection standing behind donkey.

3000 BCE — Egypt: Historical recordings of women and men copulating with goats. Arabs: Historical recordings of human sex with baboons.

1800–1500 BCE — Swedish rock carvings depict scenes in zoophilia.

490 BCE — Greeks: Men have sex with goats, mares, sows. Romans: Women insert snakes into vagina; suckle on women's breasts. Lowest of 12 categories of prostitution is the prostitute who performs with animals.

313–316 AD — First gathering of Christian leaders decide the Church's position with regard to zoophilia.

500 AD — Roman games and circus: The most explicit recorded incidents of public sex involving humans and animals.

1100s–1700s — Biblical prohibitions enforced; zoophilia met with execution. Thousands of female "witches" in Europe and the U.S. accused of having sex with animals; court records indicate it was mostly males.

1820 — Asia: "Dream of the Fisherman's Wife," Hokusai woodcut depicts woman sexually engaged with an octopus.

Modern Era — Netherlands, Denmark, Mexico, Thailand: Live sex shows between women and symbolic animals take place until recently.

TABLE 15.2
Other Types of Paraphilias

Source: Based on http://www.depression-guide.com/sexual-disorders.htm

Frotteurism	sexual arousal and gratification by rubbing one's genitals against others in public places or crowds
Coprophilia	sexual excitement focused on feces
Klismaphilia	sexual pleasure from enemas
Urophilia	sexual excitement from urine or urination
Acrotomophilia	erotic arousal from a partner who is an amputee
Troilism	obtaining sexual arousal and gratification by sharing a sexual partner while watching
Gerontophilia	specific sexual inclination toward the elderly
Mysophilia	sexual arousal and gratification by smelling, chewing, or otherwise utilizing sweaty or soiled clothing or articles of menstrual hygiene
Necrophilia	sexual arousal from corpses
Zoophilia	sexual arousal from and sexual activity with animals
Transvestite fetishism	heterosexual men who are aroused by wearing, fondling, or seeing female clothing
Hypoxyphilia	desire to achieve an altered state of consciousness to enhance orgasm through use of a drug such as nitrous oxide to produce hypoxia, or a "high" due to a lack of oxygen to the brain

behaviors, mental illnesses, and/or as dangerous, criminal acts (see Table 15.2). In the section that follows, we review the more common types of paraphilias.

FETISHISM: AROUSED BY OBJECTS

It's normal to be sexually aroused by objects. For example, you might become aroused when you see someone wearing a certain type of clothing. But if seeing or touching that type of clothing is the *only* way you can become aroused, you may have a fetish. **Fetishism** is sexual arousal and behavior with nonliving objects; the person becomes sexually aroused by wearing or touching the object. To be clinically diagnosed with having a fetish, the *DSM-IV-TR* specifies that these fantasies, urges, or behaviors must be recurrent for at least six months. Common objects include women's lingerie, shoes, things made of rubber or leather, and gloves. Scent or texture may also often contribute to the sexual arousal (Lowenstein, 2002). **Partialism**, a related disorder, involves becoming sexually aroused by a body part. Fetishism and partialism are legal.

>>> Autoerotic asphyxiation (AEA) refers to intentionally cutting off oxygen **for sexual arousal.**

The fetish may be integrated into sexual activity with a willing partner; someone with a fetish can still have sex with a person, but generally is only satisfied if the object of the fetish is present (Benuto, 2009a). For example, a man with a shoe fetish might need his partner to wear sexy shoes during sex. The fetish can also totally replace sexual activity with a partner.

Most people with fetishes are male (Bhugra, 2000; Lowenstein, 2002) and often use their fetish objects while masturbating alone or with another as a type of foreplay (Lowenstein, 2002). Fetishes tend to start early, even in childhood, and generally persist throughout life (Lowenstein, 2002). It's difficult to estimate how many people have fetishes because people do not often divulge this information.

In his review of literature on fetishes, L. F. Lowenstein (2002) lists popular types of fetishes, including those involving feet, panty hose, and hair. **Transvestite fetishism**, another common type, occurs when a heterosexual male derives sexual arousal from wearing women's clothing. Research has shown that, overall, people with transvestite fetishes do not differ from people with other types of fetishes. Therefore, transvestites may be considered fetishists (Lowenstein, 2002). This is distinct from cross-dressing, which involves a heterosexual male dressing in women's clothing as a way to express the feminine side of his personality, rather than for sexual arousal.

SADISM AND MASOCHISM: RECEIVING AND/OR INFLICTING PAIN

In 1890, Krafft-Ebing was the first to introduce the terms "masochism" and "sadism" in the medical literature. **Sexual masochism** is a paraphilia in which individuals are aroused by fantasies, urges, or behaviors that involve the infliction of psychological or physical suffering on them. **Sexual sadism** is when the person becomes sexually aroused through fantasies and/or behavior that involve inflicting psychological or physical suffering on another person (Wylie et al., 2008). These paraphilias emphasize dominance and submission more than pain (Weinburg, 2006). However, at its most extreme, sadism may involve illegal activities, such as rape

<<< What do these things have in common?

They are all often fetish objects.

and torture; it also sometimes may involve murder, after which the victim's death produces sexual arousal.

Sadism and masochism often exist together. **BDSM** is a form of consensual sex between two or more people that includes three subdivisions: *bondage and discipline (B&D, B/D, or BD)*; *dominance and submission (D&s, D/s, or Ds)*; and *sadism and masochism (S&M, S/M, or SM)*. SM is also referred to as **sadomasochism**. SM activities are interrelated, but there are generally four main types of behavior: *hypermasculinity* (cockbinding, catheters); *administration of pain* (whips or sandpaper on genitals); *humiliation* (face slapping, verbal humiliation); and *physical restriction* (using restraints such as chains or handcuffs) (Alison et al., 2001). Females tend to engage in more humiliation-related behaviors, and males, particularly homosexual males, tend to engage in more hypermasculinity behaviors (Alison et al., 2001).

A review of sadomasochism literature described what is currently known about sadomasochists (Weinburg, 2006). Sadomasochists tend to view their SM activity as recreation that is separate from the rest of their lives; they function well in society and many engage in nonsadomasochistic sex. SM activities are generally planned and consensual, and forced participation is not accepted in the SM world. Also, those who practice SM have what is referred to as a prearranged *safe word*—as soon as one partner uses the safe word, the activity immediately ends. People who engage in SM activities use a number of props that add to the symbolic nature of SM. These might include black leather costumes, whips, and restraints. Homosexuals and bisexuals tend to engage in SM behaviors more than heterosexuals, but heterosexual individuals participate in SM practices as well. Both men and women engage in SM activities; they generally begin to recognize this interest and "come out" in their early 20s.

There are communities available for those participating in SM, such as organizations, bars, parties, and online communities. These communities can help provide a sense of belonging, an outlet for SM activities, and an opportunity to socialize with people in the SM world (Weinburg, 2006).

∧
∧ BDSM is legal in the United States. A
∧
∧ 2003 landmark U.S. Supreme Court case,
Lawrence v. Texas, **determined that states cannot place prohibitions on the private sexual behavior of consenting adults.**

Something New? A Little S&M?

Bob and Hillary met while they were in graduate school and have been a couple for 14 years. They have always been able to talk openly about sex and have had what many would consider a healthy, normal, and satisfying sex life. Neither party has ever felt a desire to have sex outside the relationship. Hillary has wanted to try something different in the bedroom, however Bob doesn't quite understand this new desire and is afraid that he no longer satisfies Hillary. He is committed to Hillary and their relationship, so he wants to understand what Hillary needs to be happy.

Her side: I just thought we might want to try to spice things up a little. It's not that I'm not satisfied or that I'm bored; I was just being adventurous. We don't have to do anything he isn't comfortable with, and please don't think I no longer find him attractive. I was reading in one of my women's magazines about a couple who tried tying each other up, some spanking, and hair pulling, and it got them really excited. They said they had some of the best sex of their lives and that their orgasms were more intense. The author suggested it was more about doing things that were taboo than the actual acts that made it exciting.

His side: Maybe I was just shocked by her suggestions or maybe I felt threatened. I have always thought of myself as being sexually adventurous, and as a man, I thought I should be the one to suggest "new things." I have never even thought about doing those things. Now I'm afraid if I don't, she will start to get bored or she will go some place else to experiment. I guess I just thought of those things as being weird, so the people who did them were weird, too.

Your side: If you were Hillary, would Bob's comments about your suggestion being "weird" hurt your feelings? If you were Bob, would you feel threatened by Hillary's interest in trying something different? Use the following to help you think about your own feelings related to "normal" sexual behaviors.

1. What do you consider to be normal sexual behaviors?

2. How far would you be willing to deviate from "normal" to satisfy someone you love?

3. Can you think of anything in your life that you enjoy doing that you formerly thought was weird or that others think is weird?

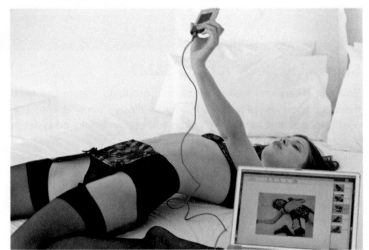

>>> Flashing is a crime, typically a misdemeanor offense. Currently, *indecent exposure* laws are being considered at the federal level (Kulbarsh, 2008).

EXHIBITIONISM AND VOYEURISM

Exhibitionism is a persistent mental disorder characterized by the achievement of sexual excitement/arousal through the compulsion to show one's genitals to an unsuspecting stranger (*DSM-IV-TR*, 2000); sometimes the exhibitionist masturbates simultaneously (Wylie et al., 2008).

Commonly referred to as *indecent exposure*, *flashing*, or *weenie wagging*, exhibitionism is one of the three most common illegal sexual offenses, and exhibitionists make up about one-third of all sex offenders (Kulbarsh, 2008). Almost all reported cases involve male perpetrators in their 20s, and their victims are almost always women and children (Carnes & Schneider, 2000); most exhibitionists are married and often make no attempt to hide their identity (this is thought to heighten their sexual arousal) (Kulbarsh, 2008). About 35 percent are re-offenders.

Table 15.3 describes three types of exhibitionists, and Figure 15.2 shows us the various types of behaviors associated with exhibitionism. Reactions from victims range from fear to laughter (Kulbarsh, 2008).

Exhibitionists tend to thrive on fear, anger, and shock reactions; victims are encouraged not to laugh at an exhibitionist, because it may result in further hostility.

Some maintain that the increasing popularity of reality television shows such as *Survivor* and *Big Brother* is a sign that we have become a nation of voyeurs who are obsessed with other people's lives (Metzl, 2004). **Voyeurism**, according to the *DSM-IV-TR* (2000), is a paraphilia in which someone becomes recurrently sexually excited or aroused by watching unsuspecting people undress, people who are nude, or people having sex. Voyeurism is one of the three most common criminal sexual offenses (Kulbarsh, 2008), and **voyeurs** (those who watch) are almost always male; their victims are usually strangers (de Silva, 1999). Even though a voyeur may return again and again to watch the same victim, rarely is there any physical contact with the victim. In pop culture, voyeurs are known as *peeping Toms*. **Scopophilia** or **scoptophilia** refers to the act of deriving sexual pleasure from looking at erotic objects, such as erotic photographs, pornography, naked bodies, or others engaging in sexual activity (Rye & Meaney, 2007). Exhibitionism and voyeurism are acts of sexual victimization, even though these paraphilias are non-contact acts (Violence Against Women, 2009).

So what is the difference between voyeurism as a mental illness and voyeurism that is deemed acceptable in today's society? Part of the

^^^ How does mooning someone or flashing breasts during Mardi Gras differ from exhibitionism? **Society and culture determine what constitutes exhibitionism.** While the acts of exposing one's buttocks or breasts is indecent exposure, Western society doesn't frown upon these behaviors.

^^ There is nothing wrong with taking photos of or recording your sex life as long as each partner consents. **But without consent from the subject, this is illegal (Women Against Violence, 2009).**

difference may lie in the potential harm to those who are being watched. In the case of reality television shows, participants know they will be watched. Similarly, openly watching your boyfriend or girlfriend undress is OK if he or she has consented. However, it is not acceptable to look through people's windows, sneak into the locker room at the gym, or otherwise watch people who are unaware that you are there.

Regardless of whether the voyeurism is consensual, a need for social approval exists (Forsyth, 1996). In a study of more than 300 college students, researchers found that just over 67 percent of students said they would watch someone whom they found attractive undress if there was no chance of getting caught; 45 percent said they would watch this person have sex with another attractive person if again there was no chance of getting caught (Rye & Meaney, 2007). However, when the students were told that there was a chance of getting caught, they said they were less likely to engage in either voyeurism or scoptophilia. Additionally, men and women were just as likely to say they would watch someone undress, but men were more likely than women to watch others having sex.

In a national Swedish population survey, researchers discovered that nearly 4 percent of women and nearly 12 percent of men reported at least one episode of voyeuristic behavior (Langström & Seto, 2006). The prevalence of exhibitionistic behavior was a bit lower, with about 2 percent of women and 4 percent of men reporting at least one episode in their lifetime. Results of this same study indicated that those who had reported exhibitionistic and/or voyeuristic behavior were more likely to have psychological problems, lower life satisfaction, and a greater likelihood of a current mental disorder than those in the study who had not engaged in exhibitionistic or voyeuristic behaviors. Finally, exhibitionistic or voyeuristic behaviors were positively associated with frequency of masturbation in the last month, pornography use in the last year, and feeling more easily sexually aroused.

So far, our study has focused on consensual behaviors, such as BDSM, non-invasive behaviors such as fetishism, and the typically non-contact behaviors such as exhibitionism and voyeurism. We have yet to discuss a paraphilia that has become an issue of great societal concern—pedophilia.

Figure 15.2 Behaviors Associated with Exhibitionism

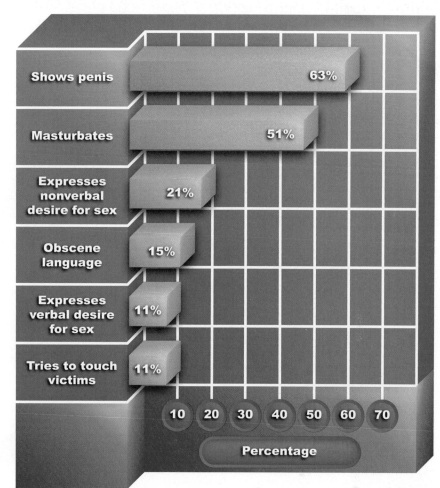

Source: Kulbarsh, 2008.

TABLE 15.3
Types of Exhibitionists

Source: Based on Kulbarsh, P. (2008)

There are three groups of exhibitionists. Types 1 and 2 are commonly more dangerous to themselves than they are to others.

1. *Inhibited/Introverted:* Typically socially awkward, often anxious, impulsive, obsessive, and sexually confused or immature.

2. *Unaware:* Some may have a mental illness or handicap, organic brain disorder, or traumatic brain injury; some may also have extreme alcohol or drug intoxication.

3. *Assaultive:* Almost always uses masturbation, and often has concurrent paraphilias such as **scatologia** (impulsive use of obscene language) and **frotteurism** (touching and rubbing against a nonconsenting person); often progresses to more aggressive sexual crimes, such as rape.

PEDOPHILIA: CHILDREN AS VICTIMS

Pedophilia, a term coined by Krafft-Ebing in 1886, is the paraphilia with which people tend to have the most familiarity and the one that they often find the most disturbing (DiChristina, 2009). The term **pedophilia** denotes the erotic preference for prepubescent children (Blanchard et al., 2009). By diagnostic criteria set forth in the *DSM-IV-TR*, a **pedophile** sexually fantasizes about, is aroused by, and/or has sexual urges toward children, typically under the age of 13. These characteristics must persist for at least six months to warrant a clinical diagnosis of pedophilia (*DSM-IV-TR*, 2000; Hall & Hall, 2007). To meet the criteria for pedophilia, an individual must be at least 16 years old and at least five years older than his or her "juvenile of interest." Pedophilia is *not* a legal/criminal term—it is a mental health diagnosis (Hall & Hall, 2007).

Pedophiles almost never force children into sexual acts (Hall & Hall, 2007); instead, they employ a number of methods. Referred to as *grooming*, pedophiles desensitize their victims, often first engaging them in harmless touching and eventually progressing to other invasive acts (Lanning, 2001; Murray, 2000; Cohen & Galynker, 2002). A majority of pedophiles (50 to 70 percent) have concurrent paraphilias and thus engage in a wide range of sexual behaviors with children (Hall & Hall, 2007):

- *Exhibitionism:* A pedophile may expose his or her genitals to a child.

- *Voyeurism:* Some pedophiles look at naked children, both in person and online; they may also undress a child. Voyeurism may or may not include touching the child.

Figure 15.3 What makes a pedophile? A number of theories have been proposed, and they center on the nature/nurture debate (Hall & Hall, 2007).

Biological Factors (Nature)

Much research points to neurological/brain differences in pedophiles. Pedophiles tend to have decreased gray matter, as well as differences in the frontal and temporal lobes. Changes in gray matter are often also seen in people who have impulse control disorders, such as addiction. Temporal lobe conditions can lead to hypersexual behavior. Neurochemical imbalances, are also linked to pedophilia.

Environmental Factors (Nurture)

If a person is sexually abused as a child, he/she has an increased risk to become an offender; this is known as the victim-to-abuser cycle, or the abused-abuser cycle. Some speculate an arousal pattern is imprinted at the time of abuse, and this is why an abuser prefers children as an adult. However, most abused people do not become abusers.

- *Frotteurism:* Pedophiles may rub their genitalia, buttocks, or breasts against a child; some engage in masturbation in front of a child or coerce the child into mutual masturbation.

- *Sexual intercourse:* Some eventually progress to oral, anal, and vaginal intercourse.

Ephebophilia (attraction to males), and **hebephilia** (attraction to females), is distinguished from pedophilia in that the erotic preferences,

∧∧∧ Would you want to know if a

pedophile moved in next door?

sexual fantasies, and/or sexual behaviors of the *ephebophile/hebephile* are directed to young adolescents, about ages 11 to 14 (Glueck, 1955; Hall & Hall, 2007). **Infantophilia** describes individuals who have erotic preferences for children younger than 5 (Greenberg, Bradford, & Curry, 1995). However, these terms are not in widespread use, even among those who work with sex offenders; most tend to lump them all under the broad category of pedophilia (Blanchard et al., 2009).

The term *child molester* is often used interchangeably with pedophile, but the two are different. A **child molester** is an individual who engages in a sexually motivated act against a prepubescent child (before age 13), but who does not meet the *DSM-IV-TR* diagnostic criteria of having erotic preferences for children for at least six months (Kingston et al., 2007). *Forcible sexual offense* is the legal term used to describe acts of sexual violence against children, whether by a child molester or a pedophile (Snyder, 2000). Not all child molesters are pedophiles, and not all pedophiles act on their fantasies or urges. This is one of the reasons it is so difficult to know just how many pedophiles there are (Cohen & Galynker, 2009).

Most pedophiles are male, but female pedophiles could be underrepresented in the estimates because it is socially acceptable for women to spend time with younger boys, such as being a Cub Scout leader, soccer coach, or tutor (Cohen & Galynker, 2009). As with other paraphilias, nobody is completely sure what causes pedophilia, but the mental health disorder is likely a combination of biological and environmental factors (DiChristina, 2009). For example, research continues to support the finding that a pedophile may have been sexually abused at some point (Cohen & Galynker, 2009; DiChristina, 2009). In support of a biological link, some studies have found higher rates of pedophiles among families already including pedophiles (DiChristina, 2009). There is also some evidence of deviant factors that affect the motivation of a pedophile, including impulsivity, or factors that inhibit appropriate sexual relationships with adults such as poor self-esteem or social anxiety (Cohen & Galynker, 2009). Figure 15.3 shows the biological and cultural factors that may contribute to pedophilia.

So far in our study in this chapter we have focused our attention on the different types of paraphilias. Before we move on, it's important to once again emphasize that not all paraphilias are "abnormal," and not all are harmful; this is why the behaviors are often referred to as sexual variations, and why we refrain from calling people sexual deviants. However, paraphilias often cause a lot of concern because the behaviors are outside the social norm. If a person desires treatment, there are options available. In the next section, we'll take a look at treatment methods for paraphilias.

TREATING PARAPHILIAS: IS THERE HELP OR HOPE?

Because the causal factors associated with paraphilias are not known for sure, treatment of paraphilias is difficult. Additionally, there is a great deal of stigma associated with paraphilias, which influences the lack of knowledge and consistency in the way paraphilias are addressed and treated.

sexual life now

Are Paraphilias Mental Disorders?

Throughout history, societies have attempted to control the sexual behaviors of their members. One way they have done this is to define specific sexual acts or interests as mental disorders or as symptoms of mental disorders. The sexual interests that are defined as such vary from culture to culture, and these definitions have changed over time. Having a diagnosis of a mental disorder can affect many rights and privileges.

The primary influence in the United States and abroad on what is considered a disorder is the *Diagnostic and Statistical Manual (DSM)*, published by the American Psychiatric Association (APA). The *DSM* describes the diagnostic criteria and defining features of all formally recognized mental disorders. Beginning with the 1980 revision, objective research was the basis for these criteria as opposed to previous versions, which were based on theory and conjecture. The APA removed homosexuality from the *DSM* more than 30 years ago because of a lack of scientific evidence supporting its inclusion. Should paraphilias be included as mental disorders in the next version of the *DSM*?

YES!

For a disorder to be classified as a paraphilia in *DSM-IV-TR*, three things must be present:

- There must be a clearly deviant form of sexual enjoyment.

- There must be evidence of a pattern of arousal (e.g., sexual urges and sexually arousing fantasies) in response to this deviant form of gratification that is recurrent and intense and occurs over a period of at least six months.

- The person must have acted on his or her paraphilia urges; otherwise, the urges or fantasies must have caused significant distress or interpersonal difficulty.

For paraphilias that do not involve non-consenting victims, the diagnosis is made if the paraphilia fantasies, urges, or behaviors cause clinically significant distress or impairment in social, occupational, or other important areas of functioning. All three are essential to the diagnosis, no matter how uncommon or unusual the paraphilia (APA, 2000).

>>> WHAT DO YOU THINK?

1. Should paraphilias be removed from the *DSM*?
2. Why do you think paraphilia behaviors might cause distress or interpersonal difficulty?
3. Are behaviors by themselves enough to characterize someone as having a mental illness?

NO!

Charles Moser and Peggy J. Kleinplatz (2005) have questioned the categorization of the paraphilias as mental disorders. Noting, "The equating of unusual sexual interests with psychiatric diagnoses has been used to justify the oppression of sexual minorities and to serve a political agenda," they assert that a "review of this area is not only a scientific issue, but also a human rights issue" (Moser & Kleinplatz, 2003, p. 93). They argue:

- Paraphilias are mental disorders, noting that research has not supported this classification.

- That there are inconsistencies and contradictions within the *DSM* classification.

- That there are specific instances in which statements appearing as fact in the section are not supported by research.

Moser and Kleinplatz note that although the *DSM* editors claim to have carefully reviewed the appropriate literature, the paraphilia section is inconsistent with the current state of knowledge, recommending the removal of the paraphilia category altogether (p. 96).

Sources: American Psychiatric Association. (2000). *Diagnostic and statistical manual of mental disorders* (4th ed., Text Revised). Washington, DC: APA; Moser, C., & Kleinplatz, P. J. (2005). DSM-IV-TR and the paraphilias: An argument for removal. *Journal of Psychology & Human Sexuality, 17(3/4)*, 91–109.

In the late 19th century, **eugenics**, or surgical castration, was the first method used to treat paraphilias (Gordon, 2008). By the 1940s, paraphilias were often treated with hormonal medications. Initially, estrogens were used in males. This resulted in feminizing side effects, such as smaller testicles and a lower sex drive. Medications then shifted to the use of drugs that inhibited or reduced testosterone production. Drugs such as these are still used today (often in combination with other medications that help with impulse control), but usually in conjunction with psychotherapy or cognitive behavioral therapy (Gordon, 2008).

Psychologist and sexologist Lorraine Benuto (2009a) outlines some treatments for paraphilias that have been used with varying degrees of success:

- *Victim Identification:* This has been helpful for individuals with exhibitionism, frotteurism, voyeurism, sexual sadism, and for some pedophiles. With the help of a therapist, paraphiliacs are helped to realize that the objects of their sexual behaviors are *victims*. The goal of this approach is for the client to develop empathy toward the victims, which may in turn reduce the harmful behavior.

- *Covert Conditioning:* Also called *shame aversion*, the client is asked to imagine feeling shame when friends or family members observe him engaging in the paraphilia behavior, rendering it less desirable.

- *Orgasmic Reconditioning/Masturbatory Extinction:* The individual is asked to either masturbate to a paraphilia fantasy or to an appropriate fantasy. The aim of both techniques is to reinforce the appropriate fantasy through orgasm and to extinguish the inappropriate fantasy.

- *Aversion Therapy:* This treatment involves pairing a deviant fantasy or arousal with either a mild electric shock or unpleasant smells. The pairing of unhealthy fantasies, urges, or behaviors with unpleasant experiences may decrease the unhealthy ones.

Each semester in my sexuality class, students ask whether treatments for paraphilias really work. As you have seen in our study, sexual offenders have a high rate of re-offending, and *no* treatment for pedophilia is effective unless it is ongoing (Hall & Hall, 2007). Even in instances of chemical castration (see the THINK Reading 5), some go on to offend again (Stone, Winslade, & Klugman, 2000).

Most of us desire to be "normal." To be sure, normal is not always easy to define. This is particularly true when it comes to the frequency of having sex. In the next section, we'll take a look at what it means to be "oversexed." We'll also explore sexual addictions, including sexual addiction involving the Internet.

There are several signs that can indicate **that one is a sex addict.**

2) the sexual behavior has significant negative contributions, but the individual still cannot stop the behavior (Briken et al., 2007).

Addiction and recovery expert Patrick Carnes (2001) outlines 10 types of sexually compulsive behaviors. These types of behaviors are presented in Figure 15.5, along with a description of each and how it might be

SEXUAL ADDICTIONS

Magazines, television shows, and movies might lead you to believe that people are having sex all the time, and that if you don't have sex several times a week, then you aren't "normal." As with every other facet of sexuality, sexual frequency exists on a continuum. On one end of this continuum are those who have little or no interest in sexuality. This condition is referred to as **hyposexuality**. On the other end are those who engage in frequent sexual activity to the point of addiction or compulsion, **hypersexuality**.

HYPERSEXUALITY AND SEXUAL ADDICTION

Sexual addiction (see Figure 15.4) refers to a lack of control over sexual behavior, and it is a concept that has only been around since the 1980s (Levine & Troiden, 1988). The idea of sexual addiction is modeled after alcoholism and first emerged in the context of the 12-step program model similar to that of Alcoholics Anonymous (Levine & Troiden, 1988). Sexual addiction has many names: nymphomania, hypersexuality, sexual addiction, sexual impulsivity, and compulsive sexual behavior. Sexologists, however, simply refer to unregulated sexual behavior as "out of control sexual behavior" (Bancroft & Vukadinovic, 2004).

Part of the confusion surrounding the terminology is related to a lack of clarity about the actual behaviors that are exhibited by those with a sexual addiction. It is widely accepted that sexual addiction has two defining features: 1) The individual is not able to control the behavior; and

Stage 1: Preoccupation

Characterized by all-consuming thoughts about sex and an obsessive search for sexual stimulation.

Stage 2: Ritualization

The sex addict's routine(s) that lead up to the sexual behavior, the preoccupation of the addict is intensified during this stage, which adds arousal and excitement.

Stage 3: Compulsive Sexual Behavior

The addict participates in the sexual behavior, which he or she is unable to control or stop; compulsive sexual behavior is the end goal of the preoccupation and ritualization stages.

Stage 4: Despair

The sex addict experiences hopelessness and recognizes the powerlessness that he or she has over the behavior; in an effort to cope, the addict may begin to engage in the preoccupation stage again, restarting the addiction cycle.

Figure 15.4 Sexual Addiction Cycle Sexual addicts appear to go through a four-step addiction cycle, which intensifies each time it is repeated (Carnes, 2001).

Figure 15.5 Ten Types of Sexually Compulsive Behavior

Types of Sexually Compulsive Behavior	What does this behavior look like?	Compulsive Behavior on the Internet
Fantasy Sex 	• safety in staying in the fantasy world • disassociate from reality • can become obsessed • masturbating is common and may become compulsive	• e-mails, chat rooms, pornography sites
Voyeurism 	• move beyond fantasy to searching out sexual objects in the real world • looking at people who do not know they are being viewed • may move to using pornography compulsively which leads to isolation	• voyeur and mini-cam sites
Exhibitionism 	• eroticism in being looked at • power of realizing they have captured the other's attention • forcing their sexuality on the other • obsessed and compulsive	• exposing oneself by sending unwanted pictures • participating in nude photo posting sites
Seductive Role Sex 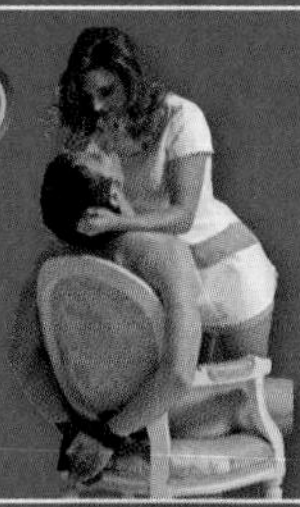	• relationships are about power and conquest • hooked on falling in love • win the attention of the other and then sexual interest subsides • may have multiple relationships simultaneously • have difficulty forming a deeper lasting relationship	• chat rooms, e-mail romance, dating services, swapping bulletin boards with the goal of conquest and not a relationship
Trading Sex 	• goes beyond the exchange of sex for money as a way to earn money • sex with clients is more pleasurable than in personal relationships • hooked on the power and life of prostitution	• use of Internet to post and schedule sexual services with the goal of conquering the client
Intrusive Sex 	• using others for sexual arousal with little chance of being caught • touching people in crowds or making obscene calls • stolen intrusion becomes the obsession	• unwanted intrusion through the computer • files of nude pictures or stores of sexual fantasy hidden in a hard drive
Paying for Sex 	• compulsive prostitution • focused on the touching, foreplay, and intercourse without the hassle of relationship	• finding a prostitute through online mechanisms
Anonymous Sex 	• focus is on sex with no need to attract, seduce, or pay for sex • associated with loneliness and isolation • part of the high is the risk of unknown persons and situations	• creating online personas
Pain Exchange Sex 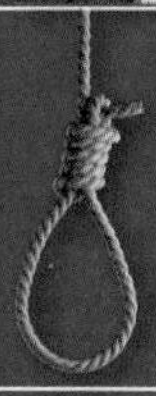	• compulsively into painful, degrading, or dangerous sexual practices such as blood sports (creating wounds that bleed as part of sex) or asphyxiation • enduring relationships are difficult to build given these arousal needs	• use of pornography sites, bulletin boards, and interest groups that depict violent or humiliating behavior
Exploitive Sex 	• exploiting vulnerable individuals • arousal is dependent on the vulnerability of another • sex offenders who rape • nonviolent predators who use seduction	• chat rooms and e-mail are ways to search for potential victims

manifested in an Internet addiction. Carnes paralleled this progression of behaviors with courting behaviors found in non-paraphilia relationships. This helps therapists and patients alike recognize that sex addiction is an intimacy disorder as well as an addiction.

SEX ADDICTS: WHO ARE THEY?

Estimates show that 4 to 6 percent of the population experience sexual addiction, and men seem to have higher rates than women (Black, 2000). Gay and bisexual men have higher rates of sexual addiction than lesbian and bisexual women, and gay and bisexual men are more likely than lesbian and bisexual women to engage in substance abuse along with the sexual behavior (Kelly et al., 2009). Sexual offenders in the prison system tend to have a greater problem than the general population with sexual addiction, being three times more likely to be classified as sex addicts (Marshall & Marshall, 2006).

Although at this time no one knows for sure what causes hypersexuality, researchers have found some support for the idea that depression and anxiety seem to be associated with those who were considered sex addicts (Bancroft & Vukadinovic, 2004); however, there seems to be many other factors associated with out-of-control sexual behavior. Additionally, people with a sexual addiction often exhibit low self-esteem, loneliness, guilt, and impaired social skills (Kelly et al., 2009).

Peer Briken and his colleagues (2007) found in their survey of German sex therapists that the most common symptoms of sexual addiction were a dependence on pornography, compulsive masturbation, and extended periods of promiscuity. Dependence on pornography tends to be more common in men, whereas promiscuity is more common in women. Many sex addicts have other conditions along with the sex addiction; men tend to have substance abuse problems, and women tend to have eating disorders (Briken et al., 2007).

In a review of research conducted on sexual addiction, Mark Bird (2006) found that sexual addiction has a direct and negative impact on marital or family relationships. Although addicts experience negative consequences to their personal life and their relationships, they can't stop participating in sexual behaviors. Many of the studies that Bird (2006) reviewed indicated that most addicts hide their compulsive sexual behaviors from their spouses. When discovered, the spouses experience a wide range of emotions including betrayal, anger, and confusion. These patterns are consistent regardless of whether the addiction is with online sex or with live sex. In these situations, couple therapy might be a good treatment approach (Bird, 2006). Individual and group therapy are common forms of treating sexual addiction, but couples therapy might be more appropriate for some addicts who are in a partnership (Bird, 2006).

In Chapter 8, we took a look at how some people use the Internet to meet their mates and intimate partners, and how some couples today grow their relationships online. Because of the ubiquity of the Internet today, it's not surprising that this medium plays a role in sexual addiction.

INTERNET SEXUAL ADDICTION

The concept of Internet sexual addiction is relatively new, and because of this, it is not yet formally recognized by the *DSM-IV-TR* as a mental disorder. However, some people have a sexual addiction specific to the Internet. **Cybersexual addiction** involves accessing sites for pornography and cybersex, whereas **cyber-relationship addiction** is an over-involvement in online relationships (Young, 1999). People are often less inhibited on the Internet, and the medium's anonymous nature may add excitement to the sexual activity (Griffiths, 2001). In addition, cybersex may accelerate addictive behavior that is already present, and those who engage in cybersex may move to sexual compulsive behaviors in the real world (Carnes, 2001, Perry, Accordino, & Hewes, 2007).

Studies have found that men are more likely than women to report viewing sexual material or seeking a sexual partner online (Perry, Accordino, & Hewes, 2007). In their study of more than 300 college

sex talk

Variety in sexual expression is normal, and there are many healthy expressions. However, it is important that you and your partner share the same ideas about how you want to express your sexuality. Often, talking about sexual desires and sexual expression can be a difficult conversation. Reflecting on these questions might facilitate a conversation with your partner about sexual expression.

I would be uncomfortable if you ever asked me to _____.

Besides sexual intercourse, I enjoy _____ as a form of sexual expression.

A sex toy that I would like to try is _____.

Watching another couple in the room have sex would/would not turn me on because _____.

I would/would not like to take photographs or videos of our sexual times together. This is because _____.

I have/have not wondered at times if my sexual behaviors were "normal." This is because I _____.

The thought of S&M makes me _____.

The thought of bondage makes me _____.

If I found out that you had a fetish, I would/would not want you to incorporate this into our sex life. I feel this way because

_____.

When I hear the term "paraphilias," I think _____.

students' attitudes toward Internet sexuality, researchers discovered that men were more likely to exhibit sexual compulsive and risk-taking behaviors than women.

Although some may feel like cyber-relationships are not harmful, Jennifer Schneider (2000) found through surveys with family members that there are harmful effects of cybersex on the family. First of all, cybersex participants withdrew from their families. Additionally, partners of a cybersex addict reported feelings of betrayal, loss of self-esteem, anger, and a variety of relationship problems. Schneider asked why online sex was a problem for family members. They revealed that they were concerned that the addiction might escalate and have cumulative negative effects on their relationships. Family members also expressed insecurities about competing with online sexual fantasies, and they noted that online sexual addictions constitute cheating and unfaithfulness to the relationship.

So, how does someone know what is healthy and what is unhealthy Internet use? The best measure is if online activities get in the way of offline life. An online sex addict may experience the following (University of Texas, 2009):

1. *Losing track of time:* Are you late to class, appointments, and work? Do you become irritated if your time online is interrupted?

2. *Isolation from family and friends:* Are you neglecting your family and friends? Is your online life becoming your "real" life? Do you ever feel that your online partners understand you/accept you better than your "real" partner, family, and friends?

3. *Feeling guilty or defensive:* Do you hide your Internet use and lie about your interactions? Do you lie about how much time you spend online or what sites you're visiting? Do you look over your shoulder often, worrying that your partner will "discover" your activities?

4. *Inability to quit:* Do you feel anxious, depressed, or angry when your "computer time" is interrupted? Have you had unsuccessful attempts at quitting or limiting your time on sex sites? Is the Internet becoming your means of sexual gratification? When you're not on the computer, are you anxious to get back to it?

Because Internet sexual addiction is a relatively new phenomenon, it is difficult to pinpoint just who may be an addict and who may not be.

If you exhibit any of the general warning signs discussed above, a visit to your campus health center would be advisable. As with all addictions, there are a number of therapeutic techniques and medications that can help someone overcome the addiction and get his or her life back on track.

SEXUAL LIFE EDUCATION

At the start of this chapter, a college student asked if his sexual behaviors were "normal." To come to an answer, we devoted our time to looking at certain variations in sexual expression and behaviors. In answering his question, we first have to remember what we have learned throughout our study together in this textbook: that the three domains of sexuality identified in Chapter 1 (biology, culture, and psychosocial/psychosexual) are intricately interwoven, and only by looking at all three domains can we find answers to our questions.

First, sexual norms exist in every society, and these norms are what define and dictate our sexuality; culture determines what is acceptable and what is not. For example, although our culture has zero acceptance of pedophilia, certain behaviors are given some slack, such as exhibitionism or voyeurism during spring break, looking at sex sites on the Internet, and perhaps even young men who have a lingerie fetish. We also have to consider biological forces; is this young man somehow predisposed to his sexual behaviors due to some hormonal cause? Finally, we must look at the psychosocial aspects associated with his actions. For example, is the college student's ability to form and maintain intimate relationships with others affected? If we look back at his story, we see that he has been dealing with his attraction to lingerie since he was a young boy; we also see that he is resorting to theft to satisfy his sexual fantasies and urges. By using the *DSM-IV-TR*'s criteria for classifying paraphilias, we can see that because his behaviors are persistent and because they are beginning to cause him significant problems in his life, his behaviors could possibly be classified as a paraphilia.

As we leave our discussion, it is important to keep in mind that as long as variations in sexual expressions do not affect the rights, health, and safety of others, the definition of what is "normal" is left to the relationship between two people.

Healthy Selves / Healthy Sex

Are You a Sex Addict?

You are not alone if you have wondered if you are a sex addict. You may enjoy sex and seek out opportunities for sex whenever you can. You may also enjoy looking at pornography. These two things alone do not make you a sex addict, and chances are you are perfectly healthy. However, if you feel that your sexual behavior is out of control, then you may want to look at the questions below that are posed by the Society for the Advancement of Sexual Health (SASH), an organization that helps those who suffer from out-of-control sexual behavior. Three basic things to consider when you define sexual addiction:

1. Do I have a sense that I have lost control over whether or not I engage in my specific out-of-control sexual behavior?

2. Am I experiencing significant consequences because of my specific out-of-control sexual behavior?

3. Do I feel like I am constantly thinking about my specific out-of-control sexual behavior, even when I don't want to?

These three factors help define sexual addiction and compulsivity. The range of behaviors can include masturbation and pornography through sexual exploitation of others. If you answered "yes" to these three questions, then you may want to see a health professional.

Source: The Society for the Advancement of Sexual Health. Retrieved September 12, 2009, from http://sash.net/index.php/Am-I-a-sex-addict.html

Summary

WHAT ARE PARAPHILIAS, AND ARE THEY VARIANT OR DEVIANT? 318

• Paraphilias are when sexual arousal is caused by objects, situations, or individuals; these behaviors are not considered socially or culturally acceptable and therefore cause problems in the lives of paraphiliacs. Whether or not a behavior is considered variant or deviant is often determined by society. Common paraphilias include fetishism, sadism and masochism, exhibition and voyeurism, and pedophilia.

HOW ARE PARAPHILIAS TREATED? 324

• While what is considered "normal" behavior has changed over time, so have the methods people have used to treat paraphilias. Some methods used include victim identification, covert conditioning, orgasmic reconditioning/masturbatory extinction, and aversion therapy.

WHAT IS SEXUAL ADDICTION? 326

• Sexual addiction, or hypersexuality, is when a person engages in sexual activity so frequently that it has gotten to the point of compulsion. People suffering from sexual addiction often feel that they have no control over their behaviors, and the Internet can factor prominently into hypersexuality. Like alcoholics, sex addicts can participate in a 12-step program to treat their addictions.

Key Terms

paraphilia a medical or psychological term that is used to describe sexual arousal caused by objects, situations, or individuals 318

paraphiliac a person who engages in paraphilia 318

necrophilia paraphilia in which someone has a sexual attraction to or sexual intercourse with dead bodies 318

sexual deviance term that encompasses paraphilias and is often extended to include sexual assault and rape 319

sexual variations a term that is sometimes used to refer to paraphilia behaviors, because it is a more neutral term and does not imply that each of the behaviors is deviant or illegal 319

zoophilia paraphilia characterized by an erotic attraction to or sexual contact with an animal 319

fetishism sexual arousal and behavior with non-living objects; the person becomes sexually aroused by wearing or touching the object 320

partialism disorder related to fetishism that involves becoming sexually aroused by a body part, such as feet, breasts, or buttocks 320

transvestite fetishism fetishism in which a heterosexual male derives sexual arousal from wearing women's clothing 320

sexual masochism paraphilia in which individuals are aroused by fantasies, urges, or behaviors that involve the infliction of psychological or physical suffering on them 320

sexual sadism paraphilia in which the person becomes sexually aroused through fantasies and/or behavior that involve inflicting psychological or physical suffering on another person 320

autoerotic asphyxiation (AEA) the practice of intentionally cutting off oxygen (through strangulation, hanging, or putting a plastic bag over the head) for sexual arousal; subcategory of masochism 320

BDSM a form of consensual sex between two or more people that includes three subdivisions: bondage and discipline (B&D), dominance and submission (Ds), and sadism and masochism (SM) 321

sadomasochism four main types of behavior: *hypermasculinity* (cockbinding, catheters); *administration of pain* (whips or sandpaper on genitals), *humiliation* (face slapping, verbal humiliation), and *physical restriction* (using restraints such as chains or handcuffs) 321

exhibitionism persistent mental disorder characterized by the achievement of sexual excitement/arousal through the compulsion to show one's genitals to an unsuspecting stranger 322

voyeurism paraphilia in which someone becomes recurrently sexually excited or aroused by watching unsuspecting people undress, people who are nude, or people having sex 322

voyeurs people who engage in voyeurism 322

scopophilia or **scoptophilia** the act of deriving sexual pleasure from looking at erotic objects, such as erotic photographs, pornography, naked bodies, or others engaging in sexual activity 322

scatologia impulsive use of obscene language 323

frotteurism touching and rubbing against a non-consenting person 323

pedophilia erotic preference for prepubescent children 323

pedophile a person who sexually fantasizes about, is aroused by, and/or has sexual urges toward children, typically under the age of 13 323

ephebophilia attraction to young adolescent males 324

hebephilia attraction to young adolescent females 324

infantophilia erotic preferences for children younger than 5 years of age 324

child molester an individual who engages in a sexually motivated act against a prepubescent child (before age 13), but who does not meet the *DSM-IV-TR* diagnostic criteria of having erotic preferences for children for at least six months 324

eugenics surgical castration 325

hyposexuality condition in which sufferers have little or no interest in sexuality 326

hypersexuality condition in which sufferers engage in frequent sexual activity to the point that it is an addiction or compulsion 326

sexual addiction a lack of control over sexual behavior 326

cybersexual addiction addiction that involves accessing sites for pornography and cybersex 328

cyber-relationship addiction an over-involvement in online relationships to the detriment of live relationships 328

Sample Test Questions

MULTIPLE CHOICE

1. Which type of theory about the origins of paraphilias suggests that testosterone plays a part?
   a. Biological
   b. ADHD
   c. Psychoanalytic
   d. Learning

2. Gerontophilia is sexual arousal caused by:
   a. Corpses
   b. Elderly people
   c. Children
   d. Animals

3. A sexual inclination toward which of the following is considered partialism?
   a. Stilettos
   b. Leather
   c. Feet
   d. Lingerie

4. Whips are used as a part of which type of sadomasochism?
   a. Humiliation
   b. Hypermasculinity
   c. Physical restriction
   d. Administration of pain

5. Which type of exhibitionist engages in frotteurism?
   a. Assaultive
   b. Unaware
   c. Inhibited/introverted
   d. All of the above

6. What term is used to describe a person who is sexually aroused by adolescent girls?
   a. Ephebophile
   b. Hebephile
   c. Pedophile
   d. Infantophile

7. Which term is not used for sexual addiction?
   a. Nymphomania
   b. Sexual impulsivity
   c. Hyposexuality
   d. Hypersexuality

8. Sexual addiction is treated with:
   a. Masturbatory extinction
   b. Covert conditioning
   c. Aversion therapy
   d. A 12-step program

SHORT RESPONSE

1. What three factors make a sexual behavior abnormal and why?

2. Explain the difference between exhibitionism and voyeurism.

3. Why is mooning not considered exhibitionism?

4. Would you want to know if a convicted sex offender moved into your neighborhood? Why or why not?

5. What factors into determining whether or not someone is actually suffering from sexual addiction?

Answers: 1.a; 2.b; 3.c; 4.d; 5.a; 6.b; 7.c; 8.d

Remember to check www.thethinkspot.com for additional information, downloadable flashcards, and other helpful resources.

SEXUALITY AND AGING

We must

have missed the memo that says when we got older we were supposed to have less sex and stop enjoying it! We've just kept doing what we have always done; sex was always important to us then, and it is just as important to us now. I guess if we looked back to how we were when we first met nearly 40 years ago, we could definitely say that the sex is different, but the change has been so gradual that we haven't really noticed. Throughout our relationship, there have been periods when we've had sex more or less frequently—but isn't that the nature of all relationships? Ebb and flow? Good times and bad? I would say that now that we are retired and have no children in the house that we are more sexually active today than we were at other points in our lives.

We do have to plan a little more and we often have to use lubrication. It may take me a little longer to get an erection and it is not always as firm as it was when I was younger. We don't do it as frequently as we used to, but when we do have sex it usually lasts longer. And the emotional connection is *so much more intense* than it was when we were younger. I guess you could say we have traded quantity for quality. I still chuckle a bit at the commercials for erectile dysfunction drugs—I guess that I'm just lucky that I have not had to use those—yet!

One of the biggest differences is, when we were younger it was expected that we were sexual. But now, if we're affectionate in public you can see the look on younger couples' faces, like they're shocked that we still like to "frolic." Our culture still holds on to the stereotype that "old people" don't have sex. I guess no one wants to think that grandma and grandpa still do it! To be honest, I can't imagine not being able to have sex; just the thought depresses me. I know the day may come when I can't, but that won't mean that I won't want to . . . and won't still try my damnedest!

Source: Author's files

CHAPTER 16

The United States is going gray! Today, there are significantly more aging Americans (those over the age of 65) than young people, with one in eight individuals 65 years or older (U.S. Census Bureau, 2007).

Our nation is moving into an unprecedented time in its history; by the year 2030, there will be 72 million people (roughly 20 percent of the population) over the age of 65 living in the United States, more than ever before (He et al., 2005). In Figure 16.1, the U.S. Census Bureau (2007) provides a current portrait of the age structure of the United States' older population. What accounts for this surge in the aging population? Baby boomers are getting older. **Baby boomers** are those who were born between 1946 and 1964. During this time in U.S. history, the birth rates rose sharply because of the economic prosperity that followed World War II. The first baby boomers will turn 65 years old in 2011. By 2030, one in six Americans will be 65 years or older (Citron, 2003). Table 16.1 illustrates the characteristics of aging America.

One hundred years ago, few people made it past the age of 70; the average life expectancy was 47. Today, it is anywhere from 68 to 80, depending on a person's race and gender (He et al., 2005).

This entire generation is growing old. After the age of 40 or so, is it really downhill until we die? And what about sex—is it a forgotten memory?

Throughout our study together, we have come to understand that sexuality and the need for human intimacy are essential throughout life—we are born sexual beings and we die as such. To this end, most of our study in this textbook has been focused on sexuality throughout early adulthood. As we age, we tend to experience a decrease in sexual interest (Arajuo, Mohr, & McKinlay, 2004; Lindau et al., 2007; Nicolosi et al., 2006). But why? In this chapter, we'll discuss some of the biological changes that take place as we age. We'll then take a look at changes in relationships. Finally, we'll examine the differences we experience in sex and sexuality as we get older, and we'll explore the increasing trend among older adults of STIs and HIV/AIDS.

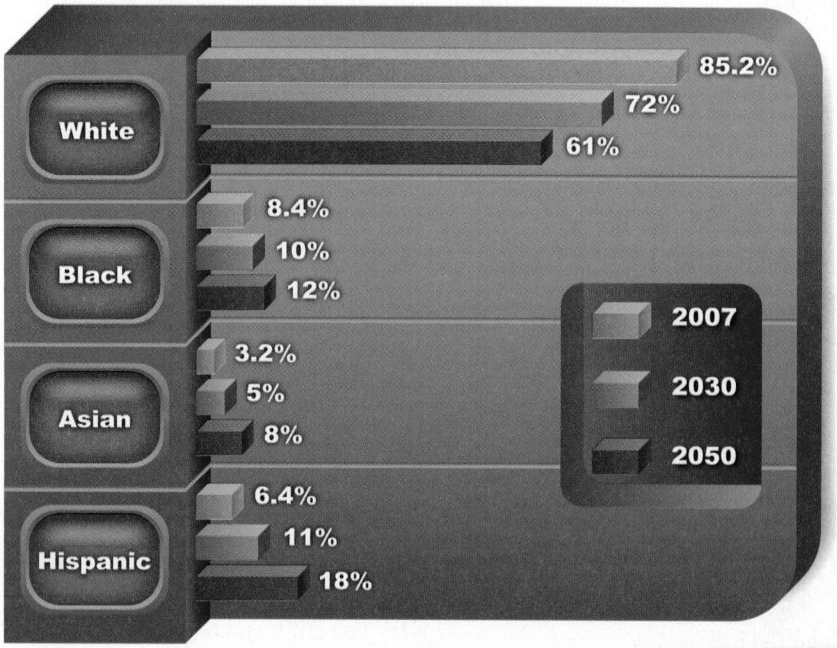

TABLE 16.1
The Portrait of Age in the U.S.

Source: U.S. Census Bureau (2007).

The face of America is changing.

- *Gender:* Females outnumber males in the elderly population: 58 percent of those over 65 are female, while 42 percent are male.

- *Diversity:* There is great diversity among older adults. Compared with African American and white older adults, Hispanics are experiencing significantly large increases. By the year 2050, the percentage of older Hispanic Americans will nearly double (U.S. Census Bureau, 2005).

- *Education:* In 2007, about 19 percent of those ages 65 and over had a college degree. By the year 2030, 75 percent will have a college degree.

- *Life expectancy:* Children born in 2001 will have an average life expectancy of 77.4 years (74.8 years for men, 80 for women), an all-time record.

Figure 16.1 U.S. Population Aged 65 and Over by Race, 2007, 2030, 2050

Sources: He et al. (2005); U.S. Census Bureau (2007).

WHAT IS AGING?

Most of us have heard the cliché, "you are as young as you feel!" But are we? Aging is not a uniform process for all; there are certainly universal aging processes that ultimately affect our sexuality, but individual experiences and lifestyle choices also affect how we age (Crosnoe & Elder, 2002).

PRIMARY AGING

To better understand the aging process and how it affects our sexuality, we first need to look at biological, age-related declines. Researchers, gerontologists (those who study aging and the aged), and developmentalists alike distinguish between primary aging and secondary aging.

Primary aging refers to the basic biological processes that are genetically programmed and that take place with the passage of time; some of the changes in sexuality during the later years in life are the result of primary aging, such as erectile functioning and vaginal lubrication (Cavanaugh & Blanchard-Fields, 2002). These aging processes represent the core aspects of aging, and they are summarized in Table 16.2.

It appears as though each species in the animal kingdom, including human beings, has a genetically programmed time limit, because at a certain point in time, cells lose their ability to replicate, which accounts for the aging process (Hayflick, 1994). There is little a person can do to prevent aging. Are there things we can do, however, to slow the process?

SECONDARY AGING

Although the characteristics associated with primary aging cannot be delayed, to a very large extent, we have control over age-related declines that are associated with

TABLE 16.2
Primary Aging: Biological Changes Associated with Aging

Source: Adapted from Cavanaugh & Blanchard-Fields (2002).

These changes are genetically programmed and take place over time, and all the changes are irreversible. Eventually, the biological changes lead to death. Death by primary aging factors is referred to as "death by natural causes."

- *Age-related anatomical and functional changes:* These include changes in the immune system and the ability to fight infection or disease, changes in vision and hearing, changes in the function of joints, and changes in memory retention.

- *Progressive changes:* Starting at about the age of 30, we begin to lose brain neurons. By age 50, our brain size is reduced to 97 percent, and by 70, our brain size is reduced to about 92 percent.

- *Inevitable changes:* This category includes declines in sensory functions. Hearing, vision, taste, and balance become less acute. Reaction times become slower because the speed of nerve impulses slows.

- *Universally experienced changes:* Regardless of one's society or culture, everyone experiences all primary aging changes.

^^^ **From Woodstock to Medicare:** Just 28 years old at Woodstock, rock and roll musicians Crosby, Stills, and Nash are 70 today. **Iconic, youthful America is turning gray.**

secondary aging, which is physiological declines that are the result of environmental and behavioral influences that significantly impact how we age. Among other things, secondary aging is influenced by lifestyle choices such as smoking, nutrition, exercise, sun exposure, alcohol/substance use, and sexual behaviors (Lemme, 2005). Secondary aging affects sexuality in a number of ways, and we'll explore those throughout this chapter.

But as you can see from the opening vignette, getting older doesn't necessarily imply a decline in sexual desire or sexual health. There are many sexual stereotypes and myths that persist regarding older adults, such as grumpy old men and dried-up old women who don't have sex. These examples illustrate the concept of ageism.

AGEISM: NEGATIVE ATTITUDES

Ageism refers to the stereotypical attitudes people hold about the aging and the elderly. People who are **ageist** have a fixed and negative mindset about older people. As a result of these attitudes, the aging population is often subject to bias and unfair treatment. The biggest problem associated with ageism is that it limits the things people can accomplish and denies them the respect they deserve (Lemme, 2005).

Researchers recently conducted a study in which participants with a mean age of 28 rated the attractiveness of various men and women (Teusher & Teusher, 2007). Overall, younger men and women were considered more attractive regardless of whether they were male or female. The study's findings suggest that *age* is more important than *sex* in determining attractiveness.

<<< Attitudes toward aging and sexuality may be changing, as illustrated by the increasing trend of older women dating younger men, like Demi Moore and Ashton Kutcher. **This has popularized the slang term, cougar, for a woman 40 or over who sexually pursues and engages younger men.**

How do older Americans rate the quality of their sexual experiences? Is sex better as we age? Worse? The same as when we were younger? How people experience their sexuality involves a complex interaction between mind, body, and emotions. As people get older, age-related changes influence the physical and psychological aspects of their sex life. And, as the opening vignette illustrates, perhaps cultural and societal attitudes even affect older peoples' sex lives.

PRIMARY AGING: THE DECLINE IN REPRODUCTIVE CAPABILITY

Climacteric is the long-term process of physiological change that results in the gradual decline in women and men's reproductive capacities. These physiological changes can affect the sexual response of men and women and may inhibit or enhance sexual functioning as people age. Beginning some time in their 40s, both men and women begin to experience declines in their sex hormones. For males, the reduction of testosterone is gradual, and they become no longer capable of reproduction much later in life. For women, estrogen reduction is more dramatic, and they tend to lose their ability to reproduce at a younger age than men. For both men and women, these physiological changes are often accompanied by psychological and psychosocial changes.

SEXUALITY AND AGING IN WOMEN: MENOPAUSE

The female climacteric is often referred to as **menopause**, which is the cessation of *menses*, the regular (monthly) shedding of the uterine lining. This process can be natural or surgical (see Figure 16.2). Menopause occurs anywhere between the ages of 40 and 60, but prior to menopause, women go through a 10- to 15-year period known as perimenopause. **Perimenopause**, the result of decreasing or erratic female sex hormone levels (see Chapter 4), is the time in a woman's life when physiological changes associated with primary aging that begin her transition to menopause gradually occur. A woman is still capable of becoming pregnant during perimenopause because she still ovulates. A woman who has had no menstrual periods for 12 consecutive months is in menopause (ACOG, 2010). Since medieval times, the median age of menopause has not significantly changed (Butler & Lewis, 1986).

Although no two women experience perimenopause/menopause the same way, many women begin to experience perimenopause as early as their 30s. Symptoms of early menopause, which

signal changes in estrogen and progesterone levels, include (ACOG, 2010; Woods & Mitchell, 2005):

- Irregular periods or heavy bleeding during periods
- Headaches
- Weight gain
- Fuzzy thinking
- Loss of sex drive
- Fatigue

Hot flashes, when skin temperature rises up to 7 degrees higher than normal, are common among 75 to 85 percent of perimenopausal women (ACOG, 2010). A hot flash is a sudden feeling of heat that rushes to the face, and it lasts from a few seconds to several minutes. If hot flashes happen at night, many women experience *night sweats*, during which their clothing may become drenched in sweat. This, in turn, causes sleep

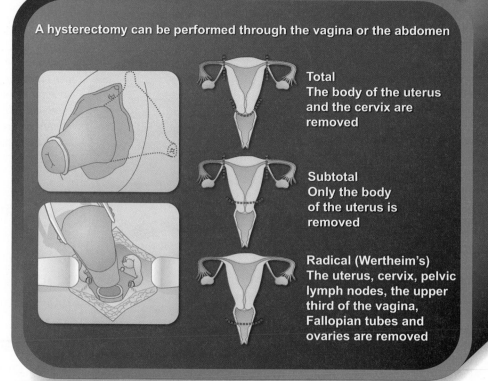

As depicted here, a **hysterectomy** is a surgical procedure in which the uterus is removed. This is done for a number of different health reasons. After the uterus is removed, a woman will no longer have monthly menstrual periods; however, she still has her ovaries and fallopian tubes, so she will continue to ovulate and to maintain her hormone levels. If a woman also has her ovaries and/or fallopian tubes removed, she will no longer produce estrogen. This surgical removal of her ovaries is known as an **oopherectomy** or **ovariectomy**. **Surgical menopause** refers to the fact that the surgery, rather than nature, induced menopause.

A hysterectomy can be performed through the vagina or the abdomen

Total
The body of the uterus and the cervix are removed

Subtotal
Only the body of the uterus is removed

Radical (Wertheim's)
The uterus, cervix, pelvic lymph nodes, the upper third of the vagina, Fallopian tubes and ovaries are removed

Figure 16.2   What Is Surgical Menopause?

TABLE 16.3
Physical Changes Associated with the Loss of Estrogen

Source: Based on ACOG (2010).

Loss of estrogen produces many changes in a woman's reproductive anatomy and physiology.

- *Vaginal lubrication:* As women age, vaginal lubrication during sexual arousal begins to take longer or may diminish to the point where a woman barely notices its presence. A lack of sufficient vaginal lubrication may make intercourse painful. Some women have increased burning and itching, and infections may occur more often.

- *Vaginal atrophy:* This refers to the physiological changes in the vaginal walls. During the aging process, the lining of the vagina becomes thinner, making the walls less elastic. This physiological change makes women more susceptible to irritation and tears during intercourse—and to STIs and HIV/AIDS. The shape of the vagina may also become shorter and narrower.

- *Clitoris changes:* After about age 75, a woman's clitoris becomes slightly reduced in size, and because of the loss of the mons, the clitoris is less protected. As a result, a woman may experience more irritation.

> ʌ
> ʌ So severe are hot flashes, some women
> ʌ resort to temporarily **sticking their**
> **heads in freezers, attempting to cool off.**

disruptions and feelings of sluggishness the next day. Every woman experiences perimenopause and menopause, due to primary aging of the reproductive system. However, not all women experience all of these symptoms, and the ones who do suffer them on a wide range.

As you learned in Chapter 4, from puberty onward, a woman experiences monthly changes in estrogen and progesterone, and these cyclical changes in her sex hormones bring about menstrual bleeding each month. As a woman ages and approaches menopause, estrogen production slows; because there is not enough estrogen to thicken the uterine lining, over time, monthly menstrual periods stop (ACOG, 2010). Ovulation also stops, rendering a woman infertile. This change in hormone production is why perimenopausal women experience erratic periods. A woman is said to be **postmenopausal** when lower estrogen and progesterone levels cause the permanent cessation of her menstrual cycle. The loss of estrogen produces many changes within a woman's body and may significantly affect her sexual desire and response. These sex-related changes are presented in Table 16.3.

> >>> After the age of 25, both women and
> men begin to lose calcium. But during
> perimenopause, women lose calcium faster,
> increasing the risk of osteoporosis. **It is vitally**
> **important for women to have a regular**
> **calcium intake from childhood onward.**

<<< A popular stereotype associated with aging is of the menopausal woman shifting from raging, angry moods into depressive, doleful slumps with no reason or warning. **But the specific connection of mood to the hormonal changes of menopause is unclear.**

The decrease in estrogen that occurs with menopause can also have an effect on nearly every body system. Loss of estrogen can place a woman at increased risk for osteoporosis and heart disease and can have major impacts on a woman's overall health and quality of life (Cleveland Clinic, 2008). **Osteoporosis** occurs when the bones lose density, making them more fragile and likely to fracture. Estrogen plays an important role in pre-serving bone mass, because it signals cells in the bones to stop breaking down. Women lose an average of 25 percent of their bone mass from the time of menopause to age 60, partly due to the loss of estrogen (Cleveland Clinic, 2008). Similarly, a woman's risk for heart disease increases after menopause. This increase may be linked to the loss of estrogen; the hormone helps maintain healthy levels of cholesterol in the blood and helps with blood flow to the heart muscle (Cleveland Clinic, 2008). Also, women are more likely to experience poor bladder function, poor brain function, poor skin elasticity, poor muscle power and tone, some deterioration in vision, and some weight gain.

At this point, you may be thinking, "Then it really *is* downhill as we begin to age!" But in reality, most women have a healthy attitude toward menopause because they feel they are in the "prime" of their lives. They find menopause to be a sexually freeing time, because they no longer have to worry about pregnancy. Also, because the children are usually out of the house, meno-pausal women have more privacy to express themselves sexually (National Institute on Aging, 2010). Further-more, there are a number of meno-pausal treatment options for women today. Treatment of menopausal

Benefits and Risks of Hormone Replacement Therapy	Women with a Uterus Estrogen + Progestin	Women Without a Uterus Estrogen Only
BENEFITS		
Relieves hot flashes/night sweats	Yes	Yes
Relieves vaginal dryness	Yes	Yes
Reduces risk of bone fractures	Yes	Yes
Improves cholesterol levels	Yes	Yes
Reduces risk of colon cancer	Yes	Don't know
RISKS		
Increases risk of stroke	Yes	Yes
Increases risk of serious blood clots	Yes	Yes
Increases risk of heart attack	Yes	No
Increases risk of breast cancer	Yes	Possibly
Increases risk of dementia, when begun by women age 65 and older	Yes	Yes
Unpleasant side effects, such as bloating and tender breasts	Yes	Yes
Pill form can raise level of triglyce-rides (a type of fat in the blood)	Yes	Yes

Figure 16.3 Hormone Replacement Therapy Hormone replacement therapy (HRT) is a pharmacology treatment program in which a woman takes estrogen and possibly progestin to relieve the symptoms of menopause. **Today, many women are given small doses of testosterone to boost their sex drives. HRT may be prescribed as a pill that is taken daily or as a patch that is worn on the skin.** It is important to weigh the benefits and risks of HRT (National Heart, Lung, and Blood Institute, 2004).

symptoms can include nutritional supplements, a low cholesterol diet, exercise, topical lubricants, and hormone replacement therapy (see Figure 16.3) (National Institute on Aging, 2009).

The end of fertility in midlife ushers in the third part of a woman's life, known as the *third age* in popular culture. Generally, women raised or living in Western countries live long enough so that nearly half of their adult life is spent after menopause. For some women, the menopausal transition represents a major life change, similar to menarche in the magnitude of its social and psychological significance. Today, older women from many religions now celebrate menopause and aging with a ritual known as croning. **Croning ceremonies** signify a major rite of passage and originated in the Jewish faith to honor aged women as wise and dignified (Kraus, 2003).

SEXUALITY AND AGING IN MEN: ANDROPAUSE

Is there such a thing as a male climacteric, or male menopause? Physician and professor of internal medicine Steven Lamberts (1997) believes that aging men experience andropause. Androgen decline in the aging male, or **ADAM**, is thought to be a gradual decrease in the production of testosterone (Morales, Heaton, & Carson, 2000). ADAM is commonly referred to as **andropause**, an age-related decline of testosterone in men. Beginning around age 40, androgen decline accounts for changes in men's erection patterns as they age. Changes, also described in Figure 16.4, include, for example, erections occurring more slowly, the increase in the length of the refractory period, and the inability to achieve or maintain an erection. An ADAM diagnosis is based on clinical signs and symptoms supported with laboratory confirmation of low serum testosterone levels.

Andropause is difficult to recognize because the signs and symptoms are often unclear and share common characteristics with other common symptoms of aging. Along with decreases in sexual function, the decline in testosterone can be associated with decreases in lean body mass, muscle strength, bone density, and changes in energy, mood, and cognition. Testosterone levels decline very gradually as men age, so the symptoms are often attributed simply to the aging process or stressors associated with day-to-day life. Studies have demonstrated that total testosterone concentrations decrease approximately 1 to 2 percent per year after the age of 40 (Harvey & Berry, 2009).

As with menopause, the link between andropause and psychological changes are not clear. It seems that andropause is not characterized by specific psychological symptoms, but may be associated with depressive symptoms that are not considered serious enough to require treatment (Delhez, Hamsenne, & Legros, 2003).

Treatment for andropause is similar to that of menopause— hormone replacement. The

Most men typically begin to worry about sexual aging sometime in their 40s; these concerns pick up in their 50s, and peak in their 60s (Butler & Lewis, 1986). As men begin to notice that their sexual organs don't work the way they used to, they often assume that primary aging changes indicate a decrease in sexual potency. This is not the case, despite the following age related changes (Butler & Lewis, 1986):

● *Erections*: Sometime during their 40s, men notice that it takes them longer to obtain an erection. In their 50s and 60s, men notice their erections are not as large or as rigid in years past. Once a man becomes erect, it is less likely to be reliable. Testes may also become smaller and less firm.

● *Lubrication*: The lubrication secreted by the Cowper's glands greatly reduces as men age, but this doesn't have much effect on male sexual performance. Men in their 40s notice a one-half reduction in the volume of seminal fluid; this results in a decrease in ejaculate and less "explosive" ejaculations. This reduction is a great advantage, however; it allows older men to delay ejaculation and extend their lovemaking experiences.

● *Orgasms*: Younger men are often unable to control or delay ejaculation, but with the changes associated with aging, some men experience an extended length of "ejaculatory inevitability." The length of the refractory period is extended.

Figure 16.4 Sexual Aging in Men Japanese folklore maintains that the angle of a man's erection as he ages corresponds with the angles of the outstretched fingers on his hand.

Figure 16.5 Various Types of Relationships by Age and Gender

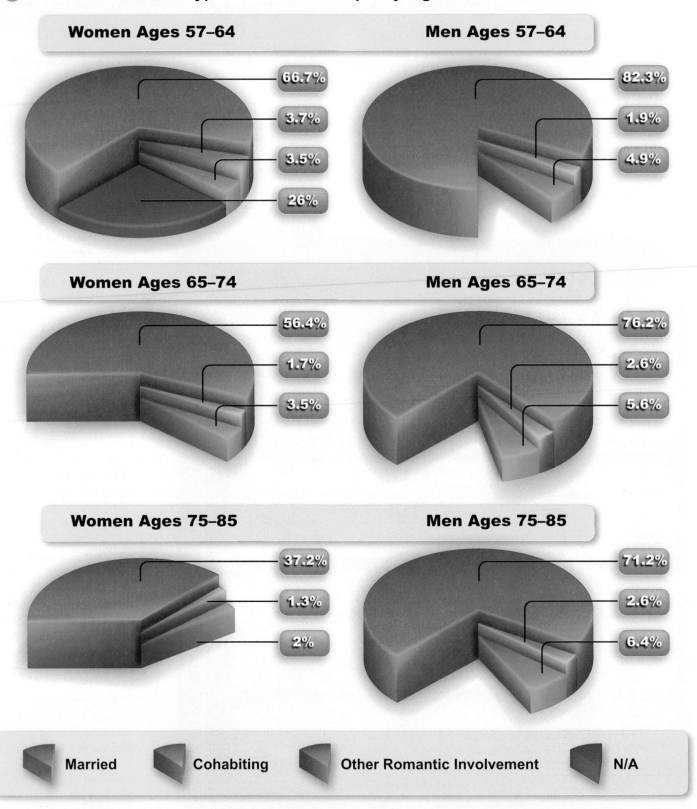

Women Ages 57–64
66.7%
3.7%
3.5%
26%

Men Ages 57–64
82.3%
1.9%
4.9%

Women Ages 65–74
56.4%
1.7%
3.5%

Men Ages 65–74
76.2%
2.6%
5.6%

Women Ages 75–85
37.2%
1.3%
2%

Men Ages 75–85
71.2%
2.6%
6.4%

Married   Cohabiting   Other Romantic Involvement   N/A

*Note: Numbers do not equal 100 percent.
Women : n = 1,550
Men: n = 1,455

Source: Waite, L. J. et al. (2009).

benefits of **testosterone replacement therapy (TRT)** include an increase in muscle mass strength, bone mineral density, and body fat, with a decrease in visceral fat, and an improved sense of well-being, improvement in cognition, improved quality of life, maintenance of secondary sexual characteristics, and improvement in sex drive and sexual function (Hijazi & Cunningham, 2005). The risks of TRT include fluid retention, especially in patients with cardiac failure or hypertension, enlarged breasts, acne or oily skin, increase in cholesterol level, sleep apnea, aggravation of prostate cancer, and aggressive behavior (Hijazi & Cunningham, 2005).

Although universal primary aging factors affect sexual functioning, it does not mean that these biological forces have to determine it (Kontul & Haavio-Mannila, 2009). Regardless of our age and gender, expression of our sexuality is fundamentally important to our mental health and overall well-being (Malatesta, 2007). Despite the common misconceptions people have about sex and sexuality in aging, throughout adulthood and into later adulthood, sexual activity plays an important role in intimate relationships (Welch, 2007). In the section that follows, we'll explore the sexual lives of older adults.

THE RELATIONAL LIVES OF OLDER ADULTS

Despite the fact that older adults experience physical changes that may affect their sexuality and sexual response, sex is still very important to them. For example:

- A study of nearly 1,700 middle-aged and later-aged adults indicated that two-thirds of the men and about one-half of the women polled believed that a satisfying sex life was important to their overall quality of life (American Association of Retired People, 2004).

- In a recent study of 1,549 people, ages 45 to 74 years, researchers discovered that, despite primary aging factors, sexual desire in middle to late adulthood is linked to good health, good sexual functioning, positive sexual self-esteem, and a skilled sex partner (Kontula & Haavio-Mannila, 2009).

- Another recent study found that sex is an important and positive aspect in the lives of 70-year-olds, even if sexual dysfunctions are present (Bechman et al., 2008).

Clearly, despite physical declines, throughout adulthood and into later adulthood, sexual activity plays an important role in intimate relationships. But unlike younger adults, sexual activity is dependent upon relationship types among older adults.

RELATIONSHIPS, AGING, AND SEX

Have you ever wondered how couples stay together for 40, 50, or even 60 years? As the man observed in the opening vignette, relationship and sexual life experiences ebb and flow throughout the course of a relationship, both good and bad. So as couples age, it is not surprising that their relationships continue to undergo changes, which in turn influence relationship and sexual life quality and experiences.

Although older couples experience an array of partnership types, today marriage provides the context for the majority of aging couples' sexual expression (Waite et al., 2009). As seen in Figure 16.5, among people ages 57 to 85, marriage is still the prevailing relationship type in which sexuality is expressed; other intimate relationships include cohabitation or other romantic/intimate partners (Waite et al., 2009). Another large-scale sexuality study also found that age (75 to 85 years) impacts the availability of an intimate partner; 40 percent of women have a spouse or intimate partner compared with 78 percent of men who do (Lindau et al., 2007). These differences are due to the fact that women are much more likely to outlive their husbands, and because men are more likely than women to remarry after the death of a spouse (Lemme, 2005).

Although divorce is relatively infrequent among America's elderly population, as baby boomers reach old age, divorce rates are on the rise. Figure 16.6 depicts the marital status of people over age 65. Slightly more than one-half are married, about one-third are widowed, and only about 10 percent are divorced or separated. Sexuality among older persons encompasses not just partnerships, but also activities and behaviors (Lindau et al., 2007).

HOMOSEXUAL RELATIONSHIPS IN LATER LIFE

There is a common stereotype that gays and lesbians engage in sexual activity with many different people and they are unable to maintain committed

Figure 16.6 Marital Status of Those Aged 65 and Older, 2007

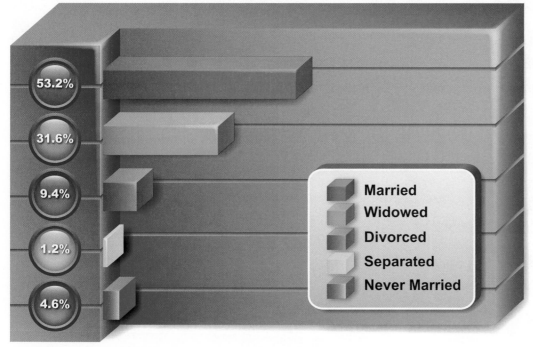

53.2%
31.6%
9.4%
1.2%
4.6%

Married
Widowed
Divorced
Separated
Never Married

Source: U.S. Census Bureau (2007).

<<< Grumpy old men? Often, senior citizens are characterized as inflexible and grouchy. **But research shows many older people are adaptable and seldom angry.**

What does differ as gays, lesbians, and bisexuals age is the level of social support and services that are available to them. For example, when a spouse dies, there are templates built into our culture to help the grieving spouse. These same systems might not be available for a gay or lesbian person who is struggling with the loss of his or her partner (Fullmer, 1995). Another area that may cause concern is long-term care arrangements. Many lesbians, gay men, and bisexuals resist long-term care settings because these settings traditionally do not recognize the sexual orientation of an individual (McMahon, 2003).

relationships. Although study in this area of intimate life is scant, available research shows that this perception is false (Fullmer, 1995). Many gay men and lesbian women experience long-term committed relationships until older age, and these relationships do not differ significantly from long-term heterosexual relationships (Fullmer, 1995).

Figure 16.7 The Importance of Sex by Age and Gender

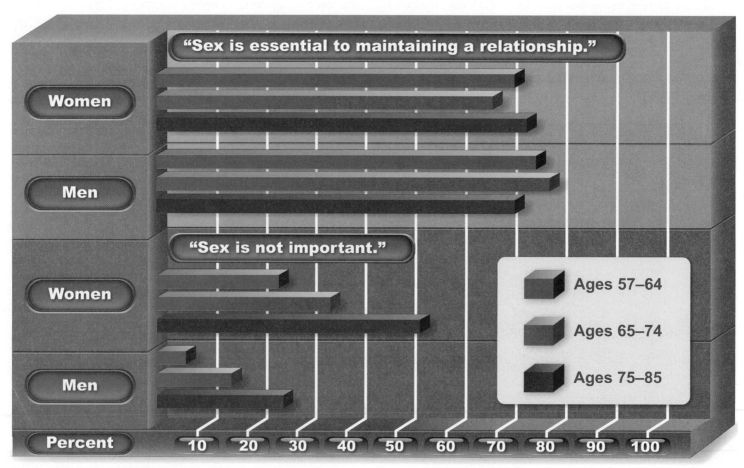

Source: Waite, L. J. et al. (2009).

>>> Many gay and lesbian couples **enjoy committed long-term partnerships.**

Gay men tend to view the aging process in a more negative light and express more ageism than do lesbian women. This fear of growing older among gay men might be an indication of a fear of being alone in their old age (Schope, 2005). Despite the presence of many long-term committed relationships, many lesbian, gay, bisexual, and transgender adults are more likely to live alone compared with other heterosexual adults, and this phenomenon continues into older adulthood (McMahon, 2003). Older single homosexuals who might wish to meet someone have limited opportunities to meet a partner when compared to older single heterosexuals (Fullmer, 1995).

Now that we have an understanding of the relational lives of older adults, let's turn our attention to their sexual lives. To be sure, older adults are not just talking about sex and its importance (see Figures 16.7 and 16.8), they are engaging in it. In the sections that follow, we'll explore the sexual frequency of older persons, their sexual behaviors, and certain sexual dysfunctions that may be associated with primary aging.

Figure 16.8 Sexual Frequency by Age and Gender

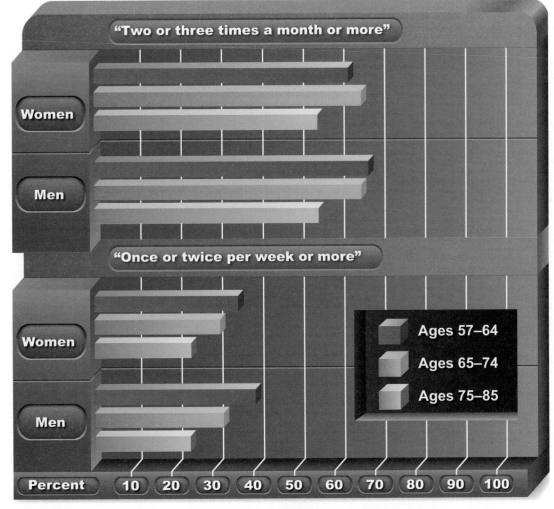

Source: Waite, L. J. et al. (2009).

THE SEXUAL LIVES OF OLDER ADULTS

Many older adults are sexually active, despite the fact that women are less likely than men to have an intimate partner. As Figure 16.8 shows, more than one-half of women and men over the age of 75 still enjoy sex two or three times a month or more; some couples still have sex once or twice a week or more (Waite et al., 2009). These findings may be surprising to some, because they negate the common notion that older men and women don't have sex. They may also speak to the cultural aspects of aging. Some of the respondents, for example, who are baby boomers, would have been young adults during the 1960s sexual revolution. Is it possible that their freer sexual attitudes of the 1960s are still prevalent some 40 or 50 years later?

QUALITY OVER FREQUENCY

As people age, they tend to define sexual satisfaction less by *frequency* and more by the *quality* of sexual

Healthy Selves | Healthy Sex

The Keys to Great Sex in Later Life

Many of the health-related problems people commonly experience as they get older cause concern for older adults with regard to sexual activity. For instance, after a heart attack, men and women are often concerned that the physical demands of the sex act may place additional stress on their hearts; consequently, they avoid sexual activity. A healthy lifestyle is key to enjoying satisfying sexual relations. Indeed, what is good for a person's overall health is also good for their sexual health. Thus, adults should:

- Eat a nutritious, well-balanced diet
- Stop smoking
- Consume alcohol only in moderation
- Engage in regular exercise, which lowers blood pressure (helping erection health), helps control weight, and improves lung capacity
- Receive regular medical checkups
- Reduce stress (stress and anxiety decrease sexual arousal)

Equipped with sound knowledge and realistic expectations about sexuality through aging and good health, sexual fulfillment later in life is a healthy, positive, and attainable goal.

---

activity (Christopher & Sprecher, 2000). In talking with menopausal women, researchers determined that many women feel that the quality of their sexual activity is higher, even if the quantity has diminished (Goberna et al., 2009). Also, when an older couple engages in sex, they may take longer and enjoy the experience more, thereby increasing their sexual satisfaction.

Older adults are also likely to expand their definitions of sexuality and intimacy and to express affection in a variety of ways. Besides sexual intercourse, other sexual activities that are prevalent among older adults with partners include kissing, hugging, sexual touching, and/or caressing (AARP, 2004). Even among those aged 75 to 85, foreplay appears to be a very important aspect of sex (Waite et al., 2009). This expanded definition of intimacy may increase the emotional connection that may, in turn, lead to higher relationship and sexual satisfaction. Many couples, particularly those who have been together for 40 years

or more, report satisfaction with their level of intimacy (Kontula & Haavio-Mannila, 2009).

Another national study reports similar numbers (Lindau et al., 2007). In a study of slightly more than 3,000 men and women (57 to 85 years of age), about 59 percent of men and 54 percent of women in the youngest age bracket surveyed (45 to 49) had intercourse at least once a week. Over age 70, about one-third still had sex at least once a week.

SEXUAL BEHAVIORS AMONG OLDER ADULTS

More so than in younger ages, among older participants, sexual activity consists primarily of kissing, hugging, and sexual touching (Waite et al., 2009). However, other sexual behaviors are common among older persons, as Figure 16.9 shows us.

Two recent studies indicate that vaginal intercourse is the sexual activity of choice for most older people most of the time (Lindau et al., 2007; Waite et al., 2009). In fact, a significant majority of individuals note that vaginal sex is still usually or always a part of sexual activity. Researchers are also interested in the frequency of masturbation, because this practice tends to indicate a person's underlying level of sexual interest (Waite et al., 2009). Contrary

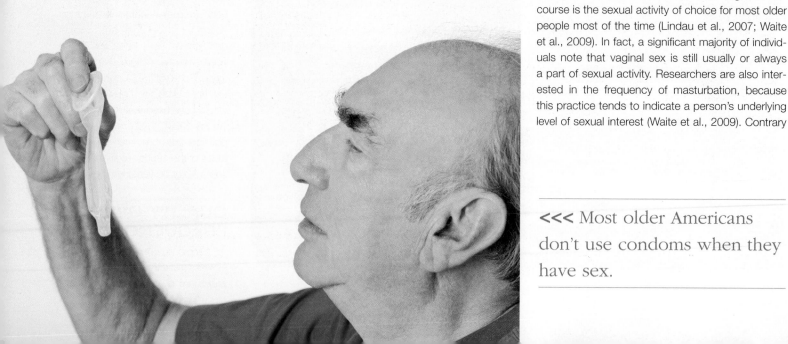

<<< Most older Americans don't use condoms when they have sex.

Figure 16.9 Sexual Behaviors by Age and Gender

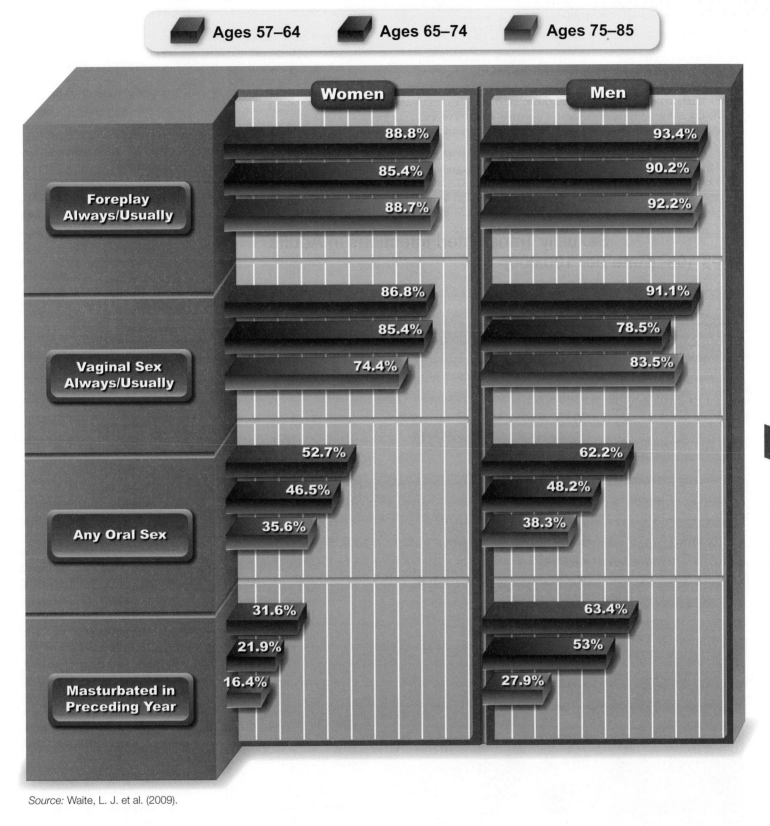

Ages 57–64 Ages 65–74 Ages 75–85

Women

Foreplay Always/Usually
- 88.8%
- 85.4%
- 88.7%

Vaginal Sex Always/Usually
- 86.8%
- 85.4%
- 74.4%

Any Oral Sex
- 52.7%
- 46.5%
- 35.6%

Masturbated in Preceding Year
- 31.6%
- 21.9%
- 16.4%

Men

Foreplay Always/Usually
- 93.4%
- 90.2%
- 92.2%

Vaginal Sex Always/Usually
- 91.1%
- 78.5%
- 83.5%

Any Oral Sex
- 62.2%
- 48.2%
- 38.3%

Masturbated in Preceding Year
- 63.4%
- 53%
- 27.9%

Source: Waite, L. J. et al. (2009).

to popular assumptions, masturbation does not replace vaginal sex as people age. Another study found that about one-half of men and a quarter of women surveyed indicated that they masturbated in the past year; these rates don't vary depending on relationship status (Lindau et al., 2007).

Oral sex is popular, too. In fact, among 75- to 85-year-olds, more than a quarter of men and a third of women say they either gave or received oral sex in the past year (Lindau et al., 2007). A newer study also determined that oral sex is a popular sexual activity among middle-aged and older adults.

IS ELDER SEX SAFE SEX?

In Chapters 13 and 14, we saw how important it is for sexually active people to protect their sexuality and to practice their sexuality safely. Are older people protected from STIs and HIV/AIDS?

1. *Physiological changes:* Due to the physiological changes in the vagina associated with aging, women's vaginal tissues become thinner, and natural lubrication decreases. These changes increase the likelihood of small vaginal tears during intercourse and increase the risk of the transmission of sexual diseases. Also, as people age, their immune system weakens and becomes less effective, increasing the risk for an STI.

2. *Sexual attitudes:* As people age, they are less likely to use condoms because they don't believe they are at risk for STIs. Also, many older persons have not had sexual education and are not aware of the importance of using condoms. A recent study of older Americans revealed that no more than 5 percent use a condom during vaginal or anal sex (Waite et al., 2009).

3. *Health care:* Although health care providers routinely check for STIs in younger adults, there is a lack of screening among older adults. If an older person has an STI, it may go unnoticed and untreated for years. Not only does this lead to potentially serious health problems, but it also increases the likelihood of infecting others.

Just how many people ages 40 and over acquire an STI or HIV/AIDS each year? The U.S. Department of Health and Human Services (2009) does track STIs, but even so, the difficulty in finding this information perhaps speaks to how marginalized the sexual health of this population is. As Figure 16.10 shows us, thousands of cases of STIs are diagnosed in middle- and later-age adults each year in the U.S.

The estimated numbers of older persons living with AIDS in the United States continues to increase, as Table 16.4 shows us. Today, over one-fourth of those who are infected with HIV are aged 50 and older (Population Reference Bureau, 2009). As you saw in Chapter 14, antiretroviral medications and the prevention/treatment of opportunistic infections enable those infected with HIV/AIDS to live longer; because of this, the number of HIV-infected older persons will likely continue to increase. In the United States, those aged 50 and up accounted for 28 percent of people living with HIV/AIDS in 2007, and over one-third of those living with AIDS in 2007, up from 24 percent in 2003 (Population Reference Bureau, 2009).

When patients are diagnosed with AIDS/HIV at older ages, the prognosis is not as good as it is for younger people; survival time after diagnosis is shorter, and the mortality rates are higher. Researchers believe this is because the already-weakened immune systems of older people make them more vulnerable to opportunistic infections and death (Effros et al., 2008).

With the increasingly older population in the United States, the U.S. Department of Health and Human Services and CDC recommend that adults over the age of 50 be screened for HIV/AIDS; it is also suggested that HIV screening tests be covered by Medicare, a federal program that pays for

Figure 16.10 Sexually Transmitted Infections in Adults Ages 40+ (Rate per 100,000)

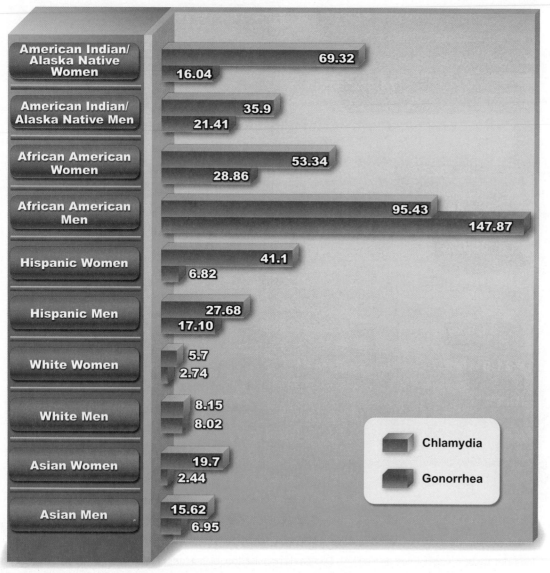

Source: U.S. Department of Health and Human Services, CDC, National Center for HIV, STD, & TB Prevention. (2009). *Sexually transmitted disease morbidity for selected STDs by age, race/ethnicity and gender, 1996–2008.* CDC WONDER On-line Database, November 2009. Retrieved February 16, 2010, from http://wonder.cdc.gov/std-v2008-race-age.html

sexual life now

Are Men's Aging Experiences the Equivalent of Women's Menopause?

Often, the symptoms that men experience as they age are similar to women's menopause experiences. This has led some to speculate that men experience a male menopause. However, others argue that these symptoms are natural aging processes and are not necessarily caused by a decline in testosterone among aging men. Are men's aging experiences the equivalent of women's menopause?

YES!

The changes men experience at midlife are often viewed as the natural consequence of aging, making it difficult to diagnose menopause in men. However, men's aging processes are similar to women's:

- Like menopause, andropause usually occurs from 50 years onward.

- There is an undeniable hormonal decline, which accelerates the aging process.

- Men experience physiological, psychosexual, psychological, and cognitive changes as they age.

NO!

Hormone changes are natural. John McKinlay, one of the nation's leading men's health experts, is a critic of the idea that men experience menopause, noting that:

- Declining hormone levels in men are gradual. They do not cause the symptoms women experience as their estrogen decreases; this is a natural aging process.

- Lifestyle habits like smoking, heavy drinking, and poor nutrition affect testosterone declines; women's lifestyle choices do not affect their estrogen decline.

- After the age of 70, men may experience a 50 percent loss in testosterone; women experience a 100 percent loss of estrogen sometime in their 50s.

>>> WHAT DO YOU THINK?

1. Do you believe that some men may experience a type of menopause?
2. Do you personally know a male who has been or is going through "a midlife crisis"? How might the idea of a "male menopause" help both of you understand what is or was going on?
3. Is male menopause a cultural conception?

Sources: Gould, D. C., Petty, R., & Jacobs, H. S. (2000). For and against: The male menopause—does it exist? / Against. British Medical Journal, 320(7238), 858–61. Retrieved September 22, 2009, from Health Module. (Document ID: 52236640); O'Donnell, A. B., Araujo, A. B., & McKinlay, J. B. (2004). The health of normally aging men: The Massachusetts Male Aging Study (1987–2004). Experimental Gerontology, 39(7), 975–984.

TABLE 16.4

Persons Ages 50 and Older Living with AIDS in the U.S., 2003–2007

Source: Population Reference Bureau (2009).

Age at end of year	2003	2004	2005	2006	2007
<40	123,763	119,456	115,185	111,829	109,831
40–44	86,383	91,397	94,026	94,735	93,297
45–49	71,286	77,390	84,045	90,325	97,017
50–54	46,661	53,125	59,045	66,003	72,991
55–59	23,976	28,149	33,279	38,626	44,298
60–64	11,224	13,232	15,265	17,878	21,196
>65	8,842	10,450	12,232	14,386	17,005

Figure 16.11 Prevalence of Sexual Problems, by Gender and Age

	Age 57–64	Age 65–74	Age 75–85
♀ Women			
Lack of sexual interest	44.2%	38.4%	49.3%
Vaginal lubrication problems	35.9%	43.2%	43.5%
Premature orgasm	9.2%	6.9%	8.5%
No orgasm	34.0%	32.8%	38.2%
Pain during intercourse	17.8%	18.6%	11.8%
Lack of sexual pleasure	24.0%	22.0%	24.9%
Avoided sex due to problems	34.3%	30.5%	22.7%
♂ Men			
Lack of sexual interest	28.2%	28.6%	24.2%
Erectile problems	30.7%	44.6%	43.5%
Premature orgasm	29.6%	28.1%	21.3%
No orgasm	16.2%	22.7%	33.3%
Pain during intercourse	3.0%	3.2%	1.0%
Lack of sexual pleasure	3.8%	7.0%	5.1%
Avoided sex due to problems	22.1%	30.1%	25.7%

Source: Waite et al., 2009

TABLE 16.5
Possible Age-Related Sexual Changes in Women and Men

Source: Based on *Understanding sexuality*. (2008). Harvard Health Publications. Retrieved September 16, 2009, from http://www.aarp.org/health/conditions/articles/harvard__sexuality-in-midlife-and-beyond_1.html

	Women	Men
Physical changes	Decreased blood flow to the genitals. Lower levels of estrogen and testosterone. Thinning of the vaginal lining. Loss of vaginal elasticity and muscle tone.	Decreased testosterone. Reduced blood flow to the penis. Less sensitivity in the penis.
Desire	Decreased libido. Fewer sexual thoughts and fantasies.	Decreased libido. Fewer sexual thoughts and fantasies.
Arousal	Slower arousal. Reduced vaginal lubrication and less expansion of the vagina during arousal. Less blood congestion in the clitoris and lower vagina. Diminished clitoral sensitivity.	Greater difficulty achieving an erection, maintaining an erection, or both. Erections aren't as rigid.
Orgasm	Delayed or absent orgasm. Less intense orgasms. Fewer and sometimes painful uterine contractions.	Longer time required to reach orgasm. Smaller volume of semen and less forceful ejaculation. Less intense orgasms.
Resolution	Body returns more rapidly to an unaroused state.	Body returns more rapidly to an unaroused state. More time is needed between erections.

certain health care expenses for those 65 or older (Population Reference Bureau, 2009).

SEXUAL PROBLEMS IN LATER LIFE

Although we know that many older adults continue to have and enjoy sex, decline in sexual activity is a normative experience for them (Kontula & Haavio-Manilla, 2009). What are some factors that might influence whether or not an older person is having sex? Figure 16.11 shows the prevalence of sexual problems in older adults while Tables 16.5 and 16.6 describe some of the factors, both internal and external.

Declining health has an effect on sexual activity and satisfaction (AARP, 2004; Lindau et al., 2007). Men's declining physical health is the most common reason men and women give for not having sex (Lindau et al., 2007). Another reason for not having sex is declining interest; women (51 percent) are more likely than men (24 percent) to report a lack of interest, particularly those women who were not in an intimate relationship. There are many other factors that influence desire, which in turn influence frequency of sexual activity. Just as with any other sexual experiences across the life span, older persons' sexuality is influenced not just by physiological factors, but by emotional and cultural forces, too.

As our study in this chapter has shown us, with increasing age there are varying degrees of reduced sex hormones in men and women. In men, this reduction in testosterone, as well as other physiological changes, can result in erectile dysfunction (ED), the inability to achieve or maintain an erection (see Chapter 11). Prior to 1983, the prevailing medical thought was that ED was the result of psychological problems, such as stress or depression. But today, with a better understanding of erection processes, medications are available. These medications, such as Viagra, Cialis, and Levitra, only cause an erection when a man is sexually aroused.

Recall from Chapter 5 and Chapter 11 that erections are the result of pressurized blood in the penis: A man becomes sexually aroused, the penis becomes erect by blood flow to the corpora cavernosa and corpus spongiosum under the influence of an enzyme, *cGMP*, and penile stimulation results in ejaculation. In men with ED, due to diminished levels of

TABLE 16.6
Factors That Influence Sexual Desire in Older Age

Many factors affect our sexuality as we age.

- *Women and sexuality:* Sexual desire, valuing sexuality, and having a healthy partner are important to women's sexuality as they age (Kontula & Haavio-Mannila, 2009; Waite et al., 2009). Women also experience many social and family issues, such as providing care to aging parents, fatigue, and issues with adult children (Goberna et al., 2009). These factors appear to affect women's sexuality more than their climacteric experiences.

- *Men and sexuality:* High sexual self-esteem, good health, and an active sexual history are important to men's sexuality in older age (Lindau et al., 2007). Men's sexuality appears to be less affected by social and emotional factors than women's sexuality is.

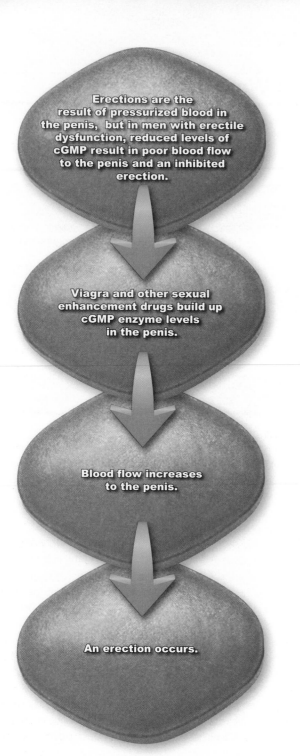

Erections are the result of pressurized blood in the penis, but in men with erectile dysfunction, reduced levels of cGMP result in poor blood flow to the penis and an inhibited erection.

Viagra and other sexual enhancement drugs build up cGMP enzyme levels in the penis.

Blood flow increases to the penis.

An erection occurs.

Figure 16.12   How Erectile Dysfunction Drugs Work

> \^ \^ \^ Does this photo contradict societal stereotypes of sex and aging?

the cGMP enzyme, the arteries in the penis do not widen and enlarge enough—the man becomes sexually aroused, but poor blood flow to the penis inhibits erection. Viagra and other **sexual enhancement drugs** work by helping build up cGMP enzyme levels in the penis, and blood flow increases to the penis, resulting in an erection. Figure 16.12 illustrates the process by which ED drugs work.

OWN IT! When Will You Stop Having Sex?

Our desire to have sex does not have an expiration date, as evidenced by the fact that nearly half of all older adults are sexually active.

1. How would you feel if someone told you tomorrow that you could no longer have sex? Would it affect your quality of life?

2. Sex is generally considered such an important part of our relationships when we are young. Should that change as we get older?

Sexual Goals for Old Age

The things we do now will likely influence our health and our sexuality in older age. As such, it may be beneficial to think about what your sexual goals are as you age and how they relate to your life now.

When I think of sex in older age, I think _____ .

I can/cannot think of myself having sex when I'm older because _____ .

Medically, I would be willing to _____ to continue to be sexually active.

To stay sexually healthy as I age, I need to _____ .

When I am older, I think that sex will be _____ to my relationship.

When we are older, I hope we still _____ .

Ways that we can show intimacy besides sexual intercourse include _____ .

_____ are things that will help me feel sexy as I age.

Today, I can _____ to ensure that I am still having sex when I am old.

I do/do not believe my attitudes toward sex will change when I am older. This is because _____ .

I think my parents are/are not still sexually active. This makes me feel _____ .

I think my grandparents are/are not still sexually active. This makes me feel _____ .

Finally, many people subscribe to the old adage "Use it or lose it!" Recent research suggests that there is a physiological basis for this argument. Juha Koskimaki and his colleagues (2008) studied almost 1,000 Finnish men, ages 50 to 75. The researchers surveyed men regarding their erections and the frequency of sexual intercourse, waited five years, and then contacted the men again. Findings revealed that those who had sex at least once a week had one-half the incidence of erectile dysfunction as those who had sex less often. Knowing that health conditions affect sexuality, the researchers made sure that things such as heart disease or diabetes were not accounting for the observed differences. It is thought that regular erections are so important to continued sexual activity because when erect, the penis is getting the benefits of oxygen. With these findings in mind, it may be worth thinking about your sexual activity now and how it might affect your sexual activity later in life!

SEXUAL LIFE EDUCATION

We are nearing the end of our study together, but you have seen that each of us is a sexual being from the time that we are born until the time we die. Although we know this to be true, there are surprisingly few resources or opportunities for helping people understand their sexuality throughout the aging process. Media images are full of sex, but most portray people who are young and beautiful.

Psychologists, sociologists, and family life and sexuality educators can play a pivotal role in facilitating a change in attitudes and knowledge regarding sexuality as people age. Life changes such as loss of a partner, illness and disability, new relationships, or the need for long-term residential care require aging couples to adopt a broader view of their sexuality and of themselves as a sexual persons. Yet myths, stigma, and stereotypes regarding sexuality and aging—that older people aren't physically attractive, that they're uninterested in sex, and that they are incapable of sexual feelings—are persistent barriers to this dynamic view of sexuality. Is it any wonder that this misinformation leads people to have a pessimistic attitude toward late-life sexuality?

As a nation, we are moving to unprecedented times. Today's oldest of the old were probably socialized to view sexuality as an act reserved for married couples for the purpose of childbearing. But the youngest of the old were socialized during the sexual revolution, an environment that embraced the interpersonal and individual aspects of sexuality. Is society ready for this new brand of elder sex?

16

Summary

WHAT IS AGING?   334

- With baby boomers turning gray, America is aging. Aging has two components; these are primary and secondary aging. Primary aging is the result of internal and natural biological processes, while secondary aging is the result of external environmental and behavioral influences.

HOW DOES AGING AFFECT THE REPRODUCTIVE CAPABILITIES OF WOMEN AND MEN?   336

- Climacteric is the long-term process of physiological change that results in the gradual decline in women and men's reproductive capacities. Women experience menopause, rendering them infertile, while men undergo andropause, an age-related decline of testosterone in men.

WHAT IMPACT DOES AGING HAVE ON THE RELATIONAL AND SEXUAL LIVES OF OLDER ADULTS?   340

- Although there is a common misconception that sex decreases with age, both men and women continue to value sex as they age. Studies show that there is an emphasis on quality over frequency, and although both men and women may experience physiological problems, there are different options available to keep sexual lives thriving. Just like young men and women must protect themselves against sexually transmitted infections and HIV/AIDS, so must older adults.

Key Terms

baby boomers portion of U.S. population born between 1946 and 1964   *334*

primary aging the basic biological processes that are genetically programmed and that take place with the passage of time; these processes represent the core aspects of aging   *334*

secondary aging physiological declines that are the result of environmental and behavioral influences that significantly impact how we age   *335*

cougar a woman aged 40 or over who sexually pursues and sexually engages with younger men (often in their 20s)   *335*

ageism stereotypical attitudes people hold about the aging and the elderly   *335*

ageist a person who has a fixed and negative mindset about older people   *335*

climacteric long-term process of physiological change that results in the gradual decline in

the reproductive capabilities of women and men   *336*

hysterectomy surgical procedure in which the uterus is removed   *336*

oopherectomy or **ovariectomy** surgical removal of ovaries   *336*

surgical menopause menopause induced by surgery rather than nature   *336*

menopause cessation of menses   *336*

perimenopause 10- to 15-year period before menopause that women undergo   *336*

postmenopausal time at which lower estrogen and progesterone levels cause the permanent cessation of a woman's menstrual cycle   *337*

osteoporosis degenerative condition in which bones lose density, which makes them more fragile and likely to fracture   *338*

hormone replacement therapy (HRT) pharmacological treatment program in which a woman takes estrogen to relieve the symptoms of menopause   *338*

croning ceremony a major rite of passage that serves as a way for postmenopausal women to acknowledge the wisdom and maturity that comes with age   *339*

ADAM androgen decline in the aging male   *339*

andropause age-related decline of testosterone in men   *339*

testosterone replacement therapy (TRT) hormone replacement therapy for men experiencing andropause   *341*

sexual enhancement drugs drugs that help build up cGMP enzyme levels in a man's penis, which positively affects blood flow and therefore the erection   *350*

Sample Test Questions

MULTIPLE CHOICE

1. Which change is NOT an example of primary aging?
   a. Erectile dysfunction
   b. Decrease in vaginal lubrication
   c. Lung problems caused by smoking
   d. Increase in reaction times

2. Which stage of menopause is characterized by a woman experiencing primary aging and decreasing or erratic sex hormone levels?
   a. Perimenopause
   b. Climacteric
   c. Postmenopause
   d. Menopause

3. Osteoporosis affects a woman's:
   a. Estrogen
   b. Bones
   c. Uterus
   d. Testosterone

4. Which is NOT a possible symptom of andropause?
   a. Decline in testosterone
   b. Increase in androgen
   c. Slower erections
   d. Increased refractory periods

5. What type of partnership is the prevailing majority for most older adults?
   a. Cohabiting
   b. Non-cohabiting, non-married romantic involvement
   c. Marriage
   d. None of the above

6. When it comes to contracting STIs or HIV/AIDS, older adults are at:
   a. A lower risk.
   b. The same risk.
   c. A higher risk.
   d. It is unknown.

7. Which is NOT a sexual enhancement drug?
   a. Levitra
   b. Viagra
   c. Cialis
   d. cGMP

8. What is a possible age-related sexual change in men?
   a. Increase in blood flow to the penis
   b. Decreased libido
   c. Decreased time needed to reach orgasm
   d. Increased testosterone

SHORT RESPONSE

1. Explain why there are more older people living in the U.S. today than younger people.

2. What is the difference between primary and secondary aging? What are some examples of each?

3. Explain how sexual enhancement drugs work.

4. Describe an example of ageism.

5. What is one idea about sexuality and aging that you were surprised to learn? What did you originally think?

THINK READINGS

THE NEW YORK TIMES

Europeans Debate Castration of Sex Offenders

By DAN BILEFSKY

Published: March 10, 2009

PRAGUE — Pavel remembers the violent night sweats two days before the murder. He went to see a family doctor, who said they would go away. But after viewing a Bruce Lee martial arts film, he said, he felt uncontrollable sexual desires. He invited a 12-year-old neighbor home. Then he stabbed the boy repeatedly.

His psychiatrist says Pavel derived his sexual pleasure from the violence.

More than 20 years have passed. Pavel, then 18, spent seven years in prison and five years in a psychiatric institution. During his last year in prison, he asked to be surgically castrated. Having his testicles removed, he said, was like draining the gasoline from a car hard-wired to crash. A large, dough-faced man, he is sterile and has forsaken marriage, romantic relationships and sex, he said. His life revolves around a Catholic charity, where he is a gardener.

"I can finally live knowing that I am no harm to anybody," he said during an interview at a McDonald's here, as children played loudly nearby. "I am living a productive life. I want to tell people that there is help."

He refused to give his last name for fear of being hounded.

Whether castration can help rehabilitate violent sex offenders has come under new scrutiny after the Council of Europe's anti-torture committee last month called surgical castration "invasive, irreversible and mutilating" and demanded that the Czech Republic stop offering the procedure to violent sex offenders. Other critics said that castration threatened to lead society down a dangerous road toward eugenics.

The Czech Republic has allowed at least 94 prisoners over the past decade to be surgically castrated. It is the only country in Europe that uses the procedure for sex offenders. Czech psychiatrists supervising the treatment—a one-hour operation that involves removal of the tissue that produces testosterone—insist that it is the most foolproof way to tame sexual urges in dangerous predators suffering from extreme sexual disorders.

Surgical castration has been a means of social control for centuries. In ancient China, eunuchs were trusted to serve the imperial family inside the palace grounds; in Italy several centuries ago, youthful male choir members were castrated to preserve their high singing voices.

These days it can be used to treat testicular cancer and some advanced cases of prostate cancer.

Now, more countries in Europe are considering requiring or allowing chemical castration for violent sex offenders. There is intense debate over whose rights take precedence: those of sex offenders, who could be subjected to a punishment that many consider cruel, or those of society, which expects protection from sexual predators.

Poland is expected to become the first nation of the European Union to give judges the right to impose chemical castration on at least some convicted pedophiles, using hormonal drugs to curb sexual appetite; the impetus for the change was the arrest of a 45-year-old man in September who had fathered two children by his young daughter. Spain, after a convicted pedophile killed a

---

Recall from an earlier discussion that eugenics sometimes refers to the forcible sterilization of social "undesirables." Are **violent sex offenders**—people who engage in crimes involving sex, rape, and/or molestation— "undesirables?" In your opinion, is surgical castration torture or treatment? Are there other methods by which to rehabilitate sex offenders?

Surgical castration refers to the surgical removal of the testicles to stop the production of androgen sex hormones. Without these hormones, it is difficult for a male to become sexually aroused. But are crimes that involve sex always about sex? Or are they about power and control? If someone is castrated, do they still have the propensity toward violence?

A **chemical castration** is the administration of hormonal drugs that inhibit the function of a man's testes. Intended to have the same effects of surgical castration, it reduces or eliminates a man's sexual impulses.

Whose rights take precedence? Sex offenders, who, with surgical or chemical castration are subjected to "cruel and unusual" punishment? The molestation or rape victim? The family of a child who is raped and killed? Society?

child, is considering plans to offer chemical castration.

Last year, the governor of Louisiana, Bobby Jindal, signed legislation requiring courts to order chemical castration for offenders convicted of certain sex crimes a second time.

In the Czech Republic, the issue was brought home last month when Antonin Novak, 43, was sentenced to life in prison after raping and killing Jakub Simanek, a 9-year-old boy who disappeared last May. Mr. Novak, who had served four and a half years in prison for sexual offenses in Slovakia, had been ordered to undergo outpatient treatment, but had failed to show up several months before the murder. Advocates of surgical castration argued that had he been castrated, the tragedy could have been prevented.

Hynek Blasko, Jakub's father, expressed indignation that human rights groups were putting the rights of criminals ahead of those of victims. "My personal tragedy is that my son is in heaven and he is never coming back, and all I have left of him is 1.5 kilograms of ashes," he said in an interview. "No one wants to touch the rights of the pedophiles, but what about the rights of a 9-year-old boy with his life ahead of him?"

Ales Butala, a Slovenian human rights lawyer who led the Council of Europe's delegation to the Czech Republic, argued that surgical castration was unethical, because it was not medically necessary and deprived castrated men of the right to reproduce. He also challenged its effectiveness, saying that the council's committee had discovered three cases of castrated Czech sex offenders who had gone on to commit violent crimes, including pedophilia and attempted murder.

Although the procedure is voluntary, Mr. Butala said that he believed some offenders felt they had no choice.

"Sex offenders are requesting castration in hope of getting released from a life of incarceration," he said. "Is that really free and informed consent?"

But government health officials here and some Czech psychiatrists counter that castration can be effective and argue that by seeking to outlaw the practice, the council is putting potential victims at risk.

Dr. Martin Holly, a leading sexologist and psychiatrist who is director of the Psychiatric Hospital Bohnice in Prague, said none of the nearly 100 sex offenders who had been physically castrated had committed further offenses.

A Danish study of 900 castrated sex offenders in the 1960s suggested the rate of repeat offenses dropped after surgical castration to 2.3 percent from 80 percent.

But human rights groups say that such studies are inconclusive because they rely on self-reporting by sex offenders. Other psychiatric experts argue that sexual pathology is in the brain and cannot be cured by surgery.

Dr. Holly, who has counseled convicted sex offenders for four decades, stressed that the procedure was being allowed only for repeat violent offenders who suffered from severe sexual disorders. Moreover, he said, the procedure is undertaken only with the informed consent of the patient and with the approval of an independent committee of psychiatric and legal experts.

Jaroslav Novak, chief of urology at the Faculty Hospital Na Bulovce in Prague, said: "This is not a very common procedure. We carry it out maybe once every one to two years at most."

Several states, including Texas, Florida and California, now allow or mandate chemical castration for certain convicted sex offenders.

Dr. Fred S. Berlin, founder of the Sexual Disorders Clinic at Johns Hopkins University, argued that chemical castration was less physically harmful than surgery and that it provided a safeguard, because a psychiatrist could inform the courts or police if the patient ordered to undergo treatment failed to show up. A surgically castrated patient, Dr. Berlin said, can order testosterone over the Internet.

For Hynek Blasko, the father of Jakub Simanek, neither form of castration is the answer. "These people must be under permanent detention where they can be monitored," he said. "There has to be a difference between the rights of the victim and the perpetrator."

In July 2008, Louisiana Governor Bobby Jindal signed "The Sex Offender Chemical Castration Bill" into law. This law authorizes the mandatory chemical castration of reoffending sex offenders; the court has the freedom to impose surgical castration. If a sex offender voluntarily agrees to surgical or chemical castration, is it really free and informed consent? Why or why not?

USING SEX AS A WEAPON:
Sexual Coercion, Rape, and Abuse

WHAT IS SEXUAL CONSENT?

WHO RAPES AND HOW DOES RAPE AFFECT THE VICTIM?

WHAT ARE THE CHARACTERISTICS OF INTIMATE PARTNER VIOLENCE?

WHAT ARE THE EFFECTS OF SEXUAL ABUSE ON CHILDREN?

My

2-year-old son was napping, so I decided to leave my door open and step out on the main balcony to have a smoke.

I put my cigarette out and turned to go back into my apartment . . . I stepped inside of my apartment, and when I put my hand on the door to shut it, suddenly this guy was in my apartment. One minute I was alone and the next minute he was there telling me to be quiet or he would hurt me. All I could think of was [my son], so I didn't yell or cry out. I didn't want him to know I had a baby and I didn't want him to hurt us.

He pushed me into the bathroom and over the next hour he forced me to go down on him and do other things to him. It had to be what hell is like. I remember trying to memorize every detail that I could. He had shaved off all of his pubic hair, but I memorized where his moles were. He came in my mouth and for some reason he immediately left the bathroom. I spit [his ejaculate] into the toilet. He came back and pulled me out into the living room, and I thought he was going to kill me. He was aggressive with me, and he kept threatening that he would kill me if I yelled or made any noise. He found my cell phone and took it, and he told me to stay put for 10 minutes and that if I called anyone he would come back and hurt me again. After he left, I remember sitting on the floor, crouched down. I didn't have a clock in front of me and I kept thinking, "Has it been 10 minutes yet?"

I eventually left the apartment and started screaming for help. The bastard had apparently tried to break into another woman's apartment [in the same apartment complex], but she was able to shut him out and call the police. By the time I was running through the parking lot screaming for help, the police were already there. They found him nearby and arrested him.

I didn't flush the toilet, so his [semen] was still in there. I also had not brushed my teeth or washed my hands or face. I don't know how I remembered all of the things I had been taught, but the little things like spitting out his cum and saving it were huge in prosecuting him. He's in prison now, and he won't be eligible for parole for 40 years.

I was a 4.0 student before this happened, and now most days I barely function. People expect me to just get over this and go on with my life because the asshole is in prison. What they don't understand is that in one hour that man took my life. He took "who" I am away . . . probably forever.

Source: Author's files

Sex is sometimes used as a weapon to control and/or harm someone whom a perpetrator perceives as vulnerable, as the opening vignette illustrates. When someone uses verbal pressure or physical force to engage in a sexual activity with someone who is unwilling, **sexual coercion** occurs (Faulkner, Kolts, & Hicks, 2008; Hartwick, Desmarais, & Henning, 2007). Sexual activity may include anything from unwanted sexual touch to oral, vaginal, and/or anal penetration, and coercion ranges from the use of teasing, taunting, and humiliation to physical threats or actions (Glenn & Byers, 2009). Today, the terms **sexual violence (SV)** and **sexual assault (SA)** are used interchangeably to refer to any sexual activity in which consent is not obtained or freely given (CDC, 2009a). There is not a one-size-fits-all description of a *perpetrator*, the person who commits the act of violence. The offender can be a current or past intimate partner, a family member, a person in a position of power or trust, a friend, an acquaintance, or a stranger (CDC, 2009b).

Sexual violence is a serious and pressing issue in the United States. Consider these unsettling facts:

- *Children and youth (under age 17):* Nearly two-thirds of female victims and nearly 70 percent of male victims were first raped before age 18

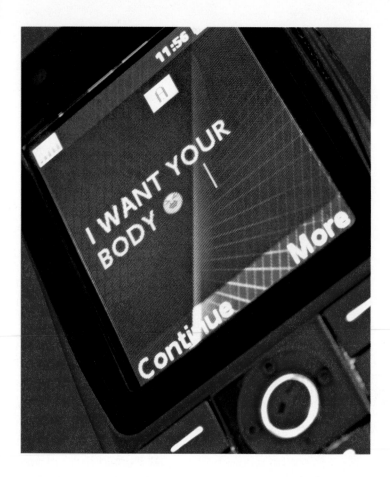

>>> Sexual assault encompasses a wide range of behaviors from direct physical contact to explicit e-mails and text messages. **Any remarks that are sexual and unsolicited are considered verbal sexual assault.**

TABLE 17.1
Types of Victimization

Source: The Sexual Victimization of College Women. U.S. Department of Justice (2010).

Completed rape	Unwanted completed vaginal, oral, or anal penetration of a body part or object by force or the threat of force.
Attempted rape	Unwanted attempted vaginal, oral, or anal penetration of a body part or object by force or the threat of force.
Completed sexual coercion	Unwanted completed vaginal, oral, or anal penetration of a body part or object involving the nonphysical punishment, promise of reward, or pestering/verbal pressure.
Attempted sexual coercion	Unwanted attempted vaginal, oral, or anal penetration of a body part or object involving the nonphysical punishment, promise of reward, or pestering/verbal pressure.
Completed sexual contact with force or threat of force	Unwanted completed sexual contact (not penetration) of the breasts, buttocks, or genitals, over or under clothes; kissing; licking; sucking; or any other unwanted sexual contact that is achieved through force or the threat of force.
Completed sexual contact without force	Unwanted completed sexual contact (not penetration) of the breasts, buttocks, or genitals, over or under clothes; kissing; licking; sucking; or any other unwanted sexual contact that is achieved through the threat of nonphysical punishment, promise of reward, or pestering/verbal pressure.
Attempted sexual contact with force or threat of force	Unwanted attempted sexual contact (not penetration) of the breasts, buttocks, or genitals, over or under clothes; kissing; licking; sucking; or any other unwanted sexual contact that is achieved through force or the threat of force.
Attempted sexual contact without force	Unwanted attempted sexual contact (not penetration) of the breasts, buttocks, or genitals, over or under clothes; kissing; licking; sucking; or any other unwanted sexual contact that is achieved through the threat of nonphysical punishment, promise of reward, or pestering/verbal pressure.
Threat of rape	Threat of unwanted vaginal, oral, or anal penetration of a body part or object by force or the threat of force.
Threat of contact with force	Threat of unwanted sexual contact (not penetration) of the breasts, buttocks, or genitals, over or under clothes; kissing; licking; sucking; and/or any other unwanted sexual contact that is achieved through force or the threat of force.
Threat of contact without force	Threat of unwanted sexual contact (not penetration) of the breasts, buttocks, or genitals, over or under clothes; kissing; licking; sucking; or any other unwanted sexual contact that is achieved through the threat of nonphysical punishment, promise of reward, or pestering/verbal pressure.

(Basile et al., 2007). Another survey found that 11 percent of girls and 4 percent of boys (grades 9–12) were forced to have sexual intercourse during their lifetimes (CDC, 2006).

- *College students:* An estimated 20 to 25 percent of college women experience attempted or completed rape while in college (CDC, 2008).

- *Adults:* A survey of nearly 10,000 adults found that 11 percent of women and 2 percent of men have experienced forced sex at some point in their lives (Basile et al., 2007).

There are many types of SV. Some involve physical contact, and some do not. In this chapter, we'll first discuss what it means to consent to sexual acts, and then we'll explore the many aspects of rape, as well as intimate partner violence and sexual harassment. We'll then examine child sexual abuse, and conclude with a discussion about the ways we can keep ourselves safe.

Given the incidence trends in sexual violence, it is likely that some of you have been victimized. If you find the content in this chapter difficult, I encourage you to reach out to your instructor or professor, or to a campus health care provider.

WHAT IS SEXUAL CONSENT?

In the United States, someone is sexually assaulted every two minutes (U.S. Department of Justice, 2007). In 2008, victims aged 12 or older experienced 203,830 sexual assaults (Rand, 2009). Adolescents and young adults are at the greatest risk of SA—the rate of sexual victimization for those ages 16 to 24 is at least double that of every other age group (U.S. Department of Justice, Office of Justice Programs, 2007). There are many types of sexual assault in which people are victimized, and these are summarized in Table 17.1. As you can see, SA includes both *attempted* acts and *completed* acts, and all acts are unwanted.

sexual life now

Honor Killings: Exemption from Punishment?

Each year across the world, 5,000 women and girls are killed as a means of preserving the family's honor (Human Rights Watch, 2009). *Honor killings* are defined as "acts of violence, usually murder, committed by male family members against female family members who are held to have brought dishonor upon the family" (HRW, 2009). There are many reasons a woman can be accused of dishonoring her family, including refusing to enter into an arranged marriage; seeking a divorce; being the victim of rape; or adopting customs outside of a given group's approval.

In the name of preserving family honor, many countries exempt honor killers from prosecution. According to the United Nations, a number of countries still fully or partially exempt people who kill for honor from punishment (United Nations, 2009). In some cases, the perpetrators are admired and given special status within their communities. Because honor killings are centuries-old practices in different cultures, should honor killers be exempt from punishment under the law?

YES!

A 2009 Turkish study, *Honor Killings in the Media and Their Impact on Students and Parents,* assessed the responses of 440 high school students and their parents in regions where honor killings were prevalent. According to the study:

- Nearly 27 percent of parents and over one-fourth of the students said they support such killings.

- Of the parents, 13 percent had witnessed an honor killing, and 10 percent of the students had.

- About 29 percent of parents and students believe that the media is not impartial/close to reality when portraying honor killings in the news.

In 2009, the President of Syria abolished a section of the Penal Code that waived punishment for a man who killed a female family member; however, the law still allows for lesser punishments for honor killings, requiring two-year prison sentences.

NO!

The United Nations (2009) and Human Rights Watch (2009) maintain that honor killings are extreme acts of discrimination against women and girls, and as such are human rights violations:

- Under international laws and standards, each country has clear responsibilities to uphold women and children's rights to ensure freedom from gender-based discrimination.

- Each country has the responsibility to protect its citizens, regardless of a person's lower status in a family.

- Governments need to reform all criminal codes that treat those who kill for honor differently from other murderers.

To circumvent new laws, many countries are encouraging *honor suicides*, where "dishonored women" are encouraged (and sometimes ordered) by male family members to kill themselves.

>>> **WHAT DO YOU THINK?**

1. Have you ever heard of honor killings or suicides? What is your reaction?

2. What is the best way for human rights groups to help reduce these occurrences?

3. *Should* human rights activists become involved in other cultures' beliefs and practices? Why or why not?

Sources: Human Rights Watch. (2009). Retrieved March 5, 2010, from http://www.hrw.org/en/news/2009/07/28/syria-no-exceptions-honor-killings; United Nations. (2009). *Violence against women: Good practices in combating and eliminating violence against women.* Retrieved March 5, 2010, from www.khafagy.honorcrimes.pdf.

We know that inherent to sexual violence/sexual assault is the lack of consent by the victim to the sexual activity. But what is consent? And if we give consent once, does that mean it applies to all future sex acts?

SEXUAL CONSENT: A VOLUNTARY AGREEMENT

Sexual assault is an intentional act that can occur in any of these ways: 1) The perpetrator ignores the objections of the other person; 2) the offender intentionally causes the victim's intoxication or impairment through the use of drugs or alcohol; and/or 3) the perpetrator takes advantage of someone's incapacitation, feelings of intimidation, helplessness, or any other ability to consent (U.S. Department of Justice, 2000). **Sexual misconduct** occurs when the offender did not intend to harm the other person and he or she unreasonably believed that consent was given; however, the offender did not meet his or her responsibility to gain consent (U.S. Department of Justice, 2000).

Each semester when I present these definitions in class, a student will inevitably ask, "Does that mean I could be charged with sexual misconduct if I don't have consent? I have to ask him/her for consent for *every single sex act*, *every single time*? When it comes to gaining consent, what is my responsibility?"

Sexual consent (see Figure 17.1) refers to the words or actions we use to show our voluntary, freely given agreement to engage in mutually agreed-upon sexual activities (U.S. Department of Justice, 2000); consent must be given at the time of the act (Washington State University, 2009). In other words, legal sexual consent happens when two people agree to do the same thing at the same time, in the same way, with each other (Kansas State University, 2010). It is also important to note that sexual consent is for *everyone*. It applies to all persons, regardless of age, gender, sexual orientation, and relationship status.

We must also consider that consent is not a one-time event; instead it is an ongoing process of mutual communication as sex progresses from one act to the next (Washington State University, 2009). For example, kissing a partner does not imply sexual consent for other sexual acts; oral sex is not consent for vaginal or anal sex. We've learned throughout our study that all sexual relationships require clear and direct communication, whether a couple is hooking up, dating, cohabiting, or married. When it comes to sexual consent, then, each person in the sexual relationship is responsible for clearly giving and receiving consent (Washington State University, 2009). Silence and submission are not consent.

THE ABSENCE OF CONSENT: THE LACK OF FREE WILL

The words "voluntarily" and "freely" are key to the legal definition of sexual consent; a person must give consent without feeling threatened or coerced by another person. For example, the agreement to participate is not considered consensual if it is given at gunpoint or any other situation that presents a threat. But the threat does not have to be physical. If a 14-year-old girl performs oral sex on her 19-year-old boyfriend because he claims that he will break up with her if she does not comply with his wishes, the girl isn't acting freely, and the consent isn't real.

The second example of consent introduces the element of power. In instances in which one person has power over the other, the more powerful party cannot obtain true consent (Cowling & Reynolds, 2004). A gap in power can occur in a relationship when there is a significant difference in age, a legitimate or distorted sense of seniority, or any other element that results in the perception that one person has authority over the other.

A student–teacher relationship like the one between 24-year-old middle school teacher Debra Lafave and her 14-year-old student, is a prime example of this type of power. Because teachers are in the position of authority when interacting with students and hold inherent power over students, is it truly possible for a student to give "consent" to a sexual act? The element of power also comes into play when a person does not have the mental capacity or maturity to understand what giving his or her consent entails. For example, a mentally disabled child may agree to let an adult neighbor touch his or her genitals, but it cannot be considered legal sexual consent if the child is incapable of understanding the implications of the touching. This situation can also occur when children are too young to comprehend sexual contact, making them powerless.

Sometimes, it is tough to determine whether sexual consent has been given. Realistically, it's not as if one person always asks the other, "Do you consent to me touching your breast?" and the other person responds, "Yes, I consent to you touching

Consent is based on a freely decided choice:
Drugs and/or alcohol make this legally impossible.

Consent is limited:
Consent to one form of sexual activity does not imply consent to other forms of sexual activity.

Consent is not an assumption:
You cannot assume what your partner does or doesn't want. Absence of clear signals means stop. Without clear consent, a crime takes place.

Figure 17.1 What is Sexual Consent?

Figure 17.2 History of Rape in the United States

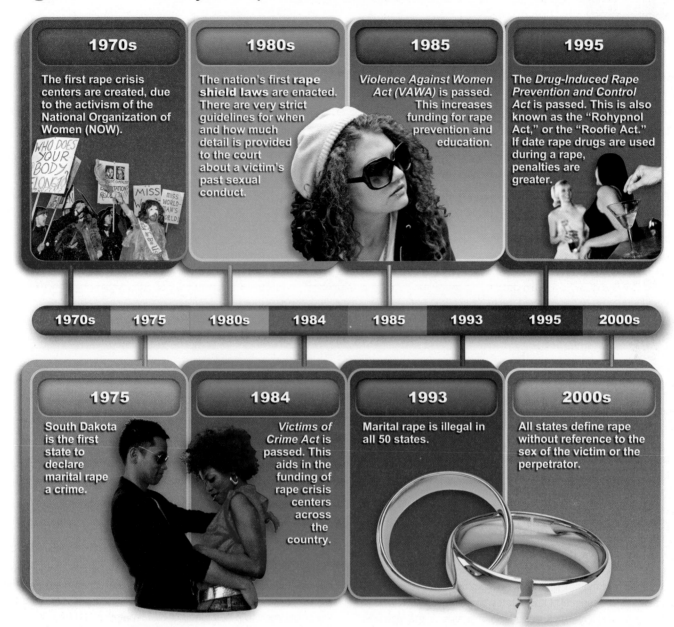

1970s

The first rape crisis centers are created, due to the activism of the National Organization of Women (NOW).

1980s

The nation's first **rape shield laws** are enacted. There are very strict guidelines for when and how much detail is provided to the court about a victim's past sexual conduct.

1985

Violence Against Women Act (VAWA) is passed. This increases funding for rape prevention and education.

1995

The *Drug-Induced Rape Prevention and Control Act* is passed. This is also known as the "Rohypnol Act," or the "Roofie Act." If date rape drugs are used during a rape, penalties are greater.

| 1970s | 1975 | 1980s | 1984 | 1985 | 1993 | 1995 | 2000s |

1975

South Dakota is the first state to declare marital rape a crime.

1984

Victims of Crime Act is passed. This aids in the funding of rape crisis centers across the country.

1993

Marital rape is illegal in all 50 states.

2000s

All states define rape without reference to the sex of the victim or the perpetrator.

my breast." This is because consent is not typically given in a formal fashion; often, it is given through one simple comment or through body language. There are many shades of gray when it comes to establishing true consent, which can make it difficult to determine whether sexual assault has occurred. If in doubt, *ask*!

All nonconsensual sexual offenses involve the violation of the victim's autonomy. Consent is an important concept to understand, because it isn't just about taking away a victim's sexual rights; it's a key player in the legal picture of what constitutes rape (McGregor, 2005).

RAPE

Defined by the Federal Bureau of Investigation, **rape** is oral, anal, or vaginal intercourse or other forms of penetration by one person (the accused) with or against another person (the victim) without the consent of the victim (Federal Bureau of Investigation, 2009). Although the definition of rape varies from state to state, all states consider rape to involve forcible sexual relations against a person's will; all states consider rape a criminal offense. As Figure 17.2 shows us, forced sex

>>> Debra Lafave was sentenced to three years' house arrest, later reduced to probation. **If it had been a male teacher with a female student, would the consequences have been the same?**

Sexual Coercion

You may not have been directly affected by sexual coercion or assault, but chances are, someone you know has been. Because it has become a pervasive problem in our society, it is helpful to examine some of our attitudes and misconceptions about rape and sexual abuse.

In order for sex to be consensual, _____ must happen.

I have had _____ consensual/nonconsensual sexual experiences.

Based on the opinion of my culture, sexual coercion is _____.

Based on my upbringing, I believe sexual coercion is _____.

A victim of sexual assault is at fault when _____.

I would expect the typical rapist to be _____.

When the perpetrator and the victim are in a relationship, sex is _____.

When I hear about children being sexually abused, it makes me feel _____.

Rape is primarily motivated by _____.

If a friend came to me and told me he or she had been sexually assaulted, I would _____.

Men who are victims of rape are _____.

within marriage and forced sex against men has not conventionally been considered rape; however, as of the early 2000s, all states define rape without reference to marital status or the sex of the victim and the offender.

Forcible rape is the term used to describe attempted or completed rape, but statutory rape occurs without force. **Statutory rape** is intercourse by an adult with a person below a legally designated age (Coccoa, 2004). By law, minors are not capable of giving consent; the legal age of sexual consent varies from state to state. For example, some states specify an *age differential*, meaning that there is an age span between the victim and the perpetrator. Other states focus on the *age of the victim*, meaning that in many states, as long as a victim is at least 16 years old and the sex partner is no more than four years older, sex is considered consensual. Other states focus on the *age of the defendant*, and consider the sex to be nonconsensual if the victim is under the age of 16 and the defendant is at least 18. The annual rape data exclude statutory rape cases.

In 2008 an estimated 89,000 forcible rapes occurred in the United States (FBI, 2009). Down almost 2 percent from the previous year, this is the lowest number of rapes in the past 20 years (see Figure 17.3). But these numbers probably do not tell the entire story, because many cases are not reported (2009b).

WHO ARE THE RAPISTS?

As with all other aspects of sex, rape is the result of individual, relationship, and cultural factors (NCWSV, 2008). Because of the complex interplay of these forces, it is nearly impossible to come up with a characterization of every rapist. Through crime statistics, however, we know that rapists are more likely to be longtime criminals than they are to be serial rapists. For example, within three years of release from prison, 46 percent of rapists are arrested for other crimes, such as drug offenses and property crimes (U.S. Department of Justice, Bureau of Justice Statistics, 2002).

There are certain individual-level factors that put someone at a greater risk to be a sexual offender. Risk factors for perpetration include (Abbey & McAuslan, 2004; CDC, 2009b; Zawacki et al., 2003):

- Being male
- Witnessing or experiencing violence/sexual violence as a child
- Alcohol or drug use/abuse
- Holding attitudes or beliefs that support sexual violence
- Holding more traditional gender roles
- Holding beliefs that it is acceptable to manipulate a relationship partner

Social factors also come into play. For example, some men may believe that women put up "token resistance" when pressured for sex; they believe that women actually want to be overcome forcefully, but feel the social need to protect their sexual reputations (Abbey, 2002).

In 1979, in his seminal research, Nicholas Groth classified three main patterns of rapists: *anger rapists*, *power rapists*, and *sadistic rapists*. According to Groth, the **anger rapist** uses more force than necessary. The individual's motivation comes from the anger or rage he or she feels for the victim or for the person the victim represents. This type of rapist is likely to cause bodily injury.

The **power rapist** needs to assert strength and dominance over the victim. The level of physical or psychological force that the power rapist uses is dependent upon the victim's level of resistance. In comparison, the **sadistic rapist** has an erotic association with violence. This type of rapist becomes sexually aroused by the pain, suffering, humiliation, and mutilation of the victim. He or she is likely to inflict serious physical and psychological harm to the victim and, in some cases, may cause death (Kocsis, 2008).

Although some women do not know their attacker, as in the opening vignette, many women do. **Date rape** or **acquaintance rape** is a criminal act that is perpetrated by a social acquaintance, a friend, or a dating or intimate partner of the victim (FBI, 2009).

The *National College Women Sexual Victimization (NCWSV)* survey (2008) indicates that all forms of sexual assault commonly occur on

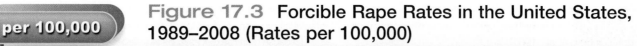

Figure 17.3 Forcible Rape Rates in the United States, 1989–2008 (Rates per 100,000)

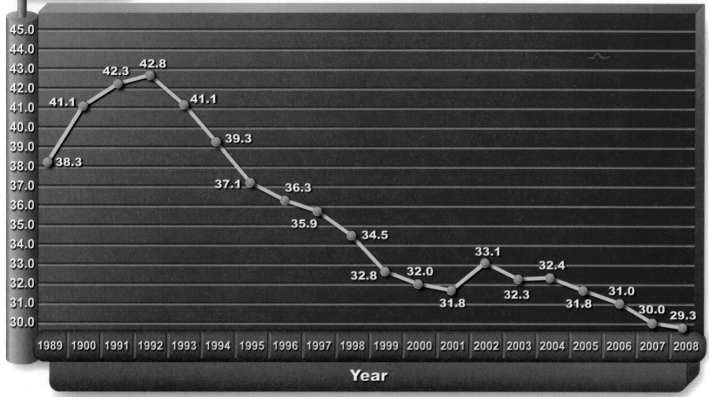

per 100,000

Source: FBI (2009).

college campuses in the United States. Sponsored by the U.S. Department of Justice, the NCWSV survey found that in nine out of 10 cases reported, rape victims knew the offenders (NCWSV, 2008). According to the NCWSV survey, nearly 13 percent of completed rapes, 35 percent of attempted rapes, and almost 23 percent of threatened rapes took place during a date. Overall, two-thirds of victims who report the rape already know their attackers in some capacity; 38 percent of

rapists are friends or acquaintances; 28 percent are intimate partners; and 7 percent are relatives (U.S. Department of Justice, 2006).

Where do rapes take place? Rapes typically occur in the victim's residence (60 percent). About 31 percent occur in other housing areas, and 10 percent take place in fraternities.

RAPE SCRIPTS OF MEN AND WOMEN

Throughout our study, we have looked at the development of *sex scripts* and how these scripts influence every facet of sex and sexuality. Part of our sex scripts is rape scripts. Our **rape scripts** include information about types of conduct that make up "rape," conduct and characteristics of "perpetrators," and the sequence of events that take place in a rape (for a review of the literature, see Clark & Carroll, 2007). Do men and women share similar rape scripts?

Men and women have different perceptions of what constitutes rape or forced sex. When hearing or reading about "rape," men and women have different conceptualizations about what took place (Clark & Carroll, 2007). For example, in a recent study that examined the responses of 417 college men and women, researchers found that in certain situations, women are more likely than men to indicate that a rape occurred, whereas men are more likely to say that women make false assumptions and it isn't rape. Also, men tend to place the responsibility of the event on the victim. Previous research showed that in rape situations, men tend to identify more with the male, while women are more apt to identify with the victim (Popovich et al., 1995).

Males are also more likely than females to believe myths about rape, such as a girl who dresses seductively is "asking for it" or it's not rape unless the victim fights back. Men are more likely to have negative views of rape victims and to blame them for the crime. Even when they do consider the act to be rape, males are also less likely than females to

People often think of rapists as angry men hiding in the bushes or lurking in the shadows, waiting to grab a victim by surprise. **But in reality, the victim generally knows the attacker.**

anticipate the ensuing damaging psychological effects. Not every man feels this way, but men tend to hold these opinions more often than their female peers do (Holcomb et al., 1991).

RACE, ETHNICITY, AND ATTITUDES TOWARD RAPE

Ethnicity also affect a person's attitudes toward rape. In a study conducted by the University of California, Fullerton, researchers found that among a group of college-aged Asian and Caucasian male and female students, Asian students were more likely to have a negative view of rape victims and were less likely to hold the rapist responsible for the crime than the white students were (Mori et al., 1995). A follow-up study in which the study participants and the victims had ethnicity in common showed that Asians were still more likely to hold negative views toward the victims, regardless of whether the victim was Asian or Caucasian (Brouillard, Wheeler, & Mori, 2002).

Although incidences of rape are on the decline, sexual violence is a problem on many college and universities and campuses today. In the section that follows, we'll look at the aspects associated with rape on campus.

RAPE ON CAMPUS

College students are four times more likely to be sexually assaulted than any other age group (RAINN, 2009b). Colleges and universities remain dangerous places, particularly for women:

- 12 percent of women attending American colleges and universities have been raped, but only about 12 percent of rapes of college women are actually reported to law enforcement (Kilpatrick et al., 2007).

- 14 percent of undergraduate women were victims of at least one completed sexual assault since beginning college (Krebs and others, 2007).

- 5 percent of undergraduate women were victims of forced sexual assault (Krebs et al., 2007).

- 8 percent were sexually assaulted while voluntarily incapacitated due to alcohol or drugs (Krebs et al., 2007).

Most of these sexual crimes, particularly rapes and physical sexual coercion, occur in on-campus student living quarters. Also, college-age sexual assault victims are four times more likely to be victimized by someone they know, not by a stranger (Baum & Klaus, 2005).

But why do collegiate rape incidences seem to be on the rise, while rape in the general population is on the decline? Some recent research suggests that institutional practices may put some women at a greater risk than others. For example, on your college campus is there a dorm or residence hall that is known for partying? Is there a "party floor" in your dorm or residence hall? **Party rape**, or rape that occurs as the result of alcohol and/or drug intoxication, occurs more frequently at schools where there are larger numbers of "party-oriented" students, and where such partying is either permitted or overlooked by the college (Armstrong, Hamilton, & Sweeney, 2006). Additionally,

white women tend to experience rape while intoxicated more than other racial/ethnic women do (Mohler-Kuo et al., 2004).

Because many sexual assaults at colleges and universities go unreported, the statistics used to track campus sexual assault trends don't always tell the whole story. According to a 2005 study conducted by the U.S. Justice Department, fewer than 5 percent of completed and attempted rapes of college women are reported (U.S. Department of Justice, 2006). Figure 17.4 presents some of the reasons women don't tell.

Contrary to common beliefs, many college students' rape scripts hold that rape involves violent tactics by the offender (Littleton & Axsom, 2003). This is not true. Most rapes that involve college students have low-level assailant violence because the rapist is able to take advantage of a woman who is incapacitated due to alcohol or drugs (Littleton et al., 2009). College students sometimes also fail to understand this is still rape.

INTOXICATION BY DRUGS

Passing out does not imply sexual consent. **Drug-facilitated assault** occurs when drugs or alcohol are used to compromise an individual's ability to consent to sexual activity or minimize the resistance or memory of the victim. **Diminished capacity** is the term used when a person does not have the ability to give consent due to the influence of drugs or alcohol. Diminished capacity is an important concept for college students to understand; many victims blame themselves for doing drugs or drinking too much rather than blaming their assailants, who took advantage of their impairment (RAINN, 2009c).

Substances commonly used in sexual assault include Rohypnol, GHB, and GBL. These drugs are typically odorless, colorless, and tasteless when placed in a liquid (except for GBL). Effects can take place anywhere from five to 30 minutes after ingestion. Drugged individuals may struggle to walk, talk, or stay awake making them very vulnerable to assault.

Figure 17.4 Why Women Don't Tell A rape victim may remain silent for many reasons (CDC, 2009b).

She is afraid to tell the police, friends, or family about the violence.

She may be ashamed or embarrassed.

She believes her case will not hold up in court or that the police cannot or will not help her.

She may believe she is to blame for the assaults.

She is worried that her sexual past will be brought to light.

She may have been threatened by the perpetrator to keep quiet.

She may not understand that sex that involves coercion or threats–psychological or physical–is considered rape.

<<< While victims are not typically "slipped" alcohol like they are pills, they can be pressured into drinking more than intended. **Even if a person has willingly consumed alcohol or drugs, he or she cannot give proper consent with diminished capacity.**

Rohypnol, also known as **roofies** or the **date rape drug**, is one of the most common drugs used in sexual assault (RAINN, 2009c). The makers of the drug, which is intended for use as a potent sedative, have changed the chemistry of the pill so that it changes the color of clear drinks to a bright blue and the color of dark drinks cloudy in an effort to decrease the use of the drug in sexual assaults.

INTOXICATION BY ALCOHOL

Alcohol is the most common chemical used in sexual assaults, with as many as two-thirds of victims reporting that they consumed alcohol prior to being assaulted (Littleton, Grills-Taquechel, & Axsom, 2009). There tends to be greater acts of violence used in the assault and higher rates of rape completion when the offender consumes alcohol, and victims tend to receive more serious injuries if the assailant has been drinking (for a full review, see Littleton, Grills-Taquechel, & Axsom, 2009). Many times, both the victim and the perpetrator consume alcohol prior to episodes of sexual assault (Zawacki et al., 2003).

The **Federal Clery Act** (also known as the **Student Right-to-Know** or **Campus Security Act**) was passed in an effort to decrease the rate of sexual assaults on campus and to improve student awareness. The act requires all colleges and universities that participate in federal financial aid programs to make public statistics regarding on-campus crime, which includes sexual assault and rape. The act was named for Jeanne Clery, a 19-year-old freshman at Lehigh University, who, in 1986, was raped and murdered in her dorm room. It aims to make university officials and students more aware of the crime trends in their communities (RAINN, 2009c).

Rape abuses a victim both physically and emotionally because it violates both a person's body and emotional connection to sexuality. In the next section, we'll explore the effects of rape on the victim, as well as its effect on the victim's partner and family.

THE EFFECTS OF RAPE

For most victims, the effects of rape are long lasting. Similar to victims of other crimes, rape victims may suffer from *posttraumatic stress disorder (PTSD)*, an anxiety disorder resulting from a traumatic event that can have a debilitating effect on a person's quality of life (Foa & Riggs, 1995). *Trauma* is both a medical and a psychiatric definition; certainly when women or men are raped, both types of trauma can occur. **Rape trauma syndrome (RTS)** is a form of PTSD that occurs in victims of rape. Victims can work toward healing by moving through the three phases of RTS, presented in Table 17.2.

WOMEN'S RESPONSES TO RAPE

Each victim has his or her own unique responses to rape, but there are some common symptoms that female victims experience. For years, the negative effects of rape have been documented by research. Depression is a common reaction to rape, and sexual assault victims are three times more likely than those who have not been raped to suffer from depression (Atkeson et al., 1982; American Psychiatric Association, 2000). Depression resulting from a rape is more than just having the blues or being sad or upset about the event. It involves intense, prolonged, and pervasive feelings of sorrow. Symptoms may include frequent crying spells, loss or gain of appetite, extreme fatigue, changes in sleeping patterns, social withdrawal, feelings of worthlessness, and/or thoughts of suicide or death (American Psychiatric Association, 2000). Some women may also resort to destructive behaviors following a rape, such as drug or alcohol abuse.

Rape victims also report fear, anxiety, social phobia (such as a college classroom), sexual dysfunction, and sleep disorders (for a full review, see McMullin & White, 2006). A recent longitudinal study of 754 female college students revealed that whether a victim labels her experiences as rape or

TABLE 17.2
The Phases of Rape Trauma Syndrome

Source: Rape trauma syndrome. RAINN: Rape, Abuse & Incest National Network (2009).

	Phase	Time Frame	Process
Step 1	Acute Phase	Takes place immediately after the assault and can last from a few days to a couple weeks	When talking about the crime, victims may be 1) expressive, showing agitated or hysterical behavior; 2) controlled, they may claim that "everything is fine"; or 3) disbelieving, showing a disconnect from the crime and difficulty recounting the details.
Step 2	Outward Adjustment Phase	Takes place when the victims try to get back their daily lives	Victims may deal with the effects of the crime by either minimizing or dramatizing the effects of the crime, suppressing feelings, analyzing the assailant's actions, or escaping all elements of their previous life such as jobs or residences.
Step 3	Resolution Phase	Takes place when the crime is no longer the central focus of the victim's life	Although victims do not learn to forget the crime in this phase, they learn to move past the pain of the crime. They are able to accept the rape as an event that occurred and to move forward.

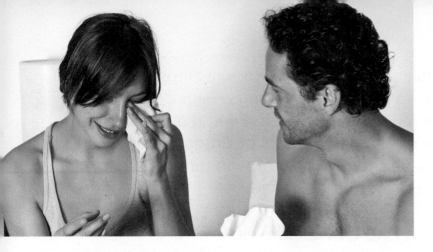

<<< A partner's reactions to rape can be so strong **that he or she takes on the role of the primary victim (Monterey Rape Crisis Center, 2009).**

of the rape, or the victim may avoid social contact with people who are aware of the crime. Intoxicated or incapacitated victims often experience more self-blame, and because of this they tend to avoid talking about their rape experiences (Ullman et al., 2007). **Avoidance strategies** focus on avoiding any thoughts or feelings associated with the sexual violence, as well as any problems that result from the rape (Littleton, Grills-Taquechel, & Axsom, 2009).

WHEN MEN ARE RAPE VICTIMS

Although women are more likely to be victims of rape than men are, in 2008, about 19 percent of sexual assault victims were males who were raped either by males or females (Rand, 2009). Nationally, it is estimated that one in every 33 men has been a victim of attempted or completed rape (U.S. Department of Justice, Bureau of Justice Statistics, 2006). Male sexual assault is almost always perpetrated against minors: 71 percent of

not has no bearing on the effects of her sexual assault. Women who were raped—regardless of how they defined the experiences—reported similar amounts of post-assault psychological distress (McMullin & White, 2006). This is a very important finding, because often women who do not consider their SA rape do not seek counseling, despite the fact that they experience physical and psychological trauma.

Other victims deal with rape by not saying anything at all. **Silent rape reaction** occurs when a victim chooses not to speak about or, in some cases, even acknowledge that the crime even happened (RAINN, 2009c). Victims may quickly change the subject when the conversation turns to a discussion

Healthy Selves / Healthy Sex

Know the Signs of an Abusive Partner

Becky lives in fear. She has been living with her boyfriend, Tony, for three years. They have a child together, and another one is on the way. Instead of enjoying affection and security with her mate, Becky suffers emotional abuse and physical violence. Tragically, she is caught between her love for the way things used to be with Tony and the desire for her and her children to live free from abuse. She wants out, but Tony has threatened great harm, and worse, if she leaves or if the authorities are brought in. Everyone has a right to not be abused in a relationship. *Abuse is not inevitable*, and there are ways to minimize your risk of encountering abuse in your relationships.

Is Your Partner Abusive?

The following are signs that you are in an abusive relationship. Pay attention to these signs; they don't go away, and they don't get better. If he promises it will never happen again, just remember it will.

- **Overly protective mannerisms**: Your boyfriend belittles your friends and tries to keep you from seeing them. He repeatedly asks for detailed descriptions of who you were with, where you went, and why you were with them.

- **Problems with anger**: Trivial and mundane things set him off. He has random and erratic mood swings, putting you at the whim of his emotional states.

- **Rigidity and belligerence**: Instead of a balanced view of relationship roles, he insists on defining the relationship on his terms, and his terms only. He ignores your needs and forges ahead with only his desires in mind.

- **Highly critical**: He is always making comments about your appearance. Healthy relationships are affirming relationships.

If you are currently in an abusive relationship, it is important that you take measures to ensure your own safety and that of any children that are in the home. Finances, counseling, and possible reconciliation are all details that can be worked out later. *It is imperative that you remove yourself from the abuse.*

- Put together a list of people you can call (family, friends, clergy, etc.) when faced with an abusive situation.

- Make known to your list of friends a clue, sign, or code word that will discreetly notify them that you are being abused and need assistance immediately.

- When an argument occurs, find a safe place to have it. Rooms with no exits, kitchens with knives, or rooms without phones are not good places to have an argument with an abusive partner.

Once you have left an abusive situation, seek help to ensure the abuse never happens again. In addition to counseling for you and any children involved, you may want to contact your local law enforcement office for suggestions on personal safety after you have left.
Source: National Coalition Against Domestic Violence. (2005). *Safety plan*. Retrieved February 26, 2010, from www.ncadv.org/protectyourself/SafetyPlan_130.html

men who indicated they were raped were victims of the crime before age 18; about half were younger than 12 (Tjaden & Thoennes, 2006).

The rape and sexual violence experiences of men are often marginalized and neglected, because it is a cultural assumption that men can "fend" for themselves. This stigma is the result of the myths and stereotypes associated with male-victim rape, including the beliefs that men are immune to victimization and that men always enjoy sex no matter what the circumstances. Because these myths are commonly accepted as truth, male victims of rape may not report the crime or may have difficulty dealing with the traumatic effects of their victimization. These myths may also be why there is such limited research about male victims of rape (Masho & Anderson, 2009).

In a recent study of male sexual assault victims, the researchers found that, similar to women, a significant number of men (68 percent) were raped by an intimate partner, friend, or someone that they knew (Masho & Anderson, 2009). The study found that common reactions to male sexual assault include depression and suicidal thoughts. Unlike women, however, men typically do not seek counseling for their depression. Men who have been sexually victimized may also experience feelings of shame, anger, or guilt; exaggerated self-blame; dramatic loss of self-esteem or sense of masculinity; sexual difficulties; self-destructive behavior; and symptoms associated with rape trauma syndrome (U.S. Department of Justice, 2003).

In instances of rape involving a heterosexual male victim and a male assailant, the victim may have more difficulty recovering from the crime due to possible feelings of being less of a man or fear that the attack will turn him into a homosexual. In the same respect, homosexual male victims may cultivate feelings that they are being punished for their sexual orientation, adding an additional level of victimization (U.S. Department of Justice, 2003). Women perpetrators, similar to male offenders, use a wide array of tactics to sexually assault their victims: seduction of unwilling partners, manipulation, alcohol and/or drugs, and the use of physical force (Schatzel-Murphy et al., 2009).

REPORTING A RAPE

Reporting rape is a vital and necessary part of preventing sexual assault. It not only helps imprison rapists that may attack again, but it also helps provide more information to public safety officials that can eventually lead to better rape-prevention programs.

Rape victims are not required to inform police about the crime. They may only confide in friends or family about the crime or tell no one at all.

If a victim chooses to report the crime, he or she can do so at virtually any time. The laws that specify the time within which victims must take judicial action vary from state to state, but typically last for several years. The chances of apprehending and prosecuting the criminal, however, decrease the longer the victim waits to report the crime.

If you or a loved one is raped, immediately call 911, the local police, or the campus police. If you do not want to call the police, immediately go to the nearest hospital emergency room; health care personnel will alert law enforcement. It is important that the victim does not discard any evidence. It is also vitally important that the victim does not shower, wash her or his hands or face, or change her or his clothing. Things that are not visible to her or him may provide valuable evidence.

The hospital will perform a sexual assault forensic examination, commonly referred to as a *rape kit*. This step is important to the prosecution process because there may be physical evidence such as semen, hair, or fibers that might connect the rapist to the crime; all of these improve the chances of a conviction. Women will be given emergency contraception and will be tested for STIs about two weeks after the assault. They will also be tested for HIV about three months after the attack.

The police will obtain a statement from the victim. Although this is a difficult process for most victims, it is necessary for prosecution. This entire process may take several hours. At the victim's request, the social worker or counselor will call the victim's family members, a significant other, a friend, or members of the clergy. Today, many campuses have advocates who help the rape victim navigate the process—first at the hospital and in the later months to come.

Sexual violence is traumatic and devastating for victims and their loved ones, and it is an experience that leaves emotional scars. Navigating the experiences of sexual assault is often a long and arduous journey. If you're a sexual assault survivor, surround yourself with people who love you, and access community resources for information, counseling, and support.

Another type of violence to address is violence against intimate partners.

RELATIONSHIP VIOLENCE

Violence that takes place between intimate partners (see Tables 17.3 and 17.4) is a prevalent, multifaceted social ailment in the U.S. It happens among gay and straight couples as well as young and elderly.

TABLE 17.3
Categories of Intimate Partner Violence

There are four broad categories of IPV (CDC, 2009c):

- *Physical violence* includes such acts as hitting, punching, pushing, slapping, biting, or throwing something at the victim.

- *Emotional violence* includes such acts as controlling the amount of contact a family member has with family and friends, name-calling, constant criticism, threats to leave the partner or throw him or her out, displays of intense jealousy/accusations that one is being unfaithful, controlling the spending and distribution of money, excessive rule-making, and threats of physical or sexual harm.

- *Sexual violence* includes marital rape, battering rape, and forced sexual acts.

- *Threats* of physical or sexual violence include the use of words, gestures, or weapons.

TABLE 17.4
Partner Rape

When IPV involves sexual abuse it is referred to as **partner rape**. There are three main types of partner rape (Based on Texas Association Against Sexual Assault, 2009):

- **Battering rape**: rape along with other acts of physical violence.

- **Forced sexual acts**: the perpetrator asserts power over the victim by forcing her or him into certain sexual acts.

- **Obsessive/sadistic rape**: the abuse involves torture and perverse sexual acts and can lead to physical injury (Based on Texas Association Against Sexual Assault, 2009).

Intimate partner rape can result in the same physical injuries associated with other types of rape including bruises, broken bones, physical pain, and reproductive problems. It can also involve the same emotional injuries, including shock, depression, posttraumatic stress disorder, and thoughts of suicide. Victims of intimate partner abuse may also suffer from feelings of betrayal and a loss of trust in the individuals who are close to them.

INTIMATE PARTNER VIOLENCE

Intimate partner violence (IPV) is an umbrella term that encompasses any behavior that intentionally inflicts harm on a partner (married or unmarried, a previous partner, or cohabiting partner). People sometimes refer to IPV as *domestic violence*, although this term also encompasses physical violence perpetrated against children. Demographers measure IPV in two ways: through survey interviews with the victims and through statistics gathered by police. The statistics are staggering:

- In 2007, IPV accounted for nearly one-fourth of all violent crimes against females and 3 percent against males (U.S. Department of Justice, Bureau of Justice Statistics, 2007).

- 15 percent of teens in relationships report being hit, slapped, or pushed by a boyfriend or girlfriend (Teen Research Unlimited, 2006).

- In 2008, IPV was the cause of 35 percent of female murder victims and 2 percent of male murder victims (FBI, 2009). Each day in the United States, four women become murder victims of their intimate partners.

- In 2007, more than 3,000 lesbians, gays, bisexuals, or transgender people (LGBT) reported that they were victims of crimes committed by their intimate partners (National Coalition of Anti-Violence Programs, 2008).

- 47 percent of LGBT IPV victims are male, 48 percent are female, and 5 percent are transgender (National Coalition of Anti-Violence Programs, 2008).

Although no one is immune from violence, there are specific factors that place some at a greater risk for experiencing violence than others. In the next sections we'll look at those who are harmed—the battered—and those who harm—the batterers.

THE BATTERED

Women who have less education, come from a lower socioeconomic status, or are single parents or young teenage parents are more likely to be victims of violence (National Coalition Against Domestic Violence, 2008). Also, women who have witnessed a parent being battered experience a higher risk of being victims themselves. Generally, women who have low self-esteem, feel a sense of inferiority, are passive, or believe that they are responsible for the batterer's actions are more likely to be abused.

No gender or racial/ethnic group is immune from violence, as the data in Figure 17.5 illustrate. Although women are victimized more frequently than men, women perpetrate about 3 million acts of IPV against men every year (National Coalition Against Domestic Violence, 2008). In addition, intimate

Figure 17.5   IPV by Race/Ethnicity and Gender

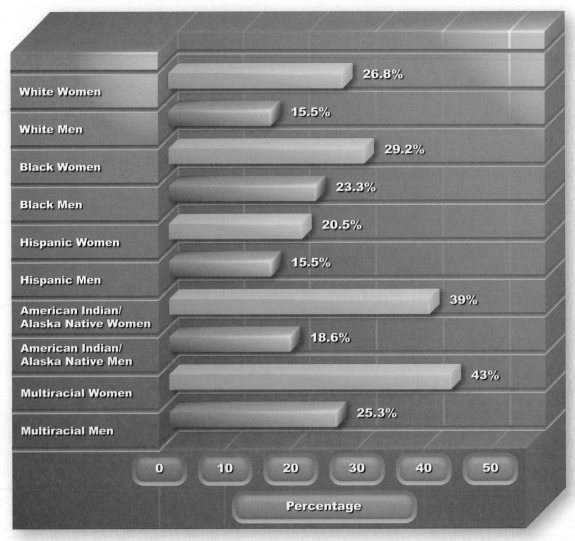

White Women	26.8%
White Men	15.5%
Black Women	29.2%
Black Men	23.3%
Hispanic Women	20.5%
Hispanic Men	15.5%
American Indian/Alaska Native Women	39%
American Indian/Alaska Native Men	18.6%
Multiracial Women	43%
Multiracial Men	25.3%

Percentage: 0 10 20 30 40 50

Source: Centers for Disease Control (2009d).

Figure 17.6 Primary Populations Served by Abuse Shelters

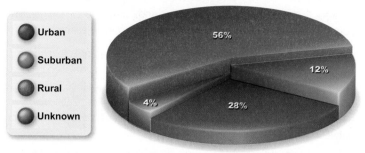

- Urban
- Suburban
- Rural
- Unknown

56%
12%
4%
28%

Source: National Network to End Domestic Violence (2007).

partner violence crosses every socioeconomic and educational level and every family type, including married, single-parent, gay, straight, and cohabiting families. In America, one in four women and one in nine men suffers physical and/or emotional violence at the hands of an intimate partner (CDC, 2008). Females who are 20 to 24 years of age are at the greatest risk of intimate partner violence (U.S. Department of Justice, 2009); however, as shown in Figure 17.6, women in rural areas seek the services of domestic violence shelters more than women from suburban or urban areas.

These trends are alarming. But *why* do people batter? What are the characteristics of those who abuse their family members? We'll examine these questions in the following section.

THE BATTERER

Those who abuse their partners share some common characteristics (see Figure 17.7). The National Coalition Against Domestic Violence (2008) notes that most batterers have low self-esteem and tend to blame everyone else for their behaviors. Batterers are also typically extremely jealous and often use sex as their weapon of aggression and ultimate instrument of control. Although violence is the way they express their anger or frustration, they underestimate or even deny that their behaviors are violent or harmful. Batterers have the need to

Figure 17.7 The Power and Control Wheel

Minnesota Program Development, Inc. interviewed hundreds of battered and sexually abused women to better understand how the men in their lives controlled them. **The Power and Control Wheel depicts behaviors that batterers use to dominate their intimate partners and/or children.**

control and dominate, and they become master manipulators—they can manipulate their partners' weaknesses and their strengths.

There is a common misconception that IPV results from an argument that "got out of hand," then escalated into physical blows. Most often, this is not the case. Many abused women note that the violence appeared to have no trigger or cause and appeared to come out of the blue. Another common misconception is that alcohol use or substance abuse is almost always associated with acts of family violence. In the 5.3 million cases of intimate partner or domestic violence in a five-year period in the United States, more than one-half of the victims indicated that there was no drug or alcohol use by the family offender (Durose et al., 2005). On the surface, domestic violence appears to be acts of physical, emotional, or sexual aggression against a victim, but the central issues in IPV are not the acts of aggression at all. Rather, the central issues of domestic violence are *control* and *domination* and are commonly perpetuated by the stronger against the weaker (McGoldrick, Broken Nose, & Potenza, 1999).

THE CYCLE OF VIOLENCE

In 1979, a professor of psychological studies, Lenore Walker, pioneered research that resulted in her **cycle of violence model**. Although not every abusive relationship experiences every phase of this cycle in every instance of abuse, Walker's research shows how abusive relationships are cyclical in nature.

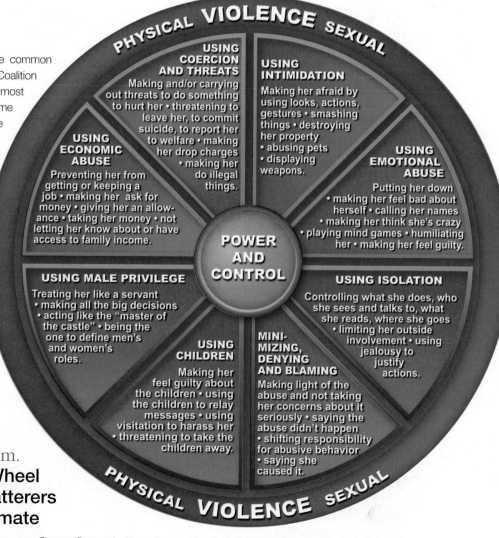

Source: Domestic Abuse Intervention Project, 202 E. Superior Street, Deluth, MN 55802.

What Constitutes Sexual Coercion?

Mark and Ann have been dating since college, and when they graduated last year, Mark asked Ann to marry him. They are engaged now and living together, and to add to Ann's busy wedding planning schedule, she recently began a new job. She enjoys her job, but the hours are long and the work is demanding. When she comes home, she is exhausted, and the last thing she's in the mood for is sex. But just because Ann is too tired for sex doesn't mean that Mark is. He feels that as Ann's significant other, he is justified in demanding sex whenever he feels like it. He believes that as Ann's future husband, it is not considered coercion if he demands that Ann has sex with him even if she doesn't want to. Ann wants to keep him happy, but she also doesn't want to get in trouble for dozing off at her desk at her first job.

His side: I love Ann, and I know she knows that. That's why I asked her to marry me. But part of a woman's job is to keep her man happy. I know she says she's just tired from working, but when she doesn't want to have sex with me, it makes me feel like she doesn't want me anymore, and that makes me second guess our plans to get married. I've never been violent with her, and I would never hurt her. Still, I don't think our sex life should be limited just to the weekends.

Her side: It's not personal. The last thing I want is to lose him. I really am just tired, but I still love him. And I thought our relationship was based on more than just sex. When we stay up late together, I sometimes oversleep and am less functional at work. But I realize relationships are based on compromise; I just wish we could find some kind of balance between what he wants and what I want.

Your side: With whom do you more strongly identify: Mark or Ann? What would you do if you were in this same situation? Is a compromise possible?

1. Do you think that Mark is correct in believing that he has a right to Ann's body simply because they're in a relationship?

2. If Mark and Ann get married, and Mark persuades her to have sex when she doesn't want to, do you consider that rape or sexual coercion? Why or why not?

3. Have you ever engaged in a sexual behavior at a time when you didn't want to?

The cycle of violence, shown in Figure 17.8, illustrates three phases of violence commonly seen in abusive relationships: the *tension-building* phase, the *acute battering* or violent act, and the *respite* (nonviolent) phase.

- **Tension-building**: The victim senses that an explosive, violent incident is about to take place. The batterer begins to isolate his partner, threaten her, slap her, belittle her, and withdraw affection. As the victim begins to feel tension and fear, her fear builds, and in response, she tries to keep her partner calm and happy by being agreeable, nurturing, and kind. All of her efforts have one goal: to keep the batterer from becoming violent. The psychological anguish may become so unbearable that many women antagonize or provoke the batterer to "just get it over with."

- **Acute battering incident**: Savage. Destructive. Out of control. Brutal. The violence from the tension-building phase escalates into an acute battering incident in which the violence can become deadly. The battered woman cannot control when the episode will end. The victim usually does not fight back. If she attempts to leave, she is at a greater risk of being killed by her partner.

- **Respite phase**: This is often called the loving phase or the "honeymoon" or "flower" phase because the abuser apologizes profusely. He may cry, beg for forgiveness, and vow that he will never harm her again. He will often give her gifts to express his regret and lavish her with attention and love. For instance, Brooke Mueller called 911 in December 2009 asking them to save her from her husband, actor Charlie Sheen, who had been holding a knife to her throat. Once he was arrested, Mueller asked law enforcement to drop the charges, a common example of the behavior of a battered woman in the respite stage. The battered woman's renewed sense of hope leads her to believe that it won't happen again. But it will.

Figure 17.8 Lenore Walker's Cycle of Violence

Source: Walker, (1979).

>>> Brooke Mueller and Charlie Sheen

CHILD SEXUAL ABUSE

Much like the sexual abuse of an adult, child sexual abuse involves unwanted sexual contact. **Child sexual abuse (CSA)** is any sexual activity that a child cannot consent to (American Academy of Pediatrics, 2010). In cases of child sexual abuse, the sexual contact is often achieved through force, trickery, or bribery and involves an imbalance in age, size, power, and knowledge. Sexual contact can include fondling of the breasts, buttocks, or genitals; vaginal, anal, or oral intercourse; exhibitionism; forced masturbation or forced viewing of masturbation; obscene gestures or comments; prostitution; or any other sexual activity that is harmful to the child's mental, emotional, or physical welfare (Finkelhor et al., 2009). When these forms of abuse are inflicted on a child by a relative, it is **incest**.

HOW ARE CHILDREN AFFECTED?

Children are greatly affected both physically and emotionally by sexual assault and abuse. Unfortunately, it is not easy to recognize an abused child. Often, children are afraid to tell anyone because they fear they may be blamed, or because the abuser is someone whom they love. Also, it often goes unreported or overlooked for long periods of time due to the child's inability to understand what is happening. CSA is often overlooked because of an adult's inability to notice the signs of abuse or unwillingness to admit that the abuse took place (American Academy of Pediatrics, 2010). Who is more likely to sexually abuse children? Risk factors include adult mental health issues or depression, a parental history of childhood abuse, and intimate partner violence (American Academy of Pediatrics, 2010). Table 17.5 presents the physical and emotional signs that a child has been abused.

The effects of CSA are often long-term. Later on, those who are sexually victimized may turn to alcohol and drugs as coping mechanisms, and a sexually abused child/adolescent may run away or abuse others. As an adult, CSA survivors sometimes develop sexual and relationship difficulties, depression, or suicidal behaviors (Child Welfare Information Gateway, 2009). The younger the child is at the age of abuse, the longer the CSA continues, and the closer the child's relationship with his or her abuser, the more significant the long-term emotional damage will be.

HELPING VICTIMS HEAL

Helping a child heal from sexual abuse can be a difficult task, especially for non-abusing parents. They are often so overcome by feelings of shock, anger, sadness, and guilt that they are unable to be a stable source of support for their child (American Academy of Pediatrics, 2010). Organizations such as Safe Harbor, which serves more than 350,000 victims of violence each year, offer families individual and group counseling. Although the emotional scars never go away completely or become invisible, counselors help reduce some of the impact of the CSA. If a parent, caregiver, teacher, youth group leader, family friend, or community member suspects that a child has been sexually abused, the individual should immediately contact the local child protective agency or a pediatrician. Doctors, health care providers, and social services can help coordinate a treatment plan that includes medical treatment for physical injuries, as well as counseling that addresses behavioral and emotional consequences.

SEXUAL LIFE EDUCATION

Although sex can be an expression of love and a pleasurable experience for many, it can also be used as a weapon in cases of sexual coercion, rape, and abuse. Rapists are sometimes random strangers, but most of the time they are not.

Different people have different perceptions about what rape is and how it should be handled. If you or someone you know has been sexually assaulted, first know that sexual assault is *never the fault of the victim. Ever*. After a sexual assault, the Rape, Abuse, & Incest National Network (2009d) suggests taking the following steps:

- **Find a safe environment** anywhere away from the attacker.

- **Report the attack** to police by calling 911. If you want more information, a counselor on the National Sexual Assault Hotline at 1-800-656-HOPE can help you understand the process; this organization also provides free, confidential counseling 24 hours a day.

- **Preserve evidence of the attack**. Don't bathe or brush your teeth.

- **Get medical attention**. Even with no physical injuries, it is important to determine the risks of STIs and pregnancy.

Just as one person views sexual assault differently than the next, one victim is affected differently than the next. The effects of sexual assault can be debilitating and long lasting, regardless of the victim's age, sex, or relation to the attacker.

Healing from sexual assault takes time. If you, a loved one, or a friend has been victimized, give yourself/the victim all the time necessary, and remember there are professionals available to help victims navigate the process.

TABLE 17.5
Signs and Symptoms of CSA

In 2007, 6 percent of children and youth from birth to 17 years were victims of sexual assault (Child Maltreatment, 2007). Over one-half of victimized children ages 6 to 11 knew their perpetrators; in those ages 12 to 17, two-thirds knew their offenders. Strangers are the least likely perpetrators of sexual assault against children; only 3 to 11 percent of victims are sexually assaulted by strangers (Finkelhor and others, 2009). There are a number of physical and emotional signs of child sexual abuse (Child Welfare Gateway Information 2007).

Genital pain or bleeding

Sexually transmitted disease

Fearful behavior (nightmares, depression, unusual fears)

Abdominal pain, bed-wetting

Attempts to run away

Inappropriate sexual behavior for the child's age

Sudden change in self-confidence

Headaches or stomachaches with no medical cause

Abnormal fears

School failure

Extremely passive or aggressive behavior

Desperately affectionate behavior or social withdrawal

Summary

WHAT IS SEXUAL CONSENT?   359

- Sexual consent encompasses the words or actions we use to show our voluntary, freely given agreement to engage in mutually agreed-upon sexual activities. Agreeing to one sex act does not necessarily imply consent for other sexual activities or future sexual activities, and consent is not viable if a person is incapacitated or powerless to give it.

WHO RAPES AND HOW DOES RAPE AFFECT THE VICTIM?   361

- Rape is oral, anal, or vaginal intercourse or other forms of penetration by one person with or against another person, the victim, without the consent of the victim. Legally, there are different types of rape from forcible to statutory, and these definitions vary by state. It's impossible to characterize all rapists, but they tend to be longtime criminals and have a certain number of risk factors in common. Rapists often fall into the categories of anger rapists, power rapists, sadistic rapists, and they often know their victims.
- Men and women tend to hold different ideas about what constitutes rape, and attitudes toward rape vary across races and ethnicities. The prevalence of alcohol and drug use often contributes to higher rates of rape on college campuses. Many rape victims experience rape trauma syndrome, a form of posttraumatic stress disorder, and every victim copes in his or her own way.

WHAT ARE THE CHARACTERISTICS OF INTIMATE PARTNER VIOLENCE?   367

- Violence that takes place between intimate partners is a prevalent, multifaceted social ailment in the United States, and it's present among people of all different races, ethnicities, religions, ages, and sexual orientations. It can include physical violence, emotional violence, sexual violence, and threats. Battered women often experience a cycle of violence, in which the hope that their partners will change keeps renewing the relationship.

WHAT ARE THE EFFECTS OF SEXUAL ABUSE ON CHILDREN?   371

- Child sexual abuse is any sexual activity to which a child cannot consent. The sexual contact is often achieved through force, trickery, or bribery and involves an imbalance in age, size, power, and knowledge. The effects of CSA vary depending on the age of the child during the abuse, the length of the abuse, and the relationship between the child and his or her abuser, but the impacts are often both short term and long term, and have a detrimental impact on the child's life.

Key Terms

sexual coercion the use of verbal pressure or physical force to engage in a sexual activity with someone who is unwilling   *358*

sexual violence (SV), sexual assault (SA) sexual activity in which consent is not obtained or freely given; an intentional act that can occur in any of these ways: a) the perpetrator ignores the objections of the other person; b) the offender intentionally causes the victim's intoxication or impairment through the use of drugs or alcohol; and/or c) the perpetrator takes advantage of someone's incapacitation, feelings of intimidation, helplessness, or any other ability to consent   *358*

verbal sexual assault acts such as catcalls, sexual innuendoes, or any other remarks that are sexual in nature and cause unwanted attention toward the victim   *358*

sexual misconduct crime in which the offender did not intend to harm the other person and he or she unreasonably believed that consent was given; however, the offender did not meet his or her responsibility to gain consent   *360*

sexual consent the words or actions we use to show our voluntary, freely given agreement to engage in mutually agreed-upon sexual activities   *360*

rape oral, anal, or vaginal intercourse or other forms of penetration by one person with or against another person (the victim) without the consent of the victim   *361*

forcible rape attempted or completed rape   *362*

statutory rape intercourse by an adult with a person below a legally designated age   *362*

anger rapist uses more force than necessary; motivation comes from the anger or rage he or she feels for the victim or for the person the victim represents   *362*

power rapist needs to assert strength and dominance over the victim   *362*

sadistic rapist has an erotic association with violence   *362*

date rape or **acquaintance rape** a criminal act that is perpetrated by a social acquaintance, a friend, or a dating or intimate partner of the victim   *362*

rape scripts information about the types of conduct that make up "rape," conduct and characteristics of "perpetrators," and the sequence of events that take place in a rape   *363*

party rape rape that occurs as the result of alcohol and/or drug intoxication; occurs more frequently at "party-oriented" schools   *364*

drug-facilitated assault when drugs or alcohol are used to compromise an individual's ability to consent to sexual activity or to minimize the resistance or memory of the victim   *364*

diminished capacity when a person does not have the ability to give consent due to the influence of drugs or alcohol   *364*

Rohypnol (roofies, date rape drug) one of the most common drugs used in sexual assault *365*

Federal Clery Act (Student Right-to-Know or Campus Security Act) passed in an effort to decrease the rate of sexual assaults on campus and to improve student awareness *365*

rape trauma syndrome (RTS) a form of PTSD that occurs in victims of rape and has three phases *365*

silent rape reaction situation in which a victim chooses not to speak about or, in some cases, even acknowledge that the rape even happened *366*

avoidance strategies strategies to avoid any thoughts or feelings associated with the sexual violence, as well as any problems that result from the rape *366*

partner rape intimate partner violence that involves sexual abuse *367*

battering rape rape along with other acts of physical violence *367*

forced sexual acts sexual assault in which the perpetrator asserts power over the victim by forcing him or her into certain sexual acts *367*

obsessive/sadistic rape abuse involving torture and perverse sexual acts and can lead to physical injury *367*

intimate partner violence (IPV) term that encompasses any behavior that intentionally inflicts harm on a partner (married or unmarried, a previous partner, or cohabiting partner) *368*

Power and Control Wheel depiction of behaviors that batterers use to control and dominate their intimate partners and/or children *369*

cycle of violence model cycle consisting of three phases of violence commonly seen in abusive relationships: the tension-building phase, the acute battering or violent act, and the respite (non-violent) phase *369*

child sexual abuse (CSA) any sexual activity to which a child cannot consent *371*

incest form of abuse inflicted on a child by a relative *371*

Sample Test Questions

MULTIPLE CHOICE

1. When was marital rape first declared a crime?
   a. 1970
   b. 1975
   c. 1984
   d. 1993

2. According to Groth, which type of rapist has a need to assert strength and dominance over the victim?
   a. Sadistic rapist
   b. Forcible rapist
   c. Power rapist
   d. Anger rapist

3. The majority of rapes occur in:
   a. The victims' residences
   b. The rapists' residences
   c. Fraternities
   d. Other housing areas

4. Which date rape drug is most commonly used in sexual assault?
   a. GHB
   b. Rohypnol
   c. GBL
   d. Ecstasy

5. During which phase of rape trauma syndrome do victims move past the pain of the crime?
   a. Acute phase
   b. Respite phase
   c. Outward adjustment phase
   d. Resolution phase

6. Constant criticism can be a characteristic of which category of intimate partner violence?
   a. Physical violence
   b. Emotional violence
   c. Sexual violence
   d. Threats

7. Which phase of the Cycle of Violence gives the battered hope that the batterer will change for the better?
   a. Intimidation phase
   b. Acute battering incident
   c. Respite phase
   d. Tension-building phase

8. Which term describes child sexual abuse inflicted on a child by a relative?
   a. Sexual coercion
   b. Incest
   c. Sexual misconduct
   d. Intimate partner violence

SHORT RESPONSE

1. What is required for consent? When is consent not viable?
2. Explain the differences between forcible rape and statutory rape.
3. What are rape scripts? What do you think your rape script is?
4. Describe some of the reasons women may stay silent about having been raped.
5. What are some of the ways a male rape victim may cope with the crime?

Answers: 1. b; 2. c; 3. a; 4. b; 5. d; 6. b; 7. c; 8. b

Remember to check www.thethinkspot.com **for additional information, downloadable flashcards, and other helpful resources.**

PLAYBOY

$ELLING $EX:
The Sex Industry and Sex Work

WHAT ROLES HAVE EROTICA AND PORNOGRAPHY PLAYED THROUGHOUT HISTORY, AND HOW HAVE THEY CHANGED?

HOW IS SEX AND SEXUALITY PORTRAYED IN THE MEDIA?

WHO BECOMES A PROSTITUTE?

HOW HAS HUMAN SEXUAL TRAFFICKING BECOME A DOMESTIC AND GLOBAL PROBLEM?

I'm

25 years old, a college graduate, and I'm starting my career as an architect. I don't consider myself much of a ladies' man, but I do think I'm normal. I've had four significant relationships in my lifetime, and right now I'm in a steady relationship with [my girlfriend].

I think the first time I saw *Playboy* I was 11 or 12 . . . my brother and I found it hidden in the back of my dad's closet (an entire stack of them!). But of course, the *Sports Illustrated* swimsuit edition was in our house for as long as I can remember (but I don't know if anyone necessarily considers that to be "porn"). I "came of age" in the 1990s, about the time families began to have personal computers in their homes. I found it very easy to access porn sites on the Web . . . it was a lot easier than sneaking into my parents' bedroom and looking at the mags!

Today I subscribe to *Maxim* and *Playboy*. I consider *Maxim* a lifestyle magazine, kind of like my girlfriend's *Cosmo*, so I usually keep that out in the living room. But I keep the *Playboy* magazine in my bedroom or the bathroom, because I do think that's porn. My girlfriend and I disagree on this, though—she thinks they are both types of pornography. My question to her is, if she thinks my magazines are porn, what about her calendar with 12 months of nearly nude Matthew McConaughey pictures? Isn't that porn, too?

Other than the magazines, sometimes I'll watch some porn on cable or hit a few free porn sites on the Internet. And sometimes my girlfriend and I will watch movies that are sexually explicit. [My girlfriend] doesn't really like watching movies that have sexual content. She says porn flicks embarrass her and make her uncomfortable, and she thinks they are demeaning to women. But she doesn't care if I watch them because she thinks that's typical for guys my age.

So, to answer your question, "What is porn?" I think I would have to say that porn is whatever the person thinks it is. Really conservative people might think that the *Sports Illustrated* swimsuit edition is porn, and really liberal people might think that anything goes.

Source: Author's files

CHAPTER **18**

Today, perhaps one of the most polarizing sociological issues the United States faces is its booming sex industry. The **sex industry** refers to the commercial enterprises or businesses related to selling or purchasing sex-related services. The industry is often referred to as **adult entertainment**. It employs people who provide sexual services, such as prostitutes, escorts, pornography models, actors who engage in sexual behaviors that are filmed, phone and Web cam sex, and erotic dancers. In 1980, activist Carol Leigh coined the term **sex worker** to describe those who work in the sex industry (Weitzer, 2000). Today, sex workers are commonly referred to as *adult service providers (ASP)* or *adult sex providers*.

In this chapter we'll examine the sex industry in the U.S. First, we'll explore the history of pornography and erotica. We'll then briefly look at theories about the sex industry and then turn our attention to sexuality on television, in advertising, and in other forms of media, such as music and the Internet. Next, we'll examine whether the sex industry should be censored. Before we conclude, we'll focus on the age-old concerns associated with prostitution, and then we'll discuss a new area of concern, human sex trafficking.

EROTICA THROUGHOUT HISTORY

Depictions of sex and sexuality intended for sexual arousal are certainly not something unique to the 20th and 21st centuries; many examples date back thousands of years ago (Hyde, 1964). **Erotica** is literature or art that is intended to arouse sexual desire. The term *erotica*, however, typically applies to works in which the sexual elements are regarded as part of the larger aesthetic characteristic. For example, the *Kama Sutra* dates back to fifth century BCE. Other famous works, such as the Persian lyric poems known as ghazals, the 16th-century Chinese novel *Chin p'ing*, William Shakespeare's novel *Venus and Adonis*, and the many writings of French nobleman Marquis de Sade are also considered erotic.

EARLY EROTICA: ARTISTIC AND PHILOSOPHICAL

Eroticism in artwork also dates back to ancient times. The erotic representations found in Hindu and Buddhist artwork from 700 to 1200 BCE were closely connected to the ideas of fertility and Tantrism, a mystical Buddhist philosophy. The erotic scenes found on the walls of ancient Hindu temples were used to encourage sexual activity and reproduction ("India," 2009).

Rococo-style eroticism emerged in the 18th century with the works of French painters Nicolas Lancret and Jean-Baptiste Pater. The paintings were decorative with delicate sketch-like techniques and wistful images of sexual fantasies. Works from this period were playful and seductive and were often admired for both their beauty and their ability to be sexually arousing ("Western painting," 2009).

MODERN EROTICA: SEXUALLY AROUSING

Mainstream erotic art (see Figure 18.1) took the form of illustrations in the late 19th century with the introduction of the Gibson Girls, the creation of American illustrator Charles Dana Gibson. The models were tall and slender with a sophisticated, sensual appeal, representing the feminine ideal of beauty and refinement.

To "please" the men of the era, in the late 1800s, photographs of women's backsides, heterosexual sex acts, and lesbian sex were produced. In 1870, the first pornography postcard was created using these pictures, and from 1890 until the 1930s these types of postcards were popular. They were the first type of mass-produced and distributed "lewd" images (Hyde, 1964).

Not surprisingly, the stuffy attitudes of the Victorians did not jibe with the production and consumption of erotica. Legislation in the 19th century outlawed the publication and retail of what the Victorians deemed pornography (Beck, 2003). The Comstock laws (see Chapter 13) came about in the late 1800s. These laws not only made it illegal to send information about contraceptives and abortion through the mail, but sending "obscene, lewd, and/or lascivious materials" by mail was also criminalized (Boyer, 2002).

Many of these works of erotic art were the forerunners to the modern pinup girl. One of the original pinup photos, a 1943 image of film actress Betty Grable in a bathing suit, with a "hello, boys" smile, had thousands of men saying "hello" right back. The image of the leggy blonde could be found in boys' bedrooms and footlockers across the country. It was even posted in the cockpit of bomber planes (*Betty Grable*, 2009).

And while Grable was posing in her swimsuit, camera clubs were springing up across the United States in the 1940s. Although these clubs claimed they existed to promote the artistry of photographs, they were actually underground organizations created to circumvent the legal restrictions on nude photos (Hyde, 1964).

In 1953, actress Marilyn Monroe became famous when she posed for the first edition of *Playboy* and became the publication's first *Playboy Bunny*. The pinup became even more risqué in 1954 when Bettie Page took the idea of a man's physical ideal and added to it the elements of sexual fantasy, fetish, and S&M. Known as the first bondage model, the extra dose

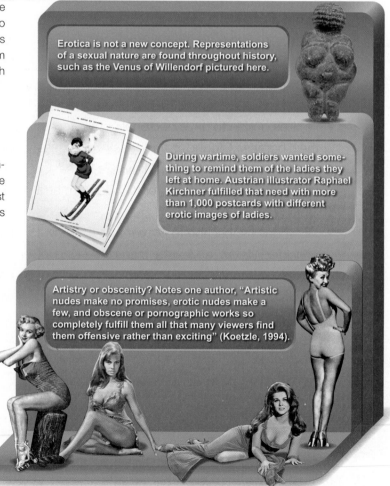

Erotica is not a new concept. Representations of a sexual nature are found throughout history, such as the Venus of Willendorf pictured here.

During wartime, soldiers wanted something to remind them of the ladies they left at home. Austrian illustrator Raphael Kirchner fulfilled that need with more than 1,000 postcards with different erotic images of ladies.

Artistry or obscenity? Notes one author, "Artistic nudes make no promises, erotic nudes make a few, and obscene or pornographic works so completely fulfill them all that many viewers find them offensive rather than exciting" (Koetzle, 1994).

Figure 18.1 Erotica Throughout Time

of sex that Page added to these photos moved them from being erotic to pornographic. From there, a $57 billion global industry was born.

PORNOGRAPHY OR OBSCENITY?

"I can't define pornography," a judge once said, "but I know it when I see it" (Justice Stewart in *Jacobellis v. Ohio* 378 US 184 [1964]). What is pornography? Is it art that portrays a sensual and philosophical aesthetic? Or is it offensive and demeaning?

PORNOGRAPHY: SEXUALLY STIMULATING

Pornography, **porn**, and **porno** are popular terms for printed or visual material that contain explicit descriptions of sexual organs or activities with the intention of stimulating erotic feelings. Unlike erotica, which is intended for both sexual and aesthetic appeal, pornography is meant solely for sexual appeal. But who determines whether something has aesthetic appeal? One person may look at a photo in *Playboy* and see artistic qualities, while another person may see only an object of sexual gratification.

One way that people distinguish pornography from obscenity is by defining what type of porn the material portrays. **Soft-core pornography**, also referred to as *soft porn*, shows more indirect and non-graphic sexual images. Most images of pinup models in the 1950s are considered soft porn. Although pornographic magazines like *Playboy* had been part of mainstream society since the 1950s, the sweeping changes ushered in by the sexual revolution in the 1960s and 1970s gave way for pornography to take more far-reaching forms in subsequent decades.

Unlike soft porn, **hard-core pornography**, or *hard porn*, shows direct and explicit sexual images.

^
^ *Deep Throat* **was the**
^ **story of a woman looking to satisfy her sexual desires.**

^
^ In 1991, Paul Reubens was arrested
^ for masturbating in an adult movie
theater in Florida. **Successful as Pee-wee Herman, his career took a hit when his arrest was publicized.**

In the United States, hard porn took the form of a feature film in 1972 with the release of *Deep Throat*. The storyline and dialogue in the movie are largely overshadowed by the graphic sexual sequences, which showed penetration as the main actress engaged in sexual intercourse with several male characters. This display of penetration and ejaculation, referred to in the porn industry as the *money shot*, is what distinguishes *Deep Throat* as hard-core pornography from soft porn, such as *Playboy* (Gubar & Hoff, 1989).

Child pornography refers to sexually explicit photographs, videos, films, or audio of prepubescent children; these images often depict explicit sex acts involving children (Wortley & Smallbone, 2006). Because children are sexually abused, in 2008, the World Congress III against the Sexual Exploitation of Children and Adolescents adopted the term **child abuse images**. "This is to reflect the seriousness of the phenomenon and to emphasize that pornographic images of children are in fact records of a crime being committed" (Mathew, 2009). Although the production and distribution of child porn is illegal in all Western societies, it is a multi-billion dollar industry, particularly on the Internet (Ferraro et al., 2004). Those who are found in possession of child pornography face criminal charges that usually include imprisonment (Yaman, 2008).

AMERICA: PORN NATION

Both soft- and hard-core pornography have become widely accepted in the United States and abroad. Although the sex industry is a $57 billion dollar industry worldwide (Adult Video News, 2006), the United States is the "pornography capital of the world," generating about $20 billion per year: America produces and consumes more porn than any other nation (Procida & Simon, 2003). The reason for this growth is multifaceted.

With advances in technology such as VCRs, DVD players, and the Internet, people no longer have to go to a porn theater to view adult films (Leung, 2004). And, yes, there is an app for that: with the advent of *Pink Visuals*, people can access porn on their iPhones. As Figure 18.2 shows

Source: AVN (2006).

Figure 18.2 Distribution of Pornographic Films

us, DVD sales and rentals account for the majority of pornography consumed in the United States.

Pornography consumption has skyrocketed in the past decade, due in large part to the growth of the Internet. There are currently 4.2 million pornographic Web sites and 40 million Americans who regularly visit them (Family Safe Media, 2009). Watching pornography seems to be the most popular American pastime; currently, porn revenues are larger than the combined revenues of all professional football, baseball, and basketball franchises (Family Safe Media, 2009). The Internet would generate even more profit if all pornographic Web sites generated revenue. Although many may assume that viewing pornography is a typically male behavior, one in three adult Web visitors is a woman. The increasing prevalence of pornography has lifted some, but not all, of the stigma placed on women who view pornography; 70 percent of those women who visit adult Web sites still keep their sexual cyber activity a secret (Family Safe Media, 2009). Because of these advances in media, porn has become more popular and more mainstream (Leung, 2004).

Still, what is the difference between pornography and obscenity?

OBSCENITY: OFFENSIVE AND DISGUSTING

The line between erotica and pornography is often determined by what is decent and what is obscene. Around the time the sex industry began to gain popularity, the U.S. Supreme Court established the obscenity standard. As with other aspects of sex and sexuality, the Supreme Court's definition of "obscenity" has changed over time, as has the differing views on pornography of younger generations (see Figure 18.3).

The First Amendment to the U.S. Constitution prohibits Congress from making any laws that restrict citizens' rights to free speech and to freedom

∧
∧ President Johnson's and
∧ President Reagan's commissions

show the controversy surrounding what is and isn't obscene.

of the press. Because pornography involves each of these freedoms, the Supreme Court has been influential in determining pornography production and distribution.

As you can see in Figure 18.4, in 1896 the Court defined "obscenity" as something depraved and corrupt, and in 1957, the test for obscenity became whether the materials aroused a person's "unwholesome interest" in sexual matters. By the late 1960s, pornography legislation was contingent on whether someone had the right to have materials in the privacy of his or her home. In the early 1970s, the Supreme Court ruled that mailing obscene material was not protected by the Constitution (Tuman, 2003).

Today, **obscenity** is viewed as the state or quality of being offensive or disgusting by accepted social standards of decency. Again, this is a matter of opinion, as an individual's tendency to be offended or disgusted can vary from another's. In a legal sense, however, pornography is defined as any sexually explicit work deemed obscene according to legal criteria.

With the hope of finding ways to control obscene materials, Congress authorized $2 million to fund a presidential commission to study the effects of pornography in the United States. In 1969, President Lyndon B. Johnson appointed the 18 members of the President's Commission on Obscenity and Pornography. When the results of the study were released, members of Congress were shocked to discover that there was no conclusive evidence to link pornography to discrimination or violence against women. It also recommended educating children about healthy sexual attitudes and behaviors and placing restrictions on children's access to pornography but removing restrictions on adult access (Baker, 1986). The conservative community did not welcome those ideas, and many dismissed them altogether.

Figure 18.3 Views on Pornography, by Generation

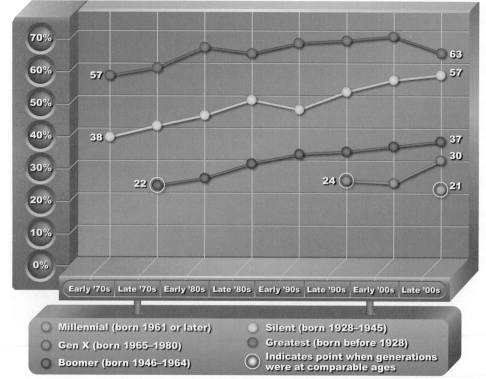

Percent saying pornography should be illegal for people of all ages.

Source: Pew Public Form on Religion and Public Life. Retrieved February 27, 2010, from http://www.pewforum.org/docs/?DocID5510

Figure 18.4 Timeline of U.S. Supreme Court Decisions on Pornography

Ronald Reagan's administration took another crack at making a connection between pornography and crime in 1985. Attorney General Edwin Meese headed the 11-member panel that wrote The Attorney General's Commission on Pornography, commonly referred to as the Meese Report. The report concluded that pornography is dangerous on many levels, increasing discrimination and violence against women and helping fund organized crime. Social scientists criticized these findings because the panel was primarily made up of politicians, many of whom had already expressed anti-pornography views. The controversy surrounding the Meese Report resulted in the general public dismissing the report as well. The effect of pornography continues to be studied by social scientists, but reliable results are still difficult to come by, as even the most straightforward research finding can be misconstrued or intentionally distorted (Wilcox, 1987).

The U.S. Supreme Court established legal criteria in 1973 that continue to guide legal action in cases that involve sexually explicit materials today. Figure 18.5 presents the three-pronged test that determines whether materials meet the Supreme Court's elements of obscenity. If so, materials lose all First Amendment rights and must be used under the restrictions put in place by state and federal governments. For the most part, however, the Court provides Constitutional protection for pornography, making regulation difficult (Procida & Simon, 2003).

Rosen v. United States
In this ruling, the Supreme Court determined that printed material is obscene if it tends to "deprave or corrupt those whose minds are open to such immoral influence, and into whose hands a publication of this sort may fall."

Stanley v. Georgia
The Court protects personal possession of obscene materials in a person's private home.

New York v. Ferber
Child pornography is not subject to any state laws regarding the distribution of pornography; the government's interest in protecting children is paramount.

1896 · 1957 · 1969 · 1973 · 1982

Roth v. United States
The test for obscenity became: "whether to the average person, applying contemporary community standards, the dominant theme of the material, taken as a whole, appeals to the prurient interest."

Miller v. California
Referred to as the *Miller test*, the U.S. Supreme Court rules that the First Amendment does not protect mailing obscene material. However, the Court notes the "dangers of undertaking to regulate any form of expression," and rules that laws that regulate obscene materials must be carefully limited.

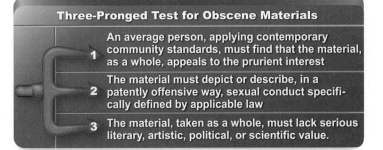

Three-Pronged Test for Obscene Materials

1. An average person, applying contemporary community standards, must find that the material, as a whole, appeals to the prurient interest

2. The material must depict or describe, in a patently offensive way, sexual conduct specifically defined by applicable law

3. The material, taken as a whole, must lack serious literary, artistic, political, or scientific value.

Figure 18.5 What Is Obscene by Law?

PORNOGRAPHY IN OTHER CULTURES

The United States produces as many as 150 new sexual adult films each week, making it the leading exporter of pornographic films (Procida & Simon, 2003). It is clear from our study so far that selling sex is a major U.S. industry, and that in determining citizens' rights regarding the production and consumption of porn, the Supreme Court protects people's First Amendment rights. But how do other cultures treat pornography? Global perspectives on pornography vary, but by and large, most Western cultures permit it (Procida & Simon, 2003).

PORNOGRAPHY: THEORETICAL ISSUES

Other than money as a possible incentive, why do people choose to go into the sex industry? Isn't it demeaning and degrading to those who participate, especially to women? Are they forced into it?

There are many myths and stereotypes about sex workers and the sex industry. Table 18.1 shows us that there are still cultural generalizations about sex workers, mainly that they are oppressed. Sociologist Ronald Weitzer (2009) provides a review of the key dimensions of contemporary sex workers and the sex industry. He notes that there are two schools of thought about the sex industry: Workers are either oppressed, or they are empowered.

SEX WORKERS ARE OPPRESSED

The **oppression paradigm** asserts that the sex industry and sex work are expressions of patriarchal gender roles. In other words, cultures that allow prostitution and pornography adhere to gender roles that promote male dominance, as well as gender attitudes that exploit women and bring them under the control of men. This is why people often hold stereotypical beliefs about sex workers. Another glance at Table 18.1 shows that most of the

TABLE 18.1
Myths about Sex Workers

Source: Based on For a full review, see Weitzer, R. (2009).

There are many stereotypes about sex workers, but by and large these are fallacies. Myths maintain that most or all sex workers:

- Were abused (physically, emotionally, sexually) as children
- Became sex workers in early adolescence, at 13 or 14
- Were or are addicted to drugs
- Were runaways
- Work under horrific conditions
- Are routinely abused their pimps or customers
- Want to leave the sex industry but are forced to stay

Old Habits Die Hard

Patrick and Becca have been in a happy relationship for two years, and when Patrick's lease on his apartment was up, Becca asked him to move in with her. Satisfied with their relationship, he readily agreed, looking forward to the prospect of being able to spend more time with Becca. One night after Patrick moved in, Becca woke up in the middle of the night to find Patrick masturbating to pornographic images on the Internet. She found this disturbing, and Patrick's penchant for porn has become a contentious point in their relationship.

Her Side: I'm not naïve. I know he probably spent a good deal of time in his single days looking at porn, either on TV or the Internet. And I know he probably continued to do so throughout our relationship, particularly when we didn't have time to see each other. But now we're living together, and our sex life has only gotten better, so I don't understand why he still needs to look at dirty photos on the Internet. Not only that, I find it insulting that he looks at these images with me right there in the room. It's like I'm not fulfilling some of his sexual needs.

His Side: It's not a reflection of our sexual relationship. She knows I love being with her, and I feel like moving in together has helped strengthen our bond. It's just that watching porn late at night or looking at pictures on the Internet turns me on. It's been a part of my life since long before I met her, and it's not something I am interested in giving up. It doesn't mean she's not good enough in bed; it's just something I enjoy doing—like a hobby. I'd ask her to watch a movie with me or look at some photos with me, but I already know she would feel uncomfortable with that.

Your Side: Have you ever been in a similar situation to Becca and Patrick's? Would it make you uncomfortable if your partner was unwilling to give up looking at porn even after you both agreed that you have a satisfying sexual relationship?

1. Do you think it's unreasonable for Becca to question Patrick's behavior? Do you think Patrick should compromise his habit in an effort to maintain his relationship with Becca?

2. Do you think Becca's conclusion that this behavior reflects badly on their sex life is an accurate one?

3. Have any issues surrounding pornography ever come up in one of your relationships? Did a conversation about it harm or help your relationship?

---

myths surrounding porn and prostitution imply that women don't enter the trade voluntarily and that they cannot leave when they want to. All of these generalizations imply that dominant men control victimized, abused, helpless women (for a review, see Farley, 2004). When writing about prostitution, for example, authors will use such terms as "paid rape" and "prostituted women." Weitzer (2009) notes that when terms like these are used, it implies that prostitution is something that is *done* to a person, not something a person chose to do.

Prominent feminists Catherine MacKinnon and Andrea Dworkin adhere to the oppression paradigm. They believe that the sex industry promotes sex discrimination and that it threatens women's safety; they also believe that much of what is produced in the sex industry is hate propaganda (Procida & Simon, 2003).

As with nearly every other aspect of sex and sexuality, society tends to try to place experiences into tidy either/or categories, and theoretical explanations are no exception. Although some believe that sex workers are oppressed, others believe they are empowered.

SEX WORKERS ARE EMPOWERED

The **empowerment paradigm** is the opposite of the oppression viewpoint. This framework puts forth the idea that sex work is no different from all other employer/employee transactions, because there is mutual gain to both parties. Adherents of this theory believe that sex work enhances a person's economic position because it is lucrative; it also gives women freedom to control their work hours. Others believe that sex work has the potential to enhance self-esteem of the individual worker (for a review, see Agustin, 2007).

But do feminists support this viewpoint? Unlike those who support the oppression perspective, some feminists are not critical of pornography or prostitution because they don't believe that coercion, exploitation, and/or dominance exist in all types of sex work. *Pro-sex* or *sex-positive* feminists, such as Jill Nagle (2001), assert that the sex industry can be a positive, beneficial experience for women and men who make informed decisions to engage in sex work. Sex workers' rights movements have developed outreach groups for sex workers, such as the International Prostitutes Collective, COYOTE, and the Sex Workers Outreach Project.

In the section that follows, we'll take a look at how television, advertising, the music business, and the Internet use sex today.

∧∧∧ Many would argue that Americans view dozens of soft porn images **every night on television.**

OWN IT! The Power of Pornography

Politicians and experts may not have been able to come to an agreement over whether pornography has a negative impact on people and their sex lives. Inarguably, pornography is one of the main representations of sexual life in our society. Respond to the following questions:

1. Do you think pornography is demeaning to women? Is this always the case? When is it and when is it not?

2. Has pornography had an impact on your sex life? Has it influenced your ideas about what sex should be like?

3. Do you feel that pornography has led people to develop skewed ideas about the different roles men and women should play in their sex lives?

SEX AND SEXUALITY IN THE MEDIA

Determining the percentage of people who view pornography may be futile because the definition of pornography varies among decades and individuals. But one thing is certain: Sexually explicit images are readily available on television today.

SEX AND TELEVISION

According to a survey conducted by the Kaiser Family Foundation, 70 percent of television programs in 2005 had some sexual content, up from 56 percent in 1998. Sexual content can include talking about sex or showing sexual behavior (Kaiser Family Foundation, 2009). With this definition in mind, we could say that 4 million people view pornography each week when they tune in to watch *Gossip Girl* on the WB network. By some standards, the sexual subject matter and visual representation on this show can be considered soft-core porn.

The Federal Communications Commission (FCC) has established a viewer rating system to help identify television shows that may have sexual content. The viewer ratings TV-Y, TV-Y7, and TV-Y7-FV are used to identify children's shows that do not contain any sexual content. TV-G indicates a show that is suitable for general audiences. The ratings TV-PG, TV-14, and TV-MA are given additional labels that indicate whether violence (V), a sexual situation (S), harsh language (L), or suggestive dialogue (D) is used in a program (Federal Communications Commission, 2009).

Cable channel HBO is well known for many of its mature audience-oriented shows. The majority of its currently top-rated original series such as *Entourage*, *Big Love*, and *Curb Your Enthusiasm* and concluded series such as *Sex and the City* and *The Sopranos* are rated TV-MA (mature audiences).

Not all sexual content on television is intended to be purely for entertainment; some of it is intended to be educational. The show *Talk Sex with Sue Johanson* airs on the Oxygen Network and covers a variety of topics regarding sex with the intention of educating viewers (*Talk Sex with Sue Johanson*, 2009). Similarly, education networks such as the Discovery Channel and the Learning Channel show fact-based programming that can contain graphic sexual content. The Discovery Channel series *Anatomy of Sex* portrays the processes of male and female sexual response, including the detailed processes of orgasms. The Discovery Channel series has a rating of TV-MA.

Selling Sex

Thinking of sex as a commodity to be bought and sold usually elicits strong feelings one way or another. In the context of your sexuality, what are some of your feelings on selling sex?

For material to be pornographic, it must _____

The difference between erotica and porn is _____

Pornography makes me feel _____

Sexuality on TV and in advertising makes me feel _____

Sexually explicit material should be censored when _____

Prostitutes and pimps are _____

People who pay for sex are _____

Prostitution should/should not be legalized because _____

A person is likely to become a prostitute if _____

Male prostitutes are _____

The obvious questions arise: What content constitutes "sexuality education," and what content comprises "pornography?" Could both be considered pornography? Neither? Many viewers might consider the *Anatomy of Sex* to be educational and therefore not pornography. But if one follows that school of thought, then any program with sexual content that claims to be educational should be viewed in the same respect.

SEX AND ADVERTISING

It is estimated that 10 to 20 percent of mainstream U.S. advertising contains sexual information. And for good reason: $ex $ells. The estimate, however, only considers advertisements that have blatantly available representations of sex. Sex in advertising can come in various forms, as illustrated in Figure 18.6. But regardless of whether sex in advertising persuades consumers to pick up a product, it certainly gets people to look, and it has kept people looking for more than 150 years.

Sex in advertising is the use of sexual imagery, referred to as **sex appeal**, to make a product appealing to a consumer (Reichert, 2003). Almost always, it uses images that are not connected to the advertised product, such as a scantily clad woman standing next to a boat, motorcycle, or sports car. Advertisers use sex appeal because of its "grabbing value," to get the attention of the consumer (Liu, Cheng, & Li, 2009). Research reveals that sex appeal in ads helps audiences remember the ad better and evokes emotional responses such as excitement or even lust (for a review, see Liu, Cheng, & Li, 2009). In other words, these ads are more persuasive than those without sexual imagery.

This concept is nothing new. Erotic images were used in advertisements even in the 1800s. Muted sexual images were used to sell anything from vices, such as tobacco and alcohol, to household necessities, like soap and toothpaste. One of the first companies to utilize the attention-grabbing powers of erotic images was U.S. cigarette producer W. Duke and Sons Company. The company's president, James Buchanan Duke, realized that promotion was the key to the company's growth, and what better image was there than the female form to catch the eye of its predominantly male consumer base? Like a stick of gum in a pack of baseball cards, the company used erotic trading cards, inserted in the back of each cigarette pack, as an extra incentive for consumers to purchase the brand's cigarettes. The campaign was wildly successful; more than 100 different trading cards were produced, and as a result of the public's desire to collect a full set, W. Duke, Sons & Co. became one of the leading cigarette manufactures in America (Reichert, 2003).

Sex in advertising can include the use of subliminal messages. **Subliminal messages** are used in advertisements to deliver subtle messages about a product to consumers without their knowledge. A classic example of subliminal advertising took place in 1957 at a movie theater in Fort Lee, New Jersey, where the messages of "Drink Coca-Cola" and "Hungry? Eat Popcorn" were projected across the screen multiple times for a fraction of a second each

Figure 18.6 What Does Sex Look Like in Advertising?

Nudity/Dress: Models are wearing revealing or tight clothing, lingerie, or no clothing at all.

Sexual Behavior: Individual sexual behavior is displayed, including flirting, eye contact, and sensual body language. Interpersonal sexual behavior can be displayed as well, including kissing, hugging, and other intimate behaviors.

Physical Attractiveness: The model or spokesperson is chosen for his or her physical beauty.

Sexual Referents (Innuendo): Allusions or references to objects or activities that can be considered sexual are present. Factors that enhance or contribute to sexual meanings can be present as well.

Sexual Embeds (Subliminal Advertising): Content interpreted as sexual on a subconscious level, which can include objects that can connote sexual body parts or actions.

time. In theory, these messages were supposed to persuade consumers to purchase these products without their conscious knowledge, but substantial research could not support their effectiveness.

Wilson Bryan Key, PhD, popularized the idea of sexual subliminal advertising in the 1970s with his book *Subliminal Seduction* (1973). Key claims that companies profit from embedding the image, or objects that can be interpreted as images, of sexual body parts or actions in advertisements. In theory, subliminal messages will persuade consumers to purchase a product, but there has been no substantial research that supports the idea that subliminal messages alone can result in increased purchasing (Reichert & Lambiase, 2003).

> ^ ^ ^ With some of today's song lyrics, **we don't have to go any further than iTunes for a good dose of sex.**

SEX TO GO: SEXUALITY IN MUSIC, ON THE PHONE, AND ON THE INTERNET

Like movies, television, and advertising, music can display sexual content. Sexual content in music is typically associated with the hard rock, hip hop, or rap music of the past few decades, but sexual content has been part of music even before the invention of the record player. *Bawdy songs*, or playful and humorous songs with lyrics about sex, are one of the first forms of mainstream pornography. Singing bawdy songs was a popular pastime for young Englishmen and Scotsmen in the 18th century. Songs such as "Roll Me Over in the Clover" contained lyrics about the popular theme of men and women having sexual relations in the countryside (Bullough & Bullough, 1994).

The 1950s and 1960s music of Motown and rock and roll are filled with sexual innuendo in many of the era's most famous tracks. The 1959 song "Long Tall Sally" by Little Richard appears to be an

<<< Phone sex hotlines gained popularity in the 1980s. **For a fee, men and women could call and have sexual conversations with live people.**

25 percent of the total search engine requests (Family Safe Media, 2009). Like the popular phone sex hotlines in the 1980s, today, the Internet allows people from various locations to connect and discuss sex. Adult chat rooms serve as a place for individuals or groups to talk, or type, about sexual activities. Technologies such as Web cams have taken some of the anonymity out of this sexual exchange, but they also bring in a visual element.

The volume of available sexual materials, the accessibility of those materials, and the ability to view them 24 hours a day from any location has led some individuals to develop an addiction to Internet pornography. Sexual additions can be as harmful and debilitating as addictions to tobacco and alcohol. Approximately 10 percent of adults admit to an Internet sexual addiction (Family Safe Media, 2009).

Sexting

Today, more than 80 percent of teens over the age of 17 own a cell phone, and nearly 60 percent of 12-year-olds own one (Pew Research Forum, 2010). There is no question that texting is significant in teens' and young adults' lives. But there is a new trend, sexting, that has the worried attention of parents, educators, and lawmakers. **Sexting** is the creation, sharing, and forwarding of sexually suggestive nude or semi-nude images (Pew Research Forum, 2010).

Between 2008 and 2010, several agencies (Cox Communication, the National Center for Missing and Exploited Children, and The National Campaign to Prevent Teen Pregnancy) undertook studies that examined sexting among teens and young adults. The results of all the studies are similar; one in 10 young adults between the ages of 14 and 24 has shared

upbeat song about a tall, slender girl named Sally, but certain lyrics allude to a woman's physical and sexual abilities.

Subtle or overt, the government issued no warnings on sexual messages in music until the late 1980s. Former Vice President Al Gore, a U.S. Senator at the time, and his wife Tipper Gore, spearheaded a program to limit the release of music with explicit lyrics. Their organization, Parents' Music Resource Center, ultimately led to the establishment of parental advisory labels and industry regulations. Rap group 2 Live Crew became the first music group to have its lyrics from the album "As Nasty as They Wanna Be" deemed obscene by the government in 1990 (Hall & Bishop, 2007). The ruling put the 2 Live Crew album in the same category as pornographic movies.

The Internet

Images of sex teem on the Internet. Pornographic Web sites make up 12 percent of the total number of sites on the Internet. With the use of search technology, these sites are not hard to find. There are more than 68 million pornographic search engine requests made each day, which makes up

Healthy Selves / Healthy Sex

Are You a Sex Addict?

Because sexuality is experienced on a continuum, and different upbringings result in different ideas about what is normal and what is not, it may sometimes be difficult to discern if one's sexual behaviors cause problems. Sex should be an enjoyable experience, but using sex to compensate for something else missing in your life isn't a healthy behavior. Much like addictions to alcohol or gambling, both men and women can experience addictions to sex (see Chapter 15).

Often, sex addicts experienced some form of sexual abuse in their childhoods. But even if they haven't, sex addiction is hard to identify because sex addicts act out in many different ways; they engage in a wide range of behaviors, from compulsive masturbating, to a preoccupation with Internet porn, to enlisting the services of prostitutes. Sex Addicts Anonymous (2009) has identified five common threads that may characterize a sex addict:

1. Powerlessness over addictive behavior

2. Resulting unmanageability of his/her life

3. Feelings of shame, pain, and self-loathing

4. Failed promises and attempts to stop acting out

5. Preoccupation with sex leading to ritual

If you are worried that you are suffering from a sexual addiction, visit saa-recovery.org for more information.

Source: Sex Addicts Anonymous. (2009). *Are you a sex addict?* Retrieved November 10, 2009, from http://saa-recovery.org/IsSAAForYou/AreYouASexAddict/

In 2009, six female Pennsylvania high school students faced child pornography charges for taking nude and semi-nude cell phone pictures of themselves and sharing them with classmates. >>>

naked images of themselves with someone else; up to 30 percent have received such pictures on their cell phones.

The Pew Research Forum tracks teen cell phone use through its Internet & American Life Project (2010). This organization found that there are three main scenarios in which teens send nude images of themselves to someone: 1) the exchanges are private, between two intimate partners; 2) exchanges occur between intimate partners, but are later shared with others outside the relationship; and 3) some people send images in hopes of getting into a relationship with another person (Pew Research Forum, 2010).

Lawmakers and law enforcement are changing policies and enforcing existing ones to deal with the increase in sexting. Teens and young adults can be prosecuted for illegally creating and disseminating pornography; if someone is under the age of 18, the images can be considered child porn, and the offenders can face harsh penalties.

So far, we have seen that sex sells. There is also no doubt that a person can sell sex. The prostitution industry, both legal and illegal, is big business in the United States and across the world. In the sections that follow, we'll take a look at the practice of prostitution, as well as laws that govern prostitution. We'll conclude this section by looking at a growing concern in the United States and abroad: sexual trafficking.

PROSTITUTION

Prostitution is the practice or occupation of engaging in sexual activity with another person in exchange for money. Referred to as the world's

oldest profession, prostitution dates back to ancient Mesopotamia around 18th century BCE. There have been many names for prostitutes over the years, but the job description has stayed relatively the same—engage in sexual activity for money.

Like any other occupation, prostitution incorporates professional hierarchies, business associates, and corporate partners into the business. Table 18.2 shows the different types of prostitution and the characteristics associated with each type of sex worker. For example, **streetwalker** is the term typically used to describe a prostitute who walks the streets looking to find a *trick*, or client: A streetwalker may or may not work with a **pimp**, a man or woman who controls prostitutes and sets up clients in exchange for a portion of the payment. Although a pimp may just seem like a business manager, the pimp-prostitute relationship is sometimes abusive, and the prostitute is treated like a product instead of a person.

While streetwalkers work the streets for their clients, **call girls** have the clients come to them. They are referred to as call girls because traditionally,

TABLE 18.2
Types of Female Prostitutes

Source: Weitzer, R. (2009).

Type of Prostitute	Business Location	Prices Charged	Exploitation by Third Parties	Risk of Violent Victimization	Public Visibility	Impact on Community
Call girl	Independent operator, private premises/hotels	High	Low to none	Low	None	None
Escort	Escort agency, private premises/hotels	High	Moderate	Low to moderate	Very low	None
Brothel worker	Brothel	Moderate	Moderate	Very low	Low	None, if discreet
Massage parlor worker	Massage parlor	Moderate	Moderate	Very low	Low	Little, if discreet
Bar or casino worker	Bar/casino contact, sex elsewhere	Low to moderate	Low to moderate	Low to moderate	Moderate	Equivalent to impact of bar or casino
Streetwalker	Street contact, sex in cars, alleys, parks, etc.	Low	High	Very high	High	Adverse

clients, or *johns*, make appointments by telephone. Independent call girls earn between $200 to $500 per hour, and some who work in higher end brothels make as much as $1,000 to $6,000 per hour or per session (Weitzer, 2009).

A **brothel** is a place where men can visit prostitutes. Brothels have existed as long as sex as a trade has. Starting in 16th-century France, the term **madam** was coined to describe a female head who runs a brothel. An **escort service** works in a similar fashion to a brothel, but it sends its prostitutes, or **escorts**, out to clients' homes, hotel rooms, or other meeting places. Individuals who want to be discreet about the exchange typically use this type of service because it does not involve entering a place that sells sex or combing the streets for random prostitutes.

Streetwalkers typically serve individuals in a lower tax bracket and can charge anywhere from a few dollars to a few hundred per trick. Prostitutes who work in brothels, particularly high-end brothels, may bring in $1,000 a day, but a significant portion of that will go to the madam as a form of commission and rent (Cosby, 2005). Although many people hold a common belief that most prostitutes are streetwalkers, this isn't the case; in many countries, such as the United States, Britain, and Australia, streetwalkers aren't as common as indoor workers (Weitzer, 2009).

Why and how does someone become a prostitute?

WHO BECOMES A PROSTITUTE?

It is important to note that streetwalkers do commonly fit the stereotype of the underpaid, violently victimized, runaway, drug using, male-dominated hooker, and for many of these women and men, there is little hope of escaping the "lifestyle" (Weitzer, 2009). But as Table 18.3 shows us, other people enter prostitution for different reasons.

Some people leave mainstream jobs to become prostitutes, and others moonlight in the sex trade when they are not at their nine-to-five jobs. Dennis Hof, owner of the Moonlite Bunny Ranch, a legal brothel in Carson City, Nevada, states that he has had many well-educated and successful women leave their "regular" jobs to work at the brothel.

Women who work at the ranch can make $2,000 to $5,000 a day. One Moonlite Bunny Ranch employee said she decided to become a

prostitute because, "I put two and two together. Men liked me, and I needed to make a lot of money. And you know, I could date men and waste my time with dinners and flowers and everything else, or I could actually charge them to spend time with me" (Cosby, 2005).

These prostitutes probably do not reflect the image of most average prostitutes, as this establishment is legal and has a high profile, but it does accurately depict the idea that many prostitutes view themselves as potentially lucrative businesses. Some prostitutes say they enjoy their work, but most deny that they receive pleasure during their sexual transactions, dispelling the idea that individuals go into prostitution because they are sex addicts (Weitzer, 2009).

MEN AS PROSTITUTES

Although the majority of prostitutes are women, there is a significant population of male prostitutes in the United States. Commonly referred to as **gigolos** or **male escorts**, male prostitutes may serve men or women, and their experience of sex work is often different than that of their female counterparts, as illustrated by Table 18.4.

TABLE 18.3
Pathways to Prostitution

Source: Based on Weitzer, R. (2009).

- By *recruitment or coercion:* Pimps often coerce and recruit streetwalkers, because many are runaways without resources. Their choices are often limited to theft, or selling drugs or their bodies.

- By *drifting from other sex work:* Many prostitutes begin as sex workers in other industries, such as stripping, phone sex, or Internet sex. They decide to experiment with prostitution.

- By *choice:* Many indoor workers experience high levels of job satisfaction because of continuous reinforcement from customers; they also feel they provide valuable services to their customers and often compare their work to that of sex therapists. They believe prostitution gives them power and control.

TABLE 18.4
How Men and Women Experience Prostitution

Source: Based on Weitzer, R. (2009).

Just like female streetwalkers, male streetwalkers share similar characteristics; they are often runaways or support a drug habit. Unlike women, though, males tend to:

- Be more sporadic and transitory, tending to drift in and out of the business.

- Leave the trade sooner than women.

- Be less likely to be coerced into the business by pimps.

- Be less likely to experience violence from customers and pimps.

- Be in greater control over their work and working conditions.

- Be less stigmatized in the gay community.

- Be more stigmatized by the wider community because they engage in both homosexual and heterosexual sex acts.

sexual (life) now

Should Prostitution Be Legalized?

Considered the "world's oldest profession," prostitution has undergone many changes over time, going from being an acceptable and even revered occupation to being considered criminal and degrading. It is currently illegal in the United States in all but 11 counties in Nevada. According to ProCon.org, approximately 1 percent of American women have engaged in prostitution at some point in their lives. Despite its status as a prosecutable crime, selling sex has been and likely will always be a mainstay of societies everywhere. Should prostitution be legalized? ProCon.org presents both sides of the story (ProCon.org, 2009).

YES!

- At its most basic level, prostitution is an exchange of skills for money. No other such exchange results in prosecution. Applying labor laws to prostitution can provide protection against exploitation, violence, and coercion.

- A person's right to agree to sex should not be subject to government interference, even if that consent is contingent upon the exchange of money. The choice to have sex, whether recreational or otherwise, is a private matter.

- If prostitution is legalized, the government will be better able to control any problems. The spread of STIs can be stunted by hygiene regulations, such as those placed on doctors and massage therapists. And with prostitution made public, crimes committed within the industry are easier for law enforcement to detect.

NO!

- Even if prostitution takes place between two consenting parties, it turns someone's sexuality into a commodity that is bought and sold, which compromises its moral integrity. When a client reduces a prostitute to a product, sex becomes an assertion of power and violence. It reduces the sex worker to nothing but body parts, rendering a person not whole.

- Although legalizing prostitution may make identification of abuses easier for law enforcement, it may also cause human trafficking to increase and go undetected.

- According to the U.S. Department of State's 2004 article, "The Link Between Prostitution and Sex Trafficking," 60 to 75 percent of female prostitutes have been raped, 70 to 95 percent have been assaulted, and 68 percent suffered from posttraumatic stress disorder. Additionally, prostitution takes a psychological toll on the people involved.

>>> WHAT DO YOU THINK?

1. What sets prostitution apart from another exchange of skills for money, such as washing dishes at a restaurant?
2. Do you think prostitution should be legalized? Why or why not?
3. If law enforcement has never successfully controlled prostitution, could legalizing it change that? Why or why not?

The idea of a woman paying a man for sex goes against many longstanding social norms that assume that women can find sex whenever they want and therefore would have no need to pay a prostitute for sex. This concept also assumes that women do not enjoy sex as much as men and would not benefit from a "professional's services."

Most often, the male prostitute performing the homosexual act is not a homosexual himself. Only 18 percent of male prostitutes identify themselves as gay; 36 percent identify as being bisexual (Altman & Aggleman, 1999; Miller, Klotz, & Eckholdt, 1998). This "gay for pay" practice is a result of the overwhelming number of men and limited number of women who are willing to pay for sex.

PROSTITUTION AND THE LAW

Currently, prostitution is illegal in the U.S. It is considered a Class 1 misdemeanor that can come with a one-year jail sentence and a $2,000 fine. It is in the same class as petty thievery and vandalism. Whom does prostitution really hurt? Some consider it a victimless crime, while others say the victims are the prostitutes themselves. It is currently legal in other countries such as Germany and the Netherlands as well as some counties in Nevada. So, should prostitution be legalized nationwide?

Those who support legal prostitution believe that legal-

>>> **Former New York Governor Eliot Spitzer attempted to hide his infidelity by using an escort service, but he was ultimately unable to avoid the press.** Emperor's Club V.I.P., is said to have charged nearly $5,500 an hour for sexual services (Buettner, 2008).

ization would reduce crime, improve public health, create more tax revenue, and allow individual freedom over one's body. Legalizing prostitution would also prevent prostitutes from putting themselves in dangerous situations, such as getting into strangers' cars to avoid getting caught by police. Those who do not support legal prostitution believe that legalization would increase crime, transmission of STIs, and human trafficking. Opponents also feel that accepting prostitution as a legal activity is immoral.

Today, one of the most significant human rights abuses in the United States and abroad is the trafficking of young children and women for prostitution and other forms of sex work (Hodge, 2008).

HUMAN SEXUAL TRAFFICKING

One of the most upsetting trends in involuntary prostitution is human sexual trafficking. The U.S. government defines **sex trafficking** as "the recruitment, harboring, transportation, provision, or obtaining of a person for the purposes of a commercial sex act" (for a full review, see Hodge, 2008).

Each year in the United States, up to 17,500 people are brought into this country or *trafficked*, for the purposes of sexual exploitation (U.S. Department of State, 2004). Globally, anywhere from 600,000 to 800,000 people are trafficked across international borders (Hodge, 2008). Estimates indicate that about one-half are children, and 70 to 80 percent are female (U.S. Department of State, 2004). Of the female victims, approximately 70 percent are sold for prostitution and other forms of sexual exploitation (U.S. Department of State, 2004). Once in a trafficker's hands, children and women are victims of emotional, psychological, physical, and sexual abuse (Hodge, 2008). The problem is immense and ruins many families and communities.

RECRUITING AND TRANSPORTING VICTIMS

Women and children from regions such as Asia, Southeast Asia, China, Nigeria, the former Soviet Union, and parts of Europe are recruited through a number of ways (for a full review, see Hodge, 2008):

- *False-front agencies:* Traffickers use false organizations, such as modeling or employment agencies, to find their victims. They almost always promise victims a better life in another country, such as the United States. Victims frequently have no idea what they're agreeing to. They enter into a **debt bondage** agreement ("transportation costs" to the new country). Women cannot leave until this debt is paid through their sexual services, and they are often passed from organization to organization, increasing their "transportation costs," and making it impossible for them to leave.

- *Local sex industries:* Some women are already engaged in prostitution, and local sex agencies approach them for their services. Although these women may have a general understanding of what will be required of them, they are not aware that they will never be able to fulfill their debt bondage agreement.

- *Abduction:* Some traffickers kidnap their victims.

- *Families in poverty:* Some families in poverty sell their young children. Traffickers promise better lives in other countries.

THE VIOLENCE PROTECTION ACT

In 2000, the United States passed the Victims of Trafficking and Violence Protection Act. Trafficked individuals are often treated as criminals when they seek help, because they are caught in illegal sexual activities and often do not have appropriate passports or visas (Hodge, 2008). The trafficking legislation first stipulates that trafficking victims are not penalized for their activities, such as working without proper documentation. The law also provides victims temporary visas so they can stay while law enforcement prosecutes the traffickers. While in the U.S., victims are provided benefits and services, including the Witness Protection Program. Finally, the law provides that after three years, trafficked victims may be granted permanent residency (Hodge, 2008).

SEXUAL LIFE EDUCATION

For as long as people have existed, so have erotica and other representations of sex. Currently, sexuality is present in television, advertising, music, on the phone, and on the Internet. Different people have different views about what is obscene and pornographic, and experts have been unable to reach a consensus about the possible impacts and their implications.

Whether or not sex is a useful tool in selling products, there is no doubt that sex has been a commodity throughout history. Considered the world's oldest profession, prostitution is a controversial fact of life in every society around the world. Some people feel it should be legalized, and some people feel it shouldn't, but regardless of what is right or wrong, selling sex has an indisputable presence today.

Several weeks ago, we began our quest to better understand how people experience and enjoy their sexuality. Throughout our study together, we have come to know that sexuality isn't just about body parts and perfectly timed orgasms—it's about so much more! It is only fitting to leave the concluding remarks to a student, who says,

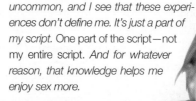

> You ask me what the most important thing is I learned this semester. We've learned about everything that affects our sex and sexuality. This has been a difficult class for me sometimes. Because of my past history with sexual abuse, I know now that I am, and might always be, afraid to fully trust and to fully give myself to my partner[s]. Sixteen weeks ago I thought that was a really crappy deal, but now I see that my experiences [with abuse] aren't that uncommon, and I see that these experiences don't define me. It's just a part of my script. One part of the script—not my entire script. And for whatever reason, that knowledge helps me enjoy sex more.
>
> Before taking this class, I think I would have said that sex is something you do. But now that we're sitting in the last class, I would have to say that sex isn't something you do—it's who you are.
>
> *Source:* Author's files

>>> Tamang girls in Nepal **have long been victims of human sex trafficking.**

Summary

WHAT ROLES HAVE EROTICA AND PORNOGRAPHY PLAYED THROUGHOUT HISTORY, AND HOW HAVE THEY CHANGED? 376

- Erotica and pornography differ in that erotica has an artistic or philosophical element in addition to its ability to arouse sexual desire, while pornography is meant only to stimulate erotic feelings. Soft-core pornography is less explicit than hard-core pornography, and child pornography involves prepubescent children.
- Because perceptions of erotica and pornography are subjective, obscenity is difficult to define. The Supreme Court's definition of obscenity has changed over time, but if something is deemed obscene, it loses its First Amendment rights and must be used under the restrictions put in place by state and federal governments. The people involved in the pornography industry are called sex workers.

HOW IS SEX AND SEXUALITY PORTRAYED IN THE MEDIA? 381

- Sexual content is present in varying degrees in most television shows, prompting the FCC to establish viewer ratings to determine the suitability for different audiences. Because sex is attention-grabbing, it is often utilized to sell different products through advertising, even if the product has nothing to do with sex at all. Sex is also readily available in music, through phone sex hotlines, and on the Internet.

WHO BECOMES A PROSTITUTE? 384

- The "world's oldest profession," prostitution is engaging in sexual activity in exchange for money. There are different types of prostitutes, and some may work with pimps, who will set up clients in exchange for a portion of the payment. Without any other resources, some prostitutes are recruited, while some come over from other sex work, and some become prostitutes by choice. Gigolos are male prostitutes who may serve both women and men.

HOW HAS HUMAN SEXUAL TRAFFICKING BECOME A DOMESTIC AND GLOBAL PROBLEM? 387

- According to the U.S. government, sex trafficking is the recruitment, harboring, transportation, provision, or obtaining of a person for the purposes of a commercial sex act. About one-half of the victims are children and most are female. Human sex trafficking results in emotional, psychological, physical, and sexual abuse, and it is an increasing international problem.

Key Terms

sex industry the commercial enterprises or businesses related to selling or purchasing sex-related services *376*

adult entertainment sex industry *376*

sex worker a person who works in the sex industry *376*

erotica literature or art intended to arouse sexual desire *376*

pornography, porn, or porno printed or visual material containing explicit descriptions of sexual organs or activities with the intention of stimulating erotic feelings *377*

soft-core pornography pornography that shows more indirect and non-graphic sexual images *377*

hard-core pornography pornography that shows direct and explicit sexual images *377*

child pornography sexually explicit photographs, videos, films, or audio of prepubescent children, usually depicting sex acts involving children *377*

child abuse images another term for child pornography *377*

obscenity the state or quality of being offensive or disgusting by accepted social standards of decency *378*

oppression paradigm paradigm that asserts that the sex industry and sex work are expressions of patriarchal gender roles *379*

empowerment paradigm framework that puts forth the idea that sex work is no different from all other employer/employee transactions, because there is mutual gain to both parties *380*

sex in advertising the use of sexual imagery to make a product appealing to a consumer *382*

sex appeal sexual imagery *382*

subliminal messages messages that go below a person's threshold of consciousness *382*

sexting creation, sharing, and forwarding of sexually suggestive nude or semi-nude images *383*

prostitution the practice or occupation of engaging in sexual activity with another person for money *384*

streetwalker the term typically used to describe a prostitute who literally walks the streets at night looking to find a trick *384*

pimp a man or woman who controls prostitutes and sets up clients in exchange for a portion of the payment *384*

call girls prostitutes whose clients come to them *384*

brothel a place where men can visit prostitutes *385*

madam a female head that runs the business of the brothel *385*

escort service service similar to a brothel, but it sends its prostitutes to clients *385*

escort a prostitute who goes to clients' homes, hotel rooms, or other meeting places *385*

gigolo, or **male escort** a male prostitute who may serve men or women   *385*

sex trafficking "the recruitment, harboring, transportation, provision, or obtaining of a person for the purposes of a commercial sex act"   *387*

debt bondage a form of indentured servitude in which women become prostitutes to pay off debts to captors   *387*

Sample Test Questions

MULTIPLE CHOICE

1. Which pinup girl is considered to be the first bondage model?
   a. Betty Grable
   b. Bettie Page
   c. Marilyn Monroe
   d. Raquel Welch

2. What accounts for the largest distribution of pornographic films?
   a. Pay TV
   b. DVD rentals
   c. DVD sales
   d. Box office

3. Which TV rating indicates that a program is not suitable for children?
   a. TV-MA
   b. TV-G
   c. TV-Y
   d. TV-Y7-FV

4. Which type of sexual content in advertising supposedly appeals to a person's subconscious?
   a. Subliminal
   b. Innuendo
   c. Physical attractiveness
   d. Nudity

5. Which type of prostitute is at the highest risk for victimization?
   a. Escort
   b. Call girl
   c. Brothel worker
   d. Streetwalker

6. More so than female prostitutes, male prostitutes are:
   a. Sporadic and transitory
   b. Likely to be coerced by pimps
   c. Likely to experience violence from customers and pimps
   d. Stigmatized in the gay community

7. A debt bondage agreement is a feature of:
   a. The relationship between a prostitute and a pimp
   b. Human sex trafficking
   c. The pornography industry
   d. Phone sex

8. Which method is NOT a means for human sex trafficking?
   a. False-front agencies
   b. Abduction
   c. Local sex industries
   d. None of the above

SHORT RESPONSE

1. Explain the differences between erotica and pornography and between soft-core and hard-core pornography.

2. Describe the oppression and empowerment paradigm theories about sex workers.

3. Explain how a debt bondage agreement works.

4. Should prostitution be legalized? Why or why not?

5. Describe the different types of prostitutes.

Answers: 1. b; 2. c; 3. a; 4. b; 5. d; 6. a; 7. b; 8. d

Remember to check www.thethinkspot.com **for additional information, downloadable flashcards, and other helpful resources.**

ENDNOTES

Abraham, J. N. (2005). Insect choice and floral size dimorphism: Sexual selection or natural selection? *Journal of Insect Behavior, 18*, 743–756.

Abramson, P. R., & Pinkerton, S. D. (1995). *With pleasure: Thoughts on the nature of human sexuality.* New York: Oxford University Press.

Abusharaf, R. M. (2001). Virtuous cuts: Female genital circumcision in an African ontology. *Differences: A Journal of Feminist Cultural Studies, 12*, 112–140.

Acs, G., & Nelson, S. (2002). *The kids are alright? Children's well-being and the rise in cohabitation* (Series B No. B-048). Washington, DC: The Urban Institute.

Addiego, F., Belzer, E. G., Comolli, J., Moger, W., Perry, J. D., & Whipple, B. (1981). Female ejaculation: A case study. *Journal of Sex Research, 17*, 1–13.

Advocates for Youth. (2008). *The facts: Effective sex education.* Retrieved August 22, 2009, from www.advocatesforyouth.org/publications/factsheet/fssexcur.htm

Afable-Munsuz, A., & Brindis, C. D. (2006). Acculturation and the sexual reproductive health of Latino youth in the United States: A literature review. *Perspectives on Sexual and Reproductive Health, 38*(4), 208–220.

Agberia, J. T. (2006). Aesthetics and rituals of the Opha ceremony among the Urhobo people. *Journal of Asian & African Studies, 41*(3), 249–260.

Ahlborg, T., Dahlof, L. G., & Strandmark, M. (2000). First-time parents' sexual relationships. *Scandinavian Journal of Sexology, 3*, 127–139.

Ahlborg, T., Lars-Gosta, D., & Hallberg, L. (2005). Quality of the intimate and sexual relationship in first-time parents six months after delivery. *The Journal of Sex Research, 42*(7), 167–174.

AIDS Infonet. (2009). Microbicides. *Fact Sheet 157.* Retrieved March 13, 2010, from http://www.aidsinfonet.org/fact_sheets/view/157

Ainsworth, M. D. S., Blehar, M. C., Waters, E., & Wall, S. (1978). *Patterns of attachment: A psychological study of the strange situation.* Hillsdale, NJ: Erlbaum.

Alan Guttmacher Institute. (2004). *U.S. teenage pregnancy statistics: Overall trends, trends by race and ethnicity, and state-by-state information.* Washington, DC: Alan Guttmacher Institute.

Alan Guttmacher Institute. (2006). *Facts on sex education in the United States.* Retrieved December 21, 2007, from www.policyinfo@guttmacher.org

Alan Guttmacher Institute. (2007). *Sex and STI/HIV education: State policies in brief.* Retrieved August 17, 2009, from www.guttmacher.org/statecenter/spibs/spib_SE.pdf

Alan Guttmacher Institute. (2008a). Abortion and women of color: The bigger picture. *Guttmacher Policy Review, 11*(3). Retrieved March 13, 2010, from http://www.guttmacher.org/pubs/gpr/11/3/gpr110302.html

Alan Guttmacher Institute. (2008b). *Facts in brief: Facts on contraceptive use.* Retrieved August 19, 2009, from www.guttmacher.org/pubs/fb_contr_use.htm

Alberta Society for the Promotion of Sexual Health. (2007). Retrieved August 19, 2009, from www.aspsh.org

Alberts, M. (2002). *The ecological model of human development: The foundation for a family policy perspective.* The University of Minnesota Children, Youth, and Family Consortium. Retrieved August 22, 2009, from www.cyfc.umn.edu/publications/connections/pubs/05summer/01-foundatoinfamilypolicy.html

Albright, J. M. (2008). Sex in America online: An exploration of sex, marital status, and sexual identity in Internet sex seeking and its impacts. *The Journal of Sex Research, 45*(2), 175–186.

Aldeeb Abu-Sahlieh, S. A. (1994). To mutilate in the name of Jehovah or Allah: Legitimization of male and female circumcision. *Medicine and Law, 13*(7–8), 575–622.

Alison, L., Santtila, P., Sandnabba, N. K., & Nordling, N. (2001). Sadomasochistically oriented behavior: Diversity in practice and meaning. *Archives of Sexual Behavior, 30*(1), 1–12.

Allen, K. R. (1997). Lesbian and gay families. In T. Arendell (Ed.), *Contemporary parenting: Challenges and issues.* New York: Sage.

Allyn, D. (2002). *The sexual revolution: An unfettered history.* London: Little Brown.

Ambert, A. M. (2009). Divorce: Facts, causes, & consequences (3rd ed.). The Vanier Institute of the Family, York University. Retrieved January 3, 2010, from http://www.vifamily.ca/library/cft/divorce_09.pdf

American Academy of Clinical Sexologists. (2007). Retrieved August 19, 2009, from www.esextherapy.com

American Academy of Family Physicians. (2008). *Circumcision.* Retrieved July 30, 2009, from www.aafp.org/or2008

American Academy of Pediatrics. (2005). Breastfeeding and the use of human milk: Policy statement. *Pediatrics, 115*, 496–506.

American Academy of Pediatrics. (2006). Menstruation in girls and adolescents: Using the menstrual cycle as a vital sign. *Pediatrics, 118*(5), 2245–2250.

American Association of Clinical Endocrinologists. (2003). Medical guidelines for clinical practice for the evaluation and treatment of male sexual dysfunction: A couple's problem—2003 update. *Endocrine Practice, 9*(1), 77–95.

American Association of Retired People. (2004). *Attitudes about aging and sexuality.* Retrieved September 17, 2009, from http://www.aarp.org/health/conditions/articles/harvard__sexuality-in-midlife-and-beyond_2.html

American Board of Plastic Surgeons. (2006). *Breast reductions and augmentations: Cosmetic plastic surgery research.* Retrieved March 12, 2010, from http://www.cosmeticplasticsurgerystatistics.com/statistics.html

American College of Obstetrics and Gynecologists. (2007). *Recommendations on routine pelvic exam, cervical cytology screening.* Retrieved July 27, 2009, from http://www.acog.org/publications/patient_education/bp150.cfm

American College of Obstetrics and Gynecologists. (2009). *ACOG Educational Pamphlet: Contraception.* Retrieved September 19, 2009, from http://www.acog.org/publications/patient_education/bp021.cfm

American College of Obstetrics and Gynecologists. (2009). Management of stillbirth. *ACOG Practice Bulletin, No. 102.* Retrieved September 12, 2009, from www.acog.org

American Congress of Obstetricians and Gynecologists. (2010). *Midlife transitions: A guide to approaching menopause.* Retrieved February 18, 2010, from http://www.acog.org/publications/patient_education/ab013.cfm

American Medical Association. (2006, March 8). *Sex: Intoxication among women more common on Spring Break.* Retrieved March 11, 2010, from www.ama-assn.org/ama/pub/category/16083.html

American Pregnancy Association. (2009). *Sexually transmitted infections during pregnancy.* Retrieved September 23, 2009, from www.americanpregnancy.org

American Psychiatric Association. (2000). *Diagnostic and statistical manual of mental disorders* (4th ed.). Washington, DC: APA.

American Social Health Association. (2008). *Vaginal infections.* Retrieved February 5, 2008, from www.emedicinehealth.com/vaginal_infections/article_em.htm

American Social Health Association. (2009). *HIV and AIDS overview: 2009.* Retrieved September 23, 2009, from www.ashastd.org/learn/learn_hiv_aids_overfirew.cfm

American Society of Plastic Surgeons. (2008). Retrieved February 5, 2008, from www.plasticsurgery.org

American Society of Plastic Surgeons. (2009). *2009 report of the 2008 statistics: National clearinghouse of plastic surgery statistics.* Retrieved July 27, 2009, from http://www.plasticsurgery.org/Media/stats/2008-US-cosmetic-reconstructive-plastic-surgery-minimally-invasive-statistics.pdf

American Society of Reproductive Medicine. (2008). *Infertility in women and in men.* Retrieved September 12, 2009, from www.asrm.org/patients/faqs.html#Q2

American Urological Association. (2008). *Introduction to premature ejaculation.* Retrieved October 17, 2008, from www.PEhomepagecom

Anad, M. (2003). *The new art of sexual ecstasy.* New York: HarperCollins.

Anand, K., & Scalzo, F. (2000). Can adverse neonatal experiences alter brain development and subsequent behavior? *Biology of the Neonate, 77*, 69–82.

Andersen, B. L., & Cyranowski, J. M. (1995). Women's sexuality: Behaviors, responses, and individual differences. *Journal of Consulting and Clinical Psychology, 63*, 891–906.

Anderson, R. U., Wise, D., Sawyer, R., & Chan, C. A. (2006). Sexual dysfunction in men with chronic prostatitis/chronic pelvic pain syndrome: Improvement after trigger point release and paradoxical relaxation training. *Journal of Urology, 176*, 1534–1538.

Angelo, E. J. (1994). The negative impact of abortion on women and families: The many faces of abortion grief. In M. T. Mannion (Ed.), *Post-abortion aftermath* (pp. 44–57). Kansas City, MO: Sheed & Ward.

Anspaugh, D. J., & Ezell, G. (2005). *Teaching today's health* (7th ed.). San Francisco: Pearson/Benjamin Cummings.

Antoniou, A., Pharoah, P. D., Narod, S., Risch, H. A., Eyfjord, J. E., Hopper, J. L., et al. (2003). Average risks of breast and ovarian cancer associated with BRCA1 and BRCA2 mutations detected in case series unselected for family history: A combined analysis of 22 studies. *American Journal of Human Genetics, 72*, 1117–1130.

APA Task Force on Appropriate Therapeutic Responses to Sexual Orientation. (2009). *Report of the task force on appropriate therapeutic responses to sexual orientation.* Washington, DC: American Psychological Association.

Arab American Institute. (2007). *Arab Americans: Demographics.* Retrieved September 14, 2009, from www.aaiusa.org/arab-americans/22/demographics

Aral, S. O., Patel, D. A., Holmes, K. K., et al. (2005). Temporal trends in sexual behaviors and sexually. *Sexually Transmitted Diseases, 32*, 710–717.

Arana, M. M. (2005). *A human rights investigation into the medical "normalization" of intersex people.* San Francisco, CA. Retrieved August 26, 2009, from www.sfgov.org/humanrights

Araujo, A. B., Mohr, B. A., & McKinlay, J. B. (2004). Changes in sexual function in middle-aged and older men: Longitudinal data from the Massachusetts Male Aging Study. *Journal of the American Geriatrics Society, 52*, 1502–1509.

Archive of Sexology. (2007). *Sexology world-wide.* Retrieved June 29, 2009, from www.sexualitystudies.net/program/111/112

Arcus, M. E., Schvaneveldt, J. D., & Moss, J. J. (1993). The nature of family life education. In M. E. Arcus, J. D. Schvaneveldt, & J. J. Moss (Eds.), *Handbook of family life education: Foundations of family life education* (Vol. 1). Newbury Park, CA: Sage.

Arnow, B. A., Desmond, J. E., Banner, L. L., Glover, G. H., Solomon, A., Polan, M. L., et al. (2002). Brain activation and sexual arousal in healthy, heterosexual males. *Brain, 125*, 1014–1023.

Aron, A., Fisher, H. E., Mashek, D. J., Strong, G., Li, H., & Brown, L. L., et al. (2005). *Love really is "All in your head."* Paper presented at the American Physiological Society Conference on Neurohypophyseal Hormones, July 16–20, Steamboat Springs, Colorado: American Physiological Association.

Atkins, D. C., Jacobson, N. S., & Baucom, D. H. (2001). Understanding infidelity: Correlates in a national random sample. *Journal of Family Psychology, 15*, 735-749.

Australian Relationship Survey. (2006). *Why do people get married?* Retrieved September 2, 2009, from www.relationship.com/au/advice/faqs/FAQ220.faq/base_view

Avari, B. (2007). *India: The ancient past.* London: Routledge.

Bachman, G. F., & Guerrero, L. K. (2006). Relational quality and communicative responses following hurtful events in dating relationships: An expectancy violations analysis. *Journal of Social and Personal Relationships, 23*(6), 943-963.

Bailey, J. M., & Pillard, R. C. (1993). A genetic study of male sexual orientation. *Archives of General Psychiatry, 50*(3), 240-241.

Baird, A. A., Colvin, M. K., VanHorn, J. D., et al. (2005). Functional connectivity: Integrating behavioral, DTI, and fMRI datasets. *Journal of Cognitive Neuroscience, 17*(4), 687-693.

Baird, A. A., & Fugelsang, J. A. (2004). The emergence of consequential thought: Evidence from neuroscience. *The Royal Society, 26*, 1797-1804.

Bakker, J., De Mees, C., Balthazart, J., & Szpirer, C. (2007). Alpha-fetoprotein protects the developing female brain from estrogen. *Endocrine Abstracts*, S14.1

Bancroft, J. (2002). Biological factors in human sexuality. *The Journal of Sex Research, 39*(1), 15-21.

Bancroft, J., Carnes, L., Jannsen, E., Goodrich, D., & Long, J. S. (2005). Erectile and ejaculatory problems in gay and heterosexual men. *Archives of Sexual Behavior, 34*(3), 285-297.

Bancroft, J., & Vukadinovic, Z. (2004). Sexual addiction, sexual compulsivity, sexual impulsivity, or what? Toward a theoretical model. *The Journal of Sex Research, 41*(3), 225-234.

Bandura, A. (1977). *Social learning theory.* Englewood Cliffs, NJ: Prentice Hall.

Banfield, S., & McCabe, M. P. (2001). Extra relationship involvement among women: Are they different from men? *Archives of Sexual Behavior, 30*(2), 119-142.

Bank, B. J., & Hansford, S. L. (2000). Gender and friendship: Why are men's best same-sex friendships less intimate and supportive? *Personal Relationships, 7*, 63-78.

Barraket, J., & Henry-Waring, M. S. (2008). Getting it on(line). *Journal of Sociology, 44*(2), 149-165.

Barrett, A. (1999). Social support and life satisfaction among the never married. *Research on Aging, 21*(1), 46-72.

Barrett, G., Pendry, E., Peacock, J., et al. (2000). Women's sexual health after childbirth. *British Journal of Obstetrics and Gynecology, 107*, 186-195.

Barsoum, I., & Yao, H. H. (2006). The road to maleness: From testis to Wolffian duct. *Trends in Endocrinology and Metabolism, 17*(6), 223-228.

Bartels, A., & Zeki, S. (2000). The neural basis of romantic love. *Neuroreport, 11*(17), 3829-3834.

Bartoli, A. M., & Clark, M. D. (2006). The dating game: Similarities and differences in dating scripts among college students. *Sexuality and Culture, 10*(4), 54-80.

Basson, R. (2001). Female sexual response: The role of drugs in the management of sexual dysfunction. *Obstetrics & Gynecology, 98*, 350-353.

Basson, R. (2002). Women's sexual desire—disordered or misunderstood? *Journal of Sex and Marital Therapy, 28*, 17-28.

Basson, R. (2005). Women's sexual dysfunction: Revised and expanded definitions. *Canadian Medical Association Journal, 172*(10), 1327-1333.

Basson, R. (2006). Sexual desire and arousal disorders in women. *New England Journal of Medicine, 354*(14), 1497-1506.

Baumeister, R. F., Cantonese, K. R., & Vohs, K. D. (2001). Is there a gender difference in strength of sex drive? Theoretical views, conceptual distinctions, and a review of relevant evidence. *Personality and Social Psychology Review, 5*(3), 242-273.

Baumeister, R. F., & Tice, D. M. (2001). *The social dimensions of sex.* Boston: Allyn & Bacon.

Baumrind, D. (1991). The influence of parenting style on adolescent competence and substance use. *Journal of Early Adolescence, 11*(1), 56-95.

Bearman, P., & Brückner, H. (2001). Promising the future: Virginity pledges and first intercourse. *American Journal of Sociology, 106*(4), 859-912.

Beckman, N., Waern, M., Gustafson, D., & Skoog, I. (2008). Secular trends in self reported sexual activity and satisfaction in Swedish 70 year olds: Cross sectional survey of four populations, 1971–2001. *British Medical Journal*, 10.1136/bmj.9279

Beck, J. G., Bozman, A. W., & Qualtrough, T. (1991). The experience of sexual desire: Psychological correlates in a college sample. *Journal of Sex Research, 28*, 443-456.

Bell, A. P., & Weinberg, M. S. (1978). *Homosexualities: A study of diversity among men & women.* New York: Simon & Schuster.

Belsky, J., Steinberg, L., & Draper, P. (1991). Childhood experience, interpersonal development, and reproductive strategy: An evolutionary theory of socialization. *Child Development, 62*(4), 647-670.

Bem, S. L., (1981). Gender schema theory: A cognitive account of sex typing. *Psychological Review, 88*, 354-364.

Bem, S. L. (1993). *Lenses of Gender: Transforming the debate on sexual inequality.* New Haven, CT: Yale University Press.

Bem, S. L. (1998). *An unconventional family.* New Haven, CT: Yale University Press.

Benkov, L. (1994). *Reinventing the family: Lesbian and gay parents.* New York: Crown Publishing.

Bensley, G., & Boyle, G. (2003). Effects of male circumcision on female arousal and orgasm. *New Zealand Medical Journal, 116*, 595-596.

Benuto, L. (2009a). *Paraphilias causes and treatments.* Retrieved September 13, 2009, from http://www.mentalhelp.net/poc/view_doc.php?type=doc&id=29729&cn=10

Benuto, L. (2009b). Sexual desire disorders: Hypoactive sexual desire disorder. Retrieved September 12, 2009, from http://www.mentalhelp.net/poc/view_doc.php?type=doc&id=29725&cn=10

Bergner, R. M. (2000). Love and barriers to love: An analysis for psychotherapists and others. *American Journal of Psychotherapy, 54*(1), 1-16.

Berkowitz, D., & Marsiglio, W. (2007). Gay men: Negotiating procreative, father, and family identities. *Journal of Marriage and Family, 69*(2), 366-381.

Bernhardt, E. (2004). Cohabitation and marriage among young adults in Sweden: Attitudes, expectations, and plans. *Scandinavian Population Studies, 13*, 157-170.

Bertone-Johnson, E. R., Hankinson, S. E., Johnson, S. R., & Manson, J. E. (2008). Cigarette smoking and the development of premenstrual syndrome. *American Journal of Epidemiology, 168*(8), 938-945.

Bhasin, S., Storer, T. W., Berman, N., Callegari, C., Clevenger, B., Phillips, J., et al. (1996). The effects of supraphysiologic doses of testosterone on muscle size and strength in normal men. *New England Journal of Medicine, 335*(1), 1-7.

Bhugra, D. (2000, February). Disturbances in objects of desire: cross-cultural issues. *Sexual & Relationship Therapy, 15*(1), 67-78. Retrieved September 25, 2009, from doi:10.1080/14681990050001574.

Bippus, A. M. (2000). Humor usage in comforting messages: Factors predicting outcomes. *Western Journal of Communication, 64*, 359-384.

Bird, J. H. (2006). Sexual addiction and marriage and family therapy: Facilitating individual and relationship healing through couple therapy. *Journal of Marital and Family Therapy, 32*(3), 297-311.

Birnbaum, G. E., Reis, H., Mikulincer, M., Gillath, O., & Orpaz, A. (2006). When sex is more than just sex: Attachment orientations, sexual experience, and relationship quality. *Journal of Personality and Social Psychology, 91*(5), 929-943.

Black AIDS Institute. (2009). *Making change real: The state of AIDS in Black America 2009.* Retrieved January 30, 2010, from www.blackaids.org/ShowArticle.aspx?pagename=ShowArticle&articletype=NEWS&articleid=663&pagenumber=1

Black, D., Gates, G., Sanders, S., & Taylor, L. (2000). Demographics of the gay and lesbian population in the United States: Evidence from available systematic data sources. *Demography, 37*(2), 139-154.

Black, D., Sanders, S., & Taylor, L. (2007). The economics of lesbian and gay families. *Journal of Economic Perspectives, 21*(2), 53-70.

Black, D. W. (2000). The epidemiology and phenomenology of compulsive sexual behavior. *CNS Spectrum, 5*, 26-35.

Blacksmith, E. (2001). Sex in the Middle Ages. *The Renaissance, 2*(1). Retrieved January 8, 2008, from www.rencentral.com/feb_mar_vol2/sexmiddleages.shtml

Blair, C. (1998). Netsex: Empowerment through discourse. In B. Ebo (Ed.), *Cyberghetto or cybertopia? Race, class, and gender on the internet.* Westport, CT: Praeger.

Blanchard, R. (2004). Quantitative and theoretical analyses of the relation between older brother and homosexuality in men. *Journal of Theoretical Biology, 230*, 173-187.

Blanchard, R., & Lippa, R. (2008, December). The sex ratio of older siblings in non-right-handed homosexual men. *Archives of Sexual Behavior, 37*(6), 970-976.

Blanchard, R., Lykins, A. D., Wherrett, D., et al. (2009). Pedophilia, hebephilia, and the DSM-IV. *Archives of Sexual Behavior, 38*, 335-350.

Blumstein, P., & Schwartz, P. (1983). *American couples.* New York: William Morrow.

Blumstein Posner, R. (2006). Early menarche: A review of research on trends in timing, racial differences, etiology, and psychosocial consequences. *Sex Roles: A Journal of Research, 54*, 315-323.

Bocij, P. (2004). *Cyberstalking: Harassment in the Internet age and how to protect your family.* Westport, CT: Praeger.

Boellstorff, T. (2005). Between religion and desire: Being Muslim and gay in Indonesia. *American Anthropologist, 107*(4), 575-585.

Bogaert, A. F. (1997). Genital asymmetry in men. *Human Reproduction, 12*(1), 68-72.

Bogaert, A. F., & Sadava, S. (2002). Adult attachment and sexual behavior. *Personal Relationships, 9*, 191-204.

Bogaert, A. F. (2006). Biological versus nonbiological older brothers and men's sexual orientation. *Proceedings of the National Academy of Sciences, 103*(28), 10771-10774.

Bogaert, A. F., Blanchard, R., & Crosthwait, L. (2007). Interaction of birth order, handedness, and sexual orientation in the Kinsey interview data. *Behavioral Neuroscience, 121*(5), 845-853.

Boies, S. C. (2002). University students' use of and reactions to online sexual information and entertainment: Links to online and offline sexual behaviour. *The Canadian Journal of Human Sexuality, 11*(2), 77-90.

Bond, B. J., Hefner, V., & Drogos, K. L. (2009). Information-seeking practices during the sexual development of lesbian, gay, and bisexual individuals: The influence and effects of coming out in a mediated environment. *Sexuality & Culture, 13*(1), 32-50.

Boonstra, H. D., Gold, R. B., Richards, C. L., & Finer, L. B. (2006). *Abortion in women's lives.* New York: Alan Guttmacher Institute.

Bos, H. M. W., van Balen, F., & van den Boom, D. C. (2004). Experience of parenthood, couple relationship, social support, and child-rearing goals in planned lesbian mother families. *Journal of Child Psychology and Psychiatry, 45*, 755-764.

Boskey, E. (2007). *Why are young women more biologically susceptible to cervical infections?* Retrieved September 25, 2009, from www.about.com

Bowlby, J. (1969/1971/1980). *Attachment and loss: Attachment* (Vols. 1-3). New York: Basic Books.

Bowlby, J. (1988). *A secure base.* London: Routledge.

Bowleg, L., Lucas, K. J., & Tschann, J. M. (2004). The ball was always in his court: An exploratory analysis of relationship scripts, sexual scripts, and condom use among African American women. *Psychology of Women Quarterly, 28*(1), 70-82.

Boyd, D., & Bee, H. (2009). *Lifespan development* (5th edition). Boston: Pearson.

Boyle, G., & Bensley, G. (2001). Adverse sexual and psychological effects of male infant circumcision. *Psychological Reports, 88*, 1105-1106.

..., Goldman, R., Svoboda, J. S., & Fernandez, E. (2002). Male circumcision: Pain, trauma, and psychosexual sequelae. *Journal of Health Psychology, 7,* 329-343.

Bramlett, M. D., & Mosher, W. D. (2002). Cohabitation, marriage, divorce, and remarriage in the United States. *National Center for Health Statistics Vital Health Statistics, 23,* 22.

Brantley, A., Knox, D., & Zusman, M. E. (2002). When and why gender differences in saying "I love you" among college students. *College Student Journal, 36*(4), 614-616.

Braveman, P. A. (2003). Monitoring equity in health and health care: A conceptual framework. *Journal of Health Population Nutrition, 21*(3), 181-192.

Brehm, S. S. (1992). *Intimate relationships.* New York: McGraw-Hill.

Brewaeys, A., de Bruyn, J. L., Louwe, L. A., & Helmerhorts, F. M. (2005). Anonymous or identity-registered sperm donors? A study of Dutch recipients' choices. *Human Reproduction, 20,* 820-824.

Briken, P., Habermann, N., Berner, W., & Hill, A. (2007). Diagnosis and treatment of sexual addiction: A survey among German sex therapists. *Sexual Addiction & Compulsivity, 14,* 131-143.

Brinley, D. E. (2000). *Improving sexual communication in marriage.* Provo, UT: Brigham Young University.

Bronfenbrenner, U. (1979). *The ecology of human development: Experiments by nature and design.* Cambridge, MA: Harvard University Press.

Brosman, S. A. (2006). *Penile cancer.* Retrieved March 5, 2008, from www.emedicine.com/MED/topic3046.htm

Brotto, L. A., Chik, H. M., Ryder, A. G., et al. (2005). Acculturation and sexual function in Asian women. *Archives of Sexual Behavior, 34*(6), 613-626.

Brown, S. L. (2004). Family structure and child well-being: The significance of parental cohabitation. *Journal of Marriage and Family, 66*(2), 351-367.

Brown, S. L. (2006). Family structure transitions and adolescent well-being. *Demography, 43*(3), 447-461.

Brown, S. L., Van Hook, J., & Glick, J. (2005). *Generational differences in cohabitation and marriage in the U.S.* Paper presented at the annual meeting of the Population Association of America, Philadelphia.

Brown, S. L., Lee, G. R., & Bulanda, J. R. (2006). Cohabitation among older adults: A national portrait. *The Journals of Gerontology Series B: Psychological Sciences and Social Sciences, 61,* S71-S79.

Brown, T. M., & Fee, E. (2003). Voices from the past. Alfred C. Kinsey: A pioneer of sex research. *American Journal of Public Health, 93*(6), 897-907.

Brückner, H., & Bearman, P. (2005). After the promise: The STD consequences of adolescent virginity pledges. *Journal of Adolescent Health, 36,* 271-278.

Brummen, H. J., Bruinser, H. W., van de Pol, G., et al. (2006). Which factors determine the sexual function 1 year after childbirth? *British Journal of Obstetricians and Gynecology, 113,* 914-918.

Buckley, T., & Carter, R. (2005). Black adolescent girls: Do gender roles and racial identity impact their self-esteem? *Sex Roles, 53*(9-10), 647-661.

Buehlman, K. T., Gottman, J. M., & Katz, L. F. (1992). How a couple views their past predicts their future: Predicting divorce from an oral history interview. *Journal of Family Psychology, 5,* 295-318.

Bullough, B., David, M., Whipple, B., et al. (1984). Subjective reports of female orgasmic expulsion of fluid. *Nurse Practitioner, 9*(3), 55-59.

Bullough, V. L. (1973). An early American sex manual or Aristotle, who? *Early American Literature, 7,* 236-246.

Bullough, V. L. (1994). *Science in the bedroom: The history of sex research.* New York: Basic Books.

Bullough, V. L. (2001). Religion, sex, and science: Some historical quandaries. *Journal of Sex Education and Therapy, 26,* 254-258.

Bullough, V. L. (2004). Sex will never be the same: The contributions of Alfred C. Kinsey. *Archives of Sexual Behavior, 33*(3), 277-237.

Bullough, V. L., & Bullough, B. (1994). *Human sexuality: An encyclopedia.* New York: Garland Publishing Company.

Bumpass, L., & Lu, H. H. (2000, March). Trends in cohabitation and implications for children's family contexts in the United States. *Population Studies, 54,* 29-41.

Burleson, B. R. (1992). Taking communication seriously. *Communication Monographs, 59,* 79-86.

Burrello, K. N. (2005). What are the strengths of interracial families? *Diversity Dating Organization.* Retrieved August 30, 2009, from www.diversitydtg.com/articles/interracial families.htm

Burrows, R., & Gane, N. (2006). Geodemographics, software, and class. *Sociology, 40*(5), 793-812.

Burton, R. (1886). The Kasîdah Of Hâjî Abdû El-Yezdî.

Busato, W., & Galindo, C. C. (2004). Topical anaesthetic use for treating premature ejaculation: A double-blind, randomized, placebo-controlled study. *British Journal of Urology, 93*(7), 1018-1021.

Bushnell, P., & Lucas, L. (2004). *Questions and answers about sex.* Kids Health. Retrieved August 30, 2007, from www.kidshealth.org/parent/emotions/feelings/sex.html

Buss, D. M. (1994). *The evolution of desire: Strategies of human mating.* New York: Basic Books.

Buss, D. M. (1999). *Evolutionary psychology: The new science of the mind.* Boston: Allyn & Bacon.

Buss, D. M., & Angleitner, A. (1989). Mate selection preferences in Germany and the United States. *Personality and Individual Differences, 10,* 269-1280.

Buss, D. M., & Schmitt, D. P. (1993). Sexual strategies theory: An evolutionary perspective on human dating. *Psychological Review, 100,* 204-232.

Bussey, K., & Bandura, A. (1999). Social cognitive theory of gender development and differentiation. *Psychological Review, 106,* 676-713.

Buster, J. E., et al. (2005). Testosterone patch for low sexual desire in surgically menopausal women: A randomized trial. *Obstetrics & Gynecology, 105,* 944-952.

Butcher, J. (1999). Female sexual problems: Loss of desire. *Western Journal of Medicine, 171*(1), 41.

Butler, R. N., & Lewis, M. I. (1986). *Midlife love life: How to deal with the physical and emotional changes of midlife and their effect on your sex life.* New York: Harper & Row.

Byers, E. S., & Demmons, S. (1999). Sexual satisfaction and sexual self-disclosure within dating relationships. *Journal of Sex Research, 36,* 180-189.

Byne, W., Tobet S., Mattiace, L. A., et al. (2001). The interstitial nuclei of the human anterior hypothalamus: An investigation of variation with sex, sexual orientation, and HIV status. *Hormones and Behavior, 40,* 86-92.

Byrne, D. (1977). Social psychology and the study of sexual behavior. *Personality and Social Psychology Bulletin, 1,* 3-30.

Cabello, F. (1997). Female ejaculation: Myth and reality. In J. J. Baras-Vass & M. Perze-Conchillo (Eds.), *Sexuality and human rights: Proceedings of the XIII world congress of sexology* (pp. 325-333). Valencia, Spain: E.C.V.S.A.

Cain, V. S., et al. (2003). Sexual functioning and practices in a multi-ethnic study of midlife women: Baseline results from SWAN. *Journal of Sex Research, 40,* 266-276.

Campbell, K. (2002). Today's courtship: White teeth, root beer, and e-mail? *Christian Science Monitor,* 1-4.

Campbell, N. (2003). *Be fruitful and multiply.* San Antonio, TX: Vision Forum.

Camperio-Ciani, A., Corna, F., & Capiluppi, C. (2004). Evidence for maternally inherited factors favouring male homosexuality and promoting female fecundity. *Proceedings Biological Sciences, 271*(15554), 2217-2221.

Canales, G. (2000). Gender as subculture: The first division of multicultural diversity. In I. Cuellar & F. A. Paniagua (Eds.), *Handbook of multicultural mental health: Assessment and treatment of diverse populations* (pp. 63-77). New York: Academic Press.

Capaldi, D. M., Crosby, L., & Stoolmiller, M. (1996). Predicting the timing of first sexual intercourse for at-risk adolescent males. *Child Development, 67*(2), 344-359.

Cardillo, M. (2005). *Intimate relationships: Personality development through interaction during early development.* Retrieved November 30, 2005, from http://www.personalityresearch.org/papers/cardillo

Carnes, P. J. (2001). Cybersex, courtship and escalating arousal: Factors in addictive sexual desire. *Sexual Addiction & Compulsivity, 8,* 45-78.

Cass, V. C. (1979). Homosexual identity formation: A theoretical model. *Journal of Homosexuality, 4,* 219-235.

Casteels, K., Wouters, C., Van Geet, C., & Devlieger, H. (2004). Video reveals self-stimulation in infancy. *Acta Paediatr, 93,* 844-846.

Catania, J. A. (1998). Dyadic sexual communication scale. In C. M. Davis, W. L. Yarber, R. Bauserman, G. Schreer, & S. L. Davis (Eds.), *Handbook of sexuality-related measures* (pp. 129-131). London: Sage.

Cavanagh, S. E. & Huston, A. C. (2006). Family instability and children's early problem behavior. *Social Forces, 85*(1), 551-581.

Cavanaugh, J. C., & Blanchard-Fields, F. (2002). *Adult development and aging* (4th ed.). Belmont, CA: Wadsworth.

Centers for Disease Control and Prevention. (2005). Births: Preliminary data for 2004. *National Vital Statistics Report, 54*(8). Retrieved March 20, 2006, from www.cdc.gov/nchs/data/nvsr/nvsr54/nvsr54_08.pdf

Centers for Disease Control and Prevention. (2006). *Sexually transmitted disease surveillance, 2005.* Atlanta: National Center for HIV, STD, and TB Prevention.

Centers for Disease Control and Prevention. (2008a). Births, marriages, divorces, and deaths: Provisional data for July 2007. *National Vital Statistics Reports, 56,* 14.

Centers for Disease Control and Prevention. (2008b). *Health risk behaviors by race/ethnicity: National YRBSS 2007.* Retrieved August 9, 2009, from www.cdc.gov/yrbss

Centers for Disease Control and Prevention. (2008c). Sexually active teens. *MMWR* 2007:57 (No. SS-4). Table 63. Retrieved August 9, 2009, from www.cdc.gov/mmwr/pfd/ss/ss5704.pdf

Centers for Disease Control and Prevention. (2008d). *Teen birth rate rises for the first time in 15 years.* Retrieved January 10, 2009, from http:// www.cdc.gov/nchs/pressroom.html

Centers for Disease Control and Prevention. (2009a). Condoms and STDs. *Fact Sheet for Public Health Personnel: 2009.* Retrieved September 23, 2009, from www.cdc.gov/condomeffectiveness/brief.html

Centers for Disease Control and Prevention. (2009b). HIV/AIDS among African Americans. *CDC HIV/AIDS Facts.* Retrieved January 31, 2010, from http://www.cdc.gov/hiv/topics/aa/resources/factsheets/aa.htm

Centers for Disease Control and Prevention. (2009c). *HIV/AIDS surveillance report, 2007* (Vol. 19). Atlanta: U.S. Department of Health and Human Services, CDC.

Centers for Disease Control and Preventions. (2009d). *Trends in the prevalence of selected risk behaviors for White students. National YRBS: 1991-2007.* Retrieved September 14, 2009, from www.cdc.gov/yrbss

Cere, D. (2001, Spring). Courtship today: The view from academia. *Public Interest, 53.*

Chang, R. H., Hsu, F. K., Chan, S. T., & Chan, Y. B. (1960). Scrotal asymmetry and handedness. *Journal of Anatomy, 94,* 543-548.

Chang, A. K. (2005). *Testicle infection.* Retrieved March 5, 2008, from www.emedicinehealth.com/script/main/art.asp?articlekey=58891&pf=3&page=2

Cheah, C. S. L., & Robin, K. H. (2004). Comparison of European American and main and Chinese mothers' responses to aggression and social withdrawal in preschoolers. *International Journal of Behavioral Development, 28,* 83-94.

Chen, J., et al. (2000). Predicting penile size during erection. *International Journal of Impotence Research, 12*(6), 328-333.

Chesney, P. J. (1989). Clinical aspects and spectrum of illness of toxic shock syndrome: An overview. *Reviews of Infectious Diseases, 11,* (Suppl. 1) 1-7.

Chevret, M., Jaudinot, E., Sullivan, K., et al. (2004). Quality of sexual life and satisfaction in female partners of men with ED: Psychometric validation of the index of sexual life (ISL) questionnaire. *Journal of Sex & Marital Therapy, 30,* 141-155.

Chiaradonna, C. (2008). The Chlamydia cascade: Enhanced STD prevention strategies for adolescents. *Journal of Pediatric and Adolescent Gynecology, 21*(5), 233-241.

Christakis, D. A., et al. (2000). A trade-off analysis of routine newborn circumcision. *Pediatrics, 105*(1), 246-249.

Christopher, F. S., & Sprecher, S. (2000). Sexuality in marriage, dating, and other relationships: EA decade review. *Journal of Marriage and the Family, 62,* 999-1017.

Chumlea, W. E., Schubert, C. M., Foche, A. F., et al. (2003). Age at menarche and racial comparisons in U.S. girls. *Pediatrics, 111,* 110-113.

Cianciatto, J., & Cahill, S. (2006). *Youth in the crosshairs: The third wave of ex-gay activism.* New York: National Gay and Lesbian Task Force Policy Institute.

Circumcision Information and Resource Pages. (2008). Retrieved February 15, 2008, from www.cirp.org

Citron, N. (2003, July 1). Demographics, health, and health services. *American Demographics.*

Clayton, A. H., et al. (2006). Reliability and validity of the Sexual Interest and Desire Inventory-Female (SIDI-F), a scale designed to measure severity of female hypoactive sexual desire disorder. *Journal of Sex and Marital Therapy, 32*(2), 115-135.

Clement, P., et al. (2005). D2-like receptors mediate the expulsion phase of ejaculation elicited by 8-hyroxy-2-(di-*n*-propylamino) tetralin in rats. *Journal of Pharmacology and Experimental Therapeutics, 316,* 830-834.

Cleveland Clinic. (2006). *Prostatitis.* Retrieved March 7, 2008, from www.cleveland clinic.org/health/

Cleveland Clinic. (2008). *Menopause: The short-term effects and long-term risks.* Retrieved September 17, 2000, from http://my.clevelandclinic.org/disorders/Menopause/hic_Menopause_The_Short-Term_Effects_and_Long-Term_Risks.aspx

Clinebell, H. J., & Clinebell, C. H. (1970). *The intimate marriage.* New York: Harper & Row.

Clinician Reviews. (2007). Amenorrhea: Signs, symptoms, and drugs. *Clinician Reviews, 17*(3), 63.

Cohan, C. I., & Kleinbaum, S. (2002). Toward a greater understanding of the cohabitation effect: Premarital cohabitation and marital communication. *Journal of Marriage and Family, 64,* 180-192.

Cohen, L. & Roth, S. (1984). Coping with abortion. *Journal of Human Stress, 10*(3), 140-145.

Cohen, L., & Galynker, I. (2002). Clinical features of pedophilia and implications for treatment. *Journal of Psychiatric Practice, 8,* 276-289.

Cohen, L., & Galynker, I. (2009, June). Psychopathology and personality traits of pedophiles. *Psychiatric Times, 26*(6), 25-30. Retrieved September 13, 2009, from Academic Search Premier database.

Coleman, E. (1987). Assessment of sexual orientation. *Journal of Homosexuality, 14*(3/4), 9-24.

Coleman, E. (1982, March). Developmental stages of the coming-out process. *American Behavioral Scientist, 25*(4), 469-482.

Collins, P. H. (2004). *Black sexual politics: African Americans, gender, and the new racism.* New York: Routledge.

Collins, S., et al. (2002). Effects of circumcision on male sexual function: Debunking a myth? *Journal of Urology, 167*(5), 2111-2112.

Connell, R. W. (1987). *Gender and power: Society, the person, and sexual politics.* Stanford, CA: Stanford University Press.

Connell, K., et al. (2005). Effects of age, menopause, and comorbidities on neurological function of the female genitalia. *International Journal of Impotence Research, 17*(1), 63-70.

Connolly, A., Thorp, J., & Pahel, L. (2005). Effects of pregnancy and childbirth on postpartum sexual function: A longitudinal prospective study. *International Urogynecological Journal of Pelvic Floor Dysfunction,* Epub ahead of print. Retrieved September 12, 2009, from http://www.ncibi.nlm.nih.gov/entrez/query.fcgi?cmd=retrieve&db=pubmed&dopt=Abstract&list_uids=15838587&query_hl=53

Cook, E. (2005). Commitment in polyamory. *Electronic Journal of Human Sexuality,* 8 (Annual 2005): NA. *Expanded Academic ASAP.* Gale. Kansas State University Libraries. Retrieved September 2, 2009.

Coontz, S., & Folbre, N. (2002) *Marriage, poverty and public policy: a discussion paper from the council on contemporary families.* Presented at the Fifth Annual CCF Conference, April 26-28, 2002. Retrieved January 3, 2010, from http://www.comtemporaryfamilies.org/briefing

Cooper, A. (2000). *Cybersex and sexual compulsivity: The dark side of the force.* New York: Brunner-Mazel.

Cooper, A., Delmonico, D. L., & Burg, R. (2000). Cybersex users, abusers, and compulsives: New findings and implications. *Sexual Addiction & Compulsivity: The Journal of Treatment and Prevention, 71*(1-2), 5-29.

Cooper, A., & Griffin-Shelley, E. (2002). The Internet: The next sexual revolution. In A. Cooper (Ed.), *Sex and the Internet: A guidebook for clinicians* (pp. 1-15). New York: Brunner-Routledge.

Corley, D. (2003). *Cybersex addiction: As lethal as crack cocaine.* Retrieved June 16, 2007, from http://www.santecenter.com/cybersex_addiction.htm

Cornog, M. (1986). Naming sexual body parts: Preliminary patterns and implications. *Journal of Sex Research 22,* 393-398.

Costello, C., et al. (2002). The effect of interval tubal sterilization on sexual interest and pleasure. *Obstetrics and Gynecology, 100,* 511-517.

Coville, J. (1999). *The perfumed garden of sensual delight* (translation). London: Kegan Paul International.

Crosnoe, R., & Elder, G. H. (2002). Successful adaptation in the later years: A lifecourse approach to aging. *Social Psychology Quarterly, 65*(4), 309-328.

Cummings, A. M., & Kavlock, R. J. (2004). Function of sexual glands and mechanisms of sex differentiation. *Journal of Toxicological Sciences, 29*(3), 167-178.

Cupach, W. R., & Comstock, J. (1990). Satisfaction with sexual communication in marriage: Links to sexual satisfaction and dyadic adjustment. *Journal of Social and Personal Relationships, 7,* 179-186.

Cyranowski, J. M., & Andersen, B. L. (1998). Schemas, sexuality, and romantic attachment. *Journal of Personality and Social Psychology, 74,* 1364-1379.

Daling, J. R., et al. (2005). Penile cancer: Importance of circumcision, human papillomavirus and smoking in situ and invasive disease. *International Journal of Cancer, 116*(4), 606-616.

Daneback, K., Cooper, A., & Mansson, S. A. (2004). An Internet study of cybersex participants. *Archives of Sexual Behavior, 34*(3), 321-328.

Daneback, K., Mansson, S. A., & Ross, M. W. (2007). Using the Internet to find offline sexual partners. *Cyberpsychology & Behavior, 10*(1), 100-107.

Darroch, J., Myers, L., & Cassell, J. (2003). Sex differences in the experience of testing positive for genital Chlamydia infection: A qualitative study with implications for public health and for a national screening programme. *Sexually Transmitted Infections, 79,* 372-376.

Davidson, J. (2002). Working with polyamorous clients in the clinical setting. *Electronic Journal of Human Sexuality, 5,* (Annual 2002). Retrieved September 2, 2009, from www.find.galegroup.com.er.lib.ksu.edu/itx/start.do?prodId=EAIM

Davidson, J., Darling, C. A., & Norton, L. X. (1995). Religiosity and the sexuality of women: Sexual behavior and sexual satisfaction revisited. *Journal of Sex Research, 32,* 235-243.

Davidson, J. K., Sr., & Darling, C. A. (1989). Self-perceived differences in the female orgasmic response. *Family Practice Research Journal, 8,* 75-84.

Davidson, J. K., & Hoffman, L. E. (1986). Sexual fantasies and sexual satisfaction: An empirical analysis of erotic thought. *The Journal of Sex Research, 22,* 184-205.

Davis, D., Shaver, P. R., & Vernon, M. L. (2003). Physical, emotional, and behavioral reactions to breaking up: The roles of gender, age, emotional involvement, and attachment style. *Personality and Social Psychology Bulletin, 29*(7), 871-884.

Davis, S. (2006). *Protect your sexual health.* Retrieved August 17, 2009, from www.medicinenet.com/sexual_health/article.htm

Deans, E. I. & Grimes, D. A. (2009). Intrauterine devices for adolescents: A systematic review. *Contraception, 79,* 419-423.

Deaux, K., & Hanna, R. (1984). Courtship in the personals column: The influence of gender and sexual orientation. *Sex Roles, 11,* 363-375.

Dekker, A., & Schmidt, G. (2002). Patterns of masturbatory behaviour: Changes between the sixties and the nineties. *Journal of Psychology and Human Sexuality, 14,* 35-48.

DeLamater, J. D., & Hyde, J. S. (1998). Essential versus social constructionism in the study of human sexuality. *The Journal of Sex Research, 35,* 10-18.

DeLamater, J. D., & Friedrich, W. N. (2002). Human sexual development (statistical data included). *Journal of Sex Research, 39*(1), 10-14.

Delhez, M., Hansenne, M., & Legor, J. J. (2003). Andropause and psychopathology: Minor symptoms rather than pathological ones. *Psychoneuroendocrinology, 28*(7), 863-874.

Demchak, M. A., Rickard, C., & Elquist, M. (2001). Providing cues to enhance receptive communication. *Nevada Dual Sensory Impairment Project Newsletter, 12*(2).

Denniston, G. C. (2004). Circumcision and sexual pleasure. In G. C. Denniston, F. M. Hodges, & M. F. Milos (Eds.), *Flesh and blood: Perspectives on the problem of circumcision in contemporary society* (pp. 44-55). New York: Kluwer.

de Silva, W. P. (1999). Sexual variations. *British Medical Journal, 318,* 654-656.

DeSteno, D., Valdesolo, P., & Bartlett, M. Y. (2006). Jealousy and the threatened self: Getting to the heart of the green-eyed monster. *Journal of Personality and Social Psychology, 91,* 626-641.

Diamant, A. L., Lever, J., & Schuster, M. A. (2000). Lesbians' sexual activities and efforts to reduce risk for sexually transmitted diseases. *Journal of the Gay and Lesbian Medical Association, 4,* 41-48.

Diamond, L. (2008). *Sexual fluidity: Understanding women's love and desire.* Boston: Harvard University Press.

Diamond, M. (2004). Pediatric management of ambiguous and traumatized genitalia. *Contemporary Sexuality, 38*(9), i-viii.

Diaz, R. M., Ayala, G., & Bein, E. (2001). Sexual risk as an outcome of social oppression: Data from a probability sample of Latino gay men. *Sexually Transmitted Infections, 85*(1), 65-69.

Dickerson, L. M., Mazyek, P. J., & Hunter, M. H. (2003). Premenstrual syndrome. *American Family Physician, 67,* 1743-172.

DiChristina, M. (2009, June). Abnormal attraction. *Scientific American Mind, 20*(3), 76-81. Retrieved September 13, 2009, from Academic Search Premier database.

Dindia, K., & Allen, M. (1992). Sex-differences in self-disclosure: A meta-analysis. *Psychological Bulletin, 112,* 106-124.

Dion, K. L., & Dion, K. K. (1993). Individualistic and collectivist perspectives on gender and the cultural context of love and intimacy. *Journal of Social Issues, 49,* 53-69.

Discovery Health Channel. (2008). *Freebirthing.* Retrieved March 13, 2010, from http://health.discovery.com/tv/crib-notes/freebirthing.html

Disease Management. (2008). Dysmenorrhea in adolescents can generally be treated successfully with NSAIDS or hormonal contraception. *Drugs & Therapy Perspectives, 24*(11), 18-20.

Dobson, J. (2005). *Courtship is an alternative to the dating model.* Retrieved October 20, 2005, from http://www.uexpress.com/focusonthefamily/index.html?uc_full_date=20020428

C. (2005). *Male-female sex differences in cross-sex and same-sex adolescent friendships.* Retrieved November 27, 2005, from http://www.students.haverford.edu/cdolich/final%20paper.htm

Donor Sibling Registry. (2008). *Redefining family.* Retrieved March 15, 2008, from www.donorsiblingregistry.com

Donovan, B. (2004). Sexually transmissible infection other than HIV. *Lancet, 363,* 545–556.

Doosje, B., Rojahn, K., & Fischer, A. (1999). Partner preferences as a function of gender, age, political orientation and level of education. *Sex Roles, 40,* 45–60.

Dorey, G., et al. (2004). Randomized controlled trial of pelvic floor muscle exercises and manometric biofeedback for erectile dysfunction. *British Journal of General Practice, 54,* 819–825.

Dover, K. J. (1989). *Greek homosexuality.* Cambridge, MA: Harvard University Press.

Doyle, C., Ewald Swain, H. A., & Ewald, P. W. (2007). Premenstrual syndrome: An evolutionary perspective on its causes and treatment. *Perspectives in Biology and Medicine, 50*(2), 181–203.

Drasin, H., et al. (2008). Age cohort differences in the developmental milestones of gay men. *Journal of Homosexuality, 54*(4), 381–399.

Dubois, S. L. (1997). Gender differences in the emotional tone of written sexual fantasies. *The Canadian Journal of Human Sexuality, 6*(4), 307.

Dunphy, D. C. (1963). The social structure of urban adolescent peer groups. *Sociometery, 26,* 230–246.

Durex. (2007). *Global sex survey.* Retrieved December 19, 2008, from http://www.about.com

Dutton, M. A. (1998, March/April). Cultural issues in trauma treatment. *Centering Newsletter, 3*(2).

Echlin, B. (2003). When two just won't do. *The Guardian* (November 14, 2003). Retrieved September 1, 2009, from www.guardian.co.uk.women/story.html

The Economist (2007). *Sex and the Internet.* April 19, 2007.

Edin, K. (2000). Few good men: Why low income single mothers don't get married. *American Prospect II,* January 2000, 26–31.

Edwards, J. N., & Booth, A. (1994). Sexuality, marriage, and wellbeing: The middle years. In A. S. Rossi (Ed.), *Sexuality across the life course* (pp. 233–259). Chicago: University of Chicago Press.

Edwards, R., & Hamilton, M. A. (2004). You need to understand my gender role: An empirical test of Tannen's model of gender and communication. *Sex Roles, 50,* 491–504.

Effros, R. B. et al. (2008). Workshop on HIV infection and aging: What is known and future research directions. *Clinical Infectious Diseases, 47*(4), 542–553.

The Egypt Exploration Society. (2007). *Philaenis, "The art of love."* Retrieved August 19, 2009, from http://papyrology.ox.ac.uk

Eisen, A. et al. (2005). Breast cancer risk following bilateral oophorectomy in BRCA1 and BRCA2 mutation carriers: International case-control study. *Journal of Clinical Oncology, 23*(30), 7491–7496.

Eisenberg, M. E., et al. (2004). Parents' beliefs about condoms and contraceptives: Are they medically correct? *Perspectives on Sexual and Reproductive Health, 36*(2), 50–57.

Eisenman, R. (2001). Penis size: Survey of female perceptions of sexual satisfaction. *BMC Women's Health, 1*(1).

Eisinger, F. (2007). Prophylactic mastectomy: Ethical issues. *British Medical Journal, 81–82*(1), 7–19.

Elliot, A. J., & Reis, H. T. (2003). Attachment and exploration in adulthood. *Journal of Personality and Social Psychology, 85,* 317–331.

Ellis, B. J., & Symons, D. (1990). Sex differences in sexual fantasy: An evolutionary psychological approach. *Journal of Sex Research, 27,* 527–56.

Ellison, C. (2000). *Women's sexualities.* Oakland, CA: New Harbinger Publications.

Elnashar, A. M., et al. (2006). Female sexual dysfunction in lower Egypt. *British Journal of Obstetrics & Gynecology, 114,* 201–206.

Emans, S. J. (2000). Physical examination of the child and adolescent. In *Evaluation of the sexually abused child: A medical textbook and photographic atlas* (2nd ed., pp. 64–65). London: Oxford University Press.

Engender Health. (2003). Teaching the client how to perform a genital-self exam. *Management of Men's Reproductive Health Problems.* Appendix F.

England, P., & Thomas, R. (2007). The decline of the date and the rise of the college hook up. In A. Skolnick & J. Skolnick (Eds.), *Family in Transition* (14th ed.). Boston: Allyn & Bacon.

Erber, R., & Erber, M. W. (2001). *Intimate relationships: Issues, theories, and research* (2nd ed.). Boston: Allyn & Bacon.

Erikson, E. H. (1950). *Childhood and society.* New York: Norton.

Erikson, E. H. (1963). *Childhood and society* (2nd ed.). New York: Norton.

Ernst, E., & Pittler, M. (1998). Yohimbine for erectile dysfunction: A systematic review and meta-analysis of randomized clinical trials. *Journal of Urology, 159,* 433–436.

Eskridge, W. N., & Hunter, N. D. (1997). *Sexuality, gender, and the law.* Westbury, NY: Foundation Press.

Evans, B. A. (2004). *Androgen insensitivity syndrome (AIS).* Intersex Society of North America. Retrieved July 19, 2009, from www.isna.org/html

Eveleth, P. B., & Tanner, J. M. (1990). Sexual development: In P. B. Eveleth (Ed.), *Worldwide Variation in Human Growth* (pp. 161–175). Cambridge, England: Cambridge University Press.

Everaerd, W., Both, S., & Laan, E. (2006). The experience of sexual emotions. *Annual Review of Sex Research, 17,* 183–199.

Fagan, P. F., & Hanks, D. B. (1997). *The child abuse crisis: The disintegration of marriage, family, and the American community.* Washington, DC: The Heritage Foundation.

The Family Research Council. Retrieved August 19, 2009, from www.frc.org

Family Violence Prevention. (2006). *The facts on reproductive health and violence against women.* Retrieved August 1, 2009 from http://www.endabuse.org/resources/facts/ReproductiveHealth.pdf

Farley, D. (1999). On the teen scene: TSS, reducing the risk. *FDA Consumer Magazine,* October 1999.

Feeney, J. A., & Noller, P. (1990). Attachment style as a predictor of adult romantic relationships. *Journal of Personality and Social Psychology, 58,* 281–291.

Fehr, B. (1988). Prototype analysis of the concepts of love and commitment. *Journal of Personality and Social Psychology, 55,* 557–579.

Feierman, J. R., & Feierman, L. A. (2000). Paraphilias. In L. T. Szuchman & F. Muscarella (Eds.), *Psychological perspectives on human sexuality* (pp. 480–518). New York: John Wiley & Sons, Inc.

Feijoo, A. N. (2007). Trends in sexual risk behaviors among high school students—United States, 1991 to 1997 and 1999 to 2003. *Advocates for Youth,* November 4. Retrieved September 14, 2009, from www.advocatesforyouth.org/PUBLICATIONS/factsheet/fstrends.htm

Feingold, A. (1992). Gender differences in mate selection preferences: A test of the parental investment model. *Psychological Bulletin, 112,* 125–139.

Feldman, H. A., Johannes, C. B., Derby, C. A., et al. (2000). Erectile dysfunction and coronary risk factors: Prospective results from the Massachusetts male aging study. *Preventive Medicine, 30*(4), 328–338.

Feldman, R. K. (2010). *Discovering the life span* (3rd ed.). Boston: Pearson Education.

Ferree, M. C. (2003). Women and the web: Cybersex activity and implications. *Sexual and Relationship Therapy, 18*(3), 385–393.

Ferris, C., et al. (2004). Activation of neural pathways associated with sexual arousal in non-human primates. *National Institute of Health, 19*(2), 168–175.

Field, A. E., et al. (2005). Exposure to the mass media, body shape concerns, and use of supplements to improve weight and shape among male and female adolescents. *Pediatrics, 116,* e214–e220.

Fields, J. (2004). America's families and living arrangements: 2003. *United States Census Bureau current population reports* (pp. 20–537). Retrieved July 5, 2008, from http://www.census.gov/prod/2004pubs/p20-553.pdf

Figard, A., & Figard, J. (1992). Personal Communication, International Childbirth Educators Association Conference. June, 1992.

Finer, L. B. & Henshaw, S. K. (2006). Disparities in rates of unintended pregnancy in the United States, 1994 and 2001. *Perspectives on Sexual & Reproductive Health, 38*(2), 90–96.

Fink, K., Carson, C., & DeVillis, R. (2002). Adult circumcision outcome study: Effect on erectile function, penile sensitivity, sexual activity, and satisfaction. *Journal of Urology, 167,* 2113–2116.

Firestone, R., & Catlett, J. (2000). *Fear of intimacy.* Santa Barbara, CA: Glendon.

Firestone, R. W., & Firestone, L. (2004). Methods for overcoming the fear of intimacy. In D. J. Mashek & A. P. Aron (Eds.), *Handbook of closeness and intimacy* (pp. 375–395). Mahwah, NJ: Erlbaum.

Fissell, M. (2003). Hairy women and naked truths: Gender and the politics of knowledge in *Aristotle's Masterpiece. The William and Mary Quarterly, 60*(1).

Flaman, P. (2001). Christian sexual ethics: A comparison of three approaches by contemporary Catholic scholars. University of Alberta. Retrieved September 14, 2009, from www.ualberta.ca/~pflaman/cse.html

Fleiss, P. M., Hodges, F. M., & Van Howe, R. S. (1998). Immunological functions of the human prepuce. *Sexually Transmitted Infections, 74,* 364–367.

Fleiss, P. M., & Hodges, F. M. (2002). *What your doctor may not tell you about circumcision.* New York: Warner Books.

Florsheim, P., et al. (2003). The transition to parenthood among young African American and Latino couples: Relational predictors of risk for parental dysfunction. *Journal of Family Psychology, 17,* 65–79.

Follingstad, D. R., & Kimbrell, C. D. (1986). Sex fantasies revisited: An expansion and further clarification of variables affecting sex fantasy production. *Archives of Sexual Behavior, 15*(6), 475–486.

Food and Drug Administration. (2009). *Gardasil.* Retrieved March 13, 2010, from http://www.fda.gov/BiologicsBloodVaccines/Vaccines/ApprovedProducts/UCM094042

Forbes, G. G., Adams-Curtis, L. E., White, K. B., & Holmgren, K. M. (2003). The role of benevolent sexism in women's and men's perceptions of the menstruating woman. *Psychology of Women Quarterly, 27,* 58–63.

Forsyth, C. J. (1996). The structuring of vicarious sex. *Deviant Behavior: An Interdisciplinary Journal, 17,* 279–295.

Fortenberry, J. D., et al. (2002). Relationship of stigma and shame to gonorrhea and HIV screening. *American Journal of Public Health, 92,* 378–381.

Fortenberry, J. D., et al. (2005). Daily mood, partner support, and partner interest and sexual activity among adolescent women. *Health Psychology, 24*(3), 252–257.

Foster, L. R. & Byers, S. E. (2008). Predictors of stigma and shame related to sexually transmitted infections: Attitudes, education, and knowledge. *The Canadian Journal of Human Sexuality, 17*(4), 193–202.

Foucault, M. (1976). *The history of sexuality* (Vol. 1): *The will to knowledge.* London: Penguin.

Foucault, M. (1984). *The history of sexuality* (Vol. 2): The care of self. London: Penguin.

Foucault, M. (1992). *The history of sexuality* (Vol. 3): *The use of pleasure.* London: Penguin.

France, D. (2007, June 25). The science of gaydar. *New York, 40*(23), 32–99.

Francoeur, R. T. (2000). *The complete dictionary of sexology.* The Continuum Publishing Company.

Freud, S. (1905). *Three essays on the theory of sexuality.* London: Hogarth Press, 1960.

Friedrich, W. N., et al. (1991). Normative sexual behavior in children. *Pediatrics, 88*(3), 456-464.

Friedrich, W. N., et al. (1998). Normative sexual behavior in children: A contemporary sample. *Pediatrics, 101*(4), 1-13.

Fugate Woods, N., & Sullivan Mitchell, E. (2005). Symptoms during the perimenopause: Prevalence, severity, trajectory, and significance in women's lives. *The American Journal of Medicine, 118*(12), 14-24.

Fullmer, E. M. (1995). Challenging biases against families of older gays and lesbians. In G. Smith, S. S. Tobin, E. Robertson-Tcabo, & P. W. Power (Eds.), *Strengthening aging families.* Thousand Oaks, CA: Sage.

Furman, W. (2002). The emerging field of adolescent romantic relationships. *Current Directions in Psychological Science 11*(5), 177-180.

Furman, W., & Buhrmester, D. (1992). Age and sex differences in perceptions of networks and social relationships. *Child Development, 63,* 103-115.

Furukawa, T., Yokouchi, T., Hirai, T., Kitamura, T., & Takahashi, K. (1999). Parental loss in childhood and social support in adulthood among psychiatric patients. *Journal of Psychiatric Research, 22,* 165-169.

Gagnon, J. H., & Simon, W. (1973). *Sexual conduct: the social sources of human sexuality.* Chicago: Aldine Publishing Co.

Galvin, K. M., Bylund, C. L., & Brommel, B. J. (2008). *Family communication: Cohesion and change.* Boston: Allyn & Bacon.

Garcia-Mayor, R. V., et al. (1997). Serum leptin levels in normal children: Relationship to age, gender, body mass index, pituitary-gonad hormones, and pubertal stage. *Journal of Clinical Endocrinology and Metabolism, 82,* 2849-2855.

Garza-Mercer, F., Christensen, A., & Doss, B. (2006). Sex and affection in heterosexual and homosexual couples: An evolutionary perspective. *Electronic Journal of Human Sexuality, 9.*

Gass, M. S., Dunn, C. D., & Stys, S. J. (1986). Effect of episiotomy on the frequency of vaginal outlet lacerations. *Journal of Reproductive Medicine, 31*(4), 240-244.

Gates, G. J. (2006). Same-sex couples and the gay, lesbian, bisexual population: New estimates from the American Community Survey. *The Williams Institute on Sexual Orientation Law and Public Policy.* Los Angeles, CA: UCLA School of Law. Retrieved September 2, 2009, from www.law.ucla.edu

Gates, G. J., Lee Badgett, M. V., Macomber, J. E., & Chambers, K. C. (2007). Adoption and foster care by gay and lesbian parents in the United States. Retrieved September 1, 2009, from http://www.law.ucla.edu/WilliamsInstitute/publications/FinalAdoptionReport.pdf

General Social Science Survey & Gallup Polls. (1997-2009). *Prevalence of sexual prejudice.* Retrieved March 22, 2010, from http://psychology.ucdavis.edu/rainbow/html/prej_prev.html#gss4_text

Georgia Reproductive Specialists. (2005). Reproductive technology. Retrieved September 2, 2009, from www.ivf.com/index.php

German, K. (2002). *Effects of intimacy on adult development.* Retrieved August 20, 2007, from www.oberlin.edu/faculty/darling

Gerressu, M., Mercer, C. H., Graham, C. A., et al. (2008). Prevalence of masturbation and associated factors in a British National Probability Survey. *Archives of Sexual Behavior, 37,* 266-278.

Getzfeld, A. R. (2006). *Essentials of abnormal psychology.* Hoboken, NJ: John Wiley & Sons, Inc.

Gibson-Davis, C., Edin, K., & McLanahan, S. (2005). High hopes but even higher expectations: The retreat from marriage among low-income couples. *Journal of Marriage and Family, 67,* 1301-1312.

Gil, V. (1990). Sexual fantasy experiences and guilt among conservative Christians: An exploratory study. *The Journal of Sex Research, 27,* 629-638.

Gilbart, V. L., et al. (2006). Factors associated with heterosexual transmission of HIV to individuals without a major risk within England, Wales, and Northern Ireland: A comparison with national probability surveys. *Sexually Transmitted Infections, 82*(1), 15-20.

Giles, J. (2004). *The nature of sexual desire.* Westport, CT: Praeger.

Gilmour-Bryson, A. (2007). Sexuality in medieval Europe: Doing unto others; Love, sex and marriage in the Middle Ages: A sourcebook; and, Gender and sexuality in the Middle Ages: A medieval source documents reader (review). *Journal of the History of Sexuality, 16*(1), 134-143.

Ginsberg, T. B., Pomerantz, S. C., & Kramer-Feeley, V. (2005). Sexuality in older adults: Behaviours and preferences. *Age & Ageing, 34*(5), 475-480.

Glendon Association. (2005). *Parent-child relationships.* Retrieved December 1, 2005, from http://64.82.2.174/glendon_compass.html

Glenn, N., & Marquardt, E. (2001). *Hooking up, hanging out, and hoping for Mr. Right: College women on dating and mating today.* Institute for American Values. Retrieved October 20, 2005, from http://www.americanvalues.org/Hooking_Up.pdf

Glueck, B. C. (1955). Final report: Research project for the study and treatment of persons convicted of crimes involving sexual aberrations. New York: New York State Department of Mental Hygiene.

Goberna, J., et al. (2009). Sexual experiences during the climacteric years: What do women think about it? *Maturitas, 62,* 47-52.

Goldstein, A. (2007). *Urology: Pre-ejaculate or pre-cum.* Retrieved July 30, 2009, from http://en.allexperts.com/q/Urology-Male-issues-989/pre-ejaculate-pre-cum.htm

Goleman, D. (1991). Theory links early puberty to stress. *New York Times, 150,* B5. July 30.

Goodson, P., McCormick, D., & Evans, A. (2001). Searching for sexually explicit materials on the Internet: An exploratory study of college student's behavior and attitudes. *Archives of Sexual Behavior, 30*(2), 101-118.

Gordon, H. (2008). The treatment of paraphilias: An historical perspective. *Criminal Behaviour and Mental Health, 18*(79-87), Published online in Wiley InterScience, Retrieved from http://www.interscience.wiley.com, DOI: 10.1002/cbm.687

Gordon, K. C., Baucom, D. H., & Snyder, D. K. (2004). An integrative intervention promoting recovery from extramarital affairs. *Journal of Marital and Family Therapy, 30,* 213-232.

Gottman, J. M. (1994a). *What predicts divorce? The relationship between marital process and marital outcomes.* Hillsdale, NJ: Erlbaum.

Gottman, J. M. (1994b). *Why marriages succeed or fail.* New York: Simon & Schuster.

Gottman, J. M. (1999). *The marriage clinic: A scientifically based marital therapy.* New York: Norton.

Gottman, J. M., & Gottman, J. (2007). *Ten lessons to transform your marriage.* New York: Three Rivers.

Gottman, J. M., Ryan, K. D., Carrere, S., & Erlye, A. M. (2002). Toward a scientifically based marital therapy. In H. A. Liddle, D. A. Santisteban, R. F. Levant, & J. H. Bray (Eds.), *Family psychology: Science-based interventions* (pp. 147-174). Washington, DC: American Psychological Association.

Gould, D. C., Petty, R., & Jacobs, H. S. (2000). For and against: The male menopause—does it exist? *British Medical Journal, 320,* 858-861.

Government Accountability Office. (2007). *Anabolic steroid abuse: Federal efforts to prevent and reduce anabolic steroid abuse among teenagers.* Retrieved March 12, 2010, from www.gao.gov/new.items./d0815.pdf

Green, A. I. (2007). Queer theory and sociology: Locating the subject and the self in sexuality studies. *Sociological Theory 25*(1), 26-45.

Greenberg, D. M., Bradford, J., & Curry, S. (1995). Infantophilia—a new subcategory of pedophilia? A preliminary study. *Bulletin of the American Academy of Psychiatry Law, 23,* 63-71.

Greene, K., & Faulkner, S. L. (2005). Gender, belief in the sexual double standard, and sexual talk in heterosexual dating relationships. *Sex Roles: A Journal of Research, 53*(3-4), 239-252.

Gregory, K. (2005). Update on nutrition for preterm and full-term infants. *Journal of Obstetrics and Gynecological Neonatal Nursing, 34,* 98-108.

Griffiths, M. (2001 November) Sex on the Internet: Observations and implications for Internet sex addiction. *The Journal of Sex Research, 38*(4), 333-342.

Griffitt, W., & Hatfield, E. (1985). *Human sexual behavior.* Glennview, IL: Scott Foresman & Company.

Grunebaum, H. (2003). Thinking about romantic/erotic love. In M. Coleman & L. Ganong (Eds.), *Points and counterpoints* (pp. 88-91). Los Angeles: Roxbury.

Guo, B., & Huang, J. (2005). Marital and sexual satisfaction in Chinese families. Exploring the moderating effects. *Journal of Sex & Marital Therapy, 31,* 21-29.

Guralnik, D. B. (Ed.). (1982). *Webster's new world dictionary of the American language.* New York: Simon & Schuster.

Gurman, T., & Borzekowski, D. L. G. (2004). Condom use among Latino college students. *Journal of American College Health, 52*(4), 169-179.

Gurin, P. (1999). New research on the benefits of diversity in college and beyond: An empirical analysis. *Diversity Digest, 5*(15).

Haavio-Mannila, E., & Kontula, O. (1997). Correlates of increased sexual satisfaction. *Archives of Sexual Behavior, 26,* 399-419.

Haeberle, E. J. (1983). The birth of sexology: A brief history in documents. *The Kinsey Institute.* Retrieved August 17, 2009, from www.indiana.edu/~kinsey/resources/sexology.html

Haffner, D., & Schwartz, P. (1998). *What I've learned about sex.* New York: Penguin Putnam, Inc.

Haider-Markel, D., & Joslyn, M. (2008). Beliefs about the origins of homosexuality and support for gay rights. *Public Opinion Quarterly, 72*(2), 291-310.

Hall, J. A. Y., & Kimura, D. (1994). Dermatoglyphic asymmetry and sexual orientation in men. *Behavioral Neuroscience, 108*(6), 1203-1206.

Hall, J. A., Coats, E. J., & Smith LeBeau, L. (2005). Nonverbal behavior and the vertical dimension of social relations: A meta-analysis. *Psychological Bulletin, 131,* 898-924.

Hall, P., & Schaeff, C. (2008, February). Sexual orientation and fluctuating asymmetry in men and women. *Archives of Sexual Behavior, 37*(1), 158-165.

Hall, R. C. W., & Hall, R. C. W. (2007). A profile of pedophilia: Definition, characteristics of offenders, recidivism, treatment outcomes, and forensic issues. *Mayo Clinic Proceedings, 82,* 457-471.

Hallowell, N., et al. (2004). High-risk premenopausal women's experiences of undergoing prophylactic oophorectomy: A descriptive study. *Genetic Testing, 8,* 148-156.

Halpern-Felsher, B. L., Cornell, J., Kropp, R. Y., & Tschann, J. (2005). Oral versus vaginal sex among adolescents. *Pediatrics, 115,* 845-851.

Halpert, S. (2002). Suicidal behavior among gay male youth. *Journal of Gay & Lesbian Psychotherapy, 6*(3), 53-79.

Handa, V. L., et al. (2004). Sexual function among women with urinary incontinence and pelvic organ prolapse. *American Journal of Obstetrics and Gynecology, 191*(3), 751-756.

Hankins, C. (2007). Male circumcision: Implications for women as sexual partners and parents. *Reproductive Health Matters, 15*(29), 62-68.

Hanson, S. L. (1992). Involving families in programs for pregnant teens: Consequences for teens and their families. *Family Relations, 41,* 303-311.

Harding, R., & Golombok, S. E. (2002). Test-retest reliability of the measurement of penile dimensions in a sample of gay men. *Archives of Sexual Behavior, 31*(4), 351-357.

Harndwerk, B. (2006). Effectiveness often in the eye of the beholder. *National Geographic News,* February 14, 2006.

L. (2000). Child sexual development. *Electronic Journal of Human Sexuality,* (Annual 2000): NA. *Expanded Academic ASAP.* Thomson Gale. Kansas State University Libraries. Retrieved August 4, 2007, from http://find.galegroup.com

Harris, C. R., & Christenfeld, N. (1996). Gender, jealousy, and reason. *Psychological Science, 7,* 364-366.

Harrison, T. W. (2003). Adolescent homosexual concerns regarding disclosure. *Journal of School Health,* (01 March).

Harvard Family Research Project. (2006). *Family involvement makes a difference.* Cambridge, MA: Harvard Graduate School of Education, Spring 2006.

Harvey, J., & Berry, J. A. (2009). Andropause and the aging male. *The Journal for Nurse Practitioners, 5*(3), 207-212.

Hassebrauck, M., & Feher, B. (2002). Dimensions of relationship quality. *Personal Relationships, 9,* 253-270.

Hatcher, R., & Nelson, A. (2004). Combined hormonal contraceptive methods. In R. A. Hatcher, et al. (Eds.), *Contraceptive technology* (pp. 361-460). New York: Irvington.

Hatfield, E. (1988). Passionate and companionate love. In R. L. Sternberg & M. L. Barns (Eds.), *The psychology of love.* New Haven, CT: Yale University Press, 191-217.

Hatfield, E., Brinton, C., & Cornelius, J. (1989). Passionate love and anxiety in young adolescents. *Motivation and Emotion, 13,* 271-289.

Hatfield, E., & Sprecher, S. (1986). Measuring passionate love in intimate relations. *Journal of Adolescence, 9,* 383-410.

Hatfield, E., & Sprecher, S. (1995). Men's and women's preferences in marital partners in the United States, Russia, and Japan. *Journal of Cross-Cultural Psychology, 26,* 728-750.

Hatzichristou, D., et al. (2004). Clinical evaluation and management strategy for sexual dysfunction in men and women. *Journal of Sexual Medicine, 1,* 49-57.

Hauck, E. W., Diemer, T., Schmelz, H. U., & Weidner, W. (2006). A critical analysis of non-surgical treatment of Peyronie's disease. *European Urology, 49*(6), 987-997.

Haveman, R., Wolfe, B., & Pence, K. (2001). Intergenerational effects of nonmarital and early childbearing. In B. Wolfe (Eds.), *Out of wedlock: Causes and consequences of nonmarital fertility* (pp. 287-316). New York: Russell Sage Foundation.

Hayflick, L. (1994). *How and why we age.* New York: Ballantine Books.

Hazan, C., & Shaver, P. (1987). Romantic love conceptualized as an attachment process. *Journal of Personality and Social Psychology, 52,* 511-524.

Hazan, C., Zeifman, D., & Middleton, K. (1994, July). *Adult romantic attachment, affection, and sex.* Paper presented at the 7th International Conference on Personal Relationships, Gronigen, the Netherlands.

He, W., Sangupta, M., Velkoff, V. A., & DeBarros, K. A. (2005). 65+ in the United States: 2005. *United States Census Bureau Current Population Reports* (pp. 23-209). Retrieved from http://www.census.gov/prod/2006pubs/p23-209.pdf

Healy, D. L. (2004). *Menorrhagia heavy periods.* Retrieved January 30, 2008, from www.med.monash.edu.au/ob-gyn/research/menorr.html

Heard, H. (2007). Fathers, mothers, and family structure: Family trajectories, parent gender, and adolescent schooling. *Journal of Marriage and Family, 69*(2), 435-450.

Heath, D. (1984). An investigation into the origins of a copious vaginal discharge during sexual intercourse: "Enough to wet the bed"—that "is not urine." *Journal of Sex Research, 20,* 194-210.

Heaton, T. B. (2002). Factors contributing to increased marital stability in the United States. *Journal of Family Issues, 23*(3), 392-409.

Hebert, S., & Popadiuk, N. (2008). University students' experiences of nonmarital breakups: A grounded theory. *Journal of College Student Development, 49*(1), 1-14.

Heiman, D. R., & LoPiccolo, J. (1988). *Becoming orgasmic: A sexual and personal growth program for women.* New York: Simon & Schuster.

Heller, P., & Wood, B. (1998). The process of intimacy: Similarity, understanding, and gender. *Journal of Marital and Family Therapy, 24*(3), 273-288.

Heller, P., & Wood, B. (2000). The influence of religious and ethnic differences on marital intimacy: Intermarriage versus intramarriage. *Journal of Marital and Family Therapy, 26*(2), 241-252.

Hellerstedt, W. L., Peterson-Hickey, M., Rhodes, K. L., & Garwick, A. (2006). Environmental, social, and personal correlates of having ever had sexual intercourse among American Indian youths. *American Journal of Public Health, 96*(12), 2228-2234.

Hellstrom, W. J., & Usta, M. F. (2003). Surgical approaches for advanced Peyronie's disease patients. *International Journal of Impotence Research, 15*(5), 121-124.

Henderson-King, D. H., & Veroff, J. (1994). Sexual satisfaction and marital well-being in the first years of marriages. *Journal of Social and Personal Relationships, 11,* 509-534.

Hendrick, C., & Hendrick, S. (1986). A theory and method of love. *Journal of Personality and Social Psychology, 50,* 392-402.

Henningsen, D. D. (2004). Flirting with meaning: Examining miscommunication in flirting interactions. *Sex Roles, 50,* 481-489.

Henningsen, D. D., Henningsen, M. L. M., & Valde, K. S. (2006). Gender differences in perceptions of women's sexual interest during cross-sex interactions: An application and extension of Cognitive Valance Theory. *Sex Roles: A Journal of Research, 54,* 821-830.

Hensel, D. J., et al. (2004). A daily diary analysis of vaginal bleeding and coitus among adolescent women. *Journal of Adolescent Health, 34,* 391-394.

Hensel, D. J., Fortenberry, D., & Orr, D. P. (2007). Situational and relational factors associated with coitus during vaginal bleeding among adolescent women. *The Journal of Sex Research, 44*(3), 269-276.

Herbst, K., & Bhasin, S. (2004). Testosterone action on skeletal muscle. *Current Options in Clinical Nutrition and Metabolic Care, 7,* 271-277.

Herek, G. M. (2002). Gender gaps in public opinion about lesbians and gay men. *Public Opinion Quarterly, 66*(1), 40-66.

Herek, G. M. (2009). Hate crimes and stigma-related experiences among sexual minority adults in the United States: Prevalence estimates from a national probability sample. *Journal of Interpersonal Violence, 24,* 54-74.

Higgins, J. A., Hoffman, S., Graham, C., & Sanders, S. (2008). Relationships between contraceptive method and sexual pleasure and satisfaction: Results from the Women's Wellbeing and Sexuality Study. *Sexual Health, 5*(4), 321-330.

Hijazi, R. A., & Cunningham, G. R. (2005). Andropause: Is androgen replacement therapy indicated for the aging male? *Annual Review of Medicine, 56,* 117-137.

Hilliges, M., Falconer, C., Ekman-Ordeberg, G., & Johansson, O. (1995). Innervation of the human vaginal mucosa as revealed by PGP 9.5 immunohistochemistry. *Acta Anatomy, 153,* 119-126.

Hines, T. M. (2001). The G-spot: A modern gynecologic myth. *Journal of Obstetrics and Gynecology, 185*(2), 359-362.

Hitchcock, C., & Johnston-Robledo, I. (2007). Menstruation is NOT a disease. *Society for Menstrual Cycle Research.* Retrieved July 27, 2009, from http://menstruation-research.org/research/2007-conference-papers/

Hjollund, N. H. I., et al. (2002). The relationship between daily activities and scrotal temperature. *Human Reproduction, 16,* 209-214.

Hock, R. (2010). *Human sexuality.* (2nd ed.). Upper Saddle River, NJ.

Hoff, T., Greene, L., & Davis, J. (2003). *National survey of adolescents and young adults: Sexual health knowledge, attitudes, and experiences.* Menlo Park, CA: The Henry J. Kaiser Family Foundation.

Hofmeyr, G. J., &, Sonnedecker, E. W. (1987). Elective episiotomy in perspective. *South African Medical Journal, 71*(6), 357-359.

Hogben, M., & Byrne, D. (1998). Using social learning theory to explain individual differences in human sexuality. *Journal of Sex Research, 35,* 58-71.

Hollander, D. (2003). Among young adults, use of the internet to find sexual partners is rising. *Journal of Sex Research, 40,* 129-133.

Holmberg, D., & Blair, K. L. (2009). Sexual desire, communication, satisfaction, and preferences of men and women in same-sex versus mixed-sex relationships. *The Journal of Sex Research, 46*(1), 57-66.

Holstein, A. F., Schulze, W., & Davidoff, M. (2003). Understanding spermatogenesis is a prerequisite for treatment. *Reproductive Biology and Endocrinology, 1*(107).

Honig, A. (1998). Sociocultural influences on sexual meanings embedded in playful experiences. In D. P. Fromberg & D. Bergen (Eds.), *Play from birth to twelve and beyond: Contents, perspectives, and meanings* (pp. 338-347). New York: Garland Press.

Hook, M. K., Gerstein, L. H., Detterich, L., & Gridley, B. (2003). How close are we? Measuring intimacy and examining gender differences. *Journal of Counseling and Development, 81*(4), 462-473.

Horowitz, S. M., Weis, D. L., & Laflin, M. T. (2001). Differences between sexual orientation behavior groups and social background, quality of life, and health behaviors. *The Journal of Sex Research, 38,* 205-218.

Hostetler, A. J. (2001). Single gay men: Cultural models of adult development, psychological well-being, and the meaning of being "single by choice." Doctoral Dissertation. University of Chicago.

Hostetler, A. J. (2004). Old, gay, and alone? The ecology of well-being among middle-aged and older single gay men. In G. Herdt & B. deVries (Eds.), *Gay and lesbian aging: A research agenda for the 21st century* (pp. 143-176). New York: Springer.

Hostetler, A. J. (2009) Single by choice? Assessing and understanding voluntary singlehood among mature gay men. *Journal of Homosexuality, 56,* 499-531.

Howard, J. A., & Hollander, J. A. (1997). *Gendered situations, gendered selves: A gender lens on social psychology.* Newbury Park, CA: Sage.

Hudson, T. (2006). Menstrual cramps (dysmenorrhea): An alternative approach. *Townsend Letter: The Examiner of Alternative Medicine, 279,* 130-135.

Huebner, A. (2000). Adolescent growth and development. *Virginia Cooperative Extension Publication Number, 350-850.*

Huhtaniemi, I., & Poutanen, D. M. (2008). Male reproductive health, mechanisms of hormone action. *Centre of Reproductive and Development Medicine.*

Human Rights Campaign Foundation. (2004). *Answers to questions about marriage equality* (pp. 164-172). Washington, DC: Author.

Human Rights Campaign Foundation. (2006). *A Resource Guide to Coming Out.* Retrieved August 28, 2009, from http://www.hrc.org/about_us/7092.htm

Humphreys, T. P. (2004). Understanding sexual consent: An empirical investigation of the normative script for young heterosexual adults. In M. Cowling & P. Reynolds (Eds.), *Making sense of sexual consent.* Aldershot, UK: Ashgate.

Humphreys, T. P. (2007). Perceptions of sexual consent: The impact of relationship history and gender. *The Journal of Sex Research, 44*(4), 307-316.

Hunt, M. (1959). *The natural history of love.* New York: Minerva Press.

Hunt, M. (1974). *Sexual behavior in the 1970s.* Chicago: Playboy Press.

Hymowitz, K. S. (2003). What to tell kids about sex. *The Public Interest* (Fall 2003), 1-18.

Impett, E. A., & Peplau, L. A. (2002). Why some women consent to unwanted sex with a dating partner: Insights from attachment theory. *Psychology of Women Quarterly, 26,* 359-369.

Impett, E. A., Peplau, L. A., & Gable, S. L. (2005). Approach and avoidance sexual motivation: Implications for personal and interpersonal well-being. *Personal Relationships, 12,* 465-482.

Impett, E. A., Strachman, A., Finkel, E. J., & Gable, S. L. (2008). Maintaining sexual desire in intimate relationships: The importance of approach goals. *Journal of Personality and Social Psychology, 94*(5), 808-823.

Institute for Advanced Study of Human Sexuality. (2007). Retrieved August 17, 2009, from www.iashs.edu

Iwawaki, S., & Wilson, G. D. (1983). Sex fantasies in Japan. *Personality and Individual Differences, 4,* 543-545.

Jaccard, J. (2009). Unlocking the contraception conundrum: Reducing unplanned pregnancies in emerging adulthood. *The National Campaign to Prevent Teen and Unplanned Pregnancy.* Retrieved August 14, 2009, from www.thenational-campaign.org/resources/pdf/pubs/Unlocking_Contraceptive.pdf

Jaccard, J., Dittus, P. J., & Gordon, V. V. (2000). Parent-teen communication about pre-marital sex. Factors associated with the extent of communication. *Journal of Adolescent Research, 15,* 187-208.

Jackson, M. (1983). Sexual liberation or social control? *Women's Studies International Forum, 6*(1), 1-17.

Jacob, K. A. (1981). The Mosher report: The sexual habits of American women, examined half a century before Kinsey. *American Heritage Magazine, 32*(4). Retrieved August 23, 2009, from www.amiercanheritage.com/aritcles/magazine/ah/1981/4/1981_4_56.shtml

Jandt, F., & Hundley, H. (2007). Intercultural dimensions of communicating masculinities. *Journal of Men's Studies, 15*(2), 216-231.

Janssen, D. F. (2002). Growing up sexually. *The Sexual Curriculum* (Vol. 2). Amsterdam, The Netherlands. Retrieved August 22, 2007, from http://www2.hu-berlin.de/sexology/GESUND/ARCHIV/GUS/GUSVOLIIAPPII.html

Janus, S., & Janus, C. (1993). *The Janus report on sexual behavior.* New York: John Wiley & Sons, Inc.

Jenny, C., Roesler, T. A., & Poyer, K. L. (1994). Are children at risk for sexual abuse by homosexuals? *Pediatrics, 94,* 41-44.

Johnson, F. L., & Aires, E. J. (1983). Conversational patterns among same-sex pairs of late-adolescent close friends. *The Journal of Genetic Psychology, 142,* 225-238.

Johnson, M. H. (2007). *Essential reproduction* (6th ed.). London: Blackwell Publishing.

Johnson-Mallard, V., et al. (2007). Increasing knowledge of sexually transmitted infection risk. *The Nurse Practitioner: The American Journal of Primary Health Care, 32*(2), 26-32.

Johnson, T. (1991). Understanding the sexual behaviors of young children. *SEICUS Report, August/September,* 8-15.

Johnson, T., et al. (2005). The relation between culture and response styles: Evidence from 19 countries. *Journal of Cross-Cultural Psychology, 36*(2), 264-277.

Johnston, L., Bachman, P., O'Malley, J., & Schulenberg, J. (2004). *Monitoring the future: National results on adolescent drug use: Overview of key findings 2003.* National Institute on Drug Abuse, U.S. Department of Health and Human Services. NIH Publication No. 04-5506.

Johnston-Robledo, I., Barnack, J., & Wares, S. (2006). Kiss your period goodbye: Menstrual suppression in the popular press. *Sex Roles, 54,* 353-360.

Jones, J. C. & Barlow, D. H. (1987). *Self-reported frequency of sexual urges, fantasies, and masturbatory fantasies in heterosexual males and females.* Paper presented at the Annual Association for the Advancement of Behavior Therapy, November 1987.

Jones, J. M. (2002). *Public divided benefits of living together before marriage.* Gallup News Service, August 16, 2002. Retrieved September 2, 2009, from www.gallup.com/poll/releases/pr02081.asp

Jones, R. (1999). To store or mature spermatozoa? The primary role of the epididymis. *International Journal of Andrology, 22*(2), 57-67.

Jones, R. K., Darroch, J. E., & Henshaw, S. K. (2002). Patterns in the socioeconomic characteristics of women obtaining abortions in 2000-2001. *Perspectives on Sexual and Reproductive Health, 34*(5), 226-235.

Jones, R. K., Fennell, J., Higgins, J. A., & Blanchard, K. (2009). Better than nothing or savvy risk-reduction practice? The importance of withdrawal. *Contraception, 79,* 407-410.

Joseph, S., & Najmabadi, A. (2006). *Encyclopedia of women and Islamic cultures: Family, body, sexuality, and health.* The Netherlands: Brill.

Jung, A., Schill, W. B., & Schuppe, H. C. (2002). Genital heat stress in men and barren couples: A prospective evaluation by means of a questionnaire. *Andrologia, 34,* 349-355.

Kaestle, C. E., & Tucker-Halpern, C. (2007). What's love got to do with it? Sexual behaviors of opposite-sex couples through emerging adulthood. *Perspectives on Sexual and Reproductive Health, 39*(3), 134-141.

Kaiser Family Foundation, National Public Radio, and John F. Kennedy School of Government. (2004). *Sex education in America: General public/parents survey.* Menlo Park, CA: Kaiser Family Foundation.

Kass, L. R. (1997). The end of courtship. *Public Interest, 126,* 39-64.

Kaunitz, A. M. (2005). Depo-Provera's black box: Time to reconsider. *Contraception, 72*(3), 165-167.

Kehoe, M. (1986). A portrait of the older lesbian. *Journal of Homosexuality, 12*(3-4), 157-161.

Kelly, B. C., et al. (2009). Sexual compulsivity and sexual behaviors among gay and bisexual men and lesbian and bisexual women. *Journal of Sex Research, 46*(4), 301-308.

Kennedy, H. (1981). The "third sex" theory of Karl Heinrich Ulrichs. *Journal of Homosexuality, 6*(1), 103-111.

Kettmann, S. (2001). *1,001 Arabian nights of sex.* Retrieved June 16, 2007, from http://www.wired.com/culture/lifestyle/news/2001/04/43243

Kigozi, G., Watya, S., Polis, C. B., et al. (2008). The effect of male circumcision on sexual satisfaction and function, results from a randomized trial of male circumcision for human immunodeficiency virus prevention, Rakai, Uganda. *British Journal of Urology International, 101*(1), 65-70.

Killian, K. D. (2001). Reconstituting racial histories and identities: The narratives of interracial couples. *Journal of Marital and Family Therapy, 27*(1), 27-42.

Kim, A., Adams, J., Adams, T., & O'Hara, S. (2003). An uncommon finding: Ovotestes in a true hermaphrodite. *Journal of Diagnostic Medical Sonography, 19*(1), 51-54.

Kimuna, S. R., & Kjamba, Y. K. (2005). Wealth and extramarital sex among men in Zambia. *International Family Planning Perspectives, 31,* 83-89.

Kingston, D., Firestone, P., Moulden, H., & Bradford, J. (2007, June). The utility of the diagnosis of pedophilia: A comparison of various classification procedures. *Archives of Sexual Behavior, 36*(3), 423-436. Retrieved September 13, 2009, from doi:10.1007/s10508-006-9091-x

Kinsey, A. C., Pomeroy, W. B., & Martin, C. E. (1948). *Sexual behavior in the human male.* Philadelphia: W.B. Saunders.

Kinsey, A., Pomeroy, W., Martin, C., & Gebhard, P. (1953). *Sexual behaviors in the human female.* Philadelphia: W.B. Saunders Company.

Kirby, D. (2008). The impact of programs to increase contraceptive use among adult women: A review of experimental and quasi-experimental studies. *Perspectives on Sexual and Reproductive Health, 40*(1), 34-41.

Kirby, J. S., Baucom, D. H., & Peterman, M. A. (2005). An investigation of unmet intimacy needs in marital relationships. *Journal of Marital and Family Therapy, 31*(4), 313-325.

Kirkpatrick, R. C. (2000). The evolution of human homosexual behavior. *Current Anthropology 39*(1), 385-413.

Kleier, J. S. (2004). Nurse practitioners' behaviors regarding teaching testicular self-exams. *Journal of the American Academy of Nurse Practitioners, 16*(5), 206-218.

Klerman, L. V. (2004). *Another chance: Preventing additional births to teen mothers.* Washington, DC: National Campaign to Prevent Teen Pregnancy.

Klinkenberg, D., & Rose, S. (1994). Dating scripts of gay men and lesbians. *Journal of Homosexuality, 26*(4), 23-35.

Kluwer, E. S. & Johnson, M. D. (2007). Conflict frequency and relationship quality across the transition to parenthood. *Journal of Marriage and Family, 69,* 1089-1106.

Knight, K. R., et al. (2005). Sexual risk taking among HIV-positive injection drug users: Contexts, characteristics, and implications for prevention. *AIDS Education and Prevention, 17*(Suppl.A), 76-88.

Knöfler, T., & Imhof, M. (2007). Does sexual orientation have an impact on nonverbal behavior in interpersonal communication? *Journal of Nonverbal Behavior, 31,* 189-204.

Knoth, R., Boyd, K., & Singer, B. (1988). Empirical tests of sexual selection theory: Predictions of sex differences in onset, intensity, and time course of sexual arousal. *The Journal of Sex Research, 24,* 73-89.

Knox, D., Breed, R., & Zusman, M. (2007). College men and jealousy. *College Student Journal, 41*(2), 494-499.

Knox, D., Sturdivant, L., & Zusman, M. E. (2001). College student attitudes toward sexual intimacy. *College Student Journal, 35,* 241-243.

Knox, D., & Zusman, M. (2002). When and why gender differences in saying "I love you" among college students. *College Student Journal,* 614-615.

Kochakian, C. D., & Yesalis, C. E. (2000). Anabolic-androgenic steroids: A historical perspective and definition. In C. E. Yesalis (Ed.), *Anabolic steroids in sport and exercise.* (2nd ed.) (pp. 17-49). Champaign, IL: Human Kinetics.

Koerner, A. F., & Fitzpatrick, M. A. (2002). Nonverbal communication and marital adjustment and satisfaction: The role of decoding relationship relevant and relationship irrelevant affect. *Communication Monographs, 69,* 33-51.

Kohl, J. V. (2002). Homosexual orientation in males: Human pheromones and neuroscience, neuroendocrinology. *The Bulletin for Section #44 (Psychotherapy) of the World Psychiatric Association and the Across-Species Comparisons and Psychopathology Society, 3*(2), 19-24.

Kolodny, R. C. (2001). In memory of William H. Masters. *Journal of Sex Research, 38*(3), p. 274-276.

Kontula, O., & Haavio-Mannila, E. (2002). Masturbation in a generational perspective *Journal of Psychology and Human Sexuality, 14,* 49-83.

Kontula, O., & Haavio-Mannila, E. (2009). The impact of aging on human sexual activity and sexual desire. *Journal of Sex Research, 46*(1), 46-56.

Koshimaki, J., et al. (2008). Regular intercourse protects against erectile dysfunction: Tampere aging male urologic study. *The American Journal of Medicine, 121,* 592-596.

Kost, K., et al. (2008). Estimates of contraceptive failure from the 2002 National Survey of Family Growth. *Contraception, 77,* 10-21.

Koukounas, E., & McCabe, M. (1997). Sexual and emotional variables influencing sexual response to erotica. *Behaviour Research and Therapy, 35,* 221-231.

Krafft-Ebing, R. (1896). *Psychopathia sexualis.* Unknown binding.

Krahe, B., Bieneck, S., & Scheinberger-Olwig, R. (2007). The role of sexual scripts in sexual aggression and victimization. *Archives of Sexual Behavior, 36*(5), 687-701.

Kratochvil, S. (April, 1994). Orgasmic expulsions in women. *Ceskoslovenaka Psychiatrie, 90*(2), 71-77.

Kraus, M. (2003). *Aging ceremony.* Retrieved February 18, 2010, from http://www.acfnewsource.org/religion/aging_ceremony.html

Kulbarsh, P. (2008). *Indecent exposure: Exhibitionism.* Retrieved February 12, 2010, from www.lawofficer.com

Kupperbusch, C., et al. (1999). Cultural influences on nonverbal expressions of emotion. In P. Philppot, R. S. Feldman, & E. J. Coats (Eds.), *The social context of nonverbal behavior* (2nd ed., Vol. 1), (pp. 17-44). Cambridge: Cambridge University Press.

Kurdek, L. A. (2004). Are gay and lesbian cohabiting couples really different from heterosexual married couples? *Journal of Marriage and Family, 66,* 880-900.

Kurdek, L. A. (2006). Differences between partners from heterosexual, gay, and lesbian cohabiting couples *Journal of Marriage and Family, 68*(2), 509-528.

Kuttler, A. F., LaGreca, A. M., & Prinstein, M. J. (1999). Friendship qualities and social-emotional functioning of adolescents with close, cross-sex friendships. *Journal of Adolescent Research, 9*(3), 339-366.

n, M., Edelman, A., Nichols, M. D., & Jensen, J. T. (2003). Bleeding patterns patient acceptability of standard or continuous dosing regimens of a low-dose contraceptive: A randomized trial. *Contraception, 67*, 9-13.

Laan, E., Everaerd, W., & Evers, A. (1996). Assessment of female sexual arousal: Response specificity and construct validity. *Psychophysiology, 32*, 476-485.

Ladas, A. K., Whipple, B., & Perry, J. D (1982). *The G spot and other discoveries about human sexuality* (1e). New York: Holt, Rinehart, and Winston.

Lamberts, S. (1997). The endocrinology of aging. *Science, 278*(5337), 419-424.

Lancaster, R. N. (2003). *The trouble with nature. Sex in science and popular culture.* Berkeley: University of California Press.

Landen, M., Walinder, J., & Lundstrom, B. (1996). Incidence and sex ratio of transsexualism in Sweden. *Acta Psychiatrica Scandinavica, 93*, 261-263.

Laner, M. R., & Ventrone, N. A. (1998). Egalitarian daters/traditionalist dates. *Journal of Family Issues, 19*, 468-477.

Langström, N., & Seto, M. C. (2006). Exhibitionistic and voyeuristic behaviour in a Swedish National Population survey. *Archives of Sexual Behavior, 55*(4), 427-435.

Lanning, K. (2001). *Child molesters: A behavioral analysis* (4th ed.). Alexandria, VA: National Center for Missing & Exploited Children.

Larson, N. C. (2004). Parenting stress among adolescent mothers in the transition to adulthood. *Child and Adolescent Social Work Journal, 21*(5), 457-476.

Latthe, P., et al. (2006). Factors predisposing women to chronic pelvic pain: A systematic review. *Reproductive Health Matters, 14*(28), 216-218.

Laumann, E. O., Gagnon, J. H., Michael, R. T., & Michaels, S. (1994). *The social organization of sexuality: Sexual practices in the United States.* Chicago: University of Chicago Press.

Laumann, E. O., Masi, C. M., & Zuckerman, M. A. (1997). Circumcision in the United States: prevalence, prophylactic effects and sexual practice. *Journal of American Medical Association, 277*, 1052-1057.

Laumann, E. O., et al., for the GSSAB Investigators' Group. (2005) Sexual problems among women and men aged 40-80: Prevalence and correlates identified in the Global Study of Sexual Attitudes and Behaviors. *International Journal of Impotency Research, 17*, 39-57.

Lawrance, K. A., & Byers, S. (2005). Sexual satisfaction in long-term heterosexual relationships: The interpersonal exchange model of sexual satisfaction. *Personal Relationships, 2*(4), 267-285.

Leber, M. J. (2006). *Balanitis.* Retrieved March 5, 2008, from www.emedicine.com/EMERG/topic51.htm

Lee, J. A. (1973). *The color of love: An exploration of the ways of loving.* Don Mills, Ontario: New Press.

Lee, J. K., Jackson, H. J., Pattison, P., & Ward, T. (2002). Developmental risk factors for sexual offending. *Child Sexual Abuse and Neglect, 26*, 73-92.

Lehrman, G. (2001). *The history of private life: Courtship in early America.* The Gilder Lehrman Institute of American History. Retrieved June 4, 2004, from http://yalepress.yale.edu

Leiblum, S. R. (2002). Reconsidering gender differences in sexual desire: An update. *Sexual and Relationship Therapy, 17*, 57-68.

Leichliter, J. S., et al. (2007). Prevalence and correlates of heterosexual anal and oral sex in adolescents and adults in the United States. *The Journal of Infectious Diseases, 196*(12), 1852-1859.

Leitenberg, H., & Henning, K. (1995). Sexual fantasy. *Psychological Bulletin, 117*, 469-496.

Lemme, B. H. (2005). *Development in adulthood* (5th ed.). Boston: Pearson Education.

Lengermann, P. M., & Brantley, J. N. (1988). Feminist theory. In G. Ritzer (Ed.), *Sociological Theory,* pp. 400-443. New York: Knopf.

Lerner, J. V., Lerner, R. M., & Finkelstein, J. (Eds.). (2001). *Adolescence in America: An encyclopedia* (Vol. 1). Santa Barbara, CA: ABC-CLIO.

Lerner, R. (2004). Can abstinence work? An analysis of the Best Friends program. *Adolescent and Family Health, 3*(4), 185-192.

Levant, R., et al. (2007). The Femininity Ideology Scale: Factor, structure, reliability, convergent and discriminate validity, and social contextual variation. *Sex Roles, 57*, 373-383.

LeVay, S. (1991). A difference in hypothalamic structure between heterosexual and homosexual men. *Science, 253*(5023), 1034-1037.

Lever, J. (1995, August 22). Lesbian sex survey. *The Advocate,* 21-30.

Lever, J., Frederick, D. A., & Peplau, L. A. (2006). Does size matter? Men's and women's views on penis size across the lifespan. *Psychology of Men & Masculinity, 7*, 129-143.

Levine, M. P., & Troiden, R. R. (1988). The myth of sexual compulsivity. *The Journal of Sex Research, 25*, 347-363.

Levine, L. A. (2003). Review of current nonsurgical management of Peyronie's disease. *International Journal of Impotence Research, 15*(5), 113-120.

Levinger, G. (1982, August). *A systems perspective on the development of close relationships.* Presented at the Annual American Psychological Association Meeting, Washington, DC.

Levkoff, L. (2007). *Third base ain't what it used to be: What your kids are learning about sex today and how to teach them to become sexually healthy adults.* New York: Penguin.

Levy, B., et al. (2007). Older persons' exclusion from sexually transmitted risk-reduction clinical trials. *Sexually Transmitted Diseases, 34*(8), 541-544.

Lewis, D. A. (2000). Chancroid: From clinical practice to basic science. *AIDS Patient Care and STDs, 14*(1), 19-36.

Lewis, L. J., & Kertzner, R. M. (2003). Toward improved interpretation and theory building of African American male sexualities. *The Journal of Sex Research, 40*(4), 383-396.

Lewis, W. J. (1997). Factors associated with post abortion adjustment problems: Implications for triage. *Canadian Journal of Human Sexuality, 6*(1), 9-16.

Li, N. P., Bailey, L. M., Kenrick, D. T., & Linsenmeier, L. A. W. (2002). The necessities and luxuries of mate preferences: Testing the tradeoffs. *Journal of Personality and Social Psychology, 82*, 947-955.

Lichter, D. T., Graefe, D. R., & Brown, J. B. (2003). Is marriage a panacea? Union formation among economically disadvantaged unwed mothers. *Social Problems, 50*(1), 60-86.

Lightfoot-Klein, H. (1989). The sexual experience and marital adjustment of genitally circumcised and infibulated females in the Sudan. *The Journal of Sex Research, 26*(3), 375-392.

Lindau, S. T., et al. (2007). A national study of sexuality and health among older adults in the U.S. *New England Journal of Medicine, 357*(8), 762-774.

Lindberg, C., Lewis-Spruill, C., & Crownover, R. (2006). Barriers to sexual and reproductive healthcare: Urban male adolescents speak out. *Issues in Comprehensive Pediatric Nursing, 29*, 73-88.

Lindberg, L. D., Jones, R., & Santelli, J. S. (2008). Non-coital sexual activities among adolescents. *Journal of Adolescent Health* (July 2008), 1-14.

Lindley, L. L., Joshi, P., & Vincent, M. L. (2007, November 3-7). *Personal and family factors associated with virginity among African American male and female high school students.* Paper presented at the 135th American Public Health Association Annual Meeting, San Diego, CA.

Lindley, L., et al. (2008). STDs among sexually active female college students: Does sexual orientation make a difference? *Perspectives on Sexual and Reproductive Health, 40*(4), 212-217.

Lindlof, T. R., & Taylor, B. C. (2002). *Qualitative communication research methods* (2nd ed.). Thousand Oaks, CA: Sage.

Lippa, R. A. (2003). Handedness, sexual orientation, and gender-related personality traits in men and women. *Archives of Sexual Behavior, 32*, 103-114.

Lippa, R. (2005). Sexual orientation and personality. *Annual Review of Sex Research, 16*, 119-153.

Liu, C. (2000). A theory of marital sexual life. *Journal of Marriage and Family, 62*, 363-374.

Liu, D. L., & Ng, M. L. (1995). Sexual dysfunction in China. *Annals of the Academy of Medicine—Singapore, 24*, 728-731.

Long, B. (2007). *The Hottentot "apron" and "Venus."* Retrieved March 13, 2010, from http://www.drbilllong.com/CurrentEventsX/HottentotIII.html

Lowenstein, L. F. (2002). Fetishes and their associated behavior. *Sexuality and Disability, 20*(2), 135-147.

Lowndes, C. M., & Fenton, K. A. (2004). Surveillance systems for STIs in the European Union: Facing a changing epidemiology. *Sexually Transmitted Infections, 80*(4), 264-271.

Luan Fauteck Makes Marks, (2007). Great mysteries: Native North American religions and participatory visions. *ReVision, 29*(3), 29-37.

Luster, T., & Small, S. A. (1994). Factors associated with sexual risk-taking behaviors among adolescents. *Journal of Marriage and Family, 56*(3), 622-632.

Ma, L. (2004). How to have great sex. *Psychology Today,* March 8, 2004.

Maccoby, E. E. (1998). *The two sexes: Growing up apart, coming together.* Cambridge, MA: Harvard University Press, Belknap Press.

MacGeorge, E. L, Graves, A. R., Feng, B., & Gillihan, S. J. (2004). The myth of gender cultures: Similarities outweigh differences in men's and women's provision of and responses to supportive communication. *Sex Roles: A Journal of Sex Research, 50*(3-4), 143-175.

Mackey, R., Diemer, M., & O'Brien, A. (2000). Psychological intimacy in the lasting relationships of heterosexual and same-gender couples. *Sex Roles: A Journal of Research, 43*(4), 201-227.

MacNeil, S., & Byers, E. S. (2005). Dyadic assessment of sexual self-disclosure and sexual satisfaction in heterosexual dating couples. *Journal of Social and Personal Relationships, 22*, 169-181.

Madden, M., & Lenhart, A. (2006). Online dating. *Pew Internet & American Life Project,* Washington, DC.

Maffesoli, M. (1996). *The time of the tribes: The decline of individualism in mass society.* London: Sage Publications.

Maher, B. (2004). Abstinence until marriage: the best message for teens. The Family Research Council. Retrieved August 19, 2009, from www.frc.org

Major, B., et al. (2000). Psychological responses of women after first trimester abortion. *Archives of General Psychiatry, 58*, 777-784.

Malatesta, V. J. (2007). Sexual problems, women and aging: An overview. *Journal of Women and Aging, 19*(1/2), 139-154.

Manning, W. D., Giordano, P. C., & Longmore, M. A. (2006). Hooking up: The relationship contexts of 'nonrelationship' sex. *Journal of Adolescent Research, 21*(5), 459-483.

Manning, W. D., & Jones, A. J. (2006). *Cohabitation and marital dissolution.* Paper presented at the annual meeting of the Population Association of America, Los Angeles, CA (March 30–April 1, 2006).

Manning, W. D., & Smock, P. J. (2003). *Measuring and modeling cohabitation: New perspectives from quantitative data.* Paper presented to the Population Association of America, May 3, 2003.

Manning, W. D., Smock, P. J., & Majudmar, D. (2004). The relative stability of cohabiting and marital unions for children. *Population Research and Policy Review, 23*(2), 135-159.

Marano, H. E. (2003). When men suffer low sex drive. *Psychology Today,* March 4, 2003.

Marcell, A. V. (2006). Making the most of the adolescent male health visit Part 2: The physical exam. *Contemporary Pediatrics,* June 1, 2006.

March of Dimes. (2009). *Stillbirth: Pregnancy and newborn health education center.* Retrieved September 12, 2009, from www.marchofdimes.com

Margolis, A. D., MacGowan, R. J., Grinstead, O., et al. (2006). Unprotected sex with multiple partners: Implications for HIV prevention among young men with a history of incarceration. *Sexually Transmitted Diseases, 33*(3), 175-180.

Marieb, E. N., & Hoehn, K. (2007). *Human anatomy & physiology* (7th ed.). Boston: Benjamin Cummings.

Marieb, E.N., & Hoehn, K. (2010). *Human anatomy & physiology* (8th ed.). Boston: Benjamin Cummings.

Markeiwicz, D., Doyle, A. B., & Brendgen, M. (2001). The quality of adolescents' friendships: Associations with mothers' interpersonal relationships, attachments to parents and friends and prosocial behaviors. *Journal of Adolescence, 24,* 429-445.

Markus, H.R., & Kitayama, S. (1991). Culture and the self: Implications for cognition, emotion, and motivation. *Psychological Review, 98,* 224-253.

Marsh, J. (2006). *Votes for women and chastity for men: Gender, health, medicine, and sexuality in Victorian England.* The Victoria and Albert Museum. Retrieved January 8, 2008, from www.fathom.com/course

Marshal, M., et al. (2008). Sexual orientation and adolescent substance use: A meta-analysis and methodological review. *Addiction, 103*(4), 546-556.

Marshall, L. E., & Marshall, W. L. (2006). Sexual addiction in incarcerated sexual offenders. *Sexual Addiction & Compulsivity, 13,* 377-390.

Marshall, W.A., & Tanner, J.M. (1969). Variations in the pattern of pubertal changes in girls. *Archives of Disease in Childhood, 44*(235), 291-303.

Marshall, W.A., & Tanner, J. M. (1970). Variations in the pattern of pubertal changes in boys. *Archives of Disease in Childhood, 45*(239), 13-23.

Martinson, F. M. (1994). *The sexual life of children.* Westport, CT: Bergin & Garvey.

Masood, S., et al (2005). Penile sensitivity and sexual satisfaction after circumcision: Are we informing men correctly? *Urology International, 75*(1), 62-66.

Masters, W. H., & Johnson, V. E. (1979). *Homosexuality in perspective.* Boston: Little, Brown and Company.

Matte, N. (2005). International sexual reform and sexology in Europe, 1897-1933. *Canadian Bulletin of Medical History, 22*(2), 253-270.

Matthiesen, S., & Wenn, H. M. (2004). Summary of the recommendations on sexual development in females. *Journal of Sexual Medicine, 1,* 24-34.

Mayo Clinic (2006). *Urinary tract infection.* Retrieved February 5, 2008, from www.mayoclinic.com/print/urinary-tract-infection/DS00286?DSECTION= all&METHOD=print

Mayo Clinic. (2008a). *Kegel exercises: How to strengthen your pelvic floor muscles.* Retrieved January 25, 2008, from www.mayoclinic.com/print/kegel-exercises/ WO00119/METHOD=print

Mayo Clinic. (2008b). *Premenstrual syndrome (PMS).* Retrieved January 31, 2008, from www.mayoclinic.com/print/premenstrual-syndrome/DS00134/DSECTION= all&METHOD-print

Mayo Clinic. (2009). *Tubal ligation.* Retrieved March 13, 2010, from http://www.mayo-clinic.com/health/tubal-ligation/MY01000

Mazur, A., Mueller, U., Krause, W., & Booth, A. (2002). Causes of sexual decline in aging married men: Germany and America. *International Journal of Impotence Research, 14,* 101-106.

McArthur, L. H., Holbert, D., & Pena, M. (2005). An exploration of the attitudinal and perceptual dimensions of body image among male and female adolescents from six Latin American cities. *Adolescence, 40*(160), 801-816.

McFadden, D., et al. (2005) A reanalysis of five studies on sexual orientation and the relative length of the 2nd and 4th fingers (the 2D:4D ratio). *Archives of Sexual Behavior, 34,* 341-356.

McLaren, A. (1990). *A history of contraception: From antiquity to the present day.* Cambridge, MA: Blackwell.

McMahon, E. (2003). The older homosexual: Current concepts of lesbian, gay, bisexual, and transgender older Americans. *Clinical Geriatric Medicine, 19,* 587-593.

McNair, B. (2002). *Striptease culture: Sex, media, and the democratization of desire.* London: Routledge.

Medicine, B. (2002). Directions in gender research in American Indian societies: Two spirits and other categories. In W. J. Lonner, D. L. Dinnel, S.A. Hayes, & D. N. Sattler (Eds.), *Online readings in psychology and culture* (Unit 3, Chapter 2). Center for Cross-Cultural Research, Western Washington University. Retrieved September 14, 2009, from www.wwu.edu/~culture

Mellish, M. E., & Cherry, J. D. (1992). Staphylococcal infections. In R. D. Feiegin (Ed.), *Pediatric Infectious Diseases.* Philadelphia W.B. Saunders and Company.

Mercer, C. H., et al. (2003). Sexual function problems and help seeking behaviour in Britain: National probability sample survey. *British Medical Journal, 327,* 4267.

Merck Medical Manual (2003). *Complications of pregnancy: Women's health issues* (Section 22, Chapter 245). Retrieved September 11, 2009, from www.merck.com/ mrkshared/mmanual_home/sec22/245.jsp

Meston, C. (2000). The psychophysiological assessment of female sexual function. *Journal of Sex Education and Therapy, 25,* 6-16.

Meston, C. M., Heiman, J. R., & Trapnell, P. D. (1999). The relation between early abuse and adult sexuality. *The Journal of Sex Research, 36,* 385-395.

Meston, C. M., Trapnell, P.D., & Gorzalka, B. B. (1996). Ethnic and gender differences in sexuality: Variations in sexual behavior between Asian and non-Asian university students. *Archives of Sexual Behavior, 25, 33-71.*

Meston, C. M., Trapnell, P .D., & Gorzalka, B. B. (1998). Ethnic, gender, and length-of-residency influences on sexual knowledge and attitudes. *Journal of Sex Research, 35,* 176-188.

Metts, S., & Cupach, W. R. (1989). The role of communication in human sexuality. In K. McKinney and S. Sprecher (Eds.), *Human sexuality: The societal and interpersonal context.* Norwood, NJ: Albex.

Metts, S., & Spitzberg, B. H. (1996). Sexual communication in interpersonal contexts: A script-based approach. In B. R. Burleson (Ed.), *Communication yearbook 19* (pp. 49-91), Thousand Oaks, CA: Sage.

Metzl, J. M. (2004). Voyeur nation? Changing definitions of voyeurism, 1950-2004. *Harvard Review of Psychiatry, 12,* 127-131.

Michaud, S. L., & Warner, R. M. (1997). Gender differences in self-reported response in troubles talk. *Sex Roles: A Journal of Sex Research, 37,* 527-540.

Miller, K. S., Forehand, R., & Kotchick, B.A. (1999). Adolescent sexual behavior in two ethnic minority samples: The role of family variables. *Journal of Marriage and Family, 61*(1), 85-98.

Miller, L., & Hughes, J. P. (2003). Continuous combination oral contraceptive pills to eliminate withdrawal bleeding: A randomized trial. *Obstetrics & Gynecology, 101,* 653-661.

Miller, L., & Notter, K. M. (2001). Menstrual reduction with extended use of combination oral contraceptive pills: Randomized and controlled trial. *Obstetrics & Gynecology, 98,* 771-778.

Mills, J. K. (1990). The psychoanalytic perspective of adolescent homosexuality: A review. *Adolescence, 25*(100), 912-922.

Mincieli, L., et al. (2007). *The relationship context of births outside of marriage: The rise of cohabitation.* Washington, DC: Child Trends.

Miner, M. M., & Kuritzky, L. (2007). Erectile dysfunction: A sentinel marker for cardiovascular disease in primary care. *Cleveland Clinic Journal of Medicine, 74*(3), S30-S37.

Mohn, J., Tingle, L., & Finger, R. (2003). An analysis of the causes of the decline in nonmarital birth and pregnancy rates for teens from 1991 to 1995. *Adolescent and Family Health, 3*(1), 39-47.

Moir, A., & Jessel, D. (1991). *Brain sex: The real difference between men and women.* New York: Doubleday.

Money, J. (1975). Ablatio penis: Normal male infant sex-reassigned as a girl. *Archives of Sexual Behavior, 4*(1), 65-71.

Money, J. (1976). The development of sexology as a discipline. *The Journal of Sex Research, 12*(2), 83-87.

Monitoring the Future Study. (2007). *National results on adolescent drug use.* Retrieved July 30, 2009, from http://www.monitoringthefuture.org/pubs/mono-graphs/overview2007.pdf

Montague, D. K., et al. (2003). American Urological Association guideline on the management of priapism. *Journal of Urology, 170*(4), 1318-1324.

Montgomery, K. A., Gonzalez, E. W., & Montgomery, O. C. (2008). Self-disclosure of sexually transmitted diseases. *Holistic Nursing Practice, 22*(5), 268-279.

Mooney, J. (1985). *The destroying angel: Sex, fitness, and food in the legacy of degeneracy theory, Graham Crackers, Kellogg's Corn Flakes and American health history.* Buffalo, NY: Prometheus Books.

Mooradian, D. D., & Korenman, S. G. (2006). Management of the cardinal features of andropause. *American Journal of Therapeutics, 13*(2), 145-160.

Moore, K.A., Jekielek, S. M., & Emig, C. (2002). *Marriage from a child's perspective: How does family structure affect children, and what can we do about it?* (Child Trends Research Brief). Washington, DC: Child Trends.

Moore, K. L., & Persaud, T. V. N. (2007). *The developing human: Clinically oriented embryology* (8th ed.). Philadelphia: Saunders.

Morales, A., Heaton, J. P. W., & Carson, C. C. (2000). Andropause: A misnomer for a true clinical entity. *Journal of Urology, 163,* 705-712.

Morales, A., et al. (2004). Endocrine aspects of sexual dysfunction in men. *Journal of Sexual Medicine, 1,* 69-81.

Morgan, E., & Kuykendall, C. (2000). Spiritual intimacy. *Marriage Partnership, 17*(2), 60.

Morley, J. E. (2007). The diagnosis of late life hypogonadism. *The Aging Male, 10*(4), 217-220.

Morokoff, P.J., et al. (1997). Sexual assertiveness scale (SAS) for women: Development and validation. *Journal of Personality and Social Psychology, 73,* 790-804.

Moser, C., & Kleinplatz, P. J. (2003). *DSM-IV-TR and the paraphilias: An argument for removal.* Paper presented on May 19, 2003 at the Annual Meeting of the American Psychiatric Association.

Moser, C., & Kleinplatz, P. J. (2005). DSM-IV-TR-TR and the paraphilias: An argument for removal. *Journal of Psychology & Human Sexuality, 17*(3/4), 91-109.

Mosher, W. D., Chandra, A., & Jones, J. (2005). Sexual behavior and selected health measures: men and women 15-44 years of age, United States, 2002. *Advanced Data, 362,* 1-55.

Motofei, I. G., & Rowland, D. L. (2005a). Neurophysiology of the ejaculatory process: Developing perspectives. *British Journal of Urology International, 96*(9), 1333-1338.

Motofei, I. G., & Rowland, D. L. (2005b). The physiological basis of human sexual arousal: Neuroendocrine sexual asymmetry. *International Journal of Andrology, 28*(2), 78-87.

Muehlenhard, C. L., et al. (2003). Gender and sexuality: An introduction to the special issue. *Journal of Sex Research, 40*(1), 1-4.

Mulholland, E., & Van Wersch, A. (2007). Stigma, sexually transmitted infections and attendance at the GUM clinic: An exploratory study with implications for the theory of planned behavior. *Journal of Health Psychology, 12,* 17-31.

Murnen, S. K., & Stockton, M. (1997). Gender and self-reported sexual arousal in response to sexual stimuli: A meta-analytic review. *Sex Roles, 37,* 135-153.

Murray, J. B. (2000). Psychological profile of pedophiles and child molesters. *Journal of Psychology, 134,* 211-224.

G. (2000). Hope and happiness. In J. Gillham (Ed.), *Dimensions of optimism ...d hope* (pp. 323-336). Radnor, PA: Templeton Foundation Press.

...yers, D. G. (2008). *Social psychology* (9th ed.). New York: McGraw Hill.

Nanda, S. (1990). *Neither man nor woman: The Hijras of India*. Belmont, CA: Wadsworth.

Narod, S. A., & Offit, K. (2005). Prevention and management of hereditary breast cancer. *Journal of Clinical Oncology, 23*, 1656-1663.

National Academy of Sciences. (1995). *Research ethics*. National Academy Press, Washington, DC. Retrieved January 1, 2008, from www.nas.edu

National Campaign to Prevent Teen Pregnancy. (2008). *National data*. Retrieved August 2, 2009, from http://www.thenationalcampaign.org/national-data/default.aspx

National Cancer Institute. (2007). *Treatment regimen effective for metastatic testicular cancer*. Retrieved July 30, 2009, from http://www.cancer.gov/ncicancerbulletin/NCI_Cancer_Bulletin_080707/page4

National Cancer Institute. (2008). *Screening mammograms*. Retrieved February 2, 2008, from www.cancer.gov

National Center for Health Statistics. (2005). *Cohabitation, marriage, divorce, and remarriage in the United States*. DHHS Publication No. (PHS) 2002-1998 (July 2002). Retrieved August 12, 2009, from http://www.cdc.gov/nchs/data/series/sr_23/sr23_022.pdf

National Center for Health Statistics. (2006). *Age at menarche*. Rockville, MD: U.S. Department of Health, Education, and Welfare. Series 11, No. 133.

National Center for Health Statistics. (2007a). *Teen birth rates rise for the first time in 15 years*. Retrieved January, 10, 2009, from www.cdc.gov/NCHS/pressroom/07 newsreleases/teenbirth.htm

National Center for Health Statistics. (2007b). *Trends in circumcision among newborns*. Retrieved July 30, 2009, from http://www.cdc.gov/nchs/products/pubs/pubd/hestats/circumcisions/circumcisions.htm

National Center for Health Statistics. (2008). *Unmarried and single Americans week*. Retrieved June 29, 2009, from www.census.gov/population/www/socdemo/hh-fam/cps2008.html

National College Health Assessment. (2008). *American College Health Assessment: Spring 2008*. Retrieved August 2, 2009, from www.acha.org

National Collegiate Athletic Association Research Staff. (2001). *NCAA study of substance use habits of college student-athletes*. Indianapolis.

National Heart, Lung, and Blood Institute. (2004). Questions and answers about the WHI postmenopausal hormone therapy trials. Retrieved September 18, 2009, from http://www.nhlbi.nih.gov/whi/whi_faq.htm

National Institute on Aging. (2009). Age page: Menopause. Retrieved September 18, 2009, from http://www.nia.nih.gov/HealthInformation/Publications/menopause.htm

National Institute on Aging. (2010). *Menopause*. Retrieved February 19, 2010, from http://www.nlm.nih.gov/medlineplus/menopause.html

National Institute on Drug Abuse. (2007). *Steroids: Anabolic*. Retrieved July 30, 2009, from http://www.drugabuse.gov/drugpages/steroids.html

National Institutes of Health. (2003). *Prostatitis: Disorders of the prostate*. NIH Publication No. 04-4553. Retrieved March 7, 2008, from www.kidney.niddk.nih.gov/kudiseases/pubs/prostatitis/

National Institutes of Health (2009). *National Asian & Pacific Islander HIV/AIDS awareness day*. Retrieved January 31, 2010, from http://www.hhs.gov/aidsawarenessdays/days/asian/index.html

National Kidney and Urologic Diseases Information Clearinghouse. (2005). *Peyronie's disease*. Bethesda, MD: National Institute of Health. NIH Publication No. 07-3902.

National Vital Statistics Reports. (2006, September 26). Births, marriages, and divorces. *National Vital Statistics Reports, 55*(1), Tables 1 & 32. Retrieved July 22, 2009, from www. healthvermont.gov/research/stats/2004/documents/APPX_D.PDF-similar—

National Vital Statistics Reports. (2008). *Births, marriages, divorces, and deaths: Provisional data for June 2007. NVSR, 56*(12).

Ndovi, T. T., et al. (2006). Quantitative assessment of seminal vesicle and prostate drug concentrations by use of a noninvasive method. *Clinical Pharmacology & Therapeutics, 80*(2), 146-158.

Needham, L. B. (1999). *An investigation of exceptions to patterns of mate selection in evolutionary theory among resource dependent and independent females*. etrieved May 27, 2004, from http://mutans.astate.edu/dcline/Guide/Mate_selection.html

Neto, F. (1993). Love styles and self-representations. *Personality and Individual Differences, 14*, 795-803.

Neto, F. (1994). Love styles among Portuguese students. *Journal of Psychology, 128*, 613-616.

Neto, F. (2001). Love styles of three generations of women. *Marriage & Family Review, 33*(4), 19-30.

Neto, F. (2007). Forgiveness, personality and gratitude. *Personality and Individual Differences, 43*, 2313-2323.

Nicholas, C. (2004). Gaydar: Eye-gaze as identity recognition among gay men and lesbians. *Sexuality & Culture, 8*(1), 60-86.

Nicolosi, A., et al. (2006). Sexual behaviour, sexual dysfunctions and related help seeking patterns in middle-aged and elderly Europeans: The global study of sexual attitudes and behaviors. *World Journal of Urology, 24*, 423-428.

Noble, M. J., & Lakin, M. (2005). *Premature ejaculation*. Retrieved February 22, 2008, from www.prostateinfo.com

Nock, S. L. (1998). The consequences of premarital fatherhood. *American Sociological Review, 63*, 250-263.

Noland, C. M. (2006). Listening to the sound of silence: Gender roles and communication about sex in Puerto Rico. *Sex Roles, 55*(5-6), 283-295.

Obermeyer, C. M. (2005). The consequences of female circumcision for health and sexuality: An update on the evidence. *Culture, Health, and Sexuality, 7*(5), 443-461.

O'Connell, H. (2005). Anatomy of the clitoris. *Journal of Urology, 174*, 1189-1195.

Oda, R. (2001). Sexual dimorphic mate preference in Japan: An analysis of lonely hearts advertisements. *Human Nature, 12*, 191-206.

O'Donnell, A. B., Araujo, A. B., & McKinlay, J. B. (2004). The health of normally aging men: The Massachusetts Male Aging Study. *Experimental Gerontology, 39*(7), 975-984.

O'Donnell, L., et al. (2006). Heterosexual risk behaviors among urban young adolescents. *The Journal of Early Adolescence, 26*(87), 87-109.

O'Farrel, N., Quigley, M., & Fox, P. (2005). Association between the intact foreskin and inferior standards of male genital hygiene behavior: A cross-sectional study. *International Journal of STD & AIDS, 16*(8), 556-588.

Ogbu, J. U. (1990). Cultural model, identity, and literacy. In J. W. Stigler, R. Shedder, & G. Herd (Eds.), *Cultural Psychology* (pp. 520-541). New York: Cambridge University Press.

Oggins, J., Leber, D., & Veroff, J. (1993). Race and gender differences in black and white newlyweds' perception of sexual and marital relations. *The Journal of Sex Research, 30*, 152-160.

O'Hara, K., & O'Hara, J. (1999). The effect of male circumcision on the sexual enjoyment of the female partner. *British Journal of Urology, 83*, 79-84.

The Ohio State University. (2006). Asian American rhetoric: Histories, theories, and practices. Retrieved September 14, 2009, from http://asianamericanstudies.osu.edu/dsp_news.cfm?NewsID=34dabbd0-29cb-458c-bd53-3a549c8d78e4

Okami, P. (1991). Self-reports of "positive" childhood and adolescent sexual contacts with older persons: An exploratory study. *Archives of Sexual Behavior, 20*, 437-457.

Okami, P., & Shackelford, T. K. (2001). Human sex differences in sexual psychology and behavior. *Annual Review of Sex Research, 12*, 186-241.

Okazaki, S. (2002). Influences of culture on Asian Americans' sexuality. *Journal of Sex Research, 39*, 34-41.

Okun, B. F. (2002). *Effective helping: Interviewing and counseling techniques* (6th ed.). Monterey, CA: Brooks/Cole.

Oliver, M. B., & Hyde, J. S. (1993). Gender differences in sexuality: A meta-analysis. *Psychological Bulletin, 114*, 29-51.

Olson, D. H., & Olson-Sigg, A. (2007). *Overview of cohabitation research*. PREPARE/ENRICH. Retrieved September 2, 2009, from www.prepare-enrich.com

Omarzu, J. (2000). A disclosure model: Determining how and when individuals will self-disclose. *Personality and Social Psychology Review, 4*(2), 174-185.

Omole, F., Simmons, B. J., & Hacker, Y. (2003). Management of Bartholin's duct cyst and gland abscess. *American Family Physician, 68*(1), July 1.

Oosterhuis, H. (2000). *Stepchildren of nature: Richard von Krafft-Ebbing, psychiatry, and the making of sexual identity*. Chicago: University of Chicago Press.

Openshaw, D. K. (1998). Resiliency. In C. A. Smith (Ed.), *The encyclopedia of parenting*. Westport, CT: Greenwood.

Openshaw, D. K. (2004). *The psychosocial development of adolescence: Intimacy*. Retrieved August 30, 2009, from www.usu.edu/openshaw

Oppenheimer, M. (2007). Recovering from an extramarital relationship from a nonsystemic approach. *American Journal of Psychotherapy. 61*(2), 181-191.

Ortner, S. (1978). The virgin and the state. *Feminist Studies, 4*(3), 19-35.

Orzack, M. H. (2004). *Computer compulsion services*. Retrieved July 7, 2007, from http://www.computercompulsion.com/

Osborne, C. (2005). Marriage following the birth of a child among cohabiting and visiting parents. *Journal of Marriage and Family, 67*, 14-26.

Osborne, C., & McLanahan, S. (2007). Partnership instability and child well-being. *Journal of Marriage and Family, 69*(4), 1065-1083.

Ozcan, U., et al. (1998). Controversy on prophylactic oophorectomy. *Journal of Medical Sciences, 28*, 461-467.

Ozretich, R., & Bowman, S. (2001). Middle childhood and adolescent development. *Oregon State University Extension Service, EC1527*.

Pan, S. (1993). Chinese wives: Psychological and behavioral factors underlying their orgasm frequency. Unpublished manuscript. Beijing: Renmin University.

Panfilov, D. E. (2006). Augmentative phalloplasty. *Aesthetic Plastic Surgery, 30*(2), 183-198.

Parmet, S. (2004, June 23-30). Male sexual dysfunction. *Journal of American Medical Association, 291*(24). Retrieved August 1, 2009, from http://jama.amaassn.org/cgi/content/full/291/24/3076

Patterson, C. J. (1996). Lesbian mothers and their children: Findings from the Bay Area Families Study. In J. Laird & R. J. Green (Eds.), *Lesbians and gays in couples and families: A handbook for therapists* (pp. 420-437). San Francisco: Jossey-Bass.

Pauls, R., et al. (2006). A prospective study examining the anatomic distribution of nerve density in the human vagina. *The Journal of Sexual Medicine, 3*(6), 979-987. Peel Public Health. Retrieved August 6, 2007, from www.region.peel.on.ca/health/commhlth/bodyimg/media.htm

Peplau, L. A. (2003). Human sexuality: How do men and women differ? *Current Directions in Psychological Science, 12*, 37-40.

Peplau, L. A., & Fingerhut, A. W. (2007). The close relationships of lesbians and gay men. *Annual Review of Psychology, 58*, 405-424.

Peplau, L. A., & Spalding, L. R. (2000). The close relationships of lesbians, gay men, and bisexuals. In C. Hendrick & S. S. Hendrick (Eds.), *Close relationships: A sourcebook* (pp. 111-124). Thousand Oaks, CA: Sage.

Perrottet, T. (2007). Ancient Greek temples of sex. *The Smart Set: Drexel University*. Retrieved November 21, 2007, from http://www.thesmartset.com/article/article11210701.aspx

Perry, M., Accordino, M. P., & Hewes, R. (2007). An investigation of Internet use, sexual nonsexual sensation seeking, and sexual compulsivity among college students. *Sexual Addiction & Compulsivity, 14*, 321–335.

Peven, D. A., & Shulman, B. H. (1999). The issue of intimacy in marriage. In J. Carlson & L. Sperry (Eds.), *The intimate couple* (pp. 276–283). New York: Bruner/Mazel.

Pew Research Center. (2007). *Purpose of marriage*. Retrieved September 2, 2009, from www.pewsocialtrends.org/pubs/?chartid=447

Pew Research Center. (2009). *Public takes conservative turn on abortion, gun control*. Retrieved September 19, 2009, from http://pewresearch.org/pubs/1212/abortion-gun-control-opinion-gender-gap

Philaretou, A. G., Mahfouz, A. Y., & Allen, K. R. (2005). Use of Internet pornography and men's well-being. *International Journal of Men's Health, 4*, 149–169.

Piaget, J. (1955). *The Child's Construction of Reality*. London: Routledge & Kegan Paul.

Pickover, S. (2002). Breaking the cycle: A clinical example of disrupting an insecure attachment system. *Journal of Mental Health Counseling, 24*, 358–367.

Piediffero, G., Colpi, E. M., Castiglioni, F., & Scroppo, F. I. (2004). Premature ejaculation. *Therapy Archives of Italian Urology and Andrology, 76*, 192–198.

Pinel, J. P. (1997). *Biopsychology* (3rd ed.). Boston: Allyn & Bacon.

Pinkerton, S. D., Bogart, L. M., Cecil, H., & Abramson, P. R. (2002). Factors associated with masturbation in a collegiate sample. *Journal of Psychology and Human Sexuality, 14*, 103–121.

Planned Parenthood. (2009). *Birth control allows us to prevent pregnancy and plan the timing of pregnancy*. Retrieved September 19, 2009, from www.plannedparenthood.org/health-topics/birth-control-4211.htm

Pommerville, P. J., & Zakus, P. (2006). Andropause: Knowledge and awareness among primary care physicians in Victoria, BC, Canada. *The Aging Male, 9*(4), 215–220.

Pope, H. G., Phillips, K. A., & Olivardia, R. (2000). *The Adonis complex: The secret crisis of male body obsession*. New York: The Free Press.

Population Reference Bureau. (2005). *U.S. attitudes toward interracial dating are liberalizing*. Retrieved March 20, 2010, from http://www.prb.org/Articles/2005/USAttitudesTowardInterracialDatingAreLiberalizing.aspx

Population Reference Bureau. (2009). World population highlights: Key findings from PRB's 2009 world population data sheet. *Population Reference Bureau, 64*(3). Retrieved March 20, 2010, from www.prb.org

Porter, T. F., et al. (2008). Early pregnancy loss. In R. S. Gibbs et al. (Eds.), *Danforth's obstetrics and gynecology* (10th ed., pp. 62–70). Philadelphia, PA: Lippincott Williams & Wilkins.

Poulson-Bryant, S. (2006). The politics of penis size (Hung: A meditation on the measure of black men in American). *The Gay & Lesbian Review Worldwide, 13*(1), 38–40.

Prager, K. J. (1995). *The psychology of intimacy*. New York: Guilford.

Prager, K. J. (1998). The multi-layered contexts of intimacy. In J. Carlson & L. Sperry (Eds.) *The intimate couple*. New York: Brunner/Mazel.

Prager, K. J., & Buhrmester, D. (1998). Intimacy and need fulfillment in couple relationships. *Journal of Social and Personal Relationships, 15*(4), 435–469.

Price, J. H., Allensworth, D. D., & Hillman, K. S. (1985). Comparison of sexual fantasies of homosexuals and of heterosexuals. *Psychological Reports, 57*, 871–877.

Prieto Castro, R. M., et al. (2003). Combined treatment with vitamin E and colchicine in the early stages of Peyronie's disease. *British Journal of Urology International, 91*(6), 522–524.

Primary Children's Medical Center. (2004). *Circumcision procedures*. Retrieved July 30, 2009, from http://intermountainhealthcare.org/hospitals/primarychildrens/Pages/home.aspx

Purnine, D. M., Carey, M. P., & Jorgensen, R. S. (1994). Gender differences regarding preferences for specific heterosexual practices. *Journal of Sex and Marital Therapy, 20*(4), 271–278.

Quilliam, S. (2005). *Staying together: From crisis to deeper commitment*. London: Vermillion.

Quinlivan, J. A., Tan, L. H., Steele, A., & Balck, K. (2004). Impact of demographic factors, early family relationships and depressive symptomatology in teenage pregnancy. *Australian and New Zealand Journal of Pyschiatry, 38*(4), 197–208.

Radiological Society of North America. (2008). *Mammography*. Retrieved February 2, 2008, from www.radiologyinfo.org/en/info.cfm?pg=mammo&bhcp=1

Ralph, D., & Christopher, N. (2007). Augmentive phalloplasty. In J. Barrett (Ed.), *Transsexual and other disorders of gender identity: A practical guide to management* (pp. 229–247). Oxford, England: Radcliffe Publishing.

Read, J. G. (2003). The sources of gender role attitudes among Christian and Muslim Arab-American women. *Sociology of Religion, 64*(2), 207–223.

Rebbeck, T. R., Friebel, T., Lynch, H. T., et al. (2004). Bilateral prophylactic mastectomy reduces breast cancer risk in BRCA1 and BRCA2 mutation carriers: The PROSE study group. *Journal of Clinical Oncology, 22*(6), 1055–1062.

Reddy, U. M. (2007). Prediction and prevention of recurrent stillbirth. *Obstetrics and Gynecology, 110*(5), 1151–1164.

Regan, P. (2000). The role of sexual desire and sexual activity in dating relationships. *Social Behavior and Personality, 28*(1), 51–60.

Regan, P. C. (1999). Hormonal correlates and causes of sexual desire: A review. *The Canadian Journal of Human Sexuality, 8*(1), 1–16.

Regan, P. C., & Berscheid, E. (1999). *Lust: What we know about human sexual desire*. Thousand Oaks, CA: Sage.

Rempel, J. K., & Baumgartner, B. (2003). The relationship between attitudes towards menstruation and sexual attitudes, desires, and behavior in women. *Archives of Sexual Behavior, 32*(2), 155–164.

Renaud, C. A., & Byers, E. S. (2001). Positive and negative sexual cognitions: Subjective experience and relationships to sexual adjustment. *The Journal of Sex Research, 38*, 252–262.

Renaud, C. A., Byers, E. S., & Pan, S. (1997). Sexual and relationship satisfaction in mainland China. *The Journal of Sex Research, 34*(4), 399–411.

Resnick, M. D., et al. (1997). Protecting adolescents from harm: Findings from the National Longitudinal Study on Adolescent Health. *Journal of the American Medical Association, 278*(10), 823–832.

Resnik, D. (1998). *The ethics of science: An introduction*. New York: Routledge.

Rice, P. F. (1993). *Intimate relationships, marriage, and families*. Mountain View, CA: Mayfield.

Richards, M. H., Crowe, P. A., Larson, R., & Swarr, A. (1998). Developmental patterns and gender differences in the experiences of peer companions during adolescence. *Child Development, 69*, 154–163.

Richardson, P. (1981). Women's perceptions of their important dyadic relationships during pregnancy. *Journal of Maternal and Child Nursing, 10*(3), 159–174.

Richters, J., et al. (2006). Circumcision in Australia: Prevalence and effects on sexual health. *International Journal of STD and AIDS, 17*, 547–554.

Richters, J., de Visser, R., Rissel, C., & Smith, C. (2006). Sexual practices at last heterosexual encounter and occurrence of orgasms in a national survey. *The Journal of Sex Research, 43*(3), 217–227.

Ridley, M. (2003). *Nature via nurture: Genes, experience, and what makes us human*. New York: Harper Collins.

Rieger, G., Linsenmeier, J., Bailey, J., & Gygax, L. (2008). Sexual orientation and childhood gender nonconformity: Evidence from home videos. *Developmental Psychology, 44*(1), 46–58.

Ries, L. A. G., et al. (2007). *SEER cancer statistics review, 1975–2004*. Bethesda, MD: National Cancer Institute.

Rocca, W. A., et al. (2008). Increased risk of parkinsonism in women who underwent oophorectomy before menopause. *Neurology, 70*, 200–209.

Roisman, G. I., et al. (2008). Adult romantic relationships as contexts of human development: A multimethod comparison of same-sex couples with opposite-sex dating, engaged, and married dyads. *Developmental Psychology, 44*, 91–101.

Roloff, M. E., Soule, K. P., & Carey, C. M. (2001). Reasons for remaining in a relationship and responses to relational transgressions. *Journal of Social and Personal Relationships, 18*, 362–385.

Romer, D., et al. (1994). Social influences on the sexual behavior of youth at risk for HIV exposure. *American Journal of Public Health, 84*(6), 977–985.

Romero, A. J., et al. (2004). Associations among familism, language preference and education in Mexican-American mothers and their children. *Journal of Developmental and Behavioral Pediatrics, 25*, 35–40.

Rose, S., & Frieze, I. H. (1993). Young singles' contemporary dating scripts. *Sex Roles, 28*, 499–509.

Roselli, C., Larkin, K., Schrunk, J., & Stormshak, F. (2004). Sexual partner preference, hypothalamic morphology and aromatase in rams. *Physiology & Behavior, 83*(2), 233–245.

Roselli, C., et al. (2004). The volume of a sexually dimorphic nucleus in the ovine medial preoptic area/anterior hypothalamus varies with sexual partner preference. *Brain Research, 1249*, 113–117.

Rosenbaum, J. E. (2009). Patient teenagers? A comparison of the sexual behavior of virginity pledgers and matched nonpledgers. *Pediatrics, 123*(1), e110–e120.

Rosenbaum, T. Y. (2007). Pelvic floor involvement in male and female sexual dysfunction and the role of pelvic floor rehabilitation in treatment: A literature review. *Journal of Sex Medicine, 4*, 4–13.

Rosenthal, D. A., & Feldman, S. S. (1999). The important of importance: Adolescents' perceptions of parental communication about sexuality. *Journal of Adolescence, 22*(6), 835–851.

Ross, M. R. (2005). Typing, doing, and being: Sexuality and the Internet. *The Journal of Sex Research, 42*(4), 342–352.

Ross, M. R. & Kauth, M. R. (2002). Men who have sex with men and the internet: Emerging issues and their management. In A. Cooper (Ed.), *Sex and the internet: A guidebook for clinicians*. New York: Brenner-Routledge.

Rosser, B. R. S., Bockting, W. O., Rugg, D. L., et al. (1991). A randomized controlled intervention trial of a sexual health approach to long-term HIV risk reduction for men who have sex with men: Effects of the intervention on unsafe sexual behavior. *AIDS Education and Prevention, 14* (Suppl. A), 59–71.

Rotter, J. B. (1954). *Social learning and clinical psychology*. New York: Prentice Hall.

Royal Australian College of Physicians. (2004). *Policy statement on circumcision*. Retrieved July 30, 2009, from www.racp.edu.au/hpu/paed/circumcision/print.htm

Rudacille, D. (2005). *The riddle of gender: Science, activism, and transgender rights*. New York: Pantheon.

Rule, N. O., & Ambady, N. (2008). Brief exposures: Male sexual orientation is accurately perceived at 50ms. *Journal of Experimental Social Psychology, 44*(4), 1100–1105.

Rule, N. O., Ambady, N., & Hallett, K. C. (2009). Female sexual orientation is perceived accurately rapidly, and automatically from the face and its features. *Journal of Experimental Social Psychology, 45*(4), 603–613.

Rupp, T. J. (2006). *Testicular torsion*. Retrieved March 6, 2008, from www.emedicine.com/EMERG/topics573.htm

F. & Zierk, K. I. (1992). Abortion, childrearing, and women's well-being. *Professional Psychology: Research and Practice, 23*, 269-280.

..e, B. J., & Meaney, G. J. (2007). The pursuit of sexual pleasure. *Sexuality & Culture, 11*(1), 28-51.

Rye, B. J., & Meaney, G. J. (2007) Voyeurism: It is good as long as we do not get caught. *International Journal of Sexual Health, 19*(1).

Sadovsky, R. (2000). Management of dyspareunia and vaginismus. *American Family Physician, 61*(8), 2511.

Saikhun, J., Kitiyanant, Y., Vanadurongwan, V., & Pavasuthipasit, K. (1999). Effects of sauna on sperm movement characteristics of normal men measured by computer-assisted sperm analysis. *International Journal of Andrology, 6*, 358-363.

Salmela-Aro, K., et al. (2006). Couples share similar changes in depressive symptoms and marital satisfaction anticipating the birth of a child. *Journal of Social and Personal Relationships, 23*(5), 781-803.

Sanches, D.T., & Kiefer, A. K. (2008). Body concerns in and out of the bedroom: Implications for sexual pleasure and problems. Retrieved October 20, 2008, from www.disanche@rutgers.edu

Sanders, J. S., & Robinson, W. L. (1979). Talking and not talking about sex: Male and female vocabularies. *Journal of Communication, 29*(2), 22-30.

Sanders, S. A., Graham, C. A., & Milhausen, R. R. (2008). Predicting sexual problems in women: The relevance of sexual excitation and inhibition. *Archives of Sexual Behavior, 37*(2), 241-251.

Sandnabba, N. K., Santtila, P., Wannas, M., & Krook, K. (2003). Age and gender specific sexual behaviors in children. *Child Abuse and Neglect, 27*(6), 579-605.

Sarkis, M. (2003). Female genital cutting (FGC): An introduction. *The FGC Education and Networking Project.* Retrieved January 22, 2008, from www.fgmnetwork.org/intro/fgmintro.html

Sato, T., et al. (2004). Brain masculinization requires androgen receptor function, *Proceedings of the National Academy of Sciences of the United States of America, 101*(6), 1673-1678.

Savin-Williams, R. C. (2005). *The new gay teenager.* Cambridge, MA: Harvard University Press.

Savin-Williams, R. C., & Esterberg, E.G. (2000). Lesbian, gay, and bisexual families. In D. H. Dmo, K. R. Allen, & M. A. Fine (Eds.), *Handbook of family diversitry.* New York: Oxford University Press.

Savin-Williams, R. C., & Ream, G. L. (2003). Sex variations in the disclosure to parents of same-sex attractions. *Journal of Family Psychology, 17*(3), 429-438.

Sax, L. J. (2008). *The gender gap in college: Maximizing the developmental potential of women and men.* San Francisco: Jossey-Bass.

Schachner, D.A., & Shaver, P.R. (2004). Attachment dimensions and sexual motives. *Personal Relationships, 11*, 179-195.

Schenk, J., Pfrang, H., & Rausche, A. (1983). Personality traits versus the quality of the marital relationship as the determinant of marital sexuality. *Archives of Sexual Behavior, 12*(1), 31-42.

Schmitt, D. P., & Buss, D. M. (2001) Human mate poaching: tactics and temptations for infiltrating existing mateships. *Journal of Personality and Social Psychology, 80*, 894-917.

Schmitt, D. P., et al. (2001). The desire for sexual variety as a tool for understanding basic human mating strategies. *Personal Relationships, 8*, 425-455.

Schneider, J. P. (2000). Effects of cybersex addiction on the family: Results of a survey. *Sexual Addiction and Compulsivity, 7*, 31-58.

Schneider, J. P. (2002). The new elephant in the living room: Effects of compulsive cybersex behaviors on the spouse. In A. Cooper (Ed.), *Sex and the internet: A guidebook for clinicians* (pp. 169-186). New York: Brunner-Routledge.

Schneller, D. P., & Arditti, J. A. (2004). After the break-up: Interpreting divorce and rethinking intimacy. *Journal of Divorce and Remarriage, 42*, 1-37.

Schoen, E. J. (2006a). Ignoring evidence of circumcision benefits. *Pediatrics, 118*(1), 85-87.

Schoen, E. J. (2006b). The increasing incidence of newborn circumcision: Data from the nationwide inpatient sample. *Journal of Urology, 175*(1), 394-395.

Schoen, E. J., Oehrli, M., Colby, C., & Machin, G. (2000). The highly protective effect of newborn circumcision against invasive penile cancer. *Pediatrics, 105*(3), PE36.

Schope, R. D. (2005). Who's afraid of growing old? Gay and lesbian perceptions of aging. *Journal of Gerontological Social Work, 45*(4), 23-39.

Schwartz, M. A., & Scott, B. M. (2003). *Marriages and families: Diversity and change* (4th ed.). Upper Saddle River, NJ: Prentice Hall.

Segura, D. A., & Pierce, J. L. (1993). Chicana/o family structure and gender personality: Chodorow, familism, and psychoanalyticsociology revisited. *Signs, 19*, 62-91.

Seligman, L., & Hardenburg, S. A. (2000). Assessment and treatment of paraphilias. *Journal of Counseling & Development, 78*(1), 107-113.

Selvin, E., Burnett, A. L., & Platz, E. A. (2007). Prevalence of and risk factors for erectile dysfunction in U.S. men. *American Journal of Medicine, 120*(2), 151-157.

Senecal, S., Murad, N., & Hess, U. (2003). Do you know what I feel? Predictors and judgments of each other's emotional reactions to emotion-eliciting situations. *Sex Roles, 48*(1-2), 21-37.

Senkul, T., et al. (2004). Circumcision in adults: Effect on sexual function. *Urology, 63*(1), 155-158.

Sergios, P., & Cody, J. (1985). Importance of physical attractiveness and social assertiveness skills in male homosexual dating behavior and partner selection. *Journal of Homosexuality, 12*, 71-84.

Sexuality Information and Education Council of the United States. (2007). *Public policy.* Retrieved August 23, 2009, from www.siecus.org.

Sexuality Information and Education Council of the United States. (2009). Retrieved August 19, 2009, from www.siecus.org

Shadish, W. (1993). Effects of family and marital psychotherapies: A meta-analysis. *Journal of Consulting and Clinical Psychology, 61*(6), 992-1002.

Shafer, M.A., & Moscicki, A. B. (2006). *Sexually transmitted infections.* Retrieved March 13, 2010, from http://www.health.am/sex/more/sexually_transmitted_infections/

Shanley, L.K. (1993). *Unassisted Childbirth.* Westport, CT: Bergin & Garvey Publishers.

Sharp, E.A., & Ganong, L. H. (2000). Raising awareness about marital expectations: An unrealistic beliefs change by integrative teaching? *Family Relations, 49*, 71-76.

Shaver, P. R., & Mikulincer, M. (2006a). Attachment theory, individual psychodynamics, and relationship functioning. In D. Perlman & A. Vangelisti (Eds.), *The Cambridge Handbook of Personal Relationships* (pp. 251-271). New York: Cambridge University Press.

Shaver, P. R., & Mikulincer, M. (2006b). A behavioral systems approach to romantic love relationships: Attachment, care-giving, and sex. In R. J. Sternberg & K. Weis (Eds.), *The new psychology of love* (pp. 35-64). New Haven, CT: Yale University Press.

Shelp, S. G. (2002). Gaydar: Visual detection of sexual orientation among gay and straight men. *Journal of Homosexuality, 44*, 1-14.

Shen, Z., Chen, S., Zhu, C., et al. (2004). Erectile dysfunction evaluation after adult circumcision. *Zhonghua Nan Ke Xue, 10*(1), 18-19.

Sherwin, B. B. (1985). Changes in sexual behavior as a function of plasma sex steroid levels in post-menopausal women. *Maturitas, 7*, 225-233.

Sherwin, B. B. (1988). A comparative analysis of the role of androgen in human male and female sexual behavior: Behavioral specificity, critical thresholds, and sensitivity. *Psychobiology, 16*, 416-425.

Sheynkin, Y., Jung, M., Yoo, P., et al. (2005). Increase in scrotal temperature in laptop computer users. *Human Reproduction, 20*(2), 452-455.

Shtarkshall, R. A., Santelli, J. S., & Hirsch, J. S. (2007). Sex education and sexual socialization: Roles for educators and parents. *Perspectives on Sexual and Reproductive Health, 39*(2), 116-120.

Shulman, S., & Kipnis, O. (2001). Adolescent romantic relationships: A look from the future. *Journal of Adolescence, 24*, 327-341.

Silverman, J. S. (2003). Fallacies about love and marriage. In M. Coleman and L. Ganong (Eds.), *Points and counterpoints* (pp. 91-93). Los Angeles: Roxbury.

Simkins, L., & Rinck, C. (1982). Male and female sexual vocabulary in different interpersonal contexts. *Journal of Sex Research, 18*, 160-172.

Simmons, T., & O'Connell, M. (2003). Married-couple and unmarried-partner households: 2000. *United States Census Bureau report.* Retrieved September 2, 2009, from www.landview.census.gov/prod/2003pubs/censr-5.pdf

Simon, J., et al. (2005). Testosterone patch increases sexual activity and desire in surgically menopausal women with hypoactive sexual desire disorder. *Journal of Clinical Endocrinology & Metabolism, 90*, 5226-5233.

Simoni, J. M., Demas, P., Mason, H. R., et al. (2005). HIV disclosure among women of African descent: Associations with coping, social support, and psychological adaptation. *AIDS and Behavior, 4*(2), 1147-1158.

Simons, W., & Gagnon, J. H. (1973). Sexual scripts. *Society, 22*, 53-60.

Skelton, C., & Hall, E. (2001). *The development of gender roles in young children.* Department of Education, University of Newcastle, UK. Retrieved July 30, 2007, from http://www.eoc.org.uk/research.html

Smith, S. (1995). Family theory and multicultural family studies. In B.B. Ingoldsby and S. Smith (Eds.), *Families in Multicultural Perspective.* New York: Guilford, 5-35.

Smock, P. J., Manning, W. D., & Porter, M. (2005). "Everything's there except money": How money shapes the decision to marry among cohabitors. *Journal of Marriage and Family, 67*, August 2005, 680-696.

Smock, P. J., Casper, L., & Wyse, J. (2008). Nonmarital cohabitation: Current knowledge and future directions for research. *Population Studies Center,* Report 08-648.

Smolak, L., Murnen, S., & Thompson, J. K. (2005). Sociocultural influences and muscle building in adolescent boys. *Psychology of Men & Masculinity, 6*, 227-239.

Snyder, D. K., Gordon, K. C., & Baucom, D. H. (2004). Treating affair couples: Extending the written disclosure paradigm to relationship trauma. *Clinical Psychology: Science and Practice, 11*(1), 155-159.

Snyder, H. N. (2000). *Sexual assault of young children as reported to law enforcement: Victim incident and offender characteristics.* Washington, DC: U.S. Department of Justice, Bureau of Justice Statistics, 2000. Publication JCJ 192990.

Society of Obstetricians and Gynaecologists of Canada. (2007). *The dangers of unassisted birth.* Retrieved March 5, 2010, from ttp://www.sogc.org/index_e.asp.

Sokolow, J. A. (1983). *Eros and modernization: Sylvester Graham, health reform, and the Origins of Victorian sexuality in America.* New Jersey: Associated University Presses.

Solar, J., & Irwin, A. (2007 draft). Towards a conceptual framework for analysis and action on the social determinants of health. *WHO/Commission on Social Determinants of Health: Geneva: WHO.* Retrieved September 23, 2009, from http://www.who.int/social_determinants/resources/csdh_framework_action_05_07.pdf.

Solomon-Fears, C. (2008). Nonmarital childbearing: Trends, reasons, and public policy interventions. *CRS Report for Congress.* Order code RL 34756. Retrieved August 2, 2009, from http://ftp.fas.org/sgp/crs/misc/RL34756.pdf

Somers, C. L. (2006). Parent-adolescent relationships and adolescent sexuality: Closeness, communication, and comfort among diverse U.S. adolescent samples. *Adolescence, 41*(161), 15-38.

Spence, N. J. (2003). *Transition to first sexual intercourse: The interaction between immigrant generational status and race/ethnicity.* Paper presented at the Southern Sociological Society. New Orleans, March 27-30.

Sprecher, S. (2002). Sexual satisfaction in premarital relationships: Associations with satisfaction, love, commitment, and stability. *The Journal of Sex Research, 39*(13), 32-44.

ENDNOTES

Sprecher, S., & Cate, R. (2004). Sexual satisfaction and sexual expression as predictors of relationship satisfaction and stability. In J. Harvey, A. Wenzel, & S. Sprecher (Eds.), *Handbook of sexuality in close relationships* (pp. 235–256). Mahwah, NJ: Erlbaum.

Sprecher, S., & Regan, P. C. (1996). College virgins: How men and women perceive their sexual status. *Journal of Sex Research, 33,* 3–15.

Sprecher, S., Sullivan, Q., & Hatfield, E. (1994). Mate selection preferences: Gender differences examined in a national sample. *Journal of Personality and Social Psychology, 66,* 1074–1080.

Sprigg, P. (2004). Questions and answers: What's wrong with letting same-sex couple "marry"? (pp. 173–179). In E. Schroeder (Ed.), *Taking sides: Clashing views on controversial issues in family and personal relationships.* New York: McGraw-Hill.

Stein, P. (1981). *Single life: Unmarried adults in social context.* New York: St. Martin's Press.

Steinberg, L., Mounts, N., Lamborn, S., & Dornbusch, S. (1991). Authoritative parenting and adolescent adjustment across various ecological niches. *Journal of Research on Adolescence, 1,* 19–36.

Stephen, R. (1995). Party of one. *Men's Health* (September, 1995).

Sterk-Elifson, C. (1994). Sexuality among African American women. In A. S. Rossi (Ed.), *Sexuality across the lifecourse* (pp. 99–126). Chicago: University of Chicago Press.

Stevenson, D. B. (1996). *Freud's psychosexual stages of development.* Retrieved March 12, 2010, from http://www.victorianweb.org/science/freud/develop.html

Stoleru, S., et al. (1999). Neuroanatomical correlates of visually evoked sexual arousal in human males. *Archives of Sexual Behavior, 28,* 1–21.

Stoller, R., & Herdt, G. (1985). Theories of origins of male homosexuality: A cross-cultural look. *Archives of General Psychiatry, 42,* 399–404.

Stolp, B., Reichman-Fried, M., Abraham, L., et al. (2009). HIV-1 Nef interferes with host cell motility by deregulation of cofilin. *Cell Host & Microbe, 6*(2), 174–186.

Stone, T., Winslade, W., & Klugman, C. M. (2000). Sex offenders sentencing laws and pharmaceutical treatment: A prescription for failure. *Behavioral Science Law, 18,* 83–110.

Storms, M. (1980). Theories of sexual orientation. *Journal of Personality and Social Psychology, 38*(5), 783–792.

Strachman, A., & Impett, E. A. (2009). Attachment orientations and daily condom use in dating relationships. *The Journal of Sex Research, 46*(4), 319–329.

Strassberg, D. S., & Lockerd, L. K. (1998). Force in women's sexual fantasies. *Archives of Sexual Behavior 27*(4), 403–415.

Strauss, L. T., et al. (2007). Abortion surveillance—United States, 2004. Centers for Disease Control and Prevention. *MMWR Surveillance Summary, November 23; 56*(9), 1–33.

Striar, S., & Bartlik B. (2000). Stimulation of the libido: The use of erotica in sex and practice of sex therapy (3rd ed.). New York: Gilford.

Sturgis, F. R. (1900). The treatment of masturbation. In F. R. Sturgis (Ed.), *Sexual debility in man* (p.373). New York: E.B. Treat & Company.

Sudhir K., & Doniger, W. (2003). *Kama sutra (Oxford World's Classics).* Oxford, UK: Oxford University Press.

Sueppel, C., Kreder, K., & See, W. (2001). Improved continence outcomes with preoperative pelvic floor muscle strengthening exercises. *Urologic Nursing, 21*(3), 201.

Sun, S. S., Schubert, C. M., Chumlea, W. C., et al. (2002). National estimates of the timing of sexual maturation and racial differences among U.S. children. *Pediatrics, 110,* 911–919.

Susan G. Komen for the Cure. (2007). *Facts for life: When you discover a lump.* St. Louis, MO: Susan G. Komen for the Cure, Item No. 806–381.

Swaab, D. F., Gooren, L. J., & Hofman, M. A. (1995). Brain research, gender, and sexual orientation. *Journal of Homosexuality, 28*(3–4), 288–301.

Swanson, J., & Chenitz, W. (1993). Regaining a valued self: The process of adaptation to living with genital herpes. *Qualitative Health Research, 3*(3), 270–297.

Sylwester, R. (2007). *The adolescent brain: Reaching for autonomy.* Corwin Press.

Symons, D. (1979). *The evolution of human sexuality.* Oxford, England: Oxford University Press.

Tager, D., Good, G. E., & Bauer Morrison, J. (2006). Our bodies, ourselves revisited: Male body image and psychological well-being. *International Journal of Men's Health, 5*(3), 228–238.

Tajfel, H., & Turner, J. (1979). An integrative theory of intergroup conflict. In W. G Austin & S. Worchel (Eds.), *The social psychology of intergroup relations* (pp. 94–109). Monterey, CA: Brooks-Cole.

Tannen, D. (1990). *You just don't understand: Women and men in conversation.* New York: William Morrow.

Taves, D. (2002). The intromission function of the foreskin. *Medical Hypotheses, 59*(2), 180.

Taylor, J. R., Lockwood, A. P., & Taylor, A. J. (1996). The prepuce: Specialized mucosa of the penis and its loss to circumcision. *British Journal of Urology International, 77,* 291–295.

Tennov, D. (1979). *Love and limerence: The experience of being in love.* New York: Stein & Day.

Teusher, U., & Tuesher, C. (2007). Reconsidering the double standard of aging: Effects of gender and sexual orientation on facial attractiveness ratings. *Personality and Individual Differences, 42,* 631–639.

Thacker, S. B., & Banta, H. D. (1983). Benefits and risks of episiotomy: An interpretive review of the English language literature. *Obstetrics and Gynecological Survey, 38*(6), 322–338.

Thigpen, J. W. (2009). Early sexual behavior in a sample of low-income, African American children. *Journal of Sex Research, 46*(1), 67–79.

Thomas, F., Renaud, F., Benefice, E., et al. (2001). International variability of ages menarche and menopause: Patterns and main determinants. *Human Biology, 73,* 271–290.

Thompson, A. (1984). Emotional and sexual components of extramarital relations. *Journal of Marriage and the Family, 46,* 35–42.

Thompson, S. H. (2007). Characteristics of the female athlete triad in collegiate cross-country runners. *Journal of American College Health, 56*(2), 129–137.

Thonneau, P., Bujan, L., Multingner, L., & Mieusset, R. (1998). Occupational heat exposure and male fertility: A review. *Human Reproduction, 13,* 2122–2125.

Thorp, J. M. (1987). Selected use of midline episiotomy effect on perineal trauma. *Obstetrics & Gynecology, 70*(2), 145–286.

Thorp, J. M., & Bowes, W. A. (1989). Episiotomy: Can its routine use be defended? *American Journal of Obstetrics and Gynecology, 160,* 1027–1039.

Tingsten, H. (1966). *Viktoria ja Viktoriaanit.* Porvoo: WSOY.

Toth, P. P. (2000). Management of Bartholin's gland duct cysts and abscesses. In Saunders *Manual of medical practice.* Philadelphia: W. B. Saunders.

Townsend, J. (1995). Sex without emotional involvement: An evolutionary interpretation of sex differences. *Archives of Sexual Behavior, 24,* 173–2005.

Træen, B., & Nilson, T. S. (2006). Use of pornography in traditional media and on the Internet in Norway. *The Journal of Sex Research, 43,* 245–254.

Trask, B. S., & Koivunen, J. M. (2006). Trends in marriage and cohabitation in culturally diverse families. In B. S. Trask & R. Hamon (Eds.), *Cultural diversity and families: Expanding perspectives* (pp. 121–136). Thousand Oaks, CA: Sage Publications.

Triandis, H. C., & Suh, E. M. (2002). Cultural influences on personality. *Annual Review of Personality, 53,* 133–160.

Trost, L. W., Gur, S., & Hellstrom, W. J. (2007). Pharmacological management of Peyronie's disease. *Drugs, 67*(4), 208–215.

Trussell, J., et al. (2009). Cost effectiveness of contraceptives in the United States. *Contraception, 79*(1), 5–14.

Trybulski, J. (2005). The long-term phenomena of women's postabortion experiences. *Western Journal of Nursing Research, 27*(5), 559–576.

Turkle, S. (1995). *Life on the screen.* New York: Simon & Schuster.

Ubillos, S., Paez, D., & Gonzalez, J. L. (2000). Culture and sexual behavior. *Psiothema, 12,* 70–82.

UNAIDS. (2007a). *Regional consultation on male circumcision and HIV prevention in Nairobi, Kenya, November, 2006.* Geneva: UNAIDS.

UNAIDS. (2007b). *Safe male circumcision and comprehensive HIV prevention programming: Guidance for decision makers on human rights, ethical and legal considerations.* Geneva: UNAIDS

UNAIDS/CAPRISA. (2007). *Perspectives from social science on male circumcision for HIV prevention, Durban, January, 2007.* Geneva: UNAIDS/CAPRISA

Understanding Sexuality. (2008). Harvard Health Publications. Retrieved September 16, 2009, from http://www.aarp.org/health/conditions.articles/harvard_sexuality-in-midlife-and-beyond_1.html

University of Iowa. (2006). *Contact vulvitis.* Retrieved March 12, 2010, from http://www.uihealthcare.com/depts/med/obgyn/patedu/vulvarvaginaldisease/contactvulvitis.html

U.S. Census Bureau. (2005). Hispanic heritage month. *U.S. Census Bureau, CB05-FF.14-3.* (September 8, 2005). Retrieved March 20, 2010, from http://www.census.gov/PressRelease/www/releases/archives/facts_for_features_special_editions/005338.html

U.S. Census Bureau. (2006a). Marital status of the population by sex, race, and Hispanic origin: 1990–2006. *Current Population Reports, P20-537.* Retrieved September 2, 2009, from www.census.gov/population/www/socdemo/hh-fam.html.

U.S. Census Bureau. (2006b). *Married couple family groups, by presence of own children in specific age groups, and age, earnings, education, and race and Hispanic origin of both spouses: 2006.* Table FG4. Retrieved September 2, 2009, from www.census.gov/populatoiin/www/socdemo/hh-fam/ cps2006.html.

U.S. Census Bureau. (2007). *Population 65 years and over in the United States.* S0103. Retrieved February 28, 2010, from www.factfinder.census.gov

U.S. Census Bureau. (2008a). *Custodial mothers and fathers and their child support.* Retrieved March 13, 2010, from www.census.gov/Press-Release/www/releases/archives/children/010634.html.

U.S. Census Bureau. (2008b). *Income, poverty, and health insurance coverage in the United States: 2007.* Retrieved January 30, 2010, from www.census.gov/hhes/www/hlthins/hlthin07.html

U.S. Census Bureau. (2008c). *Unmarried and single Americans.* CB08-FF.16. Retrieved January 25, 2009, from ww.census.gov/acs/www/Products/users_guide/index.htm.

U.S. Centers for Disease Control and Prevention. (2005). *Diagnosing TSS.*

U.S. Department of Justice. (2003). *Sourcebook of criminal justice statistics.* Washington, DC: U.S. Government Printing Office.

U.S. Department of Justice. (2007). *Stalking and cyberstalking.* Retrieved July 15, 2009, from http://www.ojp.usdoj.gov/hij/topics/crime/stalking/welcome.html

University of Texas. (2009). *Self-help: Overcoming pornography addiction.* Retrieved March 12, 2010, from http://www.utdallas.edu/counseling/selfhelp/porn-addiction.html

U.S. Department of Health and Human Services. (2007). *What is premenstrual syndrome?* Retrieved July 27, 2009, from http://www.womenshealth.gov/FAQ/premenstrual-syndrome.cfm

U.S. Department of Health and Human Services. (2009). *HIV/AIDS and American Indians/Alaska Natives.* Retrieved January 31, 2010, from http://minorityhealth.hhs.gov/templates/content.aspx?ID=3026

of Health and Human Services, CDC, National Center for HIV, STD, ...tion. (2009). Sexually transmitted disease morbidity for selected ...race/ethnicity and gender, 1996-2008. CDC WEONDER On-line ...ovember 2009. Retrieved February 16, 2010, from http://wonder. ...std-v2008-race-age.html

...partment of Labor. (2008). *The gender wage gap: 2008.* Retrieved August 26, 2009, from www.iwpr.org/pdf/C350.pdf

Upchurch, D. M., Levy-Storms, L., Sucoff, C. A., & Aneshensel, C. S. (1998). Gender and ethnic differences in the timing of first sexual intercourse. *Family Planning Perspectives, 30,* 121-127.

Vaginismus. (2008). *What causes vaginismus?* Retrieved October 20, 2008, from www.vaginismus.com

van den Eijnden, R. J., Meerkerk, G. J., Vermulst, A. A., et al. (2008). Online communication, compulsive Internet use, and psychological well-being among adolescents: A longitudinal study. *Developmental Psychology, 44*(3), 655-665.

Van Kampen, M., et al. (2003). Treatment of erectile dysfunction by perineal exercise, electromyographic biofeedback, and electrical stimulation. *Physical Therapy, 83,* 536-543.

Van Wyk, P. H., & Geist, C. S. (1984). Psychosocial development of heterosexual, bisexual, and homosexual behavior. *Archives of Sexual Behavior, 13,* 505-544.

Vangelisti, A. L., & Young, S. L. (2000). When words hurt: The effects of perceived intentionality on interpersonal relationships. *Journal of Social and Personal Relationships, 17,* 393-424.

Villarruel, A. M., & Rodriquez, D. (2003). Beyond stereotypes: Promoting safer sex behaviors among Latino adolescents. *Journal of Obstetric, Gynecologic, and Neonatal Nursing, 32*(2), 258-263.

Violence Against Women. (2009). *The facts about sexual violence.* Violence Against Women Online Resources, U.S. Department of Justice. Retrieved February 14, 2010, from www.vaw.umn.edu

Vohs, D., Cantonese, K. R., & Baumeister, R. F. (2004). Sex in "his" versus "her" relationships. In J. H. Harvey, A. Wenzel, & S. Sprecher (Eds.), *Handbook of sexuality in close relationships* (pp. 455-474). Mahwah, NJ: Erlbaum.

Vohs, K. D., & Baumeister, R. F. (2004). Sexual passion, intimacy, and gender. In D. J. Mashek & A. Aron (Eds.), *Handbook of closeness and intimacy* (pp. 189-200). Mahwah, NJ: Lawrence Erlbaum.

von Sydow, K. (1999). Sexuality during pregnancy and after childbirth: A metacontent analysis of 59 studies. *Journal of Psychosomatic Research, 47,* 27-49.

Wainwright, J. L., & Patterson, C. J. (2006). Delinquency, victimization, and substance use among adolescents with female same-sex parents. *Journal of Family Psychology, 20,* 526-530.

Wainright, J. L., & Patterson, C. J. (2008). Peer relations among adolescents with same-sex parents. *Developmental Psychology, 44,* 117-126.

Waite, L., & Gallagher, M. (2001). *The case for marriage: Why married people are happier, healthier and better off financially.* New York: Random House.

Waite, L., & Joyner, K. (2001). Emotional satisfaction and physical pleasure in sexual unions: Time horizon, sexual behavior, and sexual exclusivity. *Journal of Marriage and Family, 63,* 247-264.

Waite, L. J., Laumann, E. O., Das, A., & Schumm, P. L. (2009). Sexuality: Measures of partnerships, practices, attitudes, and problems in the National Social Life, Health, and Aging Study. *Journal of Gerontology: Social Sciences, 64B*(S1), i56-i66.

Waldinger, M. D. (2005a). Lifelong premature ejaculation: From authority-based to evidence-based medicine. *British Journal of Urology International, 95*(1), 201-207.

Waldinger, M. D., et al. (2005b). A multinational population survey of intravaginal ejaculation latency time. *The Journal of Sexual Medicine, 2*(4), 492-497.

Wallace, S. G. (2007). Hooking up, losing out? The new culture of teen sex, and how to talk to your campers about it. *Camping Magazine* (March 1, 2007). Retrieved March 13, 2010, from http://www.acacamps.org/campmag/0703wallace.php

Wallen, K. (2005). Hormonal influences on sexually differentiated behavior. In K. J. Welch, Ed., *Family life now: A conversation about marriages, families, and relationships.* Boston: Allyn & Bacon.

Ward, T., Laws, D. R., & Hudson, S. M. (2003). *Sexual deviance: Issues and controversies.* London: Sage.

Waynforth, D. (2001). Mate-choice trade-offs and women's preference for physically attractive men. *Human Nature, 12,* 207-220.

Waring, E. M. (1984). The measurement of marital intimacy. *Journal of Marital and Family Therapy, 10,* 185-192.

Waters, E. (2004). *Urban tribes: Are friends the new family?* New York: Bloombury Publishers.

Weinburg, T. S. (2006). Sadomasochism and social sciences: A review of the sociological and social psychological literature. *The Journal of Homosexuality, 50*(2/3), 2006, 17-40.

Weinstein, E., & Rosen, E. (2006). *Teaching about human sexuality and family: A skills-based approach.* Belmont, CA: Thomson Wadsworth.

Weis, D. L. (1997). Childhood sexuality. In R. T. Francoeur (Ed.), *The International Encyclopedia of Sexuality.* New York: Continuum.

Weiss, H. A., Thomas, S. L., Munabi, S. K., & Hayes, R. J. (2006). Male circumcision and risk of syphilis, chancroid, and genital herpes: A systematic review and meta-analysis. *Sexually Transmitted Infections 2006, 82*(2), 101-1110.

Weiss, R. (1969). The fund of sociability. *Transaction, 6*(9), 36-43.

Welch, K. J. (1999). *The emotional, physical, and sexual responses in women following prophylactic mastectomy and breast reconstruction.* Unpublished Dissertation. Kansas State University, Manhattan Kansas.

Welch, K. J. (2007). *Family life now: A conversation about marriages, families, and relationships.* Boston: Allyn & Bacon.

Weschler, T. (2002). *Taking charge of your fertility* (Revised ed.). New York: HarperCollins.

Wessels, H., Lue, T. F., & McAnich, J. W. (1996). Penile length in the flaccid and erect states: guidelines for penile augmentation. *Journal of Urology, 156,* 995-997.

Wester, S. R., Vogel, D. L., Wei, M., & McLain, R. (2006). African American men, gender role conflict, and psychological distress: The role of racial identity. *Journal of Counseling and Development, 84,* 419-429.

Wheeler, D. L. (2006). The Internet and youth subculture in Kuwait. *Journal of Computer-Mediated Communication, 8*(2), 0-0.

Wheeless, L. R., & Parsons, L. A. (1995). What you feel is what you might get: Exploring sexual communication apprehension and sexual communication satisfaction. *Communication Research Reports, 12,* 39-45.

White, G. L. (1981). A model of romantic jealousy. *Motivation and Emotion, 5,* 295-310.

White, J. (2003, Sept/Oct). Sex and gender confusion: Our sense of being manly or womanly. *Indian Life.*

White, J. M., & Klein, D. M. (2007). *Family theories* (3rd ed.). Thousand Oaks, CA: Sage.

Whitty, M. T. (2003). Pushing the wrong buttons: Men's and women's attitudes toward online and offline infidelity. *CyberPsychology & Behavior, 6,* 569-579.

Wiederman, M. W. (1997). Extramarital sex: Prevalence and correlates in a national survey. *Journal of Sex Research, 34,* 167-174.

Wiederman, M. W. (2005). The gendered nature of sexual scripts. *The Family Journal: Counseling and Therapy for Couples and Families, 13*(4), 496-502.

Wienke, C., & Hill, G. J. (2009). Does the "marriage benefit" extend to partners in gay and lesbian relationships?: Evidence from a random sample of sexually active adults. *Journal of Family Issues, 30*(2), 259-289.

Wildermuth, S. M., & Vogl-Bauer, S. (2007). We met on the net: Exploring the perceptions of online romantic relationship participants. *Southern Communication Journal, 72*(3), 211-227.

Williams, B. G., Lloyd-Smith, J. O., Gouws, E., et al. (2006). The potential impact of male circumcision on HIV in sub-Saharan Africa. *Public Library of Science Medicine 3*(7), E262.

Williams, C. B. (2005). Counseling African American women: Multiple identities—multiple constraints. *Journal of Counseling and Development, 83*(3), 278-284.

Williams, G. B. (2000). Grief after elective abortions. *AWOHNN Lifelines, 4*(2), 37-40.

Williams, J. E., & Best, D. L. (1990). *Measuring sex stereotypes: A multination study.* Newbury Park, CA: Sage.

Williams, K. M., et al. (2009). Inferring sexually deviant behavior from corresponding fantasies: The role of personality and pornography consumption. *Criminal Justice and Behavior, 36*(2), 198-222.

Williamson, M. L., & Williamson, P. S. (1988). Women's preference for penile circumcision in sexual partners. *Journal of Sex Education and Therapy, 14,* 8-12.

Wilson, C. A., & Davies, D. C. (2007). The control of sexual differentiation of the reproductive system and brain. *Reproduction, 133*(2), 331-359.

Wilson, K. L., et al. (2005). A review of 21 curricula for abstinence-only-until-marriage programs. *Journal of School Health, 75*(3), 90-98.

Winks, C., & Semans, A. (2002). *The good vibrations guide to sex.* Cleis Press.

Wollery, L. M. (2007). Gaydar: A social-cognitive analysis. *Journal of Homosexuality, 53*(3), 9-17.

World Health Organization. (1985). Appropriate technology for birth. *Lancet, 2*(8452), 436-437.

World Health Organization. (2000). *Female genital mutilation.* Fact Sheet No. 241. Retrieved January 22, 2008, from www.who.int.mediacentre/factsheets/fs241/en/

World Health Organization. (2007). *WHO and UNAIDS announce recommendations from expert consultation on male circumcision.* Retrieved July 30, 2009, from http://www.who.int/mediacentre/news/releases/2007/pr10/en/index.html

World Health Organization. (2009). *Chlamydia trachomatis.* Retrieved March 16, 2010, from http://www.who.int/vaccine_research/diseases/chlamydia_trachomatis/en/

Wright, E. R., & Perry, B. L. (2006). Sexual identity distress, social support, and the health of gay, lesbian, and bisexual youth. *Journal of Homosexuality, 51,* 81-109.

Wu, Z. (2007). *Shacked up: A demographic profile of non-marital cohabitation.* Paper presented on the Breakfast on the Hill Seminar Series, Ottawa, Ontario, October 23, 2007.

Wylie, K. R., et al. (2008). Sexual disorders, paraphilias, and gender dysphoria. *International Journal of Sexual Health, 20*(1-2), Retrieved from http://www.haworthpress.com

Wynd, C. A. (2002). Testicular self-examination in young adult men. *Journal of Nursing Scholarship, 34*(3), 251-255.

Yang, C. C., & Bradley, W. E. (1998). Neuroanatomy of the penile portion of the human dorsal nerve of the penis. *British Journal of Urology, 82*(1), 109-113.

Yang, M. L, Fullwood, E., Goldstein, J., & Mink, J. (2005). Masturbation in infancy and early childhood presenting as a movement disorder: 12 cases and a review of the literature. *Pediatrics, 116,* 1427-1432.

Yesalis, C. C., & Bahrke, M. S. (2005). Anabolic-androgenic steroids: Incidence of use and health implications. *President's Council on Physical Fitness and Sports Research Digest, 5*(5).

Young, K. (1999). Internet addiction: Evaluation and treatment. *Student British Medical Journal, 7,* 351-352.

Young, M., Denny, G., & Young, T., et al. (2000). Sexual satisfaction among married women. *American Journal of Health Studies, 16,* 73-84.

Youth Risk Behavior Survey. (2009). *2007 national youth risk behavior survey overview.* Retrieved September 14, 2009, from www.cdc.gov/yrbss

Zahedi, A. (2007). Contested meanings of the veil and political ideologies of Iranian regimes. *Journal of Middle East Women's Studies, 3*(3), 75-99.

Zamboni, B. D. & Crawford, I. (2002). Using masturbation in sex therapy: Relationships between masturbation, sexual desire, and sexual fantasy. *Journal of Psychology and Human Sexuality, 14*, 123-141.

Zand, D., & Rose, S. (1992). *Establishing lesbian relationships.* Unpublished manuscript, University of Missouri, St. Louis.

Zaviacic, M. (1999). *The human female prostate: Vestigial Skene's paraurethral glands and ducts to woman's functional prostate.* Bratislava, Slovakia: Slovak Academic Press (SAP).

Zaviacic, M., et al. (1997). Immunohistochemical localization of human protein 1 in the female prostate (Skene's gland) and the male prostate. *Histochemical Journal, 29*(3), 219-227.

Zaviacic, Z., et al. (1994). The significance of prostate markers in the orthology of the female prostate. *Bratisl Lek Listy, 95*(11), 491-497.

Zaviacic, M., & Ablin, R. J. (2000). The female prostate and prostate-specific antigen. Immunohistochemical localization, implications of this prostate marker in women and reasons for using the term "prostate" in the human female. *Histology & Histopathology, 15*(1), 131-142.

Zaviacic, M., Jakubovska, V., Belosovic, M., & Breza, J. (2000). Ultrastructure of the normal adult female prostate gland (Skene's gland). *Anatomy and Embryology (Berlin), 201*(1), 51-61.

Zimmer-Gembeck, M. J., Siebenbruner, J., & Collins, W. A. (2001). Diverse aspects of dating: Associations with psychosocial functioning from early to middle adolescence. *Journal of Adolescence, 24*, 313-336.

Zukerman, Z., Weiss, D. B., & Orvieto, R. (2003). Does pre-ejaculatory penile secretion originating from Cowper's gland contain sperm? *Journal of Assisted Reproduction and Genetics, 20*, 157-159.

INDEX